100 GREATEST WELSHMEN

D1375875

100 GREATEST WELSHMEN

TERRY BREVERTON

Glyndŵr Publishing

Book cover design by Dave Lewis

I bob Cymru – Yr ydym eisiau gwybodaeth am hanes y Brythoniaid I achub am byth yr iaith Brydeinig

For the people of Wales – We need to know the history of the Britons to forever save the British language

About the author

Terry Breverton was educated at Manchester and Lancaster universities, and is a Fellow of the Institute of Consulting and a Fellow of the Chartered Institute of Marketing. He has spoken on Wales at the North American Festival of Wales at Vancouver and Washington and across Wales, given academic papers in Paris, Thessaloniki, Charleston and Seattle and taught in Milan and Reggio Emilia. He has given the Bemis Lecture at Lincoln, Massachusetts and been awarded a Helm Fellowship at the University of Indiana. Breverton has appeared in several television documentaries about the Welsh, including in Los Angeles, and has worked and consulted in over thirty countries.

After a career in international business and acadaemia, he is a full-time non-fiction writer of over fifty books, and has won five Welsh Books Council 'Book of the Month' awards. He has spoken across Wales upon Welsh heritage, a particular interest being Welsh pirates and privateers such as 'Black Bart' Roberts and Admiral Sir Henry Morgan. His A to Z of Wales and the Welsh was an acclaimed 'first Welsh encyclopaedia', and Archbishop Rowan Williams commented upon his The Book of Welsh Saints: 'this book is a really extraordinary achievement: a compilation of tradition, topography and literary detective work that can have few rivals. I have enjoyed browsing it immensely, and have picked up all sorts of new lines to follow up… an enormous work of research.'

Richard Booth MBE, (King Richard Coeur de Livre, the 'King of Hay'), states that 'Breverton has done more for Welsh tourism than the Welsh Tourist Board.' His books have been published across the world, and translated into over twenty languages from Polish and Turkish to Chinese and Japanese. Breverton played rugby until he was 38, and says his proudest achievement is being on the committee of Llanybydder Rugby Football Club. Breverton's 100 Great Welshmen (2001) was a Welsh Books Council Book of the Month reviewed as 'a fascinating compendium' with 'painstaking research'. His second edition of 2006 was called: 'a veritable goldmine of a book'; and 'a massive treasure chest of facts and figures which no collector of books on Wales can overlook'.

CONTENTS

vii   Preface to 3nd Edition

xi   Introduction

1   **Caradog** fl.43-51 CE - Caractacus – 'An Eternal Memory to the
      Mercy of Rome'
7   **Pelagius** c.345-c.418 - Morgan, The True Christian 'Heretic' Who
      Almost Destroyed the Roman Church
11   **Patrick** c.389-461 - Sain Padrig, The Apostle of Ireland, 'The Most
      Famous Welshman in the World'
16   **Dyfrig** c.465-546 – Bishop Dubricius, 'Dubric the High Saint, Chief
      of the Church in Britain'
18   **Illtud** fl.530 – Abbot Illtud the Warrior
22   **Arthur** d.539, 547 or 570- Arthmael ap Meurig ap Tewdrig,
      Europe's Greatest Legend
39   **Armel** d.c.570 – Arthmael, the Real Arthur?
46   **Teilo** d.c.560-580 - Bishop of Llandaff, Founder of Llandeilo
53   **Cadog** c.497-c.577- Cadfael (Battle Prince), Founder of Llancarfan,
57   **Gildas** c.498 - c.570 or 583 - The First British Historian. The
      Second Apostle of Ireland'
62   **Merlin** 5th-6th century – Arthur's Wizard
65   **Saint David** c.520-589 – Dewi Sant, 'The Waterdrinker', The
      Patron Saint of Wales
73   **Deiniol** d.c.584 – Deiniol Wyn, Deiniol the Blessed, the Founder of
      Bangor Cathedral
75   **Taliesin** late 6th century - One of the Greatest Bards
78   **Beuno** d.642 or 660 - The Patron Saint of Computer Technicians
83   **Cadwaladr** c.630-682 - Cadwaladr the Blessed, High King of
      Britain, 'the Last of the Kings of Britain'
87   **Nennius** fl.823 - The Historian of the Britons
91   **Rhodri Mawr** 820-878 – Rhodri the Great, 'The Greatest of All the
      Kings of Wales'
93   **Hywel Dda** 890-950 – Hywel the Good
98   **Gruffudd ap Llywelyn** 1007-1063 - The Head, Shield and
      Defender of the Britons
103   **Gruffudd ap Cynan** 1055-1137 - The Possessor of Britain
109   **Owain Gwynedd** 1100-1170 – 'The Bulwark of All Wales', the
      first Prince of Wales, the last King of Wales
115   **Rhys ap Gruffydd** 1132-1197 - Yr Arglwydd Rhys, The Lord
      Rhys, Prince of the Welsh, Head of All Wales
122   **Giraldus Cambrensis** 1146-1223 - Gerald of Wales, Gerald the
      Welshman

125   **Llywelyn ab Iorwerth** 1173-1240 - Llywelyn the Great

129   **Llywelyn ap Gruffudd** c.1225–1282 – Ein Lliw Olaf, Our Last Prince

146   **Llywelyn Bren** c.1270-1318 - Llywelyn the Kingly

154   **Dafydd ap Gwilym** c.1315/20-c.1370 – Wales' Greatest Poet, 'the Nightingale of Dyfed'

157   **Owain Llawgoch** c.1330-1378 - Yvain de Galles, Warlord, Chevalier de France

164   **Owain Glyndŵr** 1354/55-c.1415/20- Prince of Wales, Wales' Greatest Hero

181   **William Herbert** 1423-1469 - William ap William ap Thomas, Earl of Pembroke, 'The First Statesman of a New Era'

184   **Jasper Tudor** 1431- 1495 – 'Dynasty Maker', The Only Lord to Fight from the First to the Last Battle of the Wars of the Roses, Earl of Pembroke

193   **Henry VII** 1457-1509 - First King of the Tudor Dynasty

197   **Robert Recorde** 1510-1589 – The Mathematician Who Revolutionised Algebra and Invented the = Sign

200   **William Cecil** 1520-1598 – Lord Bughley, 'The Architect of Elizabethan England', 'The Man Who Does Everything'

203   **William Salesbury** 1520-1584 – Translator of the *New Testament*, The Most Learned Welshman of His Day

205   **John Dee** 1527-1608 – 'Black Jack', The Magus of His Age

208   **Bishop William Morgan** - 1545-1604 - The Translator of *The Bible*

211   **Inigo Jones** 1573-1652 - The Founder of Classical English Architecture, 'The First and Greatest of English Reanaissance Architects'

212   **Lord Edward Herbert** 1583–1648 - First Baron Herbert of Cherbury, 'The Father of English Deism'

216   **George Herbert** 1593–1633 – 'Holy Mr. Herbert'

219   **Henry Vaughan** 1621–1695 – '*The Silurist*'

221   **Admiral Sir Henry Morgan** c.1635-1688 – 'The Sword of England', The Greatest Privateer of All Time

225   **William Jones** 1645-1709 – The First Man to Use the Symbol π (pi) as a Mathematical Symbol

228   **Richard Nash** 1674-1761 - 'Beau' Nash, The Master of Ceremonies, The King of Bath

234   **Bartholomew Roberts** 1678-1722 - *Black Bart*, 'The Last and Most Lethal Pirate', the Origin of the *Jolly Roger*

241   **Griffith Jones** 1683-1761 - The Man Who Made Wales the Most Literate European Nation

243   **Howell Harris** 1714-1773 - The Father of Methodism in Wales, The Greatest Welshman of his Day

245   **Richard Wilson** 1714-1782 - The Founder of British Landscape Painting

247   **William Williams** 1717-1791- 'Pantycelyn', Wales' First Romantic Poet

249   **Richard Price** 1723-1791 – The Friend of the Universe, The Apostle of Liberty, The Most Original Thinker Ever Born in Wales

256   **William Williams** c.1727-1791 – America's First Novelist, Polymath, the 'Forgotten Genius'

259   **David Williams** 1738-1816 - Founder of the Literary Fund, French Citizen

260   **Thomas Jefferson** 1743-1826 - President, and Author of the Declaration of Independence

263   **Sir William Jones** 1746-1794 – 'Oriental' Jones, 'The Father of Comparative Linguistics'

266   **Iolo Morganwg** 1747-1826 - Edward Williams, Saviour of Welsh Culture

271   **John Nash** 1752-1835 - The Architect of the Regency Period, 'The Man Who Changed the Face of London'

275   **Thomas Picton** 1758-1815 - The Hero of Waterloo

279   **John Thomas Evans** 1770-1799 - The Man Who Opened Up America

284   **David Thompson** 1770-1857 – 'Koo-Koo-Sint', The Starman, 'The Greatest Land Geographer Who Ever Lived'

288   **Robert Owen** 1771-1858 - The Founder of Socialism, The Founder of Infant Schools, 'The Most Popular Man in Europe', The Modern World's First Socialist'

294   **John Frost** 1784-1877 - Pioneer of British Democracy, Chartist Leader

298   **Richard Roberts** 1789-1864 The Unknown Pioneer of Production Engineering, The Innovator of High Precision Machine Tools and the Interchangeability of Parts

304   **Dr. William Price** 1800-1893 - Chartist Freethinker, Pioneer of Cremation, Republican Doctor

307   **Jefferson Davis** 1808-1889 - The President of the Confederate States of America

310   **Richard Lewis** 1808-1831 – Dic Penderyn, 'Martyr of the Welsh Working Class'

314   **Sir William Robert Grove** 1811-1896 – 'Father of the Fuel Cell', Inventor of the Incandescent Light

317   **Henry Richard** 1812-1888 – 'The Apostle of Peace', 'The Member for Wales'

319   **David Davies** 1819-1890 – David Davies Llandinam, Dai Top Sawyer, Davies the Railway, Davies the Ocean, The Most Successful Welsh Industrialist of the Century

324   **Michael D. Jones** 1822-1899 – 'The Greatest Welshman of the 19th Century'

329   **David Hughes** 1831-1900 - The First Man to Transmit and Receive Radio Waves, Telephone Pioneer, Polymath Musician, Inventor, The Inventor of Powder Coating, The Inventor of the Microphone, The Inventor of the Printing Telegraph, The Man Who Revolutionised Communications

332   **Sir Pryce Pryce-Jones** 1834-1920 – The Man Who Changed Shopping, The Inventor of Mail Order and the Sleeping Bag

334   **H.M. Stanley** 1841-1904 - John Rowlands, 'Breaker of Rocks', The Man Who Found Livingstone and Mapped the Congo

338   **Bill Frost** 1848-1935 - The First Man To Fly, The Pioneer of Air Travel

342   **Sidney Gilchrist Thomas** 1850-1885 - The Man Who Created the Modern Steel Industry, Inventor of the Carnegie Process

345   **David Lloyd-George** 1863-1945 - The Man Who Won The War

349   **Frank Lloyd Wright** 1867-1959 - The Greatest American Architect of All Time

353   **Bertrand Russell** 1872-1970 - The 20th Century's Most Important Liberal Thinker

355   **Billy Meredith** 1874-1958 - Football's First Superstar

358   **D.W. Griffith** 1875-1948 - The Pioneer of Cinema, The Father of Film

361   **Edward Thomas** 1878-1917 – War Poet, the Poet's Poet, 'The Father of Us All'

363   **John Llewellyn Lewis** 1880-1969 – The Conscience of American Industry

367   **Frederick Hall Thomas** 1886-1927 - Freddie Welsh, The Welsh Wizard

371   **Jimmy Wilde** 1892-1969 - The Mighty Atom, The Ghost with the Hammer in his Hand, 'The Greatest Boxer of All Time'

375   **Saunders Lewis** 1893-1985 - The Greatest Figure in Welsh Literature in the 20th Century

379   **Ivor Novello** 1893-1951 - Filmstar and Musical Playwright

381   **David Jones** 1895-1974 - Poet-Painter

384   **Aneurin Bevan** 1897-1960 - The Founder and Architect of the National Health Service

388   **Llywellyn Morris Humphreys** 1899-1965 - Murray the Camel, Murray the Hump, Public Enemy Number One, The Man Who Invented Money Laundering and gave us Las Vegas

391   **Idris Davies** 1905-1953 - The Miner-Poet admired by Pound and Eliot

395   **Gwynfor Evans** 1912-2005 - One of the Great Souls of Twentieth-century Wales, Plaid Cymru's First MP

402 **R.S. Thomas** 1913-2000 - The Poet-Priest, 'The Solzhenitsyn of Wales'

407 **Dylan Thomas** 1914-1953 - Wales' Best-Known Poet, 'The Greatest Living Poet in the English Language'

410 **Tommy Cooper** 1922-1984 - The Comedian's Comedian

414 **Donald Watts Davies** 1924-1999 - The Computer Engineer Who Made Possible the Internet

416 **Richard Burton** 1925-1984 - Film Superstar

419 **Cliff Morgan** 1930-2013 – 'The Best Fly-Half There Can Ever Have Been'

423 **John Charles** 1931-1994 – The Gentle Giant, *Il Gigante Buono*, 'The Best in the World'

429 **Anthony Hopkins** 1937- - Hollywood Superstar

431 **Gareth Edwards** 1947 - The Greatest Rugby Player of All Time

435 **Aberfan** 1966 –

PREFACE

'The scrupulous and the just, the noble, humane, and devoted natures; the unselfish and the intelligent may begin a movement – but it passes away from them. They are not the leaders of a revolution. They are its victims.' - Joseph Conrad, *Under Western Eyes* 1911

There were mistakes in the earlier versions of this book, which hopefully have been corrected. However, those books were written to cover a great deal of history, without the benefit of any editor except myself. Of course, such a book is subjective, and from my previous editions of *100 Great Welshmen* I have omitted some second and third generation Welshmen, such as John Adams, John Quincy Adams, James Monroe, Samuel Adams, Meriwether Lewis, John Pierpoint Morgan, Bobby Jones and Oliver Cromwell. Others omitted for various reasons are Howel Davis, Madoc ab Owain Gwynedd, Augustus John, Tom Jones, Geraint Evans, Charles Rolls and 'The Miner'. The last is omitted and replaced by an entry upon Aberfan, to represent the legacy of mining in Wales. The separate entries upon Arthur and Arthmael are counted as one entry.

    Instead of the above, I have added Jasper Tudor, Cliff Morgan, William Jones and his son William Jones, Richard Roberts, another William Williams, Henry Vaughan, George Herbert, Edward Herbert, Richard Lewis, Pryce Pryce-Jones, David Davies, John L. Lewis, William Grove, David Thompson, and Aberfan. Also, unlike the last book, this is in chronological rather than alphabetical order, to give an idea of the flow of history.

    The terms Wales and Welsh were given to the Christian British people of Wales and England by Germanic barbarians who took over England from the fifth and sixth centuries. It comes from a common Germanic designator for Celtic and Latin-speaking peoples, in 'Old English' welisċ, wælisċ or wilisċ meaning 'foreign.' The overseas invaders termed the native British 'foreigners', calling them variously wallas, wealh, wylisc or walsci, and called the British language weallas, which became known as Welsh. The new English called the settled Celts alien, and Wales/Welsh thus has a common root with other conquered Celtic areas – we see the words Walloon in Belgium, Wallachian in Romania, Walachian in Greece, Vlach in Romania and Valais in Switzerland - outsiders in their own lands.

    Thus the Romano-British became themselves 'foreigners' in their own land, with nearly all traces of the original British people, including the language, place names and people, being wiped out in England. The British, i.e. Welsh, word for Wales is Cymru, with y Cymry the Welsh people, Cymro a Welshman, Cymraes a Welsh woman and Cymraeg is the language. The British were pushed by successive eastern invaders to the West of England, Cumbria, Ystrad Clud (Strathclyde) and Wales. These displaced peoples called themselves Cymry (literally, fellow-countrymen) to form a common bond. The Welsh for one of the invading tribes, Saxon, is Sais, and still means Englishman, and the English language is Saxon, Saesneg (the Scots Gaelic is Sassenach for an English person). However, Latin writers adopted another tribe, the Angli (Angles) as the new inhabitants of England, and over time Angle Land became England (Lloegr in Welsh).

Ynys Prydain (Prydein in Middle Welsh) is the Island of Britain. However, Prydain is usually used for the Brittonic region, south of Caledonia, stemming from the Roman conquest. Indeed, the triads Trioedd Ynys Prydein use the word ynys not as 'island' but as land or realm, referring to the southern half of the island. There is a similar occurrence in the early 10th century vaticinatory poem Armes Prydein (The Prophecy of Britain). Taliesin and Aneirin were writing in the British (i.e. Welsh) language around 600, with John Davies commenting in his History of Wales: 'This was a bold act for, throughout the territories that had been part of the Western Empire, the Latin of Rome was the sole written medium, and hardly any attempts were made to write Latin's daughter-languages, French, Spanish and Italian, until after 1000.'

Unfortunately every scriptorium, cathedral, church, library and castle was sacked in Wales during the course of hundreds of invasions and thousands of fights from Roman times to the English Civil War, when the remaining great Welsh library was burnt at Raglan Castle. The only surviving great gospel, the Book of St Teilo dating from around 730 (older than the Book of Kells) endured because it was stolen and taken to Lichfield Cathedral, being rebranded as the St Chad's Gospels. The staffordshirehoard.org.uk website tells us, quite erroneously: 'So, the St Chad Gospels and the Lichfield Angel belong to the same world as the Staffordshire Hoard. Like items of the Hoard, the Gospels and the Angel are works of exquisite craftsmanship. They show what an important cultural centre Mercia was in the 7th to 9th centuries.' Apart from the Book of St Teilo, the Staffordshire hoard itself may well have been taken from the British. Cynddylan ap Cyndrwyn was a seventh-century Prince of Powys associated with Pengwern, his Shropshire capital (variously placed at Wroxeter, Trewern, Atcham, Baschurch, Whittington or Shrewsbury). Cynddylan's sister Heledd lamented the loss of her brothers, sisters and home in the terrible sacking of Pengwern by the Mercians, in Canu Heledd. In her magnificent elegy, this first British woman poet mourns, as an eagle tears at the flesh of her brother. We can easily posit a case for much of the Staffordshire hoard coming from the sack of Pengwern, and testing the gold can prove its provenance, as with many Irish gold artefacts.

The Welsh were known in law as the Britons, and the English as the English, until the Welsh polymath John Dee suggested to Elizabeth I that there could be a legal justification for American colonial expansion, based upon the Welsh Prince Madoc's legendary discovery of America in 1170. Over the following centuries the concept of a 'British' Empire and the

'British people' emerged and developed, by also calling the English, Scots and later Irish, 'British'. By the eighteenth century, the Britons had become 'Welsh'. To be called Welsh, a foreigner, in one's own country is condescending. Thus unimaginative politicians missed a wonderful opportunity, to call the talking shop in Cardiff Bay, the British Assembly, rather than the 'Foreign' Gathering.

There is a massive and on-going threat to Welsh heritage and culture. We have a version of history taught by the conquerors, where nothing happened in Britain until the barbarians came, and in Bishop Stubbs' words, civilized the British. And language is the key to keeping a nation's history, heritage and culture. Around a third of the three million people now living in Wales do not consider themselves Welsh, because of increasing in-migration. Probably another half-million have non-Welsh parents or grandparents. Many Welsh leave Wales for better employment prospects, being replaced by non-workers and retirees, attracted by a better environment and cheaper housing. The First Minister has set an inane and insane target for a million Welsh speakers by 2050, i.e. two out of three Welsh people. Perhaps we could substitute dream or wish for 'target'. For five decades, 90% of Welsh population growth has come from outside Wales. (And why have Welsh politicians never queried why Scotland and Northern Ireland get much more per capita from the Barnett Formula than Wales?) Just about every house sold in rural Wales seems to go to incomers. No politician will speak up about the danger to one of the world's oldest nations, with one of the world's oldest languages (- France, Italy and Germany are modern constructs). This book, and its companion volume upon Welsh women, is intended to make the remaining British people proud of their past, and pass on that sense to their children and grand-children.

INTRODUCTION

Mae'n wir angenrheidiol bod Llais Werin Bobl Cymru yn gael ei glywed heddiw... ni allwn ddibynnu ar ein gwleidyddion i gynorthwyo ni.

It is truly essential that the Voice of the common Welsh People is heard today... we cannot rely upon our politicians to assist us.

There is an inherent danger in nationalism, but only when used by politicians and proponents of military force. However, nationalism, in the sense of patriotism, must be encouraged across Wales, as it is losing the knowledge of its past. Nationalism is about showing the English Government, the government of the south-east of Britain, that Cymru has not yet been killed, that the British people and its culture, language, heritage and history, is not quite extinct. Wales and its people have survived every attempt to extinguish the premier nation of the British Isles, since the Germanic invasions of the 6th century and since the Act of Union of 1573. The spirit of Cymru still lives, but is in as critical condition as its economy, one of the worst in Europe. The problem is that the people of the British Isles do not realise that to be truly 'British' is to be Welsh - Cymraeg. In many other nations the original population is honoured and protected, rather than dismissed and neglected.

Cymru needs desperately to re-find itself. It has always been a nation of literacy, poetry, pacifism and socialism, with a deep undercurrent of Christianity in the sense of brotherhood and antagonism to violence. It can easily claim to be the nation with the longest unbroken Christian heritage in the world. Wales and its people have also been important in the development of the modern world. Readers may note that the country has massively influenced the course of American, and therefore, world history. A third of the signers of the Declaration of Independence were of Welsh rigin, and five of its first six Presidents had Welsh roots. Wales (itself a Germanic-origin word, meaning foreign, and imposed by Saxon barbarian invaders) has made important contributions to science and industry, and was the home of the Industrial Revolution. The Christian, pacifist nature of the British-Welsh shines through this book. The country has no known record of torture, nor of aggression against other nations except in defence of its remnant of Britain.

This book is not meant as an academic tome, as its purpose is to show tourists the type of people the Welsh are, and also to tell the Welsh themselves what they are never taught in schools. Indeed, Welsh history is almost unknown to its people and there seem to be no courses in schools or universities which cover the two millennia of Welsh, i.e. British, history. The Welsh may know about Dr Livingstone, but not about Stanley; about Shakespeare but not about Dafydd ap Gwilym; about Tony Blair but not about David Lloyd George; about the illiterate butcher Edward I but not Owain Glyndŵr, and so on, ad infinitum.

My apologies to anyone whose favourite hero or indeed villain is not included in this listing of great Welshmen - it is, like my previous *An A-Z of Wales and the Welsh*, an eclectic listing based on the knowledge of someone who spent his years between 18 and 50 living outside Wales. I took years to have that published (albeit in a truncated and Bowdlerised form), while trying to get politicians and publishers interested in the idea of a Welsh encyclopaedia. That wish came to fruition a decade later, with a massively subsidised and vastly overpriced volume of anodyne qualities. Because of the lack of interest in books promoting Wales and uncovering its real past and achievements, I started an independent publishing company for some ten years, Glyndŵr Publishing, to publish books by myself and others which promoted Wales and its achievements.

Like my *The Book of Welsh Saints*, this publication is part of an ongoing attempt by the author to promote Wales and its people, in the face of the continuous onslaught of Anglicisation by inwards settlement and the media. The utter ineptitude of Welsh political organisations, placemen quangos and a remote, uncaring London government over the last seven decades, has depressingly failed to secure a reasonable future for Wales. There are no prospects for its young people, the best of whom are forced to emigrate for work, with no sign of any change in this scenario. Wales is the most under-privileged region of the British Isles, and one of the most economically-depressed in the European Union. There is no economic regeneration. The future is not bleak, but black, for one of the countries which has contributed most to civilisation in the true (non-violent) sense of the word. The corruption of authority and the abuse of power have seemingly affected Wales more than any other part of the UK economy, itself in relative terminal decline.

The Barnett Formula has given Scotland and Northern Ireland higher living standards than Wales over the decades, and Welsh towns and villages are in disrepair. Our children receive £600 a year less in schools than their English counterparts, which equates to around £90,000 by the time they leave at 18 years old. Our universities are among the worst in Britain. Our health is terrible, not assisted by the great inflow of the retired, unemployed, 'relocated' and ill and to the country. 90% of the population increase of Wales has been from outside for decades, leading to only 2 million of the 3 million population now saying that they are Welsh. One could indeed posit that Wales is 'Europe's Tibet', with ethical and ethnic cleansing. The brightest and best leave the nation for work prospects, and hardly ever come back. They are replaced with incomers creating massive strains upon housing, health and welfare.

The story of Wales is one of continuous external aggression for the last two-thousand years, of constant denigration by those who know nothing of its past, of the systematic stripping of its resources, of the non-representation of its people, and of a cultural settlement into England's oldest colony. Wales needs a 'great Welshman' today, to lead the country out of its past, to stimulate investment in real work, not in 'inward investment' part-time assembly jobs or in the tyranny of short-term 'call centres'. Wales deserves better from its decision-makers, but they will have to realise that the lack of any ethics in the 'free market-place' means that right-wing demagogic free-trade has no place in Wales' future prospects. The problem is that politicians do not understand economics - and neither do their economic advisers. Just like academics teaching business, less than one in a hundred has ever had any type of position in the business community.

This is a nationalist book in many senses, but nationalist in the interest of truth rather than revenge; in the interest of research rather than the acceptance of adulterated histories; and in the interest of educative literacy rather than popularity with the 'crachach', critics and politicians. Never has Iolo Morganwg's motto of *Y Gwir Erbyn Y Byd* – The Truth Against the World – been so apt. We need people not just to be proud of Wales, but to know why they should feel pride. Pride without knowledge is jingoism. Hopefully, when true Welshmen read this publication, they will want to help put something back into Wales - help with the process of rediscovering our hidden past and safeguarding our future. This is crucially important for our country. If nationalism dies, we have nothing left. A nation cannot exist without knowledge and renewal - it will otherwise fade away - we owe it to these *100 Greatest Welshmen* to build upon their achievements. *Cymru am Byth!*

CARADOG ap CYNFELYN fl.43-51 CE

CARACTACUS, CARATACUS, CARADOC, CARADAWG, 'AN ETERNAL MEMORIAL TO THE MERCY OF ROME'

Wales was never completely subdued by the Romans. Two of their three (sometimes four) British legions were permanently stationed on the Welsh borders, at Deva (Chester) and Isca Silurum (Caerleon). Just one other legion was generally required, based at York, to control all of England and much of Scotland. Isca Silurum was built, with its nearby town of Venta Silurum (Caerwent) to keep the Silures down, while Caerfyrddin (Carmarthen) Roman fort and town were built in heartland of the Demetae tribe. Wales was never completely settled, and by 78 CE, Tacitus wrote that it was necessary to exterminate almost 'the entire race' of the Ordovices of mid-Wales and Gwynedd.

Caradog may be the same person as Arviragus, the legendary British king of the same period. Caradog's father was Cynfelin, Cunobelinus (Shakespeare's *Cymbeline*), king of the strongest of the Brythonic kingdoms of England, the Catuvellauni, and the first to be attacked by Rome. Suetonius called Cunobelin son of Tasciovanus, 'Rex Britanniorum', and he was friendly with Rome. Unfortunately his death led to a power-struggle between his sons Caradog, Togodumnus and Adminius, because of the 'cyfran' principle of inheritance (gavelkind). Adminius appealed to Rome, for help. Caradog may have been the protégé of his uncle Epaticcus, who expanded Catuvellaunian territories westwards into the land of the Atrebates. Epaticcus died around 35 CE, and the Atrebates under Verica regained some of their lands. However, Caradog then conquered the Atrebates, forcing Verica to flee to Rome.

With Caradog's brother Adminius, he appealed to the Emperor Claudius to help him regain his lands. Aware of Julius Caesar's two futile attempts to conquer Britain, Claudius knew that success in battle would stabilise his precarious position. The Roman invasion of 43 CE now targeted Caradog's stronghold of Colchester (Camelodunum), formerly the seat of his father Cynfelin. Cunobelinus had died some time before the invasion, so Caradog and his brother Togodumnus led the initial defence of the country against the four legions of Aulus Plautius. They were forced to use guerrilla tactics against an army of around 40,000 men.

After losing two initial skirmishes in eastern Kent, Caradog gathered a force on the banks of the Medway further west to face the invaders. At the same time, the Romans received the surrender of the Dobunni, based around Cirencester tribe in Gloucestershire. As the Dobunni were subjects of the Catuvellauni, this was a blow to British strength. There was no bridge over the river where the battle was fought, so a detachment of specially-trained Roman auxiliaries swam across the river and attacked the chariot horses. In the chaos that followed, the bulk of the invasion force led by Vespasian, later to become emperor from 69-79 CE, crossed the river. The overall commander was Vespasian's brother, Sabinus. The first day of fighting ended without a result, but on the second day the Britons were defeated and fell back to the Thames.

Togodumnus may have died in a defeat near the future site of London, and Caradog withdrew to more defensible terrain to the west. Two months after the initial invasion of Britain, Emperor Claudius arrived to symbolically lead his army to victory. In August, the Romans captured Camulodunum, Caradog's capital.

With the whole of south-east Britain overrun, eleven British kings made their submission. Aulus Plautius, commander of the invasion force, was appointed first Roman governor of Britain, but the majority of the island would not be pacified for at least another 50 years. By Summer 44 CE, Vespasian was moving west, fighting numerous small-scale battles and capturing a string of hill forts, including Maiden Castle and Hod Hill. In 47 CE, Aulus Plautius, governor of Briain, was received as a hero in Rome, and replaced by Publius Ostorius Scapula. By this time, Caradog was leading a coalition of Silures and Ordovices, British tribes based in Wales.

Caer Caradoc, near Church Stretton

In Summer 47 CE there was an Iceni revolt against a Roman order to surrender their weapons. The Iceni tribe, based in East Anglia, were allies of Rome and had not been conquered. When ordered to surrender their weapons by the new Roman governor Scapula, some tribesmen resisted. The revolt was quickly put down and a pro-Roman king, Prasutagus, installed. By 48 CE, the Romans had effectively subdued all territory south of a line from the mouth of the Humber to the Severn Estuary.

In Summer 49 CE, a Roman citizen-colony was founded at Caradog's home of Camulodunum (Colchester), which briefly became the capital of the province of Britain.

There was now pressure for the Romans to move into Wales for its lead, silver, gold and copper – the country was incredibly rich in important minerals. Tacitus recorded that Scapula received the submission of the Deceangli of northeast Wales on the River Dee in 49 CE, enabling him to concentrate his armies upon the Silures. The great fort of Gloucester

(Caerloyw) was built to push back the belligerent Silures. In the same year others were built at Usk and Clyro.

In 51 CE Caradog was eventually brought to battle leading the Silures and Ordovices at the Battle of Caer Caradoc, perhaps at Blodwell Rocks near Llanymynech. The site of Caradog's last stand against Rome is still not known, but it appears to have been in the northeast of Wales, near the upper River Severn. Many experts place the hill-fort of Old Oswestry as the place of battle, but it may have been the Breiddin near Welshpool or Cefn Carnedd near Llanidloes. Caractacus believed that he had found an excellent defensive position, described by Tacitus as following:

'Then Caractacus staked his fate on a battle. He selected a site where numerous factors – notably approaches and escape routes – helped him and impeded us. On one side there were steep hills. Wherever the gradient was gentler, stones were piled into a kind of rampart. And at his front there was a river without easy crossings. The defences were strongly manned... The British chieftains went around their men, encouraging and heartening them to be unafraid and optimistic, and offering other stimulants to battle. Caractacus, as he hastened to one point and another, stressed that this was the day, this the battle, which would either win back their freedom or enslave them forever.... Then every man swore by his tribal oath that no enemy weapons would make them yield – and no wounds either...

This eagerness dismayed the Roman commander disconcerted as he already was by the river-barrier, the fortifications supplementing it, the overhanging cliffs, and the ferocious crowds of defenders at every point ...After a reconnaissance to detect vulnerable and invulnerable points, Ostorius Scapula led his enthusiastic forces forward. They crossed the river without difficulty, and reached the rampart. But then, in an exchange of missiles, they came off worse in wounds and casualties. However, under a roof of locked shields, the Romans demolished the crude and clumsy stone embankment, and in the subsequent fight at close quarters the natives were driven to the hilltops. Our troops pursued them closely.'

Scapula managed to capture Caradog's wife and daughter and received the surrender of his brothers. Caradog escaped, and fled north to the Brigantes in Yorkshire, but Queen Cartimandua handed him over to the Romans in chains. With the capture of Caradog, much of southern Britain was pacified and garrisoned throughout the 50s. Caradog's family was led in triumph before the Emperor Claudius in Rome, usually the precursor to a public execution of captured opponents. However, Tacitus records the famous sparing of his life by the emperor, noting Caractacus' defence:

'Had my lineage and rank been accompanied by only moderate success, I should have come to this city as a friend rather than prisoner, and you would not have disdained to ally yourself peacefully with one so nobly born, the ruler of so many nations. As it is, humiliation is my lot, glory yours. I had horses, men, arms, wealth. Are you surprised I am sorry to lose them? If you want to rule the world, does it follow that everyone else welcomes enslavement? If I had surrendered without a blow being brought before you, neither my downfall nor your triumph would have become famous. If you execute me, they will be forgotten. Spare me, and I shall be an everlasting token of your mercy.'

Caradog, was not recorded as a saint, but has an important place in the legends of early Christianity in Wales. His father Bran was supposed to have been kept hostage at Rome for 7 years, and returned with the saints Ilid, Cyndaf, Arwystli Hen and Mawan who preached the gospel in the 1st century from around 58. Caradog's daughter Eurgain, or Eigan, was recorded as the first female saint in Britain, who founded its first monastery at Llanilltud Fawr. Another daughter, Gwladys Claudia may have been extremely influential in the early Christian church in Rome. Caradog was said to have returned with Eurgain to his base at Dunraven Castle or St Donat's, and there is an ancient farm, Cae Caradog, near Dunraven. Caradog's great-grandson Lleurwg ap Cyllin was said to be the saint who erected the first church in Britain, at Llandaf, and sent to Rome for Elfan, Dyfan, Medwy and Fagan to evangelise Britain.

Whatever the truth, Christianity was well established in Wales in the second century, and remained as the religion through the Dark Ages of England and the rest of Europe. (See this author's *The Book of Welsh Saints*).

The Silures kept fighting after Caradog's capture, and actually defeated the Twentieth Legion in 52 CE. In 57 CE, Nero ordered that Anglesey, the chief centre of British discontent, be taken, and Tacitus describes the burning of the sacred Druidic groves. The Deceangli and Ordovices rose again and were almost exterminated. Huge forts had to be built at Uriconium (Wroxeter) and Deva (Chester) to attempt to subdue the Welsh tribes, and the Romans cut through to Anglesey, the heart of European druidism in 60 CE. A garrison was established on this holy island but Boadicea (Buddug) led a revolt by the Iceni in England, so the Romans could not consolidate their gains in Wales. From 69-78 CE there was another great push against the Silures and the Ordovices, led by Julius Frontinus, and then by Julius Agricola. In 71, Petilius crushed the Brigantes, and between 74 and 79 the might of Rome turned once more against the Silures of Glamorgan and Gwent. There were at least thirteen separate campaigns against Wales and its borders between 48 and 79 CE, which explains the multiplicity of Roman villas, forts, fortlets, marching camps, roads and civil ruins dotted over much of Wales.

Three of the four Roman legions were now stationed on what is now the Welsh border. The 'exceptionally stubborn' Silures kept on resisting Rome, forcing a legion to be based at the new fort of Isca (Caerleon). The XX legion was at Uriconium (Wroxeter), the XX Augusta Legion at Isca, and the XX Adiutrix Legion at Deva. The Silures agreed peace by 75 CE.

They had fought Rome from 49 and were regarded by Tacitus as courageous, stubborn, powerful and warlike. Ostorius Scapula had said that they must be annihilated or transplanted. When he had died, 'worn out with care', the Silures destroyed a Roman legion. However, the construction of Caerleon in 75 meant that the Silures came to an accommodation with the governor, leaving their hillfort capital of Llanmelin and settling in the new Roman town of Caerwent. The Silures became the most Romanised of the Welsh tribes, paving the way for Meurig and Arthur to become Pendragons in the years after the Romans left Britain.

With southeast Wales secure, Agricola moved north to avenge a Roman defeat by the Ordovices and 'cut to pieces the whole fighting force of the region'. The Ordovices were almost slaughtered out of existence by 84 CE. Again, Anglesey was ravaged. The next 300 years were by no means peaceful in Wales, but the great stone forts at Chester, Caerleon, Carmarthen (Moridunum) and Caernarfon (Segontium) controlled a semi-quiescent people until the legions left around 400 CE. Unlike more 'settled' colonies of Rome, very few Roman villas have been found in Wales, and those that have are mainly attributed to Romano-Celts.

Professor Euros Bowen noted that several Roman villas were found near the sites of Cadog's Llancarfan, Illtud's Llanilltud and Dyfrig's foundations. Tathan was also active at Caerwent, which leads to Bowen's conclusion that the group of Celtic saints largely confined to south-east Wales represent a church that was locally established in late Roman times. This was the only part of Wales where Roman urban and country house culture was rooted, and Romano-British estates carried on the Christian tradition rather than relied on missionaries from Gaul. There seems to be a mystery about the great monastery and religious centre of Llanilltud Fawr, Lantwit Major. It appears that St Illtud, after his vision on the banks of the nearby Dawen (Thaw), founded the monastery on the site of the earliest Christian monastery in Britain, which may even been still in existence at this time. Further research is needed, but if this is the case, Wales can claim something very special in world history – the oldest educational establishment in the world up until 1100 and the Norman invasion.

Uniquely, Caradog had pardoned by the Emperor Claudius, and after seven years' captivity is said to have been allowed to return to his base at St. Donat's, near Llanilltud Fawr. Caradog's residence in Rome was known as 'The British House' and was the first house used for Christian worship in Rome. It is thought that his daughter Eurgain married a Roman, as did Gwladys (Claudia). It is thought that Eurgain brought Christianity to Wales, founding a monastic settlement called Cor Eurgain in Llanilltud Fawr. Another version is that she stayed in Rome, and the Cor was set up in her honour, first at Llanilid around 60 CE then transferring to Caer Mead or Cae Mead (Cor Eurgain) Roman villa at Llanilltud. One story was that Caradog came back to St Donats with Eurgain and was buried at Llanilltud.

St Paul was said to be a friend of Eurgain and Gwladys, and in legend came as St Ilid in 61 and 68. Gwladys is mentioned in *Epistle 2 Timothy 4-21* as Claudia. (Paul was said to have visited Galicia, which may be Wales rather than the Spanish province). Other versions relate Ilid as Joseph of Arimathea.

A Welsh tradition is that Christianity first came to Britain with St Paul who came here with Eurgan (Eurgain). She had married Lucius in Rome and with him founded the first university at Llanilltud about 68 AD, known as Cor Eurgain, where Illtud's later monastery stood. King Cyllin, whose son had been converted by Eurgain, endowed the church. It was burned by Irish pirates in 322 and rebuilt by St Theodosius, Tewdws or Tewdrig. Then it was known as Cor Tewdws, or the college of Theodosius in Caer Wrgan. It was associated with Emperor Theodosius. (Other sources tell us that Tewdws is an alternative of Tewdrig, the martyred grandfather of Arthur). There is a record that the Irish attacked and destroyed Caer Wrgan in the fifth century. Caer Wrgan is the old name for Caer Mead*, the huge Romano-Celtic villa just a mile north of Llanilltud Fawr. Cor is a very early version of Llan, meaning a monastic college. Cor Tewdws is marked on an 18th century map of Llanilltud as being a field north of the monastery site of Illtud.

'Achau y Saint' notes that the College of Caerworgorn was founded by Cystennyn Fendigaid (Constantine the Blessed) and soon destroyed by the Irish, at which time its principal was Padrig. This was Padrig Maenwyn, son of Mawon of the Gower peninsula, who was taken into captivity. This tradition is possibly fictitious. However, Caer Worgan was just a few hundred yards north of Cor Tewdws (which is still marked as such on maps). Perhaps after the sacking of the villa, a new building was erected, just north of the existing church. Theodosius II, the Great, was a contemporary of Cystennin and was supposed to have founded it, but it was more likely to have been named in his honour by a Romano-British principal. Garmon then supposedly restored the foundation in 447, when he appointed Illtud as its principal and Bleiddian as its chief bishop. However, this is far too early for Illtud, who fought with Hywel for Arthur. Bleiddian was earlier, and accompanied Garmon on his first visit to Wales. The Book of Llandaf states that Illtud received the first principalship of the college that bore his name from Dyfrig. It would appear that Illtud was included in the Garmon story by mistake, and that Garmon re-consecrated the building as Cor Worgan, if he had any connection at all with it.

* It may be that, as well as the monastery (re-founded later by St Illtud) the Irish destroyed the fabulous fifteen-room Roman villa at Caer Mead, a mile from Llanilltud. After Macsen Wledig left with the legions in 383, this was taken over by the local Romano-British leader, and there is evidence of 41 Christian burials on the site in the Age of the Saints. It is thought that the kings of Glamorgan and Gwent, from Tewdrig through his son Meurig to his son Arthmael or Arthrwys,

may have used it as their palace. Arthmael, the Arthur of legend, has always been associated with being born at nearby Boverton, which claims to the Caput Bovium of the Romans (Cowbridge being Bovium). The Caer Mead site covers two acres, and one room (the court?) was a massive 60 by 50 feet. There are superb mosaics there, and coins, pottery and glass were discovered. Excavated in 1888, it has since been covered over and ignored, when it could hold the key to the legend of Arthur. A gold torc was found early in the 19th century, but sold for £100 and melted down. CADW should excavate this priceless site, at present merely humps in the ground, but is severely financially constrained.

PELAGIUS (MORGAN) c.345-c.418

THE TRUE CHRISTIAN 'HERETIC' WHO ALMOST DESTROYED THE ROMAN CHURCH

Morgan ('from the sea') was traditionally born in Bangor-is-Coed, the site of the famous early monastery, and was a lay monk there. In Montgomeryshire, however, he was said to be a native of Llanrhaeadr, who first preached his 'heretical' ideas in the churchyard at Castell Caereinion. St Augustine, Prosper, Gennadius, Orosius and Mercador wrote that he was a Briton. A respected religious teacher in Rome in the 380's, he was forced to escape from the oncoming barbarians, who eventually sacked Rome in 410. He was now living in Carthage, but the church leaders combined to get his ideas dismissed as heretical. Leaving another

possible Briton, his friend Caelestius (Celestine) at Carthage, he went to Palestine, and was there supported by Bishop John of Jerusalem.

Pelagius had a vision of Christianity far closer to the principles of humanitarian morals and ethics than the evolving Roman church of his times. In the early fifth century this Celtic monk denied the concept of 'original sin', the teaching that Adam's sin corrupted all of his descendants. This was a practical denial of the need for the established church to grant grace and salvation to mankind. He believed that men could by themselves, and their own Christian works, be taken to heaven. Pope Innocent I and Zosimus therefore condemned him, but his teachings affected European history down to Luther, Calvin and the Cathars. Pelagius preached that giving money to the Church for salvation was not the way to heaven. Following an 'infallible' leader like the Pope was not the way to Heaven.

7

Following the example of Christ was the only way for Pelagius. He taught that salvation mainly lies with the person, who by acts of will and self-control could make himself or herself better, more acceptable to God and mankind in general.

Jerome initially accepted the doctrine, and in the 4th century John of Cassian accepted it in his thirteenth conference. The Roman church later expunged this manuscript from John's writings. The supremacy of the human will over the grace of God, as decided by the power of the church, could simply not be accepted by Rome. As Augustine stated in his *Sermons*, *'Roma locutus est; causa finita est'* – 'Rome has spoken; the case is finished.'

Pelagius had followed Origen's doctrine of 'free will', and in 401 settled in Rome lecturing upon mankind's natural dignity and the absurdity of 'original sin' as preached by Augustine. Thus to Pelagius, priests who could absolve sins were unnecessary, as a true believer could reach Heaven by his acts alone. 'Everything good and everything evil, for which we are either praised or blamed, is not born with us, but done by us', he wrote.

When Alaric and his Visigoths invaded Italy, Pelagius escaped to North Africa, where he met with Augustine. Augustine later condemned Celestine, the most prominent follower of Pelagius, for heretical teachings. Pelagius now went to Palestine, where he found favour, but Augustine persuaded the Church of Rome to condemn him in 417, which the Council of Carthage confirmed in 418. Many Italian bishops supported Pelagius, and they were banished alongside him.

Pelagianism was formally pronounced heretical in 431, as it was obvious that Pelagianism threatened the very core of the moneymaking authority of Rome.

Basically, Pelagianism took money away from the Roman Church, and thence economic and political power. Pelagius told mankind that it was basically good, and the church was not needed for people to go to heaven. Mankind is God's masterpiece of creation, because it has the capacity to reason between what is a good and what is an evil act. If mankind freely chooses 'good', it deserves salvation. If mankind chooses 'evil', it breaks the contract that binds it to God. For these ideas, Pelagius was accused by Prosper of Aquitaine of denying the concept of Original Sin, and of claiming that man can avoid sin by the power of 'free-will without the aid of Divine Grace'.

It was therefore heresy to the church that infants who die unbaptised are not necessarily banned from heaven. The Roman church as a 'command and control' system replicated that of any army, and Pope Celestine (not the Pelagian disciple) saw the Pelagian Heresy as the greatest menace to the unity of the church in the West, with Britain as its stronghold. Prosper said that Pope Celestine called the Pelagians 'Enemies of Grace', as, of course, a state of grace could only be achieved by submitting to, and paying, the

Roman Church. Prosper also declared that Agricola, son of the Pelagian Bishop Severianus, was corrupting the churches of Britain around 429. Pope Celestine thus sent the bishops Germanus (Garmon) and Lupus (Bleiddian) to Britain and a Briton, Palladius, to Ireland to try to extirpate 'that noxious and abominable teaching that men had no need of God's grace'. The British had already threatened Rome's civil power with the cavalry of Macsen Wledig (Maximus) and Cystennin (Constantine) across Gaul, and Pelagius had to be stopped in his tracks.

The ascetic Pelagius wrote two tracts and several letters that have survived. In one he states that 'It is not much to set an example to pagans; what is much better is to set such an example that even the saints can learn from you.' His truth that all people, rich and poor, are created equal by God, never gained favour with the mainstream church, which preferred the North African theology of St Augustine. Augustine (354-430) insisted 'Salus extra ecclesiam non est' – 'There is no salvation outside the church' - a doctrine still followed by many 'Christian' sects, which thus condemns those born in countries outside the ecclesiastical authority of the Christian church.

As a result there is no Saint Morgan or Saint Pelagius, but there should be. His ideas, based on Druidic and Stoic thought, were so widespread in Britain that in 429 Germanus of Auxerre had been asked to suppress them, as mentioned above. Germanus returned in the 440's to try again to impose Rome's power, in the reign of Vortigern (Gwrtheyrn), a Pelagian Christian. This seems to have been the time of the famous 'Alleluiah' victory at Maes Armon, near Mold in Flint. Vortigern kept Britain independent until 442, but has been pilloried throughout history, partially because of the Germanic bias of academics since the Hanovers took the English throne, but mainly because the early chroniclers of the history of Britain were anti-Pelagians.

Anti-Pelagianism gave us the terrible deeds of the Inquisition, Simon de Montfort's dreadful 'crusade' against the Cathar 'perfecti' in France, and led indirectly to the strict Calvinism that almost destroyed a thousand years of Welsh society and culture.

It is instructive to note that Pelagianism would have destroyed the Roman Catholic Church by starving it of funding and power. The Roman system of confessions and the selling of indulgences and pardons produced a steady income stream and lands from those in power. Thus Norman barons could steal Welsh land, blind and torture children and women, but be forgiven by God, and go to Heaven in exchange for money and endowments of land. Much of church land was taken by bloody means in Wales, via Normans and Angevins, from its original owners. The author is not a theologist, but it seems that Pelagius is nearer to Christ's teachings than the established church, and his acceptance would have led to a far more peaceful 1500 years of history.

The following extracts are taken from 'The Catholic Encyclopaedia' of 1913, and are added without comment. 'As all his ideas were chiefly rooted in the old, pagan philosophy, especially in the popular system of the Stoics, rather than in Christianity, he regarded the moral strength of man's will, when steeled by asceticism, as sufficient in itself to desire and to attain the loftiest ideal of virtue. The value of Christ's redemption was, in his opinion, limited mainly to instruction and example, which the Saviour threw into the balance as a counterweight against Satan's wicked example, so that the nature retains the ability to conquer sin and to gain eternal life even without the aid of grace. By justification we are indeed cleansed of our personal sins through faith alone but this pardon implies no interior renovation of sanctification of the soul. How far the sola-fides doctrine "had no stouter champion before Luther than Pelagius" and whether, in particular, the Protestant conception of fiducial faith dawned upon him many centuries before Luther probably needs more careful investigation... To explain psychologically Pelagius's whole line of thought, it does not suffice to go back to the ideal of the wise man, which he fashioned after the ethical principles of the Stoics and upon which his vision was centred. We must also take into account that his intimacy with the Greeks developed in him, though unknown to himself, a one-sidedness, which at first sight appears pardonable. The gravest error into which he and the rest of the Pelagians fell, was that they did not submit to the doctrinal decisions of the Church.'

The article goes on to comment on the 'last traces of Pelagianism' which held on in Celtic Britain: 'After the Council of Ephesus (431), Pelagianism no more disturbed the Greek Church, so that the Greek historians of the 5th century do not even mention the controversy or the names of the heresiarchs. But the heresy continued to smoulder in the West and died out very slowly. The main centres were Gaul and Britain. About Gaul we are told that a synod, held probably at Troyes in 429, was compelled to take steps against the Pelagians. It also sent Bishops Germanus of Auxerre and Lupus of Troyes to Britain to fight the rampant heresy, which received powerful support from two pupils of Pelagius, Agricola and Fastidius. Almost a century later, Wales was the centre of Pelagian intrigues. For the saintly Archbishop David of Menevia participated in 519 in the Synod of Brefy, which directed its attacks against the Pelagians residing there, and after he was made Primate of Cambria, he himself convened a synod against them. In Ireland also Pelagius's "Commentary of St Paul" was in use long afterwards, as is proved by many Irish quotations from it.' The Synod of Brefi was in 545, not 519, which makes Wales the last stronghold of Pelagianism.

ST PATRICK c.389-461

PADRIG, 'THE MOST FAMOUS WELSHMAN IN THE WORLD'*, THE APOSTLE OF IRELAND

Born in Bannaviem Tabarniae**, Bannventa, possibly modern Banwen near Neath, (near the village of 'Enon') he was the grandson of a priest named Potitus, and the son of a deacon and decurio (town councillor) called Calpurnius. Padrig was captured as a 16-year-old by Irish pirates organised by Niall of the Nine Hostages, High King of Ireland who died around 450 CE. Patrick was treated as a slave by a Pict in Antrim for six years. He escaped or was freed, returned to Wales, received training as a priest, and returned to Ireland around 430-433. From his Armagh base, he wrote the first literature identified with the early British church, followed the simple Welsh monastic life and attempted to abolish paganism and sun worship. His Feast Date is 17 March.

Another version of the story is that Saint Patrick was born in Carmarthen or Pembrokeshire in 389, and was carried off by Irish raiders in 406, becoming Bishop of Armagh in 432, and consecrated by St Garmon at Auxerre. Recent evidence may point to his birth in Banwen. In St. Patrick's

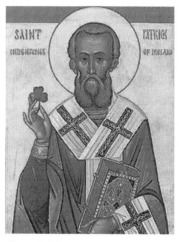

Confessio he states he was born at Banaven Taberiar, a smallholding near a Roman fort, which could be Tafarn-y-Banwen, a farm near an old Roman stronghold. This is also on the strategically important Sarn Helen, once a major Roman road through Wales. Local tradition says that Patrick came from Banwen, and there are nearby place names such as *Hafod Gwyddelig* (Irish Summerhouse) and a *Nant Gwyddelig* (Irish Stream). George Brinley Evans also points to the nearby Hirfynydd Stone, the extremely rare early Christian carving of a man in prayer, surrounded by Irish symbolic patterns. (Note that *Gwyddelig*, the Welsh for Irish, is similar to 'Goidelic'. The Welsh were the Brythonic Celts, and the Irish were the Goidelic Celts). Cressy states that Patrick was born in 'Glyn Rosina', the valley of St David, in 361, and died at Glastonbury in 472, aged 111. However many Glastonbury legends were fictions to attract pilgrims and income.

Rhigyfarch tells us that St David's father Sant was told by an angel to save some land for David, 30 years before his birth, where St Patrick was going to settle at Glyn Rhosyn (*Valis Rosina*, the Vale of Roses). Near the sea in Pembroke, near the main Pembroke-Ireland crossing, yet out of the site of pirates, this is where St David's Cathedral stands today. The angel also told Patrick to leave the area as there was a saint to be born there. Patrick was angered that God should prefer an unborn child. However, God took Patrick to the cliff-top, to the rock seat still known *as Eisteddfa Padrig* (Patrick's Seat), to show him that God wished him to look after the whole of Ireland instead.

Iolo Morgannwg names Padrig as the son of Maewan, Principal of the monastery at Bangor Illtud (Llanilltud Fawr, Llantwit Major), who was carried away by Irish pirates. Broadway, near Cowbridge, has also been linked with Patrick in legend, where he was supposed to have been born at Pedr Onen (Peter's Ash). Writing in the early 19th century, Marie Trevelyan believed that Patrick was known as Maenwyn (Holy Rock), and educated at Caerworgan (later Llanilltud Fawr, near the great Romano-British villa of Caermead). It was here that the honorary Latin name of Patricius was given to him. She wrote of an ancient folk lament, which was only remembered by two people who lived miles apart, and which was sung at 'Mal Santau' (sic). Here she means 'Mabsantau', saints' feast day festivals. The song used to be familiar in Penmark, St Tathan and Llanilltud Fawr, and commemorated a boy called Maenwyn who was born at Nant-y-Tirion, Treberfaydd ('shining place', the old Caput Bovium of the Romans, present-day Boverton). The boy was caught in a nearby bog when the Goidelic Irish burned the monastery of Caerworgan. Some people also believe that Arthur was also born at Boverton.

In Evans' *History of Glamorgan* we read '...other writers doubt the existence of Eurgain, but all agree that a college was founded by the Roman General Theodosius (called by the Welsh, Tewdws) some time between the years 368 and 395 AD. The principal and chief teacher of this college (Llanilltud) now called Cor Tewdws, was one Balerius, a learned Roman Christian. He was succeeded by Patrick, a native of Glamorgan, and a former student of the college. The college prospered exceedingly until it was attacked, despoiled, and destroyed by some Irish pirates, who, when they retired, carried Patrick with them a prisoner. Patrick continued his good work in Ireland, preaching the Gospel boldly, and he is still loved by the Irish as their patron saint.'

Under the sandy shoreline of Whitesands Bay lies the sixth century St Patrick's Chapel, which itself lies upon an older burial ground. A rectangular mound now stands in the field called Parc-y-Capel near the shore. Excavated in 1924, it is a single cell chapel with human remains below the west wall. Welsh churches were lime-washed, and Mrs Dawson mentions Tŷ Gwyn (White House) in *Archaeologia Cambrensis* in 1888: 'Tŷ Gwyn is situated above Porth Mawr, and about two miles from St David's. It stands on the south slopes of Carn Lidi, the purple rocks above it springing out of the heath, with here and there a gorse bush, like a puff of flame breaking out of the crannies of the rock. Below it, near the sea, are the foundations of St Patrick's Chapel, in the site of his embarkation. The foundations of the church of Tŷ Gwyn, the cradle of Christianity among the Southern Irish, are trodden underfoot by sheep and oxen, that wander over the wide cemetery where lie thick, in narrow coffins of unshaped stones, the bodies of the first inmates of that earliest Mission College in Britain. When we visited the spot in 1898, the farmer had torn up the grave slabs of the tombs in the cattle-yard, and the drainage of his cow stalls and pig stys [sic] soaked into the places where the bodies of the ancient fathers of the British and Irish churches had crumbled to dust.'

Candida Casa, at Whithorn in Wigtownshire, part of British Strathclyde (Ystrad Clud) followed the pattern set by Tŷ Gwyn. When books are written about the Irish saving Christianity in the Western world and not mention the fact that without Wales, Ireland would have remained pagan like England and Scotland, it is time to rethink how Wales can publicise its contribution to civilisation. There is a nearby rock at Whitesands Bay called Carn Patrick. There was also a Paterchurch, or Patrickchurch, in Monkton, Pembrokeshire. One of the gates to St David's Cathedral is still known as Porth Padrig. Cefn Padrig is a ridge of coastline between Burry Port and Llanelli.

Llanbadrig in Anglesey has probably been claimed for another Padrig, but it is recorded that the Cistercian monks of Aberconwy Abbey (destroyed by Edward I from 1283 onwards) dedicated the ancient church to St Patrick of Ireland in 1250. Llywelyn ap Gruffudd, the last Prince of Wales, had given the land to his church.

There was an old 'serpent stone' there, a carving of coiled snakes, below the base of a niche which contained a statue of the saint. Patrick was said to have driven the snakes out of Ireland, but the stone vanished in the 19th century. In the late 19th century the building was restored, and an early 'ichthus stone' of blue granite was found in the churchyard. This is not found in Anglesey and denotes a place of worship from the Age of Saints. It is today placed in the west wall with its carving exposed. A rough path from the churchyard to a cave has always been known as *Traed Padrig Sant*, 'The Footprints of St Patrick'. This cave stands in a rocky cleft underneath the church, which itself is on a headland, and at the back of the cave is a spring with fresh water. Local tradition is that Padrig was travelling between Wales and Ireland and was shipwrecked here. In gratitude for his deliverance he built the church, as it had the required local water source.

Pawl Hen traditionally founded the great monastery at Whitland in Carmarthen, variously known as Alba, Rosnat or Tŷ Gwyn (being whitewashed), but some say that Padrig founded it before he went to Ireland. Perhaps Pawl Hen founded the famous school there in Patrick's monastery, which would explain the large numbers of Irish monks said to have studied there.

Some of the other Welsh saints associated with Patrick are noted in the author's *The Book of Welsh Saints*. St Brioc was said to be a disciple of Garmon, along with Illtud and Patrick, and was a founder-saint of Brittany. St Carannog's *Vita* recounts in its 3rd lesson that the saint disguised himself as a beggar and followed Patrick to Ireland to evangelise, rather than take up his father's kingship and fight the invading pagan Irish. Sain Patrick, from the Gower Peninsula, was closely associated with Patrick and died in 493. St Seny, or Senanus, was Patrick's brother, founded Llansannan in Denbigh, Bedwellty and Llantrisant, and named his son Patrick. St Mel (d.488) was a Welsh follower of Patrick, and became Bishop of Ardagh after evangelising the area. Mechu and Muinis also left Wales with Mel to assist Patrick in his mission. All these three Welsh saints have been given Irish genealogies, just in the last two hundred years.

St Mel was possibly the son of Patrick's sister, Darerca. Patrick's British sisters, Lupida and Darerca were said to be captured with him. Darerca's son Rioch also assisted Patrick and was consecrated as a bishop. Her other sons included Secundinus (Sechnallus), Menni and Auxilius, all of whom went to Ireland. Most of these British saints are now regarded as Irish, and Darerca's life has been distorted to make her a virgin, closely associated with Patrick and Bridget. Ieuan Gwas Padrig was a saint and disciple of Patrick who founded the church at Cerrig y Druidion, and has several holy wells. Abbot Ffinian studied at Llancarfan under Cadoc, where he had a chapel, and became Ireland's leading religious leader after Patrick's death, laying out the organisation of the Irish church on the pattern of Llancarfan. Ffinian himself instructed the saints Columbus, Ciaran and Brendan.

Wherever Padrig was born, he himself claimed to have evangelised the Irish, and he visited Rome in 442 and later. According to the *Annals of Ulster*, he organised the church and founded the cathedral Church of Armagh in 444, which became the administrative centre of Christianity in Ireland. Between 412 and 415 he studied at Lerins, in France, and may have studied under St Garmon at Auxerre before he returned to Ireland in 431. St Patrice on the Loire is named after him, and local people believe him to be the nephew of Martin of Tours. Unlike St David, Patrick has never been officially canonised by the Catholic Church. In the Vatican Library, *Bibliotecha Sanctorum Vol. 10* notes that his cult started locally.

*For this quote I am indebted to Barry Tobin, a fluent Gaelic and Welsh-speaker, who has done much to pull Irish and Welsh culture together, as has Myles Pepper, the leader of the West Wales Arts Connection, based at Fishguard (Abergwaun).

**Some sources place Padrig as a Romano-Briton from Strathclyde. His *Confessio* begins: 'I am Patrick, a sinner, most unlearned, the least of all the faithful, and utterly despised by many. My father was Calpornius, a deacon, son of Potitus, a priest, of the village Bannaven Taburniae; he had a country seat nearby, and there I was taken captive.' His *Epistola* is a message to a prince named Coroticus, in Ceredigion or Pembroke, who was trying to force Irish immigrants out of his Welsh lands.

Footnotes:
1. The Breton writer Albert le Grand places Beneventum as Venta, modern Caerwent, where St Tathan taught St Cadog, and from where Dyfrig (Dubricius, q.v.) oversaw the Welsh church. Professor Bury, in his *Muirchu's Life of St Patrick* also believes the walled Roman town of Caerwent to be Bannaventum, the earliest major centre of Christian learning in Britain. The Breton Cressy noted a saint from the nearby Roman fort and camp of Caerleon, St Baccharius, who died in 460 - 'By Nation a Brittain (i.e. Welsh) and Disciple of St Patrick; he adicted himself to the study of literature at Caer-leon.' Another place associated with Bannaventum is Llansannor or the River Thaw near Llancarfan.

2. British history was rewritten in the 19th century to date from the Germanic invasions of the Saxons and Jutes. Before that were the 'Dark Ages' before Germanic civilisation came to the Isle of Britain. It is interesting that in British (not English) history, this period has always been known as 'The Age of the Saints'. (For those who wish to know why the history of Britain was rewritten, and how, please consult *The A-Z of Wales and the Welsh* by this author. In 1903, Baring-Gould and Fisher eloquently expressed what these forgotten people gave to the heritage of Britain:

'For centuries, partly due to the sneer of Bede, and partly to the proud contempt with which the Latin Church regarded all missionary work that did not proceed from its own initiative, the English Church has looked to Augustine of Canterbury as the one main source from whom Christianity in our island sprang, and Rome as the mother who sent him to bring our ancestors to Christ. That he did a good and great work is not to be denied; he was the Apostle of Kent, where the Britons had all been massacred or from whence they had been driven. But Kent is only a corner of the island. And it was forgotten how much was wrought by the Celtic Church, even for the Teutonic invaders, far more than was achieved by Augustine.

It was the Church in Wales which sent a stream of missionaries to Ireland to complete its conversion, begun by Patrick... It was from Ireland that Columcille went to Iona to become evangelist to the Picts. From Llanelwy [St Asaph] went forth Kentigern with 665 monks and clerics to restore Christianity in Cumbria, which extended from the Clyde to the Dee. It was from Iona that the missioners proceeded who converted all Northumbria, Mercia, and the East Saxons and Angles. Honour to whom honour is due, and the debt of obligation to the Celtic saints in the British Isles has been ignored or set aside hitherto.

But they did more. To them was due the conversion of Armorica. Evidence shows that nothing, or next to nothing, was done for the original inhabitants of that peninsula by the stately prelates of the Gallo-Roman Church. They ministered to the city populations of Nantes and Rennes and Vannes, and did almost nothing for the scattered natives of the province. They were left to

15

live in their heathenism and die without the light, till the influx of British colonists changed the whole aspect, and brought the people of the land into the fold of Christ.'

The Irish connection, with the Welshman Patrick and contributions from the way of Christianity in Wales, has never been truly assessed. The Irish, with their flair for publicity, can publish short books like Thomas Cahill's *HOW THE IRISH SAVED CIVILIZATION: the Untold Story of Ireland's Heroic Role from the Fall of Rome to the Rise of Medieval Europe* (Sceptre 1995 paperback) – a Welsh book could have been written with the same title and much more validity. (The book's title capitals are reproduced exactly). It totally ignores the fact that the Irish church was basically a Welsh construct upon a formerly heathen population. The church in Wales lasted from the earliest days of Christianity in the Western world through to the present day. In all other European countries the Christian church was extinguished at some time, including Ireland except for a few hermits clinging to rocks in the Atlantic. The survival of Christianity in Wales is as amazing as the survival of its language over this period, with such close proximity to England. In Ireland and Scotland, the language has all but died, despite their relatively greater distance from the power of the government of the southeast of England.

SAINT DYFRIG c. 465 - c.546

BISHOP DUBRICIUS, 'DUBRIC THE HIGH SAINT, CHIEF OF THE CHURCH IN BRITAIN'

In the *Life of Dyfrig (Vita Dubricii)*, his unmarried mother was Eurddil or Eurduila, daughter of King Peibio of Ergyng (Archenfield district in Herefordshire). He may have been born in Madley on the Wye near Hereford, which was Welsh-speaking until the eighteenth century. Other sources say that he was born at Mochros on the Wye in the same county, or on the banks of the Gwaun near Fishguard (Abergwaun) in Pembroke. He was possibly a grandson of Brychan. King Peibio was known as 'King Dribbler', and when he discovered that Eurddil was pregnant, he threw her into the river in a sack. Three times the current threw her back on the shore. He then decided to burn her, but she was found next morning unharmed, cuddling the infant Dyfrig. His Feast Dates are November 4 and 14, and translation May 29.

Dyfrig by William Burgess, Cardiff Castle

16

Dyfrig's own estate was called Ynys Eurddil, or Ynys Ebrdil (also Miserbdil) which was probably Mochros. Most sources say that his first foundation was at Archenfield, southern and west Herefordshire, (based on the Roman city of Ariconium, now Weston-under-Penyard). Archenfield was part of the Welsh kingdom of Ergyng which spread across into Monmouthshire. Another version is that he wandered along the Wye looking for the best place to live and preach, and saw a wild white sow with piglets in a meander of the river. He called the site Moch-rhos, or Mochros (Moor of the Pigs), modern-day Moccas.

Associated with teaching St Illtud and St Samson, Dyfrig was extremely important in southeast Wales and Herefordshire, and it appears that David succeeded him as primate of Wales. Dyfrig had religious centres at Hentland, Whitchurch, Madley, Moccas and Caldey Island. His chief church was centred at Hentland, just outside Ross-on-Wye, and the village itself rests on a Roman site. At a farm called Llanfrother there, were found traces of an ancient establishment. In Archenfield the church at Whitchurch, and chapels at

St David's, Llanddewi Brefi

Ballingham and Hentland are dedicated to him. It seems fairly certain that he and his disciples moved west after the battle of Dyrham, when Gloucester, Bath and probably Caerwent were destroyed. Their monasteries in Ergyng and Ewyas were wasted, and they sought refuge at Llandaff with Teilo, and at Llanilltud Fawr and Llancarfan.

In the 7th century *Life of Samson* Dyfrig is a famed churchman much older than St Samson and a little older than St Illtud. Many of the details of the Welsh saints come from such Breton *Lives*, as Welsh records were destroyed during the four-hundred year fight against Anglo-French domination. Destruction of land titles and deeds, usually recorded on church manuscripts, allowed Norman and Angevin lords to take over Welsh territories legally. Known as 'papa' Dubricius, Dyfrig was said to have ordained Samson as a deacon at Llanilltud Fawr. Some sources say that Dyfrig was taught by Germanus of Auxerre but Dyfrig was a century too late, so this may mean he was a follower of Garmon's teaching. Certainly, he seemed to have been a strong opponent of Pelagianism and persuaded his friend David to preach against it at the Llanddewi Brefi synod. It was said that he resigned his see at this meeting to pass it on to David. Samson's *Life* claims that Dyfrig was an abbot at Enlli (Bardsey Island), and Geoffrey of Monmouth claimed that Dyfrig crowned the 15-year old Arthur at Silchester.

Geoffrey of Monmouth states that there were 200 philosophers in Dyfrig's college at Caerleon, studying science and astronomy. Other later medieval records place him as bishop of Caerleon from 490 on, succeeding Tremorinus, becoming the founder of Llandaf and again as the saint who crowned Arthur. On Caldey Island was found a stone inscribed 'Magl Dubr', tonsured servant of Dubricius, where it seems Dyfrig was for some time the abbot. There are also dedications to him at Gwenddwr, south of Builth in Breconshire and at Porlock in Somerset. Porlock was formerly 'ecclesia Saint Dubricius' in a deed of 1476. Hereford's Saint Devereux is a corruption of Dubricius. There are still churches clustered in Archenfield dedicated to Dyfrig including Ballingham on the Wye; Hentland (Hen-Llan, also on the Wye); Hamnish and Whitchurch in Hereford. However, the Welsh name for Whitchurch, Llandywynnog, indicates that the relevant saint may have originally been Gwynnog. He is also remembered at Porlock in Somerset; Gwenddwr (Erwyd, on the Wye) in Breconshire; and Llanvaches in Newport. However, Llanfaches (Llanfaches) was originally dedicated to St Maches, the sister of St Cadoc.

Old and ailing, Dyfrig retired to die at Ynys Enlli (Bardsey, 'the Isle of 20,000 Saints'), but a Norman bishop of Llandaff had his bones translated to Llandaff in 1120 for the greater honour of his cathedral, where Dyfrig was one of the four titular saints. The relics reached the Llyn peninsula mainland on May 7 and arrived at Llandaf on 23 May, where his reliquaries (his head and one arm encased in silver) drew pilgrims until the Reformation. They were removed in 1538 and lost. Tennyson called him 'Dubric the high saint, Chief of the church in Britain'.

Dyfrig's most famous holy well is near the ancient monastery site of Garnllwyd at Llancarfan, where Cadog was presiding at this time. Ffynnon Dyfrig can still be found in the woods known as Coed Ffynnon Dyfrig, and nearby at Llanfeithyn he had another healing well. These survivals certainly seem to authenticate his stay, possibly with Teilo, at Llancarfan. There is a case to be made that Dyfrig founded the colleges of Llancarfan, Caerworgan (Llanilltud Fawr) and Caerleon, and that he should have been made the patron saint of Wales for the effects that these monasteries had upon Celtic Christianity. His effigy lies in Llandaff Cathedral.

SAINT ILLTUD fl.530

ABBOT ILLTUD, ILLTYD FARCHOG, ELTUT, ILDUT, HILDUTUS, ILLTUD THE WARRIOR

Illtud was said to have attended Arthur's court and was known as a knight and warrior with Cadog, before he became a saint. One source states that he trained at the monastery of Cassian near Marseilles, and was ordained by

Germanus of Auxerre. The son of Bicanus ab Emyr Llydaw, and thus of Breton origin, he built a church and later a monastery under the protection of Meirchion (Meurig) prince of Glamorgan (and Arthur's father). Illtud's wife was Trinihid, and was associated with Llanrhidian in Gower and Llantrithyd near Illtud's great monastery. Llanrhidian Church has 'The Leper Stone', a Celtic slab found embedded in the doorway in the 19th century. Illtud's name Eltut, according to a Norman source, symbolised 'Ille ab omne crimine tutus' – 'the one safe from all evil'. Illtud's Feast Dates are 6 and 7 November, and also 7 February according to Cressy.

In the *Vita* of Cadog, it is stated that Illtud became a monk when fifty soldiers under his command were swallowed up into the earth. As these were probably cavalry, this may have occurred in the swamps and marshes

around Llancarfan at the time. No less than seven named streams flow into Llancarfan and the ford is often flooded there. Llanilltud Fawr is on the site of a monastery founded (or refounded) in the late 5th or early 6th century by Illtud, and is mentioned in the 7th century *Life of Samson*. Illtud was venerated as the founder-abbot and teacher of the divinity school known as Cor Tewdws, at

St. Illtyd's Church, Llantwit Major

Llanilltud Fawr (Llantwit Major) but it may well have existed long before this time. He would have founded the monastery and college in the 6th century, and the school is believed to be Britain's earliest centre of learning. At its height, it was said to have over 1000 pupils and schooled many of the great saints of the age.

Samson was taken by his parents Bicanus and Rieingulid to Illtud's famous monastery, where 'magister Eltut' was described as: 'of all the Britons the most accomplished in his knowledge of all the scriptures, both the Old Testament and the New testament and in every branch of philosophy, poetry and rhetoric, grammar and arithmetic: and he was most sagacious and gifted with the power of foretelling future events.'

Illtud's father was a military nobleman and his mother the daughter of Anblaud, Amlawdd Wledig, king of Britain. His aunt was said to be Igerna, Arthur's mother. After serving as one of Arthur's knights, Illtud then served Paul of Penychen, king of Glamorgan and son of Glywys. Thankful for his deliverance from being swallowed up in the earth, he went to St Cadog, and left his wife. Illtud had been admonished by an angel to send his wife away into the night, and refused to ever communicate with her again. She may have founded the church at nearby Llantrithyd. Leaving Paul's residence at Penllyn or Pentre Meurig, he slept on the banks of the Naduan (-

the Dawen, or Thaw), then became a monk on the banks of the next river west, the Hodnant at Llanilltud Fawr. Named by some as the original Sir Galahad, one of the 'Sayings of the Wise' triads refers to him:

'Hast thou heard the saying of Illtud,
The studious, golden-chained knight:
Whoso doeth evil, evil betide him.'

An important saint, operating mainly in the southeast of Wales, his brother was possibly Sadwrn. His *Life*, written in 1140, is not as important as the references in *The Life of Samson* written around 650. He may have founded the monastery at Caldey Island, Ynys Pyr, which was formerly called Llan Illtud. His 'bangu' (holy bell) was recovered from King Edgar's army, and his name was called on to protect the people of North Wales from Marcher Lords in the late 11th century.

In 1080 Llanilltud's tithes and advowson were seized by Robert Fitzhamon and conferred onto the new Norman abbey of Tewkesbury, and this was confirmed by 1106 and 1180 charters. The church is unique in Wales, and was once extremely large. John Wesley noted after teaching there on 25th July 1777, 'About eleven I read prayers and preached in Llantwit Major Church to a very numerous congregation. I have not seen so large or handsome a church since I left England. It was sixty yards long but one end of it is now in ruins. I suppose it has been abundantly the most beautiful as well as the most spacious church in Wales.' Several wall paintings survive in the church, as well as the great 6th century memorial stones.

The church at Llanhamlach in Breconshire is dedicated to St Iltud and St Peter. There is also Capel Illtud (also called Llaniltud) on the Roman road between Brecon and Neath in Defynnog parish. Near Cadoxton-juxta-Neath is Llantwit-juxta-Neath (Llanilltud Nedd), and Ilston in Gower was formerly called Llanilltud Gwŷr, shortened to Eltut's Town by Flemish-Norman settlers and hence Ilston. He is also the patron of Oxwich on the Gower, and his holy well is at Llanrhidian on the peninsula. He is the patron of Penbre in Carmarthen. There is a Llanelltud near Dolgellau, and he had a cult in Brittany. Llanelltud in Merionethshire may have started with a cell of one of Illtud's disciples. Llantrisant Church in Glamorgan is dedicated to Illtud, Gwynno and Tyfodwg.

According to Ecton, Llanhari, Llantrithyd, Llantwit Fardre, and Lantwit under Neath were his foundations in Glamorgan, plus Llanhiledd in Monmouth (with nearby Mynydd Llanhilleth) and Lantwood or Llantwyd in Pembroke. Capel Illtyd under Dyfynog in Brecon and Llanelltyd under Llanfachraith in Merioneth were also his. The holy well of Ffynnon Illtud remains near the ruined cairn called Tŷ Illtyd at Llanhamlach. Another

Ffynon Illtud can be seen at Llanwonno in Glamorgan, and St Illtyd's Well at Llanrhidian, Gower, was said to have spouted milk in 1185.

Many churches and chapels in Brittany commemorate Illtud, such as Lanildut, Loc-Ildut and St Ideuc. 'Même les volailles ont leur saint: saint Ildut' (- even poulty have their saint, St Ildut, source *Bretagne, Le Culte des Saints.*) Illtud was thus the patron saint prayed to, for success with poultry. Coadout church south of Guincamp, in Treguier diocese has a statue of Ildut. A local tradition is that he used to meet and pray with Briog at a ruined dolmen near there. A song to Ildut is still sung at his pardon there. Landebaeron is dedicated to St Maudez, but also has a stature of Illtud and a silver reliquary with his skull. Doble notes several other dedications such as Ploerdut's chapel of St 'Iltut'. Aber-Ildut is northwest of Renan.

Some sources state that he taught David, as well as Samson, Maelgwn, Gildas and Pol Aurelian at Llanilltud Fawr and he was said to be buried at Bedd Gwyl Illtyd in Brecon. Bedd Gwyl Illtyd means the grave of St Illtyd's Eve. The 'bedd' lies near Llanilltyd Church and Mynydd Illtyd. It was the custom to keep watch there on the night before his feast day. At Llanilltud Fawr, there is a torchlight carnival procession featuring dragons every Bonfire night, the eve of Illtud's day, which by happy coincidence keeps the custom of his celebration alive. The Celtic carved stones in Llanilltud Church are not properly displayed, but are among the most important in the British Isles. One cross reads: 'SAMSON POSUIT HANC CRUCEM PRO ANIMA EIUS ILITET SAMSON REGIS SAMUEL ERISAR – Samson placed his Cross here for his soul, for the soul of Illtud, Samson, Rhain, Sawyl and Ebisar.'

Illtud was noted in history as having invented a special plough. The fields all around his monastery are full of limestone rock and therefore difficult to till. Before his time it was customary in Wales to cultivate fields by using a mattock and an over-treading plough (*aradr arsang*), implements used by the Irish on similar soils for centuries after. Wrmonoc's Breton *Vita of Pol Aurelian* describes in fabulous terms how Illtud regained lands from the seas to assist his cultivation, and some of the Hodnant valley and at nearby Aberddawen/Llanfabon (Aberthaw/Gileston) was reclaimed at a very early date by earthen banks acting as sea walls.

Illtud's cave on the banks of the Ewenni River can still be seen, where he slept at night. There was also supposed to have been a retreat at Llanhamlach, three miles east of Brecon, recorded by Giraldus Cambrensis, where Illtud's 'mare that used to carry his provisions was covered by a stag, and produced an animal of wonderful speed, resembling a horse before and a stag behind.' It is believed by some that he was born near Brecon. Arthurian legends place Illtud as one of the guardians of the Grail, and as Arthur's cousin. Nennius in his 8th century *Marvels of Britain* recorded that when Illtud was praying in his cave near the sea he saw the body of 'the once and future king' Arthur, whom Illtud had to bury in a secret place. This story is related to his chapel at Oxwich on the Gower peninsula. Illtud 'was praying in a cave near the sea and a boat came in bearing two men and the body of a holy man, an altar floating above his face. When Illtud went to meet them, they took out of the ship the body of the holy man, the altar still stood suspended and never moved from its position. Then the men in the boat said to Illtud "This man of God charged us to bring him to thee and to bury him with thee, and that thou should not reveal his name to anyone lest men swear by him"'. Arthur did not want anyone to swear vows at his tomb – a precursor of the 'lost' Prince of Wales, Owain Glyndŵr, eight centuries later.

It is a little-known fact that Llanilltud Fawr was earmarked for the site of the first University of Wales. However, a hotel-building project in Aberystwyth ran into difficulties, and a huge new building was suddenly made available at the right price. The site of Llanilltud monastery and church is near the first century Côr Eurgain (Caer Worgorn), succeeded by the Côr of Tewdws (Theodosius), where foundations can still be seen on the field marked Côr Tewdws in 19th century maps. The Life of Pol de Leon says that Illtud had also a monastery on Ynys Pyr, which to this author appears to more likely to be the nearer Barri (Ynys Peirio), rather than Caldey Island. A monastery site was marked upon maps of Barri until the railway station was built there, when the island was rejoined to the mainland in the docks construction.

Maen Illtud at Llanhamlach is also known as Ty Illtyd, a dolmen thought to be Illtud's hermitage. There are over 60 inscribed crosses inside the burial chamber, possibly made by a recluse. A standing stone at Illtud's Llanhamlach stands opposite Peterstone Court. There are several holy wells dedicated to Illtud. Francis Jones could not locate two in Glamorgan, but another four were noted, including those at Michaelstone, Llansamlet and Llanwynno.

ARTHUR - ARTHMAEL AP MEURIG AP TEWDRIG d. 539 after Camlan, 547* or later in 570

ARTHWYS, ATHRWYS, ARTHUS, ADRAS, ARMEL? ARZEL? - EUROPE'S GREATEST LEGEND

This is possibly the longest entry in the book, and by far the most complicated. The following entry upon Arthmael/Armel is, I believe, the same person. Time and money have never permitted me to finish my Breton researches into the links between Arthur and Arthmael. John Morris, in his magisterial *The Age of Arthur* footnotes that Arthmael was the most important of all the Welsh emigrants to Brittany in the 6th century, but 'little is known of him'. The Bretons know Armel as a warrior-prince from

Glamorgan, and his appearance there coincides with the disappearance of Arthur from Wales.

The time of Arthur is the most debated area of British history, 'The Age of Saints' in Wales, yet 'The Dark Ages' across the rest of Europe. Too much has been written upon Arthur, this most potent of Western legends, that has been based upon mediaeval French romances. In truth, he was a 6th century Romano-Celt warlord from Glamorgan and Gwent, around whom the mythology of Guinevere, Merlin, Lancelot, The Holy Grail and the Round Table revolve. He fought back the Saxon threat from the East, and the Pictish threat from the North and West, being also engaged in internal warfare against other Britons. It appears that he was Prince Athrwys, or Arthmael - the Bear Prince (Athruis ap Meurig ap Tewdrig). His son Morgan became King of Glamorgan.

Journey to Avalon - the Final Discovery of King Arthur (by C. Barber and D. Pykitt) makes a persuasive claim that Arthur's court of Gelli-

Campe d'Artis, Britanny

weg was Llanmelin Hillfort, the ancient capital of the Silures, that overlooks Caerwent Roman town. In the Welsh Triads, Gelliwig in Cernyw was one of Arthur's three principal courts. Cernyw was once part of the coastal area of South-East Wales. Cornwall was not known as Cernyw until the 10th century, hundreds of years post-dating the *Triads*. At Coed Kernew, just west of Newport, the church was founded in the sixth century by Glywys Cernyw, a son of Gwynlliw Filwr (the Warrior). Gelliwig means small grove, and Llanmelin's previous name was Llan y Gelli (church of the grove). Llanmelin is situated in Gwent-is-Coed, Gwent below the Wood (now called Wentwood), where Arthur's uncle and chief elder Caradoc Freichfras (Sir Craddock) ruled when Arthur was campaigning. Barber and Pykitt believe that Caer Melin, as the Romans knew Llanmelin, and where the Silures defeated Scapula in 53 CE, was the site of the fabled Camelot.

Nennius, from South-East Wales, wrote about Arthur and his famous twelve battles. Arthur is also referred to in *The Gododdin*, written around the end of the sixth century, early Welsh poetry, some of the *Lives of the Saints*, and in the sixth-century *Welsh Triads of the Islands of Britain*. All of these predate the Geofrey of Monmouth and Chrétien de Troyes romances. Many of the characters in Arthurian legend previously appear in Welsh legend and literature. Merlin was identified with Myrddin in Welsh history. The Latinization of Myrddin would have been Merdinus, with faecal connotations, so Geoffrey adopted Merlinus, Merlin. Both St Illtud and

Gwalchaved have bee indentified with Sir Galahad, both Gwalchmai and St. Govan with Sir Gawain, Cei with Sir Kay, and Peredur and Bedwyr in *The Mabinogion* with Sir Percival and Sir Bedivere. Peredur, who glimpses the Holy Lance and Grail in *Peredur, Son of Erawc*, has an uncle Bran the Blessed, who is the model for 'The Fisher King'. Peredur, or Pryderi, brought about the devastation of South Wales by sitting on a Perilous Mound, but as Percival, in 'Didot Perceval' causes enchantments to fall on Britain by sitting on the Seat Perilous at King Arthur's Court. Eigyr passed into legend as Igraine, the mother of Arthur, and both Gwenhwyfar and Gwendoloena the flower maiden turn into Guinevere. The Welsh prince Medraut ap Cawrdaf became Mordred, and the Druidic goddess Morgen has been associated with Morgen le Fay. Morgen was the patroness of priestesses, who lived on Avalon, Bardsey Island, with nine sisters.

Sir Lancelot may be based on Maelgwn Gwynedd, or Llwch Llawinawg, Lord of the Lakes, and Sir Tristram with Drustanus, the son of Marcus Conomorus, a prince of Glamorgan. Sir Howel is identified with Howel (Riwal) Mawr of Ergyng, who fought Lancelot, became Dux Britannorum after Arthur's death, and was buried at Llanilltud Fawr. The fabulous Castell Dinas Bran, perched high on the rocks overlooking Llangollen, is identified with Grail Castle. Both Bran (from the *Mabinogion*) and the Fisher King had wounds that would not heal, and King Bran is associated with the castle. Bran also had a magical 'cauldron of plenty', which is identified with the Holy Grail. Another of the Thirteen Treasures of Wales, *Caledfwlch*, seems to be identical with Excalibur. *Lloegr* was the Welsh name for England, and *Logres* is the name of England in Arthurian legend. Pendragon, the title first taken by Arthur's father Uther and then by Arthur, is a combination of the Old Welsh 'dragwn', dragon/leader, and the Brythonic-Welsh 'pen', or head.

At the top of Snowdon, there was a tumulus commemorating one of Arthur's victims. Arthur sailed across Snowdonia's Llyn Llydaw on his way to Avalon, after fighting Mordred at Bwlch y Saethau ('Pass of the Arrows'). Bedevere threw Excalibur into Llyn Llydau, which seems to be a continuation of the Celtic throwing away of a dead warlord's weapons into water, which was sacred to them. Avalon seems to be Afallach, the sacred and holy isle of Bardsey off the Llŷn Peninsula. Barber and Pykitt believe that Arthur recovered from his wounds at the monastery of Bardsey, and went to Brittany, where he was known as St. Armel. Barber and Pykit also state that Arthur was born in 482 at Boverton (Trebeferad), a Roman camp site in the Vale of Glamorgan, fought his final British battle at 'Cadlan' on the Llŷn Peninsula where Mordred (Medraut) had territories, recovered from his wounds at Bardsey Island, and died in 562 at St Armel des Boschaux.

A persuasive case for the final Battle of Camlan being at Maes-y-Camlan (Camlan Field), just south of Dinas Mawddwy, has been made in a little booklet by Laurence Main. This local tradition was recorded in Welsh by a local bard in 1893. In the area are two Camlans, Bron-Camlan, Camlan-uchaf and Camlan Isaf. Across the valley from Maes Camlan are Bryn Cleifion and Dol-y-Cleifion (Hill of the Wounded and Meadow of the Wounded). The nearby ridge overlooking the Dyfi River is Cefn-Byriaeth (Mourning Ridge) where graves were discovered. Five miles east is the site where Mordred's Saxon allies are said to have camped the previous night, and the stream there is still called Nant-y-Saeson (Saxon Stream). The date was 537 in the *Welsh Annals*, but the Celtic Church may have dated this from the crucifixion of Christ, instead making it 574. Arthur ap Meurig ap Tewdrig was married to Gwenhwyfar, and his son Gwydre was killed by the Twrch Trwyth (the Irish Boar, in the *Tale of Culhwch and Olwen* in the *Mabinogion*) at Cwm Cerwyn, near Nevern. Nearby are the Stones of the Sons of Arthur (Cerrig Meibion Arthur). Arthur had supposedly returned from Brittany to defeat Mordred. Again tradition states that he survived the battle, but was grievously wounded while resting after he had won (by Eda Elyn Mawr, according to *Harleian mss 4181 entry 42*). Arthur was soon succeeded as Pendragon by Maelgwn Gwynedd, sometimes identified with Lancelot.

At Ogmore Castle was found a sixth century memorial stone recording a land grant by Arthur. It is now in the National Museum, and the Latin inscription reads 'Be it known to all that Arthmail has given this field to God to Glywys and to Netart and to Bishop Fili'. And in the church of St Illtud at Llanilltud Fawr, just a few miles away, the famous Pillar of Abbot Samson reads in Romilly's 1899 translation: 'IN NOMINE DI SUMMI INCIPIT CRUX SALVATORIS QUAE PREPARAVIT SAMSONI AP ATI PRO ANIMA SUA ET PRO ANIMA IUTHAHELO REX ET ARTMALI TEC +' – '*In the name of the Most High God was begun the cross of the Saviour, which Samson prepared for his soul and for the soul of King Juthael, and for Arthmael.*'

We must remember that Armel and Samson helped Iuthael regain his throne in Brittany, and that Arthur owned the lands of Glamorgan where Ogmore and Llanilltud Fawr lie. Why no academic wishes to formally associate Arthur with the Samson Pillar and Wales is rather odd. St Illtud is known as Illtud Farchog (Illtud the Warrior-Knight) and was supposed to have fought for Arthur and for Arthur's uncle, Pawl Penychen.

Adrian Gilbert, Alan Wilson and Baram Blackett in *The Holy Kingdom* agree with much of the Barber and Pykitt research. The author is researching the area from St. Donat's Castle (the seat of Caractacus) through Llanilltud Fawr (the centre of monastic learning), Boverton (the possible birthplace of Arthur) and Llancarfan Monastery through to Caerleon, Caerwent and Llanmelin Hill Fort. This strip of the Vale of Glamorgan, the Roman forts of Cardiff and Caerleon, and the inland Church of St. Peter super Montem, seems to hold the key to all the Arthurian legends. 'The Holy Kingdom' makes the case for 'Caer Melyn' just north of Cardiff, being

Camelot. The sulphur springs nearby colour the water yellow, so Caer Melyn means Yellow Fortress. As 'mellitus' means honey-coloured in Latin, perhaps it was corrupted to Caer Mellitus and hence to Camelot. The author's preference is for Arthur to have been based at Dinas Powys fort, with a 'palace' at the great Roman villa at Caermead outside Llanilltud Fawr, but far more research will be undertaken on this topic. Cae or Caer Mead is an odd construction. Mead is a honey drink, and again Caer Mellitus could easily become Camelot. It seems also to have been named Campus Elleti, the Latin for the Field of Illtud. Again, Campus Elleti can easily become Camelot over time.

Arthur's links with the West Country are extremely tenuous, and based upon romances from the Middle Ages. The placing of Arthur, Merlin and the knights of the Round Table firmly in Wales can be a tremendous boost to the tourist industry.

St. Govan's Chapel, Pembrokeshire

All it needs is someone in power with the vision and courage to challenge and change things. English Heritage has been trumpeting the find, of a piece of slate from Tintagel in Cornwall, as proof of Arthur in the sixth century being an English reality. Cornwall was still totally British at this time, as in 936 Athelstan fixed the boundary of Saxon expansion at the Tamar. The rough inscription 'Pater Coliavificit Artnogov' means 'Artnogov, father of a descendant of Coll, has had (this building) constructed'. According English Heritage it is 'the first evidence of a link between the Arthurian legend and historical fact' (*Daily Telegraph* 7 August 1990). Yet again publicity tries to overwhelm historical truth. Arthmael ap Meurig ap Tewdrig is known and recorded in history but does not 'fit' with the English tourist industry and its promotional power. It is so easy for the relevant authorities – the Welsh Office, Welsh Tourist Board and various local councils to promote Arthurian tours and holiday breaks in Wales. Why not promote Wales as 'The Kingdom of Arthur?' It will pull in more tourists than dreamy scenes of empty beaches and deserted hills.

The *Easter Annals* describe Arthur's final battle in 539 after 12 victories, at Camlann, 'in which Arthur and Medraut (Mordred) perished.' However, we still are unsure if Mordred was his enemy or fighting alongside him, or indeed if Arthur died here. One of the problems with Arthur is that of the suspicion of the early Roman Church with this fabulous hero, known across Europe. As a result the Catholic monk writing the *Life of Cadog* describes him as being lustful and perverse, and the *Life of Padarn* makes him out to be a mean despot. There are other unflattering references in many of the later religious sources. Certainly his contemporary, the historian Gildas, had no cause to love Arthur because he executed Huail, the brother of Gildas.

In the *Triads*, Arthur is recorded as one of the 'three red chieftains of Britain' and also as one of the 'three heroic supreme sovereigns of Britain.' The 6th century Llywarch Hen, one of 'the three wise-counselling equestrians of Arthur's Court' called Arthur a great warrior, as did Nennius, writing three hundred years later. A 10th century copy of Nennius, by Mark the Hermit, called him 'dux belli' (war leader) and 'belliger Arthur' (warlike Arthur). All these references predate the mediaeval French romances.

The Genealogy of Iestyn ap Gwrgan seems to confuse Arthur ap Meurig with Adras: 'Adras, the son of Meyryg, was a very heroic sovereign, who frequently put the Saxons to flight; killing and destroying them. He enacted many laws and ordinances for civil and ecclesiastical government; and was the first who instituted a class of Equestrians (mounted knights), for the maintenance of correct comportment in war, and due discipline at arms; and also to guard well the country, watch carefully its enemies, and to establish an efficient system of communications with regard to hostilities and legislation.

Morgan, the son of Adras, called Morgan the Courteous, and Morgan of Glamorgan, was a renowned king, and an Equestrian of Arthur's court, and of the Round Table. He was Arthur's cousin; particularly handsome; extremely courteous; and so cheerfully kind and merciful, that, when he went out to war, no one, old and strong enough to bear arms, would remain at home; hence it was that he acquired the designation of – Morgan the Courteous. It was he that gave the appellation – Morganwg – to his country; which name it has retained to this very hour… He erected a Court at Margam, a place which he raised to a Bishoprick; which retained that distinction during the lives of five bishops, when it became united to Llandaff.' Morgan's grave was found between Margam and Kenfig.

It seems that Margam was originally called Morgan, and there is still a great mansion there. An important but little-known fact relating to Morgan was related by Edward Mansel of Margam, a man of Norman descent, in his *Account of the Conquest of Glamorgan* of 1591. Robert Fitzhamon was the Norman who conquered much of Glamorgan from its last prince Iestyn ap Gwrgant: 'Before the time of Robert Fitzhamon there was one Chief Lord of Glamorgan whose were the high Royalties, and he assembled the other Lords every month to his Court where all matters of Justice were determined and finally settled, these Lords sat in Judgement on all matters of Law, with twelve Freeholders from every Lordship to give opinions after what came to their knowledge, and the Bishop of Llandaff sat in the high Court as a Councellor of Conscience according to the Laws of

God, this Court was formed they say by Morgan (c.515-570?) who was Prince of the Country after King Arthur in the manner of Christ and his twelve apostles, and this form of Law was kept by Sir Robert Fitzhamon according to the old usage of the Country, after the High Court was held, which lasted three days, the Courts of the twelve Lordships were held in turn, and from them an appeal might be made to the High Court in the Country, the Lord and his yeomen in the same form and manner as in the High Court.

After the winning of the Country by Sir Robert Fitzhamon, he took to him his twelve knights to supply the places in his Courts of the Lawful and right Lords of the twelve Lordships, which caused discontent insomuch that Welsh Lords took arms under Pain Turberville and Caradock ab Iestyn and Madoc his Brother, and they came to Cardiff Castle and surrounded it insomuch that it was on the point of being taken when King Henry the first going to the top of the Raven Tower to enquire concerning the tumult which was heard, he saw the place all encompassed by fierce armed men, whereupon he called a parley when Pain Turberville told him the reason saying that if rightful orders were not made, to restore the Laws of Morgan the first, that he and Robert Fitzhamon should feel at the ears very soon of what stuff the Castle walls were of at the heart on which all in the Castle counselled together, and it was seen best to yield to the Country that request.' This may be the origin of 12 man juries.

Arthur's 'Saying of the Wise' is: 'Hast thou heard the saying of Arthur, The Emperor, the mighty sovereign? "There is no devastation like a deceiver".'

He is also named as one of 'the three red ravagers of the Island of Britain', along with Rhun ap Beli and Morgant the Wealthy. There are several triads referring to Arthur. From *Gereint fab Erbin* there is: 'At Llongborth I saw Arthur's / Brave men, they hewed with steel, / Emperor, leader in toil'. In *Mi a Wum* is recorded: 'I have been where Llachau was slain, / The son of Arthur, terrible in songs, / When ravens croaked over blood'; and also: 'What man is the porter? / "Glewlwyd Great-Grip, What man asks it?" / Arthur and Cai the Fair. / "What retinue travels with you?" / The best men in the world.'

Arthur is also mentioned in *Preidu Annwn, Cad Goddau*, and finally in this marvellously evocative verse from *Y Gododdin*, the story of the British defeat at Catraeth and the oldest extant British poem:
'He charged before three hundred of the finest,
He cut down both centre and wing,
He excelled in the forefront of the noblest host,
He gave gifts of horses from the herd in winter.
He fed black ravens on the rampart of a fortress
Although he was no Arthur.
Among the powerful ones in battle,

In the front rank, Gwawrddur was a palisade.'

* The 547 date is intriguing, for Maelgwn Gwynedd was said to have died of the Bubonic Plague (the 'Yellow Death') in this year. Arthur was recorded as having a festering wound in his groin. This is one of the classic symptoms of the plague, along with weeping yellow pustules under the armpits.

NOTE ON ARTHUR'S KNIGHTS OF THE ROUND TABLE (from *The Book of Welsh Saints*)
This is by no means completed, but it is interesting to note how many sixth-century Welsh saints were related to, or served, Arthur and Maelgwn Gwynedd in some way. A medieval text *Deuddeg Pedwar Marchog ar Hugan Llys Arthur* gives his 24 knights at court as: Gwalchmai (i.e. Gawain), Drudwas, Eliwlod, Gwrgi (i.e. Bors), Perceval, Galahad, Lancelot, Owain, Menw, Tristan, Eiddilig, Nasiens, Mordred, Hoel, Blaes, Cadog, Petroc, Morfran ap Tegid, Sanddef, Glewlyd, Cyon, Aron, Llywarch Hen and Bedwyr (Bedivere). Of these, Gwalchmai/Gawain, Bors, Perceval, Galahad, Lancelot, Tristan, Mordred and Bedwyr/Bedivere are included on the thirteenth century Winchester Castle Round Table forgery. Also of these we can count as Welsh saints Aron, Cadog, Petroc and Llywarch Hen. It is still unsure whether Arthur fought with or against Mordred at Camlan in 539. Instead, it may have been the forces of Maelgwn Gwynedd that ambushed him. Welsh sixth century saints associated with Arthur are as follows:

St Alan Frygan ab Emyr Lydaw, whose troops deserted Arthur on the eve of Camlan, married into Arthur's family;
St Allgo ap Caw appears as Calcas ap Caw in the Mabinogion, fighting for Arthur. From Glamorgan, he went to Anglesey, from which he was forced to flee by Maelgwn Gwynedd;
St Amwn Ddu ab Emyr Llydaw married into Arthur's family and may be the origin of the Black Knight;
St Angar, Angawd ap Caw is mentioned in the *Mabinogion* as Arthur's knight;
St Aron (Aaron) ap Cynfarch, father of St Ciwg, was given lands by Arthur. A saint of this name left Wales in the early 6th century and settled at St Malo;
St Baglan ab Ithel Hael is given as Sir Balan, and was related to Arthur. Baglan is culted in Brittany and therefore may have fought for Armel/Arthur there;
Bishop Bedwyn, Sir Baudwin was said to be one of Arthur's first knights, made a constable of the realm and one of the governors of Britain, but ended his life as a 'physician and hermit'. St Bedwyn was also called a 'comeregulus' (count-ruler), and Arthur had a brother called 'Comereg'. He was bishop of Cernyw (south-east Glamorgan and Gwent);
Bedwyr Bedrynant (of the perfect sinews) was Cai's companion and the model for Bedivere, mentioned in *Culhwch and Olwen*. The warrior with Cai (St Cynan) most documented with Arthur, he died fighting for him (Armel?) in France;
Bors' father was said to also be named Bors, who married Evaine, and his brother was Sir Lionel and cousin Sir Lancelot. He was said to be the father of

St Elian Wyn, but Elian's father was Gallgu Rieddog. Bors has also been identified with St Gwrgi;

St Brioc may possibly have been Arthur's brother Frioc, or Brioc the grandson of Brychan;

Sir Breunor ap Dunawd Fawr is the brother of Sir (St) Deiniol and Sir Dinadan, and is also known as the Black Knight;

St Brynach was given land by Meurig (Arthur's father), and argued with Maelgwn Gwynedd;

St Cadfan is known as a 'warrior saint' in Brittany, Armel's cousin, and possibly helped Arthur and Samson overcome Conmire (Conomorus) in battle;

St Cado ap Geraint fought for Arthur at Badon Hill, was a great friend of Caradog Freich Fras (his brother-in-law), is linked with Guinevere and fought in Brittany;

St Cadog q.v. (497-577) is linked with Arthur's family and disputed lands with Rhun ap Maelgwn and Rhun ap Brychan. He sheltered an enemy of Arthur. In a 1999 *Western Mail* article, Lawrence Main believes St Cadog to be Sir Galahad. He goes on to reason that 'since Cadoc's father was Gwynlliw and Sir Galahad was the son of Sir Lancelot, it seems obvious that Sir Lancelot was Gwynlliw, a neighbour of King Arthur and a notorious womaniser;

St Caffo ap Caw, brother of Gildas, was killed by Maelgwn Gwynedd's men in Glamorgan or Anglesey;

St Cai ap Cynyr Farchog may have became Sir Kay, and Landygai is on the north Wales coast;

St Caradog Freich Fras ab Ynyr Gwent and Madrun is mentioned in the Arthurian triads, and became 'Sir Caradoc Bris Bras'. He married Amwn Ddu's sister, and became a knight of Arthur. One of Arthur's 'three cavaliers of battle', he fought in Brittany (for Armel?) His brother 'Turquine' wanted to kill Lancelot;   .

St Carannog ap Corun was given lands by Arthur, and went with Armel to Brittany;

St Cawrdaf ap Caradog Freichfras ab Ynyr Gwent is given in the *Mabinogion* as Arthur's counsellor. His 'cor' was near Penllin, at Miskin;

St Caw fled from his kingdom in the North of England, and has 21 children listed in the tale of *Culhwch and Olwen*. Many became knights of the round table in mediaeval reworkings of the life of Arthur ap Meurig ap Tewdrig, who gave some of them lands in 'Siluria', i.e. South-East Wales;

Cedwy 'of Arthur's court' is St Cedwyn ap Gwgon Gwron ap Peredur, the half-brother of St Ceidio and Caradog Freichfras;

St Cenydd was a baby at a feast held by Arthur to celebrate Christmas;

St Cywyllog ferch Caw was the wife of Mordred, and given lands by Maelgwn Gwynedd;

St Cybi argued with Maelgwn Gwynedd, although his monastery lands were given by this king;

St Cynan Gefnhir (or Cian) ap Cynwyd may be Cyon, a 'knight-counsellor to Arthur', who in the Winchester lists is one of the 24 knights;

St Curig was a contemporary of Arthur, known as Curig the Knight, and is remembered in Brittany;

St Cynan, also known as St Kea is possibly Cai (Sir Kay) ap Lleuddyn Luydog from Lothian, who died in 550, a cousin of St Beuno. He was in Brittany at the same time as Armel;

St Cynddilig ap Nwython was summoned to Arthur's coronation, with his brother Rhun;

St Cynddilig ap Gildas attended Arthur's coronation according to Geoffrey of Monmouth;

St Cyndeyrn is mentioned as Arthur's chief bishop in the North;

St Cyngar's father, Geraint, died fighting for Arthur;

St Cynidr appears to be the St Keneder who was with Cadog in his confrontation with Arthur;

St Cynin ap Tudwal Befr was a warrior in early *Triads* and the brother of Sir Ifor who was linked with Arthur as a knight;

Cynlas Goch ab Owain was assassinated by Maelgwn Gwynedd, when he tried to break his overlordship;

St Cynwyl ap Dunawd fawr was the brother of Deiniol, and escaped from Camlan with Sandde Bryd Angel and Morfran ap Tegid;

Cystennin (Constantine) ap Cado ap Geraint took over the High Kingship from Arthur after Camlan;

Sir Danadan was possibly St Dunawd Fawr, St Dingad or St Dunwyd;

Sir Daniel was possibly St Deiniol Fawr, with a brother Sir Breunor, known as the Black Knight. Deiniol may have been with Maelgwn Gwynedd at Llaniltud Fawr. He also witnessed a land grant by Maelgwn to Cyndeyrn;

Derfel Gadarn ap Hywel Mawr ab Emyr Llydaw survived Camlan. He was said to be the brother of St Armel, and also of Christiolus, Sulien, Rhystud, Dwywan and Dwyfael;

Dewi, St David, was thought by Giraldus Cambrensis and Geoffrey of Monmouth to be Arthur's uncle. In David's time, Arthur's knight Caradog Freichfras pushed the Irish out of Menevia;

Sir Drudwas could be St Trydwas;

St Dwyfael ap Hywel Mawr was one of Arthur's knights;

St Dyfrig was said to have crowned Arthur;

St Dywel ab Erbyn fought for Arthur, mentioned in *Culhwch and Olwen* and the *Black Book of Carmarthen;*

St Edern ap Nudd is mentioned in the *Dream of Rhonabwy* and the tale of *Geraint ab Erbin*;

St Einion's father Owain Ddantgwyn was treacherously killed by Maelgwn Gwynedd;

St Elffin was rescued from Maelgwn Gwynedd's Deganwy Castle by Taliesin;

St Elidyr fought Maelgwn Gwynedd or Rhun ap Maelgwn;

Eliwlod was one of the 24 knights, a grandson of Uther and nephew of Arthur, and perhaps the original of Sir Lancelot. Could this be St Eliquid, St Eiliwedd or St Almedha?

St Endellion was said to be Arthur's goddaughter;

King Erbyn of Domnonia's sons Geraint, Dywel and Erinid fought for Arthur. Erbyn asked Arthur for Geraint to return to the West Country to take over the kingship;

St Ernin (Hernin) was linked to Conmire, who Armel fought in Brittany;

St Euddogwy was given land by Arthur;

St Eugrad ap Caw fought for Arthur in *Culhwch and Olwen*, as 'Ergyryat';

St Ffili is mentioned on a stone at Ogmore in connection with Arthmael/Arthur;

St Geraint ab Erbyn was killed at Llongborth fighting for Arthur;

St Gildas ap Caw's brother Hywel killed Gwydre ap St Gwenafwy, so he was executed by Arthur. St Gildas also arbitrated in a dispute concerning king Melwas, Gwenhwyfar and Arthur;

Gwalchmai has been associated with Gawain/Gofan, and as Arthur's nephew, killed by Lancelot or Mordred;

St Gwen has been identified with Gwenhwyfar (Guinevere);

St Gwenafwy's son was stabbed by Huail, which caused Arthur to execute Huail;

Gwenhwyfar (Guinevere, Gwenhaf) founded Amesbury Church after her affair with Lancelot (or Maelgwn Gwynedd or Medrod), and St Mylor's relics were taken there;

St Gwernabui was given land by Arthur;

Gwgan Gwron ap Peredur features in Arthurian triads and married St Madrun;

Gwrgi (Bors), the brother or son of Peredur saw the aftermath of the battle of Arderydd c.580;

St Gwrst witnessed a land grant by Maelgwn;

St Gwrthl was a chief elder who recognised Arthur as overlord, and was killed in Cardigan, possibly at Penbryn (Llongborth);

St Gwyddno was present when Arthur's son Llacheu was killed;

St Gwyndaf Hen married into Arthur's family;

St Gwynlliw 'the Warrior' has been identified with Lancelot, and is Cadog's father;

Hywel (Huail) ap Caw was killed by Arthur;

St Hywyn ap Gwyndaf was Arthur's nephew;

Sir Iddo was identified with the warrior-saint son of Cawrdaf, but he was possibly St Iddon ab Ynyr Gwent;

Sir Ifor was the brother of St Cynin, and the son of Tudwal Befr and Nefydd;

St Idloes, with St Sadwrn was one of Arthur's knights;

St Illtud Farchog (the knight) attended Arthur's court with the warrior St Cadog;

St Kea was linked with Arthur, Gildas, Gwenhwyfar and Mordred, but may be the same saint as Cai;

St Lorcan Wyddel is mentioned in Arthurian triads;

Sir Lucan (Lorcan?) was said to be the brother of St Bedwyr;

St Llywarch Hen may be a later addition to the list, but his son was Sandde who escaped the slaughter at Camlan;

St Mabon, the brother of St Teilo, was a follower and servant at Arthur's father's court;

St Maglorius went to Brittany with Samson at the same time as Armel, and was the nephew of Amwn Ddu and nephew of Arthur;

Maelgwn Gwynedd appears to have become High King (Pendragon) after Camlan, and is mentioned as Arthur's chief elder, and may have succeeded him as leader of the Britons;

St Maelog ap Caw is one of the knights in *Culhwch and Olwen*;

St Maglorius was a nephew of Arthur who went at the same time as Arthur/Armel to Brittany;

St Malo, a kinsman of Arthur, had major problems with Conmire in Brittany at the same time as Armel was there;

St Marchell was Arthur's aunt;

St Mechnyd ap Sandde was one of his 'knights';

Medrod married Cywyllog ferch Caw, who was given lands by Maelgwn Gwynedd;

St Meugan seems to have intervened in a dispute between Maelgwn and Cadog. He was related to Arthur;

St Meurig, Arthur's father has been placed as Uther Pendragon;

St Mewan was in Brocielande, a friend of Judicael (Iuthael) at the same time as Armel;

Morgan Mwynfawr ('gentle and great') was a knight, and Arthur's son, blessed by St Cawrdaf;

St Ninnoc was Arthur's grandmother;

Sir Nwython was probably St Nwythen ap Gildas, mentioned in *Culhwch and Olwen*;

Owain ab Urien Rheged was one of Arthur's knights;

St Padarn argued with Arthur and Maelgwn;

Peredur became Sir Percival, and was the Pryderi ap Dolar mentioned in *The Gododdin* and the Arthurian triads. His son was St Dwyfael. However, the Sir Dwyfael who fought for Arthur was probably Hywel Mawr's son;

St Petroc (Pedrog) was St Cadog's nephew, one of the 'three just knights of court', one of the seven knights who survived Camlan, and known as 'Paladruellt' ('splintered lance');

St Piran was mentioned in Arthurian legend as being appointed Archbishop of York;

Rhun ap Gildas was said to have been summoned to Arthur's coronation;

St Sadwrn was a knight and also the nephew of Emyr Llydaw;

St Samson of Dol was Arthur's cousin or uncle and Armel's cousin, and helped Armel overcome Conmire in Brittany;

Sandde Bryd Angel has been identified by some as St Padarn – he escaped from Camlan;

St Talhaearn is linked in a 'saying of the wise' with Arthur and was said to be the chaplain of Emrys Wledig;

St Tathan is Arthur's brother-in-law;

St Tathana's legend states that the court of Arthur's father Meurig was at Boverton;

St Tegfedd ferch Tegid Foel, of Penllyn, was with Derfel Gadarn after Camlan, and said to have been killed by Illtud so Arthur's tomb was not revealed;

St Teilo was given the land where Tegfedd was killed for settling Arthur's dispute with Cadog;

St Tewdrig was Pendragon, as was his son St Meurig, Arthur's father;

St Trillo witnessed a land grant to Maelgwn, along with Deiniol, Gwrst and Rhun ap Maelgwn;

Turquine wanted to kill Lancelot - he was the brother of St Caradog;

St Tydecho ap Amwn Ddu, the nephew of Arthur, was persecuted by Maelgwn;

St Teithfallt, Arthur's great-grandfather, is claimed to be Emrys Wledig;

St Tyfodwg, remembered at Llantrisant, is thought by Gilbert to be King Teithfallt, Arthur's great-grandfather;

St Umbrafael, the brother of St Amwn Ddu, married Arthur's sister Afrella;

St Winnoc was the son of King Judicael, helped by Armel/Arthur to regain his throne;

St Ynyr Gwent is linked with Arthur, and went to Brittany.

Thus we have around 110 saints of the early-mid 6th century whose stories intertwine around the family of Arthur ap Meurig ap Tewdrig ap Teithfallt and the legends of King Arthur and St Armel.

Taliesin's poem *The Graves of Warriors* gives us the following enigmatic lines:

'The grave of the horse, the grave of the Fierce-One,

The grave of Grim-Visaged red-sword,

The grave of Arthur, a mystery of the world.'

If Arthur was Armel, and went to Brittany to help his Breton kinsmen, this problem re-occurs. Armel's tomb at Ploermel is empty. Another translation *of Englynion y Beddau (Verses of the Graves)* is:

'There is a grave for March, a grave for Gwythur,

A grave for Gwgawn Red-Sword;

The world's wonder a grave for Arthur.'

It is a difficult translation, which either means that he had a wonderful burial-place, or that no-one will ever know where he is. The 'Pointe du Secret' on the fringe of Paimpont Forest may hold a clue to this mystery. Walter Map, writing in 1135, said that Arthur was buried in the Black Chapel, Blackfriars Monastery just outside Cardiff Castle, near the banks of the Taf.

NOTE ON ARTHUR'S SON

Lacheu fab Arthur appears in the *Black Book of Carmarthen* in battle against Cai Wyn. Also Gwyddno Garanhir claims he was present when Llacheu was killed. He is often mentioned elsewhere as a fearless warrior, and was supposed to have died 'below Llech Ysgar':

'I have been where Llacheu was killed,

Son of Arthur, marvellous in songs,

When the ravens croaked over blood ...

I have been where the warriors of Britain were slain,

From the East to the North;

I am alive, they are in their grave.'

Stones called the 'Sons of Arthur' may indicate that others of Arthur's offspring died, just leaving the young Morgan, causing the leadership of the Britons to pass to Constans (Cystennin), then to Maelgwn, or direct to Maelgwn. These two standing stones, Cerrig Meibion Arthur, stand near Cwm Cerwyn in the Preseli Hills, where Arthur fought the Twrch Trwyth and his son Gwydre and another son died. Near here is the unusually elliptical stone circle, Bedd Arthur. One tradition is that Morgan was Arthur's youngest son, born of the third of the ladies named Gwenhwyfar that Arthur married. His rise to favour irked Modred, who was Arthur's nephew, foster-son and hopeful successor. The same story tells us that Modred was the incestuous offspring of Arthur and his sister Gwyar (who may have been Morgan le Fay).

NOTE ON ARTHUR'S FATHER - Meurig ap Tewdrig ap Teithfallt, King of Morgannwg

King Tewdrig was martyred fighting the Saxons at Tintern in 470, but Meurig had taken over his kingdom prior to this date, and is thought to have been Uther Pendragon, the *Dux Bellorum* or leader in battle of the British against the Saxon and Pict invaders. Pendragon was an honorific title, and Uther's children included Arthur and Anna. Meurig was the father of King Arthur, and was excommunicated for breaking an oath and killing a rival, but canonised after his death for founding many churches. He married Onbrawst ferch Gwrgant Mawr, to reunite Glwyssing and Gwent with Ergyng. (Glamorgan, Gwent and Hereford/Worcester were the original heartland of the Silures).

His children included Arthwys (Athrwys/Arthmael/Arthur), whose son was Morgan and whose descendants ruled Glamorgan until the Norman Conquest. Meurig's daughter Anna married Amwn Ddu ab Emyr Llydaw, the dispossessed Breton prince. Amwn became a saint, and friend of Illtud and Dyfrig. Amwn's children were the important saints Tydecho, Tathan and Samson, who returned to Brittany. Another of Meurig's daughters was Afrella, who married Umbrafael ab Emyr Llydaw. Meurig's third daughter was Gwenonwy who married Gwyndaf Hen ab Emyr Llydaw, King of Brittany. Their children were Meugan (Meigant) and Hywyn. Hywyn was a confessor at the monastery on Ynys Enlli, where Arthur possibly went to recover after Camlan. The marriage of three daughters of Meurig to the three sons of Emyr Llydaw (Budic II of Brittany) gives credence to the claim that Arthur-Arthmael-Armel fought with his kinsmen in Brittany. It appears that after his three royal Breton brothers-in-law supported Arthur, he helped Hywel Mawr and Budic II regain their lands, and then overcame Conmire/Conmore for Iuthael to gain the Breton throne.

Meurig gave lands to the church around where his father Tewdrig was buried at Mathern, as recorded by Godwin, Bishop of Llandaff in 1615. Under Meurig's protection Llandaff and Llancarfan were founded, and he gave lands to both. It appears that he controlled most of Hereford, all of Monmouth and most of Glamorgan, i.e. the ancient kingdom of Siluria, and he seems to have ruled from Caerleon. After Meurig treacherously slew Cynvetu, Euddogwy summoned the bishops of Llancarfan, Llandough and Llanilltud to excommunicate him, but he was pardoned for giving lands to Llandaff, where he is buried. He may have founded the monastery at Llanfair Misgyn, Miskin. King 'Mouric ap Teudiric' is recorded as granting Roath in Cardiff (Reathr) to Gourcinnim, for a sword with a gilded hilt valued at 25 cows. A smithy of this time has been recorded at nearby Dinas Powys in the Dark Age fort. Meurig's kingdom of Glwysing may have included Brecon as a vassal kingdom. There is a 13th century church at Alltmawr in Brecon dedicated to Mauritius, which may be his foundation.

Pwll Meurig, a mile or so from Chepstow, was his holy well, famous for miracles. It ebbed and flowed with the tide like many Welsh coastal wells. The legend is that people used to stand on a magical log in the well to wash their faces. The well was flooded by the River Severn and the log floated out to sea, but always returned on the fourth day. Meurig's father Tewdrig also had a famous holy well. Barber and Pykitt believe that Meurig is buried on Mynydd y Gaer in Glamorgan, possibly on a site near Arthur's grave.

Footnote:

Dependent often upon the author's nationality, the sites of Arthur's battles as recorded by Nennius are in the West Country, the East of England, the Lake District, Yorkshire and Scotland. We could equally make a hypothesis that all of his battles were consistent with his being based in Wales, fighting against the westward aggression of the Saxons, the sea-borne invasions of the Irish, and against other Britons from North Wales and Cumbria. Even the 'lost' Vandals who sailed from North Africa, are said to have invaded Wales at this time. If nothing else, the following list may just stimulate more Welsh interest in the place-names of fields, rivers and valleys. Around 830 Nennius wrote the *Historia Brittonum*. He mentions the following battles by the 'dux bellorum', the 'magnanimous' Arthur.

'The first battle was in the mouth of the river which is called Glein' - 'Glein' stems from the Brythonic-Celtic, or Welsh, for 'clean', (today's *glân*) and there were many rivers thus named across Britain. *Glyn* is a river valley. The village Gleiniant is on the river Nant-y-Gleiniant (Gleiniant stream) just north of Llanidloes in mid-Wales. The mouth of the Gleiniant meets the river Trannon just outside Trefeglwys, where there are the remains of a Roman road from Caersws to Pennal near Machynlleth. Arthur's cavalry would have made use of Roman roads.

'The second, third, fourth and fifth (battles) on another river which is called Dubglas and is in the region Linnius' - Aberdulais outside Neath is at the mouth of the Dulais River, and Pontarddulais near Swansea spans another river Dulais. Just north of the two are Llyn y Fan Fach and Llyn y Fan Fawr, and the region 'Linnius' may refer to 'the district of lakes'. This is at the western frontier of the traditional kingdom of Glamorgan and Gwent, and there had been Irish settlement in the west of Wales. Another candidate could be Ilchester in Somerset, then British and similarly under threat from the Saxons. The area round here was the Roman 'Lindinis' which may have been corrupted to Linnuis. The men of Domnonia, the West Country, fought for Arthur. The River Dulas (Black Brook) is described in the 'Brut' as running between Caer Efrog (Wroxeter) near the Welsh border in Shrophire, and Caer Fuddai, near Machynlleth. There is an Afon Dulas (Dulas River) near Machynlleth.

'The sixth battle on the river which is called Bassas' - Some historians place this as near Baschurch, between Oswestry and Shrewsbury in Shropshire, on the Welsh borders. Bassaleg outside Newport is another contender. Many battles were fought in this area between Saxons and Britons. Barber and Pykitt make a case for the Roman fort of Letocetum, now called Wall-by-Lichfield, outside Lichfield in Staffordhire. Basingwerk upon the North-East Wales coast is also a candidate.

The seventh battle was at Cat Coed Celidon - *Cad* is Welsh for battle, *coed* for wood or forest, and Celidon has been named as Coed Celyddon, the Caledonian Forest. While this area of Scotland, like Cumbria, was still British at this time, there are candidates nearer Wales for the site. Blake and Lloyd in *The Keys to Avalon* believe the area to lie between Corwen, Cerrigydrudion and Denbigh in North Wales on the evidence of King Mark and Cernyw's association. Cernyw however was also the area just east of Cardiff, so it may have been there, between the Roman forts of Caerleon and Cardiff.

'The eighth battle was near the fort Guinnion, where Arthur bore the image of the Holy Virgin, mother of God, upon his shoulders, and through the power of our Lord Jesus Christ, and the Holy Mary, put the Saxons to flight, and pursued them with great slaughter' - Caer Guinn or Caer Gwent is the modern Caerwent, the remarkable walled Roman town near Caerleon and the Silurian camp of Llanmelin. Barber and Pykitt believe that Cats Ash near Caerleon is the site of this battle. If 'Guinnion' has been Latinised from the Welsh *gwynion*, there is a site in Denbigh known as Caeaugwynion Mawr. There is a castle mound nearby, possibly Guinnion Fort. In the Berwyn Mountains there is also a hillfort named Carreg Gwynion.

The ninth battle was fought in 'the City of the Legion' - Caerleon - Caer Legionis, or possibly the other great Roman fortress on the Welsh borders at Chester, near where a great later battle occurred in 613.

'He fought the tenth battle on the shore of the river called Tribruit' - This is properly spelt Tryfrwyd in *The Black Book of Carmarthen*. Here Cai Hir, Arthur's foster-brother, fought against Garwlwyd, presumably under Arthur. This may be on the Severn near the border at Gloucester.

'The eleventh battle was on the hill called Agned' - Sources place this battle at the Roman fort of Bravonium, modern Leintwardine on the Welsh borders between Knighton and Ludlow. Barber and Pykitt place it at Catbrain hill-fort, just north of Bristol. Blake and Lloyd believe the site to be the hillfort outside Chester known as Maidens' Castle, from evidence in the *Brut y Brenhinedd* (*Chronicle of the Kings*).

Another site given for the eleventh battle was 'Mons Beguion', (only in the Vatican ms. of the *Historia Brittonum*, and this is possibly a corruption of the 'Brewyn', where Urien Rheged fought. The Berwyn Hills or Leintwardine are candidates for this battle.

'The twelfth was a most severe contest, when Arthur penetrated to the hill of Badon. In this engagement, nine hundred and forty fell by his hand alone, no one but the Lord affording him assistance. In all these engagements the Britons were successful' - This could be outside Bath, where another crucial battle between Germans and British occurred around 603, or at Mynydd Baedan outside Bridgend in Glamorgan. It was here that the advance of the Saxons was finally halted. Lloyd and Baker suggest a hill-fort outside Buttington, North of Welshpool.

The final battle of Camlan appears to have been in Merioneth, where there are two river Camlans, and was possibly a battle between the Britons of North and South Wales for overlordship of the country. Certainly Maelgwn Gwynedd of North Wales was described as the 'Pendragon' after Arthur's disappearance after Camlan. The only other battle associated with Arthur in Britain was at Llongborth, where Geraint fell, which many have placed as Portsmouth, for some reason, but there is a Llongborth on the Ceredigion coast. *Elegy for Geraint*, said to be by Llywarch Hen, describes this battle:

Before Gereint, the enemy's scourge,
I saw white horses, tensed, red.
After the war cry, bitter the grave…
Before Geraint, the enemy of tyranny,
I saw horses white with foam,
After the war cry, a terrible torrent.
In Llongborth, I saw the clash of swords,
Men in terror, bloody heads,
Before Geraint the great, his father's son.
In Llongborth I saw spurs
And men who did not flinch from the dread of spears,
Who drank their wine from glasses that glinted…
In Llongborth I saw the weapons
Of warriors, and blood fast-falling,
After the war-cry, a fearful return.
In Llongborth I saw Arthur's
Heroes who cut with steel.
The Emperor, ruler of our labour.
In Llongborth Geraint was slain.
Heroes of the land of Dyfneint,
Before they were slain, they slew.
Under the thigh of Geraint swift chargers,
Long their legs, wheat their fodder,
Red, swooping like milk-white eagles…
When Gereint was born, Heaven's gate stood open;
Christ granted all our prayer;
Lovely to behold, the glory of Britain.

Gereint's feast date is 16 May. In the *Book of Llandaff*, Geraint founded the church at Magor near Newport. There is also Gerrans in Cornwall dedicated to Geraint, but this may be another saint. A martyr who died in battle, St Geraint is remembered in the old text 'The Sayings of the Wise':

'Hast thou heard the saying of Geraint,
Son of Erbin, the just and experienced?
"Short-lived is the hater of saints."'

The Anglo-Saxon Chronicle places Gereint's death in 501, when 'Port and his two sons, Bieda and Maegla, came to Britain at the place called Llongborth, and slew a young Welshman, a very noble man.' Some think, following Bede's mis-dating of the coming of the Saxons by 20 years, that this battle was actually fought in 480. Others believe that it was fought in 510. Welsh tradition places Llongborth at Penbryn beach, near Newquay in Ceredigion rather than Portsmouth. (Llongborth means ship door, or harbour in Welsh). A farm inland is called Perth Geraint, near Bedd Geraint, Geraint's Grave, where he was said to be buried after the battle. Nearby is a standing stone inscribed *'Corbalengi iacit Ordovs'* denoting Corbalengus of the Ordovices tribe. In this parish John Jones wrote that there is a *Llech yr Ochain* (the Stone of Grief), near a well named *Ffynnon Waedog* (the Bloody Well). However, Barber and Pykitt place the battle on the Severn Estuary, near Magor (and also to Port-is-Coed, or Porthskewett to where Geraint moved his court). Merthyr Gerein (Geraint's Martyrdom, or Shrine) was an ancient chapel on a hillock known as Chapel Tump near Magor, the church which Geraint founded.

Geraint may have held lands in Wales as well as the West Country, as there was a castle ruin named Dyngeraint (Dinas Geraint). Just seven miles from Penbryn is Cilgerran (Geraint's Retreat), with its magnificent castle overlooking a bend in the River Teifi. Provisions could be brought by boat to this site from Aberteifi (Cardigan). Cilgerran castle itself was known as Dyngeraint up to 1130 when Gilbert de Clare, first Earl of Pembroke, completed his Norman castle there.

Some claim that Geraint was the grandfather of Gildas, and also of Geraint who is mentioned in the *Life of Teilo*. A cousin or kinsman of Arthur, in legend Geraint defeated Edern ap Nudd in revenge for his slight on Gwenhwyfar (Guinevere), and married Enid, the daughter of Yniwl Iarll. In Arthurian legend, it was Geraint who encountered the 'Sparrow-Hawk Knight'. Chrétien de Troyes wrote the mediaeval poem 'Erec and Enide' about Geraint's marriage. Geraint's son Cado carried on fighting the Saxons for Arthur after his father's death. Wherever we move in the circles around the hundreds of 6th century Welsh saints, we find derivations of Arthurian legend. Wherever we look upon maps of Wales and its borders, we find the evidence for Arthur and his battles. The remarkable Kathryn Gibson is to publish a book upon Arthur, and believes that Camlan is the Bwlch Oerdrws Pass near Dinas Mawddwy, and that Baddon is Breidden near Welshpool.

ABBOT ARMEL d.c. 570 (d.552 according to Farmer)

ARTHMAEL, ARTHFAEL, ARZEL, ERMEL, HERMEL, ERMYN, ERVAN, THIARMAIL, ARMAGILLUS, THE REAL ARTHUR?

His Feast Day is 14-17 August, with 16 August being most popular in the Breton sources, and 27 July also noted in Vannes. 13 June is *'Le Passage'* feast day in St Armel. He is invoked to cure headaches, fever, colic, gout and rheumatism, and was sometimes the patron of hospitals. Saint Armel was included in my first volume of 'Eminent Britons' to stimulate discussion upon the Breton-Welsh Arthurian links. I have travelled across Brittany many times working on the theme, and hopefully this further research will

be published within five years. Princely Breton refugees fought for Arthur before some returned to Brittany to regain their lands. They married Arthur's sisters. It seems that their kinsman Arthur may have survived Camlan and returned to Armorica (Brittany) to plead their case at Childebert's court, and then with Samson dethroned the usurper king Conmire in Brittany*.

Abbot Armel was said to be the cousin of St Samson and St Cadfan, and from southeast Wales. He crossed to Brittany with many kinsfolk. Other relatives were the saints Maglorius, Malo, Padarn and Tudno. He was a member of Illtud's 'cor' (college) of monks. He went to Brittany possibly to flee the 547 Yellow Plague, and one source says that he went with Abbot Carentmail who is probably Carannog. With the assistance of King Childebert, Armel founded monasteries at Plouarmel and Ploermel. Ploermel** was formerly called Lann Arthmael. With Samson, Armel assisted in restoring the throne of Domnonia (Britanny) to King Iuthael in 555, and the famous 6th - 7th century Samson Cross in Llanilltud records the fact. There is St Armel south of Vannes, and another north-west of Bubry, near St Maurice (Meurig?). Plouarzel is west of St Renan, and another Plouarzel is near Lampaul. Ville Ermel is just north of Paimpont Forest, of Arthurian renown, as is nearby Kersamson. Samson was a kinsman of Arthur, associated with helping Armel in Brittany.

Another source states that Armel was a native of Morgannwg, in the cantref of Penychen. King Arthur was said to have been born at Boverton in Penychen, and his uncle Pawl Penychen's Penllyn Court was just five miles north. In a book of Breton names, *Tous les Prenoms Breton,* by Alain Stephan of Gissort University he states that Arzel/Armel was born in South Glamorgan, was connected to Childebert's court, and was a 'warrior-lord'. There seem to be many links pointing that Armel and Arthur were the same person. *The Iolo mss.* however record Arthmael/Armel as being the son of Hywel ab Emyr Llydaw, and the brother of Derfael Gardarn, Tudwal, Dwyfael and possibly Leonore, and cousin of Cadfan, Samson, Padarn, Maglorius and Malo. However, the more reliable *Breton mss.* would surely have recorded the fact that Armel was a grandson of Emyr Llydaw (Budic

II). The Breton saints' lives are far better documented than those of Wales, and Armel would certainly have been recounted as a Breton rather than as a native of Glamorgan. Also Barber and Pykit believe that this Arthmael ap Hywel Mawr was known as St Mael in Wales.

With Abbot Carentmail, Arthmael landed at Aber Benoit in Finistere and moved inland to found Plouarzel. Around 540, Jonas King of Domnonia had died and Conmore (Conmire, Conor, Marcus Conomorus, March) married his widow, forcing the rightful heir Prince Ithael (Judual, Iuthael) to flee. Armel/Arthmael left Wales sometime after the battle of Camlan (537 or 539) and went directly to see King Childebert in Paris to plead Ithael's cause against Conmore. Samson's arrival also compounded the religious pressure against Conmore, and together they organised an armed rising, and thus Conmore was killed in battle in 555.

In reward, Arthmael was given a vast tract of land where he

established a monastery, where the present St Armel's Church stands at Ploermel (Plouharzel) in Morbihan, seven miles south-east of Josselin. Intriguingly, Ploermel was the chosen place for the famous 'Combat of the Thirty' in 1351. Thirty knights from the English garrison at Ploermel met 30 knights from the French garrison at Josselin. Described in vivid detail by Barbara Tuchman

The battle site at Branc-Haleg

(*A Distant Mirror*), the slaughter only ended when the English leader Bemborough died.

Many Welsh princes handed on their territories or positions and retired in middle age to monasteries (even Maelgwn Gwynedd for a time). This may have been a mechanism to ensure the survival of the princedoms, rather than seeing them split up by *cyfran* (gavelkind) on the ruler's death. The strong legend that Arthur was 'unmanned' by a groin wound at Camlan may have had an effect upon his decision to seek the monastic life and hand his crown on to the son (Constans, Cystennin) of his ally Geraint ab Erbin, who had died at Llongborth. Arthur's surviving son Morgan may have been too young to take over.

In the valley of Loutehel, Armel struck the ground with his staff and supplied water for the valley. He founded the monastery at Ploermel, near a lake called l'Etang du Duc. Mont-Saint-Armel is also named after him, and his image appears in a stained glass window at St Saveur, Dinan, with a slain dragon (representing Conmore or the Saxons). He took the creature to the top of the mountain and ordered it to leap into the river below. Ergue-Armel outside Quimper was also formerly dedicated to him, as were churches at

Langoet and Languedias, and four more chapels. In the *Breviary of Leon*, Arthmael is referred to as 'Miles fortissimus' – 'the strongest of soldiers', and in the Rennes prose he is invoked as an *armigere* against the enemies of salvation. He founded the monastery of St Armel-des-Bochaux near Rennes.

St. Armel

Henry VII's glorious chapel at Westminster Abbey features a gauntleted Armel, whom Henry Tudor believed saved him from shipwreck in Brittany. Armel's mutilated statue also stands on Cardinal Morton's monument in the crypt of Canterbury Cathedral. Armel is commemorated on alabaster sculptures in Stonyhurst College and St Mary Brookfield church in London, and on the reredos at Romsey Abbey. In his Anglicised form, Ermyn, he was venerated at Westminster Abbey. St Ermyn's Hotel in Westminster stood on St Ermyn's Hill, first mentioned in records in 1496 as St Armille's Hill. Armel's chapel there is now represented by Christchurch in Westminster. Why would a Breton-Welsh Dark-Age warrior-monk, only celebrated in Brittany, be celebrated in London? St Erme in Cornwall appears to be Armel's only British foundation. Some historians state that the Roman Road, the Ermine way, was so-called because it was used by Ermyn's cavalry troops.

In the Middle Ages Armel was prayed to by people with gout and rheumatism. Sometimes a patron of hospitals, his invocation was said to cure headaches, fever, colic, gout and rheumatism. He is usually depicted in armour and a chasuble, leading a dragon with an ermine stole around its neck. He was said to have subdued a dragon – could this be the white dragon of the Anglo-Saxons rather than Conmore? As mentioned, recent researchers have placed Armel as King Arthur who went to Brittany after recovering from his wounds at Avalon (Enlli Island). If the grim Battle of Camlan happened in 539, then Arthur could have joined his Breton kinsmen to fight for them. The dragon, ermine and the placing of his saint's day in the Sarum Calendar in 1498, under the new Tudor dynasty, mean that the links with King Arthur must be explored further. Henry Tudor, for long exiled in Brittany, believed he was saved from shipwreck by praying to St Armel. In 1485, he prayed at Merevale Abbey on his way to Bosworth Field. He returned as Henry VII in 1503 to give thanks, staying at the abbey again, and stained glass of his patron saint St Armel, which can still be seen, was placed in the south isle of the gate chapel.

In Saint Armel, the last of the saltbeds were abandoned thirty years ago, and turned over to oyster basins. The first Saturday in April sees the Miss Pearl festival at neighbouring Gildas-de-Rhuys. Gildas was Arthur's contemporary. There are no dedications to Arthmael in Wales, but there was a chapel in (British) Cornwall and he was commemorated annually at Stratton. His cult spread extremely rapidly from Brittany to Normandy, Touraine and Anjou.

The website 'Catholic Online Saints' gives the following entry: 'St Armagillus d.c. 570. Feastday August 16. Welsh missionary, called Armel, Ermel and Ervan, and a cousin of St Samson. He studied under Abbot Carentmael joining the abbot in missionary journies to Brittany, France. The missionaries founded Saint-Armel-des-Boscheaux and Plou-Ermel or Plouharzel. Connor, a local chieftain, forced them to leave the mission until 555. Connor was slain in battle that year, allowing their return. Armagillus is honoured in a Cornish church, St Erme.'

Samson's mother was Anna ferch Tewdrig, the sister of Meurig, which makes him Arthur's cousin. Arthur ap Meurig disappeared from Wales around 540 after the Battle of Camlan, and Armel was known as a warrior-saint in Brittany. The dispossessed Breton family of Amwn Ddu had married into Arthur's family, and many fought for him. Arthur had given lands to Carannog who went to Brittany with monks. Probably Carannog was Carentmael. It seems that a strong case can be made for Arthur and Armel being the same person. It would not have been in the interests of the princes of Wales and Henry VII to publicise the fact, as they were of the House of Gwynedd, not of the Silurian House of Gwynlliwg and Glwyssing.

* Emyr Llydaw, also known as Budic II, was forced to flee from the throne of Cornouaille in Armorica (Brittany) by the oncoming Franks. He married Arthur's sister, although some sources state that he married St Teilo's sister. One son, St Ismael, followed Teilo as Bishop of Menevia. Another son, Euddogwy, became Bishop of Llandaff. His son Amwn Ddu married Anna, the sister of Arthmael ap Meurig, and fought for the historical Arthur. Anna has been described as 'the sister of the High King of Britain'. Budic's son Hywel Mawr, or Riwal Mawr, is featured in Arthurian legend, and it may be that his mother was Gwyar, Arthmael ap Meurig's sister. Budic's son Alan Fyrgain, also fought for Arthur. Gwyndaf Hen, another son, married into Arthur's family, his wife being Gwenonwy, Arthmael ap Meurig's sister and he fought for Arthur's knights. It also seems that Arthur's grandfather Tewdrig had helped Budoc I to regain his Breton throne, and this may be the king remembered by Margam Abbey's 6th century Bodvoc Stone. The ties between the family of Arthmael ap Meurig ap Tewdrig, the Romanised-Silurian high-kings of Britain, and the royal family of Armorica certainly bring us closer to accepting the Arthmael-Arthur-Armel connection.

** Ploermel is near the area of Brocielande and the magical Forêt de Paimpont. Brocieland was the expanse of territory given to St Armel by Ithael after Armel helped him regain his throne from Conmire. Why is Armel's land so intrinsically linked with Arthur? This area has been sympathetically developed to link Arthurian legends with the site. It is where Merlin was imprisoned in a pool by Morgan le Fay, where the knights of the Round Table met at Comper Castle, and where knights tramped across the wastelands seeking the Grail. Comper Castle has been made into an Arthurian exhibition centre, the Abbey at Paimpont features effigies of the Welsh founding saints of Brittany, and a tree in the forest has been painted gold. Sights include a wonderful walk along the Val Sans Retour (Valley of No Return), the Fontaine de Barenton, the Fontaine de Jouvence (Spring of Eternal Youth), Comper Castle and its lake, the Etang Bleu (Blue Lake), the Etang du pas du Hout, Le Temple Helouin megalith, the Lac de Tremelin and the Tombeau de Merlin (Merlin's Tomb dolmen). Le Point-du-Secret on the southern fringe of the forest may hold the clue to the burial-place of Arthur/Armel.

Footnote:

From *Les Prénoms Celtiques* by Albert Deshayes, I have translated the entry upon Saint Armel as: 'Saint Arthmael was born in 482 in Wales. He emigrated to Armorica and landed on the shore at Leon. His was the foundation of the hermitage of Plou-Arzel. He made himself close to the King of France, Childebert I, and he stayed for six years in his palace (in Paris) before coming to Brittany. One after another, he had obtained two Breton parishes which took his name: Plouarzel and Ploermel. His name is also used at Ergue-Armel in Quimper and at Saint-Armel. It was Armel, near Rennes, who accomplished a number of miracles, and he died in 552. At Ploermel, a fountain (holy well?) is dedicated, and the local church possesses a stained-glass window depicting the saint. He is invoked for the cure of gout and rheumatism, and wet nurses prayed to him to have milk. Different scenes in the life of the saint feature in the windows of Plouarzel Church. Etymology: Composed of the old Breton (Welsh) term arth (meaning 'bear', taken in the sense of being a warrior) and mael, 'prince', the name given to Arzel, Arhel but also Armel by the process of Frenchification.'

Thus this 'bear/warrior-prince' was welcome at the court of the King of France for six years, so was obviously of noble Welsh stock. Could this have been Arthur, after the Battle of Camlan in 539? Six years in honoured recuperation, at Childebert's court, before going to Brittany to repay his debt to the Breton family that supported him in Britain? Another Breton source, *Prenoms en Bretagne* tells us the following (author's translation): 'Armel is in Brittany a Christian name of masculine origin. Its etymology is 'arz': (='ours') bear and 'mael': prince. St Armel came from Wales in the 6th century. He is often represented with a dragon kept on a lead, and which is wearing a stole. The legend of the dragon is frequent in Brittany, and is found concerning other saints. He is the founder of Ploermel: Plou-Armel. (Plou, like cil and llan in Welsh means a holy foundation). He has also given his name to Saint-Armel (Ille-et-Vilaine), Saint-Armel (Morbihan), Ergue-Armel (Finistère). The Breton

44

form of his the name is Arzhel, from which Plouarzel is formed (Finistère), where he has been supplanted by Saint Eloi. The evangelisation of Brittany was not easy: persecuted, Armel was exiled for a time at the court of King Childebert 1st. Armel is honoured for several deeds; he made water come from the earth, which could cure men and animals. He is represented among other saints in the Bishop's Palace at Rennes in the Breton calvary monument *'Breiz d'ha Bugale'* of Saint Anne of Aurac. Feminine form; Armel, Arzhela, Arzela, Arzhelenn, Arzhelez, Armela. Armelle is the Frenchified form. We have also found the derived names Ermel and Hermet from Saint Armel'.

Finally, from two more Breton sources, *Une Toponomie du Finistère* and *Les Noms des Saints Bretons* (J. Loth, 1910), Plouarzel is the parish of Arthmael, and 'according to the traditional Life, he was born in Great Britain and came ashore in Armorica in the region of Ac'H, a part of lower-Leon, between the Point St-Matthieu and the Aberwrach river [- 'mouth of the witch' - Breton is identical to Welsh in this instance]. He came into the former Roman garrison town of Vorganium, Ososmi, on the Finistère coast [not Carhaix, which was Vorgium], and which is now called Coz-Castell-Ac'H. Ploermel has his relics, but his tomb is in the borough of St-Armel, where he died abbot of the second monastery founded by him. His patronage is ancient at Ergue-Armel. Arthmael is made up of 'arto', or 'ours' = bear, and 'maglo', meaning chief.'

Bruno W. Häuptli has written in German in 2006 about Armel, and the following is my partial translation: ARMEL (Armagilus, Armagillus), Welsh missionary, holy celebration: 16.8. Born 482, Pen Ohen (Vale of Glamorgan, Wales), died 570 (or 552), St-Armel-des-Boschauts (Dept. Morbihan, Brittany). Numerous name variants: Armael, Armail, Armahel, Arthmael, Arzhmael, Arzhvael, Arzhvaelig, Arzel, Arzhel, Arzhael, Arzhaelig, Ermel, Ermyl, Ermyn, Ervan, Hermel. He came according to the oldest source, in the Breviary of St-Pol-de-Léon (1516) from a distinguished Welsh house. In recent years it was with Welsh missionaries including Paulus Aurelianus (Saint Pol), a close relative, at a Welsh monastery under abbott Carentmael (Caroncinalis, Carencinal), and accompanied him on mission journeys into Brittany. The missionaries Samson and Cadfan are [said] to have been his cousins. With numerous companions he crossed in 518 the English Channel, landed in the westernmost part of Brittany (county Léon) in the bay of the L'Aber Ildut and created a monk community in the area, designated later as Plouarzel (Plou = municipality), whereby he found support with king Childebert I. (511-558) and the Breton king Hoël I the Great (the fictitious British king list by Geoffrey of Monmouth, around 1130, was converted by later Breton historians into absolute chronologies; the Reign by Hoël I after 505...

Around 540 Armel fled after the murder of the king Jona of Domnonée from his brother Conomor (Cunomorus), who took the throne. Armel went to Paris under the protection of Childebert, but returned however later to the Breton Morbihan, where he received Ländereien for a monastery after driving out Conomors, from Jona's son and successor Judual, to the west of Rennes in the forest from Brocéliande (Forêt de Paimpont). Here Armel built an Oratorium with several monk cells (later called Saint Armel des Boschauts, where he worked up to his death, which to it the day before an angel had announced...

45

The nearby city Ploërmel (in former times Plouarmel) was likewise designated after it as well as several smaller localities in Brittany (St-Armel). [There follows a series of miracles and customs associated with Armel] Armel's Sarcophagagus is to have been in the church of Saint Armel des Boschauts. His relics are to be found across Brittany: Bubry, Languédias, Langouet, Lantic, Lorient, Meslan, Plouharnel, Saint Armel, Saint Gonlay. The regionally limited cult was spread since the 12th century by the house of Anjou from Brittany to Anjou, into Normandy and into the Touraine. Heinrich VII., king of England (1485-1509), founded a church in Cornwall (at Erme), after a shipwreck at the Breton coast. He believed Armel saved him, and in Westminster Abbey (chapel Henry VII) established a statue. Armel is the national patron of Brittany; the first names Armel and for girl Armelle (Arzhela, Arzhelez, Arzhelenn, Armela, Armaela) are here this very day common. As a patron of the hospitals he is called against headache, plague, colic, fever, Rheumatism. A Glass painting in the church of Saint Armel in Ploërmel shows scenes from his life - 1. Armel leaves England, 2. Armel heals leprosy patients, 3. Armel defeats the kite. A Fresco in Saint Denis d'Anjou shows the Dragon.' This wall painting in Mayenne shows Armel and St Blaise a dragon, with Armel holding a dragon with his stole. (Blaise was a Turkish saint, celebrated at St Blaise's Church in Blaizey, Cornwall.)

Apart from the Armel connections, the Arthurian legends are incredibly embedded in early Breton literature. Much will have been taken by Britons fleeing the Saxon incursions, and other information spread by the Welsh missionaries, and intermarriages between the royal families of Wales, Cornwall and Brittany.

SAINT TEILO d.c.560-580

ELIDIUS, ELIUD, TEILIAU, TELIAUS, THELIAU, BISHOP OF LLANDAF

Teilo's Feast Dates are February 9 (then February 20 at Ffair Wyl Deilo at Llandaf and Llandeilo Fawr), November 26, and June 11. He is the Patron Saint of horses and apple trees in Brittany. Widely venerated in Wales and Brittany, Teilo was an influential religious leader who founded the monastery at Llandeilo Fawr in Carmarthenshire. He was born near Penally (Eccluis Gunnian), near

St. Teilo's Church, St. Fagans

Tenby, the son of Ensic (Enlleu) and Guenhaf*. His first name was Elios, the Welsh name for Helios, the pagan sun god. Teilo was descended from Cunedda Wledig and supposed to have accompanied Dewi and Padarn on their trip to Jerusalem, caused by the wars against the Irish invaders. At Jerusalem, the Patriarch was said to have given Teilo a magical bell, which was kept at his shrine at Llandaff with his mitre and ritual comb. On his return to Britain, he went first to Cornwall and became Geraint's confessor, but left to avoid the Yellow Plague in 547. He went to Samson's monastery at Dol, founded in 544. Geoffrey of Monmouth believed that Teilo succeeded Samson as abbot there.

Another source states that Teilo was the son of Enlleu (Usyllt) ap Hydwyn Dwn ap Ceredig ap Cunedda, and Tegfedd ferch Tegid Foel of Penllyn. His sister married Emyr Llydaw. Teilo's half-brother was Afan,

bishop of Llanbadarn. Teilo was taught by Dyfrig, and founded the college of Llandaff, which was called Bangor Deilo. Teilo was also said to have been taught by Dyfrig and Paulinus (Pol de Leon). He then went to Tŷ Gwyn, where he came into contact with David, and followed David to the new monastery at Glyn Rhosyn, the present site of St David's Cathedral. During the Yellow Plague he stayed with St Samson in Brittany for seven years and seven months, planting the great orchard that stretched three miles from Dol to Cai. Teilo was said to have helped King Budic (Emyr Llydaw) battle a great serpent there. He located a holy spring at Kerfeuntain, and is associated with the stag in Brittany. When Teilo returned to Wales, St Cadog asked seven 'fundamental questions' to the seven wise men of his college at Llancarfan. Teilo was asked what was the greatest wisdom in a man. Teilo responded 'to refrain from injuring another

St. Teilo's holy well, Llandaf Cathedral

when he has the power to do so'.

In 577 the Angles won the great battle of Dyrham near Bath, cutting off the Welsh from their fellows in Dumnonia, the West Country. The victorious army crossed the Wye to chase the defeated Welsh. Prince Iddon, son of King Ynyr of Gwent, asked Teilo as the family priest to lead his army spiritually. Teilo led the prayers on a hill near the battle site, and when Iddon's troops were victorious, Prince Iddon gave Teilo the hill for a church, which he founded at Llantilio Crosseny. The White Castle now stands where Teilo prayed. Early in the 20th century this important church at Llantilio between Monmouth and Abergavenny was still pronounced locally as Llandeilo. Croesenni is the anglicisation of Croes Ynyr, the Cross of Ynyr. The battle took place along the meadows between the church and Tre Adam, and the large field there is still known as Maes-y-Groes, after the cross, which Iddon probably raised for his father after the battle. The present church dates from the 14th century.

Teilo died at Llandeilo Fawr, from whence came the fabulous *Chartulary* that was later appropriated from Llandaff by Lichfield Cathedral. It is now wrongly known as *The Book of St Chad*. Teilo was supposed to have been the second Bishop of Llandaff, and Euddogwy (Oudoceus) was his nephew. Llandeilo, Penally and Llandaff all claimed his body, which miraculously mutiplied into three. In 1850 his tomb was opened in Llandaff cathedral and his staff and pewter 'crotcher' rediscovered.

Thirty-seven churches are associated with Teilo in south and mid-Wales. The roofless Llandeilo Abercywyn church, outside Carmarthen, stood where the little river Cywyn joins the Taff. A nearby ancient farm building is known as 'The Pilgrim's Rest', and there are mediaeval 'Pilgrims' Graves' in the facing church of Llanfihangel Abercywyn. They may be the resting places of the Lords of Llanfihangel castle, or the tombs of pilgrims on their way to St David's cathedral.

Llandeilo Tal-y-Bont church, St. Fagans

St Teilo's Church, at Llandeilo Llwydarth near Maenchlochog in the Preseli Mountains, is now totally ruined. Burial stones from the fifth or early sixth century, inscrbed to Andagellus and Coimagnus, sons of Cavetus, have been moved to Maenchlochog Church. A third slab, dedicated to Curcagnus, son of Andagellus, was moved to Cenarth. The last entry in the Baptismal Register was in 1897, but the ruins lie in a much larger, defended complex which also enclosed the farms of Prisk (Prysg) and Temple Druid, formerly called Bwlch y Clawdd - Gap in the Embankment. A few hundred yards from the church is St Teilo's Well, originally called the Oxen Well, which became a centre of pilgrimage to Teilo in the Middle Ages. In his church at Llandeilo, Carmarthenshire, are two ornately carved stone wheelheads, all that remains of the high crosses that marked his early 'clas'.

One of Teilo's holy wells, northeast of the church at Llandeilo Llwydarth, now is built into a pump-house to supply water to the neighbouring farm. Even up to this century, it was used to cure tuberculosis, whooping coughs and other chest illnesses. In World War I local people dropped pins into the well, hoping to end the slaughter. The water had to be drunk early in the morning out of part of St Teilo's skull, 'penglog Teilo'. In Carmarthen Teilo had holy wells at Llandeilo Fawr, and near Cydweli, the latter being good for curing rheumatism and sprains and next to Capel Teilo. In Pembroke, Ffynnon Deilo was near Crinow Church, Lampeter Velfrey.

From around 1057 the Mathews family were recognised as the hereditary guardians of Teilo's Llandaf shrine, saving it from vandalism and descration. In recognition of this devotion, in the 15th century they were given his skull, which they brought to Pembroke. In 1658 the Melchiors, owners of Llandeilo farm, inherited it and it became the focus for the healing waters of Teilo's holy well. This relic became shiny through constant use over the centuries, and was handed to pilgrims by the senior member of the Melchior family. It was bought back by the Mathews family in 1927 for £27. These hereditary keepers of the ancient relic were 'conned' into selling it in the 1950's by two people posing as museum officials, and Penglog Teilo vanished. It reappeared in 1994 in Hong Kong and has now been installed in its own niche in Teilo's chapel in Llandaff. The well has since been capped to provide water for a nearby house.

St Margaret's Church in Marloes, Pembrokeshire, was originally a Teilo dedication. Cilrhedyn Church on the borders of Pembroke and Carmarthen is also dedicated to Teilo. Teilo's Well by the Bishop's Palace in Llandaff came to be known as the Dairy Well, and in its wall was found the remains of a Celtic cross with knotwork, which has now been removed to the south aisle of the cathedral. If visiting Llandaff Cathedral, one can walk a couple of miles south through parkland, following the river Taff, past Cardiff Castle, to go to the National Museum of Wales. It has a room dedicated to casts of all the Welsh Celtic crosses, and some original stone carvings.

Near Waungron, between Gorseinon and Pontardulais, were the remains of St Teilo's Church, Llandeilo Tal-y-Bont. They have been moved to the Museum of Welsh Life at St. Fagans, with the remarkable wall paintings being preserved in the rebuilt church. Known locally as 'the church in the marsh', it lay near the first crossing point of the river Loughor upstream from the old Roman fort of Leucarum (Loughor). Normans built two castles on either side of the river here, for it was an important strategic site for their slow and relentless conquest of south Wales. Teilo's church at Talgarth is in an area full of megaliths. Unfortunately Croes Llechan was destroyed, sometime in the late 19th century, but Maen Llwyd on Pen Cader and Ty Isaf dolmen can still be seen. There is also a nearby stone circle, sometimes called Gader Arthur, on Pen Cader in the Black Mountains.

Teilo's churches are mainly clustered in southwest Wales, in eastern Pembrokeshire and western Carmarthenshire. However, he has dedications in Llannarth, Llandeilo Gresynni and Llandeilo Porth Haelog in Monmouthshire, Llandeilo'r Fan in Brecom and Llandeilo Graban in Radnorshire, and two in Gower among his thirty-five or so churches. Rice Rees gave the following existing churches dedicated to Teilo:

Llandeilo Fawr – 3 chapels at Taliaris, Capel yr Ywen and Llandyfaen in Carmarthenshire; Brechfa in Carmarthen; Llandeilo Abercywyn in Carmarthen; Capel Bettws in Trelech a'r Bettws; Llanddowror in Carmarthen; Cilrhedin – Capel Ifan; Llandeilo near Maenchlochog in Pembroke; Llandeilo – the chapel of St Hywel in Pembroke; Llandeilo Graban in Radnor; Llandeilo Fran in Brecon; Llandeilo Tal-y-bont in Glamorgan; Llandeilo Ferwallt (Bishopston) and Caswel in Glamorgan; Llandaf Cathedral and Whitchurch in Cardiff; Merthyr Dyfan in Glamorgan; Merthyr Mawr – St Roque's Chapel in Glamorgan; Llanarth in Monmouth; Llandeilo Bertloeu i.e Llantilio Pertholey (Porth-halawg) in Monmouth; Llandeilo Rwnnus in Llanegwad near Talley Abbey; Llwyngraddan near Llanddewi Velfrey; Trefgarn in Pembroke; Penally near Tenby; Manorbier (Maenor Byr); Lanion near Pembroke; Llandeilo Llwydiarth near Cemaes; Brechfa in Brecon; Penclecir in Castle Martin, Pembroke; Talgarth, Brecon: Elfael in Radnor; and Llowes in Radnor.

Teilo was 'claimed' by Llandaff as a saint because of his glory, and somehow the illuminated missal from Llandeilo Fawr was taken there before 850. However, later it was stolen and resurfaced in Lichfield Cathedral as

the *Book of St Chad* – possibly the greatest treasure of Wales, comparable in national importance with the *Book of Kells* and the *Lindisfarne Gospels.* It may have been taken in the time of Wynsi, Bishop of Lichfield from 974-992, but another authority believes that it was taken in the 16th century. All of the Welsh monasteries had scriptoria, even before the English and Irish were converted, but hardly anything remains after over a millennium of invasions, burning and looting. The absence of illuminated manuscripts has led to English historians believing that Wales did not have the capabilities to produce them, but Wales has suffered far more violence and destruction in its history than any of the other home nations.

Chalice, containing fragment of St Teilo's skull, Llandaf Cathedral

The Trinity College exhibition of the *Book of Kells* and the *Book of Durrow* in Dublin shows how great a tourist attraction it could be for Wales. Nearly everything else of Welsh heritage has been stripped out or melted down. Llandeilo Fawr had its own scriptorium, and in the early Middle Ages, Wales was an area of 'tremendous sanctity'. A monk named Ysgolan in the 13th century was responsible for burning those libraries of Welsh princes that had escaped Irish, Viking and Norman depredations. Not only did the writings show pre-Catholic Christianity and influence, but also they could have been 'dangerously' tainted with Pelagianism. More valuable early Welsh books were lost in the Civil War, such as the great library of the Herberts at Raglan Castle. It is little known that the Second Civil War was mainly a Welsh affair.

This *Gospel* contains the earliest known written Welsh. Llandeilo, as recorded in its *Gospel*, was a bishopric, and two stone crossheads attest to its importance. When the cult of Teilo was transferred to Llandaff, Llandeilo became a church within the diocese of St David's. Arglwydd Rhys, The Lord Rhys, founded Talley Abbey in the 12th century and passed on much of Llandeilo's wealth to it. This community of Praemonstratensian canons was based on the French model, and Normanised the Welsh 'clas' pattern of churches in the area. All Llandeilo's records have been destroyed or lost except its *Gospel*.

The boundary dispute between Llandaff and St David's for the premier bishopric in Wales lasted for a few hundred years, with both claiming Teilo. Teilo was far more associated with David, however, and may have travelled with him to Brittany and Cornwall. In Brittany Teilo is the patron saint of apple trees and horses. Chateauneuf du Faou and Lennon, near Pleyben may be his foundations. Throughout the Middle Ages, oaths were taken on Teilo's tomb. When it was opened in 1736, the remains of his staff and chalice were found. An old Glamorgan proverb is that if no snow falls before Teilo's Day (February 9), then any that falls after will clear quickly from the ground. His 'Saying of the Wise', 'while doing penance' was 'it is not wise to contend with God.'

There were four fairs a year in the churchyard at Llandeilo Fawr, about which the churchwardens were 'reticent in telling their Bishop'. The following notes are from the church's excellent parish magazine *Y Groesfaen*. 'Archdeacon Tenison tells us about these: "On the fair-days" he reported, "Horses, sheep and lambs, & casks of Ale are brought into the Churchyard and sold there." The main fair was held on St Barnabas' Day (June 11th), and indeed was the only official fair recognised by the manor court, as the court record stated in 1710: "We present no fair or markett should be kept in the church yard except Barnaby faire." It was a fair with a long history, first being mentioned in 1324, when the Black Book of St David's recorded of Llandeilo that "The Lord (of the manor) has a fair once a year, namely, on the feast of St Barnabas the apostle, and it lasts for three days."'

From *Teulu Teilo*, the church magazine of Brechfa (written by Bob Lenny and the Reverend Patrick Thomas), the author notes the following commemorative services:

Sul y Blodau (Palm Sunday) young people carry the cross to Maes-y-Groes Farm, where there is an open-air service, before returning to the church for Hot Cross Buns. Sul y Pasg (Easter Sunday) begins with the 8 am service and lighting of the Paschal Candle, then at 11 am the Easter garden is blessed and Easter eggs and butterflies given to the children. On Sul y Drindod (Trinity Sunday) there is a joint Cymanfa Ganu (singing festival) with the parishes of Abergorlech, Caio, Talley, Llansawel and Llanfihangel Rhos-y-Corn. A recent addition is the Gwyl Sant Teilo a'r Afallennau (The Feast of St Teilo and the Apple Trees) on the third Sunday in September, following the Breton custom. Lessons are read in Breton, French, Welsh and English and the church is decorated with apple branches. (This is the type of innovation based upon tradition that the author would like to see spreading across Wales). Y Cyrddau Diolchgarwch am y Cynhaeaf (Harvest Thangsgiving Services) are bilingual, in mid-October.

* Although 'Guenhaf' is given as his mother, this may be another name (White, or Holy Summer) for Tegwedd ferch Tegid Foel.

Footnote:
Further information upon the theft of *Teilo's Gospels*, and the disinformation given by present and past staff of Lichfield Cathedral is given in a wonderful article by Rhodri Pugh in *Cambria* magazine, Canol Haf 2000. His *The Lost Treasures of Wales* should be read by all Welsh people, (preferably after a blood-pressure test) and a group be set up to bring this stolen and priceless Gospel back to Wales. An early medieval Welsh poem mentions 'the book-grabbing monks of Lichfield'. The greatest expert of early Welsh script, Professor Lindsay Wallace, stated that the book should be called *The Teilo Gospels*, as it was a product of a Welsh, nor Irish or English, scriptorium. Perhaps someone at Wales' National Assembly might take an interest in its return, thereby helping Wales materially for a change. The official guide to this 9th century gospel in Lichfield Cathedral notes that 'round the edge a 9th-century Welsh hand has scribbled names' and 'the evidence is strongly against the book being a product of a Welsh scriptorium... The quality of its (Wales) artistic output was far below that of the *Lichfield Gospels*.' This last sentence is particularly moronic - as noted above, Welsh land ownership and grants were noted in holy books, Bibles and Gospels, so invading Normans destroyed all written evidence in Wales when they claimed lands and burned the churches. There is no remaining literature from this time in its original form. So how can the writer compare the so-called 'Lichfield' *Gospel* with something that has not existed for hundreds of years? What 'artistic output' is he talking about? The problem is that mendacities in print are usually unthinkingly accepted and believed, the curse of Welsh history since the Venerable Bede supported barbarian attacks upon this most Christian country in the world. The Stone of Scone was returned to Scotland, the *Lindisfarne Gospels* will go back to Northumbria, and Wales needs this lost treasure back, and on display in Cardiff. Lindsay proved that the Gospel could not possibly have been English, and concludes that it is far more likely to be Welsh than Irish. (See *Early Welsh Script* by W.M. Lindsay, published by James Parker, London 1912, St Andrew's University Publications No. X).

SAINT CADOG c.497– 577

CATWG, CADOC, CATHMAEL, CADFAEL (BATTLE PRINCE), FOUNDER OF LLANCARFAN

An important Welsh saint and missionary, who like Dyfrig, Teilo, Beuno, Gwenfrewi (Winifred) and Padarn could have been Wales' patron saint. Venerated in South Wales, he probably visited Cornwall (but less likely Scotland), and was influential in Ireland because he instructed Finnian at Llancarfan. He seems to have been a

St. Cadoc, at Ile Saint-Cadoc, Morbihan, Britanny

contemporary of Gildas, David and Samson. According to Cressy, St Tathan at Caerwent taught him. He was associated with Arthur, and was said to have attended his court with the warrior-saint Illtud. His Feast Days are September 25 and February 24, and he is Patron of the Deaf in Brittany.

Cadog's parents, King Gwynlliw (Gundleus) and Gwladys, lived at Stow Hill in Newport, where St Woolos Cathedral (a corruption of Gwynlliw) now stands on the remains of a Celtic fort. Cadog was first named Cadfael (Battle Prince or Battle Seizer), but did not take his father's crown when Gwynlliw was converted. There are two versions of his death. One is that he was killed fighting the Saxons at Weedon* in Northants, where there is now a huge church. A more plausible story is that the Welsh hid his relics during the Norman invasion of Glamorgan, and used this story as a smokescreen when the great monastery of Llancarfan was placed under St Peter's of Gloucester. King Gwynlliw is said to have left his kingdom to Meurig, the son of King Tewdrig. Meurig had married into Gwynlliw's family, and was the father of Arthur.

There are at least twenty dedications to Cadog in South Wales, and one in Cornwall. Most are found around his foundation of Nant Carban (Llancarfan) in what was Glywyssing, (East Glamorgan), and around Llangattock-juxta-Usk in Gwent. Near Llangattock-juxta-Usk were Llangattock Lenig, Llangattock Lingoed and Llangattock Feibion Afel (Llangattock Vibon Avel – referring to the sons of Abel or Afel). Pendeulwyn (Pendoylan) in Glamorgan, Llangattock (just outsde Cardiff's Pontprennau estate), Llancarfan with its two chapels at Llanfeithin and Liege Castle, Pentyrch, Llanmaes, and Cadoxton-juxta-Barri (Tregatwg) are sites of his. There are also churches at the Roman sites of Gelli-gaer (with a chapel at Brithdir) and Caerleon. Other dedications include Llangadog Crucywel, Llanysbyddyd outside Brecon, Llangadog near Llandovery and

Cadoxton-juxta-Neath. The latter church had chapels at Aberpergwm and Creinant. Llanmaes Church (near Llanilltud Fawr, Llantwit Major) also is an old Celtic foundation, now dedicated to Cadoc.

There was a St Cadog's chapel in Llawhaden and Llanrhidian. Cadog's churches are also to be found north of Cydweli and in Cheriton and Portheinon on the Gower Peninsula. Penrhos-under-Llandeilo Crosseny in Monmouth, and Trefethin-under-Llanofer in Monmouth also were his. Penrhos came for a time to be under St Michael, but somehow returned to Cadog, and the place was known as Llancaddoc Penrhos in a list of Abergavenny churches in 1348. St David is now the patron saint of Raglan church, but again this is considered a Cadog foundation. Raglan has a superb battlemented tower, and the tombs of the Marquises of Worcester and Dukes of Beaufort. Cromwell's forces destroyed many of the Somerset family monuments there, after the siege of Raglan Castle in 1640.

St. Cadoc's holy well,
Saint-Cado-Ploemel, Britanny

There are few remains of Llangadog near Amwlch in Anglesey, but a church in Cambuslang near Glasgow is still dedicated to Cadog – probably another Cadog. He had a large chapel near Harlyn Bay near Padstow, now in ruins, with one of Cornwall's most famous holy wells. There was also a holy well in St Just near the river Fal, once called Fenton Cadoc (Ffynon Cadoc) and now called Venton-Gassick.

He is celebrated in Brittany, from the Lannion Peninsula to Vannes, with a famous monastery on the Ile de Cado, off the Quiberon peninsula. A beautiful islet with a 12th century chapel on the Etel estuary in Brittany was named Saint-Cado after a 6th century 'prince de Glamorgant', who returned to Wales and was martyred. He was the patron saint of the deaf, and those afflicted used to lie on a stone 'bed' inside his chapel. The church at Pleucadeuc east of Vannes is Cadoc's. The prefix Pleu (or Plou, or Plo) dates from before the eighth century and indicates an early centre of Celtic Christianity, much as Llan does in Wales. This Cadoc may be a son of Brychan however.

Llancarfan Church is dedicated to St Cadoc who founded the 6th century Nant Carban monastery here. Here he instructed Finnian of Clonnard, and prayed with him on the island of Flat Holm. Lifris wrote that the rocks around the island, known as the 'wolves', were real wolves that were turned to stone when they swam across the water to try and take Cadoc's sheep. Robert Fitzhamon, around 1107, gave Llancarfan church to the Abbey of St Peter, Gloucester. Cromwell's soldiers broke the churchyard cross. It is very odd that no ancient stones are to be found here, unlike at nearby Llanilltud Fawr, Margam, Merthyr Mawr and Llandough. Cadoc was baptised Catmail, and it is thought that the ruined church of Lancatal (Llancadle) near Aberthaw may be his foundation.

At Cadoxton-juxta-Neath, Cadog found on the banks of the river Nedd a wild boar, bees in a hollow tree, and the nest of a hawk at the top of

St. Cado's holy well, Ile Saint-Cado, Britanny

the tree. He sent these as gifts to King Arthfael (Arthur) who granted him land to build a church. However, Llanmaes was previously dedicated to Fagan, and was called Llanffagan Fach. The parish register of Cadog's church at Llanmaes records several centenarians, including Elizabeth Yorath, who died in 1668 aged 177. Another record reads 'Ivan Yorath buried Saturdaye ye XVII day of June anno dni 1621 et anno regni vicessimo primo anno aetatis circa 180. He was a sowdiar in the fight at Boswoorthe and lived at Llantwit major and he lived mostly by fishing.' So this soldier was a veteran 44 year-old in Henry VII's Welsh forces in 1485, and lived another 136 years!

Cadoc's *Life*, by Lifris, is the most complete of all the Lives written in Wales. Lifris' father was Bishop Herwald (1056-1104) and it is probable that Lifris was the last abbot of the great Llancarfan foundation before the Normans stripped it. Gildas is said to have copied the *Life* when he stayed with Cadoc, and Caradoc of Llancarfan, who wrote Gildas' own *Life*, states that it was still in the great church of Cadoc in 1150, covered with silver and gold. The Normans probably destroyed the original to hide land ownership details. Cadoc is again linked to Arthur by giving sanctuary to a man who killed some of Arthur's men. Nine cattle of the ancient breed of Glamorgan cattle (This black and white breed died out in the 19th century. A similar breed, red cattle, with a white stripe along the backbone – can be seen at Margam Abbey Park) were given in settlement. Cadog also argued with Maelgwn Gwynedd (Arthur's successor as pendragon), his son Rhun ap Maelgwn, and Rhain Dremrydd ap Brychan. These were times of the Britons of North Wales may have been pillaging in the south, after Arthur's fateful battle at Camlan.

In the 6th or 7th century, Ilias ap Morlais, with the approval of King Ithael, gave a mansion in the middle of Abermynwy (Monmouth) with land to Dyfrig, Teilo and Euddogwy, and in the possession of Bishop Berthgwyn, the fourth Bishop of Llandaff. However, in 1075 Withnoc founded a priory there and mentions the church of Cattwg in Monmouth, and this may be the same church originally dedicated to the three saints. It seems to have been in the priory churchyard, but the present building is dedicated to the Virgin Mary. Heth, in his description of Monmouthshire, says that the school now stands on the site, and that it was known as Geoffry's Chapel – a beautiful bay window there is still called Geoffry's Window. It was a Catholic chapel until the middle of the 18th century, and is believed to have been where Geoffrey of Monmouth studied.

Between Llangaddock and Bethlehem is a six feet standing stone supported by two others. At nearby Sythfaen is a ten feet Neolithic standing stone, and Coitan Arthur lies at Pont-yr-Aber also near Llangaddock. It is said to have been thrown here by Arthur from Pen Arthur Isa Farm on Cerrig Pen Arthur. Cadoc's memorial may have been at Landyfaelog Fach, where there was once a stone inscribed CATVC. Cadog's 'Saying of the Wise' was 'let the heart be where the appearance is.' At Llangatwg in Brecon is Ffynnon Gatwg, near the church. Francis Jones also notes his Glamorgan wells at Gelligaer (near the Roman camp), Pendoylan church, Aberkenfig, 'Kibwr' Castle and Court Colman. Near Llancarfan is Dyfrig's Well and the healing well Ffynnon y Fflamwydden (Flamebearer's Well) for erysipelas (fever with an infectious skin disease). Several streams meet in Cadog's Llancarfan, under the brooding Iron Age encampment, and it is an area noted for wells. Francis Jones gives several sources to study, and mentions pin and rag wells to cure King's Evil, and a rag well still used in the early 20th century where a paste was made from soil and well water to cure erysipelas. John Aubrey of nearby Llantrithyd mentions seeing crutches by wells in Llancarfan. Its Breach Well was still being used for erysipelas before the Second World War, where rags and pins were used as well as bathing.

* This attribution to Weedon, with its remarkable church, comes from the fact that it seems to have been called Beneventum. However, the Breton writer Albert le Grand places Beventum as Venta, or Caerwent, where Tathan originally taught Cadog. Barber and Pykitt have also noted Professor Bury's identification with Caerwent in his edited *Muirchu's Life of St Patrick*. Perhaps, therefore, Patrick came from Caerwent instead of Boverton.

GILDAS c.498 - c.570 or 583

ABBOT GILDAS BADONICUS, GILDAS THE WISE, GILDAS-DE-RHUYS OF MORBIHAN, GWELTAS, THE FIRST BRITISH HISTORIAN, 'THE SECOND APOSTLE OF IRELAND'

Gildas, son of Caw, wrote *De Excidio et Conquesta Britanniae* ('Concerning the Ruin and Conquest of Britain') in 540, which was extensively used by Bede. His epithet 'Badonicus' came from the fact that he was born in the year of the great victory over the Saxons at Mount Badon. Gildas was the first British historian, and it seems more than likely that he wrote *De Excidio* at Llanilltud Fawr or nearby Caer Worgan. In *De Excidio* is quoted the letter from the Britons to Aetius in Gaul asking for assistance against the pagans. He drew lessons from the Roman occupation of Britain, and denounced five contemporary 'tyrants', the kings named as Constantinus of Domnonia, Aurelius Caninus, Vortipor of Dyfed, Cuneglasus of North Wales and the lowest of them all, Maelgwn Gwynedd (Magloconus).

Gildas wrote accusingly that the decadence of British rulers and clerics had led to Anglo-Saxon successes in Ynys Prydein, the Island of Britain. After the remaining Roman troops left in 410 to protect the Empire in Europe, the Romanised Celts of the island were increasingly subject to attacks by the Picts of Scotland, the Scots of Ireland (Goidels) and the Saxons of Germany. During these disintegrating and troubled times, the British were increasingly pushed back westwards into the areas now known as Strathclyde, Cumbria, Wales and the West of England. The brunt of the attacks upon Celtic Wales in this period was from the sea-borne Irish Goidels, and from the Germanic tribes pushing ever westwards from what is now England.

Gildas was taught by St Illtud at Llanilltud Fawr, and visited Ireland, influencing the development of its church. The Irish High King, Ainmire was so concerned about the decline of Christianity in Ireland that he had requested Gildas to organise its revival around 570. Gildas took monks from St David's (Menevia) and Llancarfan to carry out the task, including (his son?) St Aidan, who joined the King of Leinster's retinue. Gildas came to be known as 'the second apostle of Ireland.' His Feast Date is January 29 (also January 28), and Gildas is the the 'rain-saint' of Brittany.

St Columbanus wrote to Pope Gregory the Great about 'Gildas auctor' who was asked to give advice on church doctrine to 'Vennianus auctor', probably Finnian of Clonard. Finnian had founded the monastic order in Ireland before his death in 548. Cadog possibly refused to arbitrate between Gildas and David for the see of Menevia. Cadog went with Gildas to Ronech and Echni (Steep Holm* and Flat Holm). Possibly the wild leek and entire-leaved peony still found there are remnants of the early monastic settlements. On Steep Holm, where Gildas is said to have stayed, there are a well and chapel, and he lived on birds' eggs and fish. In 530-534 he stayed at Glastonbury, where he was said to have arbitrated in a dispute between Arthur, and King Melwas of Somerset who had taken Gwenwyfar – Gildas halted Arthur's siege.

He returned to Wales when he heard that his eldest brother Huail (Hywel) had been killed by King Arthur**. He was later reconciled with Arthur, who asked for his pardon, then went to Armorica (Brittany) for ten years where it is claimed that he wrote his *Epistle* admonishing the British kings for their vices***. There are also claims that it was written in Glastonbury around 540-544. It certainly seems to date from around the time of Camlan and Arthur's possible death. When Gildas returned from Brittany, Cadog asked him

St Gildas' chapel near St. Nicholas-des-Eaux, Morbihan

to direct the studies in Llancarfan for a year. Like Cadoc, he then went to a small island (perhaps Flat or Steep Holm, or even Barri Island), intending to spend the rest of his days in prayer, but was disturbed by pirates.

Gildas' lack of reference to Arthur in *De Excidio* is legendarily excused by the story that he threw the pages concerning the warrior into the sea, after Huail's death. However, it could be that the main purpose of the book was to chastise the retreating Welsh chiefs rather than praising the good Britons that fought for their country. There is also doubt that Arthur was present at Badon Hill – 498 may be too early, and it seems that Ambrosius led the British forces, possibly assisted by another chieftain called Arthmael. Arthur was around 16 at this time, probably old enough to fight (when life expectancy was far shorter), but too young to assume any real battle command.

According to Breton tradition Gildas ended his days in Brittany, founding the monastery near Rhuys near Morbihan, and dying on the Island of Houat. Gildas-de-Rhuys neighbours Saint Armel, which again shows his links with Arthur. Exiled from Paris, Pierre Abelard was abbot at Gildas-de-Rhuys in 1126, writing to Heloise 'I live in a wild country where every day brings new perils'. Showing remarkable acuity, he quickly fled as he realised that his brother monks were trying to poison him.

On the Gulf of Morbihan Gildas was known as a 'Breton' monk called Gweltas, and there is a 'Bonnes Fontaine' under the Grand Mont where his Romanesque abbey-church is situated. This well is where Gildas first stepped upon the mainland. The Rhuys Peninsula, 17 miles south of Vannes, has an exceptionally mild climate, and was renowned for its wine and its 6th century monastery. The Île St Gildas, off Treguier on the Cotes-d'Armor, has St Gildas' Chapel, two dolmens and a shrine to St Roch. In 919, because of Viking raids the monks at Rhuys fled to Locminé with the body of Gildas. The Isle of Houat, off Quiberon in Brittany, also has a church dedicated to St Gildas. With fellow Welsh saints Herve and Eloi, prayers were given to Gildas in Brittany for sick horses. His feast day is still celebrated in Vannes, and in Carhaix his festival has assumed the character of St Cerwydd's and is a fateful rain-day. (Cerwydd's legend of 40 days of rain was appropriated by Swithin, centuries later). Some other dedications include St Gildas south of Chateaulin, St Gildas-des-Bois north of St Nazaire, St Gueltas between Lamballe and Plancoat, and St Gildas north of Carhaix-Plouguer.

Llanildas near Llanilltud Fawr became Y Wig Fawr (The Great Wood) and is now known as Wick. It seems a pity that our first historian is not remembered in his own country, and perhaps Wick could re-assume its original name. His brothers were said in his *Life* to be St Allgo (Allectus), St Eugrad (Egreas), St Maelog, Guillin and he had a sister Peithien (Peteona). Old Welsh sources claim he had five sons, Cenydd, Maidoc (Aidan), Dolgan, Nwython and Gwynno. The sons of St Cenydd were St Ffili and St Ufelwy.

A wonderful fragment of one of his letters remains: 'Abstinence from bodily food is useless without charity. Those who do not fast unduly or abstain overmuch from God's creation, while being careful in the sight of God to preserve within them a clean heart (On which, as they know, their life ultimately depends), are better than those who do not eat flesh or take pleasure in the food of this world, or travel in carriages or on horseback, and so regard themselves as superior to the rest of men: to these death has entered through the windows of their pride.' He also left a 'lorica', a kind of charm prayer for every part of the human body, asking for protection of the teeth, tongue, mouth, throat, uvula, windpipe, root of tongue, etc., etc. Gildas' 'Saying of the Wise' is: 'fortune will never favour the hateful'.

It is well worth quoting parts of *De Excidio* to show the feeling with which Gildas wrote of his times. Interestingly he calls Vortigern 'unlucky' in the first extract (from Chapters 23 and 24), when he invited the Saxons into Kent to act as mercenaries, against the constant attacks from Ireland and Scotland. In the second extract, from Chapter 25, we can see his great admiration for Emrys Wledig, Ambrosius Aurelianus, who pushed back the ravaging Saxons for a time:

'They first landed on the eastern side of the island, by the invitation of the unlucky king, and there fixed their sharp talons, apparently to fight in favour of the island, but alas! more truly against it. Their mother-land, finding her first brood thus successful, sends forth a larger company of her wolfish offspring, which sailing over, join themselves to their bastard-born comrades. From that time the germ of iniquity and the root of contention planted their poison amongst us, as we deserved, and shot forth into leaves and branches'... 'For the fire of vengeance, justly kindled by former crimes, spread from sea to sea, fed by the hands of our foes in the east, and did not cease, until, destroying the neighbouring towns and lands, it reached the other side of the island, and dipped its red and savage tongue in the western ocean...

So that all the columns were levelled with the ground by the frequent strokes of the battering ram, all the husbandmen routed, together with their bishops, priests and people, while the sword gleamed, and the flames crackled around them on every side. Lamentable to behold, in the midst of the streets lay the tops of lofty towers, tumbled to the ground, stones of high walls, holy altars, fragments of human bodies, covered with livid clots of coagulated blood, looking as if they had been squeezed together in a press; and with no chance of being buried, save in the ruins of the houses, or in the ravening bellies of wild beasts and birds; with reverence be it spoken for their blessed souls, if, indeed, there were so many found who were carried, at that time, into the high heaven by the holy angels. So entirely had the vintage, once so fine, degenerated and become bitter, that, in the words of the prophet, there was hardly a grape or ear of corn to be seen where the husbandman had turned his back.'

'Some, therefore, of the miserable remnant, being taken in the mountains, were murdered in great numbers; others, constrained by famine, came and yielded themselves to be slaves for ever to their foes, running the risk of being instantly slain, which truly was the greatest favour which could be offered them; some others passed beyond the seas with loud lamentations instead of the voice of exhortation. "Thou hast given us as sheep to be slaughtered, and among the Gentiles hast thou dispersed us." Others, committing the safeguard of their lives, which were in continual jeopardy, to the mountains, precipices, thickly wooded forests, and to the rocks of the seas (albeit with trembling hearts), remained still in the country.

But in the meanwhile, an opportunity happening, when these most cruel robbers were returned home, the poor remnants of our nation (to whom flocked from divers places round about our miserable countrymen as fast as bees to their hives, for fear of an ensuing storm), being strengthened by God, calling upon him with all their hearts, as the poet says, - "With their unnumbered vows they burden Heaven," that they might not be brought to utter destruction, took arms under the conduct of Ambrosius Aurelianus, a modest man, who of all the Roman nation was then alone in the confusion of this troubled period left alive. His parents, who for their merit were adorned with the purple, had been slain in these same broils, and now his progeny in these our days, although shamefully degenerated from the worthiness of our ancestors, provoke to battle their cruel conquerors, and by the goodness of our Lord obtain the victory.' It is hardly surprising from this contemporary writing, that the Celtic Church refused to evangelise the Saxons in later years, incurring the wrath of Bede.

* On Steep Holm, on the beach near the monastery ruins, was found a small Celtic 'god-head', whose 'shouting aspect' signifies a symbol of life. It could have been placed in a wall as a talisman or fixed into the mouth of an island spring, which emerges from the cliff face. It may have been venerated by some of the Celtic soldiers who made up the Roman garrison there. Steep Holm was known as Ronech in Gildas' time, and Flat Holm as Echni. Barri (Ynys Peirio) was also a hermit island. Gildas and Cadoc probably used the Roman ruins on Steep Holm as a base for their hermitage. They were said to live on fish and the eggs of sea birds. The edible plant known as Alexanders still grows on the island, as do wild leeks and nettles, which would have complemented their diet. A few times a year one can travel to Steep Holm by the world's last ocean-going paddle steamer from Penarth, and walk around for a few hours. Flat Holm can also be reached most days of the year from Cardiff. The Saxons renamed the islands Bradanreolice and Steopanreolice ('Broad', and 'Steep Place of Burial').

The early Welsh regarded isolated offshore islands around Wales as sacred burial sites. John Leland (c.1506-1552) quoted from an old document, now lost, that Saint Cadoc the Wise stayed on Flat Holm ('Echin', sic) and Gildas on Steep Holm ('Ronnet', sic) respectively. Leland also states that on Steep Holm Gildas began writing *De Excidio*. There was a Roman signal station upon Steep Holm, in sight of the Roman harbour of Cardiff, and also within site of the Roman supply base of Classis Britannica, the Roman fleet, at Cold Knap in Barri. This latter Roman naval defence base, protecting the Channel from Irish attacks, is of great historical importance, and some remains can still be seen.

Steep Holm has the remains of a mediaeval priory, and Mary Collier's 1972 book on the *Ghosts of Dorset, Devon and Somerset* repeats a 19th century recollection: 'But although the religious house at Glastonbury was once his home, his ghost haunts Steep Holme. Maybe he loved the little island. He is not seen, but on moonlight nights he is heard nearby the ruin of the Priory, just the slow footsteps of somebody walking along, which are called "St Gilda's Tread". The 'tread' has also been heard throughout the 20th century, a noise like the 'slow crunching of gravel'; although there are no gravel paths, and the reports predate the introduction of Muntjac deer in 1977.

** In Ruthin today, Maen Huail in St Peter's Square is supposed to be the stone upon which Arthur executed Huail. It seems that Arthur may have given lands to atone for this deed, as Gallgo, Maelog, Eugrad and Peithien all had foundations in Radnorshire. Rowland's *Mona Antiqua* makes Caw the father-in-law of

61

Modred, which again would place Gildas with his kinsmen antipathetic to Arthur.

*** The tone of Gildas' attack upon the remaining kings of the British people can be seen in the following extract: 'Britain has kings, but they are tyrants; she has judges, but unrighteous ones; generally engaged in plunder and rapine, but always preying on the innocent; whenever they exert themselves to avenge or protect, it is sure to be in favour of robbers and criminals; they have an abundance of wives, yet are they addicted to fornication and adultery; they are ever ready to take oaths, and as often perjure themselves; they make a vow and almost immediately act falsely; they make war, but their wars are against their countrymen, and are unjust ones; they rigorously prosecute thieves throughout their country, but those who sit with them at table are robbers, and they not only cherish but reward them; they give alms plentifully, but in contrast to this is a whole mountain of crimes which they have committed; they sit on the seat of justice, but rarely seek for the rule of right judgement; they despise the innocent and the humble, but seize every occasion of exalting to the utmost the bloody-minded, the proud, murderers, the concubines and adulterers, enemies of God, who ought to be utterly destroyed and their names forgotten. They have many prisoners in their gaols, loaded with chains, but this is done in treachery rather than in just punishment for crimes...'

MERLIN 5th - 6th century

ARTHUR'S WIZARD

Arthur's advisor, prophet and magician is basically a construct of Geoffrey of Monmouth's *History of the Kings of Britain*. Geoffrey combined the Welsh traditions of the prophet-bard Myrddin with a story from Nennius (q.v.). Geoffrey also wrote *The Prophesies of Merlin**. The *Prophetiæ Merlini* is a Latin work circulated from about 1130. Merlin became

Dinas Emrys

a popular figure in 13th century French works, and Thomas Malory made him Arthur's advisor in the *Morte d'Arthur*, and the creator of the Round Table at Caerleon for Uther Pendragon. Tennyson made him the architect of Camelot in *The Idylls of the King*. The earliest known reference is in the prophetic poem *Armes Prydain, (The Prophecy of Britain)*, probably dating from around 900.

Myrddin Emrys, after whom Caerfyrddin, Carmarthen, was named, is the Merlin of Arthurian legend. Merlin's Oak, a leafless stump held up by iron struts, stood in the centre of Caerfyrddin until 1958 when it was removed to assist more carbon and lead pollution by modern traffic. Merlin had prophesied that Carmarthen would fall with the death of the tree, so it had been carefully preserved until the Philistines took over and uprooted it, along with fifteen hundred years of legend. His prophecies were 'Llanllwch has been, Carmarthen shall sink, Abergwili will stand', and 'Carmarthen, you shall have a cold morning; Earth will swallow you, water in your place'. Another of his prophecies was that a bull would go to the top of St. Peter's Church in Carmarthen, and a calf was found at the top centuries later. Clas Myrddin (Merlin's Enclosure), is an early name for Britain, in the early Welsh Triads.

The most famous wizard in the world, he was in Welsh folk tales long before the Arthurian cycle, where he appeared as Arthur's councillor, and foresaw that hero's downfall. He became known as Merlin because the Latinized form of Myrddin would have been *Merdinus*, linked to the Latin for dung, *merdus* (the French *merde*). He was also a poet and a prophet, forecasting that one day the Welsh would once again take over the land of Britain and drive the Saxons out. This shows remarkable scientific foresight – the east side of the British Isles is dropping into the sea at three to four times the rate of that of the west side. In future millennia, England will have disappeared and Wales and its Cornish, Cumbrian and Strathclyde cousins – the old Britons - will once again rule this island.

As a youth, Merlin was linked with Vortigern (Gwrtheyrn), King of Britain, who could not build a tower on Dinas Emrys. Merlin informed him that there was a problem because two dragons guarded an underwater lake. These red and white dragons were symbolic of the Britons against Saxons fighting for Britain. Recent archaeological excavations have shown an underground pool in the mountain. In legend, he next advised Ambrosius Aurelius, the conqueror of Vortigern, to bring back the Giant's Ring of sacred stones from Ireland and erect Stonehenge. After the death of Ambrosius, his successor Uther Pendragon became besotted with Eigyr (Igraine), wife of Gorlois, so Merlin shape-shifted Uther into Gorlois and she conceived Arthur. After the Battle of Arturet, Merlin went insane and lived in the woods. He returned to advise Arthur.

Welsh traditions say that he lies in chains in a cave under Bryn Myrddin, Carmarthen, or in a cave near Dinefwr castle, or is buried on Bardsey Island, where he took the 'Thirteen Treasures of Britain' He is also thought to have been imprisoned in Merlin's Pool in Brittany. There were probably two Myrddins, one Myrddin Wyllt, a Celtic wizard who lived in the Scottish woods at the time of Vortigern, and Myrddin Emrys from Carmarthen, who lived at the time of Arthur.

The Breton link with Merlin and Arthur is interesting. There is a scenic tour in the 'Purple Country' of Broceliande, fifty-six miles of roads criss-crossing ancient sites and megaliths. The Barenton Spring is where Merlin first met Vivian the Enchantress. Merlin's Tomb is an old passage grave where he was said to be imprisoned by Vivian. Also in the forest, the lake known as the 'Fairies' Mirror' is also supposed to be used by Vivian to hold Merlin. Morgana le Fay imprisoned Arthur's unfaithful knights in 'The Valley of No Return'. Comper Castle's lake is said to have been the home of Vivian, who brought up Lancelot under its waters, and the castle has an Arthurian exhibition. Paimpont Abbey celebrates the 6th century Welsh missionaries who were the 'founder-saints' of Brittany.

Prophecy of Merlin (Prophetiae Merlini), sometimes called *The Prophecy of Ambrosius Merlin concerning the Seven Kings*, is a 12th-century poem written in Latin hexameters by John of Cornwall, which he claimed was based or revived from a lost manuscript in the Cornish language. The original manuscript is unique and currently held in a codex in the Vatican Library. Thomas Heywood's 1812 *The Life of Merlin* links Merlin's prophecies through all the events in British history, for example the Gunpowder Plot: 'To conspire to kill the King, / To raise Rebellion, / To alter Religion, / To subvert the State, / To procure invasion by Strangers.'

* *The Prophesies of Merlin* is in the *Bodley 6943 ms, Magdalen College ms* and elsewhere, and was used by Chaucer. Part of the Magdalene version reads as follows:

'When feythe fayleth in prestys sawys (When faith fails in priestly sayings)
And lordys will be londys lawys (And lords turn against God's laws),
And lechery is prevy solas, (And lechery is held as a privy solace)
And robbery is goode purchase (And robbery is a good bargain)
Then shall the londe of Albion (Then shall England)
Be turned into confusion. (Be turned into confusion.)
When Goneway shall on Curtays call, (When rudeness calls upon courtesy)
Then Wallys shall rayke and hastely rise; (Then Wales shall wake and quickly rise)
Then Albion Skottlonde shall to hem fall; (And England and Scotland fall to them)
Then waken wonders in every wise. (Causing wonder in everyone)
The rede Irelonde foc shall rise with all (The red Irish fox shall rise with all)
With glayvys grownde, and gare men to agryse (With weapons ground and cause men to attack)
To fell and fende oure fomen all; (To fell and battle all our enemies)
Sevyn shall sytt in youre asyse.' (Seven will be sit in your assize)

Footnotes:

1. A French scribe wrote in *Vita Edward Secundi, (The Life of Edward II*), around 1330: 'The Welsh habit of revolt against the English is a long-standing madness... and this is the reason. The Welsh, formerly called the Britons, were once noble, crowned with the whole realm of England; but they were expelled by the Saxons and lost both name and country. However, by the sayings of the prophet Merlin they still hope to recover England. Hence it is they frequently rebel.'

2. Geoffrey writes: 'Mortality shall snatch away the people, and make a desolation over all countries. The remainder shall quit their native soil, and make foreign plantations.' This could refer to the 570 plague, which led, along with Saxon incursions, to many Britons settling in Brittany and giving it its language. 'The white dragon shall rise again, and invite over a daughter of Germany' could mean that after centuries of French-origin kings from 1066, the Hanoverian succession of some minor prince 58th in line to the throne has given us a German dynasty until today. The white dragon was the emblem of the Saxons. Since the time of George I, the first non-Germanic royal marriage was that of Albert (George VI) to a Scot. Their daughter married a Battenburg, and her son Charles married Diana Spencer, the first English person to marry into the royal family for centuries. Geoffrey's forecast that 'Women shall become serpents in their gait, and all their motions shall be full of pride' obviously predicts the rise of the supermodel.

SAINT DAVID, DEWI SANT 520 – 1 March 589

THE WATERDRINKER, PATRON SAINT OF WALES

Dewi Sant by John Goscombe

Feast Day March 1, July 10 in Brittany; Canonised 1119 or 1124 by Pope Calixtus; Emblem - a dove; Flag – a gold saltire on a black background; David is the only Welsh saint canonised and culted in the Western Church. Dates of birth are variously given between 460 and 520; death between 544 and 589.

Dewi ap Sant (Sanctus) ap Ceredig ap Cunedda was the great-grandson of Cunedda, who came from the North Country to settle in North Wales, and the grandson of the founder of Ceredigion. Geoffrey of Monmouth believed that David was King Arthur's uncle, as did Giraldus Cambrensis. He was possibly born in Henfynyw in Ceredigion, where the church is dedicated to him. Ffynnon Ddewi (David's Well) lies nearby. It seems that his original monastery, on land inherited from his father, was at Henllan in Dyfed, and Dewi moved to Menevia, St Davids, later. The Irish *Catalogue of the Saints* of 730 records that Irish monks 'received the mass from Bishop David, Gildas and Teilo', and they influenced monastic development in Ireland. His uncle was St Carannog and his aunt St Ina. His cousins were said to be saints Cenau, Dogfael, Pedr, Gwynlle and Afan.

Legend says that his father Sant was told by an angel to save some land for David, thirty years before he was born. Also at this time St Patrick

**St. David's shrine,
St David's Cathedral**

was going to settle in Glyn Rhosyn (Vallis Rosina, Vale of Roses) near the sea in Pembrokeshire, when an angel told him to leave it, as the place was reserved for a boy to be born in thirty years' time. Patrick was so upset at his God preferring an unborn child to him, that God had to take Patrick to a cliff rock still known as Eisteddfa Badrig (*Sedes Patricii*, Patrick's Seat), to show him that God wanted him to look after all of Ireland instead.

Many sources state that Dewi was born on the site of St Non's Chapel near St David's, baptised at Porth Clais, and educated at Hen Fynyw or Henllwyn (Vetus Rebus), with St Teilo, studying under Peulin (Paulinus). St Illtud's *Life* however says that David, Gildas, Samson and Paulinus studied under Illtud. Dewi is said to have founded twelve monasteries, from Croyland to Pembrokeshire, and Glastonbury and Bath.

It was claimed that Dewi made a pilgrimage to Jerusalem, where he was made a bishop, and took a principal part at the councils of Brefi (in Ceredigion) and Caerleon. At the Synod of Brefi he was recognised as primate of all Wales to replace Dubricius (Dyfrig), and he moved the see from Caerleon to his homeland of Menevia (Mynyw, or St David's in Pembrokeshire). Much of this information stems from Rhygyfarch's *Life of St David*, of around 1090, with which Giraldus Cambrensis (q.v.) attempted to make St David's independent of Canterbury, and may not be reliable. All sources agree, however, that his principal seat was at St David's, where he died. There is a legend that he died in the arms of his pupil and great friend, Maedoc of Ferns. The great Irish saints who are claimed to be taught by David included Maedoc, Finnian of Clonard, Senan of Scattery Island, Findbar of Cork and Brendan of Clonfert.

The most famous tradition about David is that the ground rose at his feet at the Synod of Brefi in 545. David had never preached before, but was persuaded by St Deiniol and St Dyfrig to do so, where the church now stands at Llanddewi Brefi. He was heard as clear as the bell as far away as Llandudoch (St Dogmael's, on coast). David was known traditionally as 'The Waterman' as he and his monks were ascetic teetotallers and vegetarians. His last words were said to have been 'Lords, brothers and sisters, be happy and keep the faith, and do those little things you have seen me do and heard me say.'

The legend that David went with Teilo and Padarn on pilgrimage to Jerusalem, is mentioned in the *Lives* of all the other saints. It was recounted that the Patriarch John III of Jerusalem advanced him to the Archbishopric of Mynyw, Menevia, and gave Dewi the gifts of a staff, bell, golden tunic and portable altar. In David's Welsh *Life*, however, he is consecrated Archbishop in Rome when Peulin tells the Synod of his holiness. The *Brut Dingestow* says that at this time there were just three archbishoprics in Britain and David succeeded Dyfrig (Dubricius) at Caerleon, not Mynyw (St David's). The other two cathedrals were London and York. One of Merlin's prophecies was that 'Menevia shall be dressed in the shadow of the City of the Legions'. Geoffrey of Monmouth agrees with this, but one *Triad* tells us that the three Archbishoprics of 'Ynys Prydain' (the Island of Britain) were St David's, Canterbury and York.

Dewi is culted in Hereford, Gloucester, South Wales, Devon, Cornwall and Brittany, where he seems to have travelled to escape the great plague of 547. He was invoked to cure sick children in Brittany. David was recognised as patron saint of Wales only when the bones of Gwenfrewi (Winifred) were removed to England. Bishop Asser's *Life of Alfred*, written around 893, mentions the famous monastery and parish of Holy David. About 1120 Pope Callistus II approved David's cult, and a letter sent by the Chapter of St David's to Rome around 1125-1130 claimed that St David's had been a metropolitan see since the beginnings of Christianity in Britain. Two pilgrimages to David at Mynyw equalled one to Rome, and three journeys now equalled one to Jerusalem. St David's Cathedral was rebuilt in 1275, largely from offerings taken at his shrine, which William the Conqueror, Henry II and Edward I and Queen Eleanor had visited.

David is associated with over fifty known churches in South Wales, most in the southwest. Glastonbury was claimed to be founded by David. In St David's Cathedral is a cross-slab with Latin crosses. At Llanddewi Brefi, possibly Dewi's original monastery, are four stones. Two are cross-marked, and one inscribed to Dallus Dumelus. Another inscribed stone reads: 'HIC IACET IDNERT FILIUS IACOB / I QUI OCCISUS FUIT PROPTER / PRAEDAM SANCTI DAVID' - 'Here lies Idnert son of Jacob who was killed because of the despoiling of St David'. A 1693 record fills in the defaced words David and Jacob for us. This stone dates from around the 7th century, possibly carved after St David's was ransacked.

A tall stone has been 'Christianised' and is called St David's Staff, which Dewi and Dyfrig were said to have leaned upon at the famous Synod of Brefi. At St David's Cathedral are also a number of Celtic cross-slabs. One stone had been used as a gatepost and has an inscription to 'Gurmarc'. They came from a holy well at Pen Arthur Farm a few miles away.

The church of St Mary and St David in Kilpeck in Herefordshire was formerly dedicated solely to St David. Its amazing carvings and rare 'sheel-na-gig' draw visitors from all over Britain. The present church dates from around 1140, but some Saxon stonework survives. At Llanddewi Aberarth, just north of Aberaeron, there are two Celtic stone fragments embedded in the wall of the west porch. Probably 10th century, they were found in the 1860 rebuilding of the church, and are parts of what has been called the 'finest cross in Wales.' The inscription is faded on one, and the other stone has key patterns and intricate Celtic knotwork. In the church is an 11th century 'hogback' stone, the only one in Wales and of a type only found in 'Viking' Yorkshire. 'Bangu' was David's portable bell and was kept in Glascwm Church, one of the first twelve churches he founded.
The following dedications in modern Wales can be noted:

Pembroke – St David's cathedral, Whitchurch, Brawdy, Llanychllwydog, Llanychaer, Maenor Deifi, Bridell, Llanddewi Velfrey, Hubberston, Prendergast;

Carmarthen – Abergwili, Bettws, Henllan Amgoed, Abergorlech, Llanarthney, Abergwesyn, Llangadock, St David's Carmarthen, Llanycrwys, Meidrim;

Glamorgan – Llanddewi in Gower with a holy spring, Llangyfelach, Ystalyfera, Bettws, Laleston;

Monmouth – Llanddewi Fach, Llanddewi Skirrid, Bettws, Raglan, Llanthony (formerly Llanddewi Nant Honddu), Llangeview, Trostre;

Hereford – Much Dewchurch, Little Dewchurch, Kilpeck, Dewsall;

Ceredigion – Bangor Teifi, Henllan, Blaenpennal, Bangor, Blaenporth, Henfynyw, Llanddewi Aberarth, Llanarth, Llanddewi Brefi, Blaenpenal, Capel Dewi (near Llandysul);

Brecon – Garthbrengi, Llanfaes, Llanwrtyd, Llanddewi Abergwesyn, Llywel, Trallwng, Maesmynys, Llanynys, Llanddewi y'r Cwm, Llanddulas;

Radnor – Creguna, Gladesbury, Glasgwm, Llanddewi Ystrad Enny, Llanddewi Fach, Heyope (Llanddewi Heiob), Whitton (Llanddewi yn Hwytyn).

Many churches were re-dedicated to David after he became patron saint of Wales, but there are no North Wales dedications to him in the traditional 'Six Counties', and very few in Cadog's territory of Glamorgan and

Monmouth, Glywyssing. In Monmouthshire there is Capel David near Abergafenni, Raglan, Llanddewi Rhydderch, Llanddewi Fach and Llanddewi Ysgryd. Llangadog Church in Carmarthenshire seems to have been previously dedicated to David. Llanarthne is now re-dedicated to David, and St Llywel's church at Llywel now also has dedications to David and Teilo. Near the great Carreg Cennen Castle, at Trapp on the Black Mountain, are earthworks and stone rubble of an ancient chapel dedicated to David.

In Hereford, Kilpeck, Dewsall, Little Dewchurch and Much Dewchurch are all dedicated to David. It seems that David travelled to Ireland, and also that he and Teilo evangelised parts of the West Country and Brittany. In Devon (Dumnonia was still British until around 900), there were dedications at Tilbruge (Thelbridge), Ashprington and Painsford, St David's chapel to Heavitree in Exeter and also in Cornwall at Dewstowe (Davidstow). His mother Non had dedications at Bradstone in Devon and at Altarnon and Plenynt (Pelynt, Plint) in Cornwall.

The political power of the bishops of St David's probably swayed the choice of David as the patron saint of Wales – as stated there is not one

St David's Altar Stone
St David's Cathedral

dedication to him in North Wales. Research by the Reverend Rice Rees in Wales in the 1830's showed that 'in the original Diocese of Llandaff he has but two chapels, and only three in what is supposed to have been the original Diocese of Llanbadarn; all the rest, including every one of his endowments, are in the district of which, as Archbishop of Menevia, he was himself the Diocesan. The Cathedral of St David's is in the territory of his maternal grandfather, the neighbourhood of Henfynyw appears to have been the property of his father, and Llandewi Brefi is situated on the spot where he refuted the Pelagian heresy.'

The patron saint of Wales might well have been Gwenfrewi, if not for the removal of her relics to Shrewsbury. Better claims as patron saint can possibly come from Dyfrig (especially), Beuno, Teilo, Illtud and Cadog. David's fight against the Pelagian Heresy certainly greatly assisted in his canonisation by the Roman church in the 12th century. Some of these Welsh saints' foundations were later rededicated to David, such as Llangadog in Carmarthen. To the author, Pelagius (q.v.) was a far more attractive religious thinker than any Roman Church proponent. His Christianity was based upon equality and natural goodness, rather than referent and political power, and payment for forgiveness, and would have caused fewer deaths over the centuries.

There is a tradition that Arthur allowed Dewi to move the seat of his archbishopric from Caerleon to Menevia. Geoffrey of Monmouth states that he was honourably buried on the instructions of Maelgwn Gwynedd in Menevia, soon after Arthur's death, whom he thought died in 542. Archbishop Usher thought that David died in 544 aged 82. Maelgwn Gwynedd, according to the *Annales Menevensses* died in 547 during the great plague.

In David's time's Caradog Freichfras (the son of a grand-daughter of Brychan) recovered Brecon from the Picts, and featured as Sir Carados Bris Bras in later Arthurian romances. Urien Rheged had cleared out Pictish and Irish settlers from the lands between the rivers Towy and Neath, and his descendants ruled these territories. He was known as Sir Urience in Arthurian mythology. It seems that David may have taken the opportunity in establishing churches in these reclaimed territories.

February 28 is St David's Eve, and one of the favourite nights for the Cwn Annwn (Hounds of Annwn, the Underworld) to take to the skies. They race and howl across the firmament, and are the souls of the damned, hunting for more souls to feed to the furnaces of Hell. Anyone who hears them will soon meet death. Sometimes they are seen as huge dogs with human heads. This is a pre-Christian belief that lasted in rural Wales until the nineteenth century. There was a mass sighting of this spectral pack of dogs (probably geese) in Taunton, Somerset in 1940.

In the Gwaun valley in Pembrokeshire, Old St David's Day (March 12) was the occasion where the wax candle on the table was replaced by a wooden one, signifying that supper could be eaten without candlelight. Like the same custom at Tregaron, it was a symbol of the end of the winter nights. At this time, farm workers were also entitled to three meals a day, until Michaelmas when it reverted beck to two meals.

Some old sources say that it was David who convinced the Welsh to wear a leek* in their caps to identify each other in battle. David's spirit was said to have visited King Cadwallon's army in 633, telling the men to put leeks in their hats, and Edwin of Northumbria was beaten. Certainly the Welsh had the first uniform, (green and white) in European warfare (see the author's *An A-Z of Wales and the Welsh*). Michael Drayton, in his 1612 '*Polyolbion*' however places the Welsh leek origin in a different perspective, writing of David:

'As he did only drink what crystal Hodney yields,
And fed upon the leeks he gathered in the fields.
In memory of whom, in each revolving year,
The Welshmen, on his day, that sacred herb do wear.'

70

In Shakespeare's *Henry V*, Pistol threatens the Welshman Fluellen: 'Tell him I'll knock his leek about his pate upon St Davy's Day', but later Fluellen forces him to eat the leek. In the same play, Fluellen refers to the Welsh service to the Black Prince at the battle of Poitiers: 'If your Majesties is remembered of it, the Welshmen did good service in a garden where leeks did grow, wearing leeks in their Monmouth caps; which your Majesty knows to this hour is an honourable badge of the service; and I do believe your Majesty takes no scorn to wear the leek upon St Tavy's day.' Shakespeare described the habit of Welshmen wearing leeks and daffodils on St David's Day as 'an ancient tradition begun upon an honourable request.' The Welsh for leek is *cenhinen*, but the translation of daffodil is St Peter's leek, *cenhinen Bedr.*

An interesting correlation between the leek and St David's Day is found in Hone's *Every-Day Book, Table Book and Year Book* (four Volumes, 1839) in which March 1st is the flowering day of the leek. The traditional Welsh daffodil will flower on March 7th. David's *Saying of the Wise* is as follows:

'A glywaist ti chwedl Dewi /
Gwr llwyd llydan ei deithi / Goreu defawd daioni.' (- 'Hast thou heard the saying of St David, / The venerable man of extended honour? / "The best usage is goodness".'

There are evocative remains of palaces of the bishops of St David's at Lamphey, St David's and Abergwili, adjoining Carmarthen. William Barlow, the monoglot English bishop from 1536-1548, tried to have the see moved to Carmarthen. He therefore stripped the roof of his palace at St David's to pay for his daughters' marriages, and built the 'new' palace at Abergwili. Owain Glyndŵr, in his Pennal document to Charles VI of France in 1406, wanted St David's to be accepted as a metropolitan church. Its authority would have covered the other Welsh dioceses, plus those of Exeter, Bath, Hereford, Worcester and Lichfield. Also, appropriation of Welsh churches by English monasteries would be annulled, only Welsh-speakers were to be appointed to ecclesiastical office in Wales, and two universities were to be established in North and South Wales. (The difficulties of transport and communication between the north and south in Wales are still in existence because of the nature of Welsh geography).

Maen Dewi is an eight-foot lozenge-shaped menhir on the edge of Dowrog Common in 1912, standing by a cottage known as Drws Gobiaeth (The Door of Hope). Presumably it acted as a marker to monks crossing the moorland. There was also a rocking stone, now destroyed, near St David's which was still intact in 1919. Other notable monuments in the area of the abbey include a stone circle inside the prehistoric camp on St David's Head, Trecenny Standing Stone, and two dolmens of the slopes of Carn Llidi. A seven feet Christianised standing stone can be found in Dewi's church at Bridell, made up of porphyrite greenstone from the Preselis, with Ogham and cup markings. It is inscribed 'Nettasgru Maqui Mucoi Breci' (Nettasagus son of the descendants of Breci) and was probably carved in the 5th or 6th century.

David's dedication at Abergwili in Dyfed is surrounded by standing stones such as Pentre Ynis, Pant y Glien and Merlin's Stone. The last two are both in fields called Parc y Maen Llwyd (Grey Stone Park). Carreg Fyrddin (Merlin's Stone) carried his prophecy that a raven would drink human blood off it. In the 19th century a man digging for treasure was killed when the stone fell on him. At David's Hubberston foundation, there is also a standing stone.

David had many holy wells in Wales, and the author is indebted to Francis Jones' seminal work for the following listing:

Anglesey: Llangammarch; and near Llanddewi Abergwesin Church;
Cardigan: Capel Dewi, Llandysul (used for brewing beer for the fair); Llandygwydd; near Llanarth on the ford of Afon Ffynnon Ddewi; Henfynyw; and near Gogoyam, Llanddewi Brefi, where the well was in a cottage itself called Ffynnon Ddewi; Llandysilio-go-go;
Carmarthen: Llwyn Dewi healing well near Whitland; and Pistyll Dewi near Llanarthney;
Glamorgan: Llangyfelach; Southerndown; and Newton Nottage (where there was also his chapel and Dewiscwm has been renamed The Rhyll);
Pembroke: near St David's; near St Lawrence; Mabws Fach Farm in Mathry; Llanrheithan; St Dogwell's parish (formerly called Llantydewi); Brawdy, Whitchurch; Fishguard; Llanychllwydiog; Maenclochog; Manordeifi; Llanddewi Velfrey; Pistyll Dewi at the Cathedral; Porthclais where David was baptised; Newport; Haverfordwest; Cosherston; Harglodd Isa Farm;
Radnor: Ffynon Ddewi in Llanbadarn Fynydd.

There are many traditions associated with these wells, and they are noted in Jones' work. The authorities should refurbish all of these shrines – they represent over 1400 years of history, which few other countries can show.

St David's Cathedral and its Bishop's Palace are in a hollow below the City of St David's, and it was thought that the bones of David and Justinian were still there. However, these were possibly destroyed when the shrines were smashed in the Reformation, and the relics were analysed as being only 1000 years old, which means that they may be those of St Caradog of Llancarfan. The tombs of Edmund Tudor (Henry VII's father), Bishop Gower and Rhys Gryg can be seen, as well as those attributed to the Lord Rhys and Giraldus Cambrensis.

* There is a note on the virtues of the leek in the 13th century herbal manuals of the physicians of Myddfai, 'Meddygon Myddfai': 'The juice is good against the

vomiting of blood. It is good for women who desire children to eat leeks. Take leeks and wine to cure the bite of adders and venomous beasts. The juice of leeks and women's milk is good against pneumonia. The juice with goat's gall and honey in equal parts, put warm into the ear, is good for deafness. It will relieve wind of the stomach, and engender strange dreams.' This fascinating cornucopia of mediaeval Welsh recipes gives another cure for excessive vomiting of placing one's testicles in vinegar. For irritability it recommends frequent partaking of celery juice to relieve the mood and induce joy. It also has baldness and virility cures, far too late for this author, who has recently translated the original work, adding over forty expurgated cures and correcting mistakes in the 150-year-old translation. I also discovered that the line did not die out, lasting from the time of Rhys Gryg (d.1234) to the present day.

SAINT DEINIOL d.c. 584

DEINIOL WYN, THE BLESSED, DEINIOL AIL, DANIEL, THE FOUNDER OF BANGOR CATHEDRAL

Feast Date September 10, 11, 21, 22, December 10, possibly November 21

Deiniol was a hermit who lived on Daniel's Mount in Mynyw in Pembroke, who became Bishop of Bangor. He was said to have been uneducated and illiterate, and suddenly became endowed with complete religious knowledge when he said his first mass in the cathedral. However, his parents were the famous Dunawd Fawr and Dwywe ferch Gwallog ap Llenog, which made his illiteracy unlikely. He probably assisted his father in the foundation of the great monastery at Bangor-is-Coed. Deiniol and Dyfrig were said to be the two clerics who persuaded David to take part in the Synod of Brefi in 545, which makes him an extremely important figure in the early Christian church.

We know about St. Deiniol from a Latin *Life of Deiniol*, (*Peniarth* MS226), transcribed in 1602 by Sir Thomas Williams of Trefriw. There was also a poem written in 1527 by Sir David Trevor, parson of Llanallgo. The first mention of Deiniol comes from the 9th century Irish

Martyrology of Tallaght where he is one of only three Welsh saints to be included showing the importance of his foundations in the pre-Viking period. He was the son of Abbot Dunod Fawr (Dunawd), son of King Pabo Post Prydain (Pabo, Pillar of the Britons), who lost a battle with the king of the Picts. With the defeat, the family lost its land in Southwest Scotland, but were welcomed and given land by the king of Powys, Cyngen ap Cadell. This friendship was sealed when King Pabo's daughter married a son of King Cyngen.

Deiniol's father, Abbot Dunod Fawr was the founder of the famous Bangor-is-y-coed Monastery (Bangor below the woods) on the River Dee about four miles southeast of Wrexham. Bede in his *Ecclesiastical History of the English People* said that it was so large that it was divided into seven groups each with their own superior.

Deiniol was married before becoming a monk and was father to Saint Deiniol the Younger or Deiniolen. A cousin of Saint Asaph and Saint Tysilio, Deiniol is said to have studied at his father's monastery and also under the famous Cadoc of Llancarfan and at nearby Llanilltud Fawr. He spent some of his early life as a hermit in Pembrokeshire, yet was called to be a bishop despite deficiencies in his formal education. He settled for a time at Bangor Maelor founding the brotherhood of Bangor Fawr in 525. St. Deiniol's Bangor Monastery was destroyed by the Vikings in 1073. All that remains are some geometric carvings on a few stone slabs that can be viewed in the cathedral. The 14th century Bangor Cathedral was built upon the church there and became one of Britain's earliest dioceses, along with St Asaph, St David's and Llandaff. St.Deiniol's Library at Hawarden is Britain's largest residential library, beside the site of a cell and church founded by Deiniol.

At Bangot, Deiniol became abbot but Maelgwn Gwynedd raised the place to an episcopal see, and Deiniol became its first bishop, possibly receiving the consecration from Dyfrig. As founder and first Bishop of Bangor in Arfon, Deiniol's diocese covered Gwynedd, and there is a dedication in Denbigh at Marchwiel, outside Wrexham. There are dedications at Deiniol-fab-Llanddeiniol-fab, Llanddyfnan and Llanddeiniolen in Bangor Diocese; at Eyton, Worthenbury and Llanuwchllyn in St.Asaph Diocese; at Itton in Monmouth Diocese; and at Llanddeiniol in St.David's Diocese. A great fair was held at Llanuwchllyn on 22 September until the 20th century. Wakes were held at Llanfor near Bala in Merionethshire on 11 September. Itton in Gwent was formerly called Llanddinol, and the church is dedicated to him. St Deiniol's Ash is in Clwyd. Llanddeiniol in Ceredigion is near Llanddewi Brefi, where Deiniol was associated with St David. Hawarden in Flint is dedicated to Deiniol, and there were chapels at Worthenbury in Flint, and St Daniels under Monktown (Monkton) in Pembroke. Hawarden Fair was held on 10 September, and then on the 21st when the dates changed in 1752. Llangarron in Herefordshire is dedicated to St Deinst, probably Deiniol, but it was formerly known as Lan Garran in the time of William I, so there could have been an original dedication to Caron or Caran.

Gwynfardd wrote about the privileges of St David at Brefi, that he had such joy:

'A bod o'l gylchyn, cylch ei faesydd,
Haelon, a thirion, a theg drefydd;
A gorfod gwared lliwed llonydd,
Llwyth Daniel oruchel, eu hefelydd
Nid oes, yn cadw oes, a moes, a mynudydd.'
'To have around him, about his plains,
Men liberal and kindly disposed, and fair towns;
He ensured protection to a quiet people,
The tribe of Daniel, highly exalted, their equal
Exists not, for lineage and morality and courtesy.'

At Bod-Deiniol farmhouse on Anglesey is Bedd Branwen, also sometimes called Bod-Deiniol. This is said to the burial-place of Branwen, whose tale in the *Mabinogion* involves the invasion of Ireland and the death of Bran. There is a Daniel's Well in Bangor, Caernarfon, Ffynnon Ddeiniol was in Penbryn parish, Cardigan, and Ffynnon Ddeiniol was in Bangor Monachorum parish, Denbigh. In Flint there was a Ffynnon Daniel in Bangor-is-Coed parish, and another near Llanfor churchyard in Merioneth.

Before he became a hermit, St. Deiniol had a son named St. Deiniol the Younger who succeeded him as Abbot of Bangor. The village of Llanddaniel Fab in Anglesley, eight miles southwest of Bangor is named after St. Deiniol's son. Deiniol fled the Yellow Plague in 547 to preach in Brittany and is remembered there at St Denoual and Plangenoual in the Cotes du Nord. Ploudaniel is south of Lesnevin, Kerdaniel is near St Fiacre south of Guincamp, and Pleu Daniel lies between Paimpol and Treguier. He was said to be buried on the Isle of 20,000 Saints, Bardsey (Enlli).

TALIESIN late 6th century

ONE OF THE GREATEST BARDS

Eleven of his poems survive from the sixth century, and the famous bard was believed to have sung at the courts of at least four Brythonic kings. Most of his surviving works praise King Urien of Rheged and his son Owain mab Urien, but he seems also to have been at the courts of King Brochfael Ysgithrog (the Fanged) of Powys and his successor Cynan Garwyn ap Brochfael. He wrote of the Battle of Arfderydd, which occurred around 583.

Nennius noted Taliesin writing of the Britishfighting against King Ida of Northumbria and his sons. Taliesin was a contemporary of Aneirin, who wrote the great *Y Gododdin*. The references in the *Mabinogion* show Taliesin to have been familiar with Bala and with Maeglwn Gwynedd's 6th century court at Deganwy, and his eulogy to Cynan ap Brochfael of Powys may place him as coming from northeast Wales. He then moved towards the court of Urien Rheged, Rheged being the then British region of Cumbria and Strathclyde.

Iolo Morganwg believed Taliesin to be the son of St Henwg of Caerleon, who erected the church of Llanhenwg there, and is named as 'one of the three baptismal bards of the Isle of Britain'. Taliesin may have been educated at Llanfeithyn under Cadog or Tathan, and may have died at Bangor Teifi in Ceredigion. Another tale is that he is buried at Llangynfelin. The legend of his birth is as follows.

At Llanfair Caereinion, Ceridwen, mother of Afagddu, concocted a brew of Science and Inspiration to give to her young son, to compensate for his ugliness. Gwion Bach was instructed to stir the cauldron for a year and a day, but three drops of the magic potion fell onto his fingers, which he licked clean. Being able to foresee the future, Gwion fled in fear. Ceridwen followed him, so he turned himself into a hare, whereupon she changed into a greyhound. He became a fish, and Ceridwen an otter, then he flew as a bird but Ceridwen was a hawk. Despairing, Gwion tried to hide by becoming a grain of wheat, but Ceridwen became a hen and swallowed him. She bore him for nine months and delivered him as a beautiful baby, so could not bring herself to kill him. Thus Ceridwen tied the baby in a leather bag and threw him into the sea.

The Book of Taliesin

The legend continues in that King Gwyddno, after losing his lands off the Cardigan coast, took to fishing in the Leri's estuary at Borth (Porth Wyddno). May 1st was traditionally the best day's fishing in the year, so he allowed his son St Elffin to take over his fish-weir for the day. However, there were no fish that day, just a leather bag with a baby inside it. The baby had such a beautiful head that he was named Taliesin (Radiant Brow). Being taken home in Elffin's saddlebags, the boy started singing in regular bardic metres, and grew to be Wales' most famous bard.

Bedd Taliesin, a 3000 year-old Bronze Age cairn near Llyn Geirionydd above the Conwy Valley, was supposed to mark his grave. It was opened in 1847 in the presence of the Deans of Hereford and Bangor. Traditionally he is said to have been buried above the estuary where Elffin found him, but this legend seems to date from the 9th century rather than from the 6th, and Taliesin is chronicled in the *Mabinogion*.

Taliesin prophesied the death of Maelgwn Gwynedd:

'A wondrous beast shall come up from Morfa Rhianedd, / The Sea Marsh of the Maidens, / To avenge the iniquities of Maelgwn. / Its hair and teeth and its eyes shall all be yellow, / And this beast shall be the end of Maelgwn Gwynedd!' (In 547 Maelgwn was said to have died of the Yellow Plague).

Taliesin is more famously remembered for his prophecy concerning the future of the British nation: 'Their Lord they shall praise, / Their language they shall keep, / Their land they shall lose – / Except wild Wales'.

The ancient Welsh manuscript *Llyfr Taliesin* was transcribed by monks around 1275, and it seems that much of it was originally written by Taliesin, although the contents had been amended over the year by Christian scribes to suit the Church of Rome, remove any pagan influences and references, and add praises to God. His lament for Owain ab Urien who was killed around 595 fighting seems to show that he had seen battle:

'The great host of England
Sleeps with light in its eyes,
And those who did not flee
Were braver than they were wise.
Owain dealt them doom
As the wolves devour sheep
The bright-harnessed warrior
Gave stallions to the bard.'

Taliesin wrote that Owain had killed Flamddwyn (Flamebearer), possibly the barbarian Angle King Theodric:

'When Owain slew Fflamddwyn it was no more to him than to sleep
The wide host of Lloegr [England] sleeps with the light in their eyes
And those that did not flee were braver than was needed
Owain punished them harshly like a pack of wolves chasing sheep.'

Taliesin also sang the praises of Urien Rheged ap Cynfarch, the chief leader of the Britons, who was treacherously poisoned, and some of his lines read:

'I am Taliesin, I sing perfect metre
My original country is the Land of the Summer Stars
I was with my Lord in the highest sphere
When Lucifer fell to the depths of Hell
I have borne a standard before Alexander
I know the names of the stars from north to south

I have been a blue salmon
A dog, a stag, a buck on the mountain
A stock, a spade, an axe in the hand
A stallion, a bull, a roebuck
A grain which grew on the hill
I was reaped and cast in an oven
I have been dead, I have been alive
I am Taliesin.'

His 'Saying of the Wise', 'while conversing with Merlin', was 'excessive laughter is customary with the fool', and the herb brooklime is known as Llysiau Taliesin.

SAINT BEUNO d.642 or 660

PATRON SAINT OF COMPUTER TECHNICIANS

According to Rice Rees, Beuno was the son of noble parents, Bugi (Hywgi) ap St Gwynllyw Filwr and Perfferen ferch Llewddyn Luydog of Edinburgh (Dinas Eiddyn). St Gwynlliw had been King of Glwyssing and father of St Cadog. Beuno was thus related to Cadog, and also Mungo (St Kentigern), his contemporary, and was educated at Caerwent by Tangusius. In many ways, he is the North Wales equivalent of St David. Beuno died in 660 according to Cressy, and in 642 according to Baring-Gould and Fisher. His Feast Days are 20 and 21 April.

More dedications have been made to St Beuno in North Wales than to any other saint, so it seems that he moved from a base in Powys to proselytise northwest Wales. One day, walking the banks of the river, he heard a Saxon calling to his hounds on the other bank. He rushed back to his monks and addressed them 'My sons, put on your clothes and shoes, and let us leave this place for the nation of this man I heard setting on his hounds has a strange language which is abominable and I heard his voice. They have invaded this land and will keep it in ownership.' From Montgomeryshire this early Welsh Nationalist travelled north and was given land at Clynnog, somewhat predating the 20th century movement of

St. Beuno's Church, Pistyll

R.S. Thomas from Cardiff to Aberdaron. He is associated with founding a *clas,* a unique institution of the Celtic Church, a hybrid between a monastery and a college, at Clynnog Fawr in Caernarfonshire in 616 or 630. His convert King Cadfan had given the land to him. (Other sources say Cadwallon or Cynon gave him the land.) Until the end of the eighteenth century pilgrims came to his burial place, where an oratory was built over his grave. It was excavated in 1914, and it was said that in his pelvis, the bones of a foetus were discovered. His relics had been translated to Eglwys y Bedd (the Church of the Grave), a new church nearby, and a place of great miracles.

The anchorite of Llanddewi Brefi wrote St Beuno's *Vita* in the early fourteenth century, based upon older works. As an old man, Beuno instructed Gwenfrewi with St Senan, and St Deifer continued the instruction. Leland stated that Beuno was buried in the chapel adjoining the church and that one could still see a stone with an incised cross, indented by the saint's thumb. There is a holy well nearby. There used to be seats around it, and it was especially recommended for children with epilepsy and rickets, as well as impotency. A cure would come if one slept on a tombstone above the well overnight. Babies were placed on a bed of rushes on the font.

Pennant described seeing there 'a feather bed, on which a poor paralytic from Merionethshire had lain the whole night' after first washing in the well water. Epileptics favoured bathing in the water, then covering Beuno's tomb with rushes and sleeping on it. People with eye diseases scraped debris from the chapel walls, and mixed it with his well water to drink. In the later 17th century it was still held that a sick person laid on Beuno's tomb on a Friday would either recover or die within three weeks.

Beuno's church at Clynnog Fawr became an assembly point for pilgrims making for the holy island of Bardsey. His chapel is on the south side of the church, with a great Pilgimage Cross, and *Maen Beuno* (Beuno's stone) is a large flat boulder inscribed with a Latin cross. Eben Fardd, the famous Welsh bard, held classes in the chapel until 1849. The medieval St Beuno's Chest there is carved from one piece of ash. In the cemetery, near the chapel is a sundial dating from the 10th to 12th century.

At this church at Clynnog Fawr on the Llyn, bulls bearing a certain mark were sacrificed 'the half to God and to Beuno', noted by John Ansters in 1589 – 'as that people are of the opinion, that Beuno his cattell will prosper marvellous well'. The custom finished in the 19th century. The cattle cult came down from the Celtic worship of 'Audhumla', the primal cow. In the Celtic Northern Tradition, the primal cow is responsible for the creation of the world. 'Sacred beasts' with 'Beuno's mark' were given to the churchwardens on Trinity Sunday, and the sale proceeds were placed in 'Cyff Beuno', 'Beuno's Chest'. This ancient chest gave rise to the local saying when someone tried to do something difficult: '*Cystal I chwi geisio tori Cyff Beuno*' – 'You might as well try to break into Beuno's Chest.' One of the reasons for the custom of driving local bullocks to the church to dedicate them to Beuno, was the pecuniary motive of achieving higher prices at market.

The late mediaeval church of Clynnog Fawr stands near or on the site of St Beuno's oratory. Beuno died there after seeing a vision of angels descending from and ascending back to heaven. The church and shrine stand on ancient megaliths, one of which can be seen in the nave floor, and others of which are in the foundations. The site may have been a standing circle, and many of the earliest churches were built upon such sites.

An early Christian inscribed stone, at Llanfeuno-under-Clodock (Llanveynoe) in Archenfield (Ergyng), is close to the Roman road between Gobonium (Abergafenni) and Kenchester. The Hiberno-Saxon cross reads *'Haefdur fecit crucem istam.'* This church is however now rededicated to Peter. Many British churches were rededicated by the Normans to foreign saints. Beuno is also remembered at Berriew and Betws Cedewain in Montgomeryshire near another Roman road to Caersws, and is said to have been a descendant of the princes of Powys of this area, centred on Mathrafal. North of here, Gwyddelwern near the Roman road to Caer Gai is also dedicated to Beuno, with his holy well. There is a late mediaeval 'waggon roof' in Gwyddelwern church. There is another St Beuno's Well at Betws Gwerfil Goch nearby. Further north, Whitford church was originally dedicated to Beuno, there was an old chapel of his in Llanasa, and Beuno's holy wells exist at Holywell and in Tremeirchion parish between Prestatyn and Denbigh. Many of these sites are near Roman remains.

At Tremeirchion, the church is now that of Corpus Christi, has an 800-year-old yew, and once possessed a healing cross. There is mediaeval stained glass, and a remarkable 14th century canopied tomb to Dafydd ap Hywel ap Madog, *Dafydd Ddu Arthro o Hiraddug* (Black David, teacher of Hiraddug). This vicar of Tremeirchon was a bard, writer and sooth-saying prophet, like Siôn Cent of Kentchurch. Ffynnon Beuono, Beuno's healing well lies in a nearby hollow, with water gushing from the mouth of the roughly carved stone head of unknown age. Another interesting well was Ffynnon Nantcall in Clynnog parish – it was said to cure melancholia.

In northwest Wales, Beuno is remembered at Aberffraw (the court of the princes of Gwynedd) and Trefraeth in Anglesey, and at Clynnog Fawr, Pistyll, Botwnnog and Carnguwch on the Lleyn peninsula. Aberffraw has an eleven feet dolmen called Dinas Dindryfal. There still exists Ffynnon Beuno in Malt House Lane, Aberffraw. There is also Ffynnon Bryn Fendigaid (Well of the Blessed Hill) near Aberffraw, where a fish was kept for divination purposes, near some chalybeate springs where St Gwladus was martyred at Croes Ladys. In Gwynedd, Llanycil is dedicated to Beuno, with another holy well, near Caer Gai roman fort, as is Penmorfa with a holy well, just off the Roman road between Segontium and Tomen-y-Mur. Ffynnon Ddeuno no longer flows, but his ruined chapel can be seen at

Gatwen Farm, Broughton, Brecon. In Gwyddelwern, Merioneth was Ffynnon Gwern Beuno. At Berriew (Aberrhiw), Powys, there is Beuno's standing stone, Maen Beuno, which was said to be Beuno's first pulpit.

E.G Bowen, in *The Settlements of the Celtic Saints in Wales*, draws attention to the fact that his disciples mentioned in his *Vita* founded churches near his. Llandenan and Llanwyddelan to Lorcan Wyddel; and Llwchaearn is remembered at Llanllwchaearn and Llamyrewig. Near Gwyddelwern was an old chapel dedicated to Aelhaearn, and Cwyfan's Llangwyfan is nearby. In Flintshire, the Llŷn Peninsula and Anglesey his dedications are near those of St Winifred, Gwenfrewi. In the Llŷn and Arfon, saints Aelhaearn, Cwyfan, Edern, Deiniol Fab and Twrog have dedications close to Beuno's churches, and in Anglesey churches of Cwyfan, Deiniol Fab, Dona, Ceidio, Edern and Twrog are close to his dedications.

Aelhaiarn founded churches at Llanaelhaiarn in Caernarfon and Merioneth, Berriew, and Cegidfa (now called Guilsfield, near Betws Cedewain) in Montgomery. He was a servant of St Beuno. The ascetic Beuno used to walk into a cold river to pray, and Aelhaearn followed him once, standing behind him. Beuno did not know who was behind him, and called on a pack of savage animals which tore Aelhaiarn apart. Beuno put the body together again, all except an eyebrow, which he replaced with the iron tip of his staff. Aelhaearn means 'the iron eye-brow.'

Among Beuno's dedications are: Berriew (Aber-Rhiw) and Betws in Montgomery; Llanycil and Gwyddelwern in Merioneth; Clynnog Fawr, Carngiwch Chapel, Pistyll Chapel, Penmorfa chapel, Dolbenmaen chapel in Caernarfon; Aberffraw chapel and Trefdraeth chapel in Anglesey; Llanfeuno chapel to Clydog (Clodock) Hereford; Llanfaenor near Skenfrith in Monmouthshire should be called Llanfeuno. King Ynyr of Gwent gave Beuno three estates in Ewyas including Llanfeuno. Morgan Hen, King of Glamorgan, restored Llanfaenor in 980. A new church was built on the site in 1853.

The 'Sayings of the Wise' record: 'Have you heard the saying of Beuno / To all who resort to him? / "From death, flight will not avail".'

Clynnog has an interesting cromlech with 110 cup-shaped hollows in its capstone, called Bachwen Clynnog Dolmen, and a nearby standing stone is known as Maen Dylan. Also Penarth Dolmen stands in a field named Caer Goetan. At Berriew, Maen Beuno is a leaning standing stone on the Severn's banks. Llanycil in Merioneth is dedicated to Beuno and had three standing stones, but none seem to have survived.

The loveliest of the legends surrounding Beuno is that he dropped his book of sermons walking across the Menai Strait sands from Anglesey. The strait could have been passable at this time – it appears that water levels may have risen forty to sixty feet in the last 1500 years. Stagecoaches used to cross at low water until relatively recently. When he reached Clynnog Fawr, a curlew was in Beuno's cell, sitting by the book. Beuno prayed for

God's everlasting protection of the curlew, and this is why its eggs are so difficult to find, as the colours match those of the ground upon which they have been laid.

His most famous resurrection was that of St Winifred, Gwenfrewi, at the holy well with the longest unbroken record of pilgrimage in Europe. Gwenfrewi was the daughter of Prince Tefydd and Gwenlo. Legend is that she suffered from the unwanted attentions of Prince Caradog ab Alan, from Hawarden (Penarlag in Flintshire). On Mid-Summer's Day, she fled from him but he caught up with her at the church door before she could gain sanctuary. Because she had spurned him, he cut off her head, whereupon the earth opened up and swallowed him. Her uncle, St Beuno, restored her head to her shoulders and she lived the rest of her days as a nun at Gwytherin in Denbighshire. Where her head fell to the earth at Holywell (Treffynnon, Welltown), a spring of water gushed forth. Some sources say that she became abbess of a nunnery at Holywell, and others that she then followed Beuno to Clynnog, then she moved on to Bodfari, Henllan and finally became a nun under St Eleri in Gwytherin near Llanrwst. She died fifteen years after her head was restored to her body.

A legend says that Beuno asked Gwenfrewi to send him a rain-proof woollen cloak each year on the feast day of John the Baptist, the anniversary of the day upon which she was brought back to life. She placed it on a stone in the river, and each year the stone would sail down the river and across the sea to her uncle, and reach him in a perfectly dry condition. St Beuno's chapel was erected just above where St Margaret's Chapel now stands in Holywell, but the site is now dedicated to St James.

There was an account that: 'The men of Clynnog have a tradition that St. Beuno caused the materials that were used in building the church to be landed on the shore just below it. The place where they suppose these materials were landed, is a flat sand, on each side which are mountains of pebble-stones, which oftentimes in storms entirely cover the sand, almost even with the rest, by the violence of the sea; however, it becomes in a little time as even as before, the pebbles being all swept away into their wonted places, which thing is much taken notice of by the inhabitants.'

Leland, in his *Itinerary*, says, 'Clunnok Vawr, a Monasteri sumtime of White Monkes (Cistercians), suppressed many years ago. But the original of this Monasteri was by S. Benow, of whom mention is made in S. Wenefride's Life. The White Monkes were of a newer foundation. Guithin, uncle to one of the princes of North Wales, was the first giver of Clunnok village and place to Bennow. The church that is now ther with cross isles, is almost as bigge as S. Davide's, but it is of a new worke. The old chirch wher S. Bennow liyth is hard by the new. This Clunnok stondeth almost on the shore of the maine sea, a x miles above Cair Arvon, towards the counteri of Lline [Llŷn Peninsula].

In a MS. communicated by the Rev. John Jones, Rector of Llanllyfni, 1848, entitled *Queries for Carnarvonshire*, we read: 'Q. Whether any trace of the foundation of the old monastery of Clynnoc Vawr further than in the *Monasticon*? When the church became collegiate? And whether there be not now portionists belonging to the same, and how many? I find 5 portionists temp.'

A. There is a tradition among ye vulgar that the monastery (or rather ye old church as they call it) of Clynnoc fawr was burnt, and Dr. John Davies, in his *Welsh Dictionary*, maketh mention of a book called Tiboeth, being St. Beuno's book, which was in the church of Celynnog in Arvon, with a black stone thereupon, which book had been writ by Twrog or Tauricius, Beuno's amanuensis, in the time of King Cadfan, and escaped the being burnt when the church was consumed... Thomas Willielmus Medicus, author of the Latine-Welsh part of the said Dictionary, says he saw that book anno 1594; but no tidings of it now for a long time, or rather never indeed since.

When the church was consumed I cannot tell, but I find the countries of Lleyn and Celynnog Vawr were spoiled anno 970... The chancel window of the present church there, as appeared by an inscription of late years remaining thereon undefaced, was glazed anno 1384,... but whether ye church itself might be about that time erected I know not. What time it became collegiate I cannot set forth, but that it is a collegiate church is undoubted; and there were vast possessions belonging to it, as that great and learned antiquary, Mr. Robert Vaughan of Hengwrt in county Merioneth sets forth in manner following...'

Beuno's history of bringing back to life four or five decapitated victims has made him the 'Patron of Computer Technicians', who are frequently asked to do the impossible at once. Their web page bears the motto *Illum Posse Dicere*.

KING CADWALADR ap CADWALLON c. 630 - d. 682

CADWALADR FENDIGAID, SAINT CADWALADR THE BLESSED, HIGH KING OF BRITAIN

Feast Dates November 12, October 9

Cadwaldr was the last king to hold the title of *Gwledig*, the 'High King' of Britain who had authority over the other Celtic kingdoms. His father was King Cadwallon Llew (the Lion), King of Gwynedd fron 625, the son of Cadfan ab Iago ap Beli. Edwin King of Northumbria had grown up with Cadwallon, under the protection of Iago ap Belli, but in 626 defeated Wessex and drove Cadwallon into exile. Edwin was then baptised in 627 by

Rhun ab Urien. Bede states that Edwin conquered the Brythonic kingdom of Elmet (West Yorkshire) and took Anglesey and the Isle of Man fighting Cadwallon. Cadwallon was besieged at Priestholm off Anglesey in 629, and may have escaped to Ireland before returning and defeating Edwin at Mynydd Digoll, the place where Henry Tudor symbolically gathered his troops before Bosworth.

In 633, Cadwallon resumed his title of *Dux Brittaniarum* from the *Bretwalda*, Edwin. Cadwallon had ravaged from his base in North Wales. In that year, allying with the Anglian King Penda of Mercia, King Cadwallon's army defeated and killed Edwin at Hatfield Chase near Doncaster upon 12 October. Penda and Cadwallon took Northumbria, but Cadwallon was besieged by Osric, King of Deira. Somewhere near York, Edwin's former capital, Cadwallon killed Osric and defeated an army of Angles. The new king of Bernicia, Eanfrith, was also killed by Cadwallon but he was defeated by an army under Eanfrith's brother, Oswald*. Cadwallon, 'the last hero of the British race' was killed in the last of his sixteen battles and forty skirmishes at 'Heaven's Field' near Hexham (Catscaul) in 635.

By this battle, with great losses on both sides, the British were finally pushed out of Northumbria. The Angles had attacked at night, when the British were unprepared. The Venerable Bede, who despised the Christian British, and always took the side of the pagan Anglo-Saxons in his accounts, said that Cadwallon tried to 'cut off all the race of the English within the borders of Britain... Nor did he pay any respect to the Christian religion which had newly taken root amongst them; it being to this day the custom of the Britons  not to pay any regard to the faith and religion of the English.' Bede, with his usual anti-British propaganda, criticised Cadwallon as a genocidal tyrant in the North of England, but Cadwallon's alliance with the Anglo-Saxon Penda undermines Bede's assertion that the King of Gwynedd had attempted to exterminate the English. The British saw no reason to bow to the new Roman faith, slowly being adopted by the pagans who had taken their lands and were constantly fighting them.

Cadwaladr ap Cadwallon's was around five when his father was killed, so Cadafael 'Cadomedd' ('battle-shunner') became King of Gwynedd, with Cadwaladr not taking the kingship until about 655 to 682. Geoffrey of Monmouth ends his account of the *Kings of Britain* with Cadwaladr. Despite his reluctance to face a larger army, Cadwaladr was forced to lead his people to a bad defeat, against Cenwalh, King of the West Saxons, at Peonnum in 658. This battle is mentioned in the *Anglo-Saxon Chronicle*: 'Here Cenwalh fought at Penselwood against the Welsh and drove them in flight as far as the Parret'. Cenwalh was the King of Wessex from c.641 to c.672. In this translation the original 'Peonnum' is given as Penselwood, which is on the present border between Wiltshire and Somerset, and which is the most usually accepted location of the battle. The River Parret lies further west of Penselwood in Somerset. Given its location, this battle seems to have been part of the westward expansion of Wessex, at the expense of the British Kingdom of Dumnonia, whose inhabitants were often referred to as the West Welsh or as just the Welsh.'

The tradition is that Cadwaladr was ill for most of his reign, and that Civil War raged, then a famine, then a great plague in 664, from which he may have escaped to the court of King Alain Hir in Brittany, from where he sent his son Ifwr back to regain the British throne. A mistaken tradition is that Cadawaladr went on a pilgrimage to Rome, where he died in 688. His body was brought back to his foundation at Llangadwaldr on Anglesey.

There are churches dedicated to Cadwallader in places named Llangadwaladr as far apart as Bishopston (also known as Bishton or Tref Esgob, and formerly called Llangadwaladr) under Llanwern in Monmouthshire, Llangadwaladr under Llanrhaiadr in Mochnant in Denbighshire, and Llangadwaladr in Anglesey. Magor (Magwyr) in Monmouth has been rededicated from Cadwaladr to the Virgin Mary. Michaelston-y-Fedw in Glamorgan was rededicated also away from him by the Normans, to Michael. There was also a Capel Llangadwaladr under Llanddeiniol Fab in Anglesey.

The Anglesey church, Eglwys Ael, contains a stone with a Latin epitaph to Cadwaladr's grandfather, King Cadfan. The 7th century inscription reads 'CATAMANUS REX SAPIENTISIMUS OPINATISIMUS OMNIUM REGUM'

(Cadfan the King, wisest and most renowned of all kings). Cadfan had died in 625. Cadwaladr probably died of a second great plague in 682, and was called by the bards *Bendigaid* (Blessed), being one of 'the three blessed sovereigns of Britain'. On Cadfan's tomb there are three intertwined fish, and a single fish on either side of a carved cross. His 'Saying of the Wise' is: 'Have you heard the saying of Cadwaladr, /
King of all Wales; / "The best crooked thing is the crooked handle of a plough.'

'The Red Dragon' of Cadwaladr was the standard borne by Henry VII on his way to Bosworth Field, and also used by Owain Glyndŵr as his standard and as a mark of the kingship of the Britons. Gildas referred to it, the *Insularis Draco* (Island Dragon) being carried earlier by another Gwledig, or High King, Maelgwn Gwynedd.

The Welsh national flag is not featured on the Union Flag (Union Jack) of the United Kingdom, which superimposes the blue and white saltire of St. Andrew, and the red and white crosses of St. Patrick and St. George. The British flag thus features representation from Northern Ireland, England, and Scotland, but none from Wales. The Welsh Flag consists of two horizontal stripes, white over green, with a large red dragon passant. Green and white are the traditional Welsh colours, worn by the Welsh bowmen at the Battle of Creçy. The Red Dragon, one of the most ancient badges in the world, was brought to Britain by the Romans, who had copied it from the Parthians, and it was later used by both British and Saxon kings. Traditionally it was King Arthur's flag, and it was definitely the standard of Cadwaladr, from whom the Tudors were descended.

The word *draig* or dragon was used in Welsh poetry to symbolise a warrior or leader. Pendragon, as in Uther Pendragon, meant a head, or chief leader. A legend dates from the eighth century about a fight between the Red Dragon (*Y Ddraig Goch*) representing Wales and a White Dragon representing England foretelling the triumph of the red dragon. The red dragon of the Celts was their flag and symbol against the Saxons for 600 years after the Romans left Britain.

The White Dragon of the Saxons was last seen in battle against the Normans at Hastings in 1066. *Y Ddraig Goch* was widely accepted as the oldest flag in the world at the international conference of flag makers in South Africa in 1987, according to the President of the Flag Institute. Flagmaker Robin Ashburner makes the point that it is the only flag to have remained unchanged in the last 1,000 years – 'the Welsh will be the only people to enter the next millennium with the same flag as they entered the current one'. (Denmark also claims the oldest flag, dating from 1219, but the 'father of flag science', or vexillology, Dr Whitney Smith of Massachusetts, supports the Welsh flag. The dragon came from China via the Romans, and when the Western Roman Empire was set up, the local chiefs in Britain used the dragon symbol. It was the Welsh symbol long before Offa built the dyke between the Saxon and Welsh kingdoms.

The Welshman Henry Tudur invaded England, through Wales, to end the Wars of the Roses. With the 'Red Dragon of Cadwaladr' as his standard, his smaller army defeated and killed the last Plantagenet King Richard III, at Bosworth Field. Henry used as his livery colours green and white, and on these colours his retainers painted the red dragon. When Henry became Henry VII of England in 1485, he decreed that from henceforth the Red Dragon should be the official flag of Wales. Henry even set up the official herald's position of Rouge Dragon Pursuivant to protect the flag. For a time the Dragon coexisted on the English Crown's royal crest with the Lion, but was replaced by the Unicorn of the Scottish Stuarts on the accession of James I in 1603. Thus neither the Welsh flag nor the Welsh emblems of daffodil and leek appear in a united British context. A former

Welsh Secretary of State, the South African MP for Neath, Peter Hain, wished to get rid of it.

There was no 'red rose of Lancashire' during the Wars of the Roses, and the White Rose of Yorkshire was one of several of Edward IV's badges. It seems to have been Henry Tudor's idea to amalgamate the two into the Tudor Rose when he ended the wars and married Elizabeth of York. Henry VII balanced his Greyhound emblem of Richmond and Lancaster on the Tudor royal arms, with the Red Dragon of Wales and Cadwaladr. To him the dragon showed his 'Trojan' descent and gave his kingship and the Tudor dynasty a legitimacy, which was distinct from that of the houses of Lancaster and York.

* Oswald, or Oswallt, lived from 604-64, converted to Christianity late in life, and is commemorated on August 5. This Anglian King of Northumbria was martyred at Oswestry (Croes-Oswallt) and is remembered there, just over the present border in Shropshire but under the see of St Asaf. In 635 Oswald had defeated Cadwallan at Heavenfield near Hadrian's Wall. At the age of 38 he was killed at Masefield in present-day Shropshire by the Mercian army of Penda, avenging his ally Cadwallan. Oswald's body was dismembered, but his brother Oswy later retrieved the head and hands, which he took back to Lindisfarne and Bamburgh castle respectively. An eagle took one of his arms and where it dropped King Oswald's Well bubbled forth, a place of pilgrimage renowned for healing. St Aidan, when he had originally blessed Oswald, had said 'may this hand never wither with age.' One arm was 'uncorrupted' for almost a millennium until it was destroyed in the Reformation. A wooden hand in Oswald's church at Lower Peover near Knutsford in Cheshire is a medieval 'glove' used to indicate that a free-trading fair was under way. Ffynnon Oswallt was a famous healing well in Whitford, Flintshire. It was situated in a field known as Aelod Oswald (Oswald's Limb), the name commemorating the king's dismemberment.

NENNIUS fl.823

'THE HISTORIAN OF THE BRITONS'

Nennius apparently had access to 5th and 6th century sources that no longer survive, for his early Latin compilation known as *Historia Brittonum*, giving an account of British history from Julius Caesar to the 7th century. In his preface he describes himself as a disciple of Elfoddw of Bangor, the 'chief bishop of the land of Gwynedd' in 809. Bishop Elfoddw died in that year, having acceded in 768 to pressure to alter to the Roman Church new date of Easter. Internal evidence of Nennius' work points to his being from southeast Wales, and he acknowledges his debt to Gildas (q.v.) for the events prior to 540. The author 'put together all he could find' of the remnants of writings at this time. Of course, the Celtic bardic tradition was oral, and so we are extremely fortunate that this Bangor monk pulled together various Welsh records. After the preface, the sections are as follows: *The Six Ages of the World; The History, The Anglo-Saxon Genealogie', Computations and the 28 Cities of Britain*, and *The Marvels of Britain*. The date of the compilation is given by Nennius as the 858th year of the Lord's incarnation, dating from Christ's birth. However, the *Chronicle of Ystrad Fflur* properly puts this date at 823, not 858, instead dating from Christ's death.

There is no real chronology, and Nennius is concerned to show the British, i.e. Welsh, in the most favourable light, portraying them as of noble descent, capable of heroic deeds, and treacherously driven out of their rightful territories by the Saxons. This had considerable relevance at the time, as Rhodri Mawr was later fought to consolidate the remaining Welsh lands.

The book gives some of the earliest mentions of Arthur, and has a famous passage on the earliest Welsh poets. We cannot overstate Nennius' contribution to our knowledge of British history, from a time when the nation was in terrible peril. He wrote at a time when Wales had been 'dulled' by the slaughter of monks at Bangor-is-Coed by pagans, a feat celebrated by the so-called 'Holy' Bede. Nennius is mentioned in the 9th century Irish Psalter of Cashel, and his sources include along with Gildas, Eusebius, Jerome, Isidore and Prosper.

Nennius, in his *History of the Britons*, shows how important Wales and the West were in these times. No less than 16 of his list of 28 cities are from this area of civilisation, leaving 12 spread across the rest of England and Scotland. The words 'Caer' or 'Y Gaer' normally means a camp or fortress in Welsh, and usually denotes a Roman camp ('castra') much as the suffix 'caster', 'cetter', 'cester' or 'chester' does in the English lanaauge. The Welsh word 'Dinas' meaning 'fort' is often attached to hill-camps that precede the Roman invasions. The 16 British/Welsh bases are as follows:

The History of the Britons

1 Caer-Caratauc, which is Cary Craddock [Caer Caradog] in the parish of Sellack, Hereford (not Catterick in Yorkshire). This hillfort in Ergyng was said to be a palace of Caradog Freichfras, son of King Ynyr of Gwent.
2 Caer-Costoeint - Caer Soeint - Caernarfon (Caer Segeint) or Silchester

3 Caer-Ddraiton is Din-Draithou in the Life of St Cadog, and is Dunster in Somerset. Cado entertained Arthur here, and another name was Din-Torre, the fort on the river Torre.

4 Caer-Guent is Caer Gwent or Caerwent, the Venta Silurum of the Romans. The walled Roman city became the capital of Gwent, replacing the Silures' hill-fort of Llanmelin nearby. Coin hoards from around 425 and burials denote continuing occupation throughout the 'Dark Ages'. Caerwent was 'given' by Caradog Freichfras to Tathan when he moved his main court to the more easily defended camp at Portskewett nearby. The Roman walls are remarkable at Caerwent, but it is by-passed by most visitors to Caerleon and Wales. The site covers 20 hectares and the walls once stood 20 feet high. They are around 12 feet wide at the base. The main road to South Wales ran through the East and West gates.

5 Caer-Guiragon is Worcester.

6 Caer-Guouthigorn is Little Doward hillfort at Ganarew, Hereford, supposedly the site of Vortigern's last stand, although he may have escaped to Brittany.

7 Caer-Guricon is Viroconium, Wroxeter, the capital of Powys under Vortigern but later sacked by the Anglo-Saxons, forcing the princes of Powys back to Mathrafal. The Roman remains here are excellent.

8 Caer-Legeion-guar-Uisc is Isca, Caerleon on the River Usk outside Newport, with some of the best Roman features in Europe.

9 Caer-Legion is Deva, Chester, where Arthur possibly fought. With Caerleon, this was the second great fortress on the Welsh borders as the Romans pushed out from Gloucester and Wroxeter. In 603 Augustine held his second conference with the British bishops here, and around 610 or 613 the British lost the great battle when Bangor-is-Coed was destroyed.

10 Caer-Meguaidd is Meifod at Mathrafal, the court of Powys (not Manchester).

11 Caer-Pensa-uel-Coyt is South Cadbury hillfort (not Pevensey)

12 Cae-Peris appears to be Caer Beris just outside Builth Wells, but may be Porchester

13 Caer-Segeint is the great fort at Segontium, Caernarfon the old capital of the princes of Gwynedd before they moved to Aberffraw, and forever linked with Macsen Wledig and Elen. The river Arfon flows to the sea at Caernarfon, which means 'fort on the Arfon/

14 Caer-(D)Urnac appears to be Wroxter, or possibly Dorchester

15 Caer-Luit-Coyt is Wall, outside Lichfield, retaken from the Saxons by Prince Morfael of Pengwern around 650.

16 Caer Merdin is Caerfyrddin, Carmarthen

The other towns listed by Nennius were probably Dumbarton, Canterbury, Colchester, Doncaster, York, Grantchester, Leicester, Carlisle, London, Manchester, St Albans, Ilchester and Silchester. Other towns at this time included Caer-Baddan or Aquae Sulia, Bath. King Ffernfael had his court here, and it was lost to the Saxons at the fateful battle at nearby Dyrham (Deorham) in 573 or 577. Ffernfael died, as did King Cyndyddan who had his capital at Caer-Ceri (Cirencester). Cirencester was the capital of the province of *Britannia Prima.* The third British king to die at Dyrham was Cynfael of Caer-Gloui (Gloucester). Caer-Teim was Tamium, Cardiff, where king Ynwyl was mentioned in Gereint and Enid as living in the ruined palace (the Roman fort) while the new kings of Glywyssing settled themselves at Dinas Powys hillfort just west of the city. The pagans took over Gloucester and Somerset, cutting off Wales from the Britons of Devon and Cornwall forever.

The *Prologue to the British Chronicles of Nennius* is not only a marvellous piece of writing, but mentions that he has just taken published works, even from the 'enemy' Scots and Irish and not altered them. He says it is up to the reader to sort the wheat from the chaff:

'1. NENNIUS, the lowly minister and servant of the servants of God, by the grace of God, disciple of St Elbotus, to all the followers of truth sendeth health.

Be it known to your charity, that being dull in intellect and rude of speech, I have presumed to deliver these things in the Latin tongue, not trusting to my own learning, which is little or none at all, but partly from writings and monuments of the ancient inhabitants of Britain, and the chronicles of the sacred fathers, Isidore, Hieronymus, Prosper, Eusebius, and from the histories of the Scots and Saxons, although our enemies, not following my own inclinations, but, to the best of my abilities, obeying the commands of my seniors; I have lispingly put together this history from various sources, and have endeavoured, from shame, to deliver down to posterity the few remaining ears of corn about past transactions, that they might not be trodden under foot, seeing that an ample crop has been snatched away already by the hostile reapers of foreign nations. For many things have been in my way, and I, to this day, have hardly been able to understand, as was necessary, the sayings of other men; much less was I able in my own strength, but like a barbarian, have I murdered and defiled the language of others. But I bore about within me an inward wound, and I was indignant, that the name of my own people, formerly famous and distinguished, should sink into oblivion, and like smoke be dissipated.

But since, however, I had rather myself be the historian of the Britons than nobody, although so many are to be found who might much more satisfactorily discharge the labour thus impose on me; I humbly entreat my readers, whose ears I may offend by the inelegance of my words, that they will fulfil the wish of my seniors, and grant me the easy task of listening with candour to my history. For zealous efforts very often fail. May, therefore, candour be shown where the inelegance of my words in insufficient, and may the truth of this history, which my rustic tongue has ventured, as a kind of plough, to trace out in furrows, in the ears of my hearers. For it is better to drink a wholesome draught from a humble vessel, than poison mixed with honey from a golden goblet.

2. And do not be loath, diligent reader, to winnow my chaff, and lay up the wheat in the storehouse of your memory: for truth does not come from the manner in which it is spoken, but that the thing be true: and she does not despise the jewel which she has rescued from the mud, but she adds it to her former treasures.

3. For I yield to those who are greater and more eloquent than myself, who, kindled with generous ardour, have endeavoured by Roman eloquence to smooth the jarring elements of their tongue, if they have left unshaken any pillar of history which I wished to remain. The history therefore has been compiled from a wish to benefit my inferiors, not from an envy of those who are superior to me, in the 858th year of our Lord's incarnation, and in the 24th year of Merfyn, King of the Britons*, and I hope that the prayers of my betters will be offered up for me in recompense of my labour. I shall obediently accomplish the rest to the utmost of my power.'

* Merfyn Frych was the father of Rhodri Mawr (q.v.), who became High King in 844, which confirms the date of *The History of the Britons* as 823, not 858.

RHODRI MAWR   820 - 878

RHODRI AP MERFYN FRYCH AP GWRIAD, RHODRI THE GREAT, 'THE GREATEST OF ALL THE KINGS OF WALES'

Possibly because of the lasting Roman influence in Wales, and their much later adoption of Christianity, the neighbouring Mercians and the assorted Saxons were regarded as uncultured and aggressive pagans by the Welsh, but the border held against them, albeit with some fluidity. There were also constant Pictish attacks

Dinefwr Castle

on the coastal areas of Wales. However, the next severe threat to Wales was that of the Norsemen, whose first recorded attack was in 850. Merfyn Frych spent his reign fighting against the Danes and Mercians, and fell at Cetyll against Burchred of Mercia in 844.

His son Rhodri Mawr unified most of Wales to move it towards statehood, thanks in part to the need to fight this Viking threat. A descendant of Llywarch Hen, the warrior-bard, he had succeeded his father Merfyn in 844, and it is notable that Wales achieved national unity under him, whereas England had to wait for statehood until the coronation of Edgar at Bath in 973. (The columnist Simon Heffer in the 1990s received national publicity by stating that the Wales has never been a nation. Knowledge of true history is a rare commodity). Rhodri was the only Welsh King to be called 'The Great', and earned thanks from Charlemagne for his victories against the Viking threat. The Vikings ravaged Anglesey in 854, but Rhodri killed the Viking leader Horm, off Anglesey in 856. (Orme's Head at Llandudno may be named after Horm). Rhodri's great success as a warrior was noted in *The Ulster Chronicle*, and also by Sedulius Scottus, an Irish scholar at the Liege court of the Emperor Charles the Bald. His great victory over the Vikings was acclaimed by Irish and Franks alike. In fact, Alfred and Charlemagne were the only other rulers to be bestowed with the title of 'Great' in this century, and Alfred never ruled over England. Nora Chadwick called Rhodri 'the greatest of all the kings of Wales', and he dominated Wales from the new castle he built at Dinefwr.

Until his death in battle in 878, he held Wales together for over three decades, even making an alliance with King Alfred of Wessex against the Norsemen. Rhodri had assumed the throne of Gwynedd upon his father's death, taken control of Powys upon the death of his mother's brother Cyngen (on a pilgrimage to Rome) in 856, and controlled Seisyllwg (Ceredigion, Carmarthen and Gower) from 871 when he married Angharad, the sister of its last king.

In 872 *The Chronicle of the Princes* gives Rhodri defeating the 'black gentiles', the Vikings, in Anglesey at Bangolau in 'a hard battle' and at Manegid, where the Vikings 'were destroyed.' The *Chronicle* has an 873 entry for Rhodri dying in battle at the 'Battle of Sunday' at Anglesey, but he survived. Rhodri's kingship of Powys had automatically led him into intense hostilities with the kingdom of Mercia, as Offa's Dyke proved no real frontier. In 877 he may have been defeated at Anglesey, escaping to Ireland. He allied with the Danes to return and be killed fighting Ceolwulf's Mercian invasion of Powys in 878, and his son (or brother) Gwriad fell at his side. Rhodri's dominions were divided, with Anarawd becoming King of Gwynedd, Cadell King of Deheubarth, and Merfyn King of Powys. In 881 at the Battle of Conwy, the Welsh victory under Anarawd ap Rhodri against the Mercians was known as 'Dial Rhodri' ('Rhodri's Revenge') - God's vengeance for the slaughter of Rhodri. The princes of Gwynedd henceforth always traced their ancestors to the great Rhodri.

The practice of partible inheritance, gavelkind, meant that each of Rhodri's sons had a part of Wales to control. One son seems to have been lamed at the Battle of Conwy, and by law was not allowed to inherit. Rhodri's grandson, Hwyel Dda ap Cadell ap Rhodri eventually came to rule Wales. The Viking raids carried on until 918, and the rule of Hywel Dda, and restarted two years after his death in 952, especially focusing upon Welsh monasteries. They sacked St David's Cathedral for the sixth time, as late as 1091.

The Chronicle of Ystrad Fflur records the turbulent times of Rhodri Mawr:

816 ... The Saxons ravaged Eryri and took Rhufoniog by force
817 In this year was the battle or Llan-faes
818 Coenwulf ravaged the land of Dyfed
822 Deganwy was destroyed by the Saxons and they took the kingdom of Powys into their own control
823 In this year Brother Nennius compiled his book
844 In this year Rhodri ap Merfyn was High King
848 In this year was the battle of Ffinant. And the men of Brycheiniog slew Ithel, king of Gwent
849 In this year the Saxons slew Meurig
850 In this year Cynin was killed by the Black Gentiles (Dublin Vikings)
853 In this year Mona (Anglesey) was laid waste by the Black Gentiles
855 In this year Cyngen of Powys died on pilgrimage; and Rhodri took Powys from the Saxons
864 Duda laid Glywysing (Glamorgan) waste
869 In this year was the battle of Bryn Onen
872 In this year Gwgan ap Meurig drowned and Seisyllwg came to Rhodri
874 In this year were the battles of Banolau and Ynegydd
876 In this year Rhodri was in Ireland
877 In this year Rhodri and Gwriad fell to the Saxons

HYWEL DDA 890 - 950

HYWEL AP CADELL AP RHODRI MAWR AP MERFYN FACH - HYWEL DDA - HYWEL THE GOOD OF DEHEUBARTH

By 918, it appears that Hywel ap Cadell ap Rhodri Mawr ruled Dyfed, and in 920 took over Seisyllwg when his brother Clydog died, so his lands covered the kingdom of Deheubarth, South-West Wales from the Dyfi to the Tawe. His wife was Elen ap Llywarch, by which marriage he had claimed Dyfed, and his child was Owain. Hywel made a pilgrimage to Rome in 928, and gained control of Brecon by 930. Then from his power base in Deheubarth, this grandson of Rhodri Mawr added Powys and Gwynedd to his kingdom, to largely reunify Wales in 942. In 942 Idwal Foel had been killed by the Saxons, so Hywel was now supreme among the Welsh princes. In *Brut y Tywysogion*, Hywel was described as 'the chief and most praiseworthy of all the Britons.'

The only Welsh king to earn the epithet 'the good', Hywel peacefully unified much of Wales by inheritance, marriage, alliances, and diplomatic relations with Alfred the Great of Wessex. Upon the death of Idwal Foel of Gwynedd, Hywel drove out Idwal's sons and took over Gwynedd and Powys. He led no invasions into England, and coexisted peacefully with Aethelstan upon his succession after Alfred's death. It had helped that Alfred's chief advisor, Asser, was a former monk at St. David's. Hywel understood the power of his larger neighbour, despite strong calls from the bards to ally against them. He had seen the death of Idwal Foel and witnessed the virtual extinction of the Brythonic kingdom of Cornwall, and thus wished to keep Wales intact. Hywel Dda's quiet diplomacy and conciliation helped give Wales another three centuries of independence against its larger neighbour. The nation was seen as strong enough not to be invaded, and appears to have suffered no Viking attacks during Hywel's reign – they only restarted two years after his death. Hywel seems to have felt secure enough to become the first Welsh ruler to issue his own coins, silver pennies at Chester inscribed *Howael Rex*.

Hywel Dda by F.W. Pomeroy

The assembly called by Hywel in 930 at Y Hendy Gwyn (Whitland) was one of the first of its kind in Britain. In 942 the assembly finally established a legal code for all of Wales, '*Cyfraith Hywel*', codifying the common laws of all the different kingdoms. This legislation was only destroyed in 1536 with the Act of Union with England, where laws based upon the right of the individual of any sex were replaced by laws based upon male domination, property ownership and class structure solidification. At Whitland today, one can visit the Hywel Dda Gardens and Interpretative Centre. *Cyfraith Hywel* was the name by which the native law was known to the Welsh throughout medieval times, and the extent of its use is reflected by the survival of around forty law-books dating from before 1536. The first generation of these books, some in Latin and some in Welsh, is dated from the middle decades of the 13th century. The Peniarth manuscript of this period is in the National Library of Wales and has wonderful illustrations of the king and some 24 court officials.

Welsh Law gave precedence to the woman's claim in any rape case; marriage was an agreement, not a holy sacrament, and divorce was allowed by common consent, with an equal share of land and possessions;

illegitimate children had the same rights as legitimate children; there was equal division of the land between all children upon the death of parents. (This last law contributed to the strife among Princedoms and Kingdoms - everyone had a claim somewhere, and most tried to rebuild what their parents had - the Normans were clever at playing off one heir against another and gaining in the long run). Under Hywel's Laws, farming was a communal affair (reminiscent of Robert Owen's policies eight-hundred years later), and a man did not have unrestricted control over his wife as a possession, unlike all the other 'civilised' European countries.

In the Celtic Church, as well as outside, there was a tradition in Wales that women had a real social status - a woman's rights to property under *Cyfraith Hywel* were not granted in English law until 1883. A woman also had a right to compensation if her husband hit her without any cause. In English law, the woman was the property of the husband, a chattel, whereas a divorced Welshwoman received half the property. It is typical of the Laws that the queen had special privileges - there is no mention of a queen in early English, Irish or Germanic laws.

Doctors were liable for the death of patients unless the family had agreed to the course of treatment. Contracts were stronger than legislation in civil disputes. In criminal proceedings, recompense by the offending family network, and reconciliation, took precedence over revenge. The laws tried to achieve social harmony, with none of the English elements of public whipping, trial by fire or boiling water, torturing, gibbetting, burning of witches or disembowelling being known in independent Wales. The rate of execution in 'primitive' 12th-century Wales was proportionately less than a quarter than that endured under modern English law in the 19th century. Under the entry upon John Frost we can see that the sentence given to the leading Welsh Chartists in 1839 was that they should be 'hung, drawn and quartered' – this was for asking for a movement towards democracy.

For theft there was no punishment whatsoever if the purpose was to stay alive - up to the late 18th century, children were hung in England for stealing a lamb. Children were of equal status - the law of Gavelkind meant shared inheritance amongst all children - a civilised and socially unique method of preventing massing of power and lands. Even more advanced was the law that illegitimate children received all the rights, including inheritance, of family offspring – *Cyfraith Hywel* states that the youngest son has equal rights to the oldest, and also that 'the sin of the father and his wrongdoing should not be set against the son's right to his patrimony', so illegitimate children had equal rights. A boy came of age at 14, free of parental control, and a father could be chastised for hitting him after this age. A girl came of age at 12, and like the boy could decide whether she wished to stay in the father's household. She could not be forced into marriage, nor arbitrarily divorced. Rhiannon, in the *Mabinogion* story of Pwyll, Prince of

Powys, refuses to marry, saying 'every woman is to go the way she willeth, freely.'

Professor Dafydd Jenkins noted that aspects of Hywel's laws, which were superseded by English law in 1536, were being reintroduced as enlightened reforms in the 1990's, such as reparation to the victims of crime. Compensation of the victim was more important than punishment of the  offender. For damage unwittingly done, redress had to be made. Even for murder, the Welsh state was active in seeking compensation for the victim's family, to remove the need for vengeance and feuds. Obviously, the far-extended Welsh family-clans exerted pressure on their members to toe the line, as if any of them offended, all had to pay something. All the checks and balances were in place under this system to make society enforce its own social code.

Unlike many societies, there were no differences in morality requirements for the sexes - a Welsh woman could heavily fine her husband on an increasing scale for adultery, and

Illustration from the book of Hywel Dda

also divorce him for it. A woman could even divorce her husband for 'stinking breath'. She had property rights not given under English law until the Married Woman's Property Act of 1870. In France and the rest of Britain, wife-beating was a recognised 'right' of the husband - in Wales there had to be a definite, very serious offence, and then the punishment was limited to just three strokes of a rod.

The Welsh have possibly been the most civilised race in the world in their attitudes towards women from before the Dark Ages of the fifth century to the present day. I made the old joke at an international conference that the real reason was that we feared them so much, and that we even put them on our national flag. The Laws were fair to all men and women - violence to the person was averted at all costs, and responsibility shared by the offenders' relatives, which made for social order. Not until the Act of Union in 1536 and after did we see the terribly unjust system that is known as British justice imposed on Wales. The 'torture until you confess' treatment was recently still used to get a confession in IRA bomb cases - with never a comeback on corrupt policemen, politicians, lawyers and judges who use the system to their best advantage. The twin elements that define a nation are its language and legislation - the London government wiped out a humane system of laws based upon social responsibility and replaced it with one based upon class, property, prestige, repression and violence. They almost wiped out the language by similar methods.

Hywel's death in 949 or 950* saw the end of three decades of relative peace and the resumption of Viking attacks from 952, and the laws of gavelkind meant that princes fought against princes, with no national unity until the accession of Gruffydd ap Llewellyn in 1039. There were ninety years of murder and mayhem and internal power struggles against a background of Saxon, Mercian and Norse invasions. But the *Laws* lived for six hundred years, and their ethos of human equality is slowly replacing the property-based spirit of English laws. An excellent book upon what was one of the finest legal frameworks in history is by Dafydd Jenkins, *Hywel Dda, The Law*.

* The relevant dates prior to, and after Hywel's death, from the *Chronicle of Ystrad Fflur*, show the upheaval in Wales caused by his death:

'910 In this year Cadell ap Rhodri died and Asser
914 In this year the Black Gentiles took Cyfeiliog, bishop of Ergyng
916 In this year Anarawd ap Rhodri, king of the Britons, died
918 In this year Ireland and Anglesey were ravaged by the men of Dublin (Vikings).
920 In this year Clydog ap Cadell was slain by Meurig, his brother
922 In this year was the battle of Dinas Newydd
922 In this year Hywell ap Cadell submitted to Athelstan
929 In this year Hywel ap Cadell made pilgrimage to Rome
935 In this year Gruffudd ab Owain was slain by the men of Ceredigion
942 In this year Cadell ab Arthfael was poisoned. And Idwal ap Rhodri and Elisedd, his brother, were slain by the Saxons
945 In this year Hywel ap Cadell ordered the laws to be codified
949 In this year Hywel Dda ap Cadell he head and glory of all the Britons died. And then there was the battle of Carno between the sons of Hywel and the sons of Idwal
952 In this year Dyfed was laid waste twice by the sons of Idwal, Iago and Ieuaf. And the Gentiles slew Dwnwallon
954 In this year there was a great slaughter between the sons of Hywel and the sons of Idwal at the place called Gwrgystu: the battle of Conwy Hirfawr. And after that, Ceredigion was ravaged by the sons of Idwal.

Footnote on the laws of Hywel Dda
There is a tradition that the tribal laws and customs were codified by Dyfnwal Moelmud long before Hywel, but the earliest manuscripts date from the 12th and 13th centuries, extracts made by practising lawyers, the earliest from the time of Llywelyn the Great. There were slight differences between North, West and South Wales, known as the Venetian, Dementian and Gwentian Codes, and they stayed in force in entirety until Edward I's Statute of Rhuddlan in 1283, but many provisions remained until the period of the Tudors in the 16th century.

Many Welsh laws and traditions are noted in the ancient *Triads*, expressions where objects are grouped in threes. We know of nothing similar in any other country, and some of these sayings may date back to the time of the Druids, who committed the old laws to memory. *Triads* are found in the oldest Welsh manuscripts such as the *Mabinogion*, bardic poems, the 12th century *Black Book of Carmarthen*, ancient versions of the Welsh Laws, and the 14th century *Red Book of Hergest*. Examples are:

Three things a man experiences through litigation: expense, care and trouble.
Three things which cannot be hidden: love, hatred and pride.
Three things not easily restrained are the flow of a torrent, the flight of an arrow, and the tongue of a fool.
Three things a good liar must have: a good memory, a bold face, and a fool to listen.
Three things that will take a good man unawares: sleep, sin and old age.
The strength of a bard is his muse, that of a judge is his patience, that of a lawmaker his patriotism.

The amazing fact that the laws were written in Welsh as well as Latin helped ensure that the language thrived. To keep a culture, history, laws, literature, religion, language and community must intertwine and be respected. These Welsh laws, first written down over a thousand years ago, according to Saunders Lewis fashioned: 'lively forms of the mind of every poet and writer in Wales until the sixteenth century, and also directly influenced the shape and style of Welsh prose. This implies that the language had already reached a philosophical maturity unequalled in its period. It meant that it had a flexibility and positiveness which are the signs of centuries of culture. This means that there is a long period of development behind the prose of the *Cyfreithiau* (Laws).'

From the Laws, we find that Welsh kings had a servant called a 'Foot-Holder'. This anti-stress kit consisted of a man holding the king's feet in his lap, from the moment the king sat down to eat in the evening, until he went to bed. At this time, the king had no power, as he was no longer king while his feet were off his kingdom. He could therefore relax, and not have to make any decisions, while his power passed to the 'Foot-Holder'. The 'Foot-Holder' could now grant pardons to criminals, arbitrate in disputes and the like, while the king drank quietly to oblivion and threw chicken drumsticks at the harpist.

GRUFFYDD AP LLYWELYN AP SEISYLL 1007- 5 August 1063

'HEAD, SHIELD AND DEFENDER OF THE BRITONS' - THE ONLY WELSHMAN EVER TO RULE OVER THE WHOLE OF WALES

Royal succession was extremely important in Welsh history. In direct line from Cunedda (fl.440) were Maelgwn Gwynedd (died 547), Cadwaladr ap Cadfan (defeated by Offa of Mercia in 634), Rhodri Mawr (who united

Wales against the Norse invaders, and died in 878), Hywel Dda (who established the Laws, and died in 950), and Gruffydd ap Llywelyn.

Maredudd ap Owain ap Hywel Dda briefly recreated the Kingdom of Wales from 986 to 989, after the schisms that followed his grandfather's death around 950. Later, Llywelyn ap Seisyll ruled Gwynedd and from 1018 to 1023, and had defeated the Prince of Deheubarth to establish himself as King of Gwynedd and Powys. Llywelyn's mother, Angharad, was a great-grand-daughter of Hywel Dda. Llywelyn was killed in 1023, through the jealous treachery of Madog, Bishop of Bangor. Anarchy again restarted upon his death, with all the Welsh princes reasserting their independence. Iago ab Idwal took over Gwynedd. Llywelyn's young son, Gruffydd ap Llywelyn, was also Maredudd's grandson (on his mother, Angharad's side), and seems to have fled fled to France, where he stayed for sixteen years.

Earl Robert's Mound on the site of Gruffyd's ap Llewelyn's palace at Ruddland

Brut y Tywysogion (The Chronicles of the Princes) records that between 950 and 1100 28 Welsh princes met violent deaths and four were blinded. In a hundred years, nearly fifty Welsh rulers were incarcerated, murdered or slain in battle. Wales was racked by internal warfare and invasions by the Mercians. The 31-year-old Gruffydd returned from France. In 1039, Iago ab Idwal may have been killed by his own men, or by Gruffydd. As Idwal's son was only four, he was taken into exile in Dublin, and Gruffydd regained Gwynedd.

Gruffydd next made a surprise attack on the invading the army of Earl Leofric (Lady Godiva's husband) at Rhyd y Groes near Welshpool in 1039, killing Leofric's brother Edwin. The Mercians fled, and secure in the east, Gruffydd now wished to retake his father's lands in Powys. He ravaged Ceredigion, won a battle at Pencader and carried off the wife of Hywel ab Edwin, Prince of Deheubarth. Gruffydd gathered forces and won a, before sacking Llanbadarn Fawr in 1041 to control Ceredigion for a short while. Hywel fled to Ireland.

In 1042 Prince Hywel ab Edwin returned and was said to have defeated a host of 'black gentiles' (Danes based in Dublin) at Pwlldyfarch near Carmarthen. In the same year Gruffydd is recorded as being captured by the Dublin Vikings. Perhaps having been ransomed, we next hear of Gruffydd fighting in south-east Wales, and won at Newport in 1044 to gain Gwent. Hywel now allied with Danes to gain his revenge over Gruffydd for defeat in battle and taking his wife. He landed with a fleet at the mouth of the River Tywi. Gruffydd headed west to face Hywel ab Edwin and killed the Prince of Deheubarth at the battle of Carmarthen. In 1047, around 140 of Gruffydd's *teulu*, his household guard, were killed by treachery in Ystrad Tywi. Gruffydd ap Rhydderch of Gwent took over as King of Deheubarth. Gruffydd ap Llywelyn ravaged through Ystrad Tywi and into Pembroke but could not retake the territory, and turned back towards the Welsh borders.

In 1052 he crushed the Saxons and their Norman mercenaries at the Battle of Leominster in Hereford. Gruffydd next fought and killed Gruffydd ap Rhydderch to gain the remains of Deheubarth in 1055. The ruthless Gruffydd was now master of almost all of Wales.

1055 was an eventful year for Gruffydd. Harold of Wessex, son of Earl Godwin, ensured that the Earldom of Mercia went to his brother. The deposed Earl, Leofric's son Aelfgar, allied with Gruffydd and Gruffydd married his daughter, Ealdgyth. On 24 October, Gruffydd and Alefgar defeated Ralph the Timid at Hereford. The allies burned Hereford, and Gruffydd took possession of Whitford, Hope, Presteigne, Radnor, Bangor-is-Coed and Chirk, beating a small Saxon army. These lands, across Offa's Dyke, had been in Saxon possession for three hundred years until the border stabilised. Harold was ordered to defeat Gruffydd, but instead built a castle at Longtown and Aelfgar was restored to his earldom.

Bishop Leofgar (or Bandulph) of Hereford assembled a mixed force of Norman settlers and Saxon-English. He crossed the Dyke, but was killed by Gruffydd and his army destroyed on 16 June 1056 in the valley of the Machawy, a tributary of the Wye near Paincastle in Hereford, or more likely near Glasbury on Wye. Gruffydd had now settled his court at Rhuddlan, an area heavily settled by Mercians, and from northeast Wales now re-conquered large parts of the Earldom of Chester over Offa's Dyke, including much of Flintshire and Denbighshire.

In 1056-1057 Gruffydd drove Cadwgan ap Meurig out of Morgannwg, to control the last princedom. Gruffydd ap Llywelyn became the only Welshman ever to rule over the whole of Wales. His claim to sovereignty over the whole of Wales was also recognized by the English. As John Davies wrote: he was 'the only Welsh king ever to rule over the entire territory of Wales... Thus, from about 1057 until his death in 1063, the whole of Wales recognized the kingship of Gruffudd ap Llywelyn. For about seven brief years, Wales was one, under one ruler, a feat with neither precedent nor successor.'

In 1063, Aelfgar needed Gruffydd's help to regain Mercia again, and in alliance with the Viking Magnus Barefoot's fleet, they triumphed. However, Harold of Wessex, one of the greatest generals of the time, had been occupied defeating Macbeth in Scotland and uniting Wessex, Mercia, East Anglia and Northumberland for eight years, before he unfortunately turned the Saxon war machine of the House of Godwinson against Gruffydd.

Gruffydd's brutality against rival Welsh families was well-known - he defended it as 'blunting the horns of the progeny of Wales so they do not wound their mother' (-Walter Map's *De Nugis Curialum* of 1180). As such, when Harold and his brother Tostig of Northumbria attacked by land and sea, much support faded away and the other royal houses saw the opportunity to reclaim their princedoms of Deheubarth, Morgannwg, Powys and Gwynedd. It was winter, and Gruffydd's 'teulu', or bodyguard, had returned to their lands for the winter, not expecting any attack. Harold feinted to attack from Gloucester, and raided the south Wales coast with a fleet based in Bristol. Harold then made a long forced march with lightly armed troops to the north of Wales (similar to his superb march from the Battle of Stamford Bridge in Yorkshire to Hastings three years later). Most of Gruffydd's forces were separated from him, in the south. The fast-moving Saxons had caught him out.

Harold struck so rapidly at Rhuddlan, Gruffydd's seat of government, that the unprepared Gruffydd only just escaped by sea. He was pressed back towards Snowdon, and a reward of three hundred cattle offered for his head. He was killed by one of his own men, by Cynan ap Iago, according to the *Ulster Chronicle* (the son of Iago of Gwynedd, who had himself been killed by Gruffydd). The king's death on 5 August 1063 had been made possible by the treachery of Madog, the very same Bishop of Bangor who betrayed Gruffydd's father, Llywelyn, forty years earlier.

Gruffydd's head was carried to Harold, who married his widow Ealdgyth and made Gruffydd's brothers his regional commanders in Wales. Harold refused to pay the traitor Madog, and Madog's ship was sunk carrying him to exile in Ireland. Harold did not annexe any Welsh land, and in part because of this victory, he was elected King of England over the claims of Edward the Confessor's nephew and rightful heir. Soon the Saxon enemy was to be replaced by a far more powerful force - the Normans. The *Brut y Tywysogion*, lamented Gruffydd as the 'head, shield and defender of the Briton, perished through the treachery of his own men...the man erstwhile thought invincible, the winner of countless spoils and immeasurable victories, endlessly rich in gold and silver and precious stones and purple apparel.'

The Anglo-Saxon Chronicle recalls Gruffydd ap Llywelyn as 'King over all the Welsh race.' During his reign he extended Welsh territories back into Hereford, over Offa's Dyke, and united the Welsh nation. It is to him that Wales owes its debt of lasting resistance to the Danish-French Normans who destroyed the Anglo-Saxons.

Harold went on to defeat at Hastings in 1066, and the Saxons of England were completely under the Norman yoke by 1070. The Welsh-speaking British region of Cumbria was only annexed to French-controlled England in 1170. The Welsh-speaking county of Cornwall had been annexed by the Saxons for England in 930. However, Wales kept its independence against the Normans for two centuries, until the death of Dafydd, and the 1282 Statute of Rhuddlan. From then, the Welsh were relatively subdued until the Glyndŵr rebellion gave independence again for a decade from 1400. The land was never really settled until 1485, when the Tudors took over the English crown from the Plantagenets.

Footnote:
From the *Chronicle of Ystrad Fflur*, the relevant dates of Gruffudd's time are as follows:

'1035 Maredudd ab Edwin was slain by the sons of Cynan. Afterwards a cross was raised for him at Carew (-which can be seen today outside Pembroke's Carew Castle). And the Saxons slew Caradog ap Rhydderch.
1039 Iago of Gwynedd was slain. And in his place Gruffudd ap Llywelyn rules who throughout his reign hounded the Pagans and the Saxons in many battles. And first he defeated Leofrig of Mercia at Rhyd-y-Groes.
1041 In this year was the battle of Pencadair where Gruffudd defeated Hywel ab Edwin, and he seized Hywel's wife and took her for his own
1042 In this year was the battle of Pwlldyfach where Hywel defeated the Gentiles. And in that year Gruffudd was captured by the men of Dublin [Vikings]
1043 Hywel ab Owain, king of Glamorgan, died in his old age
1044 Hywel ab Edwin gathered a fleet of the Gentiles of Ireland to ravage the kingdom. And Gruffudd encountered him and there was a mighty battle at the mouth of the Tywi. And there Gruffudd prevailed and Hywel was slain.
1045 In this year there was great treachery and deceit between the sons of Rhydderch, Gruffudd and Rhys, and Gruffudd ap Llywelyn
1047 About seven score of Gruffudd ap Llywelyn's Teulu [warband] were slain through the treachery of the leading men of Ystrad Tywi. And thereafter Gruffudd ravaged Dyfed and Ystrad Tywi.
1049 All Deheubarth was ravaged
1052 In this year Gruffudd ap Llywelyn fought the Saxons and their French allies [Norman mercenaries] at Llanllieni
1056 Gruffudd ap Llywelyn took Gruffudd ap Rhydderch's kingdom and his life. And after that Gruffudd moved a host against the Saxons, with Ranulf as their leader. And after bitter, fierce fighting the Saxons turned to flight. And Gruffudd pursued them to within the walls of Hereford and there he massacred them and destroyed the walls and burned the town. And with vast spoil he returned home eminently worthy.
1058 Magnus, son of Harold, ravaged the kingdom of England with the help and chieftainship of Gruffudd ap Llywelyn, king of the Britons
1059 In this year died Owain ap Gruffudd
1063 In this year Gruffudd ap Llywelyn was slain, after innumerable victories, through the treachery of his own men. He had been head and shield and protector to the Britons.

GRUFFYDD AP CYNAN 1055 - 1137

KING OF GWYNEDD, 'PRYDAIN BRIAWD' (THE POSSESSOR OF BRITAIN), 'HEAD AND KING AND DEFENDER AND PACIFIER OF ALL WALES' (*Brut y Tywysogion*)

From Gruffydd ap Llywelyn ap Seisyllt's death in 1063, there was almost

permanent fighting between the Welsh princes. The laws of *Gavelkind* meant that kingdoms and princedoms were constantly being broken up between all male heirs, legitimate and illegitimate. Gruffydd ap Llywelyn may killed Iago ab Idwal in 1039 to gain the crown of Gwynedd, and Iago's four-year-old son Cynan ab Iago fled to the Viking settlement in Dublin. He married Ragnhilda, the daughter of its King Olaf, and Cynan may have died soon after the birth of their son Gruffydd.

The *History of Gruffydd ap Cynan,* of perhaps 1200, details that his mother told him to reclaim his ancestry. Bleddyn ap Cynfyn of Gwynedd died, and Trahaearn ap Caradog took the lands. Gruffydd ap Cynan ab Iago, landed in Anglesey with Irish followers to reclaim his lands from Trahaiarn of Gwynedd, in 1075. Gruffydd's father Cynan may have died fighting against Gruffydd ap Llywelyn with Harold of Wessex in 1063, when Gruffydd ap Cynan was just eight years old. With the assistance of troops provided by the Norman Robert of Rhuddlan, Gruffydd defeated and killed Cynwrig ap Rhiwallon, an ally of Trahaearn who held the Llŷn.

Gruffydd ap Cynan then defeated Trahaearn at the Battle of Gwaed Erw to recover Meironydd as well as Gwynedd, and headed eastward to regain territories now held by the Normans. He destroyed Robert's castle at Rhuddlan, but there was a revolt against him because of the conduct of his Danish-Irish mercenaries in the Llyn. Trahaearn now counterattacked, defeating Gruffudd at the battle of Bron yr Erw, ear Clynnog Fawr in 1075.

Gruffydd attempted again in 1076, but was forced off Anglesey and escaped to Ireland. In 1081, he returned once more, allying himself with Rhys ap Tewdwr, Prince of Deheubarth. The Earl of Chester and vicious Robert of Rhuddlan were wreaking havoc across North Wales, but internal warfare had not relented. Rhys had been forced to flee to St David's Cathedral, after being attacked by Caradog ap Gruffydd of Morgannwg and Gwent. Gruffudd gathered an army of Irish and Danes and left Waterford, landing at St David's. Here, he was joined here by a force of his followers from Gwynedd, and he and Rhys ap Tewdwr marched north to seek Trahaearn ap Caradog and Caradog ap Gruffudd. They had made an alliance with Meilyr ap Rhiwallon of Powys, and the armies met at the Battle of Mynydd Carn. Trahaearn, Caradog and Meilyr were all killed, and Gruffydd took power in Gwynedd for the second time. William the Conqueror, on a pilgrimage to St David's in 1081, recognised Rhys ap Tewdwr's right to Deheubarth.

Gruffydd now had to turn back the Norman movement into Gwynedd, and agreed to a meeting with Red Hugh, Earl of Shrewsbury and Hugh the Fat, Earl of Chester at Rug, near Corwen. At the meeting Gruffudd was seized and taken prisoner. According to his biographer this was by the treachery of one of his own men, Meirion Goch. Earl Hugh (the Fat) had bribed Meirion Goch to bring Gruffydd to a meeting in 1081, where peace might be arranged between the Welsh and Normans. Gruffydd was imprisoned in Hugh's castle at Chester while Hugh and Robert of Rhuddlan went on to take possession of Gwynedd, building castles at Bangor, Caernarfon and Aberlleiniog. Hugh the Fat held Gruffydd as a prisoner in chains at Chester for twelve years.

In 1093, Hugh ordered that Gruffydd be displayed in chains at Chester market place so the people could see the fall of the great Prince of Gwynedd. In the bustle of the market, Cynwrig Hir rescued him. He was said to have carried the weakened Gruffydd away on his shoulders. A blacksmith had knocked Gruffydd's chains off and the small rescue party managed to escape to Aberdaron, and sail back across to Ireland. Gruffydd soon returned to Wales, following a fellow prince, Cadwgan ab Bleddyn of Powys. From 1094 they ravaged parts of Shropshire and Cheshire, attacked castles such as Aber Lleiniog, and defeated the Normans in the woods of Yspwys. The revolt spread across Wales, and William II (William Rufus) invaded northern Wales in 1095 to restore order, but the Welsh retreated to the hills, and William's army returned to Chester. In 1096, Gruffydd defeated Norman armies at Gelli Trafnant and Aber Llech. William led another full-scale invasion in 1097 against Gruffydd and Cadwgan: 'William moved a great host without number against the Britons. And the Britons, placing their trust in the Lord of Heaven, avoided the assault of the French. And the French returned home dejected and empty-handed.' *The Chronicle of Ystrad Fflur* then noted his death in 1100 thus: 'In this year died William, king of England, who would do nothing just nor anything that appertained to the commandments of God. He died without heir because he had always used concublnes.'

In Summer 1098 the earls Hugh of Chester and Hugh Shrewsbury campaigned in a concerted attack against the princes, and the Welsh retreated to Anglesey. Gruffydd and Cadwgan fled in a small boat to Ireland. They had hired a fleet from Ireland, but it changed sides after a better offer from the Normans. Norman cruelty led to a fresh Welsh revolt, and just then the Danish fleet descended upon Anglesey. The earls were beaten on the banks of the Menai River by the force led by Magnus Barefoot, King of Norway, who was said to have personally killed Red Hugh with an arrow. Gruffydd now moved back for a third time in 1099 to restore and consolidate his Gwynedd power base as the Normans retreated. Gruffydd now reigned over Anglesey and the kingdom known as Gwynedd uwch Conwy, seemingly with the agreement of Hugh the Fat.

With the death of Hugh of Chester in 1101, Gruffydd began to consolidate his position across Gwynedd, as much by diplomacy as by force. He met Henry I, who granted him the rule of Llŷn, Eifionydd, Ardudwy and Arllechwedd, extending his kingdom. However, by 1114 Gruffydd had gained enough power to induce Henry to invade Gwynedd. Henry invaded with three forces; in south Wales under Strongbow, Earl of Pembroke; in north Wales under Alexander of Scotland; and a force led by himself against Powys. In a difficult holding campaign Gruffydd fought no battles, and lost no land, but decided to parley with Henry. As a result, Gruffydd submitted to Henry, and promised to give up his son-in-law Gruffydd ap Rhys, in order to keep the peace. Gruffudd ap Rhys was the son of Rhys ap Tewdwr, the co-victor of Mynydd Carn. He later avenged the murder of his wife Gwenllian ferch Gruffudd ap Cynan, defeating the Normans outside Cardigan. However, it appears that Gruffudd ap Cynan warned Gruffudd ap Rhys of his agreement. The *Chronicles* tell us that Gruffudd ap Cynan quietly sent a messenger to Pembroke Castle to warn Nest that her brother's life was in danger, so Gruffudd ap Rhys first fled to Aberdaron. A boat then took him to the safety of the great forest of Ystrad Tywy in Deheubarth.

The cantefs of Rhos and Rhufoniog were annexed in 1118, Gruffydd was now powerful enough to ensure that his nominee David the Scot was consecrated as Bishop of Bangor in 1120. The see had been effectively vacant since a Breton incumbent had been forced to flee by the Welsh almost twenty years before, since Gruffydd and Henry could not agree on a candidate. David went on to rebuild Bangor Cathedral with a large financial contribution from Gruffydd.

Another invasion by the king of England in 1121 was a military failure, with Gruffydd's sons Owain Gwynedd, Cadwallon and Cadwaladr leading the fighting. The king had to come to terms with Gruffydd and made no further attempt to invade Gwynedd during Gruffudd's reign. Gruffudd ap Cynan ruled Gwynedd quietly until 1121, when he moved quickly to take over Powys, which was riddled with internal disputes. He later took over Deheubarth. His sons Owain Gwynedd and Cadwaladr cemented his grip on most of Wales. The death of Cadwallon in a battle against the forces of Powys near Llangollen in 1132 checked further expansion for the time being. Owain and Cadwaladr, in alliance with their brother-in-law Gruffudd ap Rhys of Deheubarth, crushed the Normans at Crug Mawr near Cardigan in 1136 and took possession of Ceredigion. During Gruffydd's lifetime, his sons also took Meirionydd, Rhos, Rhufoniog and Dyffryn Clwyd for Gwynedd.

Gruffydd ruled over a peaceful Wales until his death, blind and ailing, in 1137. The work of some poets of his time is preserved in The Black Book of Carmarthen, and the court poetry of his bard Meilyr* survives. His biography was written just twenty years after his death, declaring Gwynedd to be the 'primus inter pares' ('first among equals') of Welsh kingdoms. Gruffydd was buried in Bangor Cathedral to the left of the high altar, and his son, the heroic poet-prince Owain Gwynedd (q.v.) succeeded peacefully. He made bequests to many other churches, including one to Christ Church, Dublin, where he had worshipped as a boy prince in exile. The latter part of his reign was considered to be a 'golden age' according to his *Life*, when Gwynedd was 'bespangled with lime-washed churches like the stars in the firmament'.

Gruffudd's wife Angharad ferch Owain ab Edwin, survived him by 25 years, receiving half his goods, as was Welsh custom. The Normans executed his daughter Gwenllian after the battle of Maes Gwenllian. Her son by Gruffudd ap Rhys, Rhys ap Gruffudd (*Yr Arglwydd Rhys*) fought with Owain Gwynedd against the Normans, and took over leadership of Welsh resistance upon his death. Thus Gruffudd's descendants carried on the fight for Wales for sixty years after his passing, to the death of Rhys ap Gruffudd in 1197. Just thirteen years after this, Welsh leadership had passed to Llywelyn the Great, of the House of Gwynedd. In 1485, Gruffudd ap Cynan's descendant, Henry Tudor, became the first Welsh King of England.

Buried in Bangor Cathedral, Gruffudd ap Cynan's elegy was sung by Meilyr, his pencerdd (chief bard). In 1094, Gruffudd's 'harpist (and) chief of song' was noted in the *Life*** as being killed in the battle of Gellan, retreating from Aberlleiniog. It seems clear that Gruffudd was a cultured man, and the traditional lore of the Welsh bards was that he drew up regulations to govern their craft. This is mentioned in a statute concerning the 1523 Caerwys Eisteddfod, almost four centuries after his death.

* Meilyr Brydydd (fl. c. 1100 - c. 1137) was Gruffudd's chief court-poet at Aberffraw, the traditional seat of the kings of Gwynedd, on Anglesey. He seems to be the earliest of the *'gogynfeirdd'* (early poets) and his son Gwalchmai, and Gwalchmai's own sons Meilyr and Einion, represent the first-known line of hereditary poets. In Anglesey, the place-names Trewalchmai and Trefeilyr, Tre'r Beirdd (Place of Bards) and Pentre'r-Beirdd (Head Place of the Bards) recall these poets of a millennium ago.

** Gruffudd is the only medieval Welsh prince whose biography has survived. All the others were burned by invading land-thieves or lost. It tells us that two of his brothers were kings of Ulster, and also states 'Oh dearly beloved brother Welshmen, very memorable is King Gruffudd, who is commended by the praise of his earthly pedigree and the prophesy of Merddin (Merlin)... Intimate friends of Gruffudd say that he was a good man of middle height, fair-haired, hot-headed, with a round face of good complexion, large shapely eyes, fine eyebrows, a comely beard, a round neck, white skin, powerful limbs, long fingers, straight shanks, and fine feet. He was skilled and eloquent in several tongues. He was noble and merciful towards his people, cruel towards his enemies, and very gallant in battle... Then he increased all manner of good in Gwynedd, and the inhabitants began to build churches in every direction therein, and to plant the old woods and to make orchards and gardens, and surround them with walls and ditches and to construct walled buildings and to support themselves from the fruit of the earth after the fashion of the Romans. Gruffudd on his part, made great churches for himself in his chief places, and constructed courts and gave banquets constantly and honourably. Wherefore, he also made Gwynedd glitter ten with lime-washed churches like the firmament with stars.'

The Chronicle of Ystrad Fflur, written by the monks of Strata Florida Abbey, tell us of the turmoil following 1066, the years in which Gruffudd came to power and the 'French', i.e. Normans started to seriously attack Wales:

'1066 In this year Harold, the son of Earl Godwin, raised himself through oppression to the very height of kingship over the Saxons. And while he was enjoying the glory William the Bastard and a mighty host came after him; and after a mighty battle and a slaughter of the Saxons despoiled him of his kingdom and his life.

1069 In this year was the battle of Mechain fought between the sons of Cynfyn, Bleddyn and Rhiwallon, and the sons of Gruffudd, Maredudd and Ithel. And there the sons of Gruffudd fell and Rhiwallon ap Cynfyn. And Bleddyn ap Cynfyn rules. And Maredudd ab Owain ab Edwin ruled in the south.

1072 in this year Maredudd ab Owain was slain by the French and Caradog ap Gruffudd ap Rhydderch on the banks of the Rhymni.

1073 The French ravaged Ceredigion and Dyfed. And Menevia and Bangor were ravaged by the Gentiles [Vikings].

1074 The French ravaged Ceredigion

1075 Bleddyn ap Cynfyn was slain through the evil-spirited treachery of the princes of Ystrad Tywi; and it was Rhys ab Owain who slew him. And after him Trahaearn ap Caradog ruled over Gwynedd; and Rhys ab Owain and Rhydderch ap Caradog held the South, and Gruffudd ap Cynan took Anglesey. Thereafter was the battle of Camddwr between the sons of Cadwgan, Goronwy and Llywelyn, and Caradog ap Gruffudd, and Rhys ab Owain and Rhydderch ap Caradog. Also in this year was the battle of Bron-yr-Erw between Gruffudd ap Cynan and Trahaearn.

1076 Rhyddrch ap Caradog was slain by Meirchion ap Rhys ap Rhydderch, his cousin, through treachery

1077 In this year was the battle of Gweunytwl between the sons of Cadwgan and Rhys ab Owain

1078 In this year was the battle of Pwllgwdig in which Trahaearn obtained the victory and Rhys ab Owain fled like a wounded, frightened stag before the hounds. And at the close of the year Caradog ap Gruffudd slew Rhys and Hywel, his brother.

1079 In this year Rhys ap Tewdwr began to rule

1080 In this year Menevia (the St David's area) was pillaged

1081 In this year was the battle of Mynydd Carn, in which Trahaearn ap Caradog was slain by Rhys ap Tewdwr and Gruffudd ap Cynan. And thereafter Gruffudd ruled in Gwynedd. And William, king of England and Wales and much of France came to Menevia on pilgrimage.

1087 In this year William the Bastard, prince of the Normans and King of the Saxons and the Britons and the Scots, died after exceeding great glory in this changeable world.

1088 In this year Rhys ap Tewdwr was expelled from his kingdom by the sons of Bleddyn. And he fled to Ireland. And after he gathered a fleet there, he gave battle at Llech-y-crau and there killed two sons of Bleddyn.

1089 In this year the shrine of David was taken by stealth and despoiled

1093 In this year Rhys aop Tewdwr, king of the South, was slain by Frenchmen who were inhabiting Brycheiniog - and with him fell the kingdom of the Britons. And within two months the French over-ran Dyfed and Ceredigion - and made castles and fortified them.

1094 In this year the Britons being unable to bear the tyranny and injustice of the French, threw off the rule of the French, and they destroyed their castles in Gwynedd and inflicted slaughter upon them. And the French brought a host to Gwynedd and Cadwgan ap Bleddyn drove them to flight with great slaughter at Coes Yspwys. And at the close of the year the castles of Ceredigion and Dyfed were all taken except two

1095 William, king of England, moved a host against the Britons but he returned home empty-handed and having gained naught

1096 The French moved a host into Gwent and the Britons slew them all at Celli Tarfawg. And thereupon the French raided Brycheiniog and they were slain by the sons of Idnerth ap Cadwgan at Aber-Llech. And the war-band of Cadwgan ap Bleddyn despoiled the castle at Pembroke.

1097 William moved a great host without number against the Britons. And the Britons, placing their trust in the Lord of Heaven, avoided the assault of the French. And the French returned home dejected and empty-handed.

1098 In this year the French moved a third time against the men of Gwynedd. For fear of treahery, Gruffudd ap Cynan fled to Ireland.

1099 Cadwgan ap Bleddyn and Gruffudd ap Cynan returned from ireland. And, after making peace with the French, they received a portion of the land and the kingdom.

1100 In this year died William, king of England, who would do nothing just nor anything that appertained to the commandments of God. He died without heir because he had always used concubines. And thereupon Henry, his brother, took the kingdom.

[In 1102-1103 Henry seized Maredudd ap Bleddyn and Iorwerth ap Bleddyn by treachery and took their princedom, but Maredudd escaped in 1107 and reclaimed it. In 1106 Hywel ap Goronwy was 'slain by treachery of the French' In 1108 was noted the Flemish colony settled in Pembroke].

1114 Henry moved a host against the men of Gwynedd and above all to Powys. And Gruffudd ap Cynan made peace, paying a large tribute. And Owain ap Cadwgan did likewise and thereafter he joined the king in Normandy

1115 Henry made one from Normandy - his name was Bernard - bishop of Menevia in contempt of the clerics of the Britons [In 1116 Gruffudd ap Rhys took Narberth and ravaged the Gower, and in 1121 Henry moved into Powys, forcing Owain ap Cadwgan to pay tribute].

1137 In this year died Gruffudd ap Rhys, the light and excellence and strength of all south Wales. And Gruffudd ap Cynan, prince of Gwynedd and head and king and pacifier of all Wales, ended his temporal life in Christ after receiving extreme unction and communion and confession and repentance for his sins, and becoming a monk and making a good end in his perfect old age. And for a third time the sons of Gruffudd ap Cynan came to Ceredigion and burned castles.'

OWAIN GWYNEDD c.1109 – 23 or 28 September 1170

OWAIN AP GRUFFYDD AP CYNAN, 'KING OF THE WELSH', 'THE BULWARK OF ALL WALES'

The above entry upon Owain's father Gruffydd ap Cynan details some of Owain's fighting for his country until his father's peaceful death, aged a remarkable eighty-two. Bangor Cathedral holds a tomb believed to be Gruffydd's - the earliest tomb of a Welsh prince. During the first 200 years of battles with the Normans and Plantagenets, which lasted from 1066 until Henry Tudor's victory in 1485, three political entities in Wales had remained fairly stable and relatively independent - the princedoms of Powys, Deheubarth and Gwynedd. Owain ap Gruffydd extended his possessions over Offa's Dyke regaining lands in England, and down into the other two major princedoms, ensuring the predominance of the Princes of Gwynedd, Rhodri Mawr's descendants, in the continuing Welsh fight for independence. Owain ap Gruffydd became known as Owain Gwynedd, because another Owain ap Gruffydd was the king of southern Powys, and became known as Owain Cyfeiliog. Owain's grandson was Llywelyn ap Iorwerth, Llywelyn the Great, whose own grandson was Llywelyn ap Gruffydd, Llywelyn Olaf (Llywelyn the Last). Owain's reign saw the strongest Norman attacks so far upon Wales - his whole reign was focused upon protecting Wales from the Marcher Lords. He was also known as Owain Fawr, 'Owain the Great', and repulsed an invasion by Henry II so easily that no other Plantagenet king attempted to subjugate Wales until Owain's death. Gwalchmai, his *pencerdd* ('chief household bard'), wrote in '*The Triumphs of Owain*':

'Owain's praise demands my song
Owain swift and Owain strong;
Fairest flower of Rhodri's stem, [Rhodri Mawr's lineage]

Gwynedd's shield, and Britain's gem....
Lord of every regal art
Liberal hand and open heart...
Dauntless on his native sands
The dragon-son of Mona stands.'

Mona is the English translation of Môn (Anglesey), the holy island of Wales, where the princes of Gwynedd had their chief court at Aberffraw. From his accession to the crown of Gwynedd in 1137, Owain Gwynedd was faced with major problems from his brother Cadwaladr, and Owain's sons Hywel and Cynan defeated Cadwaladr and forced him to flee to Ireland. In 1145, aged thirty-six, Owain lost his favourite son Rhun and fell into a long period of grieving. However, two of Owain's other sons Hywel Hir and Cynan took the mighty Norman fortress of Mold (Wyddgrug) and razed it to the ground, restoring his spirits, and showing him that there was a war to be won. The castle was thought to be impregnable. In 1149 Madoc ap Maredudd, Prince of Powys, joined the Norman Earl of Chester to gain lands off Owain. Their army was slaughtered in a battle in the woods of Consyllt, but Madoc escaped to cause further trouble.

In 1156 Owain's brother Cadwaladr, and Madoc ap Maredudd, stirred the English king to invade Wales, to exterminate its over-powerful neighbour. Henry II's first campaign against Owain **Shield of Owain Gwynedd** ended in a truce in 1157. Owain, with his sons Dafydd and Cynan, had waited for Henry's army in the woods at Coed Eulo (Cennadlog) near Basingwerk, on the Dee estuary. They almost took Henry prisoner, and the Earl of Essex threw down the Royal Standard and escaped through the woods. Knights from Henry's fleet next ravaged Anglesey, trying to destroy the grain crops to starve Owain's people into submission. However, the invaders were driven back to their ships, and one of the King's sons was killed, while Henry waited for reinforcements at Rhuddlan Castle. With the 1157 truce, Owain gave King Henry hostages, promising not to attack England, and allowed the King to keep the land around Rhuddlan.

In 1160, with the death of Madoc ap Maredudd, Owain attacked Powys and extended his influence in the east. In 1166, the Council of Woodstock tried to make the Welsh princes vassals, and there was an uprising led by Owain in North Wales, and his nephew Rhys ap Gruffydd in South Wales. A monk of St. David's wrote 'All the Welsh of Gwynedd, Deheubarth and Powys with one accord cast off the Norman yoke.'

110

Henry II tried to subjugate Wales from 1164, but again failed. Henry's forces were vast, composed of Normans and mercenary Flemings, Gascons and Scots as well as English. Henry recaptured these castles, and began preparing to invade from his base at Shrewsbury. With his brother Cadwaladr back on his side, and his nephew Rhys ap Gruffydd, Owain called his forces to Corwen. Henry moved through the damp Berwyn Mountains, cutting a road through the heavy forests in Glyn Ceiriog to keep away Welsh archers and raiding parties. Even today the road is called *Ffordd y Saeson*, (The English Road). Welsh guerrilla attacks and bad weather defeated the Normans, and they retreated back to the shelter of Shrewsbury (Pengwern). One violent attack by the Welsh guerrilla forces took place at a place now called *Adwy'r Beddau* (The Pass of the Graves). Apart from Owain and his brother Cadwaladr and the men of Gwynedd, Henry was facing Rhys ap Gruffudd (The Lord Rhys) and the men of Deheubarth, and Owain Cyfeiliog's supporters from Powys and the Gwent army of the sons of Madog ab Idnerth. The English defeat at Crogen in Dyffryn Ceiriog is recorded in no English history books.

In 1165 *Brut y Tywysogion* tells us of Henry II crossing the Ceiriog Valley near Tregeiriog, en route for Ffordd Saeson across the moors in filthy weather. Welsh guerrilla tactics forced him back from his mission, which was 'to destroy all Britons.' '... The king was greatly angered; and he moved his host into Duffryn Ceiriog, and he had the wood cut down and felled to the ground. And there were a few picked Welshmen, who knew not how to suffer defeat, manfully encountered him in the absence of their leaders. And many of the doughtiest fell on both sides. And then the king, and the advanced forces along with him, encamped on the Berwyn Mountains. And after he had stayed there a few days, he was greatly oppressed by a mighty tempest of wind and exceeding great torrents of rain. And when provisions failed him, he withdrew his tents and host to the open land of the flats of England.' On his return, he destroyed all in his path, and ordered all his Welsh hostages to be blinded and castrated. He had four important hostages – Rhys and Cadwaladr, two sons of Owain Gwynedd, and Cynwrig and Maredudd, two sons of The Lord Rhys of Deheubarth. He blinded them – 'and this the King did with his own hand' according to the *Chronicles*. Few Welsh people know of this terrible event* – it is in hardly any British history books. King John was later to hang 200 Welsh children. One wonders what would have been written, if the Welsh had ever done this to English princes. As Cicero stated, 'To know nothing of what happened before you is to remain forever a child'.

Owain's son Dafydd captured the important King's castles of Basingwerk and Rhuddlan in 1166 and 1167, and Owain set about destroying the Norman castles across his lands. In 1168, diplomatic relations were established between Owain Gwynedd and King Louis VII of France, to King Henry's impotent fury. In his first two letters to Louis VII, Owain described himself as 'king of Wales' and 'king of the Welsh', although he only directly rules Gwynedd. He was also the first Welsh ruler to be known as Prince of Wales. Contemporary charters and the *Brut y Tywysogion* note these titles. Owain's ambassador to France offered Louis help against the English. Madog, a son of Owain Gwynedd, was credited as being the Welshman who discovered America, but has been omitted from this book. Madog's sister, Gwenllian, was killed after battling the Normans at Cydweli, and may have been the author of the *Mabinogion* (– see *100 Great Welsh Women* by this author). The Lord Rhys was Owain's nephew (- see the entry on Rhys ap Gruffydd). Rhys was the son of Gwenllian, and she was executed by the Normans when he was just four years old. Rhys ap Gruffydd, Prince of Deheubarth, now took the mantle of chief defender of Wales against the invading Normans.

When he died in 1170, after thirty-three years as Prince of Gwynedd, Owain was hailed as 'the king and sovereign and prince and defender and pacifier of all the Welsh after many dangers by sea and land, after innumerable spoils and victories in war... after collecting together into Gwynedd, his own country, those who had been before scattered into various countries by the Normans, after building in his time many churches and consecrating them to God'. The year 1169 in *The Chronicle of Ystrad Fflur* notes: 'At the end of this year Owain ap Gruffudd ap Cynan, prince of Gwynedd, the man who was of great goodness and very great nobility and wisdom, the bulwark of all Wales, after innumerable victories, and unconquered from his youth, and without ever having refused anyone that for which he asked, died after taking penance and communion and confession and making a good end.' Owain had encouraged monasticism, especially in Gwynedd, but he died excommunicated because he refused to divorce his wife, his cousin. Archbishop Baldwin of Canterbury, when he visited Bangor Cathedral in 1188, thus spitefully ordered Owain's bones to be moved from the Cathedral to the churchyard.

Owain had possibly twenty sons, most of them illegitimate, but they had the same standing in the succession as his legitimate offspring. There was thus mayhem after his death, with brothers fighting brothers until a grandson, Llywelyn the Great, stabilised the kingdom.

* Giraldus Cambrensis tells us of Owain's restrained behaviour towards the burning of churches and the blinding of 22 hostages, including two of his sons, and two sons of his nephew Rhys ap Gruffydd. He had been urged to burn English churches in retaliation, but replied: 'I do not agree with this opinion: rather we should be grateful and joyful because of this. For we are very unequal against the English unless we are upheld by divine aid; but they, through what they have done, have made an enemy of God himself, who can avenge the injury to himself and to us at the same time.'

VIKING ATTACKS on WALES 795-1144

While the Britons were under constant pressure from the invading Germanic tribes, and being pushed back by Saxons and then Normans, there were also many raids from the Scandinavian tribes. The first raiders were from Norway and Denmark, and also Norsemen from their kingdom of Dublin, and they were variously known as *y llu ddu* (the black host), *cenheloedd duon* (the black nations), *y Normayeit duon* (black Normans), *brithwyr du* (black Picts), *dieifyl du* (black devils), *paganaid* (pagans), *llychlynwys* (Scandinavians), *Daemysseit* (Danes) and *Llychynwyr* (men of Norway). The Norse of Dublin were often called *Gwyddyl* (Irish) or *gwyr Dulyn* (men of Dublin). Wales was called *Bretland*, Land of the Britons, in Old Norse, and Icelandic and Viking sagas note many attacks on the nation, e.g. by Eric Bloodaxe plundering in the 930's and by Sven, the son of Harald in 995. King Magnus Barefoot, in the Battle of the Menai Straits, killed Hugh, Earl of Shrewsbury in 1098 with an arrow piercing his eye. Of course, for much of this time England was either partitioned with the Danes, or later ruled by them. There were also attacks on the Welsh/Britons in Strathclyde, Cumbria and the West Country over these years. There are recorded raids or battles before 795, but just some of the influence of the Vikings is shown in the following timeline:

795 attacks recorded;
835 attacks;
850 (when Cyngen died);
850-870 along Gwent and Glamorgan coasts;
854 at Anglesey;
855 when Rhodri Mawr defeated Horm;
870 attacks;
876 at Anglesey with the fleet sheltering for the winter in south Wales;
877 when Rhodr Mawr escaped to Ireland;
877 assisting Hywel ab Ieuaf in his battle to take over Gwynedd;
879 when Vikings capture Iago ab Idwal;
890 at Castell Maldwyn;
893 at Buttington where they were defeated;
895-896 a Danish army wintered in south Wales and ravaged Glamorgan, Gwent, Brecon and Builth;
902 Dublin was captured by the Irish, forcing the Vikings into north Wales, where they were defeated by Hywel ap Cadell and driven towards Chester;
903 pitched battle with Danes under Ingimundr near Holyhead;
904 Danes kill Merfyn ap Rhodri Mawr;
905-910 raids by Eric Bloodaxe of Norway;
918 Vikings have retaken Dublin and attack Anglesey;
915 Vikings ravage Gwent, take Bishop Cyfeiliog who is ransomed by Edmund the Elder;
918-952 cessation of raids during rule of Hywel Dda;
952-1000 constant attacks on Welsh coasts;
952 two sons of the King of Glamorgan killed;
961 Holyhead ravaged;

963 Tywyn monastery and Aberffraw court attacked;

968 Limerick Norse are driven out of Ireland and defeated in Wales;

971 King Magnus of the Isle of Man and Limerick attacks Penmon monastery;

972 King Magnus's brother Godfridr conquers Anglesey;

980 Godfridr at Battle of Hirbarth;

982-1000 constant attacks on St David's;

982 St David's sacked by Godfridr who also ravages Dyfed and beats the Welsh in the battle of Llangwithenawc;

987 Godfridr again attacks Anglesey, and helps Hywel ab Ieuaf defeat Maredudd ab Owain of South Wales and take over Gwynedd at the Battle of Mannan (q.v.);

988 the monasteries of St David's, Llanbadarn Fawr, Llandudoch (St Dogmael's) near Cardigan, Llancarfan and Llanilltud are sacked;

992 St David's destroyed again and Maredudd ab Owain of Dyfed hires Norsemen to help in a war against Edwin ab Einion, King of Glamorgan;

993 Anglesey is attacked; 997-998 waves of attacks around the Severn;

999 St David's attacked for the 4th time and Bishop Morgeneu killed;

1002 Dyfed attacked; 1005 Brian Boru sends Norsemen to plunder Wales;

1012 Mercians attack St David's using Danish ships;

1022, Canute's men raid Dyfed and St David's;

1039 Meurig ap Hywel of Glamorgan captured and ransomed;

1042 Battle of Pwll Dyfach (q.v.) and also King Gruffudd ap Llywelyn of Gwynedd captured for ransom;

1044 Gruffudd ap Llywelyn had defeated King Hywel ab Edwin of Gwynedd in 1041 at Pencader to try to annexe parts of south Wales. The Norsemen supplied 20 longships and men to help Edwin, but they were beaten by Gruffudd in the estuary of the Towy and Edwin killed. He was succeeded by Gruffudd ap Rhydderch;

1044-52 Gruffudd ap Rhydderch despoiled his own villages and coastlines to make them less attractive for Norse raiders;

1049 Gruffudd ap Rhydderch of Gwynedd allied with Norse mercenaries to attack Gwent Iscoed and take it from King Meurig ap Hywel. 36 longships entered the Usk estuary and plundered the valley, including a manor in England. Bishop Ealdred of Worcester sent an army to fight Gruffudd's invaders, but was defeated after Welsh defectors from his army had alerted Gruffudd;

1053 Gruffudd raids the English border using Norsemen;

1055 Earl Aelfgar of Mercia is exiled and comes to Gruffudd ap Llywelyn's court with 18 longships full of Norse mercenaries. Gruffudd allies with him, marries his daughter, and invades Hereford. The relics of King Ethelbert are desecrated in Hereford. Edward the Confessor sends Earl Harold Godwinsson to negotiate a peace at Billingsley near Archenfield;

1056 Gruffudd and Norsemen again invade Hereford;

1058 Gruffudd and Norsemen and the again deposed Earl Aelfgar ally, to restore Aelfgar to Mercia's throne;

1063 Gruffudd ap Llywelyn killed;

1075 Gruffudd ap Cynan, raised by a Norse family, brings Norse mercenaries from Ireland and with men from Gwynedd and Robert of Rhuddlan's Normans defeats Cynwrig ap Rhiwallon of Gwynedd and Trahaearn ap Caradog of Arwystli at the battle of Bloody Acre (Gwaed Erw); In the Battle of Bron Erw, near Clynnog Fawr, Trahaearn defeated Gruffudd, and he left for Ireland, via the Skerries;

1077 Gruffudd invades with Norsemen but returns to Ireland;

1081 Norsemen attack St David's for the 5th recorded time, killing Bishop Abraham;

1087 Gruffudd uses a Danish double-edged axe in battle against the Normans of Anglesey. With his Norse followers, he sacked St Gwynlliw's Church in Newport;

1088 Rhys ap Tewdwr of Deheubarth was exiled to Ireland, but returned with Norsemen and won the battle of Penlecherau. Gruffudd ap Cynan is again in Wales with Norsemen, attacking the Normans in Rhos and Tegeingl; Robert of Rhuddlan is killed at Deganwy by Norsemen;

1093 Rhys ap Tewdwr is killed by Normans at Brycheiniog, and his son Gruffudd taken to be protected by the Irish-Norse;

1098 Gruffudd ap Cynan is hemmed in on Anglesey by the Normans and with Cadwgan forced to flee to Ireland; Hugh of Shrewsbury is killed by Magnus Barefoot on the Menai Straits;

1115 Gruffudd ap Rhys of Deheubarth returns from Ireland to try and regain his throne;

1126 Gruffudd ap Rhys is forced to flee to Ireland to join other Welsh refugees from the Norman Conquest;

1137 Gruffudd ap Cynan dies and his son Cadawladr sends of 15 Norse longships to assist his to take Cardigan castle from the Normans. The siege failed and the Norsemen attacked St Dogmael's;

1144 Civil War between Cadwaladr and his brother Owain, whose son Hywel attacked Cadawladr. Cadwaladr sent for a Norse fleet which sailed to Abermenai;

1144 Cadwgan ap Owain Gwynedd is seized for ransom by Norsemen, after hiring them to combat his brother Owain.

RHYS AP GRUFFYDD AP RHYS AP TEWDWR 1132 – 28 April 1197

YR ARGLWYDD RHYS, THE LORD RHYS, THE UNCONQUERED HEAD OF ALL WALES, PRINCE OF THE WELSH

After the death of Owain Gwynedd in 1170, the mantle of paramount Welsh ruler was taken up by his nephew Rhys ap Gruffydd of Deheubarth, who became called 'Head of all Wales' and 'Prince of the Welsh' in contemporary charters and the *Brut y Tywysogion*, upon on his death in 1197. Gwenllian, sister of the great Owain Gwynedd and daughter of the warrior Gruffydd ap Cynan, King of Gwynedd, was born in 1098, when Wales was under unceasing attack from the Normans. Owain Gwynedd had succeeded his father in leading the Welsh defence against the king and his Marcher Lords, and Gwenllian married Gruffydd ap Rhys ap Tewdwr and lived in Dinefwr Castle, with her four sons, Morgan, Maelgwn, Maredudd and Rhys. On New Year's Day, 1136, her husband joined other Welsh forces in an attack upon the Norman invaders.

Gruffydd ap Rhys was away in North Wales, trying to gain assistance from Gwenllian's father, Gruffydd ap Cynan. Noting his absence, Maurice de Londres, the detested Norman Lord of Cydweli (Kidwelly) attacked Gruffydd's lands in South-West Wales. Gwenllian led the few defenders that were left in the area, although her youngest son, Rhys ap

**The Lord Rhys,
St. David's Cathedral**

Gruffydd, was only four years old. Giraldus Cambrensis stated that 'she marched like the Queen of the Amazons and a second Penthesileia leading the army'. In 1136, Gwenllian led her small force to face the Normans at Cydweli. Another Norman army had landed in Glamorgan, and was marching to join the force of Maurice de Londres. Gwenllian stationed her rapidly assembled volunteers at the foot of Mynydd-y-Garreg, with the river Gwendraeth in front of her, and Cydweli Castle just two miles away. She sent some of her forces to delay the oncoming invasion force, but unfortunately it evaded them and her remaining army was trapped between two Norman attacks.

One son, Morgan, was killed, another, Maelgwn, imprisoned. Towards the end of the fighting, Gwenllian ferch Gruffydd ap Cynan was captured and executed, over the body of her dead son. She had pleaded for mercy, but was beheaded upon de Londres' express order. The battlefield is still called Maes Gwenllian, a mile from the castle, and a stone marks the place of her death. She left an 8-year-old son Maredudd, and a 4-year-old son, Rhys ap Gruffudd, later to be known as The Lord Rhys. Gwenllian's son Rhys was the grandson of Rhys ap Tewdwr, who was slain by the Normans at Brycheiniog in 1093, and the nephew of the great Owain Gwynedd. Gwenllian's daughter Nest married Ifor ap Meurig, the Welsh hero Ifor Bach who scaled the walls of Cardiff Castle, to kidnap Earl William of Gloucester and regain his stolen lands. Against this troubled background, Rhys' father, Gruffydd ap Rhys, Prince of Deheubarth, had avenged his wife's death, defeating the Normans at the battle of Crug Mawr in 1136. After more success, he died in unexplained circumstances within a year of Gwenllian in 1137.

Rhys ap Gruffydd was a 5-year-old orphan, and leadership of the war by Deheubarth against the invading Normans and Flemish settlers passed to his elder half-brothers Anarawd and Cadell. In 1143, Anarawd was treacherously murdered by his supposed ally, Cadwaladr of Gwynedd. Aged 13, we find Rhys and his elder full brother, Maredudd, fighting for their half-brother Cadell in 1146. Over the next decade, the kingdom of Deheubarth was bitterly reconstituted, with the expulsion of the de Clares from Ceredigion, and the Cliffords from Cantref Bychan and Llandovery. After defending the recently-captured Carmarthen Castle from a Norman counter-attack, the brothers Rhys, Maredudd and Cadell also held off an attack by the men of Gwynedd on their weakened kingdom. In 1151 Cadell was badly injured by Norman knights and archers from Tenby while out hunting and left for dead. Maredudd took over the kingship of Deheubarth from 1151, while the incapacitated Cadell lingered on until 1175, being buried at Strata Florida. After Maredudd's early death, aged just 25, the 21-year-old Rhys took the throne. Already he had seen 17 years of turbulence and death, which seems to have made him favour, given the choice, diplomatic negotiation rather than warfare.

The French King of England led another huge army into Wales in 1157, and the Welsh *Chronicles* state that Henry II's intention was 'to exterminate all the Britons completely, so that the Brittanic name should never be remembered.' However, Giraldus Cambrensis recorded an old Welshman telling Henry that Wales would never be conquered: 'No nation but this of the Welsh, not any other language, will answer for this corner of the earth on the Day of terrible Judgment before the almighty judge.' Rhys very reluctantly submitted to a truce with Henry II in 1157-58, along with his uncle Owain Gwynedd and Malcolm IV of Scotland, to avoid more bloodshed across his shattered kingdom, ceding Ceredigion and much of Ystrad Tywi. As well as this act of homage, he was forced to give up the title of King of Deheubarth, and henceforth was known as 'Yr Arglwydd Rhys', 'The Lord Rhys'. Two of his sons were also given as hostages.

When his kingdom was stronger, Rhys led a rising in 1164-65 to regain Ceredigion and Emlyn, taking the great castles of Cardigan and Cilgerran. From now until his death he retained this land, which stabilised Deheubarth as it had been on his accession in 1158. He also added parts of Dyfed after some of its Norman lords left to take part in the Irish Conquest. In 1164, Rhys met his uncle Owain Gwynedd and other Welsh leaders in the greatest assembly of Welsh forces seen thus far, and Henry's invasion force was defeated.

In 1170, Henry II was in disgrace following the murder of Thomas Beckett, and made friendly overtures to The Lord Rhys. Henry needed allies, and despite the king murdering his sons, Rhys knew that his land needed peace. Henry created Rhys Justice of South Wales, and from his main court at Dinefwr Castle he was the predominant magnate in Wales. A patron of religious orders, Whitland was under Rhys' protection, he took special care of Strata Florida and founded Talley Abbey.

The Lord Rhys held the first authenticated eisteddfod in Cardigan Castle in 1176, but the present form of eisteddfod is an early nineteenth century recreation, thanks to Iolo Morgannwg. The mediaeval meeting of the bards, called the Eisteddfod, was revived as a means of attracting patronage for Welsh cultural activity. At first the competitions were confined to the traditional poetry composition (the strict Welsh form known as *cynghanedd*) and harp playing, but today choirs, bands, acting, recitation, fiction writing and painting can also be included. The 1176 date gives Wales the right to claim the oldest European festival, one with both poetic and political overtones.

Thomas Pennant described the eisteddfod of Lord Rhys: 'In 1176, the Lord Rhys, prince of South Wales, made a great feast at Christmas, on account of the finishing of his new castle at Aberteifi (Cardigan), of which he proclaimed notice through all Britain a year and a day before; great was the resort of strangers, who were nobly entertained, so that none departed unsatisfied. Among deeds of arms, and variety of spectacles, Rhys invited all the bards of Wales, and provided chairs for them, which were placed in his hall, where they sat and disputed and sang, to show their skill in their respective faculties: after which he bestowed great rewards and rich gifts on the victors. The bards of North Wales won the prizes; but the minstrels of Rhys's household excelled in their faculty. On this occasion the Brawdwr Llys, or judge of the court, an officer fifth in rank, declared aloud the victor, and received from the bard, for his fee, a mighty drinking-horn, made of the horn of an ox, a golden ring, and the cushion on which he sat in his chair of dignity.' Among the rivals for the bardic crown were Owain Cyfeiliog, Prince of Powys, and Rhys' cousin Hywel ap Owain Gwynedd, whose poems survive today.

The last years of Yr Arglwydd Rhys were sadly spent in dispute with some of his eight sons by Gwenllian ferch Madog ap Maredudd, and in fighting the Norman barons of Richard I, who did not care for Henry II's former special relationship with the Welshman. He was buried at St David's Cathedral, where his tomb effigy can be seen.

Footnotes:
(i) In 2000 *The Sunday Times* ran an article upon the 'Richest of the Rich' of the preceding millennium. Rhys ap Gruffyd, who made his fortune from 'land and war' was rated 95th richest, with a fortune worth today £4.3 billion: 'Rhys was a marauding Welsh prince who lived - and prospered - by the sword. His military career began when he and his four brothers fought a long campaign to wrest much of their dominion of Deheubarth in southwest Wales back from Norman insurgency. By 1155 they had succeeded, but only at great cost, Rhys being the

only one to survive the struggle. He extended his land in minor wars with rival Welsh nobles and later entered into an extraordinary alliance with his old enemy, Henry II, supporting the king's expedition to curb growing baronial power in Ireland in 1171. The deal made Rhys justiciar, effectively Henry's viceroy, and established him as the predominant force in Wales. To cement his position, he bound himself to the most powerful local Anglo-Norman families through marriage and was probably responsible for the first compilation of Welsh law in book form....Rhys managed to hold onto most of his lands right up to his death, though in his final years rebellious sons challenged his authority and twice imprisoned him. Surprisingly for such a warlord, Rhys died peacefully and was worth about £5000. But over the years his territory was divided and re-divided among his ten sons and various nephews in often bloody struggles.'

(ii) From the medieval *Book of Ystrad Fflur*, written by the monks of Strata Florida Abbey, we find the following entries concerning the life of The Lord Rhys:

'1136 In this year the lady Gwenllian died, (the mother of Rhys) brave as any of the sons of Gruffudd ap Cynan. And Morgan ab Owain slew Richard fitz Gilbert. And thereupon Owain and Cadwaladr, sons of Gruffudd ap Cynan, the splendour of all Britain and her defence and her strength and her freedom, held supremacy over all Wales and moved a mighty fierce host to Ceredigion. And they burned the castles of Aberystwyth, Dineirth and Caerwedros. Towards the close of the year they came again to Ceredigion with a numerous host and against them came Stephen, the constable, and all the Flemings and all the knights. And after fierce fighting Owain and Cadwaladr honourably won the victory at Crug Mawr. And the Normans and the Flemings returned home weak and despondent, having lost about 3000 men. And Geoffrey wrote the history of the kings of Britain.

1137 In this year died Gruffudd ap Rhys (the father of The Lord Rhys), the light of excellence and strength of South Wales. (Gruffudd ap Cynan also died) ...And for a third time the sons of Gruffudd ap Cynan came to Ceredigion and burned castles.

1156 In this year when Rhys ap Gruffudd heard that Owain, prince of Gwynedd, his uncle was coming with a great host to Ceredigion, he vigorously gathered a host and he came as far as Aberteifi (Cardigan) and there he raised a ditch to give battle.

1158 In this year after all the princes of Wales had made their peace with the king, Rhys on his own carried on war against the king. And after taking counsel of his leading men, and against his will he made peace with the king.

1159 In this year Rhys ap Gruffudd conquered the castles which the French had set up all over Dyfed. And then came the earl Reginald, son of King Henry, and a vast multitude of French and Saxons and Welsh with him. And without daring to attack Rhys where he was, they returned home after a bootless journey. And they offered Rhys a truce and he accepted it.

1163 In this year Henry, king of England, came to Deheubarth with a mighty host. And after Rhys ap Gruffudd had given him hostages, he returned again to England.

1164 In this year when Rhys ap Gruffudd saw that the king would not keep aught of his promise to him, he gained possession of all Ceredigion and inflicted repeated slaughters and despoilings upon the Flemings. And thereupon all the Welsh united together to throw off the rule of the French.

1165 In this year King Henry came to Oswestry, thinking to annihilate all Welshmen. And against him came Owain and Cadwaladr, sons of Gruffudd ap Cynan, and all the host of Gwynedd with them, and Rhys ap Gruffudd and with him the host of Deheubarth, and Owain Cyfeiliog and all the sons of Madog ap Maredudd and the host of all Powys with them, and the two sons of Madog ab Idnerth and their host. And both sides stayed in their tents until the king moved his host into Dyffryn Ceiriog and there he was defeated at Crogen. And in a rage he had the eyes of 22 hostages gouged out; and these included two sons of Owain ap Gruffudd (Owain Gwynedd) and two sons of Rhys. (This was allegedly carried out personally by none other than the illiterate and vicious King of England, Henry II). And Rhys took the castles of Cardigan and Cilgerran. And through the will of God and at the instigation of the Holy Spirit, and with the help of Rhys ap Gruffudd, a community of monks came to Ystrad Fflur...

1166 In this year the French and Flemings came to Cilgerran. And after many of them had been slain, they returned again empty-handed. And in this year Basingwerk was destroyed by Owain ap Gruffudd.

1167 In this year Owain and Cadwaldadr and Rhys ap Gruffudd besieged and destroyed the castle of Rhuddlan.

1171 In this year Thomas, archbishop of Canterbury, a man of great piety and saintliness and righteousness, was slain by the counsel and at the instigation of Henry, king of England, before the altar of the Trinity in his own church in Canterbury. And Rhys ap Gruffudd forced Owain Cyfeiliog, his son-in-law, to submit to him, and took seven hostages from him. And Rhys made friends with the king [who had blinded two of his sons!] and made peace with him.

1172 In this year died Cadwaladr ap Gruffudd ap Cynan. And the king granted truce to Iorwerth ab Owain and his sons to come and discuss peace with him. And Owain ab Iorwerth was slain by the earl of Bristol's men. And after that Iorwerth and Hywel, his brother, placing no trust in the king, ravaged the lands around Gloucester and Hereford, pillaging and slaying without mercy. And the king left Rhys ap Gruffudd as justice on his behalf in all of Deheubarth and went to France.

1173 In this year many men and animals died, nor was it surprising: for there was born to Rhys a son by the daughter of Maredudd, his brother. And Iorwerth ab Owain took the castle of Caerleon by force.

1175...And Rhys ap Gruffudd took with him to the king's council at Gloucester all the princes of Wales who had incurred the king's displeasure. All those returned with Rhys, having obtained peace, to their own lands. And immediately after that Seisyll ap Dyfnwal was slain through treachery in the castle of Abergafenni by Lord de Breos of Brecon. And along with him Geoffrey his son, and the best men of Gwent were slain. And the French made for Seisyll's court; and after seizing Gwladys, his wife, they slew Cadwaladr, his son. And from that day there befell a pitiful massacre in Gwent. And from that time forth, after treachery, none of the Welsh dared place trust in the French.

1176 In this year at Christmas Rhys ap Gruffudd, Yr Arglwydd Rhys, held court in splendour at Cardigan, in his castle. And he set two kinds of contest there: one between bards and poets, another between harpists and crowthers and pibgorn-players and various classes of music-craft. And he had two chairs set for the victors. And this was the second founding of the abbey at Cwm-hir.

1177... Rhys ap Gruffudd built the castle at Rhaeadr-Gwy.

1178 In this year the sons of Cynan waged war against Rhys ap Gruffudd.

1183 In this year died king Henry the Younger

1184... At Llansantffraid Rhys ap Gruffudd confined all his gifts to the community of Ystrad Fflur.

1186...Cadwaladr ap Rhys was slain in Dyfed

1187...Maelgwn ap Rhys, the shield and bulwark of Wales, ravaged the [Fleming-settled and Norman-held] town of Tenby and burned it... the man who frequently slew the Flemings and who drove them to flight many a time.

1188 ...Rhys ap Gruffudd accompanied Baldwin Archbishop of Canterbury, and Gerald of Wales as they preached the Crusade around Wales.

1189 In this year died Henry, king of England. And Rhys ap Gruffudd took the castles of St Clears and Abercorram and Llansteffan. And Maelgwn ap Rhys - a second Gawain - was seized and imprisoned by his father and his brother.

1190...Rhys ap Gruffudd built the castle of Cydweli and Gwenllian, daughter of Rhys, the flower and beauty of all Wales, died.

1191... Rhys ap Gruffudd took the castle of Nevern

1192 In this year Maelgwn ap Rhys escaped from the prison of the Lord of Brycheiniog. And Rhys ap Gruffudd took the castle of Llawhaden.

1193...And the warband of Melgwn ap Rhys manfully breached the castle of Ystrad Meurig. And Hywel Sais ap Rhys took Wizo's castle [Wiston] by treachery.

1194 In this year Rhys ap Gruffudd was seized by his sons and imprisoned; but Hywel Sais deceived Maelgwn and released his father from prison. And the sons of Cadwallon burned the castle of Rhaeadr-Gwy.

1195...the two sons of Rhys ap Gruffudd were a second time seized through treachery by their father and imprisoned.

1196 In this year Rhys ap Gruffudd gathered a mighty host, and he fell upon Carmarthen and destroyed it and burned it to the ground. And he took and burned the castles of Colwyn and Radnor. And Roger Mortimer and Hugh de Sai arrayed a mighty host against him. And Rhys armed himself like a lion with a strong hand and daring heart, and attacked his enemies and drove them to flight. And forthwith Rhys took Painscastle in Elfael.

1197 In this year there was an exceeding great mortality in all the islands of Britain. And, on the fourth day from the calends of May, died Rhys ap Gruffudd, prince of Deheubarth and unconquered head of all Wales. Alas for the glory of his battles and the shield of his knights, the defender of his land, the splendour of arms, the arm of prowess, the hand of generosity, the eye and lustre of worthiness, the summit of majesty, the light of reason, the magnanimity of Hercules!'

GIRALDUS CAMBRENSIS c.1146 - 1223

GERALD OF WALES, GERALD THE WELSHMAN, GERALD DE BARRI

Giraldus was an extremely important figure in Welsh church and social) history. His father was William of Manorbier, and his mother was Angharad, the daughter of Gerald de Windsor and the famous Nest ferch Rhys ap Tudur. Rhys ap Tudur was Lord of Deheubarth. Gerald's family was also related to The Lord Rhys, Rhys ap Gruffudd. The youngest son of this Norman-Welsh marriage, Gerald was educated by his uncle David Fitzgerald at St David's, at St Peter's Gloucester, and then at the University of Paris. As archdeacon of Brecon, he was the favourite to succeed his uncle at St David's in 1176, but Henry II refused to recognise his nomination by the Welsh canons and enforced the election of the Englishman, Peter of Lee.

Giraldus Cambrensis by Henry Poole

Bitterly disappointed, Giraldus returned to France and became a lecturer in the University of Paris. He mediated in a dispute between Rhys ap Gruffydd and the king, and accompanied Prince John to Ireland in 1185, when he wrote *Expugnatio Hibernica* and *Topographica Hibernica*' 1188 sees him with Archbishop Baldwin touring Wales to recruit for the Crusade, the journey of which is recounted in *Itinerarium Cambriae*. In 1194 he completed *Descriptio Cambriae*, left the Crown service and went to Lincoln to further his studies.

Giraldus was offered the bishoprics of Llandaff and Bangor, and those of Ferns and Leighlin in Ireland, but he only wanted St David's. On the death of Peter de Lee in 1198, yet again the King and the Archbishop of Canterbury opposed the appointment of Giraldus, although the chapter wanted him to succeed. The dispute widened to one where Giraldus wanted the recognition of St David's as a metropolitan see, separate from Canterbury, and three times in five years Giraldus took the arduous journey to Rome to see the Pope and plead this case. The Plantagenets saw his Welshness, energy, learning and intelligence as a dangerous combination, being a French-speaking illiterate dynasty not noted for subtlety. Gerald maintained that it was the fear of the effect that it would have on the national politics in Wales that prevented his appointment. The Pope was not too anxious to have a Welsh Church independent of Canterbury, as dissent would weaken Roman power. Giraldus never succeeded in his ambition, but was buried in his beloved St David's.

Geoffrey of Monmouth's works had helped put Wales on the literary map of Europe, and Gerald helped cement this foundation of Welshmen writing important works in Latin. His writings reflect experiences gained on

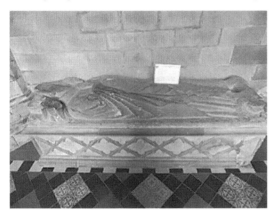

his travels as well as his knowledge of the authorities on learning. The Welshman's writings were prolific, but it is generally agreed that his most distinguished works are those dealing with Wales and Ireland, with his two books on his beloved Wales the most important. Professor Davies tells us that Giraldus, whom he calls 'an admirable story-teller', is the only source

Gerald's tomb at St David's Cathedral

for some of the most famous of the Welsh folk tales including the declaration of 'the old man of Pencader' to Henry II: 'This nation, O King, may now, as in former times, be harassed, and in a great measure weakened and destroyed by your and other powers, and it will also prevail by its laudable exertions, but it can never be totally subdued through the wrath of man, unless the wrath of God shall concur. Nor do I think that any other nation than this of Wales, nor any other language, whatever may hereafter come to pass, shall on the day of severe examination before the Supreme Judge, answer for this corner of the earth.'

It was Giraldus who also wrote [of the Welsh] that 'If they would be inseparable, they would be insuperable', and that, unlike the English hirelings, who fight for power or to procure wealth, the Welsh patriots fight for their country... In their rhymed songs and set speeches they are so subtle and ingenious that they produce, in their native tongue, ornaments of wonderful and exquisite invention both in the words and the sentences... They make use of alliteration in preference to all other ornaments of rhetoric, and that particular kind which joins by consonance the first letters or syllables of words.'

Gerald could not have predicted the later perfection of *cynghanedd*, the complex system of sound correspondence that has characterised the strict-metre poetry of the Welsh for so many centuries and that is still practised today, especially in competitions for the eisteddfod chair.

Cynghanedd did not become a formal system with strict rules until the fourteenth century, but its uniquely Welsh forms had been honed for centuries before that. Giraldus also penned the following words that give so much pride to Welsh singers of today, especially those who participate in the immensely popular Cymanfoedd Ganu (hymn-singing festivals) held throughout Wales and North America: 'In their musical concerts they do not sing in unison like the inhabitants of other countries, but in many different parts... You will hear as many different parts and voices as there are performers who all at length unite with organic melody.' This counterpart singing used to be heard at Welsh rugby internationals in wonderful hymns such *I Bob Un Sydd Ffyddlon*, but alas has been replaced by a chorus of *Hymns and Arias a*nd the pathetic Cornish miners' cry *Oggy, Oggy, Oggy*.

Gerald appears to have been a friend of Walter Map and Geoffrey of Monmouth, two other 12th century chroniclers and is one of the more attractive figures in British history. Before the Nonconformist fever, the harp was often used with a *pibgorn* (pipe) and *crwth* (Celtic violin – the surname Crowther means a crwth player). There was also a primitive Welsh bagpipe, the *pibacawd*. Giraldus Cambrensis gives us the following description: 'Guests who arrive early in the day are entertained until nightfall by girls who play to them on the harp. In every house there are young women just waiting to play for you, and there is certainly no lack of harps. Here are two things worth remembering: the Irish are the most jealous people on earth, but the Welsh do not seem to know what jealousy is; and in every Welsh court or family the menfolk consider playing on the harp to be the greatest of all accomplishments.'

The *Life* of the recluse Caradog Fyrnach, who died in 1125, was written by Giraldus Cambrensis but has been lost. This hermit-saint from Brecon was harpist and keeper of the hounds to Prince Rhys ap Tewdwr in the eleventh century, but lost the dogs. He then fled from Dyfed and Rhys ap Tewdwr to Llandaff Cathedral and was ordained. The histories attribute miracles to him, healing tumours by touching, turning fish into coins for the poor, and halting a chasing Viking longship. His tomb-effigy can now be seen in St David's Cathedral. For many years after his death, his body did not decay and lay in state in the cathedral. William of Malmesbury recounts trying to steal a finger of Caradog as a relic, but the hermit jerked his hand away. Bones were analysed in the hope that they were those of St David and St Justinian (Iestyn), but were dated at around 1000 years old, so may be those of Caradog.

St Caradog's Chapel at Newgale near St David's is now a mere hollow in the sands above the beach, but was still standing at the start of the nineteenth century. It was possibly built to commemorate Caradog's funeral procession across the sands to St David's Cathedral, when Gerald of Wales recounts that a storm failed to wet the coffin. A letter survives of Pope Innocent III in response to a request by Gerald to have Caradog canonised.

Caradog is one of the few Welshmen to have been officially sanctified by Rome, along with Dewi, Sadyrnin, Cyfelach and Gwryd, all well before the martyrs of the Middle Ages. Giraldus Cambrensis took the *Life* to read it to Pope Innocent III in Rome, to get Caradog canonized. The Pope appointed the abbots of Whitland, St Dogmael's and Strata Florida as a commission to inquire into the case, upon 8 May 1200.

On Gerald's death, Gwenwynwyn, Prince of Powys, wrote: 'Many and great wars have we Welshmen waged with England, but none so great and fierce as his who fought the king and the archbishop, and withstood the might of the whole clergy and people of England for the honour of Wales.' Even in Gerald's time he understood the factional problems of the Welsh – he wrote: 'If therefore they would be inseperable, they would be unsuperable.'

Some of his works are as follows:

1188 *The Topography of Ireland;* and *The Conquest of Ireland*
1191 *The Journey Through Wales*
1194 *A Description of Wales;* and *The Life of St David*
1195 *The Life of Galfridi* (Geoffrey) Archbishop of York
1197 *The Jewel of the Church*
1198 *The Life of St Remigius* (Remi)
1208 *De Rebus a Se Gestis* (Autobiography)
1213 *The Life of St Hugonis* (Hugh)
1216 *A Book of Invectives*; and *A Mirror of Two Men*
1218 *The Rights and Status of St David*; and *The Instruction of a Prince*
c.1220 *The Life of St Ethelbert*

LLYWELYN AP IORWERTH AB OWAIN GWYNEDD 1173 – 11 April 1240

LLYWELYN FAWR – LLYWELYN THE GREAT

Dolbadarn Castle was built by Llywelyn's father, Iorwerth, around 1170, and it was there (or at Nant Conwy) that this Prince of Wales was born in 1173. He never claimed the title, but was content to be overlord of Wales, being recognised as Prince of Gwynedd and Lord of Snowdon. His grandfather was the great Owain Gwynedd.

Professor T. Tout has called Llywelyn 'certainly the greatest of the native rulers of Wales... If other Welsh kings were equally warlike, the son of Iorwerth was certainly the most politic of them... While never forgetting his position as champion of the Welsh race, he used with consummate skill the differences and rivalries of the English... Under him the Welsh race, tongue and traditions began a new lease of life.'

Llywelyn gained possession of part of Gwynedd in 1194, when Richard I was King of England. Aged just 22, Llywelyn had defeated his uncle Dafydd at the battle of Aberconwy. On the death of his cousin Gruffydd in 1200, Llywelyn gained the rest of Gwynedd. Llywelyn now

Llywelyn's statue at Conwy

wished to push out from his Gwynedd power base, to take over the kingdoms of Deheubarth (after the death of The Lord Rhys) and Powys. To help his plans, Llywelyn first allied with King John, who became King in 1199, and he married John's daughter, Joan in 1205. John needed allies against his powerful barons, and also John wished to limit the ambitious Gwenwynwyn of Powys. Powys was traditionally the weakest of the three major princedoms of Gwynedd, Deheubarth and Powys, squeezed between the other Welsh houses and the English Marcher Barons. Llywelyn over-ran Powys while King John captured Gwenwynwyn at Shrewsbury. Llywelyn also pushed Gwenwynwyn's ally, Maelgwyn, out of Northern Ceredigion. Llywelyn then took the Marcher Earl of Chester's castles at Deganwy, Rhuddlan, Holywell and Mold. From this position of total control of North Wales, Llywelyn ap Iorwerth could then assist John on his invasion of Scotland in 1209.

However, by 1210, John saw Llywelyn as an over-powerful enemy, and with Gwenwynwyn and Maelgwn invaded Wales. Llywelyn, deserted by other Welsh nobles, fell back towards his mountain base of Gwynedd, trying a scorched earth policy to starve John's army. However, in 1211 Llywelyn eventually was forced to sign an ignominious peace treaty that just left him Gwynedd and saw his son Gruffydd being taken as a hostage by the king. The lesser Welsh rulers had preferred an absentee overlord rather than a native Welsh ruler, but the situation changed when they saw John build castles near Aberystwyth, near Conwy and in Powys.

This threat of subjugation reunited the Welsh under Llywelyn in 1212, and John's castles were attacked and taken. Pope Innocent III gave his blessing to the Welsh revolt, and King Philip of France invited Llywelyn to ally with him against the English. In retaliation John hung his 200 Welsh hostages at Nottingham, including Maelgwyn's 7-year-old son. By 1215,

Llywelyn had captured many Norman castles and was in control of Pengwern (Shrewsbury). Llywelyn joined the English barons at Runnymede, and his power was one of the major factors that persuaded John to sign the Magna Carta in that year.

Llywelyn was been Prince of Gwynedd from 1194, of Powys from 1208 and Deheubarth from 1216, thus controlling the three major princedoms. At Llywelyn's Parliament at Aberdyfi in 1216, he adjudicated on claims from rival Welsh princes for the division of Welsh territories under his overlordship, and his decisions were universally accepted. This was probably Wales' first Parliament. By 1218, Llywelyn had taken Cardigan, Cilgerran, Cydweli (Kidwelly), Llansteffan and Carmarthen castles, and was threatening the Marcher castles of Swansea, Haverfordwest and Brecon. John died in 1216, and in 1218 Llywelyn's pre-eminence in Wales was recognised by the new English king Henry III, at The Treaty of Worcester.

However William, Marcher Earl of Pembroke, seized the castles of Carmarthen and Cardigan in 1223, as the English barons moved in concert to push Llywelyn back to Gwynedd. Hubert de Burgh, justiciar of England, pushed into Powys, but was beaten by Llywelyn at the Battle of Ceri in 1228. In 1228, Llywelyn was being referred to as 'Prince of the Welsh'. Hubert consolidated his hold on Marcher Lordships, and by 1231, Llywelyn was forced to go on the offensive, pushing down to South Wales and burning Brecon and Neath. Pembroke and Abergavenny were also taken. Henry III invaded Wales, but was lucky to escape with his life when Llywelyn launched a night attack on Grosmont Castle. By the Peace of Middle in 1234, Llywelyn was once more recognised by the English as pre-eminent in Wales, content with calling himself Prince of Aberffraw and Lord of Snowdonia. He had to be conscious of the feelings of his subject rulers in the rest of Wales. Almost a quarter of a century earlier, that they had turned on him to support King John.

At this height of his powers, *Annales Cambriae* records 'The Welsh returned joyfully to their homes, but the French (i.e. the Norman-English), driven out of all their holds, wandered hither and thither like birds in melancholy wise'. Llywelyn had been very much helped in his dealings with the English through his marriage to Joan, the daughter of King John, and spent his later years building up the prosperity of Wales. Llywelyn helped religious foundations, and supported a great flowering of Welsh literature. The earliest known text of *The Mabinogion* was copied, and the imaginative brilliance of the bards can still be read today. They praised the strength and peace their lord had brought Wales against the 'French' king and his Norman barons.

Dafydd Benfras wrote Llywelyn was 'his country's strongest shield'; Einion ap Gwgan hailed him as 'the joy of armies... the emperor and sovereign of sea and land'; and Llywarch ap Llywelyn wrote 'Happy was the mother who bore thee, Who are wise and noble.'

Aged sixty-eight, this great lord of Snowdon died as a monk at Aberconwy Abbey in 1240, worn out and crippled. He was now called Prince of Wales, although he never claimed that title. Llywelyn ap Iorwerth ab Owain Gwynedd had inspired a revision of the Laws of Hywel Dda, reorganized the administrative machinery of Wales, maintained cordial relations with the Pope and the English Church, and brought peace and prosperity to a united Wales. He had also ensured that Henry III recognised his son by Joan, Dafydd, as rightful heir. His remarkable diplomatic and military skills were celebrated by all the Welsh poets of the times.

However, Gruffydd, Dafydd II's elder brother, was still imprisoned in the White Tower in London. He died on St David's Day, 1244, trying to escape on a rope of knotted sheets. In 1245 Henry III reneged upon his promises and again invaded Wales, but was defeated by Dafydd in the only significant battle at Deganwy, and retreated back to England. Upon the tragically early death of Dafydd ap Llywelyn Fawr in 1246, a new power struggle took place to control Wales, only to be resolved by Llywelyn the Last. Mystery surrounds Dafydd II's death. It may be that he was poisoned on Henry's orders.

Years later, Llywelyn's great stone sarcophagus was removed from Aberconwy Abbey, as King Edward I symbolically built his great castle of Conwy over the abbey. It was moved to the Gwydir Chapel in the Church of St Grwst in Llanrwst. The present Chapel is said to have been designed by Inigo Jones. However, Llywelyn's bones were not allowed to be taken away, and were left under the new castle of Conwy. His bard, Dafydd Benfras, wrote this moving lament at his death -
'Where run the white rolling waves
Where meets the sea the mighty river,
In cruel tombs at Aberconwy
God has caused their dire concealment from us,
The red-speared warriors,
Their nation's illustrious son.'

Annales Cambriae refers to his death... 'Thus died that great Achilles the Second, the lord Llywelyn whose deeds I am unworthy to recount. For with lance and shield did he tame his foes; he kept peace for the men of religion; to the needy he gave food and raiment. With a warlike chain he extended his boundaries; he showed justice to all... and by meet bonds of fear or love bound all men to him.' The 1240 entry in the *Chronicle of Ystrad Fflur* reads: 'In this year the Lord Llywelyn ab Iorwerth ab Owain Gwynedd, prince of Wales, a second Achilles, died after he had assumed the order of Aberconwy; and he was buried honourably there.'

LLYWELYN AP GRUFFYDD AP LLYWELYN FAWR c.1225 – 11 December 1282

EIN LLYW OLAF – OUR LAST PRINCE

The Welsh custom of 'gavelkind' meant that Llywelyn the Great's kingdom had to be divided among all his four male heirs, although Llywelyn had tried desperately for all the kingdoms to be united under his son Dafydd. Within a month of Llywelyn's death, in 1240, Henry III had moved against Dafydd, invading and reneging on an agreement with Llywelyn, and forcing Dafydd to surrender many of his father's gains. Dafydd yielded his elder brother Gruffydd, as a prisoner to the king. Incarcerated in the Tower of London, Gruffydd died trying to escape, three years later. Henry's treachery meant that Norman Marcher lords took Welsh territories, his ally Gruffydd ap

Llywelyn ap Gruffydd by Henry Pegram

Gwenwynwyn took his realm back, and the king claimed the territories of Tegeingl, Carmarthen, Cardigan and Cydweli.

Gruffydd has a particularly tragic history - he was the illegitimate son of Llywelyn the Great, and was imprisoned as a hostage by John from 1211-1215 after Llywelyn was forced to come to terms with the king. Later, Llywelyn the Great saw the illegitimate Gruffydd as a problem for Dafydd's succession and locked him up in Deganwy Castle from 1228-1234. From 1239 to 1241 both Gruffydd and his son Owain Goch were then held by Dafydd in Cricieth Castle. Finally, after Dafydd's defeat by Henry III, poor Gruffydd was to spend his last three years in the Tower of London. So Gruffydd ap Llywelyn Fawr ap Iorwerth was imprisoned by King John for four years, by his father Llywelyn the Great for six years, by his step-brother Prince Dafydd for two years, and then by King Henry III for three years, when he died trying to escape. From 1211 to 1244 Gruffydd spent fifteen of thirty-three years imprisoned. This sad history affected his son, Llywelyn ap Gruffydd, in his view of Norman-Welsh relations for the rest of his life.

Gruffydd's tragic death sparked the Welsh to react to Henry III's overlordship. Assisted by Gruffydd's vengeful son, Llywelyn, Prince

Dafydd allied with all but two of the other Welsh princes, those of Powys and Gwynllwg. They attacked the Norman lands and regained the important border castle of Mold. Dafydd also appealed to Pope Innocent IV for help, offering Wales as a vassalship in return for protection against the Norman-English. He now called himself Prince of Wales. Henry III assembled an army at Chester and beat the Welsh on the banks of the river Conwy, slaughtering all the Welsh prisoners, a despicable act to be repeated after Llywelyn's death in 1282. An English army was recalled from Ireland to lay waste to Anglesey.

Dafydd kept fighting from his Gwynedd fastnesses, and forced Henry to withdraw. One of the great tragedies of Welsh history is Dafydd's premature death in 1246, possibly from poisoning. Henry now claimed all of Dafydd's land, because he had been promised it if Dafydd died childless. A Norman army now pushed up through the South, conquering Ceredigion, Merionydd and Deganwy. The leaderless men of Gwynedd immediately accepted Llywelyn and his eldest brother Owain Goch as rulers of Gwynedd. (Owain had been imprisoned in the Tower of London with their father, Gruffydd).

However, after three years of warfare, the brothers had reached a point where the starving population could no longer support an armed force, and sued for an armistice. In April 1247 they were confirmed as lords of Gwynedd uwch Conwy (that part of Gwynedd west of the River Conwy and north of the River Dyfi) and the status of Gwynedd reduced to an English vassalship, conforming to the matters of status of an English lordship. In this year, Matthew Paris recorded that 'Wales had been pulled down to nothing'.

By 1255, Llywelyn ap Gruffydd had won total control of Gwynedd. He had defeated and imprisoned his two brothers at Bryn Derwen. Poor Owain Goch was then incarcerated in Dolbadarn Castle for twenty years to ensure stability, but the other brother Dafydd managed to escape to England. ('Red Owen' thus spent twenty-three years incarcerated, eight more than his father). In 1256, *Brut y Tywysogion* records that 'The gentlefolk of Wales, despoiled of their liberty and their rights, came to Llywelyn ap Gruffydd and revealed to him with tears their grievous bondage to the English; and they made known to him that they preferred to be slain for their liberty than to suffer themselves to be unrighteously trampled on by foreigners.'

Llywelyn now pushed out all over Wales, beating back Henry III's army, while the men of Deheubarth beat royal forces near Llandeilo in 1257. This Battle of Coed Llathen was near Llangathen west of Llandeilo, and around 3000 English knights and soldiers were slain, a higher number than were killed at Hastings. The battle-site sign of crossed swords that existed in the 1950's seems to have disappeared.

The ruling houses of Powys, Glamorgan and Deheubarth thus acknowledged Llywelyn as their lord in 1258, as he had not only pushed the Normans out of Gwynedd, but also out of most of Wales. Until 1262 there was a fragile truce, but then Llywelyn went back on the attack to gain more of Wales, first from Roger Mortimer, and then part of the lordships of Brecon and Abergavenny. In 1264, he allied with Simon de Montfort, who was now in control of England after beating the king at Lewes. By the Pipton Agreement, de Montfort recognised Llywelyn, on behalf of the crown, as Prince of Wales and overlord of the other great men of Wales.

The English chronicler Matthew Paris now wrote that 'the North Welsh and the South Welsh were wholly knit together, as they had never been before', and praised the courage and vigour of Llywelyn, saying 'Is it not better, then, at once to die [in battle] and go to God than to live [in slavery]?' Then the Treaty of Montgomery forced Henry III, in 1267, to recognize Llywelyn as Prince of Wales, who in return recognised the suzerainty of the English crown. Llywelyn now had more control and influence in Wales than any prince since the Norman Conquest of England. However, where his relations with the devious Henry had always been poor, he was soon to come up against a new king of England, who simply resented Llywelyn's very existence.

When the vicious Edward I succeeded to the English crown, Llywelyn, fearing the normal Norman-French treachery, did not attend the coronation. His father had died at the Tower of London. Llywelyn also refused to pay tribute to Edward I, and built a new castle and town, Dolforwyn, against Edward's wishes. Llywelyn had sent a letter to Edward in 1272, stating that 'according to every just principle we should enjoy our Welsh laws and custom like other nations of the king's empire, and in our own language.' Llywelyn was thus declared a rebel in 1274, and Edward invaded. Edward and his barons used violence to provoke rebellions all over Wales, which were brutally crushed, while he pursued and harried Llywelyn, even forcing him to move, starving, from his mountain stronghold of Gwynedd.

In 1277, Edward had 15,600 troops, with many foreign mercenaries, in Wales, and Llywelyn was humiliated with the Treaty of Aberconwy when he sued for peace. He was stripped of the overlordship granted at the Treaty of Montgomery. In 1278, King Edward felt secure enough to release Elinor de Montfort, the betrothed daughter of the great Simon de Montfort, from prison. He then attended her wedding to Llywelyn in Worcester Cathedral. Years previously, Elinor had been captured with her brother, on her way to marry Llywelyn – the Plantagenets feared a dynasty that would be more popular than theirs.

However, after a peaceful interlude, Llywelyn's wayward brother Dafydd attacked Hawarden (Penarlag) Castle and burnt Flint in 1282, sparking off another war. Ruthin, Hope and Dinas Bran were quickly taken. Llywelyn had the choice of assisting his brother, who had been disloyal to him before, or supporting him. He fatefully chose the latter option, agreed at a Welsh 'senedd' at Denbigh. Days before, Elinor had died on the birth of their only child, Gwenllian. Llandovery and Aberystwyth castles were soon taken as the revolt spread.

Edward now assembled 10,000 soldiers at Rhuddlan, including 1,000 Welsh archers. Navies with archers moved to the Dee and from Bristol. Other armies advanced under the Marcher Lords. The war first went well for the Welsh. Llywelyn, near Llandeilo defeated the Earl of Gloucester, and a force in Anglesey was smashed. Edward was forced back from Conwy to winter in Rhuddlan. However, more English reinforcements, including 1,500 cavalry and Gascon crossbowmen arrived. In 1282, a Welsh detachment of 18 men was entrapped at Cilmeri, near Llanfair-ym-Muallt (Builth Wells). At this place on 11 December, Llywelyn was killed. Welsh bowmen in English pay then annihilated his nearby leaderless army. It had surrendered upon hearing of Llywleyn's death, but was massacred. Anthony Edwards' *The Massacre on the Fairway* is based upon his booklet *Marwolaeth Llywelyn ap Gruffudd - Y Gwirionedd*, and contends that the surrendered army of Llywelyn, of 3000 foot-soldiers and 160 horsemen, was executed in cold blood where Builth golf course is today.

Aberedw Church, near where Llywelyn ap Gruffydd was killed

Llywelyn's head was cut off and sent to Edward at Conwy Castle, and later paraded through London with a crown of ivy, before being stuck up on the Tower of London. Llywelyn's coronet and the crown jewels of Gwynedd were offered up to the shrine of Edward the Confessor at Westminster Abbey. The *Croes Naid* of his ancestors, believed to be a fragment of the 'True Cross', and perhaps the Welsh equivalent of Scotland's Stone of Scone, was taken to Windsor Castle and vanished during the English Civil War.

There is no understanding of how Llywelyn came to be so far detached from his main forces in his Gwynedd stronghold. Edward had previously offered him exile and an English earldom in return for unconditional surrender, but Llywelyn had refused. With his small band, Llywelyn had been waiting for someone at Irfon Bridge, but longbowmen suddenly appeared and cut them to bits. Llywelyn escaped, only to be speared by Stephen de Frankton, before he could reach his main forces. Archbishop Pecham of Canterbury had been negotiating between Llywelyn and Edward on the terms of an end to the war, and much of the documentation still exists.

According to Pecham's later letters, a document was found on Llywelyn inviting him to go to the Irfon Bridge, sent by the Marcher Lords. This document disappeared, and also a copy sent by the Archbishop to the Chancellor. It looks like Llywelyn was killed by Norman treachery* – 'the treachery on the bridge' is a recurrent theme in Welsh literature, and for centuries the inhabitants of Builth were known as traitors in Wales. (*Bradwyr Buallt*, 'Builth Traitors' became a common term of abuse, but I have also seen in poetry *Bradwyr Aber Edw*). Also according to Archbishop Pecham, de Francton's spear did not kill him, and Llywelyn lived on for hours, asking repeatedly for a priest, while his army

December 11, annual remembrance, Cilmeri

was being slaughtered a couple of miles away. He was refused one, while his captors waited for the Marcher Lord Edmund Mortimer to come to the scene. According to *The Waverley Chronicle*, Mortimer executed Llywelyn on the spot. Probably he also took possession of the letter in Llywelyn's pocket at this same time. It may have been that de Franckton was given a large farmstead at Frampton, just north of Llanilltud Fawr, in the now 'safe' Vale of Glamorgan, in return for keeping quiet.

The plaque on his roadside granite monument at Cilmeri simply proclaims 'Llywelyn ein Llyw Olaf' – 'Llywelyn Our Last Leader'. His mutilated body possibly lies in the atmospheric remains of the Cistercian Abbey Cwmhir, (Abaty Cwm Hir) which had a 242-feet nave, the longest in Britain after York, Durham and Winchester Cathedrals. There is also a legend that it went to Llanrumney Priory in Cardiff, and is now in the walls of Llanrumney Hall, now a public house.

On Llywelyn's death, his brother Dafydd III pronounced himself Prince of Wales, and survived for ten months, using guerrilla tactics against Edward's forces in Snowdonia. Dafydd ap Gruffydd escaped from Dolwyddelan Castle shortly before its capture, probably moving down to Dolbadarn Castle. For a month he then operated from Llywelyn Fawr's former castle, Castell y Bere and the Cader Idris foothills. Just before four thousand troops under William de Valence reached there, he was forced back to Dolbadarn, as Castell y Bere was captured. The net was closing in on him. An army from Anglesey and a force of Basque mercenaries moved to encircle Snowdonia. Dafydd escaped to hide near Garth Celyn, the palace at Abergwyngregyn, where he was caught. After 200 years of struggle, the French-speaking Normans, with their Saxon troops and foreign mercenaries, had overcome the nation of Wales. It had taken them just months to overcome England.

With Dafydd's capture, the English tried to destroy the dynasty of the Llywelyns of Gwynedd. Llywelyn's only child, the year-old Gwenllian, was incarcerated for the rest of her life in Six Hills monastery in Lincolnshire. A plaque marks her possible resting-place. Llywelyn's nephew Owain was imprisoned for over twenty years in a cage in Bristol castle until his death. The other of Dafydd's sons, Llywelyn, also died in Bristol Castle. In 1317, Aberffraw, the traditional home of the Princes of Gwynedd, was obliterated by the English, along with all the other Welsh royal palaces except Garth Celyn, which was used by Edward while the 'Iron Ring' of castles was being built to surround Gwynedd.

Edward invented a new form of death for the wounded Prince Dafydd, which he also applied to William Wallace a few years later. The penalty for treason was being hung, and then drawn and quartered after death. Edward ensured that Dafydd would have a new punishment, the extended torture of live disembowelling. The Prince of Wales, Dafydd III, was dragged by horses through the streets of Shrewsbury, and at the High Cross he was hung until almost dead. He was then taken down, castrated and his genitals burnt in front of him. He was then cut open, and the entrails ripped from his living body. Edward

Llywelyn's Well, Cilmeri

delighted in the process lasting as long as possible. His corpse was then quartered, and his joints distributed to York, Winchester, Bristol and Northampton for display. The representatives of York and Winchester disputed over which city should have the honour of receiving the right shoulder - it went to Winchester. Dafydd's head was led on a pole through the street of London, with a crown of ivy, to the sound of horns and trumpets. It was spiked on the White Tower in London, next to his brother Llywelyn's. Conwy Castle was symbolically built on the tomb of Llywelyn the Great. By 'The Statute of Rhuddlan', in 1284, Edward finally and formally took control of Wales. His campaigns across Wales were paid for by fines and dispossession of Jews and loans from Italian bankers. He reneged on the loans, causing the bankers to fail. He loaned monies again to build his Iron Ring of castles, and again failed to repay, with the same results.

Edward I, 'The Hammer of the Scots' failed to conquer Scotland because his finances were drained in Welsh campaigns, particularly by the building of the Iron Ring of castles, including Conwy, Caernarfon and Harlech, which now form a World Heritage Site. As a youth he had cut off the ear and gouged out the eye of a young nobleman who had not bowed low enough to him. After the defeat of Simon de Montfort (the father of Llywelyn's wife) at Evesham, Edward had him killed, and his head and genitalia cut off and sent to Lady Matilda, the wife of Lord Roger Mortimer at Wigmore. The 16 year-old Edmund Mortimer and 9 year-old Roger Mortimer who witnessed this, will have known not to cross him. The 'great' historian S.B. Chrimes calls Edward a great law-giver, 'the most juristically-minded king in 14th century Europe; he was the greatest legislator in England before the 19th century...the defender of legal rights...justice according to law was his business'. The French-speaking Edward however had no scholarship and found litigation tedious, preferring torture, an illiterate brute who used the legislation created by equally revolting and rapacious Chancellor, Burnell, for his own ends.

In 1282, Gruffydd ab yr Ynad Coch's magnificent elegy to Llywelyn tells us:

'Great torrents of wind and rain shake the whole land,
The oak trees crash together in a wild fury,
The sun is dark in the sky,
And the stars are fallen from their courses,'
and ends with

'Do you not see the stars fallen?
Do you not believe in God, simple men?
Do you not see that the world has ended?
A sigh to you, God, for the sea to come over the land!
What is left to us that we should stay?'

Because of the loss of independence of Gwynedd and Powys after a thousand years, Gruffydd wrote: 'Oh God! That the sea might surge up to You, covering the land! / Why are we left to long-drawn weariness? / There is no refuge from the terrible Prison.'

In 1294 there was a serious rebellion by Madog ap Llewelyn, but Edward defeated him, and the few privileges left to the Welsh in The Statute of Rhuddlan were rescinded. The bards longed for a *Mab Darogan* to free Wales again - they had to wait a century for the great Owain Glyndŵr in 1400. Edward's Statute of Rhuddlan of 1284 bitterly punished and repressed the Welsh in their own lands, so the later rebellion by Glyndŵr, and the successful overthrow of the English monarchy by the Welsh Tudors in 1485, were massively supported by all of Wales.

* 'The Treachery at the Ford' is a recurring theme in Welsh poetry. Regarding the total annihilation of an army of 3000 Welshmen with no recorded English casualties, and the betrayal and strange death of Llywelyn, Archbishop Peckham's relevant sequence letters in his correspondence are 'missing' from official archives.

Footnotes:

1. Tŵr Llywelyn (Garth Celyn), the ancient manor house at Pen-y-Bryn, just north of Bangor, on the shores of Abergwyngregyn, overlooking the Menai Straits, is the lost palace of Llywelyn and his forebears. The Royal Commission on Ancient Monuments has called it 'the most important site discovered in Wales in this (20th) century', and the distinguished medieval archaeologist Professor David Austen has called it 'an immensely important site in the national psyche of Wales'. Llywelyn used to send letters from his court at 'Aber', or 'Garth Celyn'. Pen-y-Bryn, Abercaseg, an ancient mansion on this site, has always been known to the locals as Tŵr Llywelyn (Llywelyn's Tower). In November, 1282, Archbishop John Peckham stayed there discussing peace terms with Llywelyn. It took tremendous efforts by the owner, Kathryn Gibson, to identify the house with Llywelyn's palace, but the case is clear and evident. A sheaf of ancient letters in Latin were burned by the old lady who owned the house before Mrs Gibson - they had been found inserted into a niche in the chapel wall.

2. *Quo Warranto, 687* of 1292 seems to have been ignored by historians, and is discussed in Anthony Edwards' *Massacre at Aberedw*. In the late 19th century, 200 skeletons, mostly male and of military age, were found north-east of Aberedw Church of St Cewydd. St Cewydd's cave nearby is also known as Llywelyn's Cave. Aberedw was held by Gruffydd ab Owain, and the surrounding commotes by his brothers Madog, Llywelyn and Iorwerth. This area of Elfael had been part of Llywelyn's lands until the war of 1277, but the family then paid homage to Roger Mortimer, and from November 1282 to Edmund Mortimer. After Llywelyn's death in 1282, Elfael was given to Edmund Mortimer as 'escheat', and all the sons of Owain ap Maredudd dispossessed in December 1282. In legal terms, an 'escheat' is to take the estates of the dead. A Chancery Rolls document of 24 November 1284, dates the dispossession to December 1282 or shortly after. Llywelyn was murdered upon 11 December. It appears that the Welsh lords of Elfael and their followers may have been executed at the same tim eor just before. In the words of Anthony Edwards, 'After the defeat of Llywelyn ap Gruffudd in 1282, King Edward carried out a systematic slaughter of the Welsh in many parts of Wales, probably to reduce the Welsh manpower. For instance, the 3000 foot soldiers, the leaderless remnants of Llywelyn's army, were put to death between Llanganten and Builth, and while King Edward was at Rhuddlan very many Welsh, including priests, were put to death, bringing on him the reproof of the archbishop of Canterbury.'

3. The death of Llywelyn is a detective story, in deliberately muddied waters. A letter from John Peckham, Archbishop of Canterbury to the King, written a few days after Llywelyn's death, reads: 'Lord, know that those who were at the death of Llywelyn found in the most secret part of his body some small things which we have seen. Among the other things there was a treasonable letter disguised by false names. And that you may be warned, we send a copy of this letter to the Bishop of Bath, and the letter Edmund Mortimer has, with Llywelyn's privy seal, and these things you may have at your pleasure. And this we send to warn you, and not that any one should be troubled for it. And we pray you that no one may suffer death or mutilation in consequence of our information, and that what we send you may be secret. Besides this, Lord, know that Lady Maud Lungespeye prayed us by letter to absolve Llywelyn, that he might be buried in consecrated ground, and we sent word to her that we would do nothing if it could not be proved that he showed signs of true repentance before his death. And Edmund Mortimer said to me that he had heard from his servants who were at the death that he asked for the priest before his death, but without sure certainty we will do nothing. Besides this, Lord, know that the very day that he was killed, a white monk sang mass to him, and my lord Roger Mortimer has the vestments.' In the copy of the letter Peckham sent to the Bishop of Bath, is the amended phrase 'under the false names by certain magnates of the March.' The Bishop of Bath was the King's Chancellor and right-hand man Robert Burnell. The only reason that Roger Mortimer could have the Cistercian monk's vestments was that he had him killed as a witness to the betrayal meeting. As Edmund Mortimer kept the original letter after Peckham had copied it, probably he was its originator. Peckham appealed that the whole affair be kept secret, and the original letter has vanished.

A 1590 Welsh manuscript records that Llywelyn was killed at Aberedw, where he had come to 'meet a lady', and Lady Maude Langespey's castle of Bronllys was just ten miles away. She was a cousin of the Mortimers, and engaged to John Giffard, whose castle at Builth Llywelyn was going to attack. Maud had been seized by force in 1271, born Giffard several children, and married him in 1282. She was the heiress of Walter Clifford, owned Clifford and Bronllys castles, and possessed castles and land in Carmarthen and Cardigan. Llywelyn's wife had died six months earlier, leaving him with just his daughter Gwenllian. She was a granddaughter of Llywelyn Fawr and a cousin of Llywelyn, and was possibly seen as a future queen by Llywelyn. Traditionally Llywelyn set out unarmed from Llanganten, leaving his army, with a small party of 18 horsemen and a white monk, to meet the Mortimers, Gruffudd ab Owain (and possibly Lady Maud) at Aberedw. Welsh tradition is that lady Maud had sent Llywelyn a ring as an assurance of safe conduct, and one was unexpectedly found on his body. (In 1447, Harry Grey, lord of Powys castle, murdered Gruffydd Fychan after his wife had sent him a ring as a sign of safe conduct. The bards saw this as a repetition of the murder of Llywelyn.)

Roger Lestrange was captain of a crack troop of the King's bodyguards, involved with the capture of Llywelyn. He wrote immediately after Llywelyn's death to Edward that the flower of Llywelun's troops had been put to death in a way which he would not relate by letter, slaughtered in a manner which would be difficult to believe: 'Know Lord, that you good men whom you assigned to me from your entourage fought with Llywelyn ap Gruffudd in the country of Builth on the Friday next after the feast of St Nicholas; so that Llywelyn ap Gruffudd is dead and his men discomfited and all the flower of his troops dead, as the bearer of this letter will tell you; and believe him concerning that which he shall tell you from me.'

There is a tradition that a Welsh churchman betrayed Llywelyn. Peckham's series of peace letters to Llywelyn would have been read by Madog ap Cynwrig, Archdeacon of Anglesey, in the absence of Bishop Anian of Bangor. In 1282, Anian joined the King at Rhuddlan. Peckham wrote to his intermediary, the cleric Adda ab Ynyr, a few hours before Llywelyn's ambush, calling him back from Gwynedd. Madog remained in power in Anglesey. At the time of the murder, Peckham was just 20 miles away, at Sugwas-on-Wye, and straight afterwards moved on to Pembridge castle, just 8 miles from the Mortimers' base at Wigmore. At Pembridge he copied the incriminating letter and sent it to the king's chancellor.

At Llanganten, the *Peterborough Chronicles* tell us that the Welsh army numbered 7000 footsoldiers and 160 horsemen. It records that 3000 of his footsoldiers and all of his horsemen were killed, and Roger Lestrange implies that this was occasioned in a manner that was difficult to believe. There is no record of a single English casualty in any battle. The attack on Llywelyn's army probably occurred upon Saturday 12th, the day after he was murdered. Quite possibly his head was displayed to his army, which surrendered, expecting to be disarmed and allowed to go home.

Letter CCCLXI from John Peckham to an unknown recipient again mentions the ignominious death that the Mortimers caused Llywelyn: 'Llywelyn he aforesaid Prince of Wales, moreover having rejected all offers and plans for peace previously described, invaded the land of the lord king of England as an enemy, laying waste, burning it and pillaging; he also drew the men of that land over to his side depriving them of the benefits of the king's peace.

Nevertheless it was the prince who was killed, the first of his own army, in an ignominious death through the family of Lord Edmund de Mortimer; and his whole army was either killed or put to flight in parts of Montgomery after the feast of St Lucy, in other words the 11 December 1282 AD'. This is an absolutely critical letter, as there is no addressee, and it seems to be a fragment of a longer document, ending abruptly, and letters are missing between his warning to Adda ap Ynyr on 11 November and this date. In this context, 'ignominious' means 'disgraceful', and probably refers to a sentence of death on a captured and convicted prisoner. The missing parts of the letter may be in the Lambeth Palace archives.

Llywelyn camped near Abey Cwm Hir on 10th December, and seems to have discussed support with neighbouring Welsh lords. According to the *Welsh Chronicle*, he then gained possession of Buellt up to Llanganten just west of Builth castle.

Llywelyn 'sent his men and his steward to receive the homage of the men of Brycheiniog, and the prince was left with but a few men with him.' He left his main force with 17 or 18 men and the Welsh Chronicles say then that he was 'killed in battle' near Builth. The Annals of Chester agree that 'Llywelyn and a few followers were killed in the land of Buellt.' The *Peterborough Chronicle* states that they were killed around Vespers (dusk), and this was probably effected by the troops of Roger Lestrange, captain of the army of Montgomery, and Roger Mortimer of Chirk. William Rishanger says that Llywelyn came into the land of Buellt with just a handful of knights, and John Giffard and Edmund Mortimer came to the little band 'with nothing arousing the suspicion of the prince, himself or his allies', and the small company met their death 'like lambs', which prompts the question as to whether they were armed.

The *Welsh Chronicles* say that 'Roger Mortimer and Gruffydd ap Gwenwynwyn, and with them the king's host (the army of Montgomery), came upon them without warning; and then Llywelyn and his foremost men were slain on the 11th December.' Thomas Wykes wrote that Llywelyn's band had been tempted from their Snowdonia stronghold by 'a cleric or notary acting as a spy'. In the margin of a contemporary manuscript in the British Library, known as *Cotton Nero Ms. D II, folio 182*, is a drawing of a man in mail armour kneeling with his hands clasped, awaiting a soldier behind him to strike off his head. This is the fate of the last Prince of Wales.

4. Ian Mortimer has written a wonderful book, *The Greatest Traitor – The Life of Sir Roger Mortimer, Ruler of England 1327-1330*.' For those who doubt that Llywelyn was trapped by subterfuge, we can read the following: 'Within a few weeks Edmund (Mortimer) was leading a party of men-at-arms towards Builth in Wales. With him were his brothers – Roger, a captain in the king's army; Geoffrey and William – and other Marcher lords, including Roger L'Estange and John Giffard. Llywelyn ap Gruffydd, Prince of Wales and grandson of Llywelyn the Great, had re-established his control of North Wales, and had broken out of a siege to come south and rouse his fellow Welshmen in the Marches. Edmund, in an attempt to entrap Llywelyn, sent him a message saying he was marching to his aid, and wanted to meet with him. Llywelyn came with his army through Radnorshire, keeping to the hills. Then he made a fatal mistake. He left his army to meet the Mortimers, supposing that, if it were a trap, his men guarding Orewin Bridge would be able to hold it and protect his retreat. The Mortimer brothers, however, had heard of a ford across the river and, as Llywelyn came to meet Edmund, they sent men across to attack the bridge from the rear. Soon they had taken it, killing Llywelyn's guards, and allowing the whole Marcher army to march towards the Welsh position. Not knowing what to do, and not wanting to desert their position, the Welsh gave battle there and then. Their efforts were in vain. As they broke ranks and fled, Llywelyn, without his armour, hastened back to take charge of the situation. Unrecognised, he was stopped by the English, and run through with a sword by Stephen de Frankton, who did not stop to look more closely at his victim. Only later, when the dead bodies were being stripped of their weapons and other belongings, was Llywelyn's corpse noted. Edmund Mortimer himself confirmed it was his father's cousin, and, to the great delight of the English, Edmund's younger brother Roger set out for Rhuddlan castle with Llywelyn's head to show to king Edward. With Llywelyn's only child being a daughter in Edward's custody,

Wales was finally conquered. Thus the scholar Edmund Mortimer became a soldier. He was knighted by the king at Winchester.'

5. Without the bards' Celtic oral tradition, much of Welsh history and heritage would have been lost forever. There has been a strong oral tradition that 500 Welsh bards were slaughtered after the death of Llywelyn II, because they may have inflamed the Welsh back to rebellion against their new conquerors, the French kings of England. As well as the 'rounding up' of bards and the imprisonment and execution of their employers, Henry IV in 1403's Ordinance de Gales forbade their existence. Thus truth becomes hidden. One of the most famous and most popular Hungarian poems celebrates this story, written by the famous poet Janos Arany (1817-1882). He was Professor of Hungarian Literature at the Nagy-Koros College, a notary, actor, editor and one of the founders of modern Hungarian poetry. The Austrian Emperor Franz-Josef defeated Hungary in its War of Independence (1848-49), then made his first visit there. He asked Janos Arany to write a poem to praise him, and this was the poet's nationalistic response. (The reference to Milford Haven is to the 'Mab Darogan', the 'Son of Prophecy', Henry VII.)

A Walesi Bardok

Edward kiraly, angol kiraly
Leptet fako lovan
Hadd latom, ugymond, mennyit er
A velszi tartomany

The Bards of Wales

Edward the King, the English King,
Astride his tawny steed -
'Now I will see if Wales,' said he,
'Accepts my rule indeed.

Are streams and mountains fair to see?
Are meadow pastures good?
Do wheat-fields bear a crop more pure
Since washed with rebels' blood?'

"In truth this Wales, Lord, is a gem,
The fairest in your crown:
The streams and fields rich harvest yields
The best through dale and down."

Edward the King, the English King,
Astride his tawny steed:
A silence deep his subjects keep
And Wales is mute indeed.

The castle named Montgomery
Ends that day's travelling;
And the castle's lord, Montgomery,
Must entertain the king.

With game and fish and every dish
That lures the taste and sight
A hundred rushing servants bear
To please his appetite.

With all of worth the isle brings forth
Of splendid drink and food,
And all the wines of foreign vines
Beyond the distant flood.

'You lords, you lords, will none consent
His glass with mine to ring?
What? Each one fails, you dogs of Wales,
To toast the English king?

Though game and fish and every dish
That lures the taste and sight
Your hand supplies, your mood defies
My person with a slight!

You rascal lords, you dogs of Wales,
Will none for Edward cheer?
To serve my needs and chant my deeds,
Then let a bard appear!'

The lords amazed, at him they gaze,
Their cheeks grow deathly pale;
Not fear but rage, their looks engage,
They blanch but do not quail.

All voices cease in soundless peace,
All breathe in silent pain;
Through the door bold, a harper, old,
Enters with grave disdain.

"Lo, here I stand, at your command,
To sing your deeds, O King!"
And weapons clash and shields crash
Responsive to his string.

"Harsh weapons clash and shields crash,
And sunset sees us bleed,

Raven and wolf our dead engulf -
This, monarch, is your deed!

A thousand lie, beneath the sky,
They rot beneath the sun,
And we who live shall not forgive
This deed your hand has done!"

'Now let him perish! I must have'
(King Edward's voice is hard)
'Your softest songs, and not your wrongs!'
Up steps a youthful bard.

"The breeze is soft at eve, that oft
From Milford Haven moans;
It whispers maidens' stifled cries,
It breathes of widows' groans.

You maidens, bear no captive babes!
You mothers, rear them not!"
The fierce king nods. The boy is seized
And hurried from the spot.

Unbidden then, among the men,
There comes a dauntless third.
With speech of fire he tunes his lyre,
And bitter is his word.

"Our bravest died to slake your pride -
Proud Edward, hear my lays!
No Welsh bards live who'll ever give
Your name a song of praise.

Our harps with dead men's memories weep.
Welsh bards to you will sing
One changeless verse - our blackest curse
To blast your soul, O King!"

'No more! Enough!' - cries out the king.
Enraged, his orders break:
'Seek through these vales all bards of Wales
And burn them at the stake!'

Soldiers ride forth to South and North,
They ride to West and East.
Thus ends in grim Montgomery
That celebrated feast.

Edward the King, the English King
Spurs on his tawny steed;
Across the skies red flames arise
As if Wales burned indeed.

In martyrship, with song on lip,
Five hundred Welsh bards died;
Not one was moved to say he loved
The tyrant in his pride.

'God's Blood! What songs this night resound
Upon our London streets?
The Mayor shall feel my irate heel
If any that song repeats.'

Each voice is hushed; through silent lanes
To silent homes they creep.
"Now dies the hound that makes a sound;
The sick king cannot sleep."

'Ha! Bring me fife and drum and horn,
And let the trumpet blare!
In ceaseless hum their curses come -
I see their dead eyes glare…'

But high above all drum and fife
And trumpets' shrill debate,
Five hundred martyred voices chant
Their hymn of deathless hate…

Still now we feel the English leash
A softer type of lash
And now our politicians preach
The language will not crash

Our politicians take the place
Of military power
And 'chosen' ones will not allow
Welsh heritage to flower.
(last two verses by TDB)

Footnote on the Marcher Lords:
Edmund Mortimer's son Roger made himself ruler of the whole of Wales and
murdered Edward II, before being executed by Edward III. A later Edmund
Mortimer was captured by Glyndŵr, and ended up fighting for him against the
English crown. For most of their history they replicated the vile actions of the

Greys of Ruthin and the de Braose family, the latter family particularly featuring some of the most treacherous villains in British history.

The Chronicles of the Princes tell us of Iorwerth ab Owen, a descendant of the princes of Gwent, who controlled the lands around Caerleon. Rhys ap Gruffydd had given King Henry II free passage to cross Wales and invade Ireland in 1171. Henry took Caerleon from Iorwerth and installed a garrison. Iorwerth retook the ancient fort, and told the Normans to follow their king to Ireland. He then burnt the site so that the king would never want it again. In 1172, Henry returned, offering a pardon and the return of Iorwerth's lands. He invited Iorwerth to meet him for a peace treaty, and gave safe conducts for him and his sons. The Welsh leader was well aware of Henry's practice of blinding hostages, and sent just one son Owain, bearing gifts. Owain was killed, so Iorwerth crossed the Wye, attacking Gloucester, burning Hereford, and returned to Caerleon and rebuilt the town. His brother-in-law Seisyllt ap Dynwal captured Abergavenni Castle, and another kinsman Seisyllt ap Rhirid took the king's castle at Crickhowel (Crug Hywel), killing the garrison. In 1175, the Normans attacked suddenly and retook Caerleon from Iorwerth and his surviving son Hywel. However, The Lord Rhys arbitrated, and it was restored to Iorwerth soon after.

In 1175, William de Braose, the Norman Lord of Brecon and Abergavenny, held vast tracts of land, which he had conquered in southeast Wales. Seisyllt ap Dynwal, Lord of Upper Gwent, held the manor of Penpergwm and Castle Arnold for de Braose as his feudal overlord. The Norman invited Seisyllt and another seventy local Welsh lords to Abergavenny castle for a feast and to hear a royal declaration. Hidden outside the banqueting hall were soldiers under the command of Ranulph Poer, Sheriff of Hereford. Seated during the feast, the Welsh nobles were massacred by Norman troops. Only Iorwerth ab Owen escaped, snatching a sword and fighting his way out of the castle. The antiquary Camden noted that Abergavenny 'has been oftner stain'd with the infamy of treachery than any other castle in Wales'.

William de Braose then raced to Castle Arnold, seized Sisyllt's wife Gwladys, and murdered Seisyllt's only son, Cadwaladr, before her eyes. Norman law stated that conquest of Welsh territories by any means whatsoever was fair. Iorwerth led his men to Abergavenny, forcing De Braose to flee to his stronghold in Brecon Castle. In 1282, Seisyllt's kinfolk managed to scale the high walls of Abergavenny and took the castle, but unfortunately de Braose was absent. Seisyllt ap Eudaf had told the Constable of the castle that he would attack the castle at a certain angle, in the evening. The Normans waited all night for the attack, and were all asleep at dawn, whereupon the Welsh threw up their scaling ladders in the area that Seisyllt had said, taken the castle and burnt it to the ground.

Ranulph Poer and de Braose marched to Dingestow (Llandingat) near Monmouth to begin building another castle. The Welsh attacked and Poer was killed, and de Braose only just escaped with his life. This battle is known from the descriptions of the capacity of the bowmen of Gwent. Arrows could penetrate a width of four fingers of oak. One arrow passed through a Norman's armour plate on his thigh, through his leg, through more armour and his saddle, killing his horse. Another Norman was pinned through armour plating around his hip, to his saddle. He wheeled his horse, trying to escape, and another arrow pinned him to the saddle through the other hip.

Like his king, the Norman Marcher Lord de Braose was notable for blinding and torturing any Welshman he could lay his hands on. In 1197 he pulled Trahaiarn Fychan through the streets of Brecon behind a horse, until he was flayed alive. Maud de Valerie, his huge wife, also enjoyed seeing prisoners tortured. With the death of The Lord Rhys, de Braose pushed even more into Welsh territories. However, he fell out of King John's favour, and escaped to France in 1204, leaving his wife and eldest son behind. John took them to Corfe Castle and locked them up with just a piece of raw bacon and a sheaf of wheat – this was this Angevin king's favourite form of execution.

As for the Mortimers, the following excerpt is taken from *A Short Analysis of Welsh History* by W.J. Griffith (1911): 'Ralph (d.1104), the first of the Mortimers who held land in the middle marches of Wales, served under his kinsman Fitzosbern the Earl of Hereford, after whose fall he was a subtenant to the Earl of Shrewsbury. The fall of the latter (1102) gave him more lands.

Hugh Mortimer (d.1184) son or grandson of Ralph, lived during the troublous times of Stephen. In 1148 he blinded Rhys ab Howel, and later added Bridgnorth to his territories. The rise of Owen Gwynedd and Rhys ap Griffith had a steadying effect on the mad rapacity of the Mortimers, like other border families; while Llywelyn the Great secured their alliance and diverted their energies to aid his own policy.

Roger II (d.1282) succeeded his father as Lord of Wigmore in 1246. Next year he added considerably to his estates by marrying Matilda de Braose, daughter of William de Braose, whom Llywelyn hanged in 1230. His attachment to the king's cause brought him into trouble with his powerful kinsman Llywelyn ap Griffith. He lost Gwrtheinion (1256), Builth Castle (1260), Maelienydd (1262); and although the king was successful in 1265, Llywelyn was still powerful enough to defeat Mortimer at Brecon (1266) and to dictate terms to him. During Edward's absence he was regent, and his captain for Shrewsbury 1276. He died in 1282, when the family was entering into the heritage which he had so long coveted.

Roger, his son, participated with Warrenne in the murder of the sons of Griffith ap Madog and took the lordship of Chirk as his share of the spoil. (John de Warrenne, half-brother of Henry II, was entrusted with the care of Griffith's two sons, who they drowned. Warrenne took the lordship of Bromfield and Yale, near Wrexham). It was he that Edward I entrusted with the government of North Wales as the justice of Wales, an office which he performed in a most despotic fashion. The latter's nephew, Roger Mortimer of Wigmore, was soon to become equally powerful in the Marches. The doings of these two assume the importance of national affairs; they figure in the darkest deeds in national history.'

LLYWELYN BREN c.1270- 1318

LLYWELYN THE KINGLY, LLYWELYN AP RHYS AP GRUFFUDD AB IFOR BACH, LORD OF SENGHENYDD AND MEISGYN (MISKIN)

'People were starving to death. The Scots had torn apart the northern counties, so that manors were disappearing under the combined terrors of starvation and extortion. In the north even loyal English lords had taken to organised robbery to keep their retainers satisfied. If Robert the Bruce could ravage the country and get away with it, they reasoned, they might as well take what they could from their neighbours before Bruce did. In Wales the plight of the people was just as extreme. But there they had found a leader who not only inspired them, he inspired his enemies as well. His name was Llywelyn Bren.' (- Ian Mortimer, *The Greatest Traitor – The Life of Sir Roger Mortimer, Ruler of England 1327-1330*).

The ancient lordship of Senghenydd was the most eastern of Glamorgan's 'cantrefs', lying between the rivers Taff and Rhymney. From

the important Roman fort and port of Cardiff it headed north to include Caerphilly. In 1093 the Normans conquered Iestyn ap Gwrgant, the last king of Glamorgan (Morgannwg), and in the commote of Cibbwr, which included Cardiff, built a castle on the site of the Roman camp. The two other commotes of Senghenydd remained controlled by their Welsh

Caerphilly Castle

lord, Senghenydd-is-Caiach (Caerffili to the river Caiach), and Senghenydd - uwch-Caiach (the region north of the river).

In 1158, after an attempt by the Normans to take yet more of his lands, Ifor ap Meurig (*Ifor Bach*) scaled the walls of Cardiff Castle at night. Although 120 men-at-arms defended the castle, the Lord of Senghenydd carried off William, Earl of Gloucester, his wife Hawise and son Robert. Any Welsh rulers captured by Normans were normally tortured and blinded, but Ifor held the grabbing Norman prisoner until he had signed to give back stolen lands, and make compensation with additional lands. He then released the hostages. Senghenydd stayed in the hands of its native rulers, except for the Norman presence in Cardiff and across the Vale of Glamorgan, under Gruffudd ap Ifor (d.1211) and his son Rhys ap Gruffudd (d.1256).

Gruffudd ap Rhys was Lord in 1262, a document describing him as holding the two commotes of Senghenydd. However, because of the threat posed by Llywelyn ap Gruffudd, the last prince of Wales, Gruffudd ap Rhys was ejected by Gilbert de Clare, Lord of Glamorgan, in 1266. In 1268 the Norman began building the great fortress of Caerphilly, probably on the site of a Roman fort. This was despite the signing of the Treaty of Montgomery of 1267, when England's French rulers recognised Llywelyn as Prince of Wales. From Gwynedd, Llywelyn II therefore invaded and took over Upper Senghenydd, preparing for an attack upon the new castle rising at Caerphillyi. There was now an attempt at a treaty between Gilbert de Clare and Llywelyn at Monks' Bridge (Crickadarn in Brecon), with hostilities ceasing for a time, with no incursion by either side over the River Caiach.

However, de Clare completed his castle, which led Llywelyn to attack and destroy it on 11 October 1270. Another, much stronger, castle was erected and Llywelyn returned with his army in October 1271 and laid siege. The displaced Lord of Senghenydd, Gruffudd ap Rhys, was now in Llywelyn's army, possibly being killed in 1282. A treaty was arranged whereby the King's men took over Caerphilly, while both armies moved away. However, by a ruse Gilbert de Clare regained it from its custodians, the men of the Bishops of Lichfield and Worcester. Henry III died in 1272 without resolving the breaking of the treaty, and other Marcher Lords combined with de Clare to push Llywelyn back towards Brecon from Glamorgan. War with the new king, Edward I in 1276-77 forced Llywelyn back to Gwynedd, and his death by treachery in 1282 meant that the massive castle of Caerphilly was now safe in French hands. In 1294-95 Senghenydd was devastated in a Welsh uprising, as was the town of Caerphilly with its mills burnt, but the castle held out until the King's army came to Wales.

Not until 20 years later did Caerphilly come under siege again. Llywelyn ap Gruffydd ap Rhys, the son of the Welsh Lord of Senghenydd ejected in 1266, had a stronghold at Gelligaer, yet another Roman fort. He had considerable property in Senghenydd, holding high office under Gilbert de Clare, being 'a powerful personage in those parts... (having) great mastery in that country.' Problems started when de Clare was killed at Bannockburn in 1314. As the last of his line, the Crown took over de Clare's lands, from Neath to the Wye, the richest and most fertile part of Wales at the time.

As a vassal lord, Llywelyn had been virtually 'custos' of Glamorgan, acting as an adviser to the young Norman lord. With de Clare's death, the king appointed Ingelram de Berengar, Bartholomew de Badlesmere and Payn de Turberville in rapid succession as the king's 'keepers' in Glamorgan.

'These could be cold men, like Ingelram de Berengar, who regarded his role as having to contain the Welsh of Glamorgan through force of arms, or they could be more judicious lords, like Bartholmew de Badlesmere, whose policy was more sympathetic to local grievances. But in July 1315, when the animals started dying in the fields, and when the suffering of the people was greatly on the increase, Bartholomew de Badlesmere was removed from office and the administration of Glamorgan placed in the hands of Payn de Turberville.' (Mortimer, ibid)

There had been a spontaneous uprising, lasting from July to September 1314 across Glamorgan, forcing extra garrisons in many castles, and damage to Caerphilly Castle. Llywelyn Bren had complained to the king about the tyranny of the new land-ownership. The men of Senghenydd were no longer entitled to collect firewood, many other ancient customs had been over-ridden, and lands had been taken from him in Senghenydd and Whitchurch, where there was a Welsh castle, near Cardiff. Edward II agreed with Llywelyn's claims, ordering that the lands be given back to one of Llywelyn's sons.

Payn de Turberville, Lord of Coity, had become 'custos' of Glamorgan in 1315, succeeding Badlesmere. He hated Welshmen, being in constant conflict with Llywelyn's western kinsmen, the lords of Afan, whose territories he coveted. 'It was a decision which had terrible consequences. De Turberville's policy towards the Welsh was to beat out of the people what money he could to swell the royal coffers. Barholomew de Badlesmere's careful alliances and considerate grants were ignored. Most importantly, the middlemen who had effected de Badlesmere's policy were dismissed, and replaced with de Turberville's instruments. The most prominent of these Welshmen was Llywelyn Bren.

Bren means "royal". The epithet was given to him as a mark of respect, not just as a mark of distinguished ancestry. His proper name was Llywelyn ap Gruffydd ap Rhys, his father being one of the warriors who fought in defence of Prince Llywelyn, the last free prince of Wales. Llywelyn Bren himself was Lord of Senghenydd, and a favoured sub-lord of the dead Earl of Gloucester (de Clare, who had died at Bannockburn). Even the English chroniclers, normally biased, describe him with respect. "A great man and powerful in his own country".' (Mortimer, ibid)

Llywelyn and his followers had been removed from their offices, de Turberville was persecuting the inhabitants of Glamorgan and even taking arms against Llywelyn's men in Senghenydd. The treacherous De Turberville accused him of sedition. Llywelyn could only seek justice from the weak Edward II, who sided with his fellow-Norman. In early January 1316, appearing at Court, Llywelyn was ordered to face Parliament at Lincoln, on a charge of inciting the Welsh to rebellion. Edward II sent a message that if he were found guilty, he would be hanged. Fearing arrest on the charge of sedition, Llywelyn immediately rushed home from London, and because of Turberville's oppressive regime, found no difficulty in starting a great revolt that flashed through the Vale of Glamorgan.

It is claimed that 10,000 men joined Llywelyn, and at one time it looked as if it would develop into a national revolt. The rebellion started on 28 January, the day after Bren had been summoned to appear at Lincoln. The first target was Caerphilly Castle, where the constable was holding a court just outside the safety of its walls. Llywelyn managed to capture the constable, kill some of his men and burn the town to the ground, but the great castle remained impregnable. He and his men then swept across Glamorgan, devastating the land and destroying any symbol of English domination. Many people in Senghenydd died, and 31 burgages in Caerphilly were burnt.

'On 28 January, as Parliament gathered in the chamber of the dean's house at Lincoln, the Sheriff of Glamorgan was attending a sitting of a court outside the walls of Caerffili Castle. As the voices cut through the chill air, the sheriff and his court became aware that they were being surrounded. For those at the court it was too late. In vain they tried to retreat into the castle. Before they could do so the portcullises came down and the drawbridge was raised. The sheriff's men were slain in the outer bailey of the castle, which was then set alight. The inner castle itself, so well planned and constructed by the ancestors of the Earl of Gloucester, was impregnable (the largest castle in Europe except for the castellated palace at Windsor), but the sheriff and the constable of the castle were both captured. Then started the looting and burning as Llywelyn's men rampaged through Caerphilly with swords drawn, under the direction of Llywelyn's five sons and his adopted son, Llywelyn ap Madoc ap Hywel.' (Mortimer, ibid)

Llywelyn had returned to his base of Castell Coch, which the Normans had taken, and they refused to hand it over. Gathering around a thousand supporters, he scaled the castle walls of Castell Coch (now a restored 'fairy-tale' castle north of Cardiff) and started a revolt that lasted nine weeks. In the Vale of Glamorgan, he destroyed the castles at Sully, Barry, Old Beaupré, Kenfig, Flemingston, West Orchard and East Orchard.

'News of the attack reached Edward a few days later. His first reaction was to appoint William de Montagu and Hugh Audley, the husband of one of the three Gloucester co-heiresses, to recapture the castle. He then reconsidered and appointed the Earl of Hereford as commander-in-chief of the expedition to put down Llywelyn's revolt, and directed both Lords Mortimer to assist him. "Go quickly and pursue this traitor, lest from delay worse befall us and all Wales rise against us."' (Mortimer, ibid)

Edward, fearing that this localised disturbance might spark off more widespread Welsh uprisings, put Humphrey de Bohun, Earl of Hereford in charge of raising a force capable of squashing the revolt as quickly as possible. Hereford gathered his Marcher neighbours, including Roger de Mortimer of Chirk and Roger de Mortimer of Wigmore, Thomas of Lancaster's younger brother, Henry, and William Montagu. He was also joined by Edward's new favourites Hugh Audley and Roger Damory – the husbands of Elizabeth and Margaret de Clare (Glamorgan was part of the de Clare lands).

By February 1316, King Edward had assembled an army of mercenaries from Glamorgan, West Wales, Gloucester and the Forest of Dean at Cardiff Castle. Humphrey de Bohun approached Caerffili with another royal army, from Brecon. The Lords Mortimer marched from the north. Other marcher lords joined in, as did Badlesmere. From the east came an army under Henry of Lancaster, William de Montague and John de Hastings. The southern and eastern armies met at Cardiff Castle. On 12 March a force of 150 men-at-arms and 2000 footmen, under the command of William de Montagu, Henry Earl of Lancaster, and John Giffard of Brimpsfield marched north from Cardiff to relieve the siege of Caerffili Castle. Lady de Clare was trapped there, and there was strong opposition to the army at Thornhill. The troops seem to have flanked this opposition by way of Rudry, dislodging the Welsh from the hill-ridge as they made their way to the massive castle. In the face of two large converging armies from the north and south, and after suffering heavy losses, Llywelyn retreated to Ystradfellte in the Vale of Neath. He gathered his men there, on the edge of the great forest, for his final stand on March 18th, 1316.

The force arrayed before Bren was so formidable that he knew any further resistance was futile and fled into the hills. From there he offered to surrender as long as he was allowed to keep his life and lands. De Bohun, although sympathetic to a point, declared that any surrender had to be unconditional. Bren was now faced with a dilemma: should be fight on and risk a humiliating and bloody defeat or else surrender, as the earl of Hereford had demanded?

With two of his sons, he surrendered to de Bohun, on 20 March 1316. Knowing resistance was futile and to save his followers, he surrendered knowing his fate, saying 'I started this conflict and I will end it. I will hand over myself on behalf of all my people. It is better for one man to die than for a whole population to be killed by the sword.' His followers tried to dissuade him and fight, but their leader was insistent. Llywelyn first rode alone, in full armour, down the mountain to meet the English. He surrendered to the Earl of Hereford, Lord Roger Mortimer of Wigmore and John de Hastings.

He was taken first to de Bohun's Brecon Castle, then to the Tower of London, where he and his sons were joined by his wife Lleuci, another son, and other Welsh prisoners. Llywelyn's lands and goods were seized and the inventory of stock confiscated still exists*. Lleucu was granted an allowance of 3 pennies a day for upkeep in her captivity, and her three sons 2 pence each. Roger Mortimer especially was sympathetic to Llywelyn's cause and spoke on his behalf to the king, along with the Earl of Hereford. De Bohun and other Marcher Lords also interceded with King Edward on Llywelyn's behalf and his life was spared. They had ridden with Llywelyn to

London, getting to know him, and the Earl of Hereford had sent a letter to the king, urging him not to sentence Llywelyn until he had spoken with the Marcher Lords who had pursued him. In November 1916, with Llywelyn still imprisoned in London, Mortimer ordered John Giffard to assist Llywelyn Bren's adopted son, Llywelyn ap Madoc ap Hywel who was being attacked by the English. Meantime the terrible famine across Britain deepened.

Evans in 1908 noted that Llywelyn Bren had killed all the tax collectors in each village, ridding villagers of their unfair burdens, and 'killed so many of the English and Normans, that no Englishman even thought of remaining in Glamorgan.' The rebellion was put down by forces under the Earl of Hereford, Lord Mortimer of Wigmore and Rhys ap Gruffydd. Llywelyn Bren surrendered on condition that no harm came to his men, and they were allowed to return to their homes. After imprisonment in Brecon, Llywelyn and his two sons were taken to the Tower of London in 1316, but not treated unkindly, and set free in 1317. He received a full pardon on June 17th, 1317 and returned to Wales to lawfully recover his lands. Glamorgan had been devastated, and the heavy fines imposed upon the rebels were impossible to pay, leading to land forfeitures. Llywelyn's wife and sons seem to have been joined the barons De Bohun, Mortimer et al who invaded Despenser's territories in 1321.

The Despensers had now taken over Glamorgan, and had seized Llywelyn's estates in his absence. 'As husband of the eldest of the three heiresses of the Earl of Gloucester, Despenser was allowed to claim the largest third of his inheritance, the county of Glamorgan, in November. This was bad enough news for Mortimer, but what happened next was truly awful. Despenser celebrated his success by removing Llywelyn Bren from the Tower of London without any authority.' (Mortimer ibid) Llywelyn in fact had been granted the King's Pardon.

Hugh Despenser had appointed Payn de Turberville of Coity Castle to be Custodian of Glamorgan. Sir William Berkerolles of East Orchard was Despenser's sub-lord, given full powers over the estates of Llywelyn Bren. This had been done to evict Bren from his rightful possessions across Glamorgan. The Normans had found it far easier to subdue these flatter and richer southern parts of Wales, where reinforcements from the sea were available during their slow and uneven conquest. (The Normans only took four years to conquer England, but three hundred and fifty to completely subdue all of Wales). Ironically, Berkerolles owed Llywelyn Bren his life from 1316, as Llywelyn had previously protected him in the Welsh attack at Caerphilly, where thirteen Norman soldiers in Berkerolle's bodyguard were killed.

Llywelyn Bren was dragged through the streets of Cardiff, then slowly and barbarously executed at Cardiff Castle by the order of Despenser to Berkerolles, whose life Bren had previously saved. 'He was drawn behind two horses to a gallows by the Black Tower where he was hanged. As he was dying, the executioner cut out his heart and intestines with a knofe and threw them into a nearby fire. The limbs were hacked off and distributed throughout Glamorgan. The man to whom the king had promised mercy was no more.' (Mortimer, ibid) He was executed according to Despenser on the orders of Edward II, but Despenser had received no such authority. He wanted Bren out of the way, and had made Berkerolles execute him to distance himself from the disgusting event.

This was one of the charges by the barons that later led to Despenser's own hanging, drawing and quartering. Llywelyn's widow now led another rebellion, which led to several Norman castles being burned. Cardiff, Caerffili and St Quintin's near Cowbridge were attacked. Sir William Fleming was later hanged for carrying out Despenser's orders, and laid to rest alongside Llywelyn at Greyfriars in Cardiff. (Another version is that Fleming acted as deputy to Sir Bartholomew Badlesmere as Custos of Glamorgan in which capacity he executed Bren, but more likely he was hung for taking part in the Barons' Revolt against the Despensers.)

Iolo Morganwg gives us a note on Llywelyn Bren and his destruction of the castles of St Athan and Flemingstone, taken from the manuscript of John Philip of Treoes, near Bridgend: 'Llywelyn Bren, the Aged, called Llywelyn the Ugly, demolished many castles of chieftains, namely, the castles of St Georges, the castle of Sully, the castle of Tregogan (Cogan), the castle of Foulke Fitzwarin, the castle of Barry, the castle of St Athan, the castle of Beaupre, the castle of Kenfig, the castle of Ruthyn, the castle of Gelli Garn, and the castle of Flemingston; - and he killed such numbers of English and Normans, that no Englishman could be found who would so much as entertain, for a moment, the idea of remaining in Glamorgan. At this period, there was in each town and village a sort of land steward, called preventive mayor; but Llywelyn the Ugly had them all hanged; and the chieftains were obliged to discontinue such appointments, because no person whatever could be found to undertake such office, either for money or goods.'

Rice Merrick in 1568 makes the following entry concerning the Llywelyn Bren rebellion:

'De Johanne Flemyng:
Sir John Fflemynge, Knight, to whose lott fortuned the Lordships of Wenvo, St George's, Constantine Waules, Fflemyngstone, and Llanmays; Who gave unto his younger Sonne the Mannour of Constantine Waules and Fflemyngstone, of his name soe called, which Parcells continue at this day in his Name and lineage. The Lordshipps of Wenvo, St George's and Llanmays, discended to his eldest Sonne (and for difference was named Fflemynge of Wenvo, the other Fflemyng Melyn), whose issue Male enjoyed the same until the tyme of Edward the 2nd that Sir William

Fflemyng, being Sheriffe, and cheife Ruler of Glamorgan and Morganwg, in the tyme of Sir Hugh Spencer, the Sonne, then Lord thereof. When the fortune of Spencers altered, his misfortune approached; for hee was executed at Cardiff, for that, as it was supposed, hee had wrongfully adjudged Llewellen Brenn, of Senighenith, to death, and, as it is said, caused a Jebet to be raysed by the Black Towne, within a little Wall that enclosed about the Prison, then called Stavell & oged, and there caused him to be hanged; for which cause (as some affirmeth) hee was attaynted by the Statute of Rutland. This Sir William Fflemynge was buried in the White ffryars without the North gate of the Towne of Cardiff, whose Tombe, in a faire Stone, at the Suppression thereof, together with Llen Brenn his Tombe, made of wood, was defaced. (This is where the Pearl Building, now the Cardiff Hilton Hotel stands. Obviously the monastery was ransacked during the Reformation, and in the 1960's Cardiff Council unfortunately sold the land for development on the ruins.) Robert Ffabyan, in his CHRONICLE, alleadgeth another Cause of his death; affirming, that hee was executed at Cardiff, in Wales in the 14 yeare of Edward 2, among a great number of Barons that were in diverse places put to death. After whose death, his Inheritance discended to his only Daughter; who married Malifand, of Pembrochshire, being one of the King's Mynyons. The issue male of Malifand continued and enjoyed Fflemyng's inheritance, untill that Edmund Malifand, who married with Margarett, Daughter to Sir Mathew Cradog, Knight, in the time of H. 7. Dyed without issue.'

In 1322, Llywelyn Bren's widow and all his family were taken into custody by Despesnser on royal authority, along with all his former allies in Wales.

Despenser was later captured near Llantrisant in 1326 and executed. According to Ian Mortimer (*The Greatest Traitor – the life of Sir Roger Mortimer, Ruler of England 1327-1330*), Mortimer wanted Despenser to 'suffer a death every bit as horrific as his killing of Llywelyn Bren in 1317.' He was hung, drawn and quartered at Hereford, and his limbs distributed to Bristol, Newcastle, York and Dover. When Caerffili castle surrendered in 1326, £14,000 was found hidden in barrels that belonged to Despenser, plus tons of silver-plate. In 1327 the estates of Senghenydd were restored by Edward (under Mortimer pressure) to Llywelyn's sons, Gruffydd, John, Meurig, Roger, William and Llywelyn. Edward II was supposedly shortly after brutally put to death with a red-hot poker in Berkeley Castle, and Despenser was captured and executed as a traitor at Hereford.

* Stock included 374 cows, 114 steers and heifers, 113 sheep, 84 pigs, 71 goats, 69 oxen, 41 calves, 29 mares, 9 'affers', 7 colts and 3 bulls. Possessions included 10 gold rings, a gold clasp, military garments, brass pots, Welsh chairs, armour, brass chandeliers, a saddle and 8 silver spoons. Among Llywelyn Bren's confiscated possessions were three books in Welsh, one copy of *Roman de la*

Rose, four other books, a missal (mass book), a diurnal (service book for the day's holy offices) and two 'manuals' (office books of the medieval church).

DAFYDD AP GWILYM   c.1315/20-c.1360/70

WALES' GREATEST POET, THE NIGHTINGALE OF DYFED

A celebratory plaque marks his reputed birthplace at Brogynin near Llanbadarn Fawr. Dafydd is the most celebrated Welsh poet, said to be buried under the old yew tree, in the churchyard adjoining the ruins of Strata Florida Abbey, but there is also a tradition that he was buried 30 miles away

Dafydd's burial place, Strata Florida Abbey

at Talley Abbey. He may have died of the Black Death as early as 1350. Dafydd has been described as 'one of the greatest of all European mediaeval writers'. Many of the Welsh princes are also believed to be buried with him at Strata Florida Abbey, the Anglicised version of 'Ystrad Fflur', 'The Way of the Flowers'. He innovated in his use of language and metrical techniques, and the seven-syllabled rhyming couplet form known as the

cywydd* became his true metier. He not only developed the *cywydd* but also introduced new themes and attitudes into Welsh poetry. He was a contemporary of Boccaccio, and of the generation preceding Chaucer**.

Dafydd spent a great deal of time at his uncle Llywelyn's house, Cryngae in Castell Newydd Emlyn (Newcastle Emlyn). He described his uncle as a warrior, poet, linguist, scholar and teacher, who lived in a white-washed house with lamps burning brightly, with seats covered with gold silk, and in which fine French wine was drunk from cups of gold. Llywelyn ap Gwilym was a Constable, deputy to Earl Talbot, in charge at Newcastle Emlyn in 1343. In two *awdlau* Dafydd acknowledges his great debt to his cultured uncle, describing him as a poet, a linguist and one who possessed 'all knowledge'. Dafydd's father, Gwilym Gam ap Gwilym ab Einion, came from a powerful family which had sided with the King of England for many decades. His great-great-grandfather, another Gwilym had been Constable of Cemaes in 1241, assisting the Norman-French in their attack on Maredudd ab Owain of Ceredigion, and receiving lands as a reward.

Little is known of his life, except that he was a linguist and a member of an aristocratic family, but his *awdlau* (odes) and *cywyddau* (rhymed couplets) show that he had been trained in bardic art, and was connected historically with 'the poets of the princes'. Dafydd possibly was in exile for some of his life, but was recognised as a great poet even in his own day. He could write in the traditional manner of the older poets, the *Gogynfeirdd*, although this was difficult, and moved towards a different type of diction and choice of themes. His impact was similar to that of Wordsworth's upon the stultifying classical-based poetry of his day.

**Dafydd ap Gwilym
by W. W. Wagstaff**

Dafydd lived in the bleak years after the loss of Llywelyn the Last, when Welsh independence had been seemingly extinguished, but his work includes comic tales of amorous adventures, original nature poetry, and religious and metaphysical poems of varying form and structure. His 'new poetry' had initially been developed in Provence and France, spread by bands of young men, *troubadors* known as *clerici vagrante* or *cleri* - in Wales they were wandering scholars known as *Y Glêr*. Dafydd followed their themes of nature and love, many of his poems being devoted to the golden-haired Morfudd and the raven-haired Dyddgu.

'In the work of Dafydd ap Gwilym, almost for the first time in European literature, we find nature poetry which is the result of direct observation and of personal experience and meditation. In his nature poetry Dafydd makes use of a technique, which is chararacteristic of one type of the older traditional poetry, namely "*dyfalu*". "*Dyfalu*" is a technical term; in general it means to describe, but the "description" is carried out in many forms, by direct "word-painting", by comparison, by contrast, and in a host of other ways. Dafydd's poetry shows him to be a master of this technique; his variations on a single piece of description are almost bewildering, and throughout it all runs a vein of healthy, happy laughter.' It must be remembered that Dafydd sang his poems to the harp.

Ted Hughes and Seamus Heaney named their verse compendium for young people *The Rattle Bag* after Dafydd ap Gwilym's poem. Many of the features of his poetry cannot be translated into English, but *Morfudd fel yr Haul* (Morfudd like the Sun) in cywydd form begins with the lines:

'Gorllwyn ydd wyf ddyn geirllaes, / Gorlliw eiry man marian maes; / Gwyl

Duw y mae golau dyn, / Goleuach nog ael ewyn. / Goleudon lafarfron liw, / Goleuder haul, gwyl ydyw.' – 'I woo a softly spoken girl, / Pale as fine snow on the field edge; / God sees that she is radiant / And brighter than the crest of foam, / White as the glistening garrulous wave's edge, / With the sun's splendour; gracious is she.'

English translations cannot do justice to Dafydd ap Gwilym's mastery of the technicalities of *cynghanedd* and *cywyddau*, and how he brought light-heartedness into poetical formalities, but the following two excerpts are from The Seagull and from his famous *Merched Llanbadarn* (The Girls of Llanbadarn):

'I love her with the full force of passion;
Ah men, not Merlin, with his fine flattering lip, nor Taliesin,
Did love a prettier girl,
Sought-after like Venus, copper-haired,
Surpassing beauty of perfect form...
Oh, seagull, if you ever see
The cheek of the fairest maid in Christendom,
Unless I have the most tender greeting,
That girl will be the death of me...'
'I bend before this passion; a plague on parish girls!
Since, o force of my longing, I have never had one of them!
Not one sweet and hoped-for maiden,
Not one young girl, nor hag, nor wife,
What recoil, what malicious thoughts,
What omission makes them not want me?
What harm is it to a thick-browed girl to have me in the dark, dense wood?
It would not be shameful for her
To see me in a den of leaves...'

Sir Thomas Parry placed Dafydd in perspective: 'Dafydd is remarkable in his age for the large number of poems which he wrote about nature and about love. In this respect he far exceeded all his contemporaries, not only in amount but also in inspiration. It has been shown that he was influenced by the popular poetry of other countries, with which he probably became acquainted through sojourning among the mixed company which gathered in the towns, such as Newborough and Newcastle Emlyn. But Dafydd soars far above all influences. His view of the world around him is that of a true poet, and it is the true poet's sensibility which gives expression to it all in concrete images. His conception of the unity of the poem as the ordered production of a single mood is not matched in the works of any other Welsh poet until the present century. To communicate his vision he had the skill of one who was supreme master of the Welsh language, its vocabulary, and its terseness of idiom, and also of all the strict metrical rules of his time.'

* The *cywydd* is a Welsh verse form, a short ode in rhyming couplets, with one rhyme being accented and the other un-accented. Each line has 7 syllables and has to contain some form of *cynghanedd. Cynghanedd* itself is a complex system of alliteration and internal rhyme. The cywydd has similarities with the verse form used by French *trouvères* (troubadors) and *jongleurs* (wandering scholar-singers), and a great deal in common with the earlier *bardd teulu.* This was the poetry of the second grade of bard in the Welsh bardic system, the bard of the king or prince's 'war-band' or 'family'. The *cywydd* was the leading Welsh verse form, from the 14th until the 17th century.

** Remember that Chaucer's decision to use English, rather than Latin of French 'represented perhaps the most significant moment in our (English) national culture' (-Peter Ackroyd). English, as an 'understandable' and written language, only dates from Chaucer's work of 1400. By that time Welsh was already over a thousand years old, and Dafydd ap Gwilym's work can be read today in its original form far, far more easily than that of Chaucer.

OWAIN LLAWGOCH 1330/1335 - August 31 1378

YVAIN DE GALLES, THE LAST OF THE LINE OF GWYNEDD, 'THE LAST HEIR OF THE TRUE PRINCE OF WALES', FREEBOOTER, ADMIRAL, GENERAL, CHEVALIER DE FRANCE

Owain ap Thomas ap Rhodri was known in Wales as Owain Lawgoch, and

Owain attacking Mortagne, from Froissart's Chronicle

on the continent as Yvain de Galles, Owen of Wales. He was nicknamed *llaw goch,* 'red hand' because of his presence on battlefields across Europe from Spain to Switzerland. Owain was the grandson of Llywelyn II's brother Rhodri, and the sole heir of the Princes of Gwynedd. Rhodri ap Gruffudd had renounced his rights in Gwynedd, living safely in England as a royal pensioner. The first appearance of Rhodri ap Gruffudd in the sources after 1241 when he was a child occurs in 1272 when he quit-claimed all his paternal interest in lands in Gwynedd (and all Wales) to his brother

Llywelyn for 1,000 marks. He took no part in the subsequent wars with Edward I, having moved to Cheshire.

Then in 1278, he filed a petition seeking his rightful share of Gwynedd on the grounds that he had never been paid the promised 1,000 marks. In a hearing at the king's court at Rhuddlan attended by his brothers, Llywelyn and Dafydd, and by Edward I, Rhodri admitted that 50 marks had been paid to him but nothing more. His brothers acknowledged the unpaid debt and Dafydd offered his English lands as security for payment of the 950 marks due. Dafydd had been granted lands in England for previously helping the English fight his brother Llywelyn. The king then agreed that Rhodri had no claim to any land except as collateral for the debt. Rhodri married Beatrice, a rich daughter of John de Malpas of Cheshire and in 1294 was granted an English pension of 40 pounds a year. 'Rotheric, son of Griffin and Katherine his wife' purchased several tracts of land in Cheshire between 1299 and 1305, the same man as Roderic fitz Griffin, lord of the manor of Tatesfield'.

His son Thomas inherited estates England in Surrey, Cheshire and Gloucestershire. Records cite a Sir Thomas Roderic of Tatsfield, indicating that he was the son of the Roderic fitz Griffin, and also held Dinas in Mechain in Wales. Thomas ap Rhodri used the four lions of Gwynedd on his seal, but wisely made no attempt to win back his Gwynedd inheritance. Owain, his only son, was born in Surrey, at his grandfather's manor of Tatsfield near London. Thomas seems to have been forewarned of danger to himself and his son Owain, and quickly sent Owain to France in 1350, where Owain bound himself to the service of Jean II, King of France, and became his protégé. Froissart claims Owain fought bravely for the French against the English at Poitiers in 1356. Thomas ap Rhodri died in 1363, and Owain crossed to England in the summer of 1365 to claim his paternal inheritance. Having secured the estate, he left again for France in March 1366.

Many Welshmen followed him, including Ieuan Wyn, who took over Owain's company of soldiers in Europe after his death. Owain's company consisted largely of Welshmen, many of whom remained in French service for many years. The second in command of this company was Ieuan Wyn, known to the French as *le Poursuivant d'Amour*, a descendant of Ednyfed Fychan, Seneschal of Gwynedd. Owain also received financial support while in France from Ieuan Wyn's father, Rhys ap Robert. 'Owen of Wales' was one of the most noted warriors of the fourteenth century, the leader of one of the greatest 'Free Companies'. Described as 'high-spirited, haughty, bold and bellicose' by Barbara Tuchman (*A Distant Mirror*), after Poitiers he had campaigned in the Lombard Wars of the 1360's, and for and against the Dukes of Bar in Lorraine. In 1366, he had led the Compagnons de Galles (Company of Welshmen) to fight Pedro the Cruel in Spain. Owain developed an outstanding reputation as a mercenary leader, across France, Lombardy, independent Brittany, Alsace and Switzerland.

The truce between Edward III and Jean II of France had lasted from the Treaty of Bretigny in 1360, but in 1369 Anglo-French hostilities resumed, and Owain was to be deprived of his properties in England and Wales for adhering to the king's enemies. Though a stranger to Wales, Owain was very conscious of his hereditary claims as lineal successor of the Princes of Gwynedd, as Froissart makes clear. Owain seems to have spoken much about them in French court circles. Owain's claims were exploited by France, to divert English attacks in France, by an invasion of Wales under Owain's leadership. The English authorities were preparing for Owain's invasion of Wales as early in 1369. An Anglesey man, Gruffydd Sais was executed, and his lands confiscated by the crown for contacting 'Owain Lawgoch, enemy and traitor', for the purpose of starting a war in Wales. Charles V of France gave Owain a fleet to sail to Wales from Harfleur, but it was repulsed by storms. In 1870 all of Owain's properties were confiscated.

In May 1372 in Paris, Owain announced that he intended to claim the throne of Wales. He set sail again from Harfleur with money borrowed from Charles V. The signed treaty of Paris between Owain Llawgoch and Charles V, of 10 May 1372, still survives. It begins 'Owain of Wales, to all those to whom these letters shall come, greetings. The kings of England in past times having treacherously and covetously, tortuously and without cause and by deliberate treasons, slain or caused to be slain my ancestors, kings of Wales, and others of them have put out of their country, and that country have by force and power appropriated and have submitted its people to divers servitude, the which country should be mine by right of succession, by kindred, by heritage, and by right of descent from my ancestors the kings of that country, and in order to obtain help and succour that country which is my heritage, I have visited several Christian kings...' In this year, Rhys ap Robert's' son Ieuan Wyn, serving as Owain's right hand in France, was identified along with Owain as having received over 500 marks from Rhys to aid their fight against the English in France.

Charles now gave Owain and incredible 300,000 gold francs [estimated at over £200 million pounds in today's money], another fleet and 4,000 men to win back his land. Owain proclaimed that he owned Wales 'through the power of my succession, through my lineage, and through my rights as the descendant of my forefathers, the kings of that country'. He constantly proclaimed himself the true heir of Aberffraw, the court on Anglesey of the Princes of Gwynedd, and only de Guesclin features more highly in French literature as an enemy of the English at this time.

Owain first attacked Guernsey, and with a Franco-Castilian landing party overpowered the island's garrison at night. and was still there when a message arrived from Charles ordering him to abandon the expedition in order to go to Castile to seek ships to attack the English and Gascon forces at La Rochelle. Owain was thus forced to halt his invasion of Wales, but in Guernsey, his exploits were recorded in popular song and legend.

The Captal de Buch, Constable of Aquitaine, was a Gascon ally of the English, a friend of the Black Prince, and had distinguished himself fighting for the English at Poitiers. The French were besieging the English garrison at La Rochelle, when the Captal led an English and Gascon relief force to try to lift the similar siege at nearby Soubise. Owain led his French force from Guernsey and attacked the Captal, capturing him and Sir Thomas Percy, Seneschal of Poitou. Such was the Captal's reputation that King Charles V kept him in prison in the Temple in Paris without the privilege of ransom. Both King Edward of England and delegations of French nobles repeatedly asked Charles to ransom him if he promised not to take up arms against France, but the King refused and the noble Captal sank into depression. He refused food and drink and died in 1376.

Another invasion of Wales was planned in 1373 but had to be abandoned when John of Gaunt launched an offensive against France. Owain never had another chance to return to Wales, and in 1374 he fought in battles at Mirebau and at Saintonge. Throughout the 1370's, Owain campaigned alongside the great Bertrand du Guesclin. In 1375, Owain took part in the successful siege of Saveur-le-Comte in Normandy, where for the first time cannon were used really successfully to break the English defences. He then took a contract from the great Baron Enguerrand de Coucy, Count of Soissons and of Bedford to lead 400 men at a fee of 400 francs per month, (with 100 francs per month going to his assistant, Ieuan Wyn ap Rhys). Again, the treaty contract survives, dated 14 October 1375.

The great de Coucy wanted to win back is share of the Habsburg lands due to him as nephew of the former Duke of Austria. Any town or fortress taken was to be yielded to De Coucy. The capture of Duke Leopold

Monument at Montagne-sur-Mer

of Austria was to be worth 10,000 francs to Owain, who attracted 100 Teutonic knights from Prussia to his banner. With peace brought about by the Treaty of Bruges, English knights also came to offer their services under the leadership of Owain. Probably around 10,000 soldiers eventually formed an army for De Coucy and Owain. The knights wore pointed helmets and cowl-like hoods on heavy cloaks, and their hoods called 'gugler' (from the Swiss-German for cowl or point) gave their names to the 'The Gugler War'.

The companies making up the army plundered Alsace, and took a ransom of 3,000 florins not to attack Strasbourg as Leopold retreated, ordering the destruction of all resources in his wake. He withdrew across the

Rhine, relying upon the Swiss to stave off the attack, although the Swiss hated the Hapsburgs almost as much as they hated the Guglers. Owain's invaders were allowed entrance to Basle, but their forces became increasingly scattered as they sought food and loot in the wake of Leopold's depredations. Near Lucerne, a company of Guglers was surrounded by the Swiss and routed. On Christmas night a company of Bretons was ambushed by citizens of Berne, city of the emblem of the bear. On the next night, the Swiss attacked the Abbey of Fraubrunnen, where Owain was quartered, setting fire to the Abbey and slaughtering the sleeping 'English'. Owain swung his sword 'with savage rage' but was forced to flee, leaving 800 Guglers dead at the Abbey.

Ballads tell of how the Bernese fought '40,000 lances with their pointed hats', how 'Duke Yfo [Owain] of Wales came with his golden helm' and how when Duke Yfo came to Fraubrunnen, 'The Bear roared "You shall not escape me! I will slay, stab and burn you!" In England and France the widows all cried "Alas and woe! Against Berne no-one shall march evermore!"'

In 1377 there were reports that Owain was planning another expedition into Wales, this time with help from Castile. The alarmed English government sent a spy, the Scot John Lamb, to assassinate Owain, who had been given the task of besieging Mortagne-sur-Gironde in Poitou. The details are recounted as follows in *Froissart's Chronicles*. In 1378, Owain was conducting the siege of the castle of Mortagne-sur-Gironde near the Atlantic coast. There were chains across the river here, protecting the English-held Bordeaux from sea attacks by the French. As usual, early in the morning, Owain sat on a tree stump, having his hair combed by his new squire, while he surveyed the scene of siege. His new Scots manservant, James Lambe [according to Frossiart], had been taken into service as he had brought news of 'how all the country of Wales would gladly have him to be their lord'.

But with no-one around, following John of Gaunt's orders Lambe stabbed Owain in the back with a short spear, and escaped to the besieged Mortagne Its English commander said of the treacherous act: 'We shall incur blame thereby rather than praise.' Edward III paid £20* for the assassination of the person with the greatest claim to the Principality of Wales, the last of the line of Rhodri Fawr and Gwynedd. Norman and Angevin policy had always been to kill Welsh male heirs and put females of the lineage into remote English monasteries, as we can see in the case of Llywelyn the Last. It seems that Owain was buried at the chapel of St Leger, his possible headquarters during the siege. Owain's men swore to continue the siege and avenge their lord, but were surrounded by an English relieving army under Neville. In respect to their valour, the survivors of Owain's company were given a safe-conduct to leave Mortagne, and rejoined the main French forces. The details of the siege of Mortagne and of Owain's assassination are vividly illustrated in *Froissart's Chronicles*.

Owain Lawgoch was only second in valour to Bertrand du Guesclin in Europe through these years, a mercenary operating away from home compared to a national hero. His is an amazing story, yet he is unknown to 99% of Welshmen. His importance to Edward III of England is shown in a payment of 100 francs noted in the *Issue Roll of the Exchequer* dated 4 December 1378: 'To John Lamb, an esquire from Scotland, because he lately killed Owynn de Gales, a rebel and enemy of the King in France... By writ of privy seal, &c., £20.'

Owain Lawgoch was described by Edward Owen as 'possibly the greatest military genius that Wales has produced'.With the assassination of Owain Lawgoch the direct line of the House of Cunedda became extinct. As a result, the claim to the title 'Prince of Wales' fell to the other royal dynasties, of Deheubarth and Powys. The leading heir in this respect was another Owain, Owain ap Gruffudd of Glyndyfydrwy, who was descended from both dynasties. This Owain 'Glyndŵr' became another *mab darogan*, (Son of Prophecy) of the Welsh bards. When Glyndŵr, 26 years later in 1404, requested French help against England, he reinforced his case by referring to Owain Lawgoch's great service to the French crown. Some of Owain's free company are believed to have returned to Wales to join the war of independence of 1400-1415. Lawgoch was buried four miles away from the scene of his death, in the church of St. Leger, deeply mourned by a wide circle of associates, and commanding the admiration of some of the leading chroniclers of the age. Owain still features in the folk literature of Brittany, France, Switzerland, Lombardy and the Channel Islands.

Owain was supposed to have been buried at St Leger near Mortagne, but there are persistent legends concerning his burial at Llandybie church. He is connected with a legend at Llyn Llech Owain, a lake near Llandybie, and is also said to lie with his men in a cave under the marvellous Carreg Cennen Castle near Llandybie. He will be awoken by a bell to save Wales. There is a possibility that Ieuan ap Wynn, his second-in-command at Mortagne, returned to Wales with Owain's heart for burial. Ieuan took over the war-troop and changed his heraldic coat-of-arms to that of Owain's, adding a 'bend gules'.

Members of Owain's company were still serving in France until 1396, and French and Breton troops arrived in Wales in 1402 to fight for Owain Glyndwr. It may be that Ieuan or other veterans came with them, and Owain Glyndwr had adopted Llawgoch's heraldic badge as Prince of Wales. In early September 1378, Ieuan Wyn and Llawgoch's men met up with the main French forces at Saintes, and had taken Owain's body with them. On the way, at Cozes, they again buried his body, but kept his heart preserved in a small casket. The French-Breton force that supported Glyndŵr attacked Llandovery and Dynefwr Castles, burned Llandeilo and took Dryslwyn

Castle, before besieging Carreg Cennen. It may be that the casket-bearer was wounded, or that Llandybie was a convenient holy site for burying Llawgoch's heart in his homeland.

* As well as the £20 blood money, there were expenses to be paid. A letter from Sir John Neville, Governor of Aquitaine, to Richard Rotour, Constable of Bordeaux noted the payments made to Lamb's assassination squad, three of whom were killed by Owain's men while Lamb effected his escape. Part of the letter is translated as '...they, in the country of the French, and, especially for the great and perilous adventure in which they risked life and limb to bring about the death of Owain of Wales, traitor and enemy to the King our said Lord. By which deed they diminished the evils and destruction wrought on the lands of the subjects of the King our Lord... Owing to the great profit and service they have rendered in this recent foray to Mortagne... The said John Lamb and his companions have as outgoings the sum of 522 livres and 10 sous of current money, in payment for coats, helmets, hauberks, arm harness, gauntlets and many different harnesses and clothes purchased in the town of Bordeaux, to arm and array themselves.' There is also the receipt and letter signed by John Lamb. To put £20 in perspective, French archers were paid 4d a day at this time, so it would have been about four years pay. John Lamb died in his bed, but across Europe was despised. Even a century later a Flemish miniature was commissioned to depict the act of murder.

Footnotes:
1. The author has found an 'Edouart d'Yvain' mentioned as a minor warlord in France towards the end of Owain's life - could it be his son, and the line of Gwynedd still be extant in France? The Llawgoch Society also uncovered the intriguing information that Owain probably married a French woman, the 'Lady Elinore'. Marie Trevelyan, the early 19th century historian from Llanilltud Fawr, tells us that 'there were several Welsh military leaders at this time, and these included Edouart Yvain, probably a son of the redoubtable Yvain de Galles; Jehan Wyn, Yvain Greffin, and Gay Robin ap Ledin, Welsh deserters from the armies of Edward III appear as renowned captains of cosmopolitan banditti and freebooters, one of whom was the famous and much dreaded Chevalier Rufin'. It appears that Jehan Wyn was Ieuan Wyn, Owain's second-in-command. Gay Robin ap Ledin is probably Robin ap Bleddin who was in a company billeted at St Jean d'Angely in May 1392. The 'dreaded Chevalier Rufin' must be one of the several persons called Gruffydd (often anglicised to Griffin) who appear in muster lists of the time, possibly Gruffyd ap Madog, who was with a company at St Jean d'Angely in April 1396.

2. On the 625th anniversary of the assassination, Sunday 31 August 2003, at Mortagne-sur-Mer, south of Bordeaux, the Owain Lawgoch Society unveiled a memorial to Owain, Yvain de Galles. The site is just within what was the main land gate of the old castle, so Owain symbolically achieved his objective. The monument is a gift of the people of Wales to the people of Mortgagne and

France, and will be insured and maintained by the local council. The area surrounding has been planted with daffodils. At the centre of the festivities was the unveiling of a great hand, 8ft high, cut by a French stonemason, holding in its palm a slate disc, carved by a Welsh sculptor. This has on it the four lions of Gwynedd, the arms of Owain of the Red Hand, Owain Lawgoch, Yvain de Galles, legitimate Prince of Wales and Captain General of France. For the statue, £36,000 was provided by the French, who asked what were the Welsh contributing? Hundreds of appeals had been sent to the Welsh Development Agency, Tourist Board, politicians and the Assembly, with no response.

Bryan Davies had been the inspiration behind the appeal, assisted by Rhobat ap Steffan, who had managed to have the wonderful statue of Llywelyn ap Gruffudd Fychan commissioned at Llandovery Castle.

'Davies launched a national appeal, addressed societies from Neath to Reading, sold postcards and daffodil bulbs, and put together a touring exhibition of 20 display boards illustrating Owain's life and times. Even so, the French question became more pointed. What was the Welsh Assembly providing? News of this got out, for there now occurred a moment of black comedy unique to Welsh bureaucracy. The Assembly said it had not made a grant because it had never been asked for one. The fact that it had said there was no possibility of a grant was incidental. Davies now applied for a grant. And with the unveiling just weeks away the Assembly came up with £9,000.' Davies had dound that they people of Mortagne knew of Owain – 'Ah yes, Duke Yfo', an old lady told him. 'He was killed here by John Lambe.' The unveiling of his statue was a joint effort, on behalf of France carried out by a general. Never giving up the chance of a freeby, the Welsh unveiling was carried out by the previously disinterested chairperson of the Assembly's Cultural Committee.

OWAIN GLYNDŴR 1355 or 28 May 1354 - September 20th 1415

OWAIN AP GRUFFYDD - LORD OF GLYNDYFRDWY, PRINCE OF WALES, WALES' GREATEST HERO

For some Welshmen, Millennium Day was 16 September 2000, Glyndŵr Day, 600 years since a company of nobles gathered in his manor at Glyndyfrdwy to proclaim Owain Glyndŵr Prince of Wales. No other Welsh leader is referred to simply by his surname. Glyndŵr became the Welsh leader 'sans pareil', the name a rallying cry for all things Welsh. The group of people who regularly set alight to English holiday homes in remote areas of Wales from the 1960's to the 1980's called themselves 'Meibion Glyndŵr, 'The Sons of Glyndŵr *. Glyndŵr not only lit up Wales with a united rebellion against overwhelming odds, but also his mysterious disappearance from history left an unbeaten feeling in Welsh hearts. He was the last *Mab Darogan*, 'Son of Prophecy' for the Welsh bards, before Henry

Tudor took the English crown in 1485 from the last of the Angevins, Richard Plantagenet.

There are numerous Welsh legends about Glyndŵr's birth. They include the fact that his father's horses were standing in blood up to their fetlocks in their stables, and that the baby would cry at the sight of a weapon, and only stop when he could touch it. These legends are referred to in Shakespeare's *Henry IV, Part I*:

'... At my birth
The front of heaven was full of fiery shapes;
The goats ran from the mountains, and the herds
Were strangely clamorous to the frighted fields.
These signs have marked me extraordinary,
And all the courses of my life do show,
I am not in the roll of common men.'

Glyndŵr could trace his heritage back to Rhodri Mawr, who was head of the royal houses of Gwynedd, Powys and Deheubarth. He was born around

Statue at Corwen

1353, and some say he was educated at Oxford. He possibly studied for seven years at the Inns of Court in Westminster. Later he became squire to the Earl of Arundel and possibly Henry Bolingbroke, later Henry IV. Fluent in Latin, English, French and Welsh, he served Richard II in his 1385 Scottish campaign. He also may have fought on the Continent for the English King, but records are incomplete.

Aged around 45, after a life of service to the crown, it appears that he returned to Wales to retire to his great family estates at Glyndyfrdwy (an area of the Dee Valley, between Llangollen and Corwen), and at Cynllaith on the other side of the Berwyn Hills.

(Glyndyfrdwy means valley of the river Dee, and was shortened in his name to Glyn Dŵr, valley of water). At Sycharth, in Cynllaith, was Glyndŵr's chief house, protected by moats, with nine guest rooms, resident minstrels and bards, fishponds, a deerpark, dovecot, vineyard, orchards, mill, wheat fields and peacocks. His income from his estates, around £200 a year, had enabled him to settle down in 1398 with his wife Marged, and nine or so children.

But just four years later, in 1402, the English had burnt down both the manor houses at Sycharth and Glyndyfrdwy, of this 50-year-old nobleman. It is difficult to describe the desolation Glyndŵr must have felt about the destruction of Sycharth, in particular - all that is left is the moat, in one of the most beautiful parts of Wales. His family bard Iolo Goch (who died about 1398) has left us a full description, which ends:

'Seldom has there been seen there
Either a latch or a lock,
Or someone playing porter,
No lack of bountiful gifts,
No need, no hunger, no shame,
No one is parched at Sycharth.
The best Welshman, bold leader,
Owns this land, Pywer Lew's line,
Slim strong man, the land's finest,
And owns this court, place to praise.'

1399 had been the turning point in Glyndŵr's existence. Richard II had sailed to Ireland when he heard that the exiled Henry Bolingbroke, son of John of Gaunt, had landed in England. Richard returned via Milford Haven and made for Conwy, choosing Wales as his base for a battle. However, he was met by Henry Percy, Earl of Northumbria, who assured him that Bolingbroke meant no insurrection, and merely wanted to inherit his father's lands and title, which had temporarily been taken by Richard. Richard rode to Conwy Castle to listen to Bolingbroke's request, but was ambushed, being forced to 'abdicate' in favour of Bolingbroke, who became Henry IV.

Richard was spirited away to Pontefract Castle and disappeared from history. Richard's royal baggage train, still at Conwy, was seized by Henry's troops, but then 'liberated' by local Welshmen, who recognised treason. Henry IV developed a hatred of the Welsh, who generally stayed loyal to Richard. It also appears that Glyndŵr might have been a squire to Richard II, as well as to Bolingbroke. Owain Glyndŵr had in the past fought for King Richard, and Henry Bolingbroke was dubious as to his loyalty to a usurper king.

Richard's abduction and murder ruined Glyndŵr's idyllic existence, after just one year of retirement. In 1399 Reginald Grey, Lord of Ruthin, took advantage of the civil unrest following the new king, and stole some of his Glyndyfwrdwy lands. Glyndŵr was legally trained, and decided to fight Grey with a lawsuit in the English Parliament. A proud and loyal man, of royal blood, extremely tall for his times, he wore his hair down to his shoulders, against the prevailing fashion of cropped hair in London. His case was dismissed with the comment 'What care we for barefoot Welsh dogs!' Even Shakespeare referred to Glyndŵr as a brave and cultivated man:

'a worthy gentleman,
Exceeding well read, and profited
In strange concealments, valiant as a lion,
And wondrous affable, and as bountiful
As mines of India',
and he gives Glyndwr these lines:
'For I was trained in the English court,
Where, being but young, I framed to the harp
Many an English ditty lovely well
And gave the tongue an helpful ornament.'

We can see that Owain Glyndŵr was not the type of man to be thrown out, and treated like a dog, by an ignorant French-speaking 'English' Parliament. The new king, Henry IV now raised taxes in Wales, and his aggressive (and

Glyndŵr bust and colours - Pennal Church

illiterate) Marcher Lords like Grey urged him to settle the growing unrest there. Henry was preoccupied with Scotland, however, and instructed his barons to offer free pardons to law-breakers, hoping to defuse the situation.

Lord Grey offered a pardon and a position as master forester to Gruffydd ap Dafydd, who had stolen some of his horses. The Welshman gave himself up as requested, at Oswestry, but was lucky to escape alive. He sent a letter to Grey about the betrayal: 'I was told that you are in purpose to let your men burn and slay in any land which succours me and in which I am taken. Without doubt as many men as you slay for my sake will I burn and slay for yours. And doubt not that I will have bread and ale of the best that is in your Lordship'. Lord Grey sent a copy to the Prince of Wales, the future Henry V, together with a copy of his reply to Gruffydd, threatening him: ' I hope we shall do thee a privy thing, a rope, a ladder, and a ryng (noose), high on gallows for to hang. And thus shall be your ending.'

Grey could not be trusted, as we shall see - he desperately wanted more land in Wales. When Henry IV summoned each noble to bring a quota of men to fight in Scotland, Grey did not pass on the message to Owain

Glyndŵr. His absence from the army, just after his Parliamentary slighting, would hurt Glyndŵr's standing further in Henry's eyes. Henry's army was badly beaten, and the king now allowed Grey leave to proceed against his 'treacherous subject', Glyndŵr.

Lord Grey decided that a frontal assault was unlikely to succeed, and therefore arranged a meeting to discuss Glyndŵr's grievances. Glyndŵr agreed, but knowing Grey's record, asked for only a small band of men to accompany the Marcher Lord. Grey agreed, and arrived to open discussions at Sycharth. Luckily, Iolo Goch, the house-bard of Glyndŵr, was told of a much larger band of Lord Grey's horsemen, hidden in the woods outside the house, awaiting the signal to attack. Iolo Goch entertained the host, and singing in Welsh alerted Glyndŵr to the threat. Owain made an excuse and fled his beloved Sycharth to his other estate, further west at Glyndyfrdwy, just before Grey's troops arrived.

Here on 16 September 1400, Glyndŵr took the Red Dragon of Cadwaladr and Wales as his standard. This is now celebrated as Glyndŵr Day across Wales, with events and the wearing of red and gold ribbons - his heraldic colours. Aged around fifty, he was proclaimed Prince of Wales by Welshmen flocking to Glyndyfrdwy. Students from Oxford and Cambridge, labourers, noblemen and friars came to support him, resenting English wrongs. On 18 September, Glyndŵr's small, poorly armed force rode into Lord Grey's base of Ruthin, looted the

Newcastle Emlyn was taken by Glyndŵr

fair and fired the town. No one was killed, but fourteen rebels were captured and hanged. Glyndŵr's band soon learned about fast-moving warfare. By 24 September, they had fired and looted Denbigh, Flint, Hawarden, and Rhuddlan, and were moving on to Welshpool.

However, the Sheriff of Shrewsbury had raised men from the Border and Midlands, and beat Glyndŵr's little force decisively on the banks of the Vyrnwy River. On 25 September, Henry IV arrived in Shrewsbury with his army, and dismembered Goronwy ap Tudur, a local nobleman, sending his limbs along the Welsh borders to Chester, Hereford, Ludlow and Bristol, as an example to those thinking of supporting Glyndŵr.

Glyndŵr was now in hiding when his aggrieved cousins, Goronwy ap Tudur's kinsmen on Anglesey, Gwilym and Rhys Tudur, started a second rebellion. Near Beaumaris, at Rhos Fawr, the Tudur army was defeated but managed to melt away before it was destroyed. Henry IV then destroyed Llanfaes Abbey, as its Franciscan monks had supported the Welsh rebels. Henry marched to the coast at Mawddwy and returned to Shrewsbury. The small Welsh army watched him all the way, not strong enough to face the Plantagenet force. Henry offered a pardon to Glyndŵr's brother, Tudur, which he accepted. However, Owain Glyndŵr was excluded from terms, and all his lands given to the Earl of Somerset, John Beaufort. It looked as if Glyndŵr's days were numbered at the end of the year 1400.

The Marcher Lords were allowed to take any Welsh land that they could, by force of arms or subterfuge. As well as this, in 1401 the English Parliament passed laws that no Welsh person could hold official office, nor marry any English person. The Welsh could not live in England, and had to pay for the damage caused by the two 1400 rebellions. This racial purity enforcement enraged the Welsh of all classes. Glyndŵr was back now at Glyndwfrdwy, isolated and with few supporters, as Gwynedd had accepted the royal pardon. Other noble Welsh families now sent envoys to King Henry, complaining about the brutality and taxes of the Marcher Lords.

However, the situation looked bleak until the Tudur brothers once more decided to change the rules of the game. They emerged from hiding in their Anglesey stronghold. While the garrison of Conwy Castle was at

Carreg Cennen Castle

church outside the walls, on Good Friday 1401, two of their men posed as labourers, gained access to the castle and killed the two gatekeepers. Gwilym and Rhys Tudur, with a band of just forty men, fired the town and took control of Conwy Castle. Henry Percy, nicknamed Hotspur, controlled North Wales for the king, and needed to get them out of the castle. After weeks of negotiations, the Welsh were starving. Both sides agreed to a sad compromise. The Tudurs were guaranteed free passage back to Anglesey upon the giving up of some of their force. It is said that Gwilym selected them in their sleep - they were later drawn, hanged, disembowelled and quartered while alive by Hotspur, their remains being scattered about Wales as a warning against further rebellion.

Many Welshmen again started returning from England to Wales, and were backed by those supporters of Richard II who thought he was still alive, with donations to the Welsh cause. A man called William Clark had his tongue pulled out for daring to speak against Henry IV, then his hand cut off for writing against him, and then he was beheaded.

By May 1401, another small band of men had joined Glyndŵr, but he was routed by Hotspur, near Cader Idris. He was forced to move south to the slopes of Pumlumon and raised his standard again, where Nant-y-Moch reservoir now corrupts the land and a massive windfarm is planned. With around 400 men only, he rode down to loot and burn Llandrindod Wells, New Radnor, and Montgomery. Welshpool resisted and Glyndŵr returned with the remains of his band, now just 120 men, according to Gruffydd Hiraethog, to the safety of the Pumlumon foothills and caves.

Unknown to him, an army of 1,500 Flemings from the settlements in southwest Wales - the 'Englishry' south of the Preseli Hills - was marching to exterminate this threat to their livelihoods. They surrounded him and charged downhill at Glyndŵr's trapped army at Hyddgen on the Pumlumon foothills. Glyndŵr's army knew that they either died there and then, or would be slowly disembowelled if captured. The incentive was enough, and they halted and reversed the Flemings' charge. News spread all over Wales that the Welsh had won a real battle at last.

Hotspur, disillusioned by a lack of financial support from Henry in Wales, now took his North Wales peacekeeping army back to Northumberland. This was Glyndŵr's opportunity to traverse all Wales, hitting Marcher Lord possessions and those of their sympathisers. Sir John Wynn in his *History of the Gwydir Family* describes these years - 'beginning in Anno 1400, continued fifteen years which brought such a desolation, that green grass grew on the market place in Llanrwst... and the deer fled in the churchyard... In 1400 Owain Glyndŵr came to Glamorgan and won the castle of Cardiff, and many more. He also demolished the castles of Penlline, Landough, Flemingston, Dunraven of the Butlers, Tal-y-Fan, Llanbleddian, Llanquian, Malefant and that of Penmark. And many of the people joined him of one accord, and they laid waste the fences and gave the lands in common to all. They took away from the powerful and rich, and distributed the plunder among the weak and poor. Many of the higher orders and chieftains were obliged to flee to England'.

Llywelyn ap Gruffydd Fychan at Llandovery Castle

The king saw that Wales was turning to Glyndŵr, and that his Marcher Lords could no longer control any parts of the country. In October 1401, the king marched to Bangor in northeast Wales, then west to Caernarfon in Gwynedd, then south, looting the abbey at Ystrad Fflur (Strata Florida) near Aberystwyth. Henry carried on to Llandovery, butchering any Welshman he caught, while Glyndwr's men picked off his outriders and made constant assaults on his baggage train. At Llandovery, Henry publicly tortured to death Llywelyn ap Gruffydd Fychan for refusing to betray Glyndŵr's whereabouts. Two of Llywelyn's sons were in the Welsh army. The king personally supervised the long disembowelling. A marvellous stainless steel memorial has been erected to this loyal Welshman outside Llandovery Castle - it is time that Wales celebrated its heroes - how many people know that this event occurred? Each year a small band commemorates his killing, just as happens at Cilmeri for Llywelyn II's death.

While his supporting bands harried the King's army, Glyndŵr unsuccessfully attacked Caernarfon and Harlech castles. Facing a professional army with mere volunteers, and holding no castles of consequence, Glyndŵr made overtures to the Scots, Irish and French for desperately needed assistance against their mutual 'mortal enemies, the Saxons.' He even asked Hotspur to try to arrange a peace with Henry IV. The King was inclined to agree, but Lord Grey hated Glyndŵr, and Lord Somerset wanted more Welsh estates, so they agreed to use peace talks as a device to capture Glyndŵr. Hotspur had returned to Wales, and fortunately refused the barons' request to be part of this treacherous charade.

1402 started well for Owain Glyndŵr. On 31 January, he appeared before Ruthin Castle, challenging Grey to battle. Grey led his men and was captured, trussed up and carried away to be imprisoned in Dolbadarn Castle. Perhaps Glyndŵr should have killed the man who was the cause of all his troubles, but he quickly ransomed him for £10,000. Glyndŵr desperately needed the money to pay for provisions and arms for his troops – they did not

**Glyndŵr wall painting -
Parliament House, Machynlleth**

loot their own lands, or rely upon foreign loans to fight. Some money was raised immediately, and Grey's son was given in surety for the rest. Raising this ransom effectively ruined Grey, who signed an agreement never again to attack the man he had made an outlaw.

If positions had been reversed, the Norman Lord Grey would have tortured Glyndŵr before hanging, drawing and quartering him. The Welsh did not believe in such bestiality. We can also see that when Glyndŵr captured Lord Mortimer in battle, Mortimer eventually married Glyndŵr's daughter in captivity, and died fighting for him against the English. Soon after, Glyndŵr survived an assassination attempt by his cousin, Hywel Sele of Nannau, probably on the orders of Henry IV. The armour under his jerkin deflected an arrow, and Hywel Sele was killed and said to be placed in a hollow oak tree. Throughout the rest of the year, Glyndŵr ravaged north

Wales (leaving alone Hotspur's estates in Denbigh), and then moved against Powys, controlled by the great Marcher Earls, the Mortimers.

On St Alban's Day, 22 June 1402 at the Battle of Pilleth (near Knighton), Edmund Mortimer's English knights and Herefordshire levies charged uphill at Glyndwr's army. However, Mortimer was using Welsh archers, who poured volley after volley of deadly arrows into the English charge, apparently in an unrehearsed expression of support for Glyndŵr. Much of western Herefordshire and Worcestershire was Welsh-speaking at this time. Up to 2,000 of Mortimer's troops were killed on the slopes. Rhys Gethin, Rhys the Fierce, had drawn up his men hidden behind the top of the hill, so Mortimer had underestimated the Welsh force of 4,000, as well as having been unable to control his Welsh archers. Mortimer was captured in the battle, but Henry IV accused him of treason and would not ransom him. Hotspur, Mortimer's brother-in-law, was incensed that a villain like Lord Grey could be ransomed, whereas Henry had set his mind against the innocent Mortimer.

In Shakespeare's *Henry IV Part I*, a horrified courtier recounts:

'.... the noble Mortimer,
Leading the men of Hereford to fight
Against the irregular and wild Glendower,
Was by the rude hands of that Welshman taken;
A thousand of his people butchered,
Upon whose dead corpse there was such misuse,
Such beastly, shameless transformation
By those Welsh women done, as may not be,
Without much shame, retold or spoken of.'

Forget this propaganda against Welsh women - after this event Henry IV passed legislation banning English men marrying Welsh women. Who would have wanted to marry such harridans if the atrocity stories were true? Mortimer's dead would have been stripped after the battle of their clothes and arms. The Welsh would not have had time to bury the English, just their own near Pilleth Church, as they were so near the English border. They would have left the battlefield as quickly as possible, carting their spoils into the heartlands, leaving the foxes, badgers, kites and assorted corvids to feast upon the corpses. One just has to see how quickly a dead lamb is disposed of.

Glyndŵr at last had freedom to do whatever he wanted - he attacked and burnt Abergavenny and Cardiff, and the ruins of his sacking of the Bishop's Palace at Llandaff in Cardiff can still be seen. He besieged Caernarfon, Cricieth and Harlech castles. This forced Henry IV to totally ignore his Scottish problems and assemble three armies, totalling a massive 100,000 men, on the Welsh borders. The bards had been singing of Glyndŵr supernatural powers, and during Henry's third invasion into Wales, appalling weather conditions forced all three armies to return to England by the end of September. It was thought at the time that Glyndŵr could command the elements, and well as possessing a magic Raven's Stone that made him invisible - even the English troops ascribed magical properties to this guerrilla partisan. Again, this is referred to in *Henry IV Part 1*:

'Three times hath Henry Bolingbroke made head
Against my power. Thrice from the banks of the Wye
And sandy-bottomed Severn have I sent
Him bootless home, and weather-beaten back.'

A contemporary entry in 1402 in the *Annales Henrici Quarti* tells us of the extent of Glyndŵrs reputation at this time: '[Glyndŵr] almost destroyed the King and his armies, by magic as it was thought, for from the time they entered Wales to the time they left, never did a gentle air breathe on them, but days turned into nights, rain mixed with snow and hail afflicted them with a cold beyond endurance.'

In 1402 Sir John Scudamore of Kentchurch in Hereford was actively defending Carreg Cennen Castle, during a year-long siege. In 1416 the repair bills record that the walls had been 'destroyed and thrown down by rebels'. He secretly married Alys, a daughter of Owain, and may have harboured and supported Owain. Some of his Hereford kinsmen, such as Philip Scudamore of Troy, fought for the Welsh.

In 1402, the imprisoned Edmund Mortimer married Owain Glyndŵr's daughter, Catrin. Mortimer's own nephew, the young Earl of March, had a far better claim to the English throne than Henry IV, and no doubt Glyndŵr was hoping that Henry Bolingbroke would be killed and Wales made safe with an English king as an ally. His major problem now was that Hotspur captured the Scots leader, the Earl of Douglas, at the battle of Homildon, securing England's northern border. With his Scottish problems solved, this allowed Henry IV to plan to finally subdue Wales. Glyndŵr, on his part, wanted complete control of Wales before Henry struck.

In 1403, Owain Glyndŵr kept up his blockade of the northern Welsh castles, while attacking Brecon and Dinefwr and trying to displace the Flemings from Pembrokeshire.

Glyndŵr able lieutenants were the three Rhys's; Rhys Gethin (the Fierce), Rhys Ddu (the Black), and Rhys ap Llewellyn. The latter had real reason to hate the invading English - it was his father, Llewelyn ap Gruffydd Fychan, who had been slowly killed in front of Henry IV at Llandovery in the dark days of 1401, for refusing to lead him to Glyndŵr. Later in 1403, Lord Thomas Carew beat a Welsh army at Laugharne. Glyndŵr also sadly learned of the deliberate demolition of his manors and estates at Sycharth and Glyndfrdwy by the Prince of Wales, Henry of Monmouth, who later won undying fame at Agincourt.

Hotspur, meanwhile, wanted to ransom the Earl of Douglas, but Henry demanded him as a prisoner to secure the ransom. Coupling this insult with the argument over Edmund Mortimer's ransom, Hotspur allied with Edmund Mortimer, Douglas and Glyndŵr to form an army near Chester. At the bloody Battle of Shrewsbury, Hotspur was killed, despite the havoc wrought by his Chester archers. This tragedy happened before he could link up with Glyndŵr, who had only reached Herefordshire. Henry then went to Northumberland to suppress a small uprising by Hotspur's father, Earl Percy of Northumberland, and Glyndŵr ravaged Herefordshire in Henry's absence. The enraged King Henry now passed legislation that any Welshman found in any border town would be executed. With a fourth invasion army, the king marched through South Wales to Carmarthen, but as with the previous invasion, Glyndŵr refused a frontal battle against overwhelming odds. Henry returned to England and within a week Glyndŵr had taken Cardiff, Caerphilly, Newport, Usk and Caerleon. Some French troops were assisting Glyndwr by now, and his army had grown to at least 10,000 men-at-arms.

By 1404, Owain Glyndŵr's main focus was the taking of the seemingly impregnable 'Iron Ring' of castles in North Wales. He won over the starving Harlech garrison by pardons or bribes, when it had only sixteen men left. The great castles of Cricieth and Aberystwyth then fell, and at Machynlleth, in The Parliament House, Owain Glyndŵr held his first Parliament**. Envoys came from France and Spain, and an ambassador was sent to France. Dafydd ap Llewelyn ap Hywel, Davy Gam (squint-eyed or lame) tried to assassinate him here for Henry IV, and was surprisingly imprisoned rather than cut to pieces. This again demonstrates the humane Welsh attitude of the times towards prisoners. Davy Gam was ransomed by the king and later was knighted by Henry V, as he lay dying at Agincourt. Another Welsh Parliament was held in Dolgellau in 1404.

Glyndŵr now took a small army to again pillage Herefordshire, but the Earl of Warwick captured his standard at Campstone Hill near Grosmont Castle. Glyndŵr just escaped capture. Fortunately, the English did not pursue the defeated troops, which regrouped and then beat Warwick at Craig-y-Dorth, three miles from Monmouth, and chased them back into the fortified town. Glyndŵr was in the southeast of Wales awaiting a French invasion fleet of 60 vessels under the Count of March, who for some reason never landed. Glyndŵr now returned to his court at Harlech. In Anglesey, Owain's forces were beaten at the battle of Rhosmeirch, and also lost Beaumaris castle.

In 1405, Rhys Gethin burned Grosmont Castle in Monmouthshire, but was then decisively beaten by Prince Henry, using Welsh archers. Glyndŵr sent his almost identical brother, Tudur, and his son Gruffydd to restore the situation by attacking Usk Castle, where Prince Henry had established himself. In the battle of Pwll Melin, two miles away, Owain's brother Tudur and Abbot John ap Hywel of Llantarnam were killed. Gruffydd ab Owain Glyndŵr was imprisoned in the Tower of London in disgusting conditions until he soon died. Three hundred prisoners were beheaded in front of the citizens of Usk, as an example *pour les autres*.

After the Welsh defeats at Grosmont and Usk, Henry now offered a pardon to those who renounced the rebellion, and thereby regained full control of southeast Wales. He then gathered an army of 40,000 thousand at Hereford for a fifth invasion to advance into mid and north-Wales. Another English force took Beaumaris and control of Anglesey in the far north.

 However, at this time, Archbishop Scrope of York led a rebellion in the north of England. Henry diverted his forces to Shipton Moor where he beat back the northern rebels. This gave Glyndŵr some breathing space, and he gathered ten thousand men in Pembrokeshire to

Model of Owain's seal with rampant lion

wait for an invasion fleet of 140 French ships. Around 5,000 Frenchmen arrived at Milford, joined with Glyndŵr and sacked the English/Fleming town of Haverfordwest, but could not take the castle. They next looted Carmarthen and then took over Glamorgan, leaving Glyndŵr back in control of most of Wales again.

In August 1405, he moved on to attack England, its first invasion since 1066, and seemingly unrecorded in English history books. Henry raced to Worcester to face the threat of Glyndŵr, who was camped on Woodbury Hill. There were some skirmishes, but Glyndŵr had no lines of supply, so he retreated back to Wales, following a scorched earth policy. Henry's starving army was forced to call off the pursuit, freezing as the bitter winter took hold. Again, the terrible weather was blamed upon Glyndwr's supernatural powers. This had been Henry's sixth invasion of Wales, and still Glyndwr seemed untouchable.

1406 began with a treaty between the dead Hotspur's remaining Percy family of Northumberland, Earl Mortimer and Glyndŵr. This 'Tripartite Indenture' divided England and Wales between the three Houses, with Glyndŵr possessing Wales and gaining a 'buffer zone' on its borders. At his second Machynlleth Parliament, Glyndŵr wrote to Charles VI of France, asking for recognition, support and a 'Holy Crusade' against Henry for pillaging abbeys and killing clergymen. In turn, Glyndŵr promised the recognition by St David's of the Avignon-based Pope Benedict XIII. (Welsh Parliaments were also held in Pennal, Harlech and Dolgellau). Glyndŵr also asked Papal permission to place two universities, one each in north and south Wales, to build a future for his country. This letter was signed 'Owain by the Grace of God, Prince of Wales', and is in the French National Archives.

However, Henry IV was wasting away through syphilis or leprosy, which enabled his son Henry, the 'English' Prince of Wales to take control of the Welsh campaigns. With a seventh English invasion, hee beat a Welsh army, killing yet another of Glyndŵr's sons in March, and retook south Wales, fining the landowners heavily to support his thrust into north Wales. North Wales, being fought over for five years, had neither financial nor manpower reserves to support Glyndŵr, but he still held around two thirds of the land of Wales, and castles at Aberystwyth and Harlech. At his time, he almost disappears from history except for bardic references of him roaming the country.

In 1407, Prince Henry besieged Aberystwyth Castle with seven cannon. One, 'The King's Gun' weighed four and a half tons. Rhys Ddu held out and Henry returned to England. Glyndŵr reinforced the castle, while England unfortunately signed a peace treaty with France. In this year, Owain's great ally, Louis of Orleans, was murdered in mysterious circumstances in Paris, which was thought to be the work of English spies.

1408 saw another blow for Glyndŵr. His ally, the old Earl of Northumberland, Hotspur's father, was killed at the Battle of Braham Moor by Prince Henry's forces. There was now an eighth invasion of war-torn Wales, within nine years. The Prince re-entered Wales, finally bombarded Aberystwyth into submission, and by 1409 had also taken Harlech, Glyndŵr's last bastion, capturing his wife and family. Edmund Mortimer, the former enemy who became his son-in-law in captivity, died (probably of starvation) in Harlech, fighting for Glyndŵr. Owain had just managed to escape from Harlech as the besiegers moved in. It must have been a difficult decision to leave his family there, while he tried to round up support rather than be cornered.

A sad footnote has been the discovery noted in John Lloyd's 1931 *Owen Glendower*: – he 'left behind him in the castle one little personal relic which has recently been unearthed in the course of excavations, viz. a gilt bronze boss from a set of horse harness, bearing the four lions rampant which he had assumed as Prince of Wales'. The four lions passant, counter-changed in gold and red, were the ancient arms of the princes of Gwynedd. Owain had altered them to be rampant, erect and fighting. Glyndŵr was more a descendant of the Houses of Deheubarth and Powys than Gwynedd, but he had needed that provenance, which in effect died out with the vicious assassination of Owain Lawgoch, to be accepted throughout Wales.

The last gasp of Glyndŵr revolt occurred near Welshpool Castle when a raiding party under Phillip Scudamore of Troy, Rhys Tudur and Rhys Ddu was beaten and the leaders captured. After the usual revolting, slow, barbarous executions, Scudamore's head was placed on a spike at Shrewsbury, Rhys ap Tudur's at London, and Rhys Ddu's at Chester. This disgusting ritual torture was never practised by the Welsh when they captured prisoners, but Normans and Plantagenets believed that payment to the church would get them to heaven, whatever their sins.

In 1413, Henry of Monmouth succeeded as Henry V, and in 1415 offered a pardon to Glyndŵr and any of his men. In 1416, he tried again, through Glyndŵr's remaining son Maredudd, who himself accepted a pardon in 1421. It thus appears that Glyndŵr was still alive a few years after his last recorded sighting. Gruffydd Young, in the Council of Constance in France, was still working for Owain Glyndŵr in 1415, stating that Wales was a nation that should have a vote in ending the papal schism.

Some say Owain died in a cave in Pumlumon (Plynlimon), where it all started, mourning the death of all but one of his six sons. Other believed he ended his days with his daughter Alice and her husband John Scudamore in Golden Valley in Herefordshire. The present owner of the Great Hall of Kentchurch, Jan Scudamore, has been besieged with people asking permission to search her estate for the remains of Glyndwr. Many identify him with Siôn Cent of Kentchurch, a poet, magician and mystic whose grave can still be seen, half in and half out of Grosmont church. Other stories have him dying at Monnington Court, near Kentchurch, at Monnington-on-Wye in 1415, in the deep oakwoods of Glamorgan and on a mountain ridge in Snowdonia. The bards raided Arthurian legend to put him sleeping with his men in a cave to be awakened again (like Lawgoch) in Wales' hour of greatest need. One bard stated that Glyndŵr 'went into hiding on St Matthew's Day in Harvest (1415) and thereafter his hiding place was unknown. Very many say that he died: the seers maintain that he did not'. Probably he died at one of his daughter's houses, at Scudamore's mansion or at nearby Monnington, where he may have been disguised as a shepherd, upon 16 September 1415, aged 61, almost exactly fifteen years from the start of his war on September 20th, 1400. In 2000, the Scudamore family of Monnington Court revealed that Glyndŵr had been buried on their land, and that the family had divulged to always keep his secret.

Glyndŵr's greatest problem had been that he was up against the greatest soldier of his age, Harry of Monmouth, who within a few years was to win at Agincourt with Welsh archers, and be recognised as the future King of France. Henry cut his teeth against a massively under-resourced Glyndŵr, who had no incomes to pay his troops and relied on volunteers against a vastly superior professional force. However, Owain could still point to a career where he set up his own law-courts and chancery, tried to form the first Welsh universities, summoned parliaments, sent envoys to foreign courts and nominated bishops. However, this last battle between the 'Welsh' Prince of Wales and the 'French-Plantagenet' Prince of Wales could have only one ending.

Repressive laws were enacted after the rebellion to stop any future threat from Wales to the English crown. No one with Welsh parents could buy land near the Marcher towns, own weapons, become citizens of any towns or hold any offices. 'In lawsuits involving a Welshman and an Englishman, the Englishman decided the verdict and the sentence. Gatherings of Welsh people were forbidden, and an Englishman marrying a Welsh woman became legally Welsh, forfeiting all his rights of citizenship. No Welshman could be a juror.' These and many more impositions, on top of the already harsh regime of the Statute of Rhuddlan of 1282, ensured Henry Tudor great popular support in his move to gain the crown of England in 1485. In fact, as shown in this author's biographies of Owain, Richard III and Jasper Tudor, Wales was never settled in the seventy years from Owain's death.

Massive taxes were raised to pay for the invasions of the two Henry's, but Welshmen were not allowed to help each other to harvest their fields, causing major food shortages. If merchants of any towns were robbed in Wales, and the property was not returned within a week, they could retaliate upon any Welshman that they could seize. The best summary of Glyndwr is by the noted English historian, G.M.Trevelyan: 'this wonderful man, an attractive and unique figure in a period of debased and selfish politics'. The French historian, Henri Martin, calls Glyndŵr a man of courage and genius. Most English encyclopaedias do not mention him - one of the truly great, principled and forward-thinking men in British history. Welsh schools have not taught the history of Glyndŵr in any depth whatsoever, for over a hundred years, but his name still inspires Welshmen all over the world.

J.E. Lloyd puts Glyndŵr into his proper perspective in the Welsh national psyche:

'Throughout Wales, his name is the symbol for the vigorous resistance of the Welsh spirit to tyranny and alien rule and the assertion of a national character which finds its fitting expression in the Welsh language... For the Welshmen of all subsequent ages, Glyndŵr has been a national hero, the first, indeed, in the country's history to command the willing support alike of north and south, east and west, Gwynedd and Powys, Deheubarth and Morgannwg. He may with propriety be called the father of modern Welsh nationalism.'

Cofiwch Glyndŵr means 'Remember Glyndwr' and is a slogan for the Welsh Nationalist movement - he still lives. Glyndwr is the undefeated symbol of Wales, with his red dragon of Cadwaladr - he is the equivalent of Jeanne d'Arc and William Wallace and el Cid for Welsh people everywhere. After Owain Lawgoch's (Yvain de Galles) assassination in 1378 on the orders of the English crown, the royal House of Gwynedd was extinct. Glyndŵr was then the only 'head of Wales', as he was the direct descendant and link between the dynasties of Powys and Deheubarth. Glyndŵr symbolically adopted Owain Lawgoch's heraldic device of the lions of Gwynedd. As his ambassador had told the French king, Glyndwr was the 'rightful' heir of Lawgoch, or the princes of Gwynedd and Wales. Owain Glyndŵr united Wales both politically and symbolically.

Although Glyndŵr had briefly won political, cultural and ecclesiastical independence, before final defeat and the harshness of the laws of a revenging English king, the wars had been a personal disaster for him. His closest brother Tudur had died at the Battle of Pwll Melyn in 1405. His son Gruffydd was captured there, and spent the remainder of his years imprisoned in the Tower of London and Nottingham Castle. Some sources say that he died of the plague in the Tower of London in 1410 - he just vanished from history, like so many other captured descendants of Welsh princes. Glyndŵr's wife, two of his daughters and three grand-daughters were taken into imprisonment after the fall of Harlech Castle and soon conveniently died. His son-in-law, Edmund Mortimer, with a good claim to the English crown, died at Harlech. Mortimer's wife, Owain's daughter Catrin, died in prison with two of her daughters, and all were buried in St Swithin's Church in London around 1413. Her son Lionel, Owain's grandson and a claimant for both Welsh and English crowns, died, where or when is unrecorded. Owain Glyndŵr's closest lieutenants and comrades-in-arms, Rhys Ddu, Rhys ap Llywelyn, Rhys Gethin and Phillip Scudamore had been tortured to death.

It appears that only one relative survived the carnage, his son Maredudd, who had hidden with him when the rebellion was crushed. When Maredudd ab Owain eventually accepted the King's pardon upon 8 April 1421, it had been twenty years and six months since Owain Glyndŵr had proclaimed himself Prince of Wales. These two decades of fighting against overwhelming odds, of reclaiming Cymru from the Normans, are neglected in all British history books. This British hero has been excised from the history of Britain even more effectively than William Wallace was.

Glyndŵr had no funeral elegy from the bards – he was probably a broken man – but in Welsh mythology his disappearance from history, rather than his capture and execution, gave the poets and gives the nation a hope for the future – Glyndŵr is THE Welsh hero par excellence. This is a story of culture, humanity, nobility, treachery, courage, bitter defeat, glorious resurgence and a mysterious finale. Can anyone think of a better story for a Hollywood epic? It was not until 1948 that a Parliamentary Act, declaring Glyndŵr to be a proscribed traitor, was repealed. Perhaps a blockbuster film could start with this scene.

Cymdeithas Owain Glyndŵr attempted a geophysical survey at the mound at the deserted village of Monnington Straddel, near Monningon Court Farm, an ancestral seat of the Scudamores in Herefordshire's Golden

Valley. Sir John Scudamore of Kentchurch, a direct descendant of Sir John Scudamore and Alice ferch Owain Glyndŵr, gave affirmation of the site. A painting by Jan van Eyck at Kentchurch may be of the mystic poet-priest Sion Cent or his contemporary Owain Glyndŵr.

The Sunday Times ran a poll of 100 world leaders, artists and scientists, published on 28 November, 1999, asking for the names of the most significant figures in the last 1000 years. In 7th place was Owain Glyndŵr. (The list started with Gutenberg, Shakespeare, Caxton, da Vinci, Elizabeth I and Faraday in the first six places. Newton, Lincoln and Galileo followed Glyndŵr in the Top 10). Thus even today he is regarded above Churchill, Mandela, Darwin, Bill Gates and Einstein. Among the voters were President Clinton and Boris Yeltsin. Evan Fidel Castro paid tribute to Glyndŵr in pioneering guerilla warfare against incredible odds.

* The author is not very convinced that many of these attacks on holiday homes were carried out by Meibion Glyndŵr - at this time MI5 was at its most paranoid, and like the Brecon 'bomb-factory' incident, the political inspiration for these events seems to have come the area around Westminster.

** The author attended and contributed to the celebrations at Cardiff, Machynlleth and Corwen to mark the 600th anniversary of Wales' first Parliament and Glyndŵr's War of Independence, where the many literary and musical events were shamefully ignored by politicians and the media. There is a campaign to reinstitute a Welsh Parliament at Machynlleth. The last one was never officially dissolved. A poll run by the Welsh Assembly Government on Wales greatest hero was manipulated (according to its organisers) to show that Aneurin Bevan received more votes than Owain. This shameful act is described in my biography of Owain – Labour runs Wales, and hates any form of nationalism, as it is controlled by its HQ at Millbank. The Assembly Government has no understanding of how tourism is our only remaining industry, and that Owain is our greatest hero – look what the film *Braveheart* has done for Scotland. Wales has fewer tourists than the West Country – many just passing through on their way to Ireland.

Footnotes:
1. From Thomas Pennant's *Tour in Wales* of 1778 we are told that Glyndŵr's father was Gruffudd Fychan and his mother Elena '(of royal blood and from whom he afterwards claimed the throne of Wales). She was eldest daughter of Thomas ap Llywelyn ap Owain, by his wife Elinor Goch, or Elinor the red, daughter and heiress of Catherine, one of the daughters of Llywelyn last Prince of Wales. She probably was concealed by some friend on the death of her father, otherwise the jealousy of (King) Edward about the succession would have made her share the fate of her sister (Gwenllian) who perforce took the veil in the convent of Shrewsbury.'

2. Glyndŵr's death date has remained a mystery, but I came across three separate sources with the same date. T.J. Llywelyn Prichard wrote *The Heroines of Welsh History* in 1854, in which he quotes the Rev. Thomas Thomas, vicar of Aberporth writing *The Memoirs of Owain Glyndŵr*. 'Our hero terminated his hopes and fears on 20th of September, 1415, on the eve of St Matthew, in the 61st year of his age, at the house of one of his daughters; but whether of his daughter Scudamore or of his daughter Monnington is uncertain. Prichard also mentions *Glyndŵr's Life* in the *Cambrian Plutarch* by John Humphreys Parry, but I have been unable as yet to source either book. Marie Trevelyan of Llanilltud Fawr wrote *The Land of Arthur* in 1895, dedicated to Llywelyn ap Gruffudd, and states that Glyndŵr was born on 28 May 1354 (so we also have a birthdate!), and on 20 September 1415, this celebrated 15th century leader of the Welsh people, and last hero of Welsh independence, died in Herefordshire. According to MSS of the Harleian Collection, 'Glyndŵr's body, which was entire and of "goodly stature" was discovered at Monnington in that shire, during the restoration of the church in 1680. But his resting place remains unmarked and unrecognised.' The May birth date gives festival opportunities, and the 20 September date gives feast-week opportunities to fit in with Glyndŵr Day of 16 September. A 'penny booklet' recently acquired by the author is *Hanes Owain Glyndŵr, Tywysog Cymru,* by Thomas Pennant o'r Downing, printed by H. Humphries at Caernarfon around 1900, gives the same death date of September 20th, 1415. It points out that the king sent Sir Gilbert Talbot from Porchester to arrange a pardon for Glyndŵr and his supporters in 1415, but Owain's death delayed its implementation, until it was agreed with Meredydd ab Owain Glyndŵr in 1416.

WILLIAM HERBERT 1423 – 27 July 1469

WILLIAM AP WILLIAM AP THOMAS, EARL OF PEMBROKE, THE FIRST STATESMAN OF A NEW ERA

He was the son of William ap Thomas ap Gwilym ap Jankyn, a minor member of the Welsh gentry, who had married Elizabeth Bloet, widow of Sir James Berkeley around 1406. She was the only daughter and heiress of Sir John Bloet, whose family had held Raglan since 1174. Her son James owned Raglan Castle, which Wiliam ap Thomas held as a tenant. Elizabeth died in 1420, and in 1425 James agreed that William ap Thomas, who had sided with the English against Owain Glyndŵr, could hold the castle for the rest of his life. By this time, William ap Thomas had married Gwladys ferch Syr Dafydd Gam (a lady called by the bard Lewis Glyn Cothi, *y seren of Efenni*, 'the star of Abergafenni'). 'Davy' Gam had not only tried to kill Glyndŵr, but had been ransomed by the king, fought at Agincourt, and was said to have been knighted by the king as he lay dying. The first husband of Gwladys, Sir Roger Vaughan, had also died in 1415 at Agincourt.

181

By 1421, William ap Thomas was steward of the lordship of Abergafenni (Abergavenny). By his two marriages, William had acquired lands and wealth from heiresses, and was knighted by Henry VI when the king was just five years old. It was unusual for a Welshman to be knighted, and this border family was seen very much as a 'buffer' against future Welsh insurgencies. William ap Thomas was now known as *Y Marchog Glas o Went*, 'The Blue Knight of Gwent', and in 1432 bought Raglan Castle outright for 1,000 marks from his stepson James. He rebuilt the castle on a grand scale to match what he had seen while fighting in France in the same contingent as Davy Gam and Sir Roger Vaughan. Through his family connections to the Duke of York, William became the chief steward of his estates in Wales in 1442-1443. As Sheriff of the

The remains of William Herbert's Raglan Castle

counties of Cardigan, Carmarthen and Glamorgan, William was now a powerful man. He died in London in 1445, being buried in the Benedictine priory church of Abergafenni. His widow Gwladys died in 1454. The legend is that she was so loved that 3,000 knights, nobles and peasants followed her body from Coldbrook House to the Herbert Chapel at St Mary's Priory Church. The mighty Raglan Castle passed to William ap William.

William ap William Anglicised his name owing to royal wishes, and became known as William Herbert after a remote Norman ancestor. The Herberts became an extremely important dynasty in Britain. He married Anne, of the nearby Yorkist Devereux family, and they had four children. A prominent Yorkist, he fought in France for Henry VI's doomed claim to the French crown, and was raised to the peerage as Lord Herbert of Raglan by Edward IV for his help in usurping the kingship from the mentally troubled Henry VI. For a Welshman born of Welsh blood, a peerage was unique in these troubled times of the Wars of the Roses. (Jasper and Edmund Tudor had been made earls of Pembroke and Richmond by Henry VI, but they were his half-brothers, half French and half Welsh). Herbert's power in holding Wales for the Yorkists enabled Edward to put down rebellion in the rest of his kingdom, and Herbert's men captured Edmund Tudor in Wales, who died in prison soon after. However, Jasper Tudor, Earl of Pembroke, was Henry VI's half-brother from Owen Tudor's marriage to Henry V's widow Catherine de Valois. Jasper had custody of his nephew Henry Tudor, Earl of Richmond. In 1468, William Herbert took Tudor, the Lancastrian claimant to the English throne, and confined him with his own children at Raglan

Castle. Jasper fled to Brittany, and William was rewarded with the Jasper's title of Earl of Pembroke.

To some, Herbert now became the *mab darogan* The bard Guto'r Glyn urged Herbert to now unite Wales and free it from English rule: 'Na ad arglwydd swydd i Sais / Na'l bardwn i un bwrdais; / Barna'n iawn, brenin ein iaith / Bwrw yn tan ein braint unwaith ... / Dwg Forgannwg a Gwynedd / Gwna'n un o Gonwy i Nedd.' – 'My Lord, don't give the English office / Not pardon to a burgess; / King of our language*, be aware / Their rights were once thrown in the fire... / Join Glamorgan and Gwynedd, / Unify from Conwy to Neath.'

William Herbert's rise to power paralleled that of the Woodville family, the relations of Edward IV's wife Elizabeth. In 1466, Herbert's son and heir married Elizabeth's sister, and their daughter Maude was put forward as a possible bride for Henry Tudor, to bring him into the Yorkist fold. 'Black William' had unbroken success fighting for the usurper king Edward IV, and replaced Warwick the 'Kingmaker' as Edward's favourite, leading to Warwick changing sides. With the Lancastrian rising of 1469, Edward IV commissioned the Herberts to suppress it. The Lancastrian army was superior to Herbert's but the Welsh refused to be pushed back. On 23 July, a cavalry force led by the Earl of Devon, and by Richard Herbert, William's brother met a superior northern contingent, and after fierce fighting, fell back. They joined Herbert's main force at Banbury. Edward did not reinforce Herbert, and Lord Rivers refused to help. After heavy casualties on both sides on 25 July, an advance party of the disaffected Richard, Earl of Warwick suddenly appeared on the scene and sided with the Lancastrians. The Yorkist Earl of Devon** had not come to the battle, leaving William Herbert, Earl of Pembroke, and his brother Sir Richard Herbert of Coldbrook, alone at the Battle of Banbury, on 26 July 1469.

The chronicler Hall wrote: 'Pembroke behaved himself like a hardy knight and expert captain; but his brother Sir Richard Herbert so valiantly acquitted himself that with his poleaxe in his hand he twice by fine force passed through the battle of his adversaries and returned without mortal wound. When the Welsh were on the point of victory John Clapham, esquire, servant of the earl of Warwick, mounted on the eastern hill with only 500 men and gathered all the rascals of Northampton and other villages about, bearing before them the standard of the Earl of Warwick with the white bear, crying A Warwick! A Warwick!' Now terribly outnumbered, the 18,000-strong Welsh army of the Herberts was defeated, around 170 Welsh men of note killed and the Herbert brothers unlawfully executed by the vindictive Warwick. They were summarily beheaded at Northampton upon 27 July.

William had pleaded with Warwick the 'Kingmaker' to save Richard. Hall wrote: 'Entreaty was made for Sir Richard Herbert both for his goodly person which excelled all men there, and also for his chivalry on the field of battle. The earl when he should lay down his head on the block said to John Conyers and Clapham "Let me die for I am old, but save my brother which is young, lusty and hardy, mete and apt to serve the greatest prince in Christendom." This battle ever since has been, and yet is a continual grudge between the northernmen and the Welsh'. Sir Richard's body was immediately brought to the Herbert Chapel, and he was interned in the place meant for his brother William. The tomb-effigies can be seen today at Abergafenni. Herbert's half-brother, Tomas ap Rhosier, was also slain. His home was the mansion of Hergest, in Welsh-speaking Herefordshire. Another patron of bards, he was the keeper of the great *Llyfr Coch Hergest*, 'The Red Book of Hergest'.

The cream of Welsh aristocracy was killed at Banbury (also known as the Battle of Edgecote Moor). Guto'r Glyn wrote 'Let us hasten to the North to avenge our country. My nation is destroyed, now that the earl is slain'. And Lewis Glyn Cothi said 'this greatest of battles was lost by treachery; at Banbury dire vengeance fell upon Wales'. H.T. Evans called Herbert 'The first statesman of a new era, and the most redoubtable antagonist of the last and most formidable of the old.'

* William Herbert was said to be more fluent in Welsh than English, and a noted patron of bards and harpists. On his death, the bards sand 'Raglan was our tongue's vineyard'.

** The Earl of Devon was taken in Somerset and beheaded at Kenilworth alongside Rivers. Warwick seized King Edward near Kenilworth. Edward IV later managed to escaped and again depose Henry VI. Warwick was slain at the battle of Barnet, on Easter Day, 1471. With Edward's forces was the young son of William, the new Earl of Pembroke. Guto'r Glyn called for national rejoicing and said that the death of Warwick was just retribution for Herbert's execution.

JASPER TUDOR c.1431 – 25/26 December 1495

DYNASTY-MAKER, JASPER AB OWAIN AB MAREDUDD, EARL OF PEMBROKE, THE ONLY LORD TO FIGHT FROM THE FIRST TO THE LAST BATTLE OF THE WARS OF THE ROSES

Henry IV spent most of his reign fighting Owain Glyndŵr, and was succeeded by his son Henry of Monmouth, who died of dysentery in France shortly after. Henry V left a young attractive widow, Catherine of Valois, and a 9-month-old son Henry VI. With a 20-year-old French widow, distrusted by the English nobles, and a 9-month-old king, surrounded by royal dukes, there was bound to be conflict. A regency government was formed under the dukes of Bedford and Gloucester, and the young king was soon taken from the queen to be brought up by the Earl of Warwick and learn to ride, shoot and be educated. There were bitter arguments about who could marry Henry V's widow, as all dukes knew that whoever controlled the king could become king or make their descendants kings. The Beaufort family, led by the Duke of Somerset wanted him to marry Catherine of Valois, and this was violently opposed by Duke Richard of York. Lancastrian Henry VI, the boy-king, was the grandson of Henry IV the first Lancastrian usurper, and was opposed by Yorkist interests.

The Regency Council would not allow Catherine to marry a nobleman – and around 1428-29, when her son the king was 6 or 7, there began a relationship with a young Welshman in her employ – Owain ap Maredudd – known to us as Owain Tudor. Her son did not know, and by 1431 she was married, secretly, and had two more sons, Edmund Tudor and his younger brother Jasper*.

The boys were born at the bishops' palaces of the Bishop of London and the Bishop of Ely, away from the city. Both bishops were friends of the queen, and it seems that the young Henry VI was not aware of his half-brothers until 1432. His mother was visiting him when her waters broke at Westminster Abbey, and the baby boy, Owen, was taken into the care of monks and brought up as a monk at Westminster. The king's mother's new husband was now recognised, and Owain ap Maredudd ap Tydier was given limited rights as a citizen, and a little land by his wife. However, Catherine of Valois died in childbirth in 1437, and Owain had no friends at

Jaspar Tudor and Katherine Woodville

court. Nobles wished to punish this common Welsh upstart who had married Henry V's widow. Jasper and Edmund were taken into care of the Abbess of Barking from the ages of 6-11, while Owain was in and out of prison, trying to escape, until in 1439 the king pardoned his stepfather of whatever offences he had committed.

The brothers Edmund and Jasper were known as Edmund and Jasper ap Meredith ap Tydier at this point. In 1442, both were taken to see their half-brother the king for the first time. The young the king had no family – Henry V and Catherine of Valois were dead, and he had no siblings, so he now gave his stepfather lands, and ensured that the brothers were taught by the best priests and had military training. There was massive

185

unrest in the country, jostling for position among the nobles, and more lands were lost in France, but in 1452, the Tudor brothers, aged around 20-21 to the king's 31, were ennobled – Edmund was made Earl of Richmond and Jasper Earl of Pembroke.

They were granted estates, and had their own households at court – Jasper's close advisers at this time stayed loyal to him through the following troubles. In 1455 they were keeping the king's peace in Wales, and were jointly granted the rich wardship of the 12-year-old Margaret Beaufort, the only heiress of the dead Duke of Somerset, who may have been killed on the orders of York. Edmund, as oldest brother, married her and gained great estates and incomes.

However, that year, upon 22 May 1455 first battle of St Albans took place. York and Warwick captured Henry VI and killed the new Duke of Somerset. Deliberate policy began to kill captured nobles instead of ransom them. Edmund was in Wales, fighting the Herbert and Devereux and Vaughan Yorkist families, and taking York's castles of Carmarthen and Carreg Cennen. Jasper either escaped St Albans battlefield or was freed by York, as he had previously sided with York in his attempts to stop corruption in the country. It was the start of the Wars of the Roses. York replaced the dead Somerset at Constable of England, and Jasper supported York's party against corruption, a moderate trying to link the Lancastrian and Yorkist parties. York in turn courted Jasper, the king's half-brother, but Edmund Tudor kept out of politics.

Edmund married Margaret Beaufort in November 1455, but was captured and imprisoned in Carmarthen Castle, and died soon after from wounds or disease. Jasper now moved forever to the king's party.

In 1457 the dead Edmund's son Henry Tudor was born in Jasper's Pembroke Castle, and Jasper, Earl of Pembroke, aged 26 became the protector of Margaret Beaufort (aged 13 or 15) and his nephew Henry. Jasper was now often at court, trying to reconcile the interests of the new protector, York, and Henry VI's new queen, who was acting on behalf of her mentally unstable husband. Jasper knew that he had to safeguard his nephew Henry Tudor, and arranged for Margaret Beaufort to marry Stafford, the second son of the Duke of Buckingham. He also allied closely with Gruffydd ap Nicholas of Dinefwr, the leading lord in southwest Wales, strengthening his own position.

Jasper now began repairing castles, seemingly foreseeing the massive troubles ahead. In 1457 he organised new walls for Tenby, and made it his headquarters to return Wales to order. He took Edmund's place, working in Wales and restoring the king's castles to royal hands, fighting Herbert, Devereux and Vaughan, and in 1459 he took Carreg Cennen, Carmarthen and Aberystwyth Castles from York. He concentrated upon Harlech, Tenby and Pembroke as strategically important in any wars to connect with England, France, Burgundy, Ireland, Scotland, Flanders and Brittany. They were to be escape routes and sources of supplies and support. He also arranged for Margaret Beaufort to marry Stafford, the son of Buckingham – ensuring her safety. The sons of Gruffydd ap Nicholas, and especially a grandson, Rhys ap Thomas, were henceforth crucial to Henry Tudor taking the crown. Jasper was not thinking of the kingship at all for another two decades at least, just the survival of his only family – his nephew and sister-in-law. Hatred of the French queen and sympathy for the more efficient and people-friendly York led to resumed fighting, in 1459, at Blore Heath in Cheshire, a Lancastrian defeat. The Marcher Lords of Pembroke, Brecon and the Welsh borders would be of incredible importance in the following wars which lasted until 1487.

1460 saw the stand-off at Ludford Bridge, Ludlow. Buckingham and the Lancastrians won as Yorkists deserted Salisbury, Warwick and York. In the same year, Jasper took Denbigh Castle after 3-month siege. At Northampton, Buckingham was betrayed by defection of Lord Grey of Ruthin, and Warwick's Yorkists won. Henry VI was taken prisoner, and Jasper helped his queen, Margaret of Anjou, escape to France via his Denbigh, Harlech and Pembroke castles. Jasper was ordered by York to surrender the Welsh castles and refused. Herbert and Devereux were sent to defeat him, while York's son Edward, Earl of March was sent to Shrewsbury and the Marches to raise more troops to take Jasper.

In December 1460 York was defeated at Worksop and killed at Wakefield, along with his son Rutland and Salisbury (the father of Warwick). Jasper raised a Welsh army to try and join the victorious Lancastrian northern army, but met Edward, Earl of March, now Duke of York after his father's death. The Battle of Mortimer's Cross occurred near Wigmore Castle in 1461, where Jasper, with Wiltshire and Owen Tudor fought York, Herbert, Devereux and Vaughan. The Yorkists won and Jasper's father Owen Tudor and other Lancastrian captains were executed at Hereford after the battle. Jasper escaped and began writing letters from Tenby to rally resistance across North Wales. Most of South Wales was now controlled by Herbert and Devereux.

Next, Margaret of Anjou and Somerset defeated Warwick at the Second Battle of St Albans and Henry VI was released. Warwick escaped the battle to join Edward of York, who was crowned Edward IV in London.

In 1461 at Ferrybridge, the Yorkist vanguard was defeated but the Lancastrian Clifford killed, and it was followed by Britain's bloodiest battle at Towton, fought in a blinding snowstorm. 28,000 men died, and the only Lancastrian resistance left was Jasper Tudor, holding Tenby, Denbigh, Pembroke and Harlech castles. Jasper's estates and titles were confiscated by Edward IV and given to Herbert. Tenby and Pembroke surrendered, and at Pembroke, Henry Tudor, Earl of Richmond, aged four, was taken into the wardship of William Herbert of Raglan.

Denbigh held out until January 1462, while Harlech only surrendered in 1468, with Jasper managing to get in and out several times via its Watergate Tower. The castle is now a mile from the sea, which might prove to some experts that the climate has always changed.

In a last throw of the dice, Jasper and Exeter were defeated at Twthill outside Caernarfon Castle, and Jasper escaped in disguise to Scotland. Because of his victories, Edward IV began favouring Herbert instead of Warwick, and Herbert paid for the marriage rights of the 6-year-old Henry Tudor, wanting him to marry Maud, his daughter. In April 1462 Margaret of Anjou fled from Scotland to Brittany, where she was met by Jasper, who took her to his cousin, the new King Louis of France. He then sailed to Scotland. Jasper was continuously travelling for the next decade between Brittany, Scotland, Ireland, Wales, France, Flanders, Burgundy and he North of England – the only spark left in the Lancastrian cause.

Carreg Cennen was taken and despoiled in May 1462, while Jasper left France to again see Henry VI in Scotland.

Returned to France - Jasper was in talks with King Louis and Margaret – he secured French support.

The Northern Campaign of 2,000 French soldiers - took Bamburgh, Dunstanburgh, Warkworth and Alnwick. The greatest medieval army assembled – 39 peers (of 54) - was led by Edward IV northwards. Henry VI, Margaret and most of the French escaped to Scotland. Jasper tried to raise the sieges of the great Northern castles, but failed. He managed to get into the besieged Bamburgh Castle, but Jasper and Somerset were surrounded by 10,000 men and great cannon led to its agreed surrender. Somerset accepted pardon and helped the Yorkists, but Jasper would not accept and was escorted to Scotland in January 1463, joining the king and queen.

Margaret of Anjou now returned to her small court in Bar, Anjou, with around 200 exiles – only 13 were knights or above.

In 1463, Jasper returned to Scotland to join Somerset, then organised help from Brittany while his followers across Wales staged small risings, helped by the survival of Harlech. Somerset was beaten by Yorkists at Hedgeley Moor in 1464, and Percy (Northumberland) was killed. Somerset was then executed after another Lancastrian defeat at Hexham, while Henry VI fled into hiding. Lancastrian resistance had again collapsed. 1465 Henry VI was captured and taken to the Tower. Killing him at this point would have thrown support behind his young son Edward of Westminster. Edward IV needed both dead.

In 1466 Jasper's Harlech garrison was making sorties as far as Wrexham, and in 1467 Jasper crossed Wales, then returned to France. In 1468 Louis in France at last took up Jasper's cause and took him into his direct employ, because of fear of Edward IV's treaties with Burgundy and Brittany. Louis provided Jasper with three ships and he landed at or near Harlech. 2,000 men flocked to his banner, and Jasper burnt Denbigh walled town but could not retake castle. He then tried to raise the Herbert siege of Harlech in 1468, but Richard Herbert scattered Jasper's force near Caernarfon and Harlech at last surrendered – a punitive campaign and executions across North Wales followed. Jasper escaped to France, from Tŷ Gwyn at Barmouth.

Warwick had been disaffected by the rise of the King's wife's family, the Woodvilles, and also the Herberts. The king's younger brother Clarence was also unhappy as Edward blocked his marriage. 1469 Warwick's supporters were in open rebellion, and Clarence married Warwick's daughter against Edward's wishes. Herbert's army was defeated at Banbury (Edgcote) and both Herberts were executed. Henry Tudor was rescued from the battle and taken to Weobley Castle. He now became *mab darogan* to Herbert's supporters. Edward IV was captured, but released as there was fighting across England and Wales.

Jasper was in service of Louis XI at the royal court, October 1469 - September 1470, being paid £100 a month, around £57,000 today. Warwick inspired Welles' Rebellion, and Warwick and King Edward's brother Clarence fled to France, where Jasper and Louis managed to reconciliate Margaret of Anjou, the 11-year-old Prince Edward of Westminster, Warwick the 'Kingmaker' and Edward IV's brother Clarence. Jasper, Warwick, Clarence and Oxford now sailed from Normandy to Dartmouth and Plymouth. Jasper headed to Wales to raise an army, and Edward IV and Richard of Gloucester fled to Burgundy. Warwick entered London and Henry VI was recrowned in 1470 – the 'Readeption'. Henry Tudor was taken to see Henry VI at Westminster, and Jasper was regranted all his titles and wealth.

However, Edward returned, Clarence switched back to his brother's side and Jasper was sent to Hereford to raise troops. At Barnet in 1471 Warwick was killed and Oxford escaped. Margaret of Anjou and Edward of Westminster returned to England, not knowing of the Barnet loss. Jasper rode to join her and promised a Welsh army to join the Lancastrian survivors from Barnet. However, Margaret was prevented by floods from joining Jasper at Gloucester. At Tewkesbury, Somerset and Edward of Westminster were killed by Edward IV, Richard of Gloucester and Clarence.

Roger Vaughan, the man responsible for Owen Tudor's execution, was sent to kill Jasper and take Henry at Chepstow, but Jasper killed him, avenging his father, before escaping to Pembroke Castle with his nephew Henry Tudor. After Tewkesbury, Margaret of Anjou was captured and Henry VI murdered.

Henry Tudor was now the only adult, at just 14 years old, with a Lancastrian claim to the crown, and Edward IV was desperate to take him. Jasper and Henry were surrounded at Pembroke Castle for 8 days by Morgan ap Thomas. They escaped when the siege was raised by his brother Dafydd ap Thomas. Their younger brother, Rhys ap Thomas was crucial to Jasper's success at Bosworth. The two earls, of Pembroke and Richmond, were hidden by the White family in its Tenby cellars, sailing for France and safety on 2 June 1471.

The earls were wrecked in independent Brittany, and see as immediate value. Duke François could use them to ensure English support against France/Burgundy/Holy Roman Empire. Edward IV made constant offers of arms and money to take Jasper and Edward, as did Louis of France. Louis, François and Jasper were all around 40 years old and had known each other for years. The earls were separated, and moved away from the coast, to prevent any kidnap attempt by France, England or even Burgundy or the Holy Roman Empire taking both of them. Henry's widowed mother Lady Margaret Beaufort now married Lord Thomas Stanley, one of King Edward's most powerful supporters.

Diplomats from England came on 6 occasions to try and take Jasper and Henry back with them to a certain death. In 1476 Henry managed to feign illness and escape from a waiting ship at St Malo. In 1482, Edward promised François 4,000 archers to defend his borders, if he gave up Jasper and Henry. Edward died in 1483, and Richard III again tried to take the earls. There was national resentment against Richard taking the throne and murdering Edward V's bodyguard and Lord Hastings. Edward IV's widow fled to sanctuary and began plotting with Margaret Beaufort for Henry to marry Elizabeth, Edward's eldest daughter, and take the throne from Richard III.

In 1483 occurred the Buckingham Rebellion and risings across the south of England against the murderer of the 'princes in the Tower' (actually Edward V and Prince Richard). Many Yorkists fled to join Jasper and Henry, who learned that they are to be handed over to Richard. Richard had agreed 4,000 archers and another 2-3,000 men for Brittany in return for Henry and Jasper. Both managed to flee to France in 1484, where 400 exiles in Brittany were allowed to join them.

Jasper and Henry sent letters to supporters across Britain – to Northumberland, Herbert, the Stanleys, Grey of Ruthin, Kynaston, Shrewsbury, Rhys ap Thomas and all of Jasper's former supporters. Henry and Jasper were declared traitors in December 1484 and again in June 1485. At this time, bards were carrying messages around the courts of Wales, and indicated where Jasper should land and what route to take and meet in 1485. Henry landed near Dale with an army on 7 August made up of French, Bretons, Scots and British. His mother Margaret Beaufort has been plotting with Edward IV's widow Elizabeth Woodville, to send him money and support.

All of the Stanley family knew of his coming and mobilised their men before Richard Vergil records that the men of Pembroke 'were prepared to follow their lord Jasper'. Men joined immediately and the force headed at

20 miles a day through averfordwest to Cardigan where the Pryses, Lloyds, Lewes, Parrys, Colbys, Bowens and Phillips all come with retainers.

Aberystwyth Castle was taken with no trouble, then in Machynlleth John Savage and Richard Griffith brought messages from the Stanleys. The Tudor army crossed through the Yorkist Grey estates, guarded by the Yorkist warrior Kynaston, without hindrance to Shrewsbury. By now Rhys ap Thomas with 2,000 men and Richard ap Hywel of Mostyn have joined. Prominent Yorkists Richard Corbet, Roger Kynaston, Bourchier, Hungerford, Griffith and Walter Herbert also brought men, while Thomas Stanley's troops cleared a way along Watling Street in front of Henry to Atherstone. Henry secretly met William Stanley and Thomas Stanley.

At Bosworth Richard III had a personal army of 3,000 men – most Yorkist peers did not come. His brother had taken 39 (of c.55) to attack Jasper at Bamborough Castle in 1461-62, but just 6 peers followed Richard, of whom two were recently ennobled. Richard was killed, and soon Jasper was made Duke of Bedford, with the Crown taking Pembroke, and Henry embraced Yorkist supporters in the new regime. In November 1485, aged around 54, 30 years after his first battle, Jasper married the 27-year-old Katherine Woodville (Buckingham's widow and the sister of Edward IV's widow Elizabeth Woodville). Jasper's was the first union between York and Lancaster in 1485, followed by Henry's marriage to Elizabeth of York in 1487, Edward IV's daughter. Acts of Parliament were passed to richly reward Jasper, who stayed close to Henry in his early years of kingship.

The Vaughan Revolt at Brecon and Tretower in 1486 was put down by Jasper. In 1486-87 for the Lovell Rebellion, Jasper headed north to Yorkshire with 3,000 men with a papal bull threatening excommunication to rebels. The rising was put down without bloodshed or reprisals. Lambert Simnel had been trained to impersonate the Earl of Warwick, imprisoned in the Tower, and a continental mercenary army, supplemented by Irish forces, invaded Lancashire, following 'Warwick'. Henry displayed the real Warwick to the people of London and had his survival proclaimed in all churches. In 1487, the rebel army of 8,000 marched to York, which refused to surrender. Jasper Tudor, as Earl Marshal, gathered the king's army and met the rebels at the Battle of Stoke Field. Jasper commanded the centre, Henry the rearguard and Oxford and Rhys ap Thomas led the attack. It was the last battle of the Wars of the Roses – Jasper had fought for 32 years, from the first battle at St Albans in 1455, to this last conflict. Simnel was given a job in the royal kitchens.

Jasper was always accorded preference at state, or in banquets, and gained more estates in the Marches. His most northern estate was in Derbyshire, but his lands stretched from Milford Haven to the Thames estuary, being centred on the Severn Valley. His favoured home was Sudeley Castle, followed by Thornbury Castle and Minster Lovell Hall. Jasper mentored Prince Arthur at Ludlow, and in 1491 was in London for the birth of Henry VIII – the baby's governess was the same Jane ap Hywel who tended the baby Henry VII at Pembroke Castle. In 1492, he was one of the commanders who invaded France, but in 1494 Jasper, Lord Lieutenant of Ireland, was appointed to lead 1,000 men to deal with a rebellion in Dublin but was too ill. Jasper died at Thornbury Castle on 21 or 26 December 1495. He knew he was dying, making his will on 15 December. Attending his death were Margaret Beaufort (Henry's mother), Henry VII, Katherine Woodville and probably Queen Elizabeth, and he was buried in Keynsham Abbey.

* This author has written the first biography of this great man, *Jasper Tudor: Dynasty Maker*, published in 2014.

Footnote:
Emyr Wyn Jones: 'Hazardous undertakings involving such high stakes are not embarked upon without much careful preparatory work. Wales was emotionally prepared for Henry's arrival on its shores; the long years of encouraging prognostication by the bards had not been in vain. The long period of skilled and indefatigable political scheming, mainly in Wales, by Jasper Tudor, Henry's uncle, was about to bear fruit. It is no exaggeration to assert that Henry's arrival was an event of "messianic" significance where Wales was concerned. It was an event that culminated in the enthusiasm and prowess of the powerful army of Welshmen who accompanied "a descendant of their ancient British princes" from Dale to Bosworth, or joined him along the march...

The Welsh gentry had known Jasper operating in and around Wales for three decades, and many were related to him. They knew he was an honourable man, battle-hardened and also fortunate, perhaps destined to stay alive in these years. Across the whole of Wales, Yorkist-dominated, men flocked to join his young nephew's banner. Jasper's role in educating Henry in diplomacy and warfare in the years of exile, and his importance in taking Wales for the future king has always been underplayed. Henry's biographers and later writers have always focussed upon the king, by-passing the role of Jasper...

By the fifteenth century, national sentiment in Wales had taken deep root, finding expression in the literature and especially the prophetic literature of the period. These prophecies, cast in the cywydd metre of the period and often in allegorical form, took on a more purposeful character, and towards the end of the Wars of the Roses this literature tended to rally round Henry Tudor, who could appeal to his countrymen, both Yorkists and Lancastrians, in a truly national cause. It was this great wave of national sentiment in Wales which was to carry Henry to victory at Bosworth. As W. Watkin Davies in 1924 wrote in *Wales*: "It was as much a Welsh conquest of England, as the expedition of 1066 was a Norman conquest of England." It was more than this. It was a British conquest, and the first British royal dynasty – and without Jasper Tudor it could never have happened.'

HENRY VII OF ENGLAND AND WALES 28 January 1457 - 21 April 1509

HENRY TUDOR, EARL OF RICHMOND, THE FIRST OF THE TUDOR DYNASTY

The Welsh supported the Lancastrian cause in the Wars of the Roses, and many died in the slaughter at Mortimer's Cross in 1461. One of the Welsh captains, Owain ap Mareddud ap Tudur (Owen Tudor), was captured and

beheaded by the Yorkists, and his head placed on the steps of Hereford Cathedral. Here 'a mad woman combed his hair and washed away the blood from his face, and got candles and set them round his head, all burning, more than a hundred.' This may have been an act of clairvoyance, because Owen ap Maredudd's grandson, Henry*, founded the Tudor dynasty that united

Pembroke Castle

England and Wales. Henry's father, Edmund, died in Yorkist imprisonment in Carmarthen just three months before Henry was born in 1457.

Born in Pembroke Castle, of royal Welsh descent, one of Henry's ancestors was Llewelyn the Great's Justiciar, Ednyfed Fychan, whose heraldic arms were three severed Saxon heads. Brought up by a Welsh nurse, Henry Earl of Richmond was lucky to be alive, even before he raised the Red Dragon of Cadwaladr upon Bosworth Field. He had been born posthumously to Edmund Tudor, his mother being Margaret Beaufort, the sole inheritor of the Lancastrian claim to the crown of England.

Henry was only fourteen in 1471, the year that the Lancastrian King Henry VI was murdered and his son Prince Edward killed. Suddenly Henry was the prime Lancastrian claimant to the English crown in the continuing Wars of the Roses. His uncle Jasper Tudor (the Earl of Pembroke) only just managed to help him flee to Brittany, then still a country independent of France, and with a similar language to Welsh. Mayor Thomas White of Tenby hid young Henry in cellars which can still be seen. The new English King Edward IV asked for Henry to be handed over, but died soon after and was succeeded by Richard III of York, who killed Edward IV's two sons, the 'princes in the Tower'.

In 1483, Harri Tudor pledged his band of followers in exile that he would marry Edward IV's daughter Elizabeth of York and thus unite the warring Lancastrian and Yorkist factions. His own lineage went back through his grandfather Owain's marriage to Catherine, widow of Henry V, to the Royal Houses of Gwynedd and Gruffydd ap Cynan, and that of Dinefwr and Rhys ap Tudur. In September 1484, Henry barely escaped with his life as he was warned that a group of Breton nobles were going to take him to Richard III. He crossed the border into France, and with his uncle Jasper, the Earl of Oxford, the Bishop of Ely and the Marquis of Dorset, prepared to invade Britain. He borrowed money from France, and with 2,000 mainly Welsh, Breton and French troops, landed near his birthplace in Pembrokeshire. Tudor moved through Wales gathering support. Rhys ap Thomas gathered the men of Deheubarth and met Henry near Welshpool. So did the men of Gwynedd under Richard ap Hywel of Mostyn. While pleading his cause at Mostyn, Richard's men from nearby Flint Castle

Reconstruction of birth, Pembroke Castle

arrived and Henry had to escape by a back window. A stained glass commemoration panel in Mostyn Hall can be seen, and Henry presented the family with a silver bowl and ewer after the Battle of Bosworth, which can still be seen.

Many Welshmen believed that Henry was the promised *mab darogan*, 'son of prophecy', to free Wales from the English. Glyndŵr's rebellion had paved the way for this nationalist upsurge, and Wales had never been settled since that time. The Lancastrian forces crossed the Severn near Shrewsbury, finally meeting Richard's numerically superior army at Bosworth Field in Leicestershire. This was one of the strangest battles in history. A rag-tag army of French, Bretons and English exiles, supported by Welsh contingents, moved into the heart of England. From the west, Henry's force, watched by Richard's mounted scouts, had moved from Lichfield to Leicester, and was making its slow progress towards Bosworth Field. It had swollen from 2,500 to 4,500 soldiers on its journey across Wales. The Earl of Shrewsbury brought 500 men to the scene. From the east of England, Lord Norfolk's loyalist army of 4,000 men was approaching in the opposite direction. Percy of Northumberland was bringing Richard's 3,000 troops from the north. Richard with 6,000 followers was hurrying from the south, and another two armies of the Stanley brothers also arrived at the same time. Of the six main armies, three were uncommitted at the start of the battle. Apart from the Stanleys, related to Henry but committed by hostages to Richard, Henry's 4,500 men faced a potential 13,500 Yorkists. Henry had a fresh horse, ready to flee the battle-field and fight again, probably upon Jasper's instructions.

The Yorkist contingents under the Stanley brothers had pledged to assist Richard III, mainly as Lord Stanley's son was held hostage by Richard, but held back from the battle. The battle was started by the Earl of Oxford attacking the Duke of Norfolk's army. Lord Thomas Stanley then led his 4,000 men towards Northumberland's position on a nearby hill. Oxford's force was forced to attack because of cannon and arrow fire from Richard's higher ground. In close combat, Richard's main commander Norfolk was killed, and his son Surrey injured and captured. Richard's impressed men began falling back and some deserted. Neither Percy, Thomas Stanley nor William Stanley moved their forces to help the king. Richard was forced to move.

Around half an hour into the battle, Richard could see Henry and Jasper Tudor, with the standard of the Red Dragon, on the slopes behind Oxford's tired forces. Richard took a great gamble. At the head of a 400 men, he charged across to this position, passing William Stanley's army. Henry's flag was cut down, and the standard-bearer, Sir William Brandon was killed. In this melée, part of the army of 2,500 men under Sir William Stanley charged to help Henry. They were Denbighshire men, and this may have been

Henry VII and Elizabeth of York, alongside Jasper Tudor and Katherine Woodville at Cardiff Castle

spontaneous to help the rightful 'Welsh' king. Lord Thomas Stanley still held his 4,000 men back.

Equally, the army supporting Richard under the Earl of Northumberland refused to engage the Lancastrian army, watching the battle develop. Richard and his small force were quickly overwhelmed and Richard killed. The Yorkists left the battlefield. Rhys ap Thomas was said to have been knighted on the battlefield for killing Richard with his great battle-axe, and supposedly put Richard's crown on Henry's head. Richard III was the last king to die in battle, which was probably decided by some of Stanley's siding with Henry. Thomas Stanley, Henry's father-in-law, only threw his troops in to pursue the fleeing Yorkists. (The superbly carved medieval bed of Sir Rhys ap Thomas can be seen in St. Fagan's Castle, at The Museum of Welsh Life, Cardiff).

Henry's success had been largely due to Welsh support, and the emissary for Venice reported to the Doge that 'The Welsh may now be said to have recovered their independence, for the most wise and fortunate Henry

VII is a Welshman '. And Francis Bacon commented that 'To the Welsh people, his victory was theirs; they had thereby regained their freedom.'

Just as Richard's death effectively ended the battle, Henry's marriage and diplomacy effectively ended the Wars of the Roses. His wife Elizabeth of York was herself a descendant of Llywelyn ap Iorwerth (q.v.) A Yorkist invasion force mainly composed of Irish and Germans was bloodily defeated in 1487 at Stoke. Impostors to the throne, Perkin Warbeck and Lambert Simnel were dealt with. By the standards of the age he was extremely merciful to defeated Yorkists, with few of the executions that had followed previous battles. Despite several threats to the crown, Henry Tudur laid the basis for a stable constitutional monarchy. By the Treaty of Étaples, he took money from the French in return for not fighting them. He built trade and alliances, and under his Royal Commission John Cabot reached Nova Scotia in 1497.

Henry VII had brought up his eldest son and heir, Arthur, as a Welsh speaker. Arthur was married with great ceremony to Catherine of Aragon in 1501, cementing the Spanish alliance. Arthur's untimely death gave the nation Henry VIII and changed the course of British history – without it Britain would probably still be a Catholic country. And Henry VIII's daughter Queen Elizabeth I oversaw the greatest flowering of culture, in the British Isles, under this Tudor dynasty. For the first time Britain became a real player on the world stage in the arts. Bosworth Field marked the end of medieval England and the beginning of more modern government, with a conscious attempt to integrate Wales into England.

Aged only fifty-two, Henry Tudor died at Richmond in 1509, leaving a peaceful country, full treasury and an uneventful succession. The 'founder of the new England of the sixteenth century', Francis Bacon called him 'a wonder for wise men'. The great historian G.M. Trevelyan pointed out to the influence of Bosworth Field and the Tudors: 'Here, indeed, was one of fortune's freaks: on a bare Leicestershire upland a few thousand men in close conflict foot to foot....... sufficed to set upon the throne of England the greatest of all her royal lines, that should guide her through a century of change down new and larger streams of destiny.'

- More upon Henry is given in this author's biography *Jasper Tudor: Dynasty Maker*, and my *Henry Tudor: The Chosen King* will be published in early 2016.

ROBERT RECORDE 1510 - 1589

MATHEMATICIAN WHO REVOLUTIONISED ALGEBRA AND INVENTED THE = SIGN

A mathematician, merchant, doctor of medicine, navigator, teacher, metallurgist, cartographer, inventor and astronomer, Recorde's textbooks and their translations were studied across the Western world. Born in 1510, the son of Thomas Recorde, a Mayor of Tenby and Rose Jones of Machynlleth, he went to All Souls College. His invention of the 'equals' sign (=) revolutionised algebra, and his mathematical works were translated and read all over Europe. Recorde is commemorated in the great parish church at Tenby*.

A leading mathematician, the writer of the first English language texts on algebra and arithmetic, Recorde invented the equals (=) sign, to 'avoid the tedious repetition of equals to'. His arithmetic book went into fifty editions and was notable in being innovative in two respects. It was written as a dialogue between a master and pupil to keep it interesting

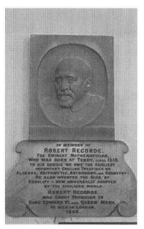

(shades of *Sophie's World*), and it used the device of pointing fingers (precursing Windows icons!) Recorde studied at Oxford, taught mathematics there and was made a Fellow of All Souls in 1531. He then qualified as a Doctor of Medicine in Cambridge, returned to Oxford to teach mathematics, and then moved to practise as a doctor in London, where he was physician to Edward VI and Queen Mary, to whom he dedicated some books.

Recorde virtually established the English school of mathematics and introduced algebra to England. He was educated at Oxford from 1525-1531, where he gained a BA and became a Fellow of All Souls, and he passed his MD in Cambridge in 1545. He seems to have been practising as a doctor in Oxford from 1533, before his medical

St. Mary's Church, Tenby

degree. In 1547 Recorde published *The Urinal of Physick*, a traditional medical work. From 1545-1547 it appears that Recorde taught mathematics privately in Cambridge and Oxford. However, although a doctor of medicine at the Royal Court, he was more noted for his astronomy and mathematics. Recorde practised medicine in London from 1547-1549.

In 1551 Recorde wrote *Pathwaie to Knowledge*, which some consider to be an abridgement of Euclid's *Elements*. It is certainly the first English translation, in which he rearranged Euclid's writings to make better sense. This is his only book that is not written in the form of a dialogue between a master and student. 1552 saw the publication of his *The Ground of Artes*, a book for learning arithmetic, dedicated to Edward VI, his patron. This was very successful commercially, 'teaching the perfect work and practice of Arithmeticke etc.' in Recorde's own words. It discusses Arabic numeral operations, counter computation, proportion, fractions and the 'rule of three', etc. Some time after this he wrote *The Gate of Knowledge*, which seems not to have been published and has been lost - it was a treatise upon measurement and the use of the quadrant. He later spoke of a quadrant that he invented (whether for mensuration or for navigation is unknown), which is probably described in this lost book.

In 1556 *The Castle of Knowledge* was published, dealing with the science of construction and the use of the sphere, using Ptolemaic astronomy, and mentioning Copernicus favourably and dangerously**. This was dedicated to his patron, Queen Mary, and its Latin version to Cardinal Pole. In 1557 appeared *The Whetstone of Witte,* his textbook of elemetary algebra. In this he invented the = sign using two parallel line segments, 'bicause noe 2 thynges can be moare equalle'. The symbol of = took some time to be accepted, with vertical parallel lines being used by some, and 'ae' by others until the 1700's. ('ae' was abbreviated from the Latin aequalis, meaning equal). The book also introduced the pre-existing + (plus) sign to English readers. *The Whetstone of Wytte* was dedicated to The Muscovy Company, for whom he planned a textbook on navigation, and to whom he was an advisor. It was the first mathematics book printed in English, rather than the traditional Latin.

After being physician to King Edward VI and then Queen Mary, which required a rapid change of religion, Recorde became Comptroller of the Bristol Mint from 1549-1551. Recorde was then made Surveyor of Mines and Monies in Ireland, based at Wexford, from 1551-53 and in 1556. He would possibly have begun life as a Catholic, averred to Protestantism under Edward VI, returned to Catholicism under Mary, and then gone back to Protestantism under Elizabeth. As Surveyor in Ireland he was in charge of the silver mines in Wexford, but the lode was not as rich as expected and they failed. For 'mismanagement' of the enterprise, Recorde was thrown into gaol by a political enemy.

His death occurred at the age of 48, at King's Bench Prison in Southwark, where he had been committed for debt, and his will was proved upon June 18th, 1558. He was shortly replaced as a polymath in Tudor society by Dr John Dee (q.v.), another brilliant mathematician. Dee published an augmentation of Recorde's *Grounde of Arts*, the mathematical textbook that ran to twenty-six editions by 1662 and wrote his own seminal *Preface to the English edition of Euclid*, which itself has been called a 'landmark in mathematical thought.'

*The Robert Recorde Memorial at the church reads:

In Memory of
ROBERT RECORDE
The Eminent Mathematician
Who Was Born at Tenby, circa 1510.
To His Genius We Owe the earliest
Important English Treatises on
Algebra, Arithmetic, Astronomy and Geometry;
He Also invented the Sign of
Equality = Now Universally Accepted
By the Civilised World
ROBERT RECORDE
Was Court Physician to
King Edward IV and Queen Mary
He Died in London
1558

** Copernicus' ideas were only around 20 years old, and 'heretical' at this time, yet the mention of him in the fourth treatise of *The Castle of Knowledge* is as follows:

Scholar: I perceive it well: for as if the earth were always out of the centre of the world, those former absurdities would at all times appear: so if at any time the earth should move out of his place, those inconveniences would then appear.

Master: This is truly to be gathered, howbeit, Copernicus, a man of great learning, of much experience, and of wonderful diligence in observation, hath renewed the opinion of Aristarchus Samius, and affirmeth that the earth not only moveth circularly about his own centre, but also may be, yea and is, continually out of the precise centre of the world 38 hundred thousand miles: but because the understanding of that controversy dependeth upon profounder knowledge than in this Introduction may be uttered conveniently, I will let it pass till some other time.

Scholar: Nay sir in good faith, I desire not to hear such vain fantasies, so far against common reason, and repugnant to the consent of all the learned multitude of Writers, and therefore let it pass forever, and a day longer.

Master: You are too young to be a good judge in so great a matter: it passeth far your learning, and theirs that are also much better learned than you, to improve (disprove) his suppositions by good arguments, and therefore you were best to condemn no thing that you do not well understand: but another time, as I said, I will so declare his supposition, that you will not only wonder to hear it, but also peradventure be as earnest then to credit it as you are now to condemn it. In the mean season, let us proceed forward to our former order...'

WILLIAM CECIL, K.G. 13 September 1520 – 5 August 1598

LORD BURGHLEY, LORD HIGH TREASURER, THE ARCHITECT OF ELIZABETHAN ENGLAND, 'THE MAN THAT DOES EVERYTHING'

Cecil came from a Welsh family whose name was anglicised from Seisyllt in the service of the Tudors, after Henry VII toppled Richard III in 1485. William's father Richard, of Burghley in Northampton married a local heiress, and thus gained the manor of Bourne. Richard was a Groom of the Wardrobe at Court, and William served as a page there, before he entered St John's College, Cambridge in 1535. He married in 1541 when he went to Gray's Inn to practise law, but his wife died in 1543, leaving him a son, Thomas. William Cecil was rewarded by Henry VIII in 1542 for defending royal policy, and given a place in the Court of Common Pleas. In 1543 he entered Parliament, aged just 23.

After a second marriage in 1545, he joined an influential Protestant circle at court. When Edward VI succeeded to the throne, Cecil joined the household of the Protector, the Duke of Somerset, becoming his secretary in 1548. However, Somerset fell from power, Cecil was caught up in his disgrace, and despatched to the Tower of London for two months in 1549. Nevertheless, the abilities of Cecil were so highly regarded that he gained royal favour and became one of two secretaries to the young king, who gave him a knighthood in 1551. Cecil had acted as a go-between between Edward Seymour, Duke of Somerset, and John Dudley, Earl of Warwick, the two main rivals for power over Edward VI, When Somerset fell from power the second time, in 1551, it was Warwick who proposed Cecil's knighthood, and Cecil committed himself to Warwick, who now became Duke of Northumberland. However, when Northumberland proposed altering the succession, Cecil sided with the judges on the Tudor side, although fearing arrest and contemplating flight. Only on the royal command of Edward VI did Cecil capitulate to Northumberland's demands. He deserted John Dudley, Duke of Northumberland directly upon Edward's death.

Cecil had met with Mary Tudor as representative of Edward's council, and she called his 'a very honest man'. Cecil was now offered a post in Queen Mary's court, but unlike most of his colleagues, preferred to withdraw from the Catholic milieu until Elizabeth's (possible) Protestant accession. His backing for Elizabeth, when it looked as if she was more likely to be executed than succeed to the throne, was something that kept the two very close throughout the next forty years. Cecil immediately became her principal secretary and chief adviser on her accession in 1558. His first act was to persuade the reluctant Elizabeth to intervene in Scotland and sign the Treaty of Edinburgh, to remove French troops from there.

Cecil was a superb statesman, but first helped Elizabeth to get the state upon a sound economic footing, including adopting a new coinage in 1561. Elizabeth operated a rotating court, spending her time at the stately homes of various subjects. With her vast army of retainers, this saved enormous sums of money, and ensured that no one individual became too rich. Her subjects vied with each other to offer the most splendid sojourn at their estates, which helped add to the pomp and panoply of the Elizabethan period, while costing her nothing. To heal the terrible religious divisions of the reigns of Henry VIII, Edward VI and Mary, Cecil and Elizabeth worked together on a compromise settlement to establish the Anglican Church in 1559. Cecil also ended the expensive war with France, organised an efficient secret service to stop Catholic attempts on Elizabeth's life, and dramatically strengthened the army and navy.

He was Chancellor of the University of Cambridge from 1559, and survived an attempt to sack him as Elizabeth's Secretary, by the jealous Lords Leicester and Norfolk in 1568. He had introduced Norfolk into the council to balance Leicester's power. Robert Earl of Leicester was John Dudley's son, whom Cecil had fallen out with politically. Leicester became emotionally close to Elizabeth, weakening Cecil's position. Cecil offered to resign, but Elizabeth trusted him implicitly and rewarded him with the lucrative mastership of the Court of Wards in 1572. She had created him first Baron Burghley in 1571.

In 1572 Cecil also became Lord Treasurer and a Knight of the Garter. His loyalty, industry and judgement were indispensable to the Queen - he was her mainstay throughout most of her reign. While opposing Leicester, Cecil was sympathetic to Protestant desires for Elizabeth to marry and produce an heir, strongly resisting Mary Stuart's claims to succeed Elizabeth. He recommended the Habsburg suitor, the Archduke Charles. In the early 1570's, Cecil was diplomatically busy, aiding the Dutch while soothing Spanish feelings, and trying to achieve a French alliance. He knew that war would overstrain England's finances, and thereby endanger the Tudor monarchy. Cecil said 'a reign gaineth more by one year's peace than ten years' war'.

In 1568, Mary Stuart, Queen of Scots, fled to England. The Ridolfi Plot to put Mary on the English throne, with a Spanish invasion, led to Norfolk's execution. The close attention paid to Mary Queen of Scots by Cecil later led to the discovery of the Babington Plot, and her trial for treason and execution in 1587.

Equally, Cecil's insight into Spanish intentions led to preparations for naval resistance that helped beat the Armada in 1588. Cecil's elder son, Thomas, commanded a ship in the English fleet. Cecil had previously offered peace negotiations to the Duke of Parma, the Spanish commander in the Netherlands, in 1585, again earning Leicester's enmity. Nonetheless, Cecil tried for peace with Spain again in 1587. The former Spanish ambassador to Elizabeth's court summed up his feelings about Britain's chief economist and diplomat as '...the man that does everything'.

Elizabeth's principal councillor now presided over the coaching of his son Robert, born in 1563, towards the post of Elizabeth's secretary, which he took in 1596. Thus the 'reign of the Cecils' continued. William Cecil retired with ill health, but still remained active, urging peace with Spain for fear of a costly war against a Franco-Spanish alliance. He died in 1598 before negotiations were concluded, and is buried at St Martin's Church, Burghley. The consummate master of Renaissance statecraft, famed over Europe, his talents as a diplomat, statesman and administrator were unparalleled.

Of himself he said 'I have gained more by my temperance and forebearing than ever I did with my wit'. A contemporary observation of Cecil showed that he kept his thoughts and feelings under control: he had no close friends, no inward companion as great men commonly have... nor did any other know his secrets; some noting it for a fault, but most thinking it a praise and an instance of his wisdom. By trusting none with his secrets, none could reveal them'.

Burghley House is probably the most magnificent Elizabethan building in Britain, built between 1565 and 1587, and still lived in by his descendants. At one point he had been offered an earldom by Elizabeth, but refused on the grounds of its great expense. Overworked and in ill health, Cecil was an expert in finances, religion and socio-economic policy. He also co-ordinated the Privy Council, which met almost every day, and was the queen's Chief Councillor and Secretary. Cecil managed Parliament and presided over the Exchequer as well as being a J.P. in five counties. He was Britain's de facto Foreign Secretary and chief diplomat, made Britain respected as a European power, and was ruthless with any opposition to his beloved queen. Without Cecil, it is difficult to envisage an Elizabethan Age.

Footnotes:
(i) Cecil's grandfather was David 'Sysill', who married Alice Dicksons. Their son was Richard 'Cyssell', who married Jane Heckington. So we appear to have transmuted through 4 generations from 'ap Seisyllt through Sysill to Cyssell and Cecil.
(ii) It appears that the Cecils were responsible for keeping the young Elizabeth away from Mary's court, in Hatfield House, for her own safety away from the intrigues of court. Elizabeth seemed to know him very well, for upon his appointment as her sole Secretary, she told him 'This judgement I have of you,

that you will not be corrupted by any manner of gift and that you will be faithful to the State and that, without respect of my private will, you will give me that counsel which you think best.' He remained her chief councillor to his death, when Elizabeth was at his bedside. 'No prince in Europe hath such a counsellor as I have in mine', she once had said. She knew that he always gave his best advice, and would not be swayed by pressure. In turn, he knew how to put up with her extremes of temper by tactically retreating - he advised a younger man 'Good my Lord, overcome her with yielding.'

WILLIAM SALESBURY c.1520 - c. 1584/99*

TRANSLATOR OF THE NEW TESTAMENT, 'THE MOST LEARNED WELSHMAN OF HIS DAY'

Given the same holy day of 10 September by the Church in Wales as William Morgan, he was born in Llansannan. He was the second son of Ffwg ap Robert ap Thomas Salbri Hen (Ffowc Salesbury) and Annes ferch Wiliam ap Gruffydd ap Robin of Cochwillan, of Y Plas Isa, Llanrwst, Denbighshire. Salesbury may have been educated at the nearby Maenan Abbey before studying at Oxford, where he seems to have converted to Protestantism.

The Act of Union of 1543 annexed Wales to England, and destroyed the humane system of Welsh laws, also threatening to extirpate the language. Without its language, it is difficult for a nation to survive, so the printing of books in Welsh became a priority for patriotic Welshmen. In 1547, Salesbury published a dictionary to instruct the Welsh to better understand English. He wrote 'And, take this advice from me; unless you save and correct and perfect the language before the extinction of the present generation, it will be too late afterwards.' This was the second book printed in Welsh**, and in the following year he published a complementary dictionary to help the English understand Welsh.

In the same year he published an edition of Gruffydd Hiraethog's Welsh proverbs, *Oll Synnwr pen Kembero ygyd,* trying to tell the Welsh people about the traditional wisdom of their nation. In this, Salesbury wrote: 'If you do not wish to be worse than animals... obtain learning in your own language, if you do not wish to be more unnatural than any other nation under the sun, love your language and those who love it. If you do not wish utterly to depart from the faith of Christ...obtain the *Holy Scripture* in your own tongue as your happy ancestors, the ancient British, had it.' He also wrote an unpublished book in Welsh, *On Rhetoric* in 1552, and not until 1916 was *Llysieulyfr* published. This was a 'herbal' translated from Latin and Welsh sources.

At Oxford he had started thinking about translating the Bible into Welsh, wanting to impart learning to the Welsh in their own language, and he appealed to the bishops to preach in Welsh. Salesbury also advocated asking the King's permission to have the Bible translated. In 1551 he published his translation of the lessons that were read in church Communion services, under the title *Kynniver Llith a Ban'*. Under Mary's Catholic reign of 1553-58 he was forced to keep silent, but under Elizabeth in 1561 it was ordained that the lessons should be read in Welsh, after they had been read in English. In 1563 a law was passed commanding that the *Bible* and the *Prayer Book* should be translated into Welsh, setting a time period of three years for this completion. It was accepted that the vast majority of the Welsh people understood no English, and a Welsh *Bible* could help the acceptance of Protestantism thorough the country.

The major reason, however, was that there was anger at the slow progress of the Welsh in taking up the English language. It was thought that, by having Welsh translations placed next to English texts in churches, the congregations would learn English. Exactly the opposite happened - why should the Welsh bother with English, when they had their own language, and a church both far more ancient than that of England? Salesbury began work with Richard Davies, Bishop of St David's, and was responsible for most of the work involved leading to the publication of the Welsh *New Testament* in 1567, while Davies contributed most to the *Prayer Book* published at the same time. Thomas Huet, precentor of St David's, also assisted Salesbury. It appears that Salesbury and Davies now began a translation of the *Bible*, but according to Sir John Wynn of Gwydir argued over the translation of one word, and the work stopped. The Welsh *Bible* thus had to wait until William Morgan's translation in 1588.

A wonderful scholar, Salesbury's strong opinions sometimes got the better of his common sense. For instance, in the printed version of the *New Testament* he ignored nasal mutations. He used a different typeface to show the part of a literary word that differed from its colloquial form. Salesbury also altered the spelling of some words to make them resemble more closely their Latin origins. However, despite contemporary criticisms, his intentions were to make the Gospels understandable to everyone, rich and poor, and Morgan's *Bible* owes a great debt to Salesbury's work. His translation 'laid a solid foundation for the translations of the next two centuries, and for modern Welsh, which is able to deal in its own idiom with the most complicated subjects.'

A master of Greek, Latin, Hebrew and modern languages, he was a 'brilliant representative of Renaissance humanism in Wales. It would be hard to find anybody who has rendered greater service to the Welsh nation than William Salesbury. His great contribution was his translation of the Bible into Welsh, thus laying the foundations of modern Welsh prose' (- *The Dictionary of Welsh Biography*).

* John Wynn of Gwydir and others have said that he lived almost until the next century, but c.1584 seems a more likely date.

** Sir John Prys of Brecon published a collection of basic religious texts, *Yn Llyvyr Hwnn* just a year previously, but Salesbury was the pioneer of Welsh publishing.

JOHN DEE 13 July 1527 - December 1608

BLACK JACK, 'THE MAGUS OF HIS AGE'

Cefn Pawl near Beguildy claims to be the home of Ieuan Ddu, John Dee, Black Jack, who became Elizabeth I's tutor, a man respected at court who was also a noted mathematician, antiquary, astronomer, philosopher, geographer, propagandist, astrologer and spy. John Dee was better known back in Powys as a magician and practitioner of the Black Arts, than as a court adviser to Queen Elizabeth. It seems he was born in Tower Ward, Mortlake, Surrey, the only child of Rowland Dee from Pilleth in Radnorshire, who worked as a 'gentleman server' to Henry VIII. However, John Dee said that he was a native of Beguildy, near Knighton in Radnorshire, and his diary shows his friendships with the Herberts, Morris Kyffin and John David Rhys (known as the grammarian-physician 'John Davies') amongst other notable Welshmen of the day. He taught the soldier-writer Morris Kyffin in London, c.1579-1580. Dee claimed descent from Rhodri Mawr, and to be a cousin of Blanche Parry. Parry was also related to William Cecil, who drew up her will and was her executor. She was 'Chief gentlewoman of the Queen's most honourable Privy Chamber and Keeper of her Majesty's jewels.

John Dee went to St John's College Cambridge in 1543, and was nominated as a foundation fellow of Trinity College Cambridge in 1546, before in 1546 moving to Louvain (Leuven)* in modern-day Belgium because science and mathematics were better established there. He believed that English humanism was not scientific enough, and made contact with some of the finest minds in mathematics and geography, such as Mercator, Ortelius and Gemma Phrysius. 'An astounding polymath... the lectures of this twenty-three-year-old at Paris were a sensation; he was to be courted by princes all over Europe. He returned to England with navigational devices like the balestila or cross-staff, was taken up by the Queen, the retinue of the Earl of Leicester and the Sidneys, and at the heart of the Elizabethan Renaissance'.

Dee was a student in Louvain until 1550. He then lectured mathematics at Paris 'to enormous acclaim' when he was twenty-three, and in 1551 returned to the court of Edward VI. By the skin of his teeth he had escaped the Marian persecution of Protestants, and returned to London to be taken into the heart of Elizabeth's court. Queen Mary had imprisoned Dee for trying to 'enchant' her, and is said to have been the model for both Shakespeare's white Prospero and Marlowe's black Faust.

With Blanche Parry and William Cecil having the queen's ear, this may have helped Black Jack to be accepted in Elizabethan court circles. He became a consultant of Elizabeth in State affairs, including giving advice on the Julian Calendar. He declined lectureships in mathematics at the College of Rheims and Oxford University in 1554.

Dee was charged with treason against Mary in 1555, but was exonerated in Star Chamber.

He presented Mary with a plan for the preservation of old books, manuscripts and records and the founding of a national library, in 1556, but his proposal was not taken up. Instead, he expanded his personal library at his house in Mortlake, tirelessly acquiring books and manuscripts in England and from Europe. Dee's library, a centre of learning outside the universities, became the greatest in England and attracted many scholars. 'With his remarkable library at Mortlake, (Dee) became the thinker behind most of the ventures of the English in their search for the North-East and North-West Passages to Cathay, pouring out treatises, maps, instructions, in his characteristic blend of technology, science, imperialism, speculation, fantasy and the occult' (- *Welsh Wizard and British Empire*, Gwyn Alf Williams). A London mob was tragically to sack his fabulous library in 1583, as the den of a black magician.

Dee invented the term 'The British Empire' for Queen Elizabeth in 1576 to justify and prove her right to North America, which had been 'discovered' by the Welsh, i.e. British prince Madoc ab Owain Gwynedd. Thus the Brythonic Celts, or the British, were the founders of her empire. His *Titles*, now lost, formed his concept of a British Empire for Elizabeth. It was based upon the polar maps of his friend, Gerard Mercator, and the work of William Lambard and the Venetian Zeno brothers

He published the seminal *Mathematical Preface* to Billingsley's translation of Euclid's *Elements* in 1570, arguing the central importance of mathematics and outlining mathematics' influence on the other arts and sciences. His preface has been called a 'landmark in mathematical thought.' Intended for an audience outside the universities, it proved to be Dee's most widely influential and frequently reprinted work. In 1577, Dee published *General and Rare Memorials pertayning to the Perfect Arte of Navigation*, a work that set out his vision of a maritime empire and asserted English territorial claims on the New World. Dee claimed Scandinavia, the Arctic and America for Elizabeth, using the Madoc story to justify the American claims. Dee also advised Drake upon his circumnavigation, and advised Gilbert upon a North-West Passage.

After being caught up in spiritualism and alchemy, Dee disappeared to Bohemia, Prague and Poland from 1584-1589. In 1587-88 Dee was spreading prophecies from Prague about 'the imminent fall of a mighty kingdom and fearsome storms'. These reached the Vatican via Dee's patron, the Emperor Rudolph, and were reprinted across Holland, undermining the morale of its Spanish occupying army. Dee's exultant letter to Queen Elizabeth on the Armada's defeat in 1588 justifies his predictions. However, James I later refused Dee's petition to clear him of the slander that he was 'a conjuror or caller or invocator of spirits'. Dee returned to Britain to be given the wardenship of Christ's College, Manchester in 1595, remaining there until 1604. His house and library in Mortlake had been sacked after his years overseas. Dee brought suspicion on himself by his intelligence across many fields of knowledge, but the whispering campaign against him started with a wonderful stage device in the Cambridge production of an Aristophanes play. People saw his brilliance as proof of collusion with the occult. *The Dictionary of Welsh Biography* states: ... it would seem certain that if he had adhered to pure science and steered clear of the esoteric or occult, he would rank amongst the foremost British pioneers of science'.

Most of his 79 treatises remain in manuscript, but his works on hieroglyphics were published across Europe, and his *Diary* in England after his death. Dee also published the work of Euclid, and prepared an edition of Robert Recorde's mathematical studies, Recorde being a fellow-Welshman and inventor of the 'equals' (=) sign. Dee's 'Memorials pertayning to the Perfect Arte of Navigation' was published in 1577.

* Even now, Leuven/Louvain is a noted university city, and having visited there over a dozen times on business, I can vouch for the fact that it has easily the best selection of beers in the world - it is also the home of Stella Artois, which is admired as a drink as much by the locals, as Mateus Rose is by the Portuguese. Dee has come back into public knowledge with the Damon Albarn opera: *Dr. Dee: An English Opera* of 2011.

Footnote:
The British rejected the Gregorian Calendar in 1583, after Secretary of State Walsingham, on behalf of the Privy Council, passed a copy of the papal bull to 'the court magus', John Dee. 'Dee was the obvious choice as advisor. One of the

leading scientific figures in England, and possessed of one of the largest private libraries in the country, he had a command of the latest astronomical learning (Copernicus included), as well as of current antiquarian and historical writing, both necessary for an understanding of the calendar issue. He had been imprisoned under Mary, had given astrological advice as to the date of the queen's coronation, had acted as an agent for Walsingham, and with him was among the advocates of a 'blue water' foreign policy combining Protestant alliances with voyages of exploration and colonisation' (-Dr Robert Poole). Dee dropped everything to work on the problem, and delivered a 62-page illuminated treatise to the Lord Treasurer Burghley (q.v. William Cecil). Cecil visited Dee to try to persuade him to advise conformity with the rest of Europe by revising the English calendar. Dee agreed to a panel of three learned university men to discuss the treatise further, one of whom, Thomas Digges, was a former pupil of Dee's and a friend of Cecil. Despite further pressure from Cecil, Dee rejected the papal calendar, as it dated from the first council of the Christian church rather than from the time of Christ.

BISHOP WILLIAM MORGAN c.1545 – 10 September 1604

TRANSLATOR OF THE BIBLE INTO WELSH

Celebrated in the Church in Wales on the anniversary of his death, Morgan was responsible for the survival of the Welsh language. William's father was John ap Morgan ap Llywelyn, and his mother Lowri ferch William ap John ap Madog. His place of birth at Tŷ Mawr, Wybrnant, Penmachno, Nant Conwy is open to the public. Educated at St Johns, Cambridge, he graduated in 1568, was ordained at Ely in the same year, took his MA in 1571, and his D.D. in 1583.

It seems that from 1572-77 William Morgan first held the ancient parish of Llanbadarn Fawr near Aberystwyth. He then became vicar of Welshpool (1575-79), holding the sinecure of Denbigh (1575-96), and vicar of Llanrhaeadr-ym-Mochnant and also Llanarmon (1578-95). From 1579 Morgan was rector of Llanfyllin, and parson of Pennant Melangell (1588-95). There was some hostility to Morgan at Llanrhaeadr, from the family of his nephew Evan Meredith, over a wedding of a wealthy heiress to Robert Wynn of Gwydir. However, the Star Chamber recorded that Morgan was a conscientious man, harassed by the malice of his enemies.

Despite his problems, the vicar completed his vast work of the translation of the *Bible* while at Llanrhaeadr, probably taking over 20 years to complete it. An Act of Parliament in 1563 was passed to allow the translation of the Bible and the Book of Prayer into Welsh 'because the English tongue is not understood of the most and greatest number of all her majesty's most living and obedient subjects inhabiting Wales'. Morgan revised Salesbury's translation of the *New Testament*, and was encouraged in his work by Archbishop Whitgift, who gave most financial support to his publishing of the Bible. John Davies and Edmwnd Prys also assisted Morgan (see footnotes).

Dr Gabriel Goodman of Ruthin had been chaplain to William Cecil and was one of Cecil's executors. As Dean of Westminster, this famous churchman assisted greatly in the production of Morgan's *Bible*, allowing Morgan to stay with him in London between 1587 and 1588. Dedicated to Elizabeth I, Morgan's work marked the beginning of modern Welsh literature and helped spur the Nonconformist movement. Also in 1588, his translation of the *Psalms* was published. In 1595, Morgan was made Bishop of Llandaff, and moved to be Bishop of St Asaph in 1601.

He died a poor man, being buried at St Asaph. After his death 'an inventorie of all and singular the goodes and chattells' of the churchman was made 'for the payment of the Debtes dewe by the said late Bishopp'. From the 'Chamber where the Bishopp lay' were taken 'two fether beddes' and 'one boulster' worth ten shillings (50p), and a 'looking glasse' worth 20 pence (8p). Also among his possessions were 40 tons of coal, and ten chickens worth three shillings. There is a memorial in the grounds of St Asaph Cathedral to the *Bible's* translators.

The 1588 *Bible* is the most important book in the history of Welsh language and literature, and its existence probably saved the language itself. At the time, there was 'alarming decay' in the Welsh language, fragmenting into different dialects, idioms and styles with the lack of any central referent source. Morgan went back to sources like the *Mabinogion* and medieval romances, to escape the current corruption of the tongue, and what emerged was a language that avoided Salesbury's pedantry. Morgan used the vigour and purity of earlier works, but added flexibility to give a wider range of expression. He gave the language a new lease of life*, providing writers with a pattern. Indeed, Meic Stephens wrote that *'The Bible* of 1588 was as influential in keeping alive the idea of an independent Wales as the defeat of the Armada was in maintaining England's independence', and that since Morgan's language was that of the poets, 'contemporary and classical, natural and dignified', his *Bible* 'ensured the purity, accuracy and strength of the poetic vocabulary should live on.' At this time the bards were facing extinction in Wales.

As the Welsh people learned to read via the *Bible,* through the schools of Griffith Jones (q.v.), and as every family tried to purchase one, the language of the *Bible* began to influence spoken Welsh. The language now was reinforced around a central core, and with the influence of preachers, gave the Welsh people a real sense of national identity. 'Every Welshman who speaks Welsh is under a deep obligation to William Morgan'. Worth noting here is the fact that 'Welsh was the only non-state language of Protestant Europe to become the medium of a published *Bible* within a century of the Reformation. Perhaps it is mainly to this fact that much of the strength of present-day Welsh is owed, compared to Irish (which did not get its own *Bible* until 1690 and where Catholic congregations did not have access to it, and Scots Gaelic (which had to wait until 1801)'.

Footnotes:

1. JOHN DAVIES 1567-1644 - Holy Day 15 May
Dr John Davies of Mallwyd is one of the greatest Welsh scholars, given a Holy Day by the Church in Wales. Born in Llanferres, the son of David ap John ap Rhys and Elizabeth ferch Lewis ap David Lloyd, he graduated from Jesus College in 1593. He was close to Bishop William Morgan of Llandaff, with whom he helped translate the *Bible*. He gained his divinity degree and doctorate from Lincoln College Oxford in 1608 and 1616 respectively. From 1604 he was rector of Mallwyd, and also gained the rector's post at Llan-ym-Mawddwy in 1614. He surrendered the sinecure of Darowen for the sinecure of Llanfor in 1621. From 1617 he was the prebendary of Llanefydd in the cathedral church of St Asaf. Davies is best known for his great *Welsh-Latin Dictionary* of 1632, which he compiled during his time as Rector at Mallwyd. His Welsh grammar, *Antiquae Lingua Britannicae*, was another magisterial work dating from 1620, and it is supposed that he was an active contributor to Richard Parry's Welsh *Bible* of 1620. He stayed at Mallwyd for 40 years, and his contribution towards the survival of the Welsh language cannot be underestimated.

2. EDMWND PRYS 1544-1623   Holy Day 15 May
Given the Holy Day of May 15th (the same as John Davies), this archdeacon of Meirionydd was possibly born at Llanfor in the same county. After St Asaph's Cathedral School, he went to St John's College, Cambridge, and in 1572 was given the living of Ffestiniog and Maentwrog. In 1576 he was appointed rector of Ludlow, and that same year made archdeacon. From 1576 until his death he lived at Tyddyn-ddu, Maentwrog. Llandenddwyn was given him in 1580, and he was made canon of St Asaph in 1602. Prys assisted William Morgan in his translation of the *Bible*, and published a book of psalms in 1621, 'the first Welsh book in which music was printed.' He also wrote 'contemplative' poetry. His first wife was Elin ferch John ap Lewis of Pengwern, and his second wife was her cousin, Gwen ferch Morgan ap Lewis of Pengwern. *The Dictionary of Welsh Biography* notes the distinguished children of the marriages.

INIGO JONES 15 July 1573 - 21 June 1652

THE FOUNDER OF CLASSICAL ENGLISH ARCHITECTURE, THE FIRST AND GREATEST OF 'ENGLISH' RENAISSANCE ARCHITECTS

Wales is about castles and churches, not great mansions and palaces. However, the great Inigo Jones has many houses and bridges attributed to him in Wales. He founded classical English architecture, designing the Queen's House at Greenwich, rebuilding the Banqueting Hall at Whitehall, and laying out Covent Garden and Lincoln's Inn Fields. He also designed two Danish royal palaces and worked with Ben Jonson, being the first to introduce the proscenium arch and movable scenery to the English stage.

Jones was the founder of the English school of classical architecture, bringing features of Rome and Renaissance Italy to Gothic England. Jones was Surveyor of the Kings Works from 1615-1635. His father was also named Inigo, a Welsh cloth worker, and Jones appears to have been apprenticed as a joiner in St Paul's churchyard before he appears in 1603 as a 'picturemaker' in the household accounts of the fifth Earl of Rutland. In 1605 he was employed by Queen Anne to provide costumes and settings for a Whitehall masque. It is fairly clear that by now he had been to Italy already, probably visiting theatres in Florence, and had acquired skills as a draftsman and architect*. In 1608 he designed the New Exchange in the Strand for the Earl of Salisbury, and a spire for St Paul's Cathedral. His main activity until 1640, however, appears to have been designing stage settings, costumes and decorations for masques for the Court, in which he worked with Ben Jonson until an argument in 1631.

In 1611, Jones was appointed Surveyor to the heir-apparent, Prince Henry, who died in the following year. In 1613 he was with the fourteenth Earl of Arundel visiting Italy again and the houses of Palladio, before returning in 1614. He was made Surveyor of the King's Works in the following year, and as an architect of outstanding skills, changed the focus of the appointment from one of maintenance to one of improvement. Jones started work of the Queen's House in Greenwich in 1617, and it was not completed until 1635. (King James' wife died in 1619, and the project was put 'on hold' for 17 years until Charles I married). In 1619 he began building the replacement Banqueting House at the palace of Whitehall, after fire had destroyed the old one. It was finished in 1622, and Rubens added the ceiling paintings in 1635. The Banqueting House was a setting for formal banquets and court masques, based on the design of a Roman basilica, and it is still used as a venue for state occasions.

Inigo Jones' most famous ecclesiastical design was the Queen's Chapel at St James Palace (1623-25, now Marlborough House Chapel). From 1625, Jones worked on converting Somerset House into a residence for Charles I's new queen, Henrietta Maria. He also made major changes to St Paul's Cathedral, but unfortunately it was destroyed in the Great Fire of London in 1666**. As the king's agent, Jones influenced the design of London houses and the development of London. He created London's first 'square' or piazza in Covent Garden in 1630, and designed the church of St Paul's on Palladian lines. Other sources state that the first square in London was his design for Lincoln's Inn. Coleshill and Amesbury were amongst the country mansions he designed. It now appears that Wilton House, attributed to Jones, was the work of his pupil and nephew, James Webb, and Jones acted as an advisor.

Civil War in 1642, and the seizure of the king's houses in 1643 meant that Jones was no longer employed. He was among the defenders at the siege of Basing House, from which he was luckily rescued wrapped in a blanket. Jones regained his properties in 1646, and was buried alongside his parents at the 'Welsh Church' of St Benet Paul's Wharf. Inigo Jones was a master of classical design, who broke the mould of Jacobean architecture in Britain. Most of his architectural drawings and masque designs survive, in collections at Worcester College, RIBA and Chatsworth House.

* It appears that he lived in Venice at this time, and Christian IV of Denmark induced him to leave Italy and accept an appointment at the Danish Court. Buildings are named as having been designed by Jones in both Denmark and Italy, but proof is difficult at present.

** In 1997, more than 70 stones from Inigo Jones 'lost' portico of the old St Paul's Cathedral were found beneath the present cathedral. Christopher Wren had used the blocks in his foundations.

LORD EDWARD HERBERT 3 March 1582 or 1583 – 20 August 1648

FIRST BARON HERBERT OF CHERBURY, 'THE FATHER OF ENGLISH DEISM'

This Welsh courtier, soldier, diplomat, historian, poet, and religious philosopher was known as 'the father of English Deism' (- Thomas Halyburton, writing in 1714). His famous work, De Veritate (On Truth), first published in 1624, in Paris, was intended to establish educated reason as a safe and reliable guide in the quest for truth. It asserted that in order for people to make decisions based on reason, they must have certain standards,

basic truths or "common notions," which all men can recognize as true once they are aware of them. Herbert identified five articles, or "common notions" of religion which he found to be present in the belief system of every religion. His work initiated a current of thought known as "deism," which accepted the creatorship of God but rejected revelatory religion and the continued involvement of the divine in the created world. His ideas were further developed by David Hume and Thomas Hobbes in England, and by Rousseau and Voltaire in France. Deism also influenced several prominent American thinkers including Thomas Jefferson (q.v.), John Quincy Adams, Ethan Allen, Benjamin Franklin and James Madison. The American deists, three of whom had Welsh origins, played a major part in creating the system of separation between church and state, and the phrases on religious freedom phrases in the First Amendment to the Constitution of the United States.

Edward Herbert of Cherbury was the eldest son of Richard Herbert of Montgomery Castle, a member of a branch of the family of the Earls of Pembroke and of Magdalen, daughter of Sir Richard Newport. His brother was the poet George Herbert (q.v.) Another brother, Sir Henry Herbert (1591-1675) was the Master of the King's Revels. As a boy he came under the tutelage of the Welsh autodidact Edward Thelwall, who apparently taught him Welsh and of whom Herbert spoke with great respect. Herbert matriculated at University College, Oxford in 1596, and in 1599 married his cousin Mary, daughter and heiress of Sir William Herbert of St. Julian's, Monmouthshire. He returned to Oxford with his wife and widowed mother, continued his studies, and learned modern languages as well as music, riding, and fencing. In 1601 he became MP for Montgomeryshire. On the accession of James I, he presented himself at court and was made a Knight of the Bath in 1603. He played the lute and composed music, and spoke several languages

In 1608, he travelled to Paris, enjoying the friendship and hospitality of the elderly Constable de Montmorency and meeting King Henri IV. In 1610, he served as a volunteer in the Low Countries under the Prince of Orange, whose intimate friend he became, and distinguished himself at the capture of Juliers from the Holy Roman Emperor. He offered to decide the war by engaging in single combat with a champion chosen from among the enemy, but his challenge was declined. During an interval in the fighting he paid a visit to Spinola, in the Spanish camp near Wezel, and to the elector palatine at Heidelberg, then traveled in Italy. At the request of the Duke of Savoy he led an expedition of 4,000 Huguenots from Languedoc into Piedmont to help the Savoyards against Spain. He returned to the Netherlands and the Prince of Orange, arriving in England in 1617. In 1619, Herbert was made Ambassador to France, but was recalled in 1621, after quarrelling with Charles de Luynes, the Chief Minister of Louis XIII, and challenging him to a duel. Herbert resumed his post in February 1622, after the death of de Luynes. He was very popular at the French court and showed considerable diplomatic ability. His chief missions were to accomplish the marriage between Charles I of England and Henrietta Maria, and to secure the assistance of Louis XIII of France for the elector palatine. He failed in the latter, and was dismissed in April 1624, returning home greatly in debt and receiving little reward for his services beyond the Irish peerage of Castle Island in 1624, and the English barony of Cherbury, or Chirbury, in May 1629. Just a mile inside the English border from Montgomeryshire, the village was formerly known as Llanffynhonwen, 'the holy place of the white (or holy) well'.

In 1632, he was appointed a member of the council of war. Herbert attended the king at York in 1639, and in May 1642 was imprisoned by Parliament for insisting on the addition of the words 'without cause' to the resolution that the king violated his oath by making war on parliament. He determined after this to take no further part in the struggle, retired to Montgomery Castle, and declined the king's summons. On 5 September1644, he surrendered the castle to Parliamentary forces in order to stop his great library being confiscated, returned to London, submitted, and was granted a pension of twenty pounds a week. In 1647, he paid a visit to Paris, and died in London, a depressed and disappointed man, in 1648. He was buried in the church of St Giles's in the Fields. Montgomery Castle, with its newly built mansion and extraordinary library were demolished a year after his death, by order of Parliament.

Edward Herbert is best known as the originator of deism. Herbert's first and most important work was the *De veritate, prout distinguitur a revelatione, a verisimili, a possibili, et a falso* (Paris, 1624; London, 1633). It combined a theory of knowledge, a methodology for the investigation of truth, and a scheme of natural religion. In *De veritate*, Herbert dismissed all past theories, and professed his intention to constitute a new and true system. There was little polemic against the received form of Christianity, but Herbert's attitude towards the Church's doctrine was distinctly negative, and he denied revelation except to the individual soul. In *De veritate,* Herbert produced the first purely metaphysical treatise written by a Briton, and in his *De religious gentilium*, one of the earliest studies in comparative theology. Both his metaphysical speculations and his religious views were highly original and provoked considerable controversy. 'Deism' refers to a view of

God which upholds the creatorship of God, but rejects a continuing divine involvement with that creation. Deism is now used to refer to the views of certain English philosophers during the Age of Reason in the late seventeenth and early eighteenth centuries. Deists understood God as an extension of generally accepted human ideas of justice, rationality and wisdom. While traditional Christianity was based on a divine revelation and was not accessible to those who lived before Christ, deism was available to all people at all times and places. He produced several additional religious treatises.

His *The Life and Raigne of King Henry VIII* (1649) is valuable because of its composition from original documents. Edward Herbert's poems, published in 1665, reflected his admiration for John Donne. Both Donne and Ben Jonson honoured Herbert in poetry. His rather self-regarding autobiography, first published by Horace Walpole in 1764, concentrated on

his duels and amorous adventures to the exclusion of more creditable incidents in his career, such as his contributions to philosophy and history, his intimacy with Donne*, Ben Jonson, John Selden and Thomas Carew, Isaac Casaubon, Gassendi and Grotius, or his embassy in France, about which he described only the

Portrait by Isaac Oliver, 1610

splendour of his retinue and his social triumphs.

Herbert's philosophical work was praised by Descartes who wrote that Herbert's 'mind had few equal'. Tommaso Campanella, Hobbes, Sir William Dugdale and Hugo Grotius held his work in high esteem. Gassendi called him 'the second Verulam' (Lord Francis Bacon) and Ben Jonson wrote of him as 'all-virtuous Herbert', who could not be contained because he was 'so many men' in one. Charles Blount hailed Herbert as 'the Great Oracle and Commander of his Time for Learning.'

* John Donne was of Welsh origins, and one of his most important poems, *Goodfriday, 1613. Riding Westwards*, 'records an intense religious meditation at a crucial turning point in the author's life – and, by extension, in the intellectual history of early modern England.' Born into a dangerously devout Catholic family in a time of heightened religious sensitivity, Donne eventually joined the Church of England and became one of the most celebrated preachers of his day. A daringly controversial erotic poet whose scandalous marriage cost him a promising secular career, he ended his life as Dean of St Paul's Cathedral, a moral compass for the nation. This 42-line poem, conceived as Donne entered

his 42nd year, was written at exactly the time Donne made his decision to take orders, in spring 1613. The poem was probably composed when Donne visited Edward Herbert at Montgomery Castle. Following his return to London, Donne announced his 'resolution of a new course of life and new profession' – divinity.

GEORGE HERBERT 3 April 1593 – 1 March 1633

'HOLY MR. HERBERT'

George Herbert was born at Montgomery Castle, the fifth son of Sir Richard Herbert and Magdalen Newport. The Herberts, since during the Wars of the Roses, had been among the greatest names in English and Welsh politics. After his father's death in 1596, George and his six brothers and three sisters were raised by their mother, patron to the London Welshman John Donne, who dedicated his *Holy Sonnets* to her. His brother was Lord Edward Herbert of Cherbury, and a cousin Sir Edward Herbert was a close associate of Charles I. Herbert  was educated at Westminster School and Trinity College, Cambridge. His first two sonnets, sent to his mother in 1609, maintained that the love of God is a worthier subject for verse than the love of woman. In the accompanying letter he wrote: *'My meaning (dear Mother) is in these sonnets, to declare my resolution to be, that my poor abilities in poetry, shall be all and ever consecrated to God's glory.'* After taking his BA and MA degrees with distinction, Herbert was elected a major fellow of Trinity. In 1618 he was appointed Reader in Rhetoric at Cambridge, and in 1620 he was elected Public Orator (to 1628). He acted as a sort of an ambassador for the school in this role, writing and delivering speeches to King James. In 1623, Herbert was the university's hero of the hour when his graceful Latin restored King James's good temper, after rash dons had performed an anti-Catholic play in front of their royal visitor.

It was expected that he would serve in some high position of state under James I. While still at the university, Herbert became an ordained deacon in 1624. In 1624 and 1625 Herbert was elected to represent Montgomery in Parliament. In 1626, at the death of Sir Francis Bacon, (who had dedicated his *Translation of Certaine Psalmes* to Herbert the year before) he contributed a memorial poem in Latin. Herbert's mother died in 1627, and her funeral sermon was delivered by John Donne. In 1629, Herbert married his step-father's cousin Jane Danvers, while his brother Edward Herbert, the noted philosopher and poet, was raised to the peerage as Lord Herbert of Chirbury.

Herbert could have used his post of orator to reach high political office, but instead gave up his secular ambitions. Herbert took holy orders in the Church of England in 1630 and spent the rest of his life as rector in Fugglestone-cum-Bemerton near Salisbury. At Bemerton, George Herbert preached and wrote poetry, cared deeply for his parishioners and helped rebuild the church out of his own funds. He came to be known as Holy Mr. Herbert' around the countryside in the three years before his death of consumption on St. David's Day, 1633.

His humble home contrasted with the great Montgomery Castle, where his bibliophile brother Edward built a luxury home inside medieval walls. Thanks to Cromwell's Roundheads, only a grassy platform remains where Edward's fantasy castle stood, but the views endure over Herefordshire and the Welsh Borders, home in the next generation to two more great Welsh poets, Henry Vaughan and Thomas Traherne, whose love of George Herbert enriched their verse.

A Priest to the Temple; or, The Country Parson, His Character and Rule of Holy Life, (published 1652), Herbert's practical manual of advice to country parsons, bears witness to the intelligent devotion with which he undertook his duties as priest. Herbert had long been in ill health. While dying of tuberculosis, he sent the manuscript of *The Temple: Sacred Poems and Private Ejaculations* to Nicholas Ferrar, asking him to publish the poems only if he thought they might do good to 'any dejected poor soul. Herbert wrote: '*It (my book) is a picture of the many spiritual conflicts that have passed between God and my soul, before I could subject mine to the will of Jesus, my Master, in whose service I have now found perfect freedom.*' The Temple was published posthumously in 1633 and met with enormous popular acclaim, having 20 printings by 1680. Some lines from *The Temple* are: 'Drink not the third glass, which thou canst not tame, / When once it is within thee'; 'Dare to be true. Nothing can need a lie: / A fault, which needs it most, grows two thereby'; 'By no means run in debt: take thine own measure. / Who cannot live on twenty pound a year, / Cannot on forty'; 'Wit's an unruly engine, wildly striking / Sometimes a friend, sometimes the engineer'; 'Be calm in arguing: for fierceness makes / Error a fault, and truth discourtesy.'

Herbert's poems are characterized by a precision of language, a metrical versatility, and an ingenious use of imagery or conceits that was favored by the metaphysical school of poets. They include almost every known form of song and poem, but they also reflect Herbert's concern with speech--conversational, persuasive, proverbial. Carefully arranged in related sequences, the poems explore and celebrate the ways of God's love as Herbert discovered them within the fluctuations of his own experience.2 Because Herbert is as much an ecclesiastical as a religious poet, one would not expect him to make much appeal to an age as secular as our own; but it has not proved so. All sorts of readers have responded to his quiet intensity;

and the opinion has even been voiced that he has, for readers of the late twentieth century, displaced Donne as the supreme Metaphysical poet George Herbert was an ordained priest and poet. In 1633, his book was published posthumously.

The Poetry Foundation website says of his poems: 'This is the stuff of humility and integrity, not celebrity. But even if Herbert does not appear to be one of the larger-than-life cultural monuments of seventeenth-century England - a position that virtually requires the qualities of irrepressible ambition and boldness, if not self-regarding arrogance, that he attempted to flee - he is in some ways a pivotal figure: enormously popular, deeply and broadly influential, and arguably the most skilful and important British devotional lyricist of this or any other time. There is, as Stanley Stewart has convincingly demonstrated, a substantial School of Herbert cutting across all ages.'

His poems are characterized by a deep religious devotion, linguistic precision, metrical agility, and the ingenious use of conceit. Coleridge wrote of Herbert's diction that 'Nothing can be more pure, manly, or unaffected,' and he is ranked with his friend Donne as one of the great Metaphysical poets. The poems are a spiritual autobiography, many describing his intensely personal struggles with faith and calling. The poems record his own doubts and faith, in a way that rings true with many readers. They are an example of the metaphysical school of poetry, which deliberately piled metaphor upon metaphor, and drew those metaphors from the cutting edge of contemporary science and philosophy. They flatter the reader by assuming a breadth and depth of political, theological and scientific knowledge. Deeply intelligent, they are also full of genuine emotion. He does not ask the reader whether something is true, but asks him to explore his feelings about the subject. He was deeply conflicted by knowing that if his former academic life was unconventional for an aristocrat, still more was being a simple parish priest.

His masterpiece, *Love III* gives us the lines: 'Love bade me welcome; yet my soul drew back, / Guilty of dust and sin. / But quick-ey'd Love, observing me grow slack / From my first entrance in, / Drew nearer to me, sweetly questioning, / If I lacked any thing.' The mystical philosopher Simone Weil described it as the most beautiful poem in the world. Ralph Vaughan Williams captured the joy and colours of Herbert's verse, and we remember the hymns from Herbert's words: 'Let all the world in every corner sing' and 'Teach me, my God and King, in all things thee to see'. On the day before his death Herbert was singing his own verse, accompanying himself on the lute.

HENRY VAUGHAN 17 April 1621 – 23 April 1695

'THE SILURIST'

Henry was the older twin brother of the hermetic philosopher and alchemist Thomas Vaughan. They were the sons of Thomas Vaughan and Denise Morgan, of Trenewydd (Newton-upon-Usk) in the parish of Llansanffraid in Breconshire, and their grandfather William Vaughan held Tretower Court. The Vaughans and Herberts were Yorkist allies in the Wars of the Roses, fighting the Lancastrian Edmund and Jasper Tudor (q.v.), and had intermarried for centuries in south-east and mid-east Wales. One of Henry Vaughan's ancestors, Sir Roger Vaughan from Tretower Court had led Jasper Tudor's father to execution, and tried to kill Jasper before being killed by Jasper. Thomas Vaghan had moved from Tretower Court to his wife's farm estate at Llansanffraid.

The brothers were educated by Matthew Herbert, rector of Llangattock, and a cousin was the noted John Aubrey. Henry Vaughan appears to have gone to the 'Welsh University', Jesus College, Oxford in 1638 but unlike his brother took no degree. In 1640 his father sent him to London to study law, but the Civil War interrupted his studies and he fought for the Royalists. He is known to have returned home by 1647. About 1650 he was converted to a religious life under the influence of George Herbert (q.v.). Parliamentary victory, the temporary confiscation of his home, the death of his brother William and his own illness distressed him, but he found consolation in the scenery of the Usk Valley. Vaughan began reading devotional works and occult philosophy, and began to practise as a physician. He was married Catherine Wise, and upon her death, her sister Elizabeth. Vaughan took his literary inspiration from his native environment and chose the descriptive name 'Silurist', derived from his homage to the Celtic Silures tribe of the region. Vaughan's chief works are: *Poems* 1646; *Silex Scintillans (Sparkling Flint)* 1650; *Olor Iscanus (The Swan of Usk)* 1651; *The Mount of Olives* 1652; *Flores Solitudinis* 1654; and *Thalia Rediviva*, 1678. Vaughan was bilingual, and there are traces of Welsh influence in his poetry, which also reflects his love of his tranquil native valley. In his fondness for solitary communion with nature and his reminiscences of childhood, he anticipates Wordsworth, whose *Ode to Intimations of Immortality* seems to have been inspired by Vaughan's works. In turn, Vaughan owes a great deal to the works of Donne and especially George Herbert.

He was 'one of the finest poets of the metaphysical school, [who] wrote verse marked by mystical intensity, sensitivity to nature, tranquillity of tone, and power of wording.' The metaphysical poets concentrated upon exploring the personal relationship with God. The period shortly preceding the publication of his greatest work *Silex Scintillans* marked an important period of his life. Certain indications in the first volume and explicit statements made in the preface to the second volume suggest that Vaughan suffered a prolonged sickness that inflicted much pain. Vaughan believed he was spared to make amends and start a new course not only in his life but in the literature he would produce. It is during this period of Vaughan's life, around 1650, that he adopts the saying *moriendo, revixi*, meaning 'by dying, I gain new life'.

Archbishop Trench stated that 'As a divine Vaughan may be inferior [to Herbert], but as a poet he is certainly superior'.

In *Silex Scintillans*, *The World* is the favourite poem by Vaughan of many people. The first verse is:

'I saw Eternity the other night,
Like a great ring of pure and endless light,
All calm, as it was bright;
And round beneath it, Time in hours, days, years,
Driv'n by the spheres
Like a vast shadow moved; in which the world
And all her train were hurled.
The doting lover in his quaintest strain
Did there complain;
Near him, his lute, his fancy, and his flights,
Wit's sour delights,
With gloves, and knots, the silly snares of pleasure,
Yet his dear treasure
All scattered lay, while he his eyes did pour
Upon a flow'r.'

The poem *Peace* from *Silex Scintillans* is demonstrative of his searching for a personal relationship with God:

'My soul, there is a country
  Far beyond the stars,
Where stands a wingèd sentry
  All skilful in the wars:
There, above noise and danger,
  Sweet Peace sits crown'd with smiles,
And One born in a manger
  Commands the beauteous files.
He is thy gracious Friend,
  And - O my soul, awake! -
Did in pure love descend
  To die here for thy sake.
If thou canst get but thither,
  There grows the flower of Peace,

The Rose that cannot wither,
  Thy fortress, and thy ease.
Leave then thy foolish ranges;
  For none can thee secure
But One who never changes -
  Thy God, thy life, thy cure.'

He spent nearly all his life in Llansantffraed and is buried in its churchyard. Henry Vaughan's *The Evening-Watch* was used for the 1924 *The Evening-Watch: Dialogue between Body and Soul* by Gustav Holst. Vaughan was acclaimed less during his lifetime than after his death but influenced Wordsworth, Tennyson and Siegfried Sassoon.

ADMIRAL SIR HENRY MORGAN 1635? – 25 August 1688

'THE SWORD OF ENGLAND', THE GREATEST PRIVATEER OF ALL TIME

'Privateering' was the practice of the state commissioning privately owned ships to attack enemy merchant ships. It came into its own with the sea-dog captains of the Elizabethan Age, men such as Drake, Hawkins, Frobisher and Raleigh. Legally sanctioned, it was fundamentally different from piracy, which preyed on all shipping, in that it focused upon enemy ships only. There was no Royal Navy as such, and the monarch had to rely upon privately owned ships to fight. The Crown often sold 'privateering' licences in return for a cut of the spoils. Many of the privateers who fought the Spaniards in the 17th century became known as buccaneers, from the French *boucaniers* in the West Indies, meaning sun-dryers of meat. The most famous and successful of all the buccaneers was a Welshman, Henry Morgan, although in reality he was a privateer.

Henry Morgan was a cousin of the Morgans that owned Tredegar Park outside Newport, the son of a gentleman farmer, from Llanrhymney Hall. He set sail from Bristol at the age of around twenty, bound for the West Indies to make his fortune. He served in the shambolic expedition sent by Cromwell to Hispaniola. Instead, in 1655 Jamaica was seized from Spain, to serve as a base for freebooting American and British privateers to operate against Spanish America. In 1662 Morgan joined a ship to plunder Spanish shipping and various enemy-occupied coastal towns.

Morgan was so successful that within two years his share of the booty enabled him to buy his own ship. Aged around twenty-nine, he now used Jamaica as his base, and from here he harassed the Spanish on the American mainland, and built up an enormous treasure trove. When the Spanish started attacking British ships off Cuba, the Governor of Jamaica asked Morgan to return and scatter the Spanish fleet.

Morgan was then made Admiral of the Jamaican fleet of ten ships and five hundred men, because of his courage and success. By 1665, Morgan had made enough money to marry Elizabeth, the daughter of Edward Morgan, Deputy-Governor of Jamaica since 1664. Edward Morgan was his uncle, and related to the great Morgan family of Tredegar House, Newport. From 1666, Morgan allied himself with Edward Mansfield, the famous buccaneer, and on Mansfield's death was elected 'admiral' of his buccaneer fleet. Governor Modyford of Jamaica gave Henry Morgan privateering 'commissions' to raise men and attack the Spanish, who were threatening Jamaica.

Morgan's exploit in the sacking of Puerto Principe (now Camaguey in Cuba) in 1668 is well documented. In the same year, he looted and ransacked the largest city in Cuba, Porto Bello, and Maracaibo in Venezuela. He took Maracaibo Castle, but the fleeing Spaniards lit a fuse to the fort's powder magazine. Morgan's men ran away, but Morgna ran to it, and stamped it out with seconds to spare, saving many lives. His fame spread as a brave leader, but he was later trapped in a lagoon 80 miles inland and had to use fireships to escape. Morgan sailed north, capturing three Spanish ships before re-entering the Caribbean. He now plundered some of Spain's richest coastal cities, but was eventually chased into open waters by the main Spanish fleet. Morgan and his privateers decided to turn and fight, and nearly annihilated the Spanish. On his return to his Jamaican base, Morgan had lost just eighteen men, and plundered a quarter of a million pieces of gold and silver coins, jewellery, silks, spices, munitions, weapons and slaves. Captain Morgan was just thirty-three years old, with a reputation that had attracted seafarers from all over the West Indies to join his flag.

After his sacking of Porto Bello in Panama, Morgan attacked a French ship. It appeared that the French had given 'notes of exchange' to an English ship previously, in return for provisions. These notes had not been 'honoured' when presented for payment in Jamaica. Morgan positioned his flagship, the *Oxford*, in a bay in south Haiti, waiting for a sighting of the French ship. When it appeared, he invited the captain and officers to dine with them and took them prisoner. Unfortunately, a spark of celebratory gunfire lit the powder magazine, and there was an explosion. Three hundred crew and the French prisoners were blown to bits. Luckily Morgan and his officers were at the stern of the ship, and survived, being furthest away from the explosion.

He returned to the site later, in the *Jamaica Merchant*, to try and salvage the ship, during which operation the *Jamaica Merchant* also sank. Also in 1669, the Spanish Capitan Pardal swore vengeance upon Morgan. After making a small raid on a Jamaican village, left the following note pinned to a tree near the smouldering village hall. 'I, Capitan Manuel Pardal, to the Chief of Privateers in Jamaica. I come to seek General Henry Morgan, with two ships and twenty-one guns. When he sees this Challenge, I beg that he will come out and seek me, that he may see the Valour of the Spaniards'. Within weeks, Pardal was caught near the east coast of Cuba by one of Morgan's captains, the Welshman John Morris, and shot through the neck in battle.

On his return to Jamaica, Morgan was placed in charge of 35 ships and 2,000 men. Aged thirty-five, he decided to break the power of Spain in the West Indies by attacking Panama, the largest and richest town in the Americas.

Meantime, Britain and Spain had negotiated peace in London and orders were despatched to him to call off any attacks on Spanish colonies. Morgan ignored the orders, reached the mainland in 1670, and marched across the Isthmus of Panama towards the city. In the course of this devastating raid, Morgan and his men succumbed to the heat and disease as they hacked their way through the jungle, destroying every fort and settlement in their path. By the time he reached Panama, in January 1671, Morgan had only a half of his original 2,000 men left, but he attacked the defending force of 20,000 Spaniards with such venom that they fled the city. One hundred and fifty mules were needed to take the booty back to the ships. Morgan had made six separate inland raids upon Spanish cities, this being the greatest achievement. It is thought that his raids throughout the Indies and Central and South America took Spanish resources from North America, enabling the British to gain a foothold and expand south.

The Spanish put a price on Morgan's head, and as the raid had occurred in peacetime, put diplomatic pressure upon Charles II. Morgan was arrested and extradited to London in 1672. Governor Modyford had already been sent home to answer charges. Luckily for Morgan, the peace did not last and he was soon released after paying out a huge part of his treasure to the Crown. The king was deeply unpopular, with the Dutch sailing up the Medway to destroy the English fleet, and the Great Fire of London and the Great Plague also being seen as God's judgment on his reign. Morgan was feted everywhere as 'the sword of England', the only good news in Charles II's reign, for which the king was duly grateful. Charles II knighted him and sent him back to Jamaica as Lieutenant Governor of the island, where Morgan died, a successful planter, at the age of 52 in 1688. Morgan was one of the greatest generals in history, having invaded inland Spanish possessions on six occasions, defeating greater forces each time. Arthur Glyn Prys-Jones's poem *Morgan's March to Panama* reads:

Morgan's curls are matted,
His lips are cracked and dry,
His tawny beard is tangled,
And his plumed hat hangs awry:

But his voice still booms like thunder
Through the foetid jungle glade
As he marches, bold as Lucifer,
Leading his gaunt brigade.

Twelve hundred famished buccaneers
Blistered, bitten and bled,
A stricken mob of men accursed
By the monstrous sun o'erhead:

Twelve hundred starveling scarecrows
Without a crumb to eat,
And not a drink for tortured throats
In that grim, festering heat.

Twelve hundred threadbare musketeers
Rotting in tropic mud
Where the reeking, fevered mangroves
Wreak havoc in their blood:

Twelve hundred febrile wretches,
A legion of the dead:
But Morgan in his blue brocade
Goes striding on ahead.

Twelve hundred tatterdemalions,
The sorriest, maddest crew
That ever the green savannahs saw
When the Spanish bugles blew:

Twelve hundred rattling skeletons
Who sprang to life, and then
Like a wild wave took Panama,
For they were Morgan's men.

Morgan's exploits are far too incredible to feature in a book of this length. The English translation publishers of Esquemeling's contemporary book, *The Buccaneers of America* were sued by Morgan for calling him a 'pirate', and questioning his upbringing, in 1685. This was the first ever recorded case of damages being paid and apologies being made for libel. This author has translated the three different foreign versions of Esquemeling's work, which were published as *The Illustrated Pirate Diaries – A Remarkable Eye Witness Account of Captain Morgan and the Buccaneers* (Apple, Collins 2008). For further information, please see this author's *Sir Henry Morgan, the Greatest Buccaneer of Them All* (2005).

WILLIAM JONES FRS 1675 – 3 July 1749

FIRST MAN TO USE THE SYMBOL π (PI) AS A MATHEMATICAL SYMBOL

William Jones was the son of a poor farmer Siôn Siôr (John George Jones) and Elizabeth Rowland, and born in Llanfihangel Tre'r Beirdd, Anglesey. He attended a charity school at Llanfechell, where his mathematical aptitude was spotted by the local landowner, who arranged for him to be given a job in London working in a merchant's counting-house. He owed his successful career partly to the patronage of the North Wales Bulkeley family, and then to the Earl of Macclesfield. Jones left the counting-house and served at sea, teaching mathematics on naval men-of-war between 1695 and 1702, when he published *A New Compendium of the Whole Art of Navigation*. He married twice, firstly the widow of his counting-house employer, whose property he inherited on her death, and secondly, in 1731, Mary, the 22-year-old daughter of cabinet-maker George Nix, with whom he had two surviving children. Their son, William Jones (q.v.), born in 1746, was the philologist who established links between Latin, Greek and Sanskrit, leading to the concept of the Indo-European language group.

He was present at the battle of Vigo in October 1702 when the English intercepted the Spanish treasure fleet. Jones then moved to London, teaching mathematics in coffee houses. Soon he was also a private tutor to Philip Yorke, later 1st Earl of Hardwicke, who became Lord Chancellor and provided an invaluable source of introductions for Jones. Jones published *Synopsis Palmariorum Matheseos or A New Introduction to the Mathematics* in 1706, based on his teaching notes and which included theorems on calculus. The history of the constant ratio of the circumference to the diameter of any circle is ancient, but the symbol for this ratio known today as π (pi) dates from Jones' book. It is thought that he chose π because it is first letter of the word for periphery (περιφέρεια) and/or because it is the first letter of the word for perimeter (περίμετρος).

The ratio had previously been referred to as: *quantitas in quam cum multiflicetur diameter, proveniet circumferencia* (the quantity which, when the diameter is multiplied by it, yields the circumference). It is still widely believed that the Swiss mathematician Leonhard Euler (1707-83) introduced the symbol π into common use, but Jones used it a year before his birth. However, the symbol π was popularised in 1737 by the Swiss Euler, but it was not until 1934 that the symbol was adopted universally. Before the appearance of the symbol π, approximations such as 22/7 and 355/113 had also been used to express the ratio, which gave the impression that it was a rational number.

Although he did not prove it, Jones believed that π was an 'irrational number', an infinite, non-repeating sequence of digits that could never totally be expressed in numerical form. He wrote: '... the exact proportion between the diameter and the circumference can never be expressed in numbers' so a symbol was required to represent an ideal that can be approached but never reached, and Jones recognised that only a pure platonic symbol would suffice. The symbol represented the platonic concept of *pi*, an ideal that in numerical terms can be approached, but never reached.

As well as his first use of the symbol pi, Jones is of great interest because of his connection to a number of key mathematical, scientific and political characters of the 18th century. He developed one of the greatest scientific libraries and mathematical archives in the country, which remained in the hands of his patrons the Macclesfield family for nearly 300 years. It was probably around 1706 that Jones first came to Isaac Newton's attention when he published *Synopsis*, in which he explained Newton's methods for calculus as well as other mathematical innovations. In 1708 Jones was able to acquire Collins's extensive library and archives, which contained several of Newton's letters and papers written in the 1670s. Collins corresponded with Newton and with many of the leading English and foreign mathematicians of the day, drafting mathematical notes on behalf of the Royal Society.

When Jones applied for the mastership of Christ's Hospital Mathematical School in 1709 he carried with him testimonials from Edmund Halley and Newton, but did not get the post. However Jones's former pupil, Philip Yorke, introduced his tutor to Sir Thomas Parker (1667-1732), who was on his way to becoming the next lord chief justice in the following year. Jones joined his household and became tutor to his only son, George (c.1697-1764), the start of his life-long connection with the Parker family.

Around the time that Jones bought Collins's library and archive, Newton and the German mathematician Gottfried Leibniz (1646-1716) were in dispute over who invented calculus first. In Collins's mathematical papers, Jones had found a transcript of one of Newton's earliest treatments of calculus, *De Analyst* (1669), which in 1711 he arranged to have published. Jones' 1711 work, *Analysis per quantitatum series, fluxiones ac differentias,* first introduced the dot notation for differentiation in calculus, and in November that year he became a Fellow of the Royal Society, later becoming its Vice-President. In 1712 Jones joined the committee set up by the Royal Society to determine priority for the invention of calculus. Jones made the Collins papers with Newton's correspondence on calculus available to the committee and the resulting report was based largely upon them, giving precedence of Newton over Leibniz.

In 1718 Jones' patron Sir Thomas Parker was made Lord Chancellor and in 1721 became Earl of Macclesfield. In 1731 Jones published *Discourses of the Natural Philosophy of the Elements.* Among the many influential mathematicians, astronomers and natural philosophers he corresponded with was Roger Cotes, the first Plumian Professor of Astronomy at Cambridge and considered by many to be the most talented British mathematician of his generation after Newton. Jones also had an extensive correspondence with the astronomer and mathematician, John Machin, who served as secretary to the Royal Society for nearly 30 years from 1718. Machin had also worked on a series for the ratio of the circumference to the diameter which converged fairly rapidly. The result of his calculation was printed in Jones's 1706 book, 'true to above a 100 places; as computed by the accurate and ready pen of the truly ingenious Mr John Machin...' frequent occurrence in those days.

In his will William Jones bequeathed his library of around 15,000 books together with some 50,000 manuscript pages, many in Newton's hand, to the third Earl of Macclesfield. Some 350 of these books and manuscripts were written in Welsh, and this portion of the original library was safeguarded in about 1900 to form the Shirburn Collection at the National Library of Wales in Aberystwyth. A hundred years later, in 2001, that part of William Jones's collection that comprised papers and notebooks belonging to Sir Isaac Newton were sold to the library of the University of Cambridge for over £6m, a sum partly raised by public subscription. The bulk of the rest of the library was sold in a series of auctions at Sotheby's in 2004 and 2005, raising many more millions: a copy of the astronomer Johann Kepler's *Harmonices mundi* raised close to £100,000 and Newton's classic *Principia mathematica* a further £60,000. William Jones's own book, *Synopsis palmariorum matheseos*, was a bargain at a mere £8,000. In one of Newton's books, edited by William Jones, and given as a gift by Jones to the Macclesfield family, there was a single loose sheet in Newton's own handwriting. This sheet alone raised £90,000.

RICHARD 'BEAU' NASH 18 October 1674 – 3 February 1761

'THE KING OF BATH', 'THE MASTER OF CEREMONIES', 'THE DANDY OF BATH'

Richard 'Beau' Nash was born in Swansea, son of Richard Nash of Pembrokeshire (possibly of Llangwm), who had settled in Swansea as a partner in a glass-works. His mother was one of the Pembrokeshire Poyer family. Educated at Queen Elizabeth's Grammar School, Carmarthen, Beau Nash went to Jesus College, Oxford, but dropped out. He joined the army but found that it was too expensive and time-consuming, then went to the Middle Temple in 1693 to study law. He hardly attended, but somehow lived a sybaritic and hedonistic life, probably through his skills in gambling. Aged just twenty-one, in 1695 Nash organised a pageant for William III at the Middle Temple, who was so impressed that he offered Nash a knighthood. Not having any real means to support a title, Nash declined. From henceforward he lived by making huge wagers and gaming, and receiving gifts from women admirers.

The small town of Bath had been exploited by the British and then the Romans for its hot mineral springs, which pump out 250,000 gallons of water a day, but it was Nash who really gave Bath its special social appeal. Queen Anne's visits in 1692, 1702 and 1703 to take the waters had improved Bath's social standing. Attracted to Bath in 1705, Nash organised a band, and took a lease of rooms 'for assembly'. A failed scholar, lawyer and soldier, Nash found his true métier, and excelled in organising social ceremonies. He was a socialite with a penchant for order, cleanliness and propriety. He was first aide-de-camp to the master of ceremonies, a Captain Webster, who was soon killed in a duel. Nash became master or ceremonies and transformed Bath into the fashionable centre of England. Nash was quickly responsible for the outlawing of the wearing of swords within the city walls, mindful of the fate of his precursor. This prompted Richard Sheridan to write in *The Rivals*: 'A sword seen in the streets of Bath would raise as great an alarm as a mad dog.'

In 1706 he raised the fortune of £18,000 by subscription, to improve the roads in the City around his 'Assembly Rooms'. The roads were now paved, so that gowns did not drag in the mud. Beggars and thieves were driven out of Bath, and sedan chair drivers were fined for insolence. Nash drew up rules against the wearing of swords, duelling, informal dress, promiscuous smoking, the cheating of 'chairmen' (sedan-chair carriers) and lodging-house keepers. Nash, champion of the 'gentlemen of fashion' took to snuff and decried the use of pipes. He prohibited all smoking in public rooms and assemblies, and manufacturers started making scented snuff, as on the Continent, to meet a massive upsurge in demand. Snuff mills across Britain, notably still in Kendal, were built by 1720 to meet the demand caused by Nash's fashion. He enforced his rules autocratically against noble and commoner alike.

Nash's 'rules' of 'polite society' were allied to a common dress code and the discouragement of 'hard drinking'. He was so successful in attracting both the aristocratic elite and the growing gentry class to his fashionable and safe town, that Bath's population grew from 3,000 in 1700 to 35,000 in 1800, swelled also by visitors in the 'Bath Season' of October to early June. Bath quickly grew to become the eighth largest city in England. The new rules and dress code encouraged sociability between the gentry and nobles, and made the less fashionably minded feel at home. His 'Rules - by general consent determined' are as follows:

'That a visit of ceremony at coming to Bath, and another at going away, is all that is expected or desired by ladies of quality and fashion - except impertinents.

That ladies coming to the ball appoint a time for their footmen's coming to wait on them home, to prevent disturbances to themselves and others.

That gentlemen of fashion never appearing in a morning before the ladies in gowns and caps, show breeding and respect.

That no person take it ill that any one goes to another's play or breakfast, and not to theirs - except captious by nature.

That no gentleman give his tickets for the balls to any but gentlewomen - N.B. Unless he has none of his acquaintance.

That gentlemen crowding before ladies at the ball, show ill-manners; and that none do so for the future - except such as respect nobody but themselves.

That no gentleman take it ill that another dances before them - except such as have no pretence to dance at all.

That the elder ladies and children be contented with a second bench at the ball, as being past or not come to perfection.

That the younger ladies take notice how many eyes observe them - N.B. This does not extend to the Have-at-Alls.

That all whisperers of lies and scandals be taken as their authors.

That all repeaters of such lies and scandal be shunned by all company - except such as have been guilty of the same crime. N.B. Several men of no character, old women and young ones of questioned reputation, are great authors of lies in the place, being of the sect of Levellers.

"Beau" Nash, 1742'

A superb conversationalist and wearing distinctive clothes, he was the arbiter of fashion and taste. From the start, he dressed the part, and moved with an exaggerated elegance, which soon earned him the nickname 'Beau'. Instead of the popular white wigs of the time, he wore a black wig, with a jewelled cream beaver-skin hat set at a rakish angle. His coat was highly decorated with lace and braid, and left open to show his splendid waistcoat and ruffled shirt. Nash made Bath the playground of the English aristocracy, the most fashionable resort in the land. He was a bon vivant, and star of the show, with his huge white hat, parading around the paved streets in a carriage drawn by six grey horses, his progress announced by the blast of French horns.

Although dismissed as a 'fop' and a 'dandy', he soon imposed his rules of polite society across the city, and encouraged the wealthy to invest in superb new buildings*. Nash initiated the buildings of the Pump Rooms, overlooking the King's Bath, where the company of rich people could assemble to gossip, as well as the Assembly Rooms, with a huge ballroom for the sparkling balls and adjoining card (gaming) room. Poor lodgings were replaced by luxurious ones. He even built a hospital, promoting the use of Bath's mineral waters. In the Pump Rooms and the Assembly Rooms, the Master of Ceremony's word was law. He ridiculed the wearing of riding boots at fashionable gatherings. One of Nash's rules forbade the wearing of boots in the rooms at evening, and a country squire tried to defy him. Nash asked him 'Why have you not also brought your horse into the ballroom, since the four-footed beast is as well-shod as its master?'

Even Princess Amelia, the daughter of George II, was refused one more dance when he had decreed that the music should stop. In Constance Hill's biography of Jane Austen we read: 'When Miss Austen and her uncle had passed in also, they would find themselves in a long, lofty room lighted by tall windows, and having at each end a large semi-circular arched recess, one containing the musicians' gallery, the other a statue of beau Nash standing in a niche above a tall clock. Beau Nash! Who for fifty years "was literally the King of Bath", and of whom Goldsmith wrote: "I have known him on a ball night strip even the Duchess of Queensberry of her costly lace apron, and throw it to one of the back benches; observing that none but abigails appeared in white aprones; and when the Pricess Amelia applied to him at 11 o'clock for one more dance he refused, his laws being as he said like those of Lycurgus - unalterable.'

Dress Balls were held once a week and began at 6pm, when the eleven musicians on the first-floor gallery struck up. Between 6 and 8 there were minuets, a stately dance performed by couples alone: 'It is often remarked by Foreigners that the English nation of both sexes look as grave when they are dancing, as it they were attending the Solemnity of a Funeral.' The more energetic country dances followed between 8 and 9 and required a freer dress, and the Rules of the Assembly Rooms noted: 'No Lady dances country-dances in a hoop of any kind and those who choose to pull the hoops off, will be assisted by proper servants in an apartment for that purpose.' At 9 the dancers moved to the Tea Room for refreshment, and the entertainment continued with further country-dances until 11, when the Master of Ceremonies ended the evening. Nash 'entering the ballroom. Orders the music to cease, and the ladies thereupon resting themselves till they grow cool, their partners complete the ceremonies of the evening by handing them to the (sedan) chairs in which they are conveyed to their respective lodgings.'

An 'Assembly' was defined in 1751 as 'a stated and general meeting of the polite persons of both sexes, for the sake of conversation, gallantry, news and play.' Guests amused themselves at cards, drank tea or walked around talking and flirting. Nash had constructed the Assembly Rooms for this purpose, with different rooms being used for tea drinking, eating, gossiping, dancing and gaming. The Tea Room was used mainly for refreshments and concerts. Meals were served throughout the day, from public breakfasts, to supper during Dress Balls. Food on the side-tables included 'sweetmeats, jellies, wine, biscuits, cold ham and turkey.' Tea was the favoured drink, usually drunk weak and without milk, but sometimes with arrack (fermented cocoa) and lemon.

A foreign visitor noted that Bath's tea parties were 'extremely gay'. Sometimes, things got out of hand: 'The tea-drinking passed as usual, and the company having risen from the tables, were sauntering in groups, in expectation of the signal to attack, when the bell beginning to ring, they flew with eagerness to the dessert, and the whole place was instantly in commotion. There was nothing but jostling, scrambling, pulling, snatching, struggling, scolding and screaming.'

In 1738 Nash welcomed the Prince of Wales to Bath, and set up an obelisk, inscribed by Alexander Pope, to mark his visit. Bath had become 'the place to be, and be seen', and Nash's presence and the social scene also drew in many of the architects who accomplished great buildings in the city. It was during his time that the city acquired its ranks of Palladian mansions and town houses, all built in the local honey-coloured Bath stone, in which all new buildings have to be clad, even today. The physical design of the wonderful city of Bath under the two John Woods is entirely due to Nash. The Woods created Queen Square, the North and South parades and the Royal Crescent. In 1820, Nash's Assembly Rooms were burnt to the ground. Also known as 'the Lower Rooms', they were situated on 'the Walks leading from the Grove to the Parades', with 'a Ball Room ninety feet long, as well as two tea rooms, a card room' and 'an apartment devoted to the games of chess and backgammon'. 'They were superbly furnished with chandeliers, girandoles, etc.'

Two meetings with the preacher John Wesley have been recorded, both to the detriment of Nash. On one occasion, Beau jested to his friends that he would attend a prayer meeting and confound the Methodist 'ranter'.

He entered the meeting, swaggering pompously, and a large audience had gathered to 'see the fun'. Nash asked Wesley by what authority he dared to preach, declaring that he was breaking the laws, and added 'Besides your preaching scares people out of their wits.' Wesley responded 'Sir, did you ever hear me preach?' and Nash replied that he had not. Wesley asked 'How the can you just of what you have never heard?' 'By common report.' answered Nash, to which Wesley responded: 'Sir, is not your name Nash? I dare not judge you by common report. I think it is not enough to judge by.' Nash then said 'I desire to know what these people come here for.' A member of the congregation answered 'Sir, let an old woman answer him. You, Mr Nash, take care of your body. We take care of our souls, and for the food of our souls we have come here'. Flustered, Nash left, and Wesley proceeded with his sermon. Desiring revenge, Beau Nash was walking down a narrow street in Bath, and saw Wesley walking through the crowds towards him. He rushed forwards, confronting the preacher, crying 'Make way, sir! I never give way to fools!' John Wesley calmly answered, 'Why sir, I always do' and graciously stepped aside to make way for the red-faced rake.

Bath became the centre for high-stakes gambling, and it was not uncommon for titled men and women to lose their entire estates at the gaming tables. The historian Lecky wrote that at Bath, gambling 'reigned supreme; and the physicians even recommended it to their patients as a form of distraction...among fashionable ladies the passion was quite as strong as among men.' The city drew large incomes - the losses of the wealthy - from the tables, which were an integral part of funding municipal works and establishing the social character of the city.

However, tighter laws against gaming, in 1740 and 1745, reduced Nash's circumstances, and his income and influence waned. When untrammelled gaming had been allowed, his position as Master of Ceremonies had made it difficult for him to absolutely ruin himself. He had to show control in the socially charged atmosphere of the gaming tables, and had restrained his own expenditure on the tables. The gambling tables were the main attraction for the idle rich, and attracted sharpsters (professional gamblers) as well, who exploited the more amateur players. Gambling was carried on at a fever pitch, as illustrated in Connely's biography of Nash: 'Not even his loss of £1400 impaired his prestige as guardian of the games. His net reputation was that he was a winner, because of his "superior skill and dispassionate attention". Players who lost £20 to £200 begged Nash to tie them up, like Ulysses, lest they succumb to the siren sound of the dice, and the Master often caught hold of a player's dice-box in mid-air.'

Living in poverty towards the end of his life, Beau wrote a letter condemning gambling as folly, and a vice to be avoided at all costs. When he was 82, the corporation voted him an allowance of £10 per month. Upon his death, aged 87, there was a lavish ceremony paid for by the Corporation, and he was buried with much pomp in Bath Abbey. The entire city mourned his passing. An article upon Beau Brummell, one of Nash's successors as arbiters of fashion, notes of Nash: '- a man of singular success in his frivolous style, made for a master of ceremonies, the model of all sovereigns of drinking-places, absurd and ingenious, silly and shrewd, avaricious and extravagant. He created Bath; he taught decency to "bucks", civility to card-players, care to prodigals, and caution to Irishmen! Bath has never seen his like again' (- *Blackwood's Edinburgh Magazine*, June 1844). Oliver Goldsmith wrote in his biography: 'The whole kingdom became more refined by lessons originally derived from him,' and that he was 'the first who diffused a desire for society and an easiness of address among a whole people.'

What is now known as Beau Nash House in Saw Close, was built in 1720 for Juliana Popjoy, his life-long mistress. Originally intended for her sole use, Nash took residence there after losing his own house in a gambling game. It is now Popjoy's Restaurant. Nash's original house St John's Court is now the Garrick's Head pub, around the corner. Beau was accused, when he moved in with Juliana, of being a 'whoremonger'. He replied that you could no more call a man a whoremonger for having one whore in his house, than you could call him a cheesemonger because he had one cheese. Born in Wiltshire in1714, Juliana Popjoy was thirty years younger than Nash. A contemporary caricature depicts her as 'Lady Betty Besom' leaping over 'the sacred boundary of Discretion' on her dapple-grey horse. She helped Beau receive Princess Mary and Princess Caroline at his magnificent house in 1740. She nursed Nash in the last years of his life, and a notice appeared in the *Gentleman's Magazine* in 1777 announcing her death. She had lived for some years 'in a large hollow tree' near Warminster, 'on a lock of straw, resolving never more to lie in a bed: and she was as good as her word unless when she made her short peregrinations to bath, Bristol and the gentlemen's houses adjacent; and she then lay in some barn or outhouse.'

* Much of the investment capital came from the Bristol slave trade. The town, possibly the first in the world built solely for pleasure, relied on the arms and cloth sent to Africa, the slaves sent from Africa to the colonies, and the tobacco, rum, sugar and raw cotton that came from the colonies. This 'triangular trade' was described in *The Book of Welsh Pirates and Buccaneers* by this author. As a result, Nash himself noted 'Bath is become a mere sink of profligacy and extortion. Every article of house-keeping is raised to an enormous price…I have known a negro-driver, from Jamaica, pay overnight, to the master of one of the rooms, 65 guineas for tea and coffee to the company, and leave Bath the next morning, in such obscurity, that not one of the guests had the slightest idea of his person, or even made the least enquiry about his name.'

1. Royal Tunbridge Wells claims that Beau Nash was also Master of Ceremonies there, and its present Master of ceremonies at the chalybeate springs dresses up as Beau Nash, but wears a white wig.

2. Not everyone was enamoured of the glories of Bath society under Nash. Smollett, in *The Expedition of Humphrey Clinker* gives a Scottish perspective: 'Imagine to yourself a high exalted presence of mingled odours, arising from putrid gums, imposthumated lungs, sour flatulencies, rank armpits, sweating feet, running sores and issues, plasters, ointments, and embrocations, hungary-water, spirit of lavender, asafoetida drops, musk, hartshorn, and sal volatile; besides a thousand frowzy streams, which I could not analyse. Such… is the fragrant aether we breathe in the polite assemblies of Bath.'

3. The rules and regulations which Nash imposed upon Bath's unruly sedan chair operators are the basis for the regulations which govern modern taxis.

BARTHOLOMEW ROBERTS 17 May? 1682 – 10 February 1722

BLACK BART, THE LAST AND MOST LETHAL PIRATE, THE ORIGIN OF THE 'JOLLY ROGER'

Somehow Roberts has disappeared from history, a man far more famous and feared across the world in his day than ever were Captain Kidd or Blackbeard. 'Black Bart' was the only pirate who deliberately attacked naval ships instead of fleeing, took over 400 ships, and amassed the greatest treasure of all pirates. Stevenson's *Treasure Island* of 1883 only mentions 5 'real' pirates – the three Welshmen Black Bart Roberts, Roberts' surgeon Peter Scudamore, Robert's former captor Howel Davis; the West Countryman Captain Edward England; and Israel Hands. Hands had served with Blackbeard, and was captured and taken to Virginia for trial. In exchange for immunity, he gave testimony against corrupt North Carolina officials in 1718. Captain Charles Johnson then states that Hands died in poverty in London.

However, the 29 year-old 'Israel Hynde' joined Black Bart Roberts' crew when the *Mercy* galley was captured in October 1721 on the Calabar River. He was captured from the *Ranger* when Black Bart Roberts was killed on February 10th, 1721. In the greatest pirate trial of all time, Hands was found guilty of piracy and sentenced to be hung in chains at Cape Corso on 13 April 1722. Of the other 3 men taken from the *Mercy* galley, the surgeon was acquitted, and the other two reprieved to serve seven years in the Royal Africa Company.

There were only 18 men sentenced to be hung in chains of the 52 sentenced to death. They were all experienced pirates, such as the members of 'the House of Lords' who had served under Howel Davis and Bart Roberts, and Scudamore who would not rescind his crimes. It thus appears that Hands did not die a beggar but returned to the sea, and also to just three months of piracy. In *Treasure Island* Israel Hands is the terrifying coxswain of the Hispaniola, whom the hero Jim has to shoot dead.

His shipmate, the surgeon Peter Scudamore, is mentioned in *Treasure Island* also, and the pirates' fate is laid upon Captain Bart Roberts' changing the name of his ship several times, and bringing bad luck. Jim recounts what he hears when hiding in the apple barrel: 'No, not I,' said Silver. 'Flint was cap'n; I was quartermaster, along of my timber leg. The same broadside I lost my leg, old Pew lost his daylights. It was a master surgeon, him that ampytated me – out of college and all – Latin by the bucket, and what not; but he was hanged like a dog, and sun-dried like the rest, at Corso Castle. That was Roberts' men, that was, and comed of changing the names of their ships – *Royal Fortune* and so on. Now what a ship's christened, let her stay, I says.'

The greatest pirate trial began on 28 March 1722 with a Vice-Admiralty Court led by Captain Mungo Herdman, against the survivors of Black Bart Roberts' crews. The court was filled with 69 prisoners taken from the *Great Ranger*, commanded by Captain James Skyrme, who was barely alive. Then the prisoners from the *Royal Fortune* came into court, of whom 87 were charged with piracy. 91 pirates were found guilty and 74 acquitted as having been forced into piracy.

'The House of Lords', the hardest and longest-serving members of the crew, had also followed Howel Davis, and regarded themselves as the 'aristocracy' of the pirate profession, giving each other honorary 'lordships'. They were not contrite at their trial. Captain Skyrme and most members of Roberts' 'House of Lords' were found 'Guilty in the Highest Degree', and the President of the Court, Captain Herdman pronounced: 'Ye and each of you are adjudged and sentenced to be carried back to the place from whence you came, from thence to the place of execution without the gates of this castle, and there within the flood marks to be hanged by the neck till you are dead, dead, dead. And the Lord have mercy on your souls'…'After this ye and each of you shall be taken down, and your bodies hung in chains.' (*Records of the High Court of the Admiralty*).

Of the 52 members of Roberts' crew hung on the Gold Coast, a third were from Wales, and a third from the West Country. (After an act of betrayal, it seems that Roberts would allow no Irish to serve with him). The oldest to be executed was forty-five, and the youngest just nineteen. As well as these men sentenced to hanging, Herdman sentenced 20 men to an effective death sentence in the Cape Coast mines, and sent another 17 to imprisonment in London's Marshalsea Prison. Of these 17, 13 died in the Weymouth in passage to London. The 4 survivors were eventually pardoned while in Newgate Prison. Two 'guilty' sentences were 'respited'. Of the 52 pirates hung at Cape Coast, nearly half were Welsh or West Countrymen, and most of the others indentured servants or poor white colonists. 15 pirates had died of their wounds on the passage to Cape Corso Castle for trial, and 4 in its slave-holes (dungeons) before the trial. 10 had been killed in the *Ranger*, and three in the *Royal Fortune*. Thus 97 of Roberts' crew had died. The 70 blacks on board the pirate ships were returned to death in slavery.

Surgeon Atkins's account of the hangings is repeated in Defoe's *History of the Pyrates*. The first six to hang were the hardened 'Lords' Sutton, Simpson, Ashplant, Moody (a former pirate captain), Magness and

Wearing the cross of the King of Portugal

Hardy. Atkins offered his services as a priest, but even Sutton, who had been suffering dysentery for days, ignored him. They called out for drinking water, and complained that 'We are poor rogues, and so get hanged while others, no less guilty in another way, escaped.' Loosened from their shackles, they walked carelessly to the gallows. 'Little David' Simpson spotted poor Elizabeth Trengrove in the huge crowd, who he had ravished when the *Onslow* was taken in August 1721. He shouted 'I have lain with that bitch three times, and now she has come to see me hanged.' The executioners did not know how to hang men, and wrongly tied their hands in front of the 'Lords'. Lord Hardy stated calmly 'I have seen many a man hanged, but this way of having our hands tied behind us I am a stranger to, and I never saw it before in my life.'

Later hangings saw many of the men admit their sins, especially surgeon Scudamore, the only ship's doctor to have willingly joined any pirate ship. He asked for two days reprieve to read the scriptures, and was allowed to sing the *31st Psalm* on the gallows before being swung off. 18 of the bodies were dipped in tar, encased in a frame of iron bands, and hung from gibbets in chains from nearby Lighthouse Hill, Connor's Hill and Catholic Mission Hill, overlooking the sea-lanes as a warning to pirates. Others were simply left hanging for the birds to eat. In Robert Louis Stevenson's *Treasure Island* is the following passage: 'You've seen 'em, maybe, hanged in chains, birds about 'em, seamen pointing 'em out as they go down with the tide… And you can hear the chains a-jangle as you go about and reach for the other buoy.'

The 'Old Roger' or 'Jolly Roger' is the most famous pirate flag, the 'skull and crossbones', but most pirates amended this to their own personal banner. Black Bart Robert's main flag had him sharing a glass of wine with the skeleton of the devil, which was holding a burning spear. His personal pennant was a picture of him with a raised sword, standing on two skulls, marked *ABH* and *AMH*. These signified a Barbadan's head and a Martinican's head, as the governors of these colonies both had sent vessels to capture Roberts. The flags were meant to strike fear into the enemy's heart, and when a merchant ship saw Roberts' flags being raised, its crew did not generally wish to fight 'the great pyrate.' This black flag was raised before battle, and if the prize did not strike its colours, the red flag would be flown, signifying 'no quarter'.

This most famous pirate in history was born John Robert, and was a lifelong teetotaller. He altered his name to Bart Roberts, presumably to distance himself from his past. It is interesting that in the 19th century, doing 'a John Roberts' in Wales, was to drink enough to keep drunk from Saturday morning until Sunday night. He was also known as 'The Great Pyrate', 'The Black Captain', and is generally regarded as the 'last and most lethal pirate'. He took over 400 recorded prizes from the coast of Africa to the Caribbean, and was by far the most successful and most feared pirate of all time (see this author's *Black Bart Roberts – The Most Famous Pirate of Them All*).

The marooned Welsh privateer William Williams wrote Llewelyn Penrose's *Journal*, possibly the earliest story of buried treasure, upon which Edgar Allen Poe based his *Gold Bug* and began his career. We have seen that Wales produced the most famous privateer in history, Sir Henry Morgan. It also produced a notable series of pirates, including Howel Davis, called by Defoe 'the Cavalier Prince of Pyrates', and John Callice, the most renowned Elizabethan priate. The 'greatest and most curious' of all pirates, Black Bart, was also Welsh. *Newsweek* called him the 'last and most lethal pirate', and he was known across the seas as 'the Black Pyrate' and 'the Great Pyrate', with no peers. Daniel Defoe called his aspect 'black', as he had black hair and a dark complexion, and he was simply the most formidable pirate in history.

To put piracy into context, the English Navy was a bitterly cruel organisation, and deserters were common. It had to press-gang most of its unfortunate seamen from British ports. Conditions were as bad in the merchant navy, and there was a constant flow of dissatisfied seamen men willing to sail under the flag of piracy.

Born John Robert in 1682 at Casnewydd Bach (Little Newcastle) in Pembrokeshire, not far from Howel Davis' origin of Milford Haven, Bartholomew Roberts went to sea as boy and became a skilled navigator, acquiring a dark complexion over his years at sea. He had probably been a former pirate in the Indian Ocean, accepting a pardon under an Act of Grace, before resurfacing as the 37-year-old third mate on the *Princess* galley, picking up slaves from the Gold Coast. He was captured by two pirate ships, captained by Howel Davis, and given the choice of joining them, which he eventually did, seemingly unwillingly.

Within six weeks, Howel Davis was dead in an ambush by the Portuguese, and Roberts was voted the new captain. His senior pirates, 'the House of Lords' could not agree on a new captain, despite having the feared former captain Christopher Moody amongst them. It may be that someone knew that the tall and imposing John Robert had been a pirate, and they needed a navigator, and Valentine Ashplant insisted that Robert be elected. Accepting, he said 'If I must be a pirate, it is better to be a commander than a common man'. Bartholomew Roberts said of his motives for becoming a pirate: 'In an honest service there is thin rations, low wages, and hard labour; in this, plenty, satiety, pleasure and ease, liberty and power; and who would not balance creditor on this side, when all the hazard that is run for it, at worst, is only a sour look or two at choking [dying]? No, a merry life and a short one shall be my motto.' This is the origin of the phrase – 'a short life and a merry one.' Black Bart's favourite oath was 'Damnation to him that ever lived to wear a halter!'

He swiftly avenged Davis' death, then sailed to attack the Portuguese treasure fleet at night, although outnumbered by 42 merchant ships and 2 men-of-war to his own two small ships. Roberts escaped with the richest merchantman, the *Sagrada Familia* and two other Portuguese treasure ships, from the Bay of All Saints, Brazil. He took 40,000 moidores and a fortune in diamonds and gold, including a gold chain and cross holding a huge emerald intended for the King of Portugal. He henceforth always wore the great cross in battle.

He allowed no boys or women on his ships, was a teetotal tea-drinker, and the ship's band played hymns for Sunday services. No drinking or gambling was allowed on board on Sundays. The band also played Black Bart into battle - he dressed in red damasks and velvet from head to toe, with a three-cornered red hat with a huge scarlet plume, armed with cutlasses and pistols. His demeanour and scarlet dress were such that French traders called him *Le Joli Rouge* – the handsome man in red, the origin of the 'Jolly Roger'.

Black Bart (Barti Ddu), captured an amazing 400 ships between 1719 and 1722, bringing commerce in North America, the West Indies, West Africa and the whole Atlantic almost to a standstill. He was known as 'pistol-proof', as he was expert in ship handling, crew control, and the tactics of naval warfare. Suffering mutinies, internal fights, and terrible deprivations at times, he was feared by all sea-going vessels. Being annoyed at the persistent attempts of the governors of Barbados and Martinique to imprison and execute him, he designed a personal flag and plate for his cabin door, with ABH (a Barbadian's head) and AMH (a Martinican's head) illustrated on them. He later captured, and hung, the Governor of Martinique in October 1720 from his yardarm.

Roberts' crew was drunk when a special convoy of Royal Navy frigates finally ambushed him. It seems that Roberts deliberately sought death. He was tired of trying to control a drunken, womanising rabble. Black Bart's drunken helmsman swung his ship the wrong way, and Bart was shot dead. His crew quickly wrapped him in chains, still wearing the King of Portugal's emerald, and threw him in the sea. Captain Ogle was knighted for his singular service in killing 'the great pirate Roberts', the only naval man honoured for service against the pirates. Black Bart was not yet 40 years old. Ogle himself made a fortune, from illicitly purloining the plundered gold dust he found in Roberts' cabin. Messages were sent by the governors of French, Dutch, Spanish and English colonies across the world celebrating the death of the man who almost brought transatlantic shipping to a standstill. The shock of the death of this most famous, brave and dreaded pirate helped end the so-called 'golden age' of piracy.

THE BALLAD OF BARTI DDU (or *Black Bart's Shanty*)
By this author, this is a reworking of the Welsh poem about Black Bart (*Barti Ddu*) by Isaac Daniel Hooson (1880-1948).

Howel Davis in the Royal Rover
Was the Cavalier Prince of Pirates
With his House of Lords he roamed the seas
To the King's discomfit.
Baa Baa Bartholomew
The great pyrate Roberts
Baa Baa Bartholomew
In his coat of scarlet
He took Bartholomew Roberts
In the Princess on the Gold Coast
And the mate from Casnewydd Bach
Soon led the Brethren's great host
Baa Baa Bartholomew
The great pyrate Roberts
Baa Baa Bartholomew
In his coat of scarlet
Cap'n Davis soon was killed
At the Isle of Princes
The House of Lords chose Bart as captain
To scour the sea's provinces.
Baa Baa Bartholomew etc.
Barti Ddu, he sailed the sea

The ship's band always playing
'A short life and a merry one'
Was his favourite saying.
Baa Baa Bartholomew etc.
Black Bart sailed the Seven Seas
In his silk scarlet costume
Crimson would not show the blood
As the Spanish met their doom.
Baa Baa Bartholomew etc.
Black Bart took 400 ships
In his great *Royal Fortune*
The House of Lords sang and caroused
While the ship's band played the old tunes.
Baa Baa Bartholomew etc.
From Africa to the Caribbean
And up to Newfoundland
He stopped Atlantic shipping
His cutlass in his hand
Baa Baa Bartholomew etc.
His ships were full of gems and gold
But Black Bart became tired
He was the lone teetotaller
He could see his funeral pyre
Baa Baa Bartholomew etc.
The House of Lords drank more and more
Black Bart was losing patience
He seemed to be seeking his death
He'd had enough of vengeance
Baa Baa Bartholomew etc.
He sailed straight for the royal ship
With his drunken crew
The cannon blew him half apart
There was nothing left to do
Baa Baa Bartholomew etc.
Le Joli Rouge still sails the seas
Teacup in one hand
Looking for adventure
And for a freer land
Baa Baa Bartholomew etc.

Footnote:
Much more on Henry Morgan, Howel Davis and Bart Roberts appeared in the author's biography of Henry Morgan (q.v.); and his *The Book of Welsh Pirates and Buccaneers* (2003); *The Pirate Handbook* (2004) and *Black Bart Roberts – The Most Famous Pirate of Them All* (2004).

GRIFFITH JONES   1683 (May 1 1684 christened) - April 8 1761

THE MAN WHO MADE WALES THE MOST LITERATE EUROPEAN NATION

Born at Pant-yr-Efel, Penboyr, Carmarthenshire to John ap Gruffydd and Elinor John, after primary education in his village, he became a shepherd. Wishing to become a clergyman, he then went to Carmarthen Grammar School. From 1707 he applied several times for ordination, but was rejected until 1708 when he was made deacon, and then a priest in 1708 at Penbryn, Ceredigion. He was curate at Penrieth, Pembroke in 1709 and Laugharne, Carmarthen in the same year. At Laugharne he became master of the SPCK. (Society for Promoting Christian Knowledge) school founded by Sir John Phillips of Picton Castle, and in 1711 was appointed rector at Llandeilo-Abercywyn, Carmarthenshire.

Jones was now known as a superb preacher, and people travelled for miles to hear him, leading to a formal complaint by the English Bishop William Ottley of St David's in 1714, about Jones 'going about preaching on weekdays in Churches, Churchyards, and sometimes on the mountains, to hundreds of auditors'. Several times between 1714 and 1716 Griffith Jones was summoned before the Bishop's Court in Carmarthen to answer charges of ignoring church laws and customs, i.e. popularising Christianity. Even today, this is frowned upon by the Church, which seems to prefer men from the grey world of pointless committees to real men of faith and action.

Becoming a corresponding member of the SPCK in 1713, Jones was chosen to become a teacher and missionary in India, but declined the appointment, and in 1716 Sir John Philipps appointed Griffith to become rector of Llanddowror, Carmarthenshire.

Jones worked hard to support the SPCK, and supported a new edition of the Welsh *Bible* for a decade. In 1718 he travelled around Wales, England and Scotland with Philipps on a preaching tour, before marrying Philipps' sister in 1720. In 1731 Griffith wrote to the SPCK proposing a 'Welch School' at Llanddowror, as the number of SPCK schools in Wales had started to decline. In response, Griffith Jones now began the 'circulating schools' movement sometime between 1731 and 1737, by which later date there were 37 schools with 2,400 scholars.

Schools were held for three months in the same place, usually in winter when farm-workers and children had more time available to study. Often the village church was used, if the rector would agree. Schools were also run in barns, storehouses and even a windmill. Night schools were also available for those who could not get any time off in the day, and pupils were taught to read the Welsh *Bible* and to learn the *Church Catechism*. SPCK religious texts were used to teach literacy, and any funds raised were spent on teaching, not on buildings. All the schoolmasters were trained by Griffith Jones personally at Llanddowror, and he insisted that they were members of the Church of England.

The movement was essential in giving the Welsh opportunities for literacy - by the time he died in 1761, it was estimated that 158,000 people between the ages of 6 and 70 had learned to read, out of an estimated Welsh population of 480,000 (in 1750). This percentage of literate Welsh people was probably higher than any other European nation of the time, and probably the world, despite the grinding poverty. The annual report, *Welch Piety*, recorded that over 3,495 schools had been set up by Jones's death, a wonderful success story. In that actual year, the 210 existing schools taught 8,023 pupils. The Miners' Institutes of the 19th century further assisted this desire for literacy, with their wonderful library collections. One has been shifted, stone by stone, to the Museum of Welsh Life at St. Fagans.

The major contribution that Jones made was to save the life of the Welsh language – he taught the nation to read, and imbued it with a sound knowledge of Bishop Morgan's wonderful Welsh translation of the *Bible*. His Holy Day in the Church in Wales is 8 April, the date of his death. Of course, some parts of Wales were not visited by the schools, and the teacher moved on after three months, and into this vacuum the Sunday schools came. This idea from England was seized upon in Wales, by the rapidly growing Nonconformist sects, and operated upon the day that everyone was available. They gave a huge impetus to the Welsh language before the provision of state education, and then became rather peripheral to education in Wales.

After Jones' death, Bridget Bevan carried on his work with training masters for the schools until her death in 1779. Griffith Jones' schools were attacked with a series of indignant pamphlets by some church dignitaries, because of his connections with Whitfield and other Methodist leaders. The schools helped the Methodist Revival in Wales, and nearly all its early leaders came into contact with Jones. Both Griffith and his wife Margaret are buried in Llanddowror Church. The circulating schools were an immense achievement, unparalleled elsewhere in the world, and created armies of readers conversant with the standard language of the *Bible*. This made possible the awakening of interest in education among the Welsh in the 19th century – Jones' input was essential in the survival of the language.

HOWELL HARRIS   January 23 1714 - July 21 1773

'THE FATHER OF METHODISM IN WALES', 'THE GREATEST WELSHMAN OF HIS AGE', 'GOD'S GIFT TO WALES'

Whether we regard the great Methodist Revival in Wales as something that destroyed much of the fabric and tradition of Welsh society, or as a unique massive spiritual upheaval in Wales that helped save the language, it is certain that it altered irrevocably the nature of Wales and its people. There was a complete renewal of the Welsh people in all aspects of the national life and character. At the core was Howell Harris, of whom the great Sir Owen M. Edwards wrote 'Whatever else can be said of Harris's oratory and genius and of his strange projects, the awakening of Wales from a sleep that was paralysing its national vigour can be attributed to him more than anybody else.'

In 1738, Harris began his mission in North Wales, as one of a trio of leaders across the nation, the others being Daniel Rowland of Llangeitho and Howell Davies, the 'Apostle of Pembrokeshire'. Harris's father had come from Llangadoc in Carmarthen, to Talgarth in Brecon, around 1700, as was known as Howell Powell alias Harris. He married Susanah Powell of Trefeca-fach in 1702, and Howell was their third son. His eldest brother Joseph went to the West Indies, wrote navigational treatises and became Assay-Master at the Royal Mint in the Tower of London, and his other brother Thomas also made his fortune in London, returning to become Sheriff of Brecknock and a land-owner.

Howell went to Llwyn-llwyd Academy (like William Williams, q.v.), and from 1732 until 1735 was schoolmaster at Llangors and Llangasty. In 1735, he was overwhelmed by the preaching of Pryce Davies, vicar of Talgarth, and became committed to evangelise. His brother Joseph Harris returned from London to take Howell to St Mary Hall, Oxford, to matriculate. However, Harris left Oxford in days and applied for holy orders in 1736, which was refused several times because he was preaching 'irregularly'. Harris consulted Griffith Jones, who had suffered the same problems, and in 1737 began working with Daniel Rowland, soon converting William Williams and Howell Davies, who was recommended by Harris to work with Griffith Jones.

1742 saw the formation of various religious societies into an Association, which formed an alliance with the English Methodist movement. This Association influenced all phases of Welsh religious life, and created as its permanent body the Calvinistic Methodist, or Presbyterian, Church of Wales. Harris sided with Whitefield when he broke with John and Charles Wesley, on the issue of Calvinism versus Armenianism. In the famous Welsh-English Calvinistic Association meeting at Watford, Caerphilly, in 1743, Whitefield presided over Harris, Williams of Pantycelyn, Rowland and John Powell. There then begane the formative years of Welsh Calvinistic Methodism, where societies were organised, regions arranged for preachers, and associations set up to control the movement. Harris was 'its organising genius, without any doubt', and the system's foundations remain today. He tried to heal the breach between Whitefield and the Wesleys, and preached at Moorfields in Whitefield's absences. Harris, unusually, always tried to attend conferences called by the Wesleys. His great contribution to British Methodism was his vision of an evangelical movement, encompassing not only the conflicting Methodist groups, but also the Moravians.

In 1744, Howell Harris married Anne Williams of Ysgrin, Radnorshire, which her parents fought to prevent, and they went to live in his mother's cottage at Trefecha. In the 1740's he had drifted towards Moravian doctrine, and in 1750 the Welsh Methodists split into two movements, the other supporting Daniel Rowland's views. Harris now appeared harden his line and became 'unmanageable'. After so many years trying to heal wounds, he now would stand no interference, and quickly lost supporters. Almost alone, he retired to Trefecha in 1752, where his health and balance were restored. After his massive work from 1735-1750 in altering the religious complexion of Wales, he turned inwards, and set up a religious community based upon the Pietistic Institution at Halle, Germany.

Harris pulled down his home, to create a larger building where he and his followers could live, work and worship together. Members of 'The Family' placed all their possessions with the community, and in a few years over a hundred people were following trades and crafts at Trefecha. Members of the Family took over local farms, and Harris helped found the Breconshire Agricultural Society, the first in Wales. By 1763, in the new spirit of revival fanned by Rowland's ministry and William Williams' hymns, a more subdued Harris was welcomed back into the evangelist fold. He again embarked upon a series of preaching tours, and massive crowds of his former converts went to see the great man. In 1768, the Countess of Huntingdon opened a college for preachers at Trefecha. Harris was now ill, and after a few years of suffering died in 1773, to be buried in Talgarth Church. *The Dictionary of Welsh Biography* concludes: 'His greatest contribution to the welfare of the people was his preaching. This was the means of waking the humbler classes of Wales from their torpid slumber and of revealing to them their spiritual endowments. He was, indeed, one of the makers of modern Wales. In spite of his cross-grained and dictatorial temper, his unceasing enthusiasm and his unbounded desire to save souls carried everything before him in the early days of the religious renaissance. The influence which he has had on the life of his people proves that he was the greatest spiritual force in his generation and many believe that he was the greatest Welshman of his age.'

The historian Dr R.T. Jenkins wrote 'It is difficult to believe that Howell Harris was not the greatest Welshman of his century.' Finally, the Rev. G.T. Roberts in his biography of Harris stated: 'This powerful evangelist, able organiser, and great Methodist was God's gift to Wales, and very few men have so deeply and so permanently influenced the religious life of the Principality as Howell Harris.'

RICHARD WILSON 1 August 1714 - 15 May 1782

THE FOUNDER OF BRITISH LANDSCAPE PAINTING, TURNER'S 'HERO'

Son of the Vicar of Penegoes, near Machynlleth, Wilson was educated by his father and showed signs of being an excellent artist. He may have been born at the Felin Crewi watermill, which is now a private house. His family was one of the old Welsh families of the Arwystli, based around Trefeglwys, Montgomery. Wilson seems to have moved to Mold with his mother when his father died, and shortly after his uncle, Sir George Wynne, took him to London in 1729. The 15-year-old Richard was placed him under the charge of the eminent painter, Thomas Wright. Wilson soon succeeded as a portrait painter, painting the young Prince of Wales and Duke of York, but wished to study Italian painting to complete his education as an artist. He had painted a few landscapes in this period, and one of Westminster Bridge is in Philadelphia. Unfortunately, the only way to make a living as an artist in England was as a portrait painter, and there was great competition with the likes of Reynolds and Gainsborough at this time.

With his own savings, and gifts from friends, Wilson went to Venice in 1750, then Rome in 1751, studying the Old Masters and the natural scenery of Italy. From Rome, he explored the Neapolitan coast, the Alban Hills and Tivoli. Zuccarelli and Vernet advised him to concentrate solely upon landscape painting. Returning to London in 1757, from 1760-68 he was at the peak of his powers, exhibiting *Niobe, View of Rome from the Villa Madama* and other works. In 1768 he was a founder member of the

Royal Academy, and was its Librarian from 1776. However, he had incurred the great enmity of the leading portrait painter of the day, Sir Joshua Reynolds, who alongside other painters conspired against Wilson. The reasons for this are unknown, but it may well be that Wilson championed landscapes over portraits.

Joseph Wright of Derby, John Crome, Constable and Turner all acknowledged their debt to Wilson, never having his experience of the foreign masters, and his inspiration from the works of Claude Lorrain and Claude and Nicolas Poussin. Wilson was forced into accepting commissions of pawnbrokers, but the quality of his artistic output never faltered. The brilliant Thomas Jones of Pencerrig (1742-1803) was a pupil of Wilson's. In 1781 Wilson returned to Wales and died at the Colomendy estate near Llanferres outside Mold, being buried in Mold churchyard next to his mother's grave. His aunt, Catherine Jones, owned the estate and the hall now belongs to Liverpool Council.

Wilson is now accepted as one of the greatest of European landscape artists, and the pioneer of the genre in Britain. Some of his works may be seen in the National Museum of Wales, and his works are exhibited in most of Europe and America's major public collections. The National Museum of Wales in Cardiff has 14 magnificent paintings, covering the whole range of his output (portraits, British and Italian landscapes, classical scenes), and an important portrait of Wilson by Mengs. The Yale Centre for British Art at New Haven, Connecticut, has one of the largest Wilson collections in the world, and Wilton House near Salisbury has nine Wilsons. According to *The Dictionary of Welsh Biography*, 'At his best, he is a master of style; as an interpreter of light he is the successor of Claude and Cuyp, and an inspirer of Constable and Turner. His own inspiration came equally from Italy and Wales, enabling him to express romantic emotion within a classical framework.'

Peter Pindar wrote in the 19th century: 'Wilson has been called the English Claude; but how unjustly, so totally different their style. Claude sometimes painted grand scenes, but without a mind of grandeur; Wilson, on the contrary, could infuse a grandeur into the meanest objects; Claude when he drew on the bank of his own ideas was a mere castrato in the art; ...Wilson on the contrary was a Hercules.'

Constable wrote many kind words about his debt to Wilson, including 'Poor Wilson! Think of his fate. Think of his magnificence' and 'One of the great men who show the world what exists in nature but which was not known till his time.' Ruskin said 'with the name of Richard Wilson the history of sincere landscape art founded on a meditative love of nature begins for England'. Turner went for inspiration to Wilson's birthplace as a young man, and the curator of the Turner Collection in the Tate stated in 1988 'For the first few years of Turner's career as a painter, Wilson was quite explicitly his hero and his chief model.' The *Encyclopedia of Wales* describes Wilson as the 'most distinguished painter Wales has ever produced and the first to appreciate the aesthetic possibilities of his country'.

WILLIAM WILLIAMS c.11 February 1717 - 11 January 1791

PANTYCELYN, 'WALES' FINEST POET', 'Y PÊR GANIEDYDD' (THE SWEET SINGER), 'THE FIRST ROMANTIC POET IN WALES', 'THE GREATEST WELSH HYMN-WRITER'

Williams was born at Cefn-y-Coed, near Abergwesyn and like Howell Harris was educated at the Llwyn-Llwyd Academy, near Hay-on-Wye. He was preparing for a career in medicine, when he heard Howel Harris preach at nearby Talgarth in 1738 and was completely converted. Williams said that 'God's word penetrated his heart'. He joined the church and was ordained as a deacon in 1740, working as a curate for Theophilus Evans at Llanwrtyd, Llanfihangel and Llanddewi Abergwesyn until 1743.

However, for 'nineteen reasons' Evans refused him ordination in 1743, and Williams turned towards the Methodist movement, becoming one of its leaders in Wales. Evans' reasons had included refusing to read parts of the service, preaching in unconsecrated places, and 'rambling into several other counties to preach'. Becoming for a time a schoolteacher, Williams was present at the early meeting of Calvinistic Methodists at Watford near Caerphilly in 1743, where George Whitefield was moderator. A resolution was passed that the Rev. Williams 'should leave his curacies and be an assistant to the Rev. Mr [Daniel] Rowland.'

Marrying Mary Francis of Llansawel in 1748, they went to live in his parents' remote old farm at Pantycelyn near Abergwesyn, hence his epithet among the many 'William Williams' of his day. In the Rowland-Harris dispute of 1751, Williams sadly decided he had to side with Daniel Rowland, because of Howell Harris's conduct and doctrinal errors, but he wrote a touching reconciliatory letter to Harris saying that the church was in great need of him, and that the church owed him a huge debt for its progress. His elegy on Harris's death contains the following (translated) lines, recalling that Harris had called him to God's service: 'This the morning, still remembered, / That I first heard Heaven's sound; / And the summons straight from glory, / By His voice my heart did wound.'

The great revival at Llangeitho in 1762 coincided with the end of the dispute, assisted by the collection of Williams' hymns *The Songs of Those upon the Sea of Glass*. Williams spent most of his life as an itinerant preacher, travelling the length and breadth of Wales. He estimated he covered more than 150,000 miles on horseback to preach, published over 90 books and pamphlets in his lifetime, and wrote over 1,000 hymns. As Methodism swept across Wales, his works became hugely popular, and he attracted massive crowds to hear him preach. His hymns were important not only for religion's sake, but a valuable contribution to the nation's literary culture. In his epic poem *Bywyd a Marwolaeth Theomemphus*, Williams interpreted the religious experience of the Methodist movement with intense feeling and sensitivity. Apart from his religious poems and prose treatises, he also attempted a

Statue by L. S. Merryfield

history of world religions from 1762 onwards, in *Pantheologia*. Some of his books were written to educate the Welsh in their own tongue, and for his own use in teaching them to read.

For much of his life, Williams lived at Llanfair-ar-y-Bryn, near Llandovery. A successful farmer and businessman, Williams also had a thriving tea-selling business. He was also successful in selling his own books. When he tired of writing he worked the farm, and was often not in bed until nearly dawn. Interestingly, he always considered himself as an Anglican clergyman, although he spent most of his life in evangelical tours as a Methodist minister. He is buried at Llanfair-ar-y-Bryn, Llandovery. Harris's view of Williams, the hymn-writer, preacher, counsellor, theologian, writer and instructor, was as follows: 'Hell trembles when he comes and souls are daily taken by Brother Williams in the gospel net…He is eminently owned by his Heavenly Master in his service: he is indeed a flaming instrument in his hands: and he is on the stretch day and night.'

William Williams of Pantycelin was renowned as Wales' finest poet, along with Dafydd ap Gwilym. His best known hymn is *Arglwydd, arwain trwy'r anialwch* (Lord, lead thou through the wilderness, adapted as *Guide me, O Thou Great Jehovah* (*Redeemer*) to the tune of John Hughes' *Cwm Rhondda*: 'Guide me O Thou Great Jehovah, / Pilgrim through this barren land; / I am weak but Thou art mighty, / Hold me with Thy powerful hand / Bread of Heaven, Bread of Heaven, / Feed me now and evermore, / Feed me now and evermore.'

Most of his writing was in Welsh. In his prose works, Williams attempts to classify the emotions and experiences which move the mind and heart of man, but his hymns and poems are more important. We see his emotions, thoughts and feelings taking expression in them. In simple language, they are unaffected, and their pure lyricism began the modern period in Welsh poetry, casting aside the 'strict' metres of the past, much as Wordsworth destroyed the formalism of his era. 'Earlier Welsh poetic tradition was almost unknown to him, and his bare metre, burning sincerity of language, mystical reflection, and spiritual longing were new to Welsh poetry.' Together with Howell Harris and Daniel Rowland, William Williams Pantycelyn is acknowledged as the leader of the Methodist Revival in Wales in the 18th century.

RICHARD PRICE 23 February 1723 - 19 April 1791

'THE FRIEND OF THE UNIVERSE, THE GREAT APOSTLE OF LIBERTY', 'THE MOST ORIGINAL THINKER EVER BORN IN WALES'

Painting by Benjamin West

Richard Price of Tŷ'n Ton, near Llangeinor in Glamorgan's Garw Valley was one of the most influential and original Welshmen in history. His father was Rhys Price, and he was educated privately before studying at the Reverend Vavasor Griffith's Academy at Talgarth, Breconshire. His strict father virtually disinherited Richard, because he did not have as orthodox religious views. In *Cadrawd's* superb history of Llangeinor, he notes the extreme parental authority of the Prices of Tynton - Richard's cousin Ann Thomas was the ill-fated *Maid of Cefn Ydfa*, her mother being Rhys Price's sister. Richard was only 16, and studying in Talgarth, when he heard the news of his father's death, and he and his mother were forced to move from Tynton by his step-brother, and live in semi-penury in Bridgend.

Richard several times walked between Bridgend and Talgarth to see his family. His mother soon died, and Richard was left with £400 from his father's estate upon this event. He nobly donated all of the money to his sisters, although he had no means of support and was aged only 18. He could no longer afford to stay in the Academy, so appealed to his uncle the Rev. Samuel Price, to be allowed to join him in London. Richard appealed to his stepbrother for assistance to reach London, but that individual merely loaned Richard a horse to reach Cardiff.

Price then walked to London, sometimes hitching a lift on farm wagons. His uncle Samuel received him unfavourably, sending Richard out to very cheap and unhealthy lodgings in Pudding Lane. The Rev. Price also placed Richard in Mr Coward's Academy in Moorfields, to be trained as a dissenting minister. However, long study and poor lodgings almost broke Richard's health, and he had to return to Glamorgan for the summer to recuperate. Upon returning to London, Price moved into better lodgings and studied Mathematics, Philosophy and Theology. He became attached to his tutor, John Eames, a friend of Isaac Newton, a noted mathematician and an FRS.

Leaving Moorfields Academy, Price became a domestic chaplain in Stoke Newington, continuing his studies for 13 years, until his employer died. Fortunately, this employer left Richard Price a house in Leadenhall Street and another smaller property. During this time Price had gained fame as a noted preacher, as from the age of 22, he had taken the lectureship at the Presbyterian Meeting House in Old Jewry. With his circumstances improved, Price was able to marry in 1757. He was devoted to his wife, who unfortunately within a few years had become a confirmed invalid. It was in 1756 that Price published his great work on moral philosophy, *'A Review of the Principal Questions and Difficulties in Morals.'*

This work notably widened his circle of acquaintances, to include the Master of Pembroke College, the Bishop of St Asaph, and the great philosopher-historian David Hume. He was now aged 33, and had the audacity to challenge the work of Locke and Hume, arguing that 'morality is a branch of necessary truth', but Hume enjoyed the openness, modesty and friendship of Price, visiting him many times at his home in Stoke Newington. Professor Fowler, in his *Principles of Morals* stated that Price had anticipated the conclusions of the German Immanuel Kant (1724-1784) by 20 years. It can be posited that the universally famous Kant, who spent his life in university pondering ethical science, knew of Price's work and plagiarised it.

Benjamin Franklin wrote to Price in 1767, congratulating him, and sending a glowing review of his work from Paris in a publication of the Bibliotheque des Sciences et des Beaux Artes. The brilliant scientist Joseph Priestley also joined Price's discussion groups, and became a great and lifelong friend. Richard Price used his influence to get Priestley a post with the Earl of Shelburne, enabling Priestley to experiment towards his position as 'the father of the science of chemistry'. Lord Shelburne had been intrigued by Price's *Dissertations* and had become a firm friend of his. One of his letters to Price begins: 'When I write to you, my heart and pen go together.' Priestley reinforced these feelings: 'For the most amiable simplicity of character, a truly Christian spirit, disinterested patriotism, and true candour no man in my opinion ever exceeded Dr Price. I shall ever reflect upon our friendship as a circumstance highly honourable, as it was a source of peculiar satisfaction to me.'

Price was also a friend of the poet Samuel Rogers, and of his parents. The poet's biographer states: 'But a man destined to European renown and worthy of it, was living near, and gave occasional help, this was Mr (afterwards Dr) Price, one of the most acute and enlightened minds the 18th century produced, the charm of whose character exerted a considerable influence on Rogers' parents, and a close friendship sprung up between them.'*

Thomas Bayes**, a friend of Price's died, leaving a problem on the *Theory of Probabilities* unsolved, and Price took two years, working intermittently, to solve it. He published his paper in 1763 in *Transactions of the Royal Society*. A supplementary paper appeared in 1764's *Philosophical Transactions*, and its importance led to the great honour of election to a Fellowship of the Royal Society in 1765 for his work on probability. Price's portrait still hangs there. Now known as a radical dissenter, Unitarian minister and moral philosopher, Price had established his reputation as a preacher in Newington Green, London and Hackney, and followed up his *Principal Questions in Morals* with *The Importance of Christianity'* 1766). 1767 saw another four volumes of his work published, *Dissertation on Miracles, Dissertation on Providence 'Dissertation on Prayer* and *Junction of Virtuous Men in a Future State.*

In 1769, he was made a D.D. by Glasgow University, and also published his celebrated *Northampton Mortality Tables*. Price had given a paper to the FRS in 1769 upon the *Expectation of Live'*, diffidently correcting errors made by the mathematician de Moivre. The difficulty of the work was said to have turned Price's hair white. In 1767 Price had been approached by a number of lawyers who had formed a plan for the provision of their widows. Price found it so defective, that he researched to correct the defective bases of many societies like that of the lawyers. His celebrated treatise on *Reversionary Payments* was dedicated to Lord Shelburne, and his *Northampton Life Tables* (the result of over 20,000 calculations on life statistics) formed the basis of new industry of 'Life Assurance' and pensions.

Price was associated with the first such society to be established, the 'Equitable Assurance Society', its success being due to his advice, and his Bridgend-born nephew William Morgan, became its first actuary. More editions followed, with the 1772 publication containing an appeal to reduce the 'grand national evil' of the National Debt. William Pitt was greatly influenced by Price's writings on the National Debt. Among his many influential books is *An Appeal to the Public on the Subject of the National Debt* (1772).

Richard Price was in touch with the political leaders in the New England colonies, the Welsh future-president John Adams, Arthur Lee and

Benjamin Franklin among others, and urged an easing of measures by the British government. It is said that in 1874, Price advised the citizens of Boston to 'throw the taxed tea into the sea rather than submit to taxation without representation' War broke out in 1775, and in 1776 Price published *Observations on the Nature of Civil Liberty - the Principles of Government, and the Justice and Policy of the War with America*, pleading for justice and putting forward a plan to pacify the colonies. This pamphlet was a sensation, having to be reprinted several times, and selling an unheard-of 60,000 copies in 12 editions by the end of 1776. He argued that each community had the right to self-government, responsible only for carrying out their electors' wishes, and that denial of this responsibility constituted treason.

How different to today, where MPs are only responsible to their lords and masters who dictate three-line-whip party policy. The pamphlet was also translated into French and Dutch and went into several editions on the Continent. John Wesley, the Archbishop of York, and the Bishop of London attacked Price in print separately. His nephew William Morgan's *Memoirs* aptly commented 'The preachers of the Gospel of peace denounced their anathemas against the friend of peace and harmony, whose only aim was to prevent the ravages of war, attempting at least to point out the folly and injustice of it.' King George III's brother, the Duke of Cumberland, supported Price, and told him at the Bar at the House of Lords that he had been 'reading the pamphlet until he was blind'. Lord Ashburton interposed 'It is rather remarkable that Your Royal Highness should have been blinded by the book which has opened the eyes of all mankind.'

Merchants in the City of London were hard-hit by the war, and the Court of Common Council gave the freedom of the City of London to Price in 1776, in a gold box to the value of £50, in recognition of his work in trying to bring peace. Crowds flocked to Hackney to see Price preach, Priestley saying that he attained a greater celebrity than any other Dissenting Minister in the past, yet Price remained humble in his dealings with everyone. In 1777 he published another pamphlet on the American War, dedicated to the Lord Mayor and notables of London. Appended were more writings on the National Debt, and work on the debts and resources of France. It demolished the arguments of the critics of his former pamphlet, as did another pamphlet aimed against Burke and the Archbishop of York in the following year.

Price supported the American Revolution with several books. He was honoured in both France and America. This 'Friend of the Universe, the Great Apostle of Liberty' was asked by the newly established American Congress, through his friend Benjamin Franklin, to accept American citizenship and to set up a financial system in the new republic. His strong moral and lobbying support of the new American democracy, and his abilities in philosophy, insurance and national financing were such that the young republic sent him the following resolution 'In Congress 6 Octr 1778

Resolved, That the Honourable Benjamin Franklin, Arthur Lee, and John Adams Esqrs or any one of them, be directed forthwith to apply to Dr Price, and inform him, that it is the Desire of Congress to consider him as a Cityzen of the united States, and to receive his Assistance in regulating their finances. That if he shall think it expedient to remove with his family to America and afford such Assistance, a generous Provision shall be made for requiting his Services.'

This wonderful offer, to be in effect the first 'Chancellor of the Exchequer' of the USA, was declined, probably because of the serious illness of Price's wife. 1780 saw collaboration with Horne Tooke to publish *Facts*, a damning indictment of Lord North's government, which helped bring about his downfall. Also in that year, Price wrote a further *Essay on the Population of England*, which influenced Malthus' works. Yale University gave Dr Price an honorary Doctor of Laws in 1781 – the sole other recipient was George Washington. President Washington commented upon another publication by Price on America in 1785 as 'being the best legacy he could leave them.' Price's friend Lord Shelburne succeeded Lord North as Prime Minister in 1782, and was advised by Dr Price upon the finances of the country. Price refused the post of Private Secretary, however. William Pitt the Younger, who also took the post of Chancellor, and leaned heavily upon Dr Price's advice, soon succeeded Shelburne. Lecky, the historian, referred to Price's original 1772 publication on the National Debt as 'destined to exercise a profound and most singular influence on English financial policy.' Pitt's major motive now in economics was the reduction of in Dr Price's term 'that monstrous accumulation of artificial debt.' Pitt worked with Price to develop his 'Sinking Fund Scheme' of 1786 to reduce the National Debt. In 1786 Price helped found a new Academy at Hackney, where he would teach Morals, Mathematics, Astronomy and Natural Philosophy to educate Ministers and the sons of Dissenting Ministers. Unfortunately, his ailing wife died in September, greatly distressing Price, and Lord Lansdowne wrote a sympathetic letter of condolence from Bowood House in Wiltshire. It is worthwhile noting its contents to show once again the character of Richard Price, the poor boy from Glamorgan, and his influence upon all levels of society:

'Though the post only allows me a moment, I cannot delay a day to assure you that you have not a relation who feels more sensibly the loss which you have sustained. Let me beseech you to command me in any shape, I will come instantly to London if I can contribute to your comfort, or will be happy to see you here, where no one shall come but as are agreeable to you. You will find Lady Lansdowne and me nearly alone. We dine at 5 o'clock as plain as you do in your own house, Lady Lansdowne plays for an hour on the harpsichord, and we go to bed at eleven. We'll consider and treat you as a father. Every person about the house reveres and respects you, and you'll make us very happy, which is the next best thing to being happy yourself.'

At home, or at his church, Price was visited by Benjamin Franklin; (the later President) Thomas Jefferson; (the later President) John Adams and his wife Abigail; the politicians Lord Lyttleton, Earl Stanhope and William Pitt the Elder; the writers David Hume and Adam Smith; the prison reformer John Howard; and William Godwin and his wife Mary Wollstonecraft. Price had continued corresponding with leading American statesmen, earning the opprobrium of the British security forces, and also wrote to the distinguished Frenchmen Turgenev, Necker (a popular minister to Louis XVI) and Condorcet. They all saw him not just as an expert on national finance, but had read his theories on liberty and civil government in their French translation. France was struggling with its economy.

As well as with his former pamphlets, Richard Price now also provoked Burke's anger with his support for the French Revolution. In his *A Discourse of the Love of Our Country* in 1789, he sermonised 'Tremble, all ye oppressors of the world... you cannot now keep the world in darkness'. Price celebrated their 'ardour for liberty', and provoked Edmund Burke to write his *Reflections on the Revolution in France*. Aged 66, and in poor health, Price had been asked to give the speech for the 'Anniversary of the English Revolution', on 4 November 1789, presided over by Earl Stanhope. Price's *Love of Our Country* speech eulogised the establishment of a free constitution for France (something that Britain still needs), stating 'Behold, the light you have struck out, after setting America free, reflected in France, and there kindled into a blaze that lays despotism in ashes, and warms and illuminates Europe!'

In the evening dinner of the London Revolution Society that followed, Doctor Price gave a congratulatory address to the National Assembly in Paris, hailing 'the glorious example given in France to encourage other nations to assert the unalienable rights of mankind, and thereby to introduce a general reformation in the governments of Europe and make the world free and happy.' Price's speeches, enunciating the principles of the Revolution, were transmitted to the Duc de la Rochefoucauld and the French Assembly, who received it with loud applause.

Rochefoucauld personally wrote thanking the doctor, addressing him as 'the Apostle of Liberty'. The discourse and speech were published in pamphlet form, and again caused a sensation. During the French Revolution, Price had corresponded closely with Thomas Jefferson (q.v.), the American Minister to France, and became a correspondent and supporter of Tom Paine. A year later, on 14 July 1790, Price made another speech to commemorate the first anniversary of the French Revolution, promoting peace forever between nations, as the French had promised. De la Rochefoucauld read the speech out to the National Assembly, who all stood to listen, their heads uncovered as a mark of respect to Richard Price. De la Rochefoucauld then read it again in his honour.

After Price's death upon April 19th, 1791, the Earl of Stanhope led the huge funeral procession, and Dr Priestley read the funeral service. The National Assembly and the Jacobins in France declared a National Day of mourning. To summarise this most remarkable man, with his friend Joseph Priestley, Price had helped found the Unitarian Society. He influenced Mary Wollstonecraft, who wrote the important *Vindication of the Rights of Women*. His *Review of the Principal Questions in Morals* put an element of realism into the philosophy of the day, and was possibly the greatest of his theological and ethical treatises. He also drew up the first budget of the new American nation, and his expertise on demography and actuarial matters influenced the financial policies of William Pitt and Shelburne. Unwavering in his support for the American colonies, despite English opposition, however Price refused an offer of American citizenship. Price was also a great supporter of the French Revolution. This statistician, preacher, liberal theorist and philosopher had a political influence upon radicals in both the Old and New Worlds. John Davies calls Price 'the most original thinker ever born in Wales'. A friend of Presidents and Prime Ministers, one of Britain's greatest thinkers, mathematicians and philosophers is little-known.

* Samuel Rogers wrote of this vastly underestimated polymath, 'He was the most humane of men; to see distress was in him to feel an impulse to relieve it. All admired and loved him for the sweetness of his disposition and the unaffected sincerity of his manners.' Price needs not just a new biography, but also an international society dedicated to his memory.

** Without Richard Price, it is possible that Bayesian statistical analysis may have been overlooked in history. His friend, the Rev. Thomas Bayes was elected a Fellow of the Royal Society in 1742, and was a mathematician but published very little. On his death aged 59 in 1761, Richard Price was executor and found among Bayes' papers an *Essay towards solving a problem in the Doctrine of Chances*. Price realised its importance, as it contains Bayes' Theorem, one of the fundamental results of probability theory. Price Price wrote an introduction to the paper which provides some of the philosophical basis of Bayesian statistics, and had it published by the Royal Society in 1763. Bayesian estimation became a statistical technique for calculating how true a proposition is likely to be. Unlike classical statistics, for the first time prior judgement is factored into the equation. Bayesian methods have grown in popularity for business forecasting, archaeological digs, court cases, in analysing the results of drugs trials and improving the service of banks, amongst other uses.

WILLIAM WILLIAMS c.1727 – 27 April 1791

THE FIRST AMERICAN NOVELIST, ANTI-SLAVERY WRITER, THE FORGOTTEN GENIUS

A truly remarkable 18th century manuscript lies in the Lilly Library, Bloomington Campus, Indiana University. This author was awarded an Everett Helm Travelling Fellowship to transcribe it, and published an academic version of 446 pages in 2007, *The First American Novel: The Journal of Penrose, Seaman by William Williams, & the Book, the Author,*

First page of Penrose's Journal

and the Letters in the Lilly Library by Terry Breverton. I transcribed it into chapters, modernising the spelling and grammar, and shortened sentences to make it more readable. It was printed in a small academic edition of 500 copies (with 350 unsold) with 800 footnotes and a biography of William Williams to protect copyright. To try and stimulate interest I again rewrote it without footnotes, replacing more antiquated words, to read as a modern version of *Robinson Crusoe* would read. This appeared as print-on-demand and e-book in 540pp in 2014 as *The Journal of Penrose, Seaman: "The New Robinson Crusoe" and The First American Novel*. No Welsh or European/American publisher wishes to publish the book, which is one of the finest and most important works in literary history.

When I finished transcribing it, I was on the point of tears – it is incredibly moving – an account of a man far before his times.

A transcript of Williams' book was first published in 1815 a quarter of a century after the writer's death. It was a literary sensation, influencing Lord Grey to abolish slavery, and keeping Lord Byron up all night either reading or dreaming about it. Proof-read by Sir Walter Scott, this was a heavily Bowdlerised edition, but highly lauded by the Poet Laureate Robert Southey. It was pirated in Germany as '*Der Neue Robinson Crusoe*', praised as vastly superior to that book, and reprinted in 1825. In 1968 the original manuscript was rediscovered, purchased by Indiana University and published as an exact copy of the original by Howard Dickason.

In my work upon privateers, I came across the work, written by an unknown Welsh privateer and polymath, William Williams, and saved to fly to America and work on the original. It is a factional account of his being marooned and living among the Rama Indians of the Miskito Coast, a superb evocation of an almost idyllic existence, and almost a natural history of the area. It is the first novel written in America by around 20 years, and should be on all academic syllabi in that country, also being suitable for a film script. Of special importance in the text is his discovery of mammoth bones in the rainforest, along with basalt pillars with hieroglyphics – both have been discovered in Nicaragua in the last 10 years. It is the first story of buried treasure and possibly the first mention of a message in a bottle in literature.

Around 1786, an impoverished artist was befriended by the literary critic Reverend Thomas Eagles, who found him lodgings in the Merchant Venturers' Almshouses in Bristol. The man had returned from living in the American colonies, escaping the War of Independence. The painter's

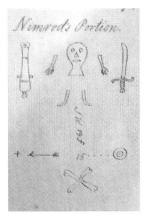

The First Treasure Map

bedroom can even today be visited. The old man had been a successful painter in colonial America, and became known to Eagles as 'Llewellin' Penrose. Penrose became very friendly with Eagles' family, and in 1791 Eagles was surprised to be Penrose's sole beneficiary in his deathbed will. His family only now discovered that Penrose's real name was William Williams.

Williams left all his possessions to Reverend Eagles, including a manuscript written in the Americas, *The Journal of Penrose, Seaman*. In 1805, fourteen years after Williams' death, the great American artist Benjamin West RA was taken to visit Thomas Eagles' London town house. Luckily, as he waited for Eagles, West happened to notice William's manuscript lying upon a table. West then borrowed the manuscript, telling Thomas Eagles' son John that he had known Williams, aka 'Penrose', both in America and London. Williams had initially inspired, and indeed then taught West to paint. West honestly believed the *Journal* to be a true account of Williams' life as a privateer, and that Williams had been marooned among the Caribbean Indians. The places mentioned in the text - the islands, reefs, caves and coastline – have all been identified in Nicaragua.

Written perhaps around 1775, the book is a factional account of being imprisoned by the Spanish, marooned and then living among the Rama Indians of the Miskito Coast. It is a superb evocation of an almost idyllic existence, and in effect an astonishing natural history of the area – its jungle, shoreline, sea and islands. There are described at least 36 different species of birds, 48 different trees, shrubs, fruit and vegetables, 36 fish, 11 crabs and shells, 14 mammals, 24 reptiles, 20 insects, 7 turtles and tortoises, plus crustaceans and invertebrates totalling around 200 known animals and plants. All these fish, plants and animals mentioned by Penrose are native to the Atlantic seaboard and rainforest of Nicaragua. The indigenous Rama tribe which supported him is now facing extinction, and their customs are described in some detail.

Williams' *The Journal of Penrose, Seaman* contains entries covering twenty-seven years in the rainforest shoreline, and reads almost as if it is written in the 21st century, with strong feelings against slavery and religious bigotry running as themes throughout the book. The author's attitudes towards racial and female equality, in a time of universal slavery, are simply astonishing, as is his positing of a 'savage' civilization being far more humane and rational than many aspects of the Christian church.

The Reverend Thomas Eagles and his son John altered the original manuscript to produce a book not published until 1815. It was a literary sensation. Proof-read by Sir Walter Scott, this was a heavily expurgated edition, but was still highly lauded by the Poet Laureate Robert Southey, who believed it to be true. The Journal was ecstatically reviewed by Lord George Byron. 'I have never read so much of a book in one sitting in my life. He (Penrose) kept me up half the night, and made me dream of him the other half... it has all the air of truth, and is most interesting and entertaining in every point of view.' It is also thought that Penrose's Journal influenced Lord Grey to later enact anti-slavery laws when he became Prime Minister. It was widely praised as being vastly superior to *Robinson Crusoe* (published in 1719), as Daniel Defoe had never experienced the vicissitudes of William Williams.

The book is a plea for racial and religious tolerance, but much more than that, a marvellous adventure story based upon its author running away from Caerphilly to sea in 1744, and being marooned in the coastal rainforests of Central America until his death in 1775. Of the author himself, in 1946 the art critic James Thomas Flexner wrote of: 'The amazing William Williams: Painter, Author, Teacher, Musician, Stage Designer, Castaway... The activities of this forgotten genius spread across almost every branch of American culture... he will stand out as a significant figure in the development of American culture.' This forgotten author was a polymath – a privateer, poet, music-teacher, naturalist, writer and painter who inspired and taught Colonial America's greatest artist Benjamin West, built America's first permanent theatre and wrote America's first novel.

The Journal of Penrose, Seaman was strongly anti-slavery at a time when Presidents Washington, Jefferson and Adams had slaves, and the reason that it is still barely known is a mystery. The book is an astounding piece of writing, an exciting adventure story worthy of international renown and would make a marvellous film to put Wales on the world map.

DAVID WILLIAMS 1738 – 29 June 1816

FOUNDER OF THE ROYAL LITERARY FUND, FRENCH CITIZEN

David Williams, who founded the Royal Literary Fund, was born at Waunwaelod (later called The Carpenter's Arms) in Eglwysilan near Caerffili. His father was William David, from Llwynybarcud, Llanhari, Glamorgan, and he was educated by the influential David Williams (1709-1784), the Dissenting minister of Trinity Chapel, Womanby Street, Cardiff, and of Watford Chapel Caerphilly. In response to the request of his dying father, David Williams became a Dissenting minister himself in 1752. He studied at Carmarthen Academy, and became Independent minister at Frome in 1758, moving on to Exeter in 1761, and Highgate, London from 1769 until 1773. Here he knew Oliver Goldsmith and David Garrick.

Generally abandoning the ministry aged 35, Williams now maintained himself on incomes from political pamphlets, teaching and

lecturing. He had not been able to survive in London on a cleric's single stipend, so he opened an expensive boarding school in Chelsea in 1774. In this year, he wrote his *Treatise on Education.* Upon 9 December 1775, a daughter Emilia was born, but his wife Mary died of childbirth complications just eleven days later. David Williams abandoned the school upon his wife's death, and it did not reopen in 1776. However, his writings on liturgy and education had attracted Benjamin Franklin's attention, and he stayed in Williams' house in Chelsea, when

Franklin 'took refuge from the political storm' in 1776. They formed the '13 Club', a group of Deists for which Williams wrote *A Liturgy on the Universal Principles of Religion and Morality.* The work was eulogised by no less than Rousseau, Voltaire and Frederick II.

A friend of many eminent thinkers, in 1777 Williams also gave shelter to Benjamin Franklin when he stayed in Wales. Williams advanced Richard Price's (q.v.) philosophy that parliamentarians are 'trustees of the people', in his *Letters on Political Liberty* in 1782. It was a defence of the American colonists, and a schedule for revolution and radical reform. Its French translator, Brissot, was imprisoned in the Bastille. However, after the Revolution David Williams, held in high esteem in France, was asked to become an honorary French citizen by the leading French revolutionaries, and to take a seat in their Convention of 1792. He accepted an invitation to criticise and amend the draft of the First Constitution of the French

Republic, by the Girondists. He remained in Paris until 1793, and was asked by the French foreign minister, Le Brun, to make overtures for peace with the English government, itself afraid of the revolutionary example being followed.

Williams maintained his income by taking private pupils, delivering courses of public lectures and by writing. He wrote a *History of Monmouthshire* in 1796, and published another 25 books. His manuscripts are in Cardiff Library and The National Library of Wales. The British Government asked Williams to visit France after the Treaty of Amiens, to report on public opinion on Napoleon Buonaparte. Williams first proposed a fund for writers in 1773. In 1790, The Literary Fund as established through his efforts to assist needy authors, and David Williams lived at its headquarters at 36 Gerrard Square, Soho, until his death in 1816.

THOMAS JEFFERSON 1743 - July 4 1826

THE AUTHOR OF THE DECLARATION OF INDEPENDENCE

Born in Albemarle County, Virginia, he inherited from his father 5,000 acres of plantations, and from his mother a position in society. Jefferson said that his father came from the Snowdon foothills, and a US State Department official unveiled a plaque at Llanfair Ceiriog in 1933, 'To the Memory of a Great Welshman, Thomas Jefferson'. After studying at the College of William and Mary, he read law, and in 1772 married a widow, Martha Waynes Skelton. He took her to live in his partly finished mountaintop home, Monticello.

'He was also an architect, builder and carpenter. Into his stately Virginia home, Monticello, went gadgets that were designed to save time and energy for its occupants. He built a circular staircase to save space. He also installed a dumbwaiter to save the servants many needless trips up and down the stairs. There were folding tables, and chairs than folded back into the walls when not in use. Sliding panels were built into some of the walls so that dishes and other small objects could be passed from one room to another with ease. He designed a trick bed. From one side he emerged to his study, from the other, to his breakfast. During the day the bed was raised out of the way.'

Jefferson's original draft of the Declaration of Independence was severely pruned by Congress, and North Carolina and Georgia were responsible for the removal of anti-slavery promises. Jefferson used all his powers when he drafted the Declaration of Independence*, imbued with the Welsh traditions of social equality. His original draft declares 'We hold these truths to be sacred and undeniable; that all men are created equal and independent, that from that equal creation they derive rights inherent and inalienable, among which are the preservation of life, and liberty, and the pursuit of happiness.' In the same year, 1786, he wrote a bill establishing religious freedom, and in the years that followed endeavoured to make his words reality. Jefferson was very proud of his Virginian statute He enshrined the separation of the church and state, as he believed in religious liberty - a politically-aligned religion would mean minority persecution. He believed that 'the care of human life and happiness... is the first and only legitimate object of good government.' This belief in the welfare of citizens is alien to present Western governments, which seem to kow-tow to the multinational business interests which control them.

Jefferson had succeeded Benjamin Franklin as Minister to France in 1785. His sympathy for the French Revolution later brought him into conflict with Alexander Hamilton, when Jefferson was Secretary of State in 1793, so he resigned from Washington's Cabinet. Two political parties began to emerge; Jefferson's Democrat-Republicans and Hamilton's Federalists, and Jefferson opposed a strong Federal government and championed the rights of states. He was a reluctant candidate for the presidency in 1796, yet came within three votes of selection. He was appointed Vice-President, although at that time an enemy of President John Adams. In 1800 he tied with Aaron Burr for the presidential candidacy, but with Hamilton's support was elected President.

As third President after George Washington, from 1801-1809, Jefferson negotiated and signed the Louisiana Purchase of vast French territories from Napoleon. For $15 million, the USA doubled in size - a cost of under 3 cents an acre. The sale included over 600 million acres, most of the 13 states in the middle of America, from the Gulf of Mexico to the Rocky Mountains and Canadian border. It was a diplomatic and political triumph, ending the threat of war with France, and opening up the land west of the Mississippi for settlement, allowing the colonies to eventually reach the Pacific. By acquiring the heart of the continent, he secured the independent future of the fledgling USA. Some objected to the purchase as it was not provided for in the Constitution, but Jefferson later admitted that he had stretched his Presidential power 'till it cracked', for 'what is practicable must often control what is pure theory.'

In his first term, Jefferson cut back upon central army and navy expenditures and slashed the government budget, allowing him not only to reduce the National Debt by one third, but also to eliminate the unpopular tax on whiskey. He also sent a naval squadron to suppress the Barbary

Pirates who were harassing American ships in the Mediterranean. In his second term he fought to keep America neutral in the Napoleonic Wars, although both England and France interfered with American merchantmen. Jefferson had been the first President to be inaugurated in Washington, and he called his new residence, The White House, 'a great stone house, big enough for two emperors, one pope and the grand lama in the bargain.' He walked to his inauguration in a homespun grey suit, as bad weather had delayed the arrival of an expensive velvet suit and a new $6,000 carriage.

The Library of Congress purchased Jeffferson's 6,500 volume book collection for almost $24,000 to replace those burned by the British, but he died in relative poverty. On July 4, 1826, there was a ceremony in the House of Representatives to celebrate 50 years of independence. Jefferson's friends were soliciting money for his relief, with little success, at the ceremony. Jefferson died that same day, along with his friend John Adams. J. F. Kennedy at a dinner honouring Nobel Prize winners said 'I think this is the most extraordinary collection of talent, of human knowledge, that has ever gathered together at The White House - with the possible exception of when Thomas Jefferson dined alone.' This greatest and most unassuming American president composed his own epitaph... 'Here was buried Thomas Jefferson, Author of the Declaration of American Independence, of the Statute of Virginia for Religious Freedom, and Father of the University of Virginia.'

* Another Welshman, the one-legged lawyer Gouveneur Morris (1755-1835), wrote the final draft of the Constitution and as such is commemorated on a plaque on Philadelphia Town Hall, along with William Penn, Jefferson, and the Welshmen Robert Morris and John Marshall. Gouveneur Morris was later Minister to France and a senator:
'Perpetuating the Welsh heritage, and commemorating the vision and virtue of the following Welsh patriots in the founding of the City, Commonwealth and Nation:
William Penn, 1644-1718, proclaimed freedom and religion and planned New Wales, later named Pennsylvania;
Thomas Jefferson, 1743-1826, third President of the United States, composed the Declaration of Independence;
Robert Morris, 1734-1806, foremost financier of the American Revolution and signer of the Declaration of Independence;
Gouverneur Morris, 1752-1816, wrote the final draft of the Constitution of the United States;
John Marshall, 1755-1835, Chief Justice of the United States and father of American constitutional law.'

SIR WILLIAM JONES 28 September 1746 – 27 April 1794

ORIENTAL JONES, PHILOLOGIST AND JURIST, THE FATHER OF COMPARATIVE LINGUISTICS

He was the son of William Jones of Anglesey (q.v.), who first used pi, but his father died when William was just three years old. Jones was a precocious child, being an outstanding talent at Harrow School and then at University College, Oxford (1764–68).

In Oxford he had already developed a reputation for his impressive scholarship, and college enabled him to increase his knowledge of Middle Eastern studies, philosophy, Oriental literature, and Greek and Hebrew. In addition, he learned Spanish and Portuguese, and also mastered the Chinese language. By the end of his life, the hyperpolygot had learned 28 languages, including Chinese, often by teaching himself. He supported himself through college with scholarships and by serving as a tutor to Earl Spencer, the seven-year-old son of Lord Althorp, who was the brother of Georgiana, Duchess of Devonshire.

Jones earned his BA in 1768. By then he had already become a well-known Orientalist, despite being only 22 years old. That same year, Jones was asked by Christian VII of Denmark to translate a Persian manuscript about the life of Nadir Shah into French. The Danish king had brought the manuscript with him on a visit to England. The Persian manuscript was a difficult one, and Jones was forced to interrupt his own postgraduate studies for a year to complete the translation. It was eventually published in 1770 as *Histoire de Nader Chah*, and it included an introduction that contained descriptions of Asia and a history of Persia. His *Grammar of the Persian Language* (1771) was authoritative in the field. The work, which went through several editions and translations, provided a model that later language scholars would follow.

During this period he took his MA in 1773 and produced three more books, including the 542-page *Poeseos Asiaticae Commentariorum* (1774), which demonstrated Jones's brilliance and helped cement his academic reputation, also earning him the nicknames of 'Persian Jones', 'Oriental Jones', and 'Linguist Jones'. His published academic and literary output provided Jones with a high professional rank and important social connections. He became a fellow of the Royal Society, and in 1773, at the age of 26, Jones was elected to Dr Johnson's Literary Club, on terms of intimacy with Johnson, Hester Thrale, Elizabeth Craven, Boswell, Reynolds, Georgiana Duchess of Devonshire, Elizabeth Vesey, Elizabeth Montagu, Franklin, Price, Adam Smith, Priestley, Burke, Hastings, Zoffany, Gibbon, Goldsmith, Percy, Sheridan, Fox, Pitt, Wilkes, Warton, Garrick, etc.

After these years in translating and scholarship, for financial reasons Jones also began studying law, entering London's Middle Temple in 1770, but he continued working on translations. He was admitted to the bar in 1774, and made a modest living as a barrister, an attorney, and an Oxford fellow. He also worked with Benjamin Franklin in Paris, trying to help resolves issues involving the American Revolution. Through his law studies, Jones also became a noted legal scholar. In 1776 he was appointed commissioner in bankruptcy, which led to his famous *Essay on the Law of Bailments* (1781), a lucid study that compared English bailments with other legal systems. The work went through several editions and became a standard for English and American lawyers. Other works included the translation of *The Speeches of Isaeus* (1779), which dealt with the Athenian right of inheritance.

Jones demonstrated a passion for social justice, pro-American sympathies, republicanism and a disdain for right-wing government polices. From 1780 to 1783, Jones wrote four political tracts, the most famous and influential of which was *An Inquiry into the Legal Mode of Suppressing Riots, with a Constitutional Plan of Future Defence* (1780). In 1782, his *The Principles of Government* was published anonymously. When it was deemed libellous by the British government, Jones decided to reprint the pamphlet, this time with his name revealed as its author. The resulting libel case resulted in the Libel Act of 1792, which helped advance the cause of freedom of the press.

His *Moallakât* (1782) was a translation of seven famous pre-Islamic Arabic odes, which influenced Tennyson and later important poets. In 1783 Jones was knighted and sailed for Calcutta as judge of the Supreme Court. In his 11 years on the Supreme Court of Calcutta he helped determine the course of Indian jurisprudence as well as preserve the rights of Indian citizens to trial by jury, as Jones considered Indians to be equal under the law with Europeans.

In 1784 he founded the Asiatic Society of Bengal to encourage Oriental studies. 'The founding of the Society grew out of Jones's love for India, its people and its culture, as well as his abhorrence of oppression, nationalism and imperialism. His goal for the Society was to develop a means to foster collaborative international scientific and humanistic projects that would be unhindered by social, ethnic, religious and political barriers.' He himself took up Sanskrit, to equip himself for the preparation of a vast digest of Hindu and Muslim law. Of this uncompleted venture, his *Institutes of Hindu Law* was published in 1794 and his *Muhammedan Law of Inheritance* in 1792.

In his 1786 presidential discourse to the Asiatic Society, he postulated the common ancestry of Sanskrit, Latin, and Greek, his findings providing the impetus for the development of comparative linguistics in the early 19th century. He is best known for his famous proposition that many languages sprang from a common source. His scholarship helped to generate widespread interest in Eastern history, language and culture, and it led to new directions in linguistic research.

While studying Sanskrit, Jones had developed the idea of a common source for languages, which proved to be his greatest achievement of all. *In The Sanscrit Language* (1786) Jones wrote of how he observed that Sanskrit had a strong resemblance to Greek and Latin, which led him to suggest that the three languages not only had a common root but they were related to the Gothic, Celtic, and Persian languages. The impact of the work was enormous, as it brought about the separation of religion from language and eschewed mythology for a more scientific approach to linguistics. His discovery was regarded as just as important, in its own way, as the scientific discoveries made by men like Galileo, Copernicus and Charles Darwin. Jones's efforts not only substantially added to the store of human knowledge; his work also generated a renewed interest among the Indian people about their own rich national and literary heritage. Notable among his contemporaries as being utterly free of racial prejudice, he was the first linguist to discover that there was a linguistic 'family tree' that diversified into different, but related, languages.

Eventually, living in Calcutta (Kolkata) took its toll on Jones and his wife. In November 1793, Anna Jones was forced to return to England for health reasons. Jones stayed to try and complete his translation of Hindu and Muslim laws so that the Indian people would be able to govern themselves under their own laws. However, five months later, Jones died in Calcutta from inflammation of the liver, a condition aggravated with overwork. Apart from his contribution to linguistics, his translations introduced the Western world to the rich heritage of the Middle East. It has been pointed out that his style, which mixed Western and Eastern elements, helped influence poets of England's Romantic movement, especially Samuel Taylor Coleridge and Lord Byron. Later writers that Jones influenced are said to have included Matthew Arnold, Rudyard Kipling, Ralph Waldo Emerson, Walt Whitman, Goethe, and T.S. Eliot. William Jones facilitated India's cultural assimilation into the modern world, helping to build India's future on the immensity, sophistication, and pluralism of its past.

IOLO MORGANWG 19 March 1747 – 18 December 1826

EDWARD WILLIAMS, SAVIOUR OF WELSH CULTURE

Upon 21 June 1792, an itinerant stonemason named Edward Williams

proclaimed a *Gorsedd of the Bards of the Island of Britain*, at Primrose Hill in London. Using his bardic name of Iolo Morganwg, he went on to lay out another circle of stones at the Ivy Bush Hotel in Carmarthen in 1819, re-starting the ancient tradition of the eisteddfod. A National Eisteddfod was held in Liverpool in 1929, and in 1900 a Gorsedd of Bards was formed in Brittany, and in 1928 a similar Gorsedd was started in Cornwall.

Born at Pennon, Llancarfan, he was the son of Edward Williams of Gileston and Ann Mathew of Llanmaes, who had married in nearby St. Tathan in 1744. The thatched cottage at Pennon was in ruins when visited by Awbery in the 1950's. Soon after Edward's birth, they moved to St Tathan, but from 1756 the family lived in a tiny thatched cottage in Flemingston, and Iolo trained as a stonemason, eventually moving to Cowbridge, where an 1826 plaque in the High Street commemorates him. It reads: 'Er cof am / Edward Williams, (Iolo Morganwg), / 1747-1826, Saer Maen, Bardd Rhyddid, / Hynafhiaethydd, ac un o Gymwynaswyr Mwyaf / Llen a Hanes Cymru. Y Gwir Erbyn Y Byd.' (- In memory of Edward Williams (Iolo Morganwg), 1747-1826, Stone Mason, Bard, Historian, and one of the Greatest Benefactors Of Welsh History and Literature. Truth Against the World.) 'The truth against the world' was Iolo's motto throughout life.

Iolo states that he learned to read by watching his father cut inscriptions on gravestones, as he did not attend any school. His mother also probably taught him, and he says that Edward Williams of Llancarfan taught him in the bardic crafts. It was thought that his mother married 'beneath her station' as her distant relatives, the Seys, in the great Boverton Place, had brought her up. Other Glamorgan bards such as Rhys Morgan, Lewis Hopkin and Siôn Bradford influenced his childhood. The Rev. Edward Pritchard also lived in Iolo's tiny Flemingstone cottage, which had one room downstairs, and two tiny box bedrooms open to the rafters. It was held on lease from Lady Charlotte Edwin, and the height of the bedrooms was only 4 feet at the sides, rising to around 6 foot in the middle. By 1850, the cottage was demolished. It had been situated in the yard of Gregory Farm, where the barn is now.

The Rev. David Williams writes: 'Edward junior was trained as a stonemason but realised that his true craft lay elsewhere, in the history and culture of Wales. He was a life-long sufferer with asthma and this, too, may well have inclined him away from manual work to more literary pursuits. Although it is sometimes stated that he was self-taught, his studies were guided by John Walters, Rector of Llandough and Vicar of St Hilary - a noted scholar and lexicographer. He was also helped in his studies by another clergyman, Thomas Richards of Coychurch, and it was through his studies with the latter that he became fascinated with the bardic tradition and saw himself as its true heir. He adopted the bardic name of Iolo Morganwg, the name by which he is best known...

His Unitarian beliefs did not prevent his having his children baptised at Flemingston Church, nor was he refused burial in the churchyard. The date of his funeral is recorded as taking place on December 20th 1826. He was buried just outside the West end of the Church and the extension of the building in 1858 meant that his burial spot now lies within the Church building. To mark the place there is a memorial wall tablet to him and his son, Taliesin. This was erected by Caroline, Countess of Dunraven among other admirers. Close to it is a memorial window depicting Christ among the doctors. This was given by Iolo's great grandson, Mr Illtyd Williams of Middlesborough whose family long maintained an interest in the Church. As a young man, Iolo had the opportunity to read ancient Welsh manuscripts, which had been collected by John Walters of Llandough and Thomas Richards of Coychurch, which gave him a great interest in the structure and vocabulary of the Welsh language.'

Professor G.J. Williams wrote the following, which was delivered posthumously on the BBC Welsh Home Service in 1963: 'Iolo was, in his early years, a romantic poet, and throughout his life, a romantic dreamer. Everybody agrees that he was the greatest authority of his day on the subject of Welsh literature and on many aspects of Welsh history. He was also an authority on such subjects as horticulture, agriculture, geology and botany and, in his old age, he was prepared to lecture on metallurgy in the school which his son had opened in the new industrial town of Merthyr Tudful. His manuscripts show that he was a musician who had composed scores of hymn tunes, and that he took great delight in collecting folk songs. He was a theologian who helped establish the Unitarian denomination in South Wales, and a politician who revelled in the excitement of the early years after the French Revolution.'

Edward Williams was responsible for retrieving much material upon early Welsh history, but has been portrayed as a fraudster by nearly all sources. As a result, the author has been extremely careful in using his material. However, it seems time for a careful study of his life's work – vitriol was heaped upon him for daring to say that British history predated the Germanic invasions. Hanoverian apologists such as Bishop Stubbs hated any church predating the Roman Catholic conversion of the pagan Saxons. He was also pilloried for his researches showing the influence of South Wales upon Welsh history. A very major reassessment of Iolo is needed as Iolo Morgannwg is a shining beacon of Welsh history. He tried to 'kick-start' the engine of a dying culture, for which the many of the 'crachach' (snobs) of the time hated him. Vitriolic attacks often have a reason that stems not from academic integrity, but from dislike of change. For many academics to change their thinking, to go back to original sources, to approach a problem differently, requires a change in our educational system. The Rev. David Williams wrote: 'The cottage in which he lived was demolished not long after his death and in the space it occupied there now stands the barn of Gregory Farm. The manuscripts which once filled the house were carefully preserved and are now kept at the National Library of Wales at Aberystwyth. They are so numerous that any scholar would find it a daunting task to read through them and they bear eloquent testimony to the man's industry.'

Apart from buying and collecting old manuscripts from across the length of Wales, Iolo noted local events: 'John Harry's age ascertained from register. A lying old devil as ever was. Swore by his God that he was 118 years of age and could remember King David.... Catherine Rees alias Jenkins of the same parish, died about 1768 at about 100 or more - an illiterate rustic. She could give no interesting account of anything that had happened in her day, only that men and women of all ages in her young days had the general habit of smoking. She remembered Morris Dances by women, all in breeches, continuing with companies of men dancers. She lamented the discontinuance of Sunday dancing.' He also noted the depopulation of the Vale in this time 'After looking at St Athan and Flimston, let the mournful (for he must be so) observer proceed to the next village of Boverton... And observe what were once populous places. The numerous farm houses and cottages in ruins will give an idea similar to no other but that of the recent depredatory approach of an invading army having passed through the country, beating down all before him.'

Little known is the fact that Iolo and John Evans of Waun-fawr planned in detail to visit the tribe of Welsh Indians, the Mandans, supposed to be descendants of Prince Madoc's 1170 expedition. The ailing Iolo dropped out in 1792, leaving Evans to explore the Missouri alone. Evans is regarded as the greatest explorer in America, along with Meriwether Lewis, the Welsh leader of the Lewis and Clark Expedition, which crossed the continent. Another point about Iolo's life is that he said that Wil Hopcyn (1700-1741) was the author of the haunting *Bugeilio'r Gwenith Gwyn* (the song known in English as *Watching the Wheat*), but it seems that Iolo himself wrote the poem. Iolo's son Taliesin later told the tragic tale of Wil Hopcyn and Ann Thomas of Llangynwyd, the *Maid of Cefn Ydfa*, and connected the song to this story.

Much has been written on Iolo, but little in this century - it seems that only in the later 1990's has a pride in being Welsh reappeared in the national psyche. It is to be hoped that dissertation students spend time quarrying among Iolo's voluminous writings rather than wasting their time reinventing the wheel in ever more abstruse and obtuse terms. Details of his life from the *Dictionary of Welsh Biography* are as follows. After training as a stonemason, he journeyed in North Wales, 1771-72, then went with his brothers to London in 1773. He met Owen Myfyr and other members of the Society of Gwyneddigion, and studied the manuscripts of the Morrises of Anglesey. The poet Robert Southey wrote: "Iolo, Iolo, he who knows / The virtue of all herbs of mount or dale, / Or greenwood shade, or quiet brooklet's bed; / Whatever lore of science or song / Sages or bards have handed down.'

In London Iolo met Prime Minister Pitt, and the great Dr Johnson, who tried to humiliate him. He worked as a mason in London and Kent, went to Bristol in 1777, married in 1783 and met financial difficulties. His father-in-law gave him some land at Tredelerch (Rumney in Cardiff) to farm, but Iolo was in Cardiff Gaol in 1786-1787. In August 1786 he had been taken to court in Cowbridge by two of his many creditors, Dr John Walton and Evan Griffith of Penllyn. Unable to pay up, Iolo was set free at the Great Sessions of August 1787.

After then spending time back in Flemingston (Trefflemin), he returned to London for most of the years between 1791 and 1795. In London he presented the Prince of Wales with a poem on his marriage in 1795, and supposedly attended the ceremony wearing a leather apron and carrying a trowel. In London he was in contact with Unitarian leaders and sympathisers of the French Revolution, and accused of preaching sedition. It is said that he was now examined by Pitt, who declared him innocent and restored his research papers to him.

In 1795 Iolo was back in Trefflemin, and in 1796 was given a contract by the Board of Agriculture, to describe the condition of lands and farms in Glamorgan and Carmarthenshire. This was his great opportunity to rescue old manuscripts and parchments from outlying farms and manors. He assisted Gwallter Mechain (Rev. Walter Davies) in a report on Welsh agriculture. Before this, Iolo had opened a shop in Cowbridge, where he sold books and groceries. Because of the fears engendered by the French Revolution, the House of Commons proscribed the selling of Tom Paine's *The Rights of Man,* which should even now be compulsory reading for politicians and employers. Iolo wrapped a *Bible* in paper, writing on the outside, *The Rights of Man*, and displayed it in his shop window. A man bought it, hoping to report Iolo to the authorities, but Iolo told him 'My friend, that book contains the best and dearest rights of man.' Tom Paine had subscribed to Iolo's publication of poems in 1794, along with two other friends, Hannah Moore the reformer, and Robert Raikes, the founder of Sunday Schools.

At his shop from 1795-1796 Iolo declined to sell any sugar that had been associated with slavery, campaigning for its abolition. His sugar, he proclaimed, was 'East India sweets, uncontaminated by human gore.' By this time, the stone-dust he had inhaled through masonry work was giving him severe breathing difficulties. Like all his contemporaries, Iolo took laudanum, the aspirin of his day, for his illnesses. He has been constantly traduced in the 20th century for this – being described as 'drug-addled' and an addict by academic scholars who have no idea of the times. Iolo walked across Wales with his mule, researching and carrying books he bought, sleeping on straw, into his 70s – he was never an addict. I have recently witnessed a famous Welsh professor of history telling an audience this in Cowbridge church – academic historians tend these days to repeat what they are told, rather than look at a wider picture.

Appointed as an editor of the *Myvyrian Archaiology*, in 1799 Iolo travelled through North Wales again, collecting materials. He was a leading figure in the formation of the Unitarian Association in South Wales in 1802, and was still in contact with friends in London until around 1805. Known now as a principal authority on Welsh history, he succeeded in making the Gorsedd of Bards an integral part of an eisteddfod in the grounds of Carmarthen's Ivy Bush Hotel in 1819. Maxwell Fraser stated that Iolo had devised the Gorsedd ceremonial at Primrose Hill in 1791. He published very little in his lifetime, and died at Trefflemin on 18 December 1826, aged 81. Many of his hymns were published after his death.

Much of the vituperation heaped upon his research was unfounded, based on the work of Hanoverian apologists such as Bishop Stubbs, who could not believe that Britain had a history before the 'civilising' Saxons came from Germany. *The Dictionary of Welsh Biography* entry concludes as follows: 'Iolo was a versatile man. He took an intelligent interest not only in the literature of Wales but also in such subjects as agriculture, gardening, architecture, geology, botany, politics, the history of religion, theology, etc. He was an excellent poet and he ahs a special place in the history of romantic verse in Wales. The most strange thing about him was his complex mind - but it would be out of place to treat that subject here. After the death of Iolo his son, Taliesin, bound his papers into volumes; those volumes are now in the National Library.' The great Nonconformist revivals swept away great swathes of Welsh culture, tradition, music and dance. Without Iolo Williams even more would have been lost, and he inspired generations to retrieve and re-enact tradition. Intriguingly, the burial registers of Flemingstone reveal that the burial immediately before Iolo's was his invalid daughter Peggy (Margaret), and the death immediately after was that of his blind wife Margaret. This author's *The Secret Vale of Glamorgan* contains a long appendix upon Edward Williams.

JOHN NASH 18 January 1752 – 13 May 1835

THE ARCHITECT OF THE REGENCY, THE MAN WHO CHANGED THE FACE OF LONDON

John Nash was the son of a Welsh millwright from Cardigan who moved to London. Aged 14, he was apprenticed to the architect Sir Robert Taylor for ten years. Leaving upon completion to pursue a career as a surveyor, builder and carpenter, he married the daughter of a surgeon. He was earning a substantial £300 a year and in 1777 established his own architectural practice.

They had two children but by June 1778 'By the ill conduct of his wife found it necessary to send her into Wales in order to work a reformation on her'. It seems that Jane Nash 'Had imposed two spurious children on him as his and her own, notwithstanding she had then never had any child', and she had incurred many debts, including one for milliners' bills of an astounding £300. The claim that Jane had faked her pregnancies and then passed babies she had acquired off as her own was brought before the court of the Bishop of London, and she wife was sent to Aberavon to lodge with Nash's cousin Ann Morgan.

In the portico of All Souls, Langham Place, London

However, Jane Nash began an affair with a local man Charles Charles before returning Nash in June 1779. Her extravagance continued to act extravagantly so Nash sent her to another cousin, Thomas Edwards of Neath. Here she gave birth, and acknowledged Charles Charles as the father. In 1781 Nash instigated divorce, and in 1782, Charles was found guilty. He was unable to pay the damages of £76 and subsequently died in prison. The divorce was finally read 26 January 1787. After inheriting £1,000 in 1778 from his uncle Thomas, Nash invested the money in building his first known independent works, 15-17 Bloomsbury Square and 66-71 However, the Georgian terraced properties failed to let and Nash was declared bankrupt on 30 September 1783. His debts were £5,000, including £2,000 he had been lent by Robert Adam and his brothers.

Nash left London in 1784 to live in Carmarthen, where his mother had retired, living near her family. In 1785 he and a local man Samuel Simon Saxon re-roofed St. Peter's church for 600 guineas and Nash began practising again. His first major work in the area was the first of three prisons he would design, Carmarthen 1789–92, a prison initially planned by the penal reformer John Howard. Nash developed new prisons for Cardigan and Hereford, the latter approved by James Wyatt. In 1789 Nash was called in to survey the failing structure of St David's Cathedral and develop a plan to save the building, his solution to the west front and chapter house completed in 1791. Nash designed Castle House Aberystwyth, and the Grade I-listed mansions at Llanerchaeron and Ffynone.

The beautiful house he designed in Llanerchaeron, near Aberaeron, is now a National Trust property. It is the finest example of a classical villa in Wales, and has been restored at a cost of over £2,000,000. The original house was remodelled by Nash, with a freestanding billiards room, home farm, superb granary, cow-byre etc., and forms the centrepiece of a rare example of a Welsh gentry estate of the period. Originally belonging to the Parry family, descendants of Llywelyn Fawr, it passed to the Lewis family in 1634, and Colonel Lewis commissioned Nash in the 1790's. John Powell Ponsonby Lewes left the estate in his bequest to the nation in 1989. Its 670 acres include two historic parks, three SSSI's, the unaltered farm complex and labourers' cottages. The estate's property manager says 'Llanerchaeron is nationally important, as estates have all but disappeared through dereliction, fragmentation, modernisation and development.' 'Ffynone was perhaps the most successful of Nash's early houses quite plain, well mannered and with a great sense of style. Inside, we see for the first time, in plan, detail and decoration, an original Nash interior; one which he was to use in the future in a variety of ways and on different scales.' Also in Wales, designed the great and beautiful houses of Nanteos (where the 'Holy Grail' was kept), Dolaucothi and Hafod.

Now successful, after his second move to London in the 1790's, he employed as his first draughtsman Auguste Charles Pugin, and also John Adey Repton, the son of his friend the garden designer Humphry Repton. One of the greatest town planners, Nash's 1779 patent for improvements to the piers and arches of bridges led the way for the introduction of steel girders in building. On his return to London, Nash had collaborated in a partnership with the landscape gardener Sir Humphrey Repton, but became employed by the Prince of Wales from 1798. The Royal Palace at Brighton was originally a large 18th century farmhouse, which Henry Holland transformed for the Prince Regent (later George IV) into a Palladian villa from 1787. However, the prince commissioned his favourite architect, John Nash in 1814 to create a more exotic vision, and by 1822 there was completed an extraordinary building, extremely different from the refined neo-Classical mode of Regency times. Said to have cost over £500,000, it is a mixture of Indian exterior and Chinese interior, with bulbous domes, minaret chimneys, silk wall hangings, and an astonishing tribute to the versatility of John Nash.

Apart from his church work, he built Gothic country houses and Palladian terraces. Nash acquired considerable wealth, and from 1798 built

East Cowes Castle on the Isle of Wight, which influenced the early Gothic Revival School of architecture. Nash's London was a mish-mash of architectures - the rich preferred to have their great houses in the countryside, and town houses in London. The city was a collection of unconnected suburbs. Prince George became Regent as George III passed further and further into insanity, and decided that Britain needed a real capital city, as had been achieved in Paris. With Napoleon's defeat, Britain was now the greatest power and major trading nation in the world. In 1811, the prince selected John Nash to expand his leased income properties in London. In this year, Marylebone Park had reverted to Crown ownership,

and the prince saw the chance to build upon it and make a rental property fortune. He loved Nash's work on the Prince's Royal Pavilion in Brighton, and asked him to design

Royal Pavilion, Brighton

Regent's Park, a new housing development on Crown lands. Nash was in competition against two government architects, who proposed an inward-looking development, but Nash proposed keeping the (former Marylebone) Regent's Park, and connecting it to the rest of the city with a sweeping new street, Regent Street. He also linked the street to existing landmarks, opening up vistas rather than closing them off. The park was given a lake, the Regent's canal, a large wood and botanical area, and on the periphery shopping arcades and picturesque groupings of residences.

The Prince Regent agreed, saying he was 'so pleased with this magnificent plan which will eclipse Napoleon's.' In his 1811 plan, Nash said the street should constitute 'a boundary and complete separation between the streets and squares occupied by the nobility and gentry, and the narrow and meaner houses occupied by mechanics and the trading part of the community.' Thus it would appeal to rich people who could afford to pay high rents to the Prince. His bold and unpopular plan led to mass destruction of slums and houses, and he was mercilessly lampooned in the press until the completion of the project. Nash sliced through the city with Regent Street and new connecting streets, lining them with new buildings and pavilions. He planned, designed, and even acted as general contractor, bartering constantly with masons, carpenters and builders. Where Regent Street joined the Park, Nash designed the long and beautiful curve of houses known as Park Crescent. Designed to look like a palace, the crescent was a row of houses in a palace façade.

The people of London came to love the 'Nash Terraces' in the area, and his system of inter-linking parks and landmarks. The Quadrant led into Piccadilly Circus. Nash gave London a shape totally unconnected to the old system of separate village squares, a garden city of villas, terraces, crescents, a canal and lakes. From Carlton House (Prinnie's home) and St James's Park to Regent's Park and its lake, on one side of Regent Street lies the original city of London, and on the other Westminster. The street was widened, and forced to twist and turn by Nash as he could not afford to buy up any of the more expensive West End properties to achieve his goal. Nash's elegant, neo-classical style, with its porticoes, pediments, statues and colonnades, became known as 'Regency' architecture. Nash laid out Regent's Park, Trafalgar Square, St James Park, Carlton House Terrace and Regent Street.

In 1820, George IV decided to reconstruct Buckingham Palace, as his Carlton House was 'antiquated, run-down and decrepit', and gave John Nash a budget of £450,000 to achieve its transformation. Nash retained the main block, but doubled its size and faced the main block with mellow Bath stone, adding a new suite of rooms facing west to the gardens. In 1827 he demolished the North and South Wings, and rebuilt on a larger scale with a triumphal arch. In 1829, he was sacked (after George IV's death) because the cost of rebuilding had reached £500,000, and Edward Blore completed the building in the 1830's. Today's palace, however, is the work of Nash. During the building work, Nash redesigned Marble Arch in 1828, inspired by Rome's Arch of Constantinus. It was supposed to be the gateway to the Mall, but was too narrow for the State Coach to pass through, and was moved to the top of Hyde Park. Nash also cleared the slums and mazes of alleys to form Trafalgar Square as a lasting monument to Admiral Nelson. Nash's career effectively ended with the death of George IV in 1830. The king's extravagance had generated resentment and Nash was now without a protector.

In his work on Regent Street, he built the remarkable All Soul's Church in Langham Place, with its needle-shaped spire and colonnades. Apart from his work on St James's Park (1827-29) and Regent's Park and its terraces (1811-25), Nash's key works are: The United Services Club, Pall Mall 1827; Regent Street 1813-25; the Brighton Pavilion 1815-21; Royal Opera Arcade 1816-1818; Haymarket Theatre 1822-25; All Souls' Church, Langham Place 1822-1825; the Marble Arch (1828); Buckingham Palace 1821-30; Carlton House Terrace 1827-33; the Royal Mews 1825 and Trafalgar Square 1826-35. In 1825 he designed the Picton Monument in Carmarthen to Sir Thomas Picton (q.v.) A generous patron of artists, Nash died at East Cowes in 1835, aged 81. He had changed the face of London forever and inspired new generations of architects. He was an almost exact contemporary of that other great architect, Sir John Soane (1753-1837), and the architects Pugin and Salvin trained under John Nash.

SIR THOMAS PICTON 24 August 1758 - June 18 1815

THE HERO OF WATERLOO

A son of Thomas Picton of Poyston, Pembrokeshire, he was commissioned (aged 13) as an ensign in 1771 in the 12th Regiment, which was under his uncle's command. He was promoted to lieutenant five years later. Picton became a half-pay captain for 12 years, remembered only for his actions when the 75th Regiment was being disbanded in Bristol at the end of the American War. Some of the men began to protest, and Picton, a burly man

Statue by J. Mewburn Crook

of over six feet tall, drew his sword and plunged into the mob to arrest the ringleader. After these years of enforced idleness, in 1794 Picton sailed without orders to the West Indies, to press his services upon fellow-Welshman, Lieutenant-General Sir John Vaughan. He was 38 years old. With several actions against the Spanish, he was rapidly promoted. However, his first 'official' active service did not come about until the capture of St Lucia in 1796, where he distinguished himself by his bravery. He was promoted from captain to lieutenant colonel. Picton was made governor of Trinidad when it was taken in 1797, and his nine-year tenure aroused much controversy.

Picton's major problem was that he lacked the resources to keep the island British - he had few men, and a paucity of funds. He literally had to rely on threats and corruption to keep control. He even entered an alliance with the island's French planters, against the threat of invasion by French and Spanish fleets. The Spanish offered a reward of 20,000 dollars for his death. In 1806, because of the complaints of new colonists entering the island, he was brought back to London to face a variety of charges. All charges were dismissed, except for the torture of a slave, which was overturned on appeal.* The inhabitants of Trinidad were so grateful for the benefits of his administration of the island, that they voted him £5,000 when he left it, as a token of their esteem and gratitude. A few years later, fire ravaged the capital of Trinidad, and Picton returned the whole £5,000 to help repair the damage.

In 1809, Thomas Picton fought on the expedition to Walcheren, and was appointed Governor of Flushing when it was taken. However, a bout of fever forced him to return to England, where Wellington personally asked that Picton be given a division to command against Napoleon in Spain. Picton's main reputation stems from his command of the 'Fighting' 3rd Division in the Peninsular War. His bravery at the terrible battles of Badajoz,

Vittoria and Ciudad Rodrigo made him popular with his men, and the public back in England.

At Bussaco on 27 September 1810, Picton caught up with the retreating Portuguese battalion on hearing of their defection from the English camp. Still wearing his coloured nightcap, he had turned them around, shouting 'Forward' and 'Hurrah' to save the day and defeat the French under Massena and Ney. After wintering defending the lines of Torres Vedras, Picton led his division, the 'Fighting Third' at the Battle of Fuentes de Onoro. In September 1811 he was given the local rank of lieutenant-general, and in the same month the division won glory by its rapid and orderly retirement under severe pressure from the French cavalry at El Bodon. In October Picton was appointed to the colonelcy of the 77th Regiment of Foot.

In the first operations of 1812 Picton and Craufurd, side by side for the last time, stormed the two breaches of Ciudad Rodrigo, where their second-in-commands were killed. A month later at Badajoz, the successful storming of the fortress was due to his courage and ability in converting the secondary attack on the castle, delivered by his 3rd Division, into a real one. He had personally led his men up the breach at the walls of Badajoz. He was wounded in this bloody engagement, and unconscious for twenty minutes, but recovering would not leave the ramparts. When he came round, his first words were: 'if we cannot win the fort, let us die upon its walls'. Wellington's attack had failed and he waited anxiously until one of Picton's officers spurred up to him in great haste. 'General Picton has taken the fort, my lord', said the officer. 'Then Picton and the Third Division have saved my honour,' replied Wellington.

The day after, having recently inherited a fortune, Picton gave every survivor of his command a guinea. His wound, and an attack of fever, compelled him to return to Britain to recoup his health, where the Prince Regent George invested him as a Knight of the Order of the Bath. As a reward for his services he was elected an MP, and when he made his first appearance in the Commons, the Speaker said: 'Whenever the story of this war comes to be written, your name will be found among the foremost in the race for glory.' Picton, moved, could only stammer a few words in reply. In June he was made a lieutenant-general and returned to the Peninsular War.

At the Battle of Vittoria, Picton led his division across a key bridge under heavy fire. According to Picton, the enemy responded by shelling his 3rd with 40 to 50 cannon. A counter-attack on his right flank, which was still open because he had captured the bridge so quickly, caused the 3rd to lose 1,800 men (over one third of all Allied losses at the battle) as they held their ground. At Vittoria, Picton's division sustained, for over four hours, an unequal attack from the main body of the French army. For this, he had received Wellington's warmest congratulations. The conduct of the 3rd division under his leadership at Vittoria and in the engagements in the Pyrenees raised his reputation even higher as a skilful fighting general. Early in 1814 he was offered, but after consulting Wellington declined, the command of the British forces operating on the side of Catalonia. He fought in the Orthez Campaign and in the final victory before Toulouse.

On the break-up of the division, Picton's officers presented him with a silver dinner service, made by the greatest of the Georgian silversmiths, Paul Storr, in 1814. It cost the enormous sum of £1400 and has just been auctioned in New York for £200,000. One of the tureens has the inscription from his officers and staff 'in testimony of their respect for his distinguished military talents uniformly displayed during the campaigns of 1810, 1811, 1812, 1813 and 1814 as a memorial of their attachment arising no less from his publick than from his private worth.' There follows a list of his battle honours - Busacco, Fuentes d'Onor, Ciudad Roderico, Badajos, Vittoria, Pyrenees, Orthez and Toulouse. He received the thanks of the House of Commons for the seventh time, and Carmarthen crowds turned out to meet him when he retired, aged 56, to Ferryside in 1814. His home was Iscoed, at Ferryside in the parish of St Ishmael's.

Picton was not included amongst the generals who were raised to the peerage, but early in 1815 he was made a GCB. Possibly because of the Trinidad scandal, his name was the only one omitted from the list of generals made a lord. Possibly another cause was Wellington's dislike of Picton's mixing with his officers and men. Wellington called him 'a rough foul-mouthed devil as ever lived,' but Picton was Wellington's favourite companion during that gruelling campaign across Spain and Portugal. Extremely disillusioned, Picton returned to Carmarthenshire, to contest an election and enter politics, but Napoleon escaped from Elba. Wellington hastily recalled the 67-year-old Picton, as one of his most trusted generals, to command the 5th Division. Picton had been knighted in the same year. He dressed in a blue frock-coat, tightly buttoned to the throat; a very large black handkerchief around his neck, showing little of no shirt collar, dark trousers and a round hat. He seemed to know that he would not return, saying 'When you hear of my death, you will hear of a day of victory.'

Wellington, in his orders for the day, named Picton as supreme commander if anything happened to himself – he needed someone who the soldiers would follow anywhere. Wellington's *Dispatches* regarding Waterloo noted: 'I had directed all of my army to march upon Les Quatre Bras; and the 5th Division, under Lieut. General Sir Thomas Picton, arrived at about half past two in the day, followed by the corps of troops under the Duke of Brunswick, and afterwards by the contingent of Nassau... At this time the enemy commenced an attack upon Prince Blucher with his whole force, excepting the 1st and 2nd corps, and a corps of cavalry under General Kellermann, with which he attacked our post at Les Quatre Bras...We maintained our position also, and completely defeated and repulsed all the enemy's attempts to get possession of it. The enemy repeatedly attacked us with a large body of infantry and cavalry, supported by numerous and powerful artillery. He made several charges with the cavalry upon our infantry, but all were repulsed in the steadiest manner...

Picton... highly distinguished [himself]... [because of Blucher's withdrawal], I retired from the farm of Quatre Bras upon Genappe, and thence upon Waterloo, the next morning, the 17th, at 10 o'clock.. [a description of the Battle of Waterloo follows]... I propose to move this morning upon Nivelles, and not to discontinue my operations... such advantages could not be gained, without great loss, and I am sorry to ad that ours has been immense. In Lieut. General Sir Thomas Picton His Majesty has sustained the loss of an officer who has frequently distinguished himself in his service, and he fell gloriously leading his division to a charge with bayonets, by which one of the most serious attacks made by the enemy upon our position was repulsed.' Picton was loved by his men, as he was

Sculpture commemorating Picton in Carmarthen Museum, Glangwili

one of that very rare breed of generals who 'led from the front' - they knew that he would not ask them to do anything that he would not do.

An account of the battle reads: 'When Buonaparte was convinced that he had failed in his design upon Hougoumont, the fire of cannon and musketry became more terrible. Columns of French infantry and cavalry, preceded by a formidable artillery, advanced from all points, ascended the eminence on which the British were stationed, and precipitated themselves upon their squares. In vain the French artillery mowed down entire ranks of their opponents. The chasms were instantly filled, and not a foot of ground was lost. "What brave troops!" exclaimed Buonaparte to his staff. "It is a pity to destroy them; but I shall defeat them at last."

The British reserved their fire until the enemy had approached within a few paces, and then, with one well-directed volley, levelled whole squadrons of the French. Other troops, however, succeeded, and the enemy pressed on to closer and more destructive combat. The principal masses of the French were now directed on the left of the British, where the divisions of Generals Picton and Kempt were posted. Napoleon's object in this attack was to turn the left of the allies, and, by separating them from the Prussians, cut off the retreat of Lord Wellington in that direction. The Scottish regiments displayed all the heroism by which they had been distinguished in that battle of the 16th (Quatre Bras), and sustained the principal brunt of the attack.

A strong column of the enemy advanced under a galling fire from the British artillery, without discharging a shot. They gained the height, and pressed on, resolved to carry the position. Sir Thomas Picton immediately formed his division into a solid square, and advanced to the charge. Appalled by the boldness of his manoeuvre, the French hesitated, fired one volley, and retreated. On this occasion, Sir Thomas Picton received a musket-ball in his temple, and expired without a struggle. After his lamented fall, it was discovered that he had received a wound in his hip, on the 16th (2 days prior to Waterloo, at Quatre Bras), which he had concealed from all except his valet, and which had assumed a serious aspect for want of surgical assistance.' His soldiers caught Picton, as he fell from his horse.

Picton must have been in terrible pain from gangrene at Waterloo, but still wished to lead the Scottish 5th Division. In bitter hand-to-hand fighting, Picton's 'thin red line' had held at Quatre Bras, which saved the day for Wellington, but he had been was severely injured. A musket ball had broken two of his ribs, and he had a hip wound. Heavily bandaged under his uniform, Sir Thomas had concealed his wound to lead the charge of his men at Waterloo. His crucial bayonet charge stopped d'Erlon's corps' attack against the allied centre left. He was the most senior officer to die at Waterloo.

Forty-five years a soldier, there are monuments to his memory in St Paul's Cathedral, where he is buried, and at Carmarthen. His place in the crypt of St Paul's Cathedral is next to Wellington's tomb, and Picton is the only Welshman buried in that Cathedral. His first monument at Carmarthen was designed by John Nash (q.v.) in 1825.

* This was a most strange affair, where it seems that a confession was sought from a slave girl, Louisa Calderon, the 10-11 year-old mistress of a Pedro Ruiz. She was supposed to have stolen money from Ruiz, in collusion with Carlo Gonzalez. Gonzalez was apprehended, and Picton imprisoned the girl, who was allegedly tortured for 55 minutes and 22 minutes to confess by a magistrate named Bagora.

JOHN THOMAS EVANS christened 14 April 1770 - May 1799

THE MAN WHO OPENED UP AMERICA

Evans was born at Gwredog Uchaf farm in Waunfawr, near Caernarfon, the son of a Methodist minister. Jefferson's friend and protégé, a fellow-Welsh-American called Meriwether Lewis, opened up the American West, with fellow explorer William Clark. Lewis commanded and completed the first overland expedition to the Pacific Coast and back (1803-1806). They had used the maps of John Thomas Evans, who had explored the Missouri

Valley in 1795-96 for the first time, looking for Prince Madoc's Welsh Indians. They almost definitely would not have discovered the route to the Pacific Ocean, a decade later, without the work of Evans. Jefferson personally sent Evans' maps to Meriwether Lewis, and used them when making 'The Louisiana Purchase'.

The plan for the young weaver, John Evans, to find 'Welsh Indians' or 'Madogwys' descended from Madoc ap Owain Gwynedd (fl.1170), had been inspired by Iolo Morganwg, who was going to go with him to America. There had been an outbreak of 'Madoc Fever' across Wales at the time, but Iolo was too ill to go. Evans arrived in Baltimore in October 1792, after paying £20 to travel 'steerage', with letters of introduction to several Welshmen of influence in Philadelphia. However, the Philadelphians warned him that the Indian tribes were dangerous, and told him to forget his quest. He wrote to Iolo Morganwg 'Either the Madogion or death', and the minister's son said to his Baltimore friends: 'God is my shield.'

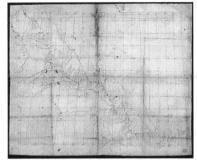

Evan's map of Missouri Basin

At this time, apart danger from the Native Americans, England, America, France and Spain were all manoeuvring to gain chunks of the sub-continent. Undeterred, in Spring 1793 the 23-year-old Evans set off through hostile territories with $1.75c in his pocket, to look for the 'white Indians.' Evans crossed the Allegheny Mountains to today's site of Pittsburgh, then travelled 700 miles through Indian territory down the Ohio in a river boat until he reached the Mississippi. Then he followed the Mississippi north to St Louis, its junction with the Missouri. During his long walk to St Louis, Evans contracted malaria, which kept recurring and eventually killed him.

St Louis was a small French-speaking frontier town controlled by the Spanish, who still had a large American empire and were hostile to Britain. He told the authorities that he wished to travel up the Missouri to contact the Mandans, who were known as the Welsh Indians. Thinking he was an English spy, the Spanish threw him into prison. They came to realise that he had no love of the English, and offered him work as an agent for Spain. He was released on the representations of John Rice Jones, a prominent New Orleans businessman who had previously employed him as a surveyor.

The French had ceded Louisiana to Spain in 1764, and before that date there had only been one expedition, under Bourgmont in 1714, partially along the Mississippi and Missouri Valleys. After this time, no European had successfully ascended the Missouri River beyond the Platte River, until Jacques d'Eglise brought back stories of incursions by English traders from

Canada into upper Louisiana. Alarmed by the threat to its sovereignty, Spain decided to promote exploration prior to settlement in the upper Missouri River. In 1793, Spain chartered the 'Company of Discoverers and Explorers of the Missouri', familiarly known as the 'Missouri Company' to exploit the fur trade in the region. A prize was offered to the first Spanish subject to reach the Pacific Ocean via the Missouri River. The Spanish sponsored four separate parties to reach the Mandan villages, before the one led by John Evans in 1795-96 finally succeeded. Incidentally, two years later the Welsh cartographer David Thompson mapped the upper Missouri and upper Mississippi for the first time.

In April 1795, the Spanish sent Evans to explore the Missouri and to try to discover a route to the Pacific Ocean from its headwaters. They wanted a route across the Rocky Mountains to its lands in California. The Spanish saw Evans as being able to take over Welsh-Indian (Mandan) territory for them, especially as he 'spoke' their language. Evans had entered the service of Spain and Jacques Clamorgan and wished to reach the Mandans, thought to be the remnant tribe of Prince Madoc's 1170 voyage. Charles Morgan (Jacques Clamorgan) is a mysterious figure, and seems to be related to the family of Morgans who were influential in the West Indies at this time.

Evans was made second-in-command under a Scot called James McKay, and in summer of 1795 a party of 30 well-armed men set off, with four large boats loaded with goods for trading. By November, the party reached the Omaha Indians, whose chief Blackbird was one of the most powerful rulers in the area. He had once murdered 60 of his own warriors by putting poison in their dog soup. The Europeans won him over with gifts of blankets, tobacco and muskets, and had his permission to build a fort on the riverbank to shelter until spring. While Mackay was building, Evans spent almost a month out on the frozen plains with an Omaha hunting party, tracking buffalo and sleeping out in subzero temperatures. In the New Year he left McKay at the fort, took a handful of men with him and rode off on horseback. Before they left, McKay gave the small party strict instructions to claim all lands they passed for the king of Spain and to make detailed notes of every new tribe, plant and animal they saw McKay warned 'Appear always on guard and never be fearful or timid, for the savages are not generally bold, but will act in a manner to make you afraid of them.' After about 300 hundred miles, they were attacked by a Sioux war party, and managed to escape back to join McKay at Fort Charles, in modern-day Nebraska. Mackay gave Evans detailed instructions to explore the river to the Mandan Villages and beyond to the Pacific. Evans left on 8 June and arrived at the Mandan villages on 23 September. There are no journal records attributed to Evans, but he gave information for the drawing of the maps of the journey up the Missouri River and its tributaries across 1,000 miles. Evans travelled up the Missouri into the barren Badlands of South

Dakota, and after 9 weeks reached the Arikara, who relieved him of most of his trade goods. Evans had high hopes of the Mandans. A French explorer had already made contact with the tribe and reported that their skin was whiter than other Indians. They lived in fixed settlements, not roaming the plains like their nomadic neighbours. They had round earth huts, not wigwams. They raised crops instead of tracking buffalo. Their bull-boats were identical to Welsh coracles.

Evans was to be disappointed – many were fair-skinned and had blue eyes, and they knew no Welsh, although a later adventurer, the painter George Catlin, truly believed that they were of Welsh stock. Evans met their

John Evans memorial at Waunfawr

chiefs, Big White Man and Black Cat, and handed over flags and medals as gifts. Then he spent winter with them, in the earth huts they shared with their horses. He stayed six months, learning about their culture and their land, occasionally entertaining his hosts on his flute. He was permanently hungry and the extreme cold affected him. The brutal winter with the Mandan broke his health forever.

Just before Evans found the Mandans, a Canadian fur trader called Rene Jessaume had arrived via a different route. Jessaume had established a small trading post, raised the Union Jack and then left. Evans lowered the British flag and replaced it with the Spanish flag, and when some other Canadians showed up some weeks later, he boldly sent them away. However, in the spring Jessaume returned with a group of hardened frontiersmen, weighed down with gear to trade. Evans tried to stop them dealing with the Indians, but by now he was a sick and isolated man and no match for Jessaume. Evans said Jessaume tried to kill him, and the Mandans protected him against Canadian traders. In ill health, Evans had nothing left to trade and had to leave the Mandans because of financial troubles in the Spanish Missouri Company, which was supporting his expedition.

Back in St Louis, he wrote to friends with the bad news. Thus having explored and charted the Missurie for 1,800 miles and by my Communications with the Indians this side of the Pacific Ocean... I am able to inform you that there is no such People as the Welsh Indians.'

However, Evans' influence and the visit 7 years later by Lewis and Clark held the Mandans for Spain against the Canadian French and English, thus helping to fix the current American-Canadian border. Evans had travelled further than any white man before him along the Missouri River, and mapped the whole of his journey. He travelled 1,800 miles in 68 days, arriving back in St Louis in July 1797. Mackay and Evans later travelled to New Orleans to procure a position for Evans with the Spanish government. Governor Gayaso de Lemos was arranging a position for him, when, later that month, May 1799, Evans had a fatal attack of malaria. Evans had never received promised lands, lost his possessions in Mississippi floods, and died in the Spanish governor's house in New Orleans, aged only 29. He may have been killed. Many sources state that he died of alcoholism but this seems not to be the case.

Evans wrote a terse note within a much longer letter to Samuel Jones of Pennsylvania that there were no Welsh Indians between latitudes 30 and 40. The brevity of this note is strange, as the discovery of the 'Madogwys' was the very raison d'être of his being in the USA. Dr Islyn Thomas made a speech in New Jersey in 1967, quoting the great-grandfather of one Arthur T. Halliday as saying that he was convinced that Evans was lying - 'he never returned to Philadelphia because he lied to his friends about the Indians'. A postscript to this 1803 memorandum, just 4 years after Evans' death, said that Evans 'when heavily in strong liquor bragged to his friends in St Louis that the Welsh Indians would keep their secret to their graves because he had been handsomely paid to keep quiet on the subject. He added that in a few more years there would be no more trace of any Welsh ancestry or language as time and disease would eventually remove all traces.' It may be that as an employee of Spain Evans may have held their line, against America being settled by the British-Welsh before Columbus' claim to the New World.

Footnote:
This author has been a member of Madoc1170 for some years, and has amassed evidence upon the Mandans and other 'white Indian' tribes, including the intriguing Modoc on the border of California and Oregon. In 1819 *The Kaleidoscope* printed a letter by Owen Williams of Cardiganshire and Baltimore, apparently based on personal knowledge. He described himself as a 'Fur-merchant', who was 'a plain man of business', and 'a native of Cardiganshire, S. Wales'. He claimed unequivocally that he had 'had dealings with some hundreds of them' (Welsh Indians), 'during a residence of forty years in different parts of the United States'. Also *Lieutenant Roberts's Account of his interview with a Chief of the Welsh Indians*, which took place in 1801, states that the Chief spoke 'the ancient British language as fluently as if he had been born and brought up in the vicinity of Snowdon'. There are dozens of similar accounts and letters.

DAVID THOMPSON 30 April 1770 - 10 February 1857

KOO-KOO-SINT, THE STARMAN, THE STARGAZER, THE GREATEST LAND GEOGRAPHER WHO EVER LIVED

Following on the work of John Evans (q.v.), this Welshman, born in Westminster of Welsh parents, whose family name was Tomos, was the first man to map the Upper Missouri and Upper Mississippi. He is honoured in

Canada, being known as 'the greatest land geographer who ever lived', mapping one-fifth of the Continent, well over two millions square miles of wilderness. His parents David and Ann had only recently moved to London for work when he was born, but when Thompson was two, his father died. The immediate financial hardship resulted in his and his brother's placement in the Grey Coat Hospital, a school for the disadvantaged children of Westminster. He eventually graduated to the Grey Coat mathematical school and was introduced to basic navigation skills which would form the basis of his future career. In 1784, at the age of 14, he entered a seven-year apprenticeship with the Hudson's Bay Company, leaving England on 28 May.

Initially working as a clerk in Manitoba and Saskatchewan, at the age of seventeen, David Thompson spent the winter of 1787 with the Peigan, where he soaked up the language, life and customs of these Plains Native Americans. He was impressed by the wisdom of Kootenay, the Peigan War Chief who became his friend and probably in later years deterred many young Blackfoot braves from killing the explorer. On 23 December 1788, Thompson seriously fractured his leg, forcing him to spend the next two winters convalescing, and he greatly refined and expanded his mathematical, astronomical and surveying skills under the tutelage of Hudson's Bay Company surveyor. Thompson remembered: 'While wintering at Manchester House I fell, breaking my leg, which by the mercy of God turned out to be the best thing ever happened to me... when Philip Turnor... taught me the art of surveying: how to determine longitude and latitude exactly for each post of trade... Now I could make of this uncharted land a known quality and to this end I kept for sixty years records of all observations of each journey made.' It was also during this time that, unknown to his employers, he lost sight in his right eye, almost definitely caused by staring at the sun while surveying.

In 1790 with his apprenticeship with nearing its end, Thompson asked for a set of surveying tools in place of the typical usual gift of fine clothes offered by the company to those completing their indenture. He received both, and then entered the service of the Hudson's Bay Company as a fur trader. In 1792 he completed his first significant survey, mapping a route to Lake Athabasca. In recognition of his map-making skills, the company promoted him to surveyor in 1794. Thompson continued working for the Hudson's Bay Company, but dissatisfied with his employers, Thompson joined its competitor the North West Company in 1797. He walked 80 miles in snow to the nearest North West Company post, to work as a fur trader and surveyor.

The North West Company wanted to explore the reaches of the North Saskatchewan River, hoping to finally find a way through the Rockies to the Pacific. His first major assignment was a vital one, to survey the 49th parallel, to ascertain whether or not any North West Company posts were now in American territory. Thompson now was given command the most experienced and hardiest *voyageurs* employed by the Company. His North Saskatchewan River expedition bore witness to many encounters with hostile Peigan and Blackfoot Indians, who deliberately denied crossings and passes to traders. David Thompson received special attention as he was believed to have special powers.

A passage in *The North Saskatchewan River 1972 White Water Report* reads: '"The remaining three miles to Saskatchewan Crossing are easy paddling, for the river again widens into a larger channel. It was in this vicinity in 1810 that David Thompson's party was attacked by a Peigan (Blackfoot) war party determined to stop Thompson from going through the mountain passes. Fortunately for Thompson, three grizzlies suddenly appeared on the scene. Since the Peigans and most of the Tribes who met David Thompson, believed that bears were Thompson's supernatural protectors, Thompson and his men were able to escape. The Indians named Thompson koo-koo-sint, "You who Look at the Stars," from his constant use of his sextant which the Indians saw as possessed of special powers.'

In 1797, the North West Company was headquartered in Montreal. Each year, they would send a large number of *voyageurs* from Montreal as soon as the ice melted in early April and arrive at Grand Portage by the end of June. They would return to Montreal before winter set in. The reason was to exchange goods from Montreal with furs brought to Grand Portage by the *voyageurs* who lived in the continental interior. These men would paddle 15 to 18 hours a day, with five minute breaks each hour for a smoke on their pipes. They covered up to 80 miles a day through rapids, around water falls, over portages, and up and down powerful rivers. David Thompson's crews were comprised of these French *voyageurs* and they could erect a big log house from the cutting of the trees in just a few days.

Each voyageur back-pack contained 90 pounds of goods, was wrapped in canvas, tied securely and labelled with its destination. 'These packs were carried... across the nine mile portage and loaded into the west bound canoes. Such was the competitive nature of these men that they never walked, but always raced over the rough, steep ground at a jog trot... Their diet was a porridge made of beans, corn, and salt pork cooked until it was stiff enough to hold a spoon erect. Few of these voyageurs knew how to swim and the most common cause of death was drowning. No voyageur carried less than two packets [back-packs]. Some carried three at the same time. These fellows were short, and over 5'6" disqualified you as a voyageur, and weighed about 150 lbs. Consider a 150 lb. man carrying 270 lbs. over rocks and unmarked trail! Or, consider them carrying their canoe which weighed 600 lbs!'

Their birch-bark canoes were constantly in need of repair, using the native materials at their disposal. These *canots du nord* were fragile, and easily damaged, but were capable of carrying 3,000 pounds of provisions or trade goods and in addition carried six paddlers. The voyageurs used a variety of canoes from their big 40-foot freight canoes to the small single canoes that David Thompson would use on occasion to either track ahead or to catch up to his canoes. 'They were great singers and were known to sing continually as they paddled sometimes to the pace of 120 strokes per minute!'

In 1797, Thompson was sent south by his employers to survey part of the Canada-US boundary, and by 1798 Thompson had completed a survey of 4,190 miles. In 1798, the company sent him to Alberta to establish a trading post. Thompson spent the next few seasons trading based in Fort George and during this time led several expeditions into the Rockies. In 1804, at the annual meeting of the North West Company, Thompson was made a full partner of the company and spent the next few seasons based there managing the fur trading operations but still finding time to expand his surveys of the waterways around Lake Superior.

However, a decision was made at the 1806 company meeting, concerned with the Lewis and Clark American expedition, to send Thompson back out into the interior. Thompson was asked, like Lewis and Clark, to find a route to the Pacific and open up the lucrative trading territories of the Pacific Northwest. He prepared for an expedition to follow the Columbia River to the Pacific. In June 1807 Thompson crossed the Rocky Mountains and spent the summer surveying the Columbia Basin, continuing to survey the area over the next few seasons. Thompson mapped and established trading posts in Montana, Idaho, Washington and Western Canada, two of which were the first trading posts west of the Rockies. These posts extended North West Company fur trading territory into the Columbia Basin drainage area. The maps he made of the Columbia River basin were of such high quality and detail that they continued to be regarded as authoritative well into the mid-20th century.

In early 1810, Thompson was returning to Montreal, but received orders to return to the Rocky Mountains and establish a route to the mouth of the Columbia. During his return, Thompson was delayed by Peigans, which forced him to seek a new route through the Athabasca Pass.

David Thompson was the first European to navigate the full length of the Columbia River. During Thompson's 1811 voyage down the Columbia River he camped at the junction with the Snake River, and erected a pole and a notice claiming the country for Great Britain. In his published journals, Thompson recorded seeing large footprints near what is now Jasper, Alberta, in 1811. It has been suggested that these prints were similar to what has since been called the *sasquatch*. Thompson noted that these tracks showed 'a small Nail at the end of each [toe]', and stated that the track 'very much resembles a large Bear's Track'.

In 1820, the English geologist, John Bigsby described a party in Montreal: 'I was well placed at table between one of the Miss McGillivray's and a singular-looking person of about fifty. He was plainly dressed, quiet, and observant. His figure was short and compact, and his black hair was worn long all round, and cut square, as if by one stroke of the shears, just above the eyebrows. His complexion was of the gardener's ruddy brown, while the expression of his deeply-furrowed features was friendly and intelligent, but his cut-short nose gave him an odd look. His speech betrayed the *Welshman* [author's italics], although he left his native hills when very young. I might have been spared this description of Mr David Thompson by saying he greatly resembled Curran the Irish Orator...'

On 10 June 1799, Thompson he married Charlotte Small, the daughter of a Cree mother and a Scottish fur trader who abandoned them. She was known as a Métis, the name then given by Canadian French to 'half-breeds'. Their marriage was formalised in Montreal in 1812. He and Charlotte had 13 children together, five being born before he left the fur trade. Their extremely happy marriage lasted 58 years, the longest Canadian pre-Confederation marriage known. David Thompson abhorred liquor at least in selling liquor to the Indians. He saw many horrible tragedies of abuse, maimings and killings that he attributed directly to the sale of liquor as a trade item. Thompson refused to use liquor as any kind of enticement to trade. He was also a God fearing man.

Retiring on a pension from the North West Company, he now worked on completing his 'Great Map', a summary of his lifetime of exploring and surveying the interior of North America. The map covered the area stretching from Lake Superior to the Pacific, and was given by Thompson to the North West Company. Thompson's 1814 map, his greatest achievement, was so accurate that 100 years later it was still the basis for many of the maps issued by the Canadian government. It now resides in the Archives of Ontario.

Thompson returned to a life as a land owner, but soon financial misfortune ruined him. By 1831 he was so deeply in debt he was forced to take up a position as a surveyor for the British American Land Company to provide for his family. Thompson carried on with surveying commissions, needing the money, and in 1843 completed his atlas of the region from Hudson Bay to the Pacific Ocean. He was forced to move in with his daughter and son-in-law in 1845. This man who had done so much for Canada, and who was still working at surveying long after his 70th birthday to make ends meet, was refused a modest pension he had requested from the British Government. The poverty worsened. Thompson was forced to sell his beloved sextant and his surveying instruments, and pawned his overcoat for a little money to buy food for Charlotte and himself. One of the last entries in his daily journal is a very poignant note: 'Have this day borrowed two shillings and six pence from a friend. Thank God for this relief.'

He began work on a manuscript chronicling his life exploring the continent, but this project was left unfinished when his sight failed him completely in 1851. Thompson died in Montreal in near obscurity on 10 February 1857, his accomplishments almost unrecognised. He never finished the book of his 28 years in the fur trade, based on his 77 field notebooks, before he died and was buried in an unmarked grave. Within three months of David Thompson's death, his grieving wife died. In the 1890s geologist J.B. Tyrrell resurrected Thompson's notes and in 1916 published them as *David Thompson's Narrative*.

Since this time, a tombstone has been placed and he has appeared upon a Canadian stamp. His prowess as a geographer is now well-recognized, and he has been called 'the greatest land geographer who ever lived.' During the 28 years that David Thompson spent in the west, in addition to his meticulous and accurate maps, his journals and field notes are filled with his observations of the Indian Tribes, their customs, their way of life, their legends and beliefs. Indeed David Thompson has become a legend himself.

ROBERT OWEN   May 14 1771 - November 17 1858

'THE FOUNDER OF SOCIALISM', 'THE FOUNDER OF INFANT SCHOOLS', 'THE MOST POPULAR MAN IN EUROPE', 'THE MODERN WORLD'S FIRST SOCIALIST'

In 1771, Trenewydd (Newtown) in Montgomeryshire produced a man who changed society across the world with his thoughts and actions. Karl Marx and Freidrich Engels both paid generous tribute to him in the development of their theories (see footnote). Engels wrote in *The Condition of the Working Class in England*, 1844, that 'English socialism arose with Owen.' The youngest son of the village postmaster, aged 10 he was apprenticed to a draper in Stamford, Lincolnshire. He spent all his spare time reading at his employer's library, before being appointed superintendent of Drinkwater's large cotton mill in Manchester, aged only 19. He soon transformed the factory into one of Britain's leading producers, making the first use in Britain of American 'sea island' cotton, and making improvements in spun cotton quality. Aged 28, in 1799 he moved to David Dale's cotton mills in Lanarkshire as manager, marrying Dale's daughter in 1800 and buying a partnership in the firm.

When Robert Owen took over these cotton mills in New Lanark in Scotland, he improved housing and sanitation, provided medical supervision, set up a co-operative shop, selling at little more than cost price, and established the first infant school in Great Britain. Owen also founded an Institute for the Formation of Character and a model welfare state for New Lanark. He reasoned that character was moulded by circumstances, and that improved circumstances would lead to goodness. 500 of his employees were

 young children from the poor-houses and charities of Edinburgh and Glasgow, and Owen set up a model factory and a model village, where hours were considerably shorter than elsewhere in Britain (a 12-hour day, including one and a half hours for meal-breaks). The *Gentleman's Magazine* recorded: 'the children live with their parents in neat comfortable habitation, receiving wages for their labour...The regulations here to preserve health of body and mind, present a striking contrast to those of most large manufactories in this kingdom.'

The mills made a commercial profit, but some of his partners were displeased with the extra expenses incurred by Owen's philanthropic socialism, and in 1813 Owen organised a new firm. Its members were content with a mere 5% return on capital, and stockholders included the Quaker William Allen and the legal reformer Jeremy Bentham. The factories not only enhanced the workers' environment, but received international interest as they actually also increased productivity and profits. 1813 also saw the publication of Owen's *A New View of Society*, pleading for education for all as the key to social reform and improving working conditions. From 1816, his school at New Lanark took children from 3 to 10 years-old, or to 13 if parents could afford for the child not to work. The 'play and learn' approach was the basis of his Utilitarian theory of education - nursery and infant schools were Owen's original concept. Owen saw national education as freeing man from narrow views and the dogmatism of the church.

His example was largely responsible for bringing about The Factory Acts of 1819, but disappointed at the slow rate of reform in Sir Robert Peel's England, Owen emigrated to America in 1821 to set up another model community. From 1817 Owen had proposed that 'villages of co-operation', self-supporting communities run on socialist lines, should be founded, to ultimately replace private ownership. He took these ideas on co-operative living to America and set up the community of New Harmony, Indiana, between 1824 and 1828, before he handed the project over to his sons and returned to Britain. Owenite community village experiments in Britain continued, in Hampshire, near Glasgow and in County Cork.

The experiment cost him £40,000, an absolute fortune in those days. The USA community failed without his inspiring idealism, but he carried on encouraging the fledgling trade union movement and co-operative societies.

School in New Lanark

From 1929, Owen took over the development of co-operatives, the first having been formed in London in 1926). 1832 saw a failed attempt to set up a National Equitable Labour Exchange. In 1833 he formed the Grand National Consolidated Trades Union. He wanted to use the unions to change the economic system, to destroy capitalism and break the overwhelming power of the state. In 1835 he founded the Association of All Classes of All Nations, for which he is known as 'the founder of the socialist movement'.

From 1834, Owen led the opposition against the deportation of The Tolpuddle Martyrs, a group of Dorset farm labourers, who had stopped working in a cry for higher living wages. Because of his criticisms of the organised religion of the day, where positions were granted as favours, he lost any support from those in power, whose families benefited from the system.

He wrote about the barbaric nature of unrestrained capitalism in *Revolution in Mind and Practice* - the glories of Thatcherite free trade, where Nike, Adidas and Reebok sportswear are made in totalitarian regimes using semi-slave labour, spring to mind today. [This last sentence was written in 2000, and has not been altered for this 2015 edition]. Owen wanted political reform, a utopian socialist system, with a transformation of the social order. People were all equal, there should be no class system, and individuals should not compete but co-operate, thereby eliminating poverty.

He was a forerunner of the co-operative movement, a great inspirer of the trades union movement, and the modern world's first socialist. Those that followed his teachings, who called themselves Owenites, gradually changed their name to Socialists, the first recorded use of the term. Owen is a Welshman of international stature, who is hardly acclaimed in his own land, but his socialism is a thread that runs through Welsh history from the *Laws of Hywel Dda* in the tenth century, to the election of the first Labour MP in Britain in 1910, to the whole-hearted support for the Miners' Strike in 1984, to the present state of left-wing support in Wales.

As the pioneer of co-operation between workers and consumers, his understanding of the 'value chain' and wealth creation has not been equalled until Michael Porter in recent years. The over-riding problem in Western society is that political leaders are insulated from the communities they represent - they are always several orders of magnitude richer than the common man, and do not understand the basic nature of wealth creation. Wealth comes from something being dug out of the ground, altered and transported, with value being added along the route. Every service is parasitic upon this process. It seems that Mrs Thatcher never realised that marrying a millionaire was not an option for most of society, and that a country cannot progress with tax-avoiding foreign-owned manufacturing and low-paid service jobs.

In April 1840, an editorial in *The Cambrian* referred to Robert Owen: 'The discontent of the lower and working classes as assumed a new form which threatens to become far more mischievous than mere political agitation, however fiercely carried on. We allude to the institution and spread of Socialism. Under pretence of improving the condition of the poor, Socialism is endeavouring, permanently, to poison their happiness, by depraving their morals, and depriving them of all those consolations flowing from the principles of religion. It is of little use to show that Mr. Owen is a lunatic.'

Incidentally, a theme in this book is that the Welsh are terrible self-publicists. In 'The Witch Doctors' a 1997 'global business book award winner', we have reference to Robert Owen, 'a Scottish mill-owner who thought there was money to be made by treating workers as if they were human beings (he would not employ any child under ten years old) and thus has been deemed to be "the pioneer of personnel management" (quote from Urwick and Breech, quoted in Clutterbuck and Crainer)... Peter Drucker's enthusiasm for the well-being of workers led Rosabeth Moss Kantner to compare him to Robert Owen, the nineteenth century Scotsman who ordered his factory managers to show the same due care to their vital human machines as they did to the new iron and steel which they so lovingly burnished.' So there we have it, the leading edge authors of *The Witch Doctors*, with other eminent management writers, all claim Owen to be Scottish. No wonder no one knows about Wales on the world stage. Many

291

websites even state that Owen was English. Robert Owen was simply one of the most noble and influential men in history.

His son, Robert Dale Owen, was prominent in the abolitionist movement in the USA, writing *The Policy of Emancipation* and *The Wrong Slavery*. He became Ambassador to Naples, but (like his father) returned to Newtown and died in 1858. 'Hiraeth' is a strong emotion. A memorial museum* is now in the house where his father was born. Owen's other sons were also notable in the history of the USA, David Dale Owen making the first geological survey of the American mid-west, and Richard Dale Owen serving with distinction in the Civil War and becoming a professor at Nashville University.

* Another museum in Newtown is in the High Street, with mementoes about W.H. Smith, the leading British newsagent chain, that started there in 1792. Newtown also saw the birth of the mail-order idea, started by Sir Pryce Pryce-Jones (q.v.) in 1861 to sell Welsh linens. One of his more famous customers was Queen Victoria, the Anglo-German queen only remarkable in that her girth exceeded her height in her latter years. His business base, the Royal Welsh Warehouse is still being used. Keeping on the subject of Newtown, in the 18th century, Sir John Pryce of Newtown passed into history as a man who loved his wife so much that he slept in bed with her embalmed body after she passed on. His second wife had to sleep on the other side of the bed from the corpse. When this second wife died, Sir John settled down at night between two embalmed women.

Footnote:
Freidrich Engels wrote in *Socialism: Utopian and Scientific*: 'At this juncture, there came forward a manufacturer 29-years-old - a man of almost sublime, childlike simplicity of character, and at the same time one of the few born leaders of men. Robert Owen had adopted the teaching of the materialistic philosophers: that man's character is the product, on the one hand, of heredity; on the other, of the environment of the individual during his lifetime, and especially during his period of development. In the Industrial revolution most of his class saw only chaos and confusion, and the opportunity of fishing in these troubled waters and making large fortunes quickly. He saw in it the opportunity of putting into practice his favourite theory, and so of bringing order out of chaos. He has already tried it with success, as superintendent of more than 500 men in a Manchester factory. From 1800 to 1829, he directed the great cotton mill at New Lanark, in Scotland, as managing partner, along the same lines, but with a greater freedom of action and with a success that made him a European reputation.

A population, originally consisting of the most diverse and, for the most part, very demoralised elements, a population that gradually grew to 2,500, he turned into a model colony, in which drunkenness, police, magistrates, lawsuits, poor laws, charity, were unknown. And all this simply by placing the people in conditions worthy of human beings, and especially by carefully bringing up the rising generation. He was the founder of infant schools, and introduced them first at New Lanark. At the age of two, the children came to school, where they enjoyed themselves so much that they could scarcely be got home again. Whilst his competitors worked their people 13 or 14 hours a day, in New Lanark the working day was only 10 and a half hours. When a crisis in cotton stopped work for four months, his workers received their full wages all the time. And with all this the business more than doubled in value, and to the last yielded large profits to its proprietors.

In spite of all this, Owen was not content. The existence which he secured for his workers was, in his eyes, still far from being worthy of human beings. "The people were slaves at my mercy". The relatively favourable conditions in which he had placed them were still far from allowing a rational development of the character and of the intellect in all directions, much less of the free exercise of all their faculties. "And yet, the working part of this population of 2,500 persons was daily producing as much real wealth for society as, less than half a century before, it would have required the working part of a population of 600,000 to create. I asked myself, what became of the difference between the wealth consumed by 2,500 persons and that which would have been consumed by 600,000?'

The answer was clear. It had been used to pay the proprietors of the establishment 5% on the capital they had laid out, in addition to over £300,000 clear profit. And that which held for New Lanark held still to a greater extent for all the factories in England. "If this new wealth had not been created by machinery, imperfectly as it has been applied, the wars of Europe, in opposition to Napoleon, and to support the aristocratic principles of society, could not have been maintained. And yet this new power was the creation of the working classes". To them, therefore, the fruits of this new power belonged. The newly-created gigantic productive forces, hitherto used only to enrich individuals and to enslave the masses, offered to Owen the foundations for a reconstruction of society: they were destined, as the common property of all, to be worked for the common good of all.

Owen's communism was based upon this purely business foundation, the outcome, so to say, of commercial calculation. Throughout, it maintained this practical character. Thus, in 1823, Owen proposed the relief of distress in Ireland by Communist colonies, and drew up complete estimates of costs of founding them, yearly expenditure, and probably revenue. And in his definite plan for the future, the technical working out of details is managed with such practical knowledge - ground plan, frond and side and bird's-eye views all included - that the Owen method of social reform once accepted, there is from the practical point of view little to be said against the actual arrangement of details.

His advance in the direction of Communism was the turning-point in Owen's life. As long as he was simply a philanthropist, he was rewarded with nothing but wealth, applause, honour, and glory. He was the most popular man in Europe. Not only men of his own class, but statesmen and princes listened to him approvingly. But when he came out with his Communist theories that was quite another thing. Three great obstacles seemed to him especially to block the path to social reform: private Property, religion, the present form of marriage.

He knew what confronted him if he attacked these - outlawry, excommunication from official society, the loss of his whole social position. But nothing of this prevented him from attacking them without fear of consequences, and what he had foreseen happened. Banished from official society, with a conspiracy of silence against him in the press, ruined by his unsuccessful Communist experiments in America, in which he sacrificed all his fortune, he turned directly to the working-class and continued working in their midst for 30 years.

Every social movement, every real advance in England on behalf of the workers links itself on to the name of Robert Owen. [author's italics]He forced through in 1819, the first law limiting the hours of labour of women and children in factories. He was president of the first Congress at which all the Trade unions of England united in a single great trade association. He introduced as transition measures to the complete communistic organisation of society, on the one hand, co-operative societies for retail and production. These have since that time, at least, given practical proof that the merchant and the manufacturer are socially quite unnecessary. On the other hand, he introduced labour bazaars for the exchange of the products of labour through the medium of labour-notes, whose unit was a single hour of work; institutions necessarily doomed to failure, but completely anticipating Proudhon's bank of exchange of a much later period, and differing entirely from this in that it did not claim to be the panacea for all social ills, but only a first step towards a much more radical revolution of society.'

JOHN FROST 25 May 1784 – 27 July 1877

PIONEER OF BRITISH DEMOCRACY

Chartist Memorial Day 10 April

It is fairly amazing that most people have heard of the 'Tolpuddle Martyrs', six English farmworkers, who were briefly transported for union activity in 1834, whereas the Newport Chartist Uprising of five years later is unknown. Welsh history has always been ignored. A new working-class militancy was a strong breeding ground for the doomed Chartist Movement, a campaign for basic human rights in the 19th century. The 1838 People's Charter called for universal male franchise, payment of MPs, equal electoral districts, secret elections and the abolition of property qualifications to vote. Most activity supporting Chartism, trying to stop wealthy landowners buying votes from the enfranchised few, took place in the industrialised parts of South Wales, and Newport's Chartist Uprising of 1839 ended when troops killed 24 Chartists. Many more were wounded, some dying in obscurity to avoid their families being persecuted by the authorities. 7,000 marchers, mainly miners, had walked down Newport's Stow Hill to be met by a hail of bullets by soldiers hiding in The Westgate Hotel.

Queen Victoria knighted the mayor, who gave the order to shoot the marchers, whose 8 ringleaders were sentenced to be hung, drawn and quartered. This is only in 1839! Michael Foot called the political show-trial 'the biggest class-war clash of the century'. Public protest led to the sentence being commuted to transportation for life, without a last meeting with their families. The historian, Macaulay, called the ringleaders ' great criminals... who would, if their attempt had not been stopped at the outset, have caused such a destruction of life and property as had not been known in England for ages.' These words come from a man who believed universal suffrage to be incompatible with civilisation, as he knew it. He thought democracy would hurt the English property-owning classes.

Just like the later important Merthyr Rising (q.v. Richard Lewis, 'Dic Penderyn'), there was negligible publicity in England. As Coupland says: 'Nothing happened in England to match the march of some five thousand Welshmen down from the coal valleys through the darkness and drenching rain of a winter night to Newport... nobody remarked that the trouble was suppressed by English soldiers who were paid to do it and shot down 22 Welshmen and wounded several others in the doing.'

The leader of the Newport Rising was born in Newport, a Welsh-speaker whose father died, and who was raised by his grandparents. After a very short time at school, John Frost was apprenticed as a boot-maker to his grandfather, but left home at 16 to become a tailor in the nearby town of Cardiff. Aged 22, he had made enough money to return home and start his own business as a draper and tailor, and just three years later, in 1809, became a burgess for Newport. Over the next 11 years he married and had 8 children, and voraciously read to catch up on his lost education. As a leading businessman and official, he read and was strongly influenced by the writings of the libertarians Tom Paine and William Cobbett. However, in 1821 he accused a Newport solicitor of being responsible for his exclusion from his uncle's will, and was sued and fined £1,000 for libel in 1822. He continued to accuse the solicitor of malpractice and in 1823 was imprisoned for 6 months. Told he would receive a long prison sentence if he repeated his allegations, Frost turned his anger against the solicitor's close friend, Sir Charles Morgan, owner of the great Tredegar House in Newport. An 1830 pamphlet accused Morgan of treating his tenants badly, and advocated that votes for all (universal suffrage) and secret ballots were the only means of curbing the power of the aristocracy. Inspired by Cobbett, Frost established a left-wing periodical, *The Welchman* in 1831.

For the next five years, Frost devoted himself to leading the movement for universal suffrage in Newport. In 1835 he was voted one of Newport's 18 councillors and also made a magistrate, in 1836 being elected mayor. However, his aggressive behaviour led to his replacement as mayor in the following year. Frost also served Newport as a Guardian of the poor and as an Improvement Commissioner. He now focussed upon campaigning for the *People's Charter*, becoming a national leader. In 1839 he made

Part of the Newport Chartist Memorial, showing troops firing on the marchers

several inflammatory speeches at the Chartists' First National Convention. Therefore Lord John Russell, Home Secretary, had Frost removed as a magistrate, because he was advocating violence to achieve democracy. Frost wrote in the *People's Charter*: 'The time is fast approaching when there must be no neutrals; the question will be who is for good and cheap Government, and who is against it'

In 1838 Henry Vincent had been imprisoned at Monmouth Assizes for 12 months, for making 'inflammatory' speeches supporting Chartism. Frost toured South Wales calling for a massive protest meetings, to show the strength of feeling against this sentence. His plan was to march upon Newport to demand Vincent's release. Queen Victoria and her ministers were frightened that such a march could be repeated across Britain, threatening the stability of the German monarchy and its government, so major preparations were made to defuse the march. Frost had asked the crowds 'Does any man expect that members put into the House of Commons by bribery, and perjury, violence and drunkenness will ever make laws favourable to the people?' (Under the 'rotten borough' system whereby very few people could vote, their voting could be 'bought' by substantial largesse including free alcohol - the richest man usually won the election - as Frost said: 'A bad system cannot produce good men. We do not look for figs from thistles').

When the 7,000 marchers arrived in Newport they discovered that several Chartists had been arrested and taken to the Westgate Hotel in the town centre. On the night of November 3, 1839, after marching down Stow Hill, they gathered outside the hotel, chanting 'free the prisoners'. After a few moments, soldiers placed inside the hotel were ordered to fire into the crowd, when at least 22 were killed and scores wounded. The marchers fled back up to the Valleys, and a manhunt started for all those involved.

1,400,000 people signed a petition asking for the pardon of the ringleaders, but most died as convicts in Australia. Lord Melbourne, after Cabinet discussions, decided to commute the sentences of hanging, drawing and quartering to transportation for life. The trial judge also asked for commutation - there was only one sentence for 'treason', which he had had to pronounce. John Frost was transported to Tasmania, where after hard labour he worked as a clerk and as a schoolteacher. In 1846 Thomas Duncombe pleaded for Frost to be freed, in the House of Commons. Years later, in 1854, Duncombe persuaded Lord Aberdeen, the Prime Minster to release Frost. Aberdeen stipulated that Frost was not to be allowed back into Britain, and Frost's daughter Catherine joined him in the USA, where Frost toured making speeches against the British system of government.

John Frost, former Mayor of Newport and JP, was fully pardoned in 1856 when he was 71 and returned to be honoured in Newport, being carted through the town in a flower-bedecked carriage. His former Chartist comrades drew it though the crowded streets. His wife Mary died just a year later, after their 17-year parting. The main square in Newport is now named after him, and you can still see bullet holes in the Westgate Hotel. He soon retired to Bristol, where he wrote articles for newspapers on subjects such as the horrors of deportation, universal suffrage and prison reform. Frost died aged 93, and is buried at Horfield Parish Church, Bristol. The Corn Laws were repealed in 1846, making bread cheaper, and 1867's Great Reform Bill doubled the electorate, adding another one million voters. At last some working people could vote - Chartism had helped change British history.

Frost himself said 'By the struggle of these men, we now enjoy five of the six demands of the people's Charter covenants in our constitution. I do hope one day the last of these will be included, whereby we can at least get rid of a third of the House of Commons every year, by vote.'

Footnotes:
(i) The Anglicisation of Newport and its environs since this time has been rapid. John Frost had addressed the Chartists in Welsh, and Gwent, even on its Herefordshire borders, was a Welsh-speaking county. A few years earlier, Iolo Morganwg had stated that Gwent had the highest proportion of monoglot Welsh speakers of all the counties in Wales.
(ii) The Chartist Mural was a mosaic of 200,000 pieces of tile and glass designed by Kenneth Budd, and created in 1978 in a pedestrian underpass at John Frost Square in Newport's centre. It commemorated the rising of 1839, was 115 feet long and 13 feet high. The mural was controversially destroyed in 2013 despite public opposition. The demolition of the mural drew national as well as local condemnation, with The Independent describing it as 'indicative of the lack of regard for Welsh history and the triumph of the brute stupidity and disregard for the views of their constituents that many in authority have.' A spokesman for

Newport council stated that the mural "has served to remind us of Newport's past, but we must now focus on Newport's future.' The council's Chief Executive apologised to councillors for not informing them in advance of when the demolition was to occur. In March 2014, former Archbishop of Canterbury Rowan Williams said that destruction of the Chartist Mural in Newport was 'a sad blow for the city... It did seem to be a sad blow to something of Newport's self image and self confidence.. There was a real need to gather up literally and figuratively what was left and ask the question: how can Newport now celebrate this crucial part of its history? ... The Chartist legacy is surely one of the great elements in the pride that people ought to take... I did think the destruction of the mural was a great sadness.' All across Wales, there have been similar occurrences of council stupidity in this author's lifetime.

(iii) In 1847, the Government's official *Report on the State of Education in Wales* apportioned some blame for the rise of Chartism 'I regard the degraded condition (of the people of Monmouthshire) as entirely the fault of their employers, who give them far less tendance [sic] and care that they bestow on their cattle, and who with few exceptions, use and regard them as so much brute force instrumental to wealth, but as no wise involving claims upon humanity'... 'Brynmawr contains 5000 people, nearly all of whom are the lowest class... Not the slightest step has been taken to improve the mental or moral conditions of this violent and vicious community'. At this time, the ironmasters and colliery owners like Crawshaw Bailey were living in heavily defended castles and mansions, guarded from the hatred of their employees.

(iv) John Humphries' remarkable *The Man from the Alamo – Why the Welsh Chartist Uprising of 1839 Ended in a Massacre* uncovers invaluable new information about Frost, Zephaniah Williams and John Rees (a.k.a. Jack the Fifer).

RICHARD ROBERTS 22 April 1789 – 11 March 1864

THE UNKNOWN PIONEER OF PRODUCTION ENGINEERING, THE INNOVATOR OF HIGH PRECISION MACHINE TOOLS AND THE INTERCHANGEABILITY OF PARTS

Roberts was possibly the most important mechanical engineer of the 19th century. Born at Carreghofa near Llanymynech in Wales, this virtually unknown inventor and innovator of high precision machine tools received only rudimentary education. Aged 20, he found a job as a pattern-maker at Bradley Ironworks, Staffordshire. To avoid being forced into the militia during the Napoleonic Wars, Roberts moved to Birmingham, Liverpool, Manchester, Salford and London, before returning to Manchester in 1816, where he set up his own

workshop. After making a successful gas meter for Manchester, where others had failed, he went on to other inventions. Through lack of finance, he could not patent his meter, and it was copied by Samuel Clegg in London as a water meter, then as a gas meter. One of Roberts' first tasks in his own business was to make himself a gear cutting machine, and a sector to measure the gear blanks accurately. His first commercial work seems to be the manufacture of letterpresses. Creating their flat surfaces inspired the invention of his metal planing machine tool of 1817, which he sold to other companies and engineers. Previously, flat surfaces were laboriously made by hand with the fitter using hammers and chisels, files and scrapers to get a true surface. Roberts also realised the potential of such machines for generating flat surfaces at angles in addition to the horizontal. He also adapted it to plane curves and spirals, so making the planer essential in engineering workshop. His planer is now in the Science Museum.

In 1817 Roberts also designed a metal-turning lathe with innovative features and in 1820, a screw cutting lathe. His centre lathe was capable of turning metal articles 6 feet long and 18 inches in diameter. It was fitted with back-gearing and was probably the first of its type. Roberts also built special lathes for screw-cutting as well as centre lathes with rack or screw traverse motions, the latter being capable of cutting screws. These again were offered for sale in a range of sizes. Both types of lathe continued in use in the Beyer-Peacock factory into the 20th century and are in the Science Museum. 1818 saw Roberts producing a breech-loading rifled cannon for a Mr. Bradbury.

In 1820 Roberts advertised 'that he has cutting engines at work on his new and improved principle, which are so constructed as to capable of producing any number of teeth required: they will cut Bevil, Spur or Worm Geer, of any size or pitch, now exceeding 30 inches diameter in Wood, Brass, Cast-Iron, Wrought-Iron or steel, and the teeth will not require fileing-up... Manufactory, New Market Buildings, Pool Fold; House 5 Water Street, Manchester.' In 1821, he placed an advertisement in the first issue of the *Manchester Guardian* for an improved gear cutting machine, one of which is preserved in the collections of the Science Museum in London.

Not content with inventing planing, turning, screw-cutting and gear-cutting machine tools, Roberts turned his attention to weaving, and in 1822 patented a power loom. Output may have reached 4,000 a year by 1825. Such a volume needed batch or semi-mass production techniques as well as special machine tools, and it was supplied to many spinning companies at home and overseas. On his power looms, pulley and gear wheels had to be secured to their shafts by keys. To cut the slots for these, Roberts introduced his '*keyway grooving machine*' in 1824, which was later improved into his more versatile '*slotter*' in 1825.

The slotting machine cut keyways in gears and pulleys to fasten them to their shafts, which previously was done by hand chipping and filing.

The tool was reciprocated vertically. By adopting Maudslay's slide rest principle, Roberts made the work table with a universal movement, both straight line and rotary, so that the sides of complex pieces could be machined. Later he developed the '*shaping machine*', where the cutting tool was reciprocated horizontally over the work, which could be moved in all directions by means of screw-driven slides. Roberts also manufactured and sold sets of stocks and dies to his range of pitches, so other engineers could cut threads on nuts and bolts and other machine parts. A blowing engine for furnaces in foundries, like an Archimedean screw, and the first of his punching and shearing machines followed soon afterwards.

Thus a power loom, slotting machines, shaping machines, punching and shearing machines were added to his portfolio of inventions. In 1825, Roberts patented his first design of a '*self acting*' (automatic) spinning mule. Because of a strike of skilled mule spinners, local mill owners had asked Roberts to make the mule work automatically, but he at first refused. He relented and, but for a disastrous fire at the Globe Works in the summer of 1825, would have had it running then. It did not prove as successful as hoped, but Roberts designed standard templates and gauges to secure accuracy in its manufacture. These became features in Roberts' later manufacture of other products such as railway

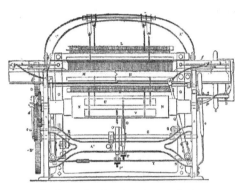

Roberts' spinning loom design

locomotives and much more. This idea was quickly copied by others. 1830 saw a further patent for the spinning mule which included his intricate '*quadrant winding mechanism*'. It brought limited financial success because of its costs of development. It was a superb solution to a complex problem, and remained little altered and in production for over one hundred years.

Roberts had carried out experiments on the friction of railway wagons in 1825, and constructed a steam road carriage capable of carrying 35 passengers, which he trialled in 1834. He next designed and built several railway locomotives, and his 1835 design of 2-2-2 tender locomotives was ordered by many railway companies both in Britain and on the Continent. Roberts invented cylindrical slide valves, patented in 1832, at the same time as a variable expansion gear for steam engines and a differential gear for road locomotives. He also invented a steam brake. His locomotives were built to high engineering standards, had strong frames and large bearing surfaces. Roberts was probably the first British engineer to apply weights to driving wheels to balance revolving masses. Demand became so great that it could not be met and a new factory had to be built. Roberts continued with his standardisation of as many parts as possible, so that they could be manufactured on specially designed (dedicated) machine tools.

As well as nut and bolt making machines, Roberts now introduced new shaping machines, plate rolling machines, and improved punching and shearing machines. He was in advance of his era as he designed tools with rotary cutters similar in principle to modem milling machines, for producing his crankshafts, with hexagon heads on bolts as well as oil grooves in bearings. He also had a wide variety of drilling machines and is credited with inventing the extremely important 'radial arm drill'. Roberts continued with patenting improvements in the textile industry, for combing machines, new looms and finishing machines. He invented a cigar rolling machine and presented a paper about a design for a floating lightship.

Roberts' most famous invention at this period was the 'Jacquard punching machine' (as it worked on the same principles as a Jaquard loom), for punching the rivet holes in the iron plates making up the railway bridge at Conwy. This plate punching machine made possible the rapid construction of the Conwy and Britannia tubular bridges. The regular rivet holes enabled the steel plates to match exactly with each other. In 1841 Roberts had taken out 22 patents. All were commercial failures although one was possibly 'the first digitally-controlled machine tool' - the heavy Jacquard-controlled plate-punching machine Roberts made in 1847 for Stephenson's Menai Bridge.

Meters for liquids, turbines, clock mechanisms, chronometers, machines for drilling watch plates and many more inventions were featured in his patents during this period. Roberts now realised that iron ships could be built on similar principles as the tubular bridges, with tubes acting as strengthening girders. He secured a patent in 1852 for a very advanced design of liner to carry 500 passengers which, if it had been built, would have been the largest ship afloat. The patent contained claims for a wide range of novelties in both merchant and naval ship design. Twin screws capable of being worked independently for greater manoeuvrability were another feature which Roberts advocated. One ship at least, the S.S. *Flora*, was fitted with his twin screws and showed great manoeuvrability when employed as a blockade runner in the American Civil War. Roberts made several visits to France to set up a factory in Alsace for a firm of textile manufacturers, which changed to manufacturing machinery. He returned to England, and then proposed designs for ships and men of war to improve their functioning and internal servicing, and to make them less vulnerable to enemy fire. Roberts had about 30 patents taken out in a space of 28 years, and worked until the end of his life, but died in poverty.

The inventions and innovations of this uneducated man are astounding to anyone who understands mechanical engineering. His primary contribution was the introduction of improved machine tools and standard manufacturing techniques, without which high standards of accuracy could not be achieved. This laid the foundation of production engineering, leading to the interchangeability of standard parts and mass production.

Footnote:
Obituary from the *Manchester Times* - Saturday 19 March 1864
'We regret to announce the dearth of Mr. Richard Roberts, the eminent mechanical engineer, formerly a partner of the celebrated firm of Sharp, Roberts, and Co., of Manchester.

Mr. Roberts will be remembered as one of the most prolific and powerful inventors in a century of which invention has been said to be the motive power. The cotton trade, especially, is indebted to him for the self-acting mule, one of the prime motors in the great development of manufacture. Mr. Roberts died yesterday, in London, and was, we believe, about 74 years of age.

When a boy he was almost without education, and his life is the familiar story of native talent forcing its way through all obstacles to fame and usefulness, if not to fortune. He was the son of a shoemaker, and was born in 1789, at Carreghova, in a house so exactly on the border of England and Wales that one door opened in Shropshire and another in Montgomeryshire.

He was early put to work as a common labourer, and it was in the intervals of occupation as a quarryman, that he began to show his quality by ingenious contrivances in mechanics. This encouraged him to search for higher employment.

We first hear of his connection with iron work, when in the service of that skilful Staffordshire mechanician, Mr. John Wilkinson, who employed Roberts as a pattern maker. After acquiring a variety of knowledge sad dexterity in different employments at Birmingham, Robert was again working as a pattern maker at Tipton, when, to his extreme disgust, he was drawn for the militia.

Serve he would not - that he was resolved upon; and it was while traversing the country on foot, in his determination to escape, that hoe first came to Manchester, weary and penniless fugitive. He got some work in Salford at lathe and tool making. But he was soon on the tramp again, from his fear of the long arm of the law, and this time he made his way (as Mr. Smiles tells us, in his memoir of Roberts) to "that great hiding-place," the metropolis.

After working some time at Maudelay's, continually developing his ingenuity and skill, he at length settled in Manchester. In 1816 he was carrying on business on his own account in Deansgate, and was already distinguished in his vocation by a variety of inventions or improvements.

In the following year, at the request of the borough reeve and constables of Manchester, he contrived an oscillating and rotating wet gas meter, which enabled them to sell gas by measure. As in that case, it is rather singular (regarding him as one of those whose brains, it is said, are so formed that we could never want for inventions, though patents were unheard of) that, in the two inventions for which afterwards he was perhaps the most famed, the achievement was rather due to instigation from others - in one instance, at least, we might almost say compulsion - than to spontaneous effort.

His great improvements in weavers' reed-making machines having led to the formation of the prosperous partnership with which his name was so long identified, it happened in the year 1824 that the cotton manufacturers of the neighbourhood, driven to bay by the turbulence of their spinners (the highest paid of workmen, but the most given to strikes), on whom the entire machinery of a cotton mill and all its other workers were then dependent - were induced to apply to Messrs. Sharp, Roberts, and Co., as to reputed magicians, for aid in their extremity. The problem to be solved was to make spinning mules self-acting. The idea was not now, for self-acting mules had been brought out more than once. Unfortunately they had failed. And now, when a mule that would do its own work unmistakeably was the article in demand, every mechanic to whom the thing was broached, not excepting Mr. Roberts, declared it out of the question.

He would hardly listen to the explanations of the applicants. He knew nothing about cotton spinning, he told them, and seemed, oddly enough in such a man, bent on ignorance perpetual. The spinners still kept everything at a stand by their strike. A second time the manufacturers called on Mr. Roberts, without effect. A third time (Mr. Smiles relates) they called, and appealed to Mr. Sharp, the capitalist of the firm. Mr. Sharp was about to try his persuasive powers on the clever but obdurate partner, but now it appeared, on the first mention of the matter, that Mr. Roberts had been revolving the subject in his own mind all along, and at last "saw his way."

To recount the success and the consequences of this well-known invention, would here be superfluous; and we have not space for a fragment of the long list of inventions which have since borne Mr. Roberts's name to all parts of the world, not only in connection with the staple manufactures of this district, but in the making of locomotives and many kinds of machinery. His Jacquard punching machine, another self-acting tool of great power, was due to the entreaties of the contractors for the Conway Tubular Bridge, in 1848, who appealed to Mr. Roberts to free them, as he had freed the cotton traders, from the combinations of their workmen.

It is sad to say, at the end of such a career, that Mr. Roberts, outside the realm of invention, did not find the path of prosperity so clear. On the death of Mr. Sharp, Mr. Roberts left the firm which had promised him so much competency as well as renown, and once more commenced business on his own account.

From his want of commercial aptitudes that undertaking was discontinued, with an unsatisfactory result.

Lately he had been residing in London with a daughter, in delicate health, dependent on him. His friends, including some of the most eminent in the land, had already begun to subscribe for a well-merited testimonial to him, and if the conclusion of their effort should yet prove to be a timely offering to the survivor, the debt of great numbers of his countrymen will be well acknowledged, though never repaid.

The funeral will take place at Kensal Green Cemetery London, on Saturday (to-day). The funeral cortege will start from his late residence, 10, Adam-street, Adelphi, at twelve o'clock, arriving at Kensal Green at two o'clock.'

DR. WILLIAM PRICE 4 March 1800 – 23 January 1893

CHARTIST FREE-THINKER, PIONEER OF CREMATION, REPUBLICAN DOCTOR

Llantrisant in Mid-Glamorgan has a superb hill fort, and a ruined medieval castle, and provided the Black Prince's finest archers for The Hundred Years' War. However, its main claim to fame is its 19th century doctor/druid, Dr. William Price, who proselytised not just vegetarianism, nudity, and free love, but also the unhealthiness of socks, the potential dangers to the environment from rapid industrialisation, revolution, republicanism and radical politics. He refused to treat patients who would not give up smoking, and prescribed a vegetarian diet instead of pills.

Price was born in a cottage at Tŷ'n-y-coedcae Farm* near Rudry, east of Caerphilly. Price learned English at school. His minister father wanted him to be a churchman, but William wished to practise medicine. He studied under Dr Evan Edwards at Caerphilly for six years, during which time his father died. His guardian uncle Thomas secured him an appointment as a schoolmaster, but William refused the offer and enrolled at the Royal College of Surgeons in London. How he supported himself is unclear, but he astonished everyone by passing the examination of both College and Hall in just 12 months, the first student in history to do so. He spent another year studying anatomy, surgery, physiology and medicine, and Dr Price returned to Wales in 1821.

Practising at Nantgarw outside Cardiff, near the world-famous porcelain works, where there is a museum today, Price acquired fluency in several languages including Hindi. A tall man, he dressed in a white tunic over a scarlet waistcoat and green trousers. Price let his hair grow into long plaits, and was of the opinion that doctors should be paid a regular wage for keeping people healthy - when they became ill, the doctor should then bear the expense of treating them. He often put patients on a natural, vegetarian diet, which he followed himself, and gave a public lecture in which he said 'Medical science has of all the sciences been the most unscientific. Its professors, with a few exceptions such as myself, have always sought to cure disease by the magic of pills and potions and poisons that attack the ailment with the idea of suppressing the symptoms rather than attacking the cause.'

Apart from the quacks and authorities of the medical profession (with their 'cursed regimes' of purging and bleeding), he also made enemies of the church, both established and Nonconformist, telling them that 'Man is greater than your God, for Man created God in his own image.' He also wrote to a friend: 'Priests are paid to teach that the world of thieves and oppressors, of landlords and coal-owners, is a just world. Their theology is always that of the doctrine that the powers that be are ordained by God.' During his practice, he also became associated with 'druidical rites' and deposited many researches into the Public Records Offices. He was the first doctor to be elected by a group of factory workers as their own general practitioner, being paid a weekly deduction out of wages paid at the Pontypridd Chainworks. This was the precursor of the miners' medical societies, which were, in turn, the origin of the National Health Service.

A skilled surgeon, he attended Chartist rallies in a cart drawn by goats. In a speech on Pontypridd Common, he stated 'we have tolerated the tyranny of those who oppress us - landlords, coal-owners, and the clergy - too long. We must strike with all our might and power. Let cowards go their way, for they have no part to play in this great struggle. Men of the valleys, remember that principle behind Chartism is the principle which acknowledges the right of every man who toils to the fruits of his labours. The points embedded in this charter are our immediate demands. But ultimately we shall demand more. Oppression, injustice and the grinding poverty which burdens our lives must be abolished for all time. We are the descendants of valiant Welshmen and we must be worthy of the traditions which they have passed on to us.' Price had moved from Nantgarw to Llantrisant by this time, and was elected leader of the Pontypridd and District section of the Charter. John Frost (q.v.) and Price's great friend William Jones were arrested after the Newport Rising, and a warrant issued for the arrest of Dr Price. He was thus forced to escape to France dressed as a female in a dress to live in 1839. The story is that Price was assisted up the gangplank at Cardiff Docks by a police inspector who was looking for him. In France, Price became convinced that an ancient prophecy predicted that he would liberate his country from English rule.

In Paris he was helped by his friend John Masklyn to set up in practice, and he consorted with the great writer-philosopher Heinrich Heine. Price spent seven years in Paris, becoming something of a society doctor, with his fresh approach to medicine, and returned to Eglwysilan near Pontypridd in 1846. He still ranted against the medical profession - 'Some call it recognised science, but I call it recognised ignorance!' A campaigner against tobacco, he threw a man's clay pipe out a railway carriage, and told the offender that he would follow it, if he complained. He held druidic ceremonies at the rocking stone near Pontypridd, which were considered satanic by the local Methodists, and began building a Druidic Temple near it. A case of trespass on the site was proven against Price, who flatly refused to pay the fine. When a warrant was issued for his arrest, William promptly fled back to Paris and resumed his practice in 1860. He spent another six years there, where he consorted with Proudhon, the anarchist and revolutionary philosopher, and returned to Wales in June 1866.

Price supported the coal-miners in their 1871 strike, writing to the newspapers against the coal-owners: 'You are the Welsh Pharaohs who think you can suck the life-blood of the colliers forever. You have grown fat and prosperous; you own the big houses; you wear the finest clothes; your children are healthy and happy; yet you do not work. Let me tell you. You have been stealing the balance of low wages which you have been paying them. Take heed, you men whose bodies and souls are bloated by the life-blood of the poor, take heed before it is too late. Remember that the oppression of the Pharaohs of Egypt did not last forever, and neither will the oppression of the blood-sucking Pharaohs of Wales.' In 1875, Dr William Price made the long journey to Dean Street, Soho, to meet Karl Marx, whom he found to be a 'fascinating personality',

His own cremation, which he sold tickets for!

but he was 'less than impressed' with Marx's phrase 'historical inevitability', as there was as yet no educated industrial proletariat in Wales which would force revolution.

He did not approve of marriage as it 'reduced the fair sex to the condition of slavery' and lived openly 'in sin' with his young housekeeper. This precursor of the Hippy Movement had a son when he was eighty-three, and named him 'Iesu Grist' (Jesus Christ). When Iesu died, aged five months, in 1884, Dr Price cremated him on an open funeral pyre. Price was dressed in flowing druidical robes, and timed the event to take place as the locals were leaving their chapels. The local population attacked him, rescuing the charred remains of the child, and the police arrested Price. The mob then went to find the mother, Price's young housekeeper, Gwenllian, but were deterred by Price's twelve large dogs. (As mentioned, Price did not believe in marriage as 'it turned women into slaves.') The doctor was acquitted after a sensational trial in Cardiff, and cremation was legalised in Britain as a result. Another infant was born, named 'Iarlles Morgannwg', the 'Countess of Glamorgan' and in one of his many lawsuits he called the child as assistant counsel to him.

He issued medallions to commemorate his legal victory, and at the age of ninety had another son, again called Iesu Grist. Aged ninety-three, Price died and was cremated in front of twenty thousand spectators at East Carlan Field, Llantrisant. This was the first legalised cremation (1893), and a ton of coal and three tons of wood were used to accomplish the mission. Price had organised the cremation himself, selling tickets to the estimated twenty thousand people that later attended it. Llantrisant's pubs ran dry.

Price, with a long flowing beard and hair past shoulder-length, habitually wore only the national colours of red, white and green. On his head was a red fox-skin pelt, with the front paws on his forehead and the tail hanging down his back. His cloak was white, his waistcoat scarlet, and he wore green trousers - the colours of Wales. He started building a druidic temple, of which the gatehouses are lived in today. One of the two round 'Druidic' towers he built in 1838 as a gatehouse for his projected eight-storey Druidic Palace was recently on the market. He had dreamed of 'a golden age' when Wales would once again be ruled by Druids.

Dr. Price's last dying act was to order and drink a glass of champagne before he moved on to his next destination. Eat your heart out, Hollywood, no-one could make up a life like this. Dr. William Price was an anti-establishment campaigner for women's rights, socialist, progressive doctor, rebel, Chartist, druid, hippy, vegetarian, consort of Heine, Proudhon and Marx, environmentalist pioneer of cremation who foresaw the dangers of smoking two-hundred years ago. His biographer Dean Powell considered Price 'the most notable individual in 19th century Wales.'

* His birthplace is said to be Tŷ'n-y-coedcae Farm near Rudry, but the old Green Meadow Inn at Waterloo, near Newport, also claimed to be his birthplace – perhaps he grew up there. Discovery Inns wished to demolish it, to put up 13 boxes that pass for living dwellings these days. CADW, the historic monuments society in Wales, washed its hands of the matter, although the local community desperately wanted to save this historic site. It has gone.

JEFFERSON DAVIS 3 June 1808 – 5 December 1889

PRESIDENT OF THE CONFEDERATE STATES OF AMERICA

John Davies emigrated from Wales to Philadelphia in 1701. His son Evan married a Welsh widow named Jane Williams, and the couple had a son, Samuel. The family moved to Augusta, Georgia, when Samuel was a boy, and her two Welsh sons by her earlier marriage enlisted in the Revolutionary Army. Young Samuel Davies followed as a mounted gunman, later forming his own infantry company, fighting the British in Georgia and the Carolinas. At the end of the war, Samuel was granted land in Georgia, then moved to

Kentucky to breed racing horses on 600 acres of land, later known as Christian County and now as Todd County. Here, in 1808, the last of his 10 children was born, named Jefferson, after the great Welshman just finishing his second term as President of the United States. At some stage the spelling of Davies changed to Davis.

The cradle in which his mother Jane rocked the infant Jefferson Davis, is in the Confederate Museum in New Orleans. When Jefferson was three years old, the family moved to Louisiana, and in 1812 to Mississippi. While Welshman Thomas Jefferson had created the new country of the United States, the Welshman Jefferson Davis grew up to almost break it in two. A graduate of West Point, Jefferson Davis served in the Indian Wars, and was wounded, becoming a hero in the Battle of Buena Vista against the Mexicans. He held his position here, saving Zachary Taylor from an  ignominious defeat. David then eloped with Taylor's daughter Sarah, who died shortly after their marriage in 1835. He later married a Welsh lady, the daughter of a Mississippi aristocrat and plantation owner.

A war-hero, Davis spent ten years as a Mississippi planter. In 1838 he was elected to the House of Representatives, during which time he again served under Zachary Taylor in the Mexican-American War, and sat in the US Senate from 1847 to 1851. Davis was Secretary of War under President Franklin Pierce from 1853 until 1857, when he returned to the Senate, becoming leader of the Southern Democrats. The German-born abolitionist Carl Schurz said that Davis met every expectation of what 'a grand personage the War Minister of this great Republic must be'. As unofficial 'spokesman for the South', Jefferson, however viewed the Southern states as 'a country within a country'.

The reasons for the coming Civil War were many, not just slavery-related. In 1860 South Carolina issued a declaration of secession from the USA. By January 1861, Georgia, Florida, Alabama, Mississippi, Florida, Louisiana, Texas and Arkansas had also seceded from the union. Virginia and North Carolina soon followed. Jefferson Davis was elected in February 1861 as President of the Confederate States of America, although he wished to lead the Confederate forces as a general in defence of his homeland. The ensuing bitter Civil War lasted from 1861 to 1865, with the vast military capability of the Union North eventually overcoming the Confederate Southern states.

The great and brutal battles of Manassas (where Davis actually took the field), Appomatox, Shiloh, Gettysburg, and the two battles at Bull Run echo through history, and the South has still not forgotten Sherman's devastation. In terms of personnel losses, the South won but its economy was destroyed by pillage. 359,528 Union and 258,000 Confederate troops had died in the young republic. The turning point in the war, more than any other, was the mass-production of the Springfield rifle in Connecticut. It had greater accuracy and three times the range of the old smoothbore rifle. On the fateful third day of Gettysburg, 12,000 Confederate soldiers had mounted one last, great, Napoleonic assault on the Union lines. All but 300 were mown down before they reached the Northerners.

John Morgan's Second Kentucky Volunteers, the 'Alligator Horsemen', were the most hated and feared of all the Confederate soldiers. Courageous guerrillas, led by a Welshman, no atrocities can be held against their name in this dirty war. By 1865, the Second Kentucky cavalry was a scattered regiment of foot soldiers, as the Union rampaged through the Southern States. Even now, they were so highly rated that they were the chosen élite troops, to assist the Welsh Confederate President Jefferson Davis, in his flight from Richmond, before his capture. After being caught near Irwinville, Georgia, Jefferson Davis was put in shackles and imprisoned. His Welsh wife, Varina Howell, fought for his early release after two years in poor conditions. (See the author's *100 Great Welsh Women*). Davis refused to request an official pardon, which would have restored his citizenship. A private businessman and author after his release, Davis died in New Orleans aged 82. Jefferson Davis Day is held on his birthday 3 June in Alabama, Florida, Georgia and Mississippi.

The *New York World*, not a Southern sympathiser, called Jefferson Davies 'the best equipped man, intellectually, of his age, perhaps, in the country'. Joseph McElroy, in his biography of Davis, says that 'Lincoln sought to save the Union; Davis did not wish to destroy the Union; he sought to preserve states' rights, under his interpretation of the Constitution.' Like Jefferson before him, the right to liberty justified revolution for Davis - for him the Civil War was not about slavery but about freedom for the states and their individuals. He 'was convinced that Lincoln's aim was to convert a Federal republic of sovereign states into a consolidated nation with the right to dominate the states, the old idea which had precipitated the American Revolution.' In the South, the Civil War is still referred to as 'The War of the States'.

This 'demon of centralisation, absolutism and despotism', which is 'well-known by the friends of constitutional liberty', has modern parallels in the formation of a united Europe with national sovereignty being subverted to central, unelected committees. A central over-riding bureaucracy could not work for Russia, so the European Union seems to be struggling against the natural flow of history. Both Thomas Jefferson and Jefferson Davis were been rightly suspicious of both centralisation of power and rule by procedure and committees. Interestingly Lincoln had said that if he could win the Civil War without freeing the slaves, he would. Lincoln's main reason for pursuing this course of action 'was not to free the slaves, but to cause discomfiture to the South in the Civil War' (Brian Walden, *BBC TV*, 13 January 1998). The distinction of Jefferson Davis being pro-slavery and Lincoln being anti-slavery has been a useful myth to help centralise power in Washington.

RICHARD LEWIS 1808 – 13 August 1831

'DIC PENDERYN', 'MARTYR OF THE WELSH WORKING CLASS'

Richard Lewis was born in Aberavon, and moved aged 11 to Merthyr Tydfil with his family in 1819, where he and his father found work in the local mines. He was literate with some chapel schooling, and his sister Elizabeth was married to the Methodist preacher Morgan Howells. He was possibly known as 'Dic' Penderyn as his lodgings were in Penderyn, but by the time of his death he was a married man living in Merthyr. However, a 1919 letter recounting a conversation with an old man who knew him in the paper *Y Drysorfa* stated that he was the son of Lewis Lewis, who lived at a cottage named Penderyn in the parish of Pyle.

The Great Depression of 1829 led to massive unemployment and wage cuts, making the working classes even more indebted to their masters. Terrible working conditions in the mines and iron works of the country were made even worse by wage cuts and, in some cases, by the laying off of men as demand for iron and coal fell away. Thanks to things like the hated truck shops (an arrangement in which employees are paid in commodities), food was always in short supply and now money was also a problem. Debts spiralled

Plaque to Dic Penderyn

out of control as women sought to feed their families and men seemed helpless to solve the problem. William Crawshay was going to lower wages at his Merthyr iron foundries even further, there was a crisis among tradesmen and shopkeepers, and the Debtor's Court confiscated workers' property to pay off debts. Thomas Llywelyn, a miner, demanded compensation and led a demonstration that released prisoners and marched on Aberdare.

At the same time in nearby Hirwaun, when the Debtors' Court had seized the goods of Lewis Lewis (said to be the cousin of Richard Lewis), miners, iron workers and tradesmen joined the political radicals - they had had enough. In 1831, hungry iron and coal workers took over Hirwaun and Merthyr from for five days, parading under a sheet daubed symbolically with the blood of a lamb and a calf. The sheet acted as a huge flag, and on its staff was impaled a loaf of bread, showing the needs of the marchers. This was the first time that the 'red flag' of revolution was raised in Britain, and perhaps in the world. Some 7,000 to 10,000 workers had marched under the flag, which was later adopted internationally as the symbol of the working classes.

After storming Merthyr, the rebels sacked the local debtors' court and the goods that had been collected. Unemployment, filthy water supplies, lack of sanitation and reduced wages had fomented the unrest, and the workers burnt court records and some of their employers' property. Account books containing debtors' details were destroyed. Among the shouts were cries of *Caws a bara* (cheese and bread) and *i lawr â'r brenin* (down with the king). On 1 June 1831, the protesters marched to local mines and persuaded the men on shift there to stop working and join their protest. Rioting began on 2 June with an attack on the house of Joseph Coffin, clerk to the Court of Requests, and the destruction of his furniture. Troops were then called for by the magistrates, and a company of the 93rd (Highland) Regiment arrived from Brecon. A number of these entered the Castle Inn. Others, who were left outside, were hemmed in by a crowd, among whom was Dic Penderyn. While worried local employers and magistrates were holding a meeting with the High Sheriff of Glamorgan at Merthyr's Castle Inn, a group led by Lewis Lewis (Lewsyn yr Heliwr) demanded a reduction in the price of bread and an increase in their wages.

The demands were rejected, and after being advised to return to their homes, the crowd attacked the Castle Inn. The tyrannical ironmasters Crawshay and Guest were locked inside Merthyr's Castle Inn, defended by Scottish soldiers. A scuffle ensued, until soldiers within the Castle Inn fired through the windows into the crowd. Around 28 protesters were killed and many more wounded, and several soldiers were injured. It is not known that Dic Penderyn took any part in the activities that followed, such as the waylaying of an ammunition-party from Brecon and the ambushing and disarming of the Swansea Yeomanry Since the crowd was now too large to be dispersed, the soldiers were ordered to protect essential buildings and people.

The 93rd Sutherland Highlanders had to be reinforced by the Glamorgan Yeomanry, and the supporting Swansea Yeomanry was forced back to Neath. Major Richards called out the equivalent of the Home Guard, the Llantrisant Cavalry, to rescue the regular soldiers, who sustained no losses.After a protracted struggle in which hundreds sustained injury, some fatal, the Highlanders were compelled to withdraw to Penydarren House, and abandon the town to the rioters. For four days, magistrates and ironmasters were under siege in the Castle Hotel, and the protesters effectively controlled Merthyr.

Penydarren House became the sole refuge of authority. With armed insurrection fully in place in the town by 4 June, the rioters had commandeered arms and explosives, set up road-blocks, formed guerrilla detachments, and had banners capped with a symbolic loaf and dyed in blood.

The workers ambushed the 93rd's baggage-train on the Brecon Road, under escort of 40 of the Glamorgan Yeomanry, and drove them into the Brecon hills. They also saw off a relief force of a 100 cavalry sent from Penydarren House. The Swansea Yeomanry were met on the Swansea Road, and driven back to Neath. The rioters sent messengers, who started strikes in Northern Monmouthshire, Neath and Swansea Valleys, and the riots reached their peak. However, panic had spread in Merthyr, and families began to flee. The rioters arranged a mass meeting for Sunday 6 June, and government representatives in Penydarren House managed to split the rioters' council. When 450 troops marched to the mass meeting at Waun above Dowlais with levelled weapons, the meeting dispersed and the riots were effectively over.

Along with Lewis Lewis, the 23-year-old collier Richard Lewis was arrested for stabbing Private Donald Black of the 93rd (Sutherland Highlanders) Regiment of Foot, using a bayonet attached to a gun. The two men were accused of riotous assault and of a 'felonious' attack upon Private Black, outside the Castle Inn. Black's injuries were not serious, and he could not identify either man, but both were convicted and sentenced to death. Penderyn was tried at Cardiff Assizes before Mr. Justice Bosanquet, and, on the evidence of James Abbott, hairdresser, and William Williams, tailor, both of Merthyr, was found guilty. The soldier, who had seen Dic in the crowd, freely admitted that he did not know who had wounded him. There is no evidence that Penderyn played any substantial part in the rising at all unlike Lewis who was definitely involved. Both were held in Cardiff gaol.

Lewis Lewis had his sentence commuted to transportation, largely thanks to the testimony of John Thomas, a special constable whom Lewis had shielded from the rioters. The people of Merthyr Tydfil were convinced that Dic Penderyn was not responsible for the stabbing, and more than 11,000 signed a petition demanding his release. The conservative *Cambrian* newspaper also objected. Joseph Tregelles Price, a Quaker ironmaster from Neath, went to console the two condemned men, and was convinced of Penderyn's innocence. He went to Merthyr to gather evidence, and persuaded the trial judge that the sentence was unsafe. The Home Secretary

Lord Melbourne delayed the execution for two weeks, but refused to reduce the sentence despite pleas not only from workers but the Welsh establishment. It seems the execution occurred solely because Lord Melbourne wanted at least one rebel to die as an example.

Four Wesleyan Methodist ministers accompanied him to the scaffold. Dic Penderyn was hung at Cardiff on 13 August, his last words being *Arglwydd, dyma gamwedd* (Lord God, what an injustice). The gallows were on St Mary Street, and a plaque commemorates the event at Cardiff Market near the spot. Legend also states that Dic's young wife was pregnant at the time and the shock of her husband's arrest, trial and subsequent execution caused her to miscarry.

Others of the 28 defendants were transported to Australia. Thousands accompanied his body through the Vale of Glamorgan from Cardiff to his grave in Aberavon, and listened to a funeral sermon from his brother-in-law Morgan Howells. He is buried in St Mary's churchyard, Aberavon, where a memorial was placed on his grave by local trades unionists in 1966. The carter who took Penderyn's body back to Aberavon asked to be, and is, buried next to Dic Penderyn in the churchyard of St. Mary's.

Over 40 years later, in 1874 an immigrant from Merthyr, Ieuan (Ianto) Evans, confessed on his deathbed in the USA to the Reverend Evan Evans that it was he that wounded the soldier. Evans had fled to America fearing capture by the authorities, thus exonerating Dic Penderyn. Another man named James Abbott, who testified against Penderyn at the trial, also later admitted to lying under oath.

The Merthyr Rising was described by John Davies as 'the most ferocious and bloody event in the history of industrialised Britain.' Gwyn Williams pointed out that 'these defeats inflicted on regular and militia troops by armed rioters have no parallel in recent British history.' Publicity was suppressed - after all the starving Welsh working class did not matter in the grand scheme of things. In June 1831, a Mrs Arbuthnot noted in her diary: 'There has been a great riot in Wales and the soldiers have killed twenty-four people. When two or three were killed at Manchester, it was called the Peterloo Massacre and the newspapers for weeks wrote it up as the most outrageous and wicked proceeding ever heard of. But that was in Tory times; now this Welsh riot is scarcely mentioned.' Gwyn Williams commented that 'bodies were being buried secretly all over north Glamorgan ...widows did not dare claim poor relief.'

Regarded as a martyr, Penderyn's death further embittered relations between Welsh workers and the authorities and strengthened the Trade Union movement and Chartism, helping foment the Newport Rising eight years later (see John Frost). In 1977 a memorial to a 'Martyr of the Welsh Working Class' was unveiled at Merthyr public library by the general secretary of the TUC. Along with the Newport Rising eight years later, the

Merthyr Rising was one of the most serious violent outbreaks witnessed on mainland Britain, yet is hardly recorded in British history compared to the minor affair of the Tolpuddle 'Martyrs' and the Peterloo 'Massacre'. Over 60 Welshmen probably died in the two events in Glamorgan and Monmouthshire, compared to 2 or 3 in England. After the Newport Rising, there were four years of the Rebecca Riots across south and mid-Wales, with nothing comparable in England.

The English Establishment took decisive measures to suppress dissent in Wales. The county's industrial capacity, particularly coal and steel made the Welsh peoples' compliance vital for profit margins. The Welsh language was singled out as an obstacle to London rule, and the following decades saw the imposition 'civilizing' measures such as the appalling 'Welsh Not' to try and finally kill the language.

SIR WILLIAM ROBERT GROVE 11 July 1811 – 1 August 1896

'FATHER OF THE FUEL CELL', INVENTOR OF THE NITRIC ACID BATTERY, INVENTOR OF THE FIRST INCANDESCENT LIGHT

Born in Swansea, Grove was educated by private tutors and then at Brasenose College, Oxford, and also studied law at Lincoln's Inn, being called to the bar in 1835. Ill health interrupted his law career, and he turned to science. A High Court judge from 1880, he was also a Fellow of the Royal Society, Privy Councillor and Professor of the London Institution, writing the seminal scientific work, *Correlation of Physical Forces.*

Grove invented two cells of major scientific significance. His contribution to battery or cell development was to devise a combination of metals and liquids that greatly reduced the loss of voltage. In the simple early cells, hydrogen bubbles collected at the poles, setting up a back voltage that greatly weakened the current, a phenomenon called 'polarization'. To solve the problem, experimenters used liquid depolarizers that destroyed the hydrogen by oxidising it into water, but this resulted in low voltage batteries. Grove experimented and instead used nitric acid as an oxidizing agent, producing a higher voltage battery. He described his results to a meeting in Birmingham. He 'hastily constructed' a battery for the meeting, placing a zinc

(positive) electrode and dilute sulphuric acid in one compartment, and a platinum (negative) electrode and strong nitric acid in another. The compartments were porous pots that allowed the easy passage of the electric current but safely contained the liquids. Grove announced the latter development to the Académie des Sciences in Paris in 1839. He was just 28.

Grove's nitric acid cell was the favourite battery of the early American telegraph (1840-1860), because it offered a strong current output. This cell had nearly double the voltage of the first Daniell cell, but by the time of the American Civil War, Grove's battery was being replaced by the Daniell battery. As telegraph traffic increased, it was found that the Grove cell discharged poisonous nitric oxide gas. Large telegraph offices were filled with gas from rows of hissing Grove batteries. As telegraphs became more complex, the need for constant voltage became critical and the Grove device was necessarily limited, because as the cell discharged, nitric acid was depleted and voltage dropped sharply. His battery had a much higher voltage and, with low internal resistance, and a stronger current than any previous battery. However, platinum was expensive, and the Grove cell was replaced by the cheaper, safer and better performing gravity cell in the 1860s.

In 1840 Grove invented the first incandescent electric light, which was later perfected by Edison, who was always more of an innovator than an inventor. At the London Institution, where he was Professor of Physics (1840–47), Grove used his platinum-zinc batteries to produce electric light for one of his lectures. At Birmingham, Grove's work came to the attention of Michael Faraday, who invited him to present his discoveries at the Royal Institution in March 1840.

Grove became the first professor of experimental philosophy at the London Institution in 1841. His inaugural lecture in 1842 was the first announcement of what Grove called the correlation of physical forces. His classic *On the Correlation of Physical Forces* (1846) enunciated the principle of conservation of energy a year before the German physicist von Helmholtz. Joule's claim, that each of the various manifestations of force and energy in nature is convertible into any other, was made originally by Grove in his *On the Correlation of Physical Forces.* Grove's theory of the correlation of physical forces is widely regarded as a precursor to one of the most important ideas in physics - the conservation of energy.

In 1842, Grove developed the first fuel cell, which he called the 'gas voltaic battery', which produced electrical energy by combining hydrogen and oxygen, and described it using his correlation theory. In developing the cell and showing that steam could be disassociated into oxygen and hydrogen, and the process reversed, he was the first person to demonstrate the thermal dissociation of molecules into their constituent atoms. He showed that steam, in contact with a strongly heated platinum wire, is decomposed into hydrogen and oxygen in a reversible reaction. The experiment was the very first proof of the thermal dissociation of atoms within a molecule. Unlike his first battery, there were no harmful gases, and it was the forerunner of modern fuel cells. He based his experiment on the fact that sending an electric current through water splits the water into its component parts of hydrogen and oxygen. Grove tried reversing the reaction - combining hydrogen and oxygen to produce electricity and water. This is the basis of a simple fuel cell. The term 'fuel cell' was coined in 1889 by Ludwig Mond and Charles Langer, who attempted to build the first practical device using air and industrial coal gas.

Fuel cells produce water, and are being used in a new generation of hydrogen-powered cars, backed by US Government funding. Fuel cells were used by NASA to power onboard systems for its Apollo and Shuttle space programmes, and Grove is known as 'The Father of the Fuel Cell' overseeing the genesis of a 'clean' power source. His work also led him to early insights into the nature of ionisation, and he is credited for the discovery of sputtering, the is a process whereby atoms are ejected from a solid target material due to bombardment of the target by energetic particles.

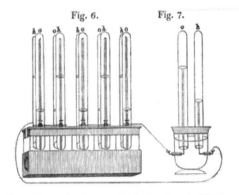

Drawing of a 'gas voltaic battery', 1843

In the 1840s Grove also collaborated with Gassiot at the London Institution on photography and the Daguerrotype and calotype processes. He saw into the future and wrote in 1942: 'It would be vain to attempt specifically to predict what may be the effect of Photography on future generations. A Process by which the most transient actions are rendered permanent, by which facts write their own annals in a language that can never be obsolete, forming documents which prove themselves, - must interweave itself not only with science but with history and legislature.'

In 1852 Grove discovered striae, the dark bands that occur in electrical breakdown, and investigated their character, presenting his work in an 1858 lecture. In an 1874 edition of *On the Correlation of Physical Forces*, he wrote of Olber's paradox, also known as the 'dark night sky paradox' which is that a static, infinitely old universe with an infinite number of stars distributed in an infinitely large space would be bright rather than dark. '... it is difficult to understand why we get so little light at night from the stellar universe, without assuming that some light is lost in its progress through space – not lost absolutely, for that would be an annihilation of force – but converted into some other mode of motion.' This could be a predictor of 'dark flow'. Indeed he speculated upon dark energy, dark matter and dark flow by writing that other forms of energy were yet to be discovered 'as far certain as certain can be of any future event... in all physical phenomena, the effects produced by motion are all in proportion to the relative motion.'

From 1846 Grove had started to reduce his scientific work in favour of his professional practice at the bar, his young family providing the financial motivation; and in 1853 became a QC. The bar provided him with the opportunity to combine his legal and scientific knowledge, in particular in patent law. His scientific career led to the practice of patent and other law after 1853. He was appointed to the court of common pleas in 1871 and was knighted in 1872. After retirement from the bench in 1887, he resumed his scientific studies. Grove, his health perpetually troubled, died at home in London after a long illness.

Footnote:
A fuel cell is an electrochemical cell that converts chemical energy from a fuel into electrical energy. Electricity is generated from the reaction between a fuel supply and an oxidizing agent. The reactants flow into the cell, and the reaction products flow out of it, while the electrolyte remains within it. Fuel cells can operate continuously as long as the necessary reactant and oxidant flows are maintained. Fuel cells are different from conventional electrochemical cell batteries as they consume reactant from an external source, which must be replenished. This is a called thermodynamically open system, whereas conventional batteries store electric energy and are a closed system. The hydrogen fuel cell uses hydrogen as its fuel, and oxygen (usually from air) as its oxidant. Fuels can include alcohols or hydrocarbons and oxidants can include chlorine and the bleaching compound, chlorine dioxide.

HENRY RICHARD 3 April 1812 – 20 August 1888

APOSTOL HEDDIWCH (THE APOSTLE OF PEACE), 'THE MEMBER FOR WALES'

Born at Prospect House, Tregaron, Henry was the son of Ebeneser Richard, a powerful Calvinistic Methodist minister, whose own father (another Henry) had been a Methodist minister and one of the circulating teachers of Griffith Jones (q.v.) Henry Richard's mother was Mary, the daughter of William Williams of Tregaron. After schooling in Llangeitho, Henry worked as a draper's apprentice in Carmarthen before deciding to enter the ministry. After attending London's Highbury College, he was ordained a minister in the Marlborough Congregational Chapel in the Old Kent Road, where he remained until retiring from the ministry in 1850.

The Society for the Promotion of Permanent and Universal Peace was a British pacifist organization, later known as the Peace Society or

Peace Union, founded in 1816 through the hard work of Joseph Tregelles Price. Price was the humanitarian Quaker who had tried desperately to save the doomed Dic Penderyn (q.v. Richard Lewis). The Society advocated a gradual, proportionate, and simultaneous disarmament of all nations and the principle of arbitration. Its first secretary was Evan Rees of Montgomeryshire, author of *Sketches of Horrors of War*. Henry Richard followed him as secretary from 1848-1885, and the secretaries for the first hundred years were all Welsh.

The pacifist Henry Richard of Tregaron was known as *Apostol Heddwch* (The Apostle of Peace) in Wales. After playing a prominent part in

a Brussels peace conference, Price became active in the promotion of such conferences in Paris, Frankfurt and elsewhere, and in the overseeing of publications for peace. He helped organize a series of congresses in the capitals of Europe, and was partly instrumental in securing the insertion of a declaration in favour of arbitration in the 1856 Treaty of Paris, settling the Crimean War. Through this work he became universally known in Europe and the United States until his resignation in 1885.

The Peace Union was the forerunner of the League of Nations, which in turn changed into The United Nations. It had been set up, mainly by Nonconformists and Quakers, as being 'principled against all war, upon any pretence', its object being to 'print and circulate Tracts and to diffuse information tending to show that War is inconsistent with the spirit of Christianity, and the true interests of mankind; and to point out the means best calculated to maintain permanent and universal peace, upon the basis of Christian principles.'

Its most important staff appointment was that of Henry Richard. With the reformers John Bright and Richard Cobden, he tirelessly carried the ideals of pacifism, peace and reconciliation into every part of England, until his retirement in 1885, aged 73. He was also the editor of the Peace Society's monthly magazine, *Herald of Peace*. Under Henry Richard's guidance, the Union opposed the Boer War (like Lloyd-George, q.v.) The Welsh connection was kept up with the appointment of Richard's successor, William Evans Darby, who held the post until 1915.

A nonconformist radical and a friend of Richard Cobden, Richard travelled widely in Europe, holding peace conferences and encouraging the use of arbitration in international disputes. Becoming involved in politics, in 1865 he withdrew from candidature as Liberal candidate for Cardiganshire. By 1866, Henry had published diaries of his European tours, many pamphlets and *Letters on the Political and Social Conditions of Wales*, and in that year married Matilda Farley. Richard was elected MP for Merthyr Tydfil at the age of fifty-six in 1868, and previously in 1847 had repudiated *The Blue Books* which had maligned Welsh education. His first act in The House of Commons was to condemn those landlords who evicted their Welsh tenants for voting Liberal. This protest facilitated the Ballot Act of 1872. He was the first proponent of Welsh Nonconformism in the House of Commons. As an MP, he was passionately interested in Welsh education, land reform, disestablishment of the English Church in Wales, and the protection of the Welsh language. His interests led to his nickname as 'The Member for Wales', and he wrote to the English press explaining why the Rebecca Riots were happening in Wales.

In July 1873, apart from his work in upholding Welsh and Nonconformist rights, Henry Richard succeeded in carrying a motion in favour of international arbitration. He was elected Chairman of the Congregational Union of England and Wales in 1877, the first layman to be chosen for this office. He became closely associated with the University of Wales in Aberystwyth, and in 1880 served on the committee studying intermediate and higher education in Wales. Henry Richard died at Treborth, near Bangor, and there is a prominent statue of this political reformer and idealist in Tregaron's main square. Tom Ellis opined that Richard was the first to represent in Parliament the new national spirit that arose in Wales in the second half of the 19th century.

DAVID DAVIES 18 December 1819 - 20 July 1890

DAVID DAVIES LLANDINAM, DAI TOP SAWYER, DAVIES THE RAILWAY, DAVIES THE OCEAN, THE MOST SUCCESSFUL WELSH INDUSTRIALIST OF THE CENTURY

The Times in 1866 noted the prevalence of English entrepreneurs (ignoring that they had initial capital unavailable to men such as David Davies): 'Wales... is a small country, unfavourably situated for commercial purposes, with an indifferent soil, and inhabited by an unenterprising people. It is true it possesses valuable minerals but these have chiefly been developed by English energy and for the supply of English wants.' Wales has been stripped of its copper, gold, silver, lead, slate, limestone, iron and recently water for two millennia, from being the most resource-rich area of Europe. In return we have among the poorest housing, education, health and infrastructure in the developed world. The only input is social dumping, with 90% of population growth in the past 40 years coming from outside Wales. People do not come to Wales to work – there are only public sector jobs available. They come to retire or be assured of benefits. It is fulfilling

England's 'green agenda' by having five times the density of wind turbines as that country, as the wind seems to stop at Offa's Dyke. These inefficient bird-choppers are hurting the small tourist industry and will remain rotting across the landscape when subsidies stop, as the blades are not recyclable and the motors have carcinogenic materials. Their owners will sell them on to token companies for a token cost, which will almost immediately declare bankruptcy, thereby avoiding any costs of clean-up.

There have been few Welsh industrialists, and this remarkable man had four separate nicknames in his career. Born the eldest of nine children in

Statue of Davies outside Barry Dock offices overlooking his new docks

Llandinam, there is a wonderful statue of David Davies outside the Docks Offices in Barry, and a replica is in Llandinam. He was known as David Davies Llandinam to distinguish himself from the many other people named David Davies, much as today's Welsh farmers are known as Harri Dolau-Duon, Rhys Pantllaethdu etc. His father ran a farm and small sawmill, and Davies' nickname from working there stayed with him all his life - Dai Top-Sawyer. Upon leaving school at the age of 11, David Davies began to work on the farm and in the sawpits of his father, also called David Davies. His nickname dates from this time as he had always had the good sense to work at the top of the sawpit and thus avoid being covered by shavings and sawdust. The top sawyer was also known as the 'top dog', and the under sawyer as the 'underdog'. For several years Davies worked as a sawyer, farmer and local contractor.

Commenting on the death of his father and brother Edward from TB when David was just 20, Davies' biographer wrote: 'The cause of death of David Davies, farmer is given as "Decline," and the next column, reserved for the signature, description and residence of the informant, bears the words "The Mark X of David Davies, Present at the Death." Eight weeks later he made his mark a second time as witness to the death of his brother Edward. Five years were to pass before he carefully wrote his name on his marriage certificate.' David Davies taught himself to read in the years between the death of his brother and his marriage to Margaret Jones of Llanfair Caereinion.

Davies was given the opportunity to create the foundations and the approaches to a new bridge across the Severn at Llandinam. The County Surveyor, one Thomas Penson, was so impressed with the work that he began to put other projects Davies' way. He was on the road to success, and soon began making money from organising labour gangs on the new railway lines that were being built across Wales.

As well as roads and bridges, Davies built several railways across mid-Wales. Starting with the construction of the Newtown & Llanidloes Railway in 1859, he became involved in the construction of a number of railways in mid-Wales, the Vale of Clwyd and Pembrokeshire, He played a major part if the construction of the Newtown to Aberystwyth railway, and a notable achievement was the crossing of the massive Tregaron Bog to finish the line between Lampeter and Aberystwyth. Building railways soon became second nature to Davies, and he even headed to the south west to construct the Pembroke to Tenby line. His greatest achievement as a railway engineer was the great Talerddig cutting on the Newtown & Machynlleth Railway, completed in 1862 and the deepest in the world at that time. As a contractor then financier, he took part in the building of seven Welsh railway lines, thereby earning another soubriquet, 'Davies the Railway', but not all of his Manchester & Milford Railway was completed.

By the late-1850s he was an important and wealthy man and could have left supervision to others, but Herbert Williams in *Davies The Ocean*, writes: 'He was still the old Davy, ready to roll up his sleeves and turn to with the lads. One morning he saw them struggling to roll heavy stones into trucks in a quarry and with a cry of 'Sweet boys, up with them!' helped them shoulder the stones into place. His effort was all the more impressive in that he was on his way to London on business and wearing a dark suit which was so covered in dust that he had to go home to change before making the journey.'

1864 marked a decisive turning point in his career when he took out a pioneering mineral lease in the south Wales valleys. He bought land in the Upper Rhondda Valley and sank the Parc and Maerdy coal pits. It took two years before the first pits were in full production. Five more collieries were opened by 1886. In the following year they were vested in a new public limited company, the Ocean Coal Co. Ltd., and at the time of Davies's death in 1890, it was the largest and most profitable coal company in south Wales. In 1865, he sank the two deepest coal shafts ever made at that time, anywhere in the world. He sank all his money into developing mines on land leased from the Crawshay family in the Rhondda. Gradually the cash ran out and Davies had still not found a profitable seam of coal. Running out of money, he addressed the workers, saying that he only had a half-crown piece left (about twelve pence in modern money), and could not afford to pay them any more wages. A man shouted 'We'll have that as well', and Davies threw him the coin. The men promised to work just one more week without wages, and in March 1866 a coal seam was found at the unheard-of depth of 660 feet - the Cwmparc mine in Treorchy became one of the richest in the world. Further mines followed, including the Garw and the Lady Windsor.

The crowning achievement of David Davies's career was the construction of the dock at Barry, south Wales. Davies and a number of fellow Rhondda colliery owners came together to solve congestion both on the Taff Vale Railway and at Cardiff's Bute Docks*. Faced with higher charges and narrowing profit margins for exporting coal through Cardiff, Davies chose to build his own docks 7 miles away in Barry. Despite fierce opposition from the Bute faction, Davies built a railway line to Barry, and built the most modern docks in history by 1889, breaking the Marquis of Bute's monopoly of the shipping of Valleys coal. His Ocean Coal wagons rolling down to Barry Docks gave him his fourth nickname, Davies the Ocean. It had taken years of persuasion and an Act of Parliament, but by 1914 Barry was a bigger port than Cardiff in tonnage exported. Barry had then been a scattering of twelve cottages, and Davies linked Barry Island to the mainland to create the great docks. Barry became possibly the busiest port in the world, shipping coal everywhere. Barry's No.1 dock in 1913 exported 11m tons of coal.

David Davies was a Liberal MP for many years, representing Newtown and then the county of Cardiganshire, but quarrelled with Gladstone over Irish Home Rule, and lost the 1886 election by a margin of just nine votes. Davies died just four years later, his personal estate being valued at over £400,000. The *Aberystwyth Observer* of 26 July 1890 published an obituary full of anecdotes from Davies' life. 'While extending the railway from Moat Lane to Aberystwyth he came, as he felt assured, to the brink of ruin. Right in his track was a huge rock. To drive through it was impossible, and there was no going around it. "There it stood," and he, speaking of it in after days, to Kilsey Jones, "the rock upon which I was to be wrecked. But he attacked it with iron will and found it laminated like the leaves of a rock, and it supplied him with excellent stone for all his bridges. "It was the rock," be added, "of my salvation."

Thenceforward Mr Davies threw himself into the rapidly developing coal industry of South Wales, associating himself with the Ocean Collieries. He was always held in the highest esteem by the workmen of all grades in fact, no master was ever more respected than Mr Davies by his workmen. He would speak to the workmen as a workman, and his kind, unassuming manner won the hearts of all. Nothing tried him more than to see work badly performed. It is said of him that during one of his visits to the collieries he was walking by a place where a number of navvies were at work, one of whom, it appears, was not an expert workman, and the way he performed his work was painful to the eyes of the old gentleman, who immediately asked for the pick and gave the navvy a lesson in the way of using that tool, much to the amusement of his fellow workmen. The navvy, with a little grumbling, took the pick in hand again, and shouted to one of his mates, "Who is that old chap?" He would hardly believe that the man who had just given him a lesson and who was so commonly dressed, with no outward show whatever, was the great "Davies yr Ocean." as the colliers would call him.

One more peculiarity of Mr Davies is worth a note. He was a man of fine physique, and on occasions when his workmen would be unable to proceed with their work, through unfavourable weather or ether circumstances, he would visit them in their sheds and go through different exercises with them, such as throwing the hammer, lifting weights, and other feats demanding strength. He was a strict total abstainer, and no intoxicants were ever supplied to his servants on the farm, even in harvest time. He, too, was as strict a Sabbatarian. At all times, if any way possible, he would return home for the Sunday, in order not to miss service with his class in the Sunday School. So, strict, indeed, were his views regarding the commandment to keep holy the Sabbath Day that he would not even open letters on Sunday. When a young man, while contracting in a small way, the road surveyor who superintended the work Mr Davies had in hand one Sunday drove from Welshpool to Llandinam, a distance of about twelve miles, to see him on some matters connected with the work. On his arrival Mr Davies was at chapel, and a messenger was despatched to him with the intelligence that the surveyor desired to see him. The reply was that Mr Davies would see the surveyor on the following day…'

A philanthropist, as a benefactor he played a major role in the establishment of the University College at Aberystwyth. David Davies was a passionate supporter of Calvinistic Methodism, a life-long Sabbatarian and teetotaller, who gave generously to religious and educational causes. His grand-daughters Gwendoline and Margaret Davies of Gregynog were responsible for the bequest of Impressionist Art, which made The National Museum of Wales at Cardiff the envy of many other European museums. His grandson David Davies, first Baron Llandinam, was the major benefactor of the first Welsh university and the National Library of Wales at Aberystwyth, as well as a chain of hospitals across Wales. The post-war nationalisation of the coal, dock and railway industries saw the family lose control of their vast undertaking. Today, all the Ocean pits have closed, as has much of the railway system created by David Davies, and Barry Dock sees little activity.

* The massive profits pouring into Cardiff saw shipping, coal, iron and steel companies needing a central exchange, and the Cardiff Coal Exchange was built between 1884 and 1888. In the 1880s Cardiff has exported 25% of the world's supplies of coal. The world's first million pound deal was said to have taken place at the Coal Exchange. Huge congestion at Cardiff, which handled 72% of Welsh coal exports, led to David Davies' successful petition in 1884 for a new dock at Barry,. There followed a rapid increase in population, making Barry the fastest-growing town in Britain. Incidentally, the Marquis of Bute had become the richest man in the world through his control of Welsh coal, docks and

shipping, via his Welsh wife's inheritance of large parts of Glamorgan and Monmouthshire.

Footnote:
The 1847 Report on education in Wales, known as the 'Blue Books', was scathing. It stated that Welsh was a 'peasant tongue, and anyone caught speaking Welsh were to be severely punished'. The 'Welsh Not' was a ban upon the speaking of Welsh in schools, and was carried out with some vehemence, in yet another attempt to exterminate the language. A wooden placard had to be worn around the neck, passed on to anyone heard speaking Welsh, with the last child at the end of the day being thrashed by the teacher. This piece of wood on a leather strap was called a *cribban*, and Irish and Breton children had their languages thrashed out of them in a similar manner. In other Welsh schools, a stick was passed on to the same effect. In others, the child was fined half-a-penny, a massive sum for poor parents. At the same time, David Davies was saying that Welsh was a second-rate language – 'If you wish to continue to eat barley bread and lie on straw mattresses, then keep on shouting *Bydded i'r Gymraeg fyw am byth* [May the Welsh language live forever, the chorus of the National Anthem]. But if you want to eat white bread and roast beef you must learn English!' Unfortunately, Davies know that the Welsh could only 'get on' by learning good English and abandoning their language in these times. The English poet and schools inspector, Matthew Arnold, declared in 1855 that the British regions must become homogeneous... 'Sooner or later the difference of language between Wales and England will probably be effaced'... an event which is socially and politically desirable'. In 1865 *The Times* called the language 'the curse of Wales...the sooner all Welsh specialities vanish off the face of the earth the better'. In years to come, older people used to recount how many times they had been caned for wearing the 'Welsh Not' at the end of the day.

MICHAEL DANIEL JONES 2 March 1822 - 2 December 1899

THE FOUNDER OF THE WELSH COLONY OF PATAGONIA, FATHER OF THE MODERN WELSH NATIONALIST MOVEMENT, 'THE GREATEST WELSHMAN OF THE 19TH CENTURY'

Jones was born in the Manse, Llanuwchllyn, Merioneth, the son of another Michael Jones, who was minister of *Yr Hen Gapel* (the old chapel) there. There was a huge theological controversy, which split the congregation, and his father left Llanuwchllyn became Principal of the Independent College at nearby Bala. After being educated by his father, Jones spent a few months as a draper's apprentice in Wrexham. However, Michael D. Jones wished to follow his father into the ministry, and went to Carmarthen Presbyterian

College (1839-43) and then Highbury College in London. In 1847, he went to America, in the midst of the great emigration caused by the poor harvests and agricultural depression of 1840-1850. He stayed with relatives in Cincinnati and was asked to stay for some time as a minister.

While in America, Jones set up a society to give financial assistance to poor people from Wales who wished to emigrate, and several branches of 'The Brython Association' started across the United States. This was to be the genesis of Jones' life mission, to establish a Welsh-speaking 'Welsh Colony' for emigrants who wished to escape from the oppression of Tory landlords across Wales. He wanted a Welsh state where: '… a free farmer could tread on his own land and enjoy on his own hearth, the song and the harp and true Welsh fellowship…There will be chapel, school, and parliament and the old language will be the medium of worship, of trade, of science, of education and of government. A strong and self-reliant nation will grow in a Welsh homeland.'

Returning to Wales, Michael D. Jones became pastor of Independent churches in Carmarthenshire. His father died in 1853, and Michael was asked to succeed him as minister of Bala, Tyn-y-Bont, Soar, Bethel and Llandderfel, and as Principal of Bala College. However, a constitutional dispute meant that for a time a rival college operated in Bala, before moving to Bangor in 1886. This was known as 'the Battle of the Two Constitutions' (1879-85). Jones wanted the subscribers to be able to control the government of the college, whereas his antagonists wanted the controllers to be representatives, appointed by the churches of each county of Wales. (Bala was the major Welsh-speaking college at this time).

The problem was exacerbated by Jones' financial support for the Patagonian Colony. He was forced to sell off Bodiwan, which was his home and also the seat of the college, to meet his debts, and the so-called 'Decapitation Committee' held at Shrewsbury dismissed Jones from the Principalship. Jones resigned from Bala College in 1892 to allow it to also move to Bangor, the new Bala-Bangor College later becoming part of the University of Wales.

In South America the existence of the Welsh-speaking colony, in Patagonia, stopped Chile claiming vast expanses of land from Argentina in 1865. 153 Welsh emigrants had boarded the sailing ship *Mimosa* and landed at Port Madryn there in the same year, trekking 40 miles to found a settlement near the Chubut River. In 1885, some families crossed 400 miles of desert to establish another settlement in Cwm Hyfryd at the foot of the Andes. *Y Wladfa* ('The Colony'), founded by the reformist preacher Michael D. Jones, was to be a radical colony, where Nonconformism and the Welsh language were to dominate. Jones was deeply concerned about the Anglicisation of Wales - to preserve the heritage his people would have to move. He is regarded as the founder of the modern Welsh nationalist movement. The Argentine government was anxious to control this vast unpopulated territory, in which it was still in dispute with Chile, so granted 100 square miles for the establishment of a Welsh state, protected by the military.

For ten years after 1865, this Welsh state was completely self-governing, with its own constitution written in Welsh. The immigrants owned their own land and farmed their own farms – there was to be no capitalist state with its hated landlord system. Females were given the vote – the first democracy in the world to show egalitarianism, and this 50 years before British suffragettes started to try to change the British system. Boys and girls aged 18 could vote, over a century before they could in Britain. Voting was by secret ballot and all were eligible – two more democratic innovations. The language of Parliament and the law was Welsh, and only Welsh school books were used.

Back home in Wales, the use of Welsh was forbidden in schools, and suppressed by the digusting 'Welsh Not.' *Y Wladfa* was 'the first example of a practical democracy in South America', and also the first example of a practical, egalitarian, non-discriminatory democracy anywhere in the world. There were massive problems in the settlement at first, until the native Teheulche Indians and their chief taught the Welsh to catch guanaco and rhea, from the prairies. Also, the Indians would exchange meat for bread, going from house to house saying *poco bara* - Spanish for 'a little' and Welsh for 'bread'. This was a 'green colony' whereby both sides gained. The Welsh taught the Indians to break in horses, and in turn they showed the Welsh how to use bolas to catch animals. By controlling the waters in the Camwy Valley, the settlers began to prosper.

Unlike unsuccessful Spanish settlers before them, they had very few problems with the native Indians, who still empathise with the Welsh. When two Welshmen were killed in the Chubut River uplands in 1883, Lewis Jones, the leader of the colony, refused to believe it. He told the messenger 'But John, the Indians are our friends. They'd never kill a Welshman.' It transpired that an Argentine patrol had trespassed on Indian land, and the Welsh were tragically mistaken for the Indians' Argentine enemies. The bodies had their sexual organs stuffed into their mouths.

The colony grew to 3,000 people by the time Welsh immigration halted in 1912, and had been the first society in the world to give women the vote. Interestingly, the Welsh code of law established by the settlers was the first legal structure in Argentina, and its 'influence in modern-day

Argentinian law can still be seen'. 400 people are currently learning Welsh in Patagonia, helping the language to survive there, and there are teacher exchanges. However, only 4,000 still speak the language regularly, most of them in their later years. The success of the colony attracted immigrants from Spain and Italy in the first decades of the twentieth century, and the Welsh influence is declining steadily. Jones was almost broken financially by the strain of supporting the settlement in Patagonia - he had envisaged it as the pattern for an independent Wales, and laboured, travelled, wrote, addressed meetings, collected money and lost his son there.

He also fought against the oppression of Tory landlords - he hated servility, and beat the candidate of Sir Watkin Williams Wynn as representative on the county council for Llanuwchllyn in 1889. This was a tremendous victory for Welsh radicalism. He is buried at Yr Hen Gapel. His vision, hope and enthusiasm helped develop Welsh patriotic feeling into a vigorous, practical nationalism. The great poet Gwenallt, in *The Historical Base of Welsh Nationalism*, described Michael D. Jones as 'a saint, a great and large-hearted Congregationalist; the greatest Welshman of the 19th century; and the greatest nationalist after Owain Glyndŵr.'

The *Eisteddfod Fawr* is still held in Chubut, financially supported by the Argentinian government. It gives around a £250,000 a year to support eisteddfodau in Gaiman, Trefelin and Trelew in recognition of the service performed by the early settlers. Gaiman is the most Welsh town in Patagonia, with signs on the road approaching 'Visit Tŷ Llwyd, the Welsh Tea House', 'Stop at Tŷ Gwyn' and 'Come to Tŷ Te Caerdydd'. In Tŷ Te Caerdydd, a costumed group from the local school sometimes dances, and Welsh-speaking, Welsh-costumed staff serve the traditional Welsh tea and cakes. Bruce Chatwin's curious travelogue, *In Patagonia*, gives some flavour of the place, with characters like Alun Powell, Caradog Williams, Hubert Lloyd-Jones, Mrs Cledwyn Hughes and Gwynneth Morgan.

In the 1920's, President Fontana was the first President of Argentina to visit the region. On horseback – there were no roads or trains – the official party could not cross the river into Trelew. A tall, strong, red-haired youngster called Gough offered to help, and lifted him up and carried him across the raging river, to the town reception. A couple of years later the boy was in the ranks of conscripts in the main square in Buenos Aires, waiting for the president to address all those required to carry out their National Service in the military. The president stepped out onto the square, surrounded by his generals and bodyguard, when a Welsh voice rang out loud and clear 'Hey, I know you!' Gough broke ranks and started striding towards the president, waving his arms. A hundred guns trained on him before President Fontana broke into a smile and shouted to his guard that this big red-haired Welsh youth was indeed not dangerous, and known to him.

I am indebted to a friend, Rene Griffiths, for the above story. He has a ranch near Butch Cassidy's* old farm in Cholila, and is fairly certain that the gang carried out a maximum of two robberies in South America, simply because of the distances involved (at Rio Gallegos, and Villa Mercedes de San Luis in 1905). Butch and Sundance, under their aliases, were accepted into the community and Welshmen helped them get started in horse breeding. Incidentally, Benetton has bought huge tracts of Patagonia to farm sheep, and Sylvester Stallone and other Hollywood stars have ranches there. Rene showed me a photograph of the lake on his land, where he wants people to come for fishing holidays. I idly asked how long it was - ten miles was the answer. There is a huge scale to these lands. I also asked if there were any problems with his cattle stock when he visited South Wales - he answered 'only mountain lions'.

* Butch Cassidy and the Sundance Kid in Patagonia were alleged to have formed a gang comprised of Welshmen, and Cassidy's old farm is still ranched. Their best friend was a Welshman called Daniel Gibbons, who helped them purchase horses. A son of Michael D. Jones, a grocer called Llwyd ap Iwan, was said to have been killed by the gang in 1909, in Arroyo Pescado in Northern Patagonia. However, it appears to have been a couple of renegade drifters from the USA that carried out this act. It was this pair, named William Wilson and Robert Evans, which were also killed in the shoot-out with the Argentine military at Rio Pico, not the famous American outlaws. The Bolivia deaths were the fiction of a screenwriter. Butch, Sundance and Etta appear to have spent their time peaceably - they had no need of money at first - and were assisted by the Welsh to settle in.

Butch Cassidy bought 12,000 acres near Cholila in 1901, and the following year Sundance and his 'wife', Etta Place arrived. However, in 1907 one of their gauchos saw Butch's picture in a Buenos Aires paper, although he could not read, and told everyone around him that this was his 'boss'. A couple of days later, Sheriff Perry (of Pinkerton's Detective Agency), heard the story and made his way down to Patagonia from the capital. The gaucho showed the outlaws the picture in the newspaper, and they escaped with Etta Place over the Andes into Chile, just two days before Pinkerton's detectives arrived on the scene. According to his sister, Butch died in the 1930's in Washington State, and Etta Place seems to have died in Denver some time after 1924.

DAVID EDWARD HUGHES FRS 16 May 1831 - 22 January 1900

THE FIRST MAN TO TRANSMIT AND RECEIVE RADIO WAVES, TELEPHONE PIONEER, POLYMATH MUSICIAN, INVENTOR, SCIENTIST AND PHILOSOPHER, THE INVENTOR OF POWDER COATING, THE INVENTOR OF THE MICROPHONE, THE INVENTOR OF THE PRINTING TELEGRAPH

A prime example of an unknown Welsh contribution to science is that of David Hughes. Hughes made the original breakthroughs in telephony,

broadcasting, telegraphy and powder coating of metals. Apart from his successful teleprinter and telegraph system of 1856-59, Hughes invented the carbon microphone vital to telephony and broadcasting in 1877. He invented the induction balance (1878), the metal detector (1878), the world's first radio wave transmission (1879) and the technology of powder coating (1879). Hughes is a prime example of an unknown inventor, a polymath and the first man to transmit and receive radio waves.

Often referred to as an 'Anglo-American' inventor, Hughes was born at the cottage now known as Green y Ddwyryd, in Corwen. His work is mentioned in biographies of the great inventors Morse, Preece (another Welshman), Heavenside and Lodge. As the *Daily Post* recorded, following an exhibit of David Hughes in Denbigh County Library in 1999, 'Italian-born Gugliemo Marconi is world famous as the inventor of the wireless radio and German scientist Heinrich Hertz attained fame by giving his name to radio frequency waves. Yet, eight years before Hertz, Welshman D.E. Hughes became the first person in the world to transmit and receive radio waves. That same year he developed a radio system to transmit signals from Lavernock near Cardiff to Bream in Somerset. His work failed to satisfy colleagues' demands for proof and his achievements went unrecognised for years.'

His father, also named David Hughes, was an accomplished musician, and all his children were considered child prodigies. He started giving concerts with Joseph Tudor (David Edward's brother), when Tudor was only five, playing in all the UK's major cities as well as before royalty. Each child, David Edward, John Arthur and Margaret (an accomplished harpist) joined the travelling concert party with their parents, and when the family emigrated to America, gave concerts in all of New England's principal venues. However, Joseph tragically drowned, and after a few months the family started touring America, Canada and the West Indies before settling in Virginia to live.

David Edward Hughes' virtuosity at the piano had attracted the attention of Herr Hast, an eminent German pianist, who procured him a professorship of music at St Joseph's College, Bardstown, Kentucky. Apart from his musical gifts, his accomplishments in physical science and mathematics made him the natural choice for the chair of natural philosophy at the same college. At the age of 19 he held two professorships, in natural philosophy and music. A polymath, from 1850-53, Hughes was Professor of Music at Bardstown College, Kentucky. Readers might note that Bardstown was where the Evan Williams family set up American bourbon whisky production, and the area has strong Welsh linkages.

Hughes invented the printing telegraph when he was just 23. His keyboard enabled the corresponding letter to be printed at a distant receiver, working a little like the '*golfball*' typewriter, before any typewriter was invented. This was patented in 1856, and this caused several small telegraph companies to merge and form Western Union Telegraph Co., to exploit telegraphy across the USA using the '*Hughes System*'. His system was thought to be better, and much cheaper than the monopoly enjoyed by American Telegraph's Morse system. The editor of the *New York Associated Press* summoned Hughes via telegram from to New York. The American Telegraph Company used Morse technology, charging exorbitant rates for the transmission of news. His editors took up Hughes' instrument in opposition to Morse, and introduced it on the lines of several companies. The Western Telegraph Company then took over those companies, and editors were once again faced with high prices Hughes' mechanism became the genesis of the modern teleprinter, telex system and even the computer keyboard is its direct descendant.

Hughes received US patents for the *Telegraph* (with alphabetic keyboard and printer) in 1856; the *Duplex Telegraph* in 1859 and the *Printing Telegraph* (with type-wheel) also in 1859. Hughes returned to Europe, where his telegraph system became the adopted standard. Hughes had travelled Europe, implementing his system, in the year after his return from America. His teleprinter (telegraph-typewriter) revolutionised reporting and communications.

Hughes' invention of the 'loose-contact' carbon microphone in 1877 made practical telephony a possibility for the first time - he refused to take out patents but gave the invention to the world. Wheatstone in 1827 had been the first to use the term 'microphone', and Hughes revived it in 1878 for his invention. He discovered that a loose contact in a circuit containing a battery and telephone receiver would give rise to sounds in the receiver, which corresponded to the vibrations impinged upon the diaphragm of the mouthpiece or transmitter. This invention was made practical telephony a possibility for the first time, and was later vital to broadcasting and sound recording. He revealed his secrets to the Royal Society at London on 8 May

1878, and to the general public in June of the same year. Hughes refused to take out patents, but gave the invention to the world.

Also in 1878 he invented the induction balance, then known as '*Hughes' Induction Balance*', to detect concealed metal such as the position of bullets in a wounded person. It is the basis of today's metal detectors. In 1879, Hughes discovered that when a stick of wood covered with powdered copper was placed in an electrical circuit, the copper would adhere when a spark was made. This started off the invaluable technology of powder coating. His research into the experimental theory of magnetism was a major contribution to electrical science, and his papers on this and other subjects brought him many honours and medals, as well as Fellowship of the Royal Society.

Also in 1879, Hughes held an experiment in Great Portland Street. At one end of the street he had a spark transmitter to generate electro-magnetic waves, and at the other a 'coherer', a piece of equipment to receive the waves. He had proposed the theory to Clark Maxwell, and the President and Secretary of the Royal Society witnessed the success of the experiment. A Welshman had proposed and demonstrated the first radio transmitter and receiver in the world, and thereby proved the existence of electro-magnetic radiation. The English committee was not impressed, however, and attributed the effects to Faraday induction rather than electro-magnetic radiation. Hughes even developed his radio system to transmit signals several miles across the Bristol Channel from Wales to England. Hughes was the first person in the world to transmit and receive radio waves, 8 years before Hertz, and was the real inventor of the wireless radio, rather than Marconi, who knew Hughes and his work well.

In 1886 he was President of the Institution of Electrical Engineers. All of this time, he was composing and playing works for concertina, violin, piano and harp, and some of his inventions had musical applications. His telegraph was internationally used until the 1930's, and his microphone is the forerunner of all the carbon microphones now in use. Hughes became one of the most highly decorated scientists of the period, honoured by most European nations. He was awarded a Grand Gold Medal at the 1867 Paris Exhibition, the Royal Society Gold Medal in 1885, and the Albert Gold Medal of the Society of Arts in 1897. No other person received all three of these distinctive honours. For inventing the microphone and printing telegraph, plus other inventions, Napoleon III created Professor Hughes a Chevalier of the Legion of Honour.

He became perhaps the most highly decorated scientists of the period, honoured by most European nations. Some of his other titles included: The Order of Saint Meurice and Saint Lazare (Italy); The Order of the Iron Crown (Austria), which carried with it the title of Baron; The Order of Saint Anne (Russia); The Noble Order of Saint Michael (Bavaria); Commander of the Imperial Order of the Grand Cross of the Medjidie

(Turkey); Commander of the Royal and Distinguished Order of Carlos III (Spain); The Grand Officer's Star and Collar of the Royal Order of Takovo (Serbia); and Officer of the Royal Order of Leopold (Belgium).

In 1900, *The Electrician* noted: 'It is with profound sorrow that we have to announce the death, on Monday evening last, of Professor D.E. Hughes. His death, at the age of 69 years, deprives the world of one of its most accomplished electricians, the electrical profession of one of its most honoured and respected members and a worldwide circle of admirers of a genial and well-beloved friend. It truly can be recorded that David Hughes lived without making a single enemy, and died mourned by all whose good fortune it has been to come within the cheery circle of his friendship.' He left a fortune to four London hospitals. Most of his £470,000 will went to the hospitals, but some smaller amounts were bequeathed to a number of technical societies.

SIR PRYCE PRYCE-JONES 16 October 1834 - 11 January 1920

THE MAN WHO CHANGED SHOPPING, THE INVENTOR OF MAIL ORDER* 1861 and the SLEEPING BAG 1876

Pryce-Jones was born in Llanllwchaiarn, just outside Newtown, Montgomeryshire. Apprenticed from the age of 12 to 21 at a draper's in Newtown, Pryce-Jones took it over aged 22 in 1856. Newtown was a centre of the Welsh woollen industry and local Welsh flannel formed the mainstay of his business. Flannel is a soft woven fabric, originally made from carded wool, and was invented in Wales in the 16th century. Its importance at the time is demonstrated by the fact that 'flannel' is one of only a handful of words in the British language which has been incorporated into the English language. The beginning of the national postal service from 1840, and the arrival of the railway network in Newtown from 1859, were the events which allowed Pryce-Jones turn his shop into a global sales concern.

Using the post and train services, he sent out promotional leaflets, from which people could choose what they wanted, with Pryce-Jones despatching them. Remember that there were no real shops with an abundance of choice at this time, as we would recognise them today. Pryce-Jones had the idea from knowing about his rural community, where farmers, farm labourers and their wives had no time to travel for a day by horse to a shop. And, and on Sunday, their only day off, shops had to be closed. It was the world's first mail order business, forever altering the nature of retailing throughout the world, and indeed the model upon which today's giant internet sellers are based. Expansion of the railways allowed Pryce-Jones to take orders from across the British Isles and the continent and then the globe, and his business grew exponentially. During the 1870's Pryce-Jones took part in exhibitions across the world, spreading the new retailing concept, winning several medals and becoming world famous.

In 1862 he received an order from Florence Nightingale, and cleverly used her name in his advertisingl. Pryce-Jones had built up a client list which included Florence Nightingale, Queen Victoria, the Princess of Wales and royal households across Europe. Pryce-Jones marketed them as his customers on his leaflets, which developed into bigger and bigger catalogues, selling house wares and clothes and well as draperies. By the 1880s his patrons included the royal houses of Britain, Germany, Hanover, Austria, Denmark, Italy, Naples and Russia. He began selling Welsh Flannel from Newtown to America, Australia and India, and several times re-located to larger premises. In 1879, he built the Royal Welsh Warehouse, the tall, massive red-brick building in Newtown which still stands today.

By 1880, Pryce-Jones had more than 100,000 customers and his success was acknowledged by Queen Victoria in 1887 with a knighthood. Sir Pryce Pryce-Jones produced 'Royal Welsh Warehouse Company' mail order catalogues from 1890, after a printing press was installed in his Newtown warehouse. In his summer catalogues, there were now many items of leisure and sporting wear available. As with modern mail order catalogues, the emphasis was on women's clothing. The men's catalogue was smaller, but featured cricket, tennis and boating outfits, along with cloth samples, pants, vests, surplices, cassocks, collars, shirts and cuffs. There were also home furnishing and children's catalogues. Pryce-Jones was elected MP for Montgomery and became High Sheriff for Montgomeryshire. However, after his death in 1920, the company was hit badly by the depression of the 1920s and 1930s, being taken over in 1938. Mail order became a global phenomenon and a way of life, especially in the United States, providing a lifeline for its sparsely populated, rural communities. Pryce-Jones changed the nature of retailing and shopping across the world. Internet shopping has damaged catalogue shopping in the last decade or so, but the underlying principle of internet marketing is the same.

* All known sources relate that Aaron Montgomery Ward started the mail-order industry in 1872, in Chicago with two employees and a catalogue of 163 products, but by this time Pryce-Jones was known across the world and also selling in the USA. Pryce-Jones had started in a small way in 1859 by sending out patterns and stock lists to the local gentry, and by arranging for local woollen manufacturers and merchants to supply goods to meet the orders he obtained. Pryce-Jones was excellent at gaining publicity for his rapidly growing

mail-order drapery business and expanded it across Britain and the Continent by 1861. A pamphlet of 1869 illustrates his company's awards for the best Welsh flannel at the Grand National Eisteddfod of Wales in 1865, 1866, 1869 and 1868, so his customers could be assured that they were buying the best. By the 1860s his sales leaflets were also offering general household goods and clothing, well before Montgomery Ward.

** Just one of Pryce-Jones' innovatory products was his patented *Euklisia Rug* - an all-in-one rug, shawl, blanket and pillow. None survive, but records show that they were used in the Australian outback, the Congo jungle, and by armies across Europe. A reproduction was recently made for the BBC series *A History of the World in 100 Objects*. An 1877 mailshot tells us that the Russo-Romanian army took the besieged Turkish-controlled Plevna, so he had a surplus of sleeping bags. They were 2 yards 11 inches long, 1 yard and 31 inches wide, and sold for 3 shillings and 11 pence:

'Pryce Jones has the honour of calling the special attention of Ladies to the following. He has on hand seventeen thousand Brown Army Blankets (fitted with an air tight pillow, as per sketch above) which were expressly made for the Russian Army. These are the remains of a Contract of Sixty thousand, delivery of which was to have taken place at the rate of 6,000 per week. Plevna fell, and the order was cancelled. These goods have remained in his possession ever since, carefully packed in bales of fifties. P.J. proposes to clear off the lot at a great sacrifice - he intends removing the air tight pillows and sewing up the slot, the space may, if required, be refilled with a pillow of feathers, wool, cotton or straw, and may in this manner, be utilized for the poor - being a bed and blanket combined.

These are much wider and longer than ordinary rugs. These Blankets may, if desired, be obtained with the patent pillow attached, the cost of each rug would then be 3/- more than price named above. As P.J. offers these goods under cost of production, he solicits and hopes to receive early orders. Royal Warehouse, Newtown, N. Wales.'

SIR HENRY MORTON STANLEY 28 January 1841 - 10 May 1904

JOHN ROWLANDS, 'BREAKER OF ROCKS', THE MAN WHO FOUND LIVINGSTONE and MAPPED THE CONGO

Sir Henry Morton Stanley, of 'Dr Livingstone, I presume' fame, was born in Denbigh, and one of his claims to fame was killing five Africans with four shots from his elephant rifle when attacked. He had loaded the gun with explosive charges as a precaution. Born in 1841 in a cottage outside Denbigh Castle, he was the illegitimate son of John Rowlands and Elizabeth Parry, and was brought up as John Rowlands in St Asaph's workhouse from the age of 6. The overcrowding and lack of supervision meant that he was

frequently abused by older boys. Robert Aldrich suggests that he was raped in 1847 by the headmaster of the workhouse, shortly after he entered the institution. Rowlands escaped to sea as a cabin boy in 1859, and was befriended by the childless Henry Hope Stanley of New Orleans. Rowlands took his benefactor's name.

He fought on both sides in the American Civil War, being injured captured at the terrible battle of Shiloh in 1862 while serving in the Confederate Army's 6th Arkansas Infantry Regiment. To escape the terrible conditions of his Illinois prison camp, he joined the Union Army in June, but was discharged 18 days later due to severe illness. Recovering, he served on several merchant ships before joining the Union Navy in July 1864. On board the *Minnesota*, he became a record keeper, which led him into freelance journalism. Stanley jumped ship in 1865 in New Hampshire. Stanley may well have been the only man to serve in the Confederate Army, the Union Army, and the Union Navy.

Becoming a journalist, he was imprisoned by the Ottoman Empire, becoming one of the *New York Herald's* correspondents in 1867. As a roving reporter, Stanley accompanied the British punitive expedition led by Napier against Theodore II of Abyssinia (Ethiopia), and was the first to relay the news of the fall of its capital, Magdala. As the *Herald's* correspondent, he had travelled across Abyssinia, Asia Minor and Spain, and was told by his editor to find the missing missionary and explorer David Livingstone in 1869. Stanley had lobbied the editor for months for finance for an expedition, and asked how much he could spend. The reply was 'Draw £1,000 now, and when you have gone through that, draw another £1,000, and when that is spent, draw another £1,000, and when you have finished that, draw another £1,000, and so on — BUT FIND LIVINGSTONE!'

The Scot had been seeking the source of the Nile and had not been heard of for years. Stanley left Zanzibar in March 1871, with a force of 200 porters, and found the ailing Livingstone at Ujiji, near Lake Tanganyika on 10 November that same year. His 700-mile expedition through the tropical forest saw many of his carriers desert, and the rest were decimated by tropical diseases. The dangerous trek through different warring tribes, each needing goods to pass through their territories, is brilliantly described in Stanley's *How I Found Livingstone*, still in print.

Stanley was unsure whether to embrace the famous lost man, in the uncharted depths of Africa in front of a crowd of Africans, instead holding back, and greeting him with the formal 'Dr Livingstone, I presume'. Staying with the doctor, Stanley nursed him back to health. He then travelled with Livingstone until February 1872, while they both explored Lake Tanganyika, but Stanley could not persuade the doctor to return home with him.

Upon news of Livingstone's death in 1873, the New York Herald and London's Daily Telegraph jointly financed an expedition to continue Livingstone's work. In 1874, Stanley was sent once again to Africa, becoming the first white man to cross Central Africa from East to West. Stanley's initial mission this time was to report on the British campaign against the Ashanti in Ghana. Stanley followed up Livingstone's researches on the Congo/Zaire and Nile systems, and examined the findings of the other explorers Speke, Burton and Baker. Stanley's further explorations are detailed in *Through The Dark Continent* and *In Darkest Africa*.

Stanley traced the course of the River Zaire (Congo) to the sea from 1874-77, visiting King Mutesa of Buganda, becoming involved in several skirmishes when circumnavigating Lake Tanganyika, and heading west to the Lualaba, a headstream of the Congo. Stanley used sectional boats to pass the great cataracts that separated the Congo into distinct tracts. The boats had to be taken apart and transported around the rapids before being rebuilt to travel on the next section of river. Navigating both rivers as far as Livingstone Falls, which Stanley named in the doctor's honour, his party reached

Stanley meeting Livingstone

the Atlantic in August 1877. He had followed the great Congo over 999 days for 2,000 miles. 242 of his 356 men had died of fever, starvation, murder, dysentery, drowning and in fights with natives. He had to leave 53 men, crippled with leg ulcers and suffering from malnutrition, at the aptly named Starvation Camp. All three of the Europeans who had accompanied him were also dead, and Stanley was to suffer recurring debilitating illnesses for the rest of his life.

Returning to London in 1878, Stanley was given a commission under the sponsorship of King Leopold of Belgium in 1879, and he returned to the Congo for another five years. He constructed a road from the lower Congo to Malebo pool, and laid the foundations for the establishment of the Congo Free State (now Zaire). The Congolese called Stanley *Bula Matari*, 'Breaker of Rocks'. As the leader of Leopold's expedition, he commonly worked with the labourers breaking rocks with which they built the first modern road along the River Congo. By 1884 he had carved out a huge colony in Central Africa for his friend and employer on this mission, King Leopold.

In yet another expedition, Stanley charted much of the unexplored African interior between 1887 and 1889, when he led an expedition to relieve Emin Pasha (the German explorer Eduard Schnitzer, governor of the Equatorial Province of the Egyptian Sudan). Emin Pasha was surrounded by rebellious Mahdist forces, but refused to return to Egypt. Not until the end of 1890 did Stanley persuade Emin Pasha to return to the coast under Stanley's escort. However, the expedition tarnished Stanley's name because of the conduct of some British gentlemen and army officers. An army major, Edmund Barttelot, was shot by an African porter, after behaving with extreme cruelty.

As Stanley's second in command Barttlot was leader of the Rear Column which was left in the jungle to wait for more porters to be brought by an Arab slave trader, while Stanley marched on to reach Emin as soon as possible. During Stanley's absence, Barttelot was unable to maintain discipline, and resorted to repeated floggings of Africans, a least two of whom died from the beatings. Large numbers of bearers from the Manyema tribe died from malnutrition and untreated illness or deserted. When he threatened a woman with his revolver after she was beating a drum during a ceremony in the early hours of the morning, he was shot dead by the woman's husband, a man named Samba. Stanley received reports about Barttelot's behaviour from other officers. One, William Bonny, said that 'the least thing caused the Major to behave like a fiend' and that he would repeatedly stab African workers with a steel-pointed cane. Another said that the Major 'had an intense hatred of anything in the shape of a black man.' A 13 year-old boy named Sudi had been beaten and kicked by him. Stanley nursed the injured Sudi, who died 6 weeks after Stanley returned. Furious, Stanley mainly blamed Barttelot for the failure of the Rear Column, though he also criticised the other officers for allowing him to 'kick, strike and slay human beings'. Adam Hochschild wrote in *King Leopold's Ghost* that after being left in charge of the Rear Column: 'Major Barttelot promptly lost his mind. He sent Stanley's personal baggage down the river. He dispatched another officer on a bizarre three-thousand-mile three-month round trip to the nearest telegraph station to send a senseless telegram to England. He next decided that he was being poisoned, and saw traitors on all sides. He had one of his porters lashed three-hundred times (which proved fatal). He jabbed at Africans with a steel-tipped cane, ordered several dozen people put in chains, and bit a village woman. After trying to interfere with a native festival, an African shot and killed Barttelot before he could do more.' Some have said that Stanley was the source for Kurtz in Joseph Conrad's novel *Heart of Darkness*, but it was Barttelot.

James Sligo Jameson, heir to Jameson's Irish whiskey, bought an 11-year-old girl and offered her to cannibals, so he could document and sketch how she was cooked and eaten. Stanley found out only when Jameson had died of fever. Stanley had found the Mountains of the Moon (the Ruwenzori Range, mentioned by Ptolemy), and discovered that the Semliki River linked Lake Albert to Lake Edward. Stanley Falls, Stanley Pool and Stanleyville have now been renamed Boyoma Falls, Pool Malebo and Kisangani. These vast lands became known as the British East African Protectorate, but not until 1899, aged 58 was Stanley awarded the GCB and became Sir H.M. Stanley.

On his return he had married Dorothy Tennant, of Cadoxton Lodge, Neath, in 1890. For a short time he was an MP for North Lambeth. Stanley travelled on lecturing tours almost until the end of his life, through America, Germany and Australia. He made one more visit to his beloved Africa in 1897. Stanley had wished to be buried in Westminster Abbey, but the dean refused, presumably because Stanley's birth certificate described him as a 'bastard' and the slur affected him all his life. Stanley was instead interred near his home at Pirbright, Surrey. This poor Welsh urchin ended up a celebrated explorer, author, MP and with the Grand Cross of the Order of the Bath. As with Glyndŵr, Bart Roberts, Llywelyn ap Gruffudd, William Williams (Penrose) and Owain Lawgoch, this Welshman's life would make a wonderful film.

BILL FROST 28 May 1848 – March 1935

THE FIRST MAN TO FLY, THE PIONEER OF AIR TRAVEL

Born in Saundersfoot, he designed an early flying machine, the Frost Airship Glider. Frost was a religious man, and became deacon of his local chapel. He was also an accomplished musician and founded the Saundersfoot Male Voice Choir.

Upon 26 July 1998, *The Sunday Times* carried a long feature 'Welsh airman beat Wrights to the skies'. Andrew Alderson wrote that Welsh carpenter, Bill Frost, flew in summer 1896: 'Until now, history has credited the Wright brothers with conquering the skies. But new evidence suggests that their famous flight was not the first. Seven years before them, Frost is said to have set off in a "flying machine" from a field in Pembrokeshire and stayed in the air for 10 seconds. Newly discovered documents reveal that Frost, from Saundersfoot, Pembrokeshire, applied to register a patent for his invention – a cross between an airship and a glider – in 1894. It was approved the following year and detailed how the invention was propelled upwards by two reversible fans. Once in the air, the wings spread and are tilted forward "causing the machine to move, as a bird, onward and downward." A fan is used to help the aircraft "soar upward", while the steering is done by a rudder at both ends.

Crucially, locals in the Welsh seaside resort insist that the aircraft was built and flown within a year of the patent being approved. Yesterday experts on both sides of the Atlantic believed that the name of William Frost, not the Wright Brothers, deserves pride of place in aviation record books as the first pioneer of manned, sustained and powered flight. Historians, descendants and a former neighbour of Frost are convinced that only his modesty – in failing to acclaim his role or having a photograph of the flight – meant his achievements went unacclaimed. Roscoe Howells, the historian and writer, used to be a neighbour of Frost in Saundersfoot and heard an account of the flight from the inventor himself. "He became airborne, so he said, and I would never believe that Bill Frost was a liar or romancer," said Howells. "His flying machine took off, but the undercarriage caught in the top of a tree and it came down into a field. If he hadn't caught it in the tree, he would have been right over the valley over Saundersfoot and it would have been death or glory." Nina Ormonde, Frost's great great-granddaughter, said: "Our family has always known that he was the first to fly, he flew for 500 to 600 yards.

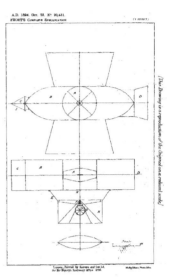

Frost's glider plans

But Bill gave up on it and there is no point in our revelling in the glory because it was his achievement." Frost's flying machine was 31 feet long and made of bamboo, canvas and wire mesh, with hydrogen-filled pouches to attain "neutral buoyancy."'

The later flight by Orville Wright in 1903 lasted just 12 seconds. Alderson describes Bill Frost as a carpenter and builder on the nearby Hean Castle estate, who was a deacon of the chapel and founded the local male voice choir. 'His determination to fly his aircraft after the initial flight was defeated by bad luck and lack of money. Although he repaired his machine after hitting the tree, it was later ripped from its moorings and damaged by gales, apparently in the autumn of 1896. He later travelled to London and tried to get funding from the government's war department.

According to Frost's descendants, he received several approaches from foreign governments for the rights to his patent, but refused on the grounds of patriotism. The revelations about Frost's design and flight have been uncovered by Jill Waters, a producer, and Patrick French, a presenter, for Radio 4's *Flying Starts*: 'The Wright Brothers had the benefit of independent witnesses, log books full of technical data and, most important, photographic evidence', said French. 'Yet there are compelling reasons for thinking that the first person to fly was Bill Frost.' In an interview given in 1932, three years before his death, Frost described himself as 'the pioneer of air travel'. Then aged 85 and blind, he spoke of his disappointment and lack of funding after St John Brodrick, Under-Secretary of State at the War Office, dismissed his efforts, writing, 'the nation does not intend to adopt aerial navigation as a means of warfare'.

'Jeff Bellingham, a Gloucester-born mechanical engineer now living in Minnesota, first discovered Frost's invention after reading Howells' local history book and deciding, on a whim, to see if the inventor had a patent. Bellingham intends to build a replica, first a quarter-size and later a full-size one, of Frost's aircraft. "I believe it will fly and that afterwards people will acknowledge history books are wrong," Bellingham said. Bellingham is looking for sponsors in the Lake Elmo area of Minnesota to build a £25,000 quarter-size model of the 1896 craft. Having tracked down the patent, Bellingham also intends to build a £180,000 full-sized replica and fly it from the same field in Saundersfoot. Bleriot crash-landed in Dover in 1909, a full thirteen years after Frost's flight. Some people claim that Gustave A. Whitehead flew in 1901 in Connecticut, before the Wright's first controlled powered flight in 1903. However, there are no claims for such a flight prior to Frost's in 1896.'

According to T.G. Sticking's *The Story of Saundersfoot*, Frost's machine was 'a triplane, but made only one flight - on a night when a gale was raging - when it took to the air, unpredictably, and landed two miles away, in pieces!' Designed to take to the air by means of a horizontal fan, with the assistance of a cylinder filled with hydrogen, once in the air the machine would glide for a while on its wings. When more height was required, the wings would be tilted upwards and the fan used again. The *Pembrokeshire Herald and General Advertiser* on 11 October 1895 stated that Frost had a provisional patent for his flying machine invention, and had been engaged on the project since 1880, a period of fifteen years. He gave a press interview in 1932, when blind and poor, just three years before his death, claiming to have flown. He said that as a carpenter aged 28, in 1876, he had been momentarily lifted off the ground in a high wind, when carrying a long plank. From then on he had become obsessed with trying to fly, and in the early 1890's had been seen by onlookers running around a filed with a sheet of zinc strapped to his head. His wife and daughter had recently died, and people put it down to temporary madness induced by grief. A devout chapel man, people believed his story that he had built the plane in his garden workshop at St Bride's Hill, and that he had flown in it.

His original patent description of 30 August 1895, reads: 'the flying machine is constructed with an upper and lower chamber of wirework, covered with light waterproof material. Each chamber formed sharp at both ends with parallel sides. The upper large chamber to contain sufficient gas to lift the machine. In the centre of the upper chamber a cylinder is fixed in which a horizontal fan is driven by means of a shaft and bevelled gearing worked from the lower chamber. When the machine has been risen to a sufficient height, then the fan is stopped and the upper chamber, which has wings attached, is tilted forward causing the machine to move as a bird, onward and downward. When low enough it is again tilted in an opposite direction which causes it to soar onward and upward, when it is again assisted if necessary by the fan. The steering is done by a rudder at both ends.'

Roscoe Howells was born in 1920, remembering Bill Frost well, and him telling his father about the flight. Locals know the field where it flew, and they can point to the tree into which it crashed. In his 2007 *A Pembrokeshire Pioneer* Howells gives a description of the flying machine as 'part balloon (gas cylinders gave it lift), part powered hang glider, foot-pedals operating helicopter-style blades.' His flight was or about 24 September 1896. Observers said the machine flew over 500 yards, then crashed into bushes, well outdistancing the 120 feet in 12 seconds by the Wright brothers in their first powered flight, which did not feature a vertical takeoff. During the night following the flight, a violent storm destroyed and scattered the flying machine. To Frost's misfortune, the event was not recorded except in local memories, and he could not afford to build a new plane. Howells checked for records of the local storm which wrecked the plane, and found in the *Tenby and County News* of 30 September 1896 the headline 'GREAT STORM'. Frost had said that his plane, tethered to a tree, was smashed irreparably in a terrible storm just a few days after his flight of 26 September.

In the book, Howells said that a man showed him the field where his grandmother had said the flight had occurred. A very old baker, who had delivered bread to his family, showed him the tree where, as a boy of three, he had seen the wreckage. A schoolmate remembered what his father had said, that Frost, after his fall into the brambles, had spent a whole day pulling thorns out of his face. Men remembered the classroom scene when a teacher, telling the children that the Wright brothers had been the first to fly, had been confronted by Frost's grand-daughter who told her very politely that no, it had been her grandfather, and, though small, would not be shaken. Although a poor working man, Frost had applied for a patent which was accepted and registered in London on 25 October 1894 under number 1894-20431. Unable to pay renewal fees, he allowed the patent to lapse four years later. He died aged 87, almost blind, without wealth or recognition in 1935. Phil Carradice wrote: 'Everyone who knew him was clear that Bill Frost was the most truthful of men. If he said that he had flown then he most certainly had done so.'

SIDNEY GILCHRIST THOMAS 16 April 1850 – 1 February 1885

THE MAN WHO CREATED THE MODERN STEEL INDUSTRY, INVENTOR OF THE CARNEGIE PROCESS

Born in Canonbury, London, Sidney Gilchrist Thomas had to give up his dreams of studying medicine when his father died in 1867. William Thomas, his father, was from Llanafan, Ceredigion, and had married Melicent Gilchrist of Cardigan before working for the Inland Revenue in London. Forced to leave Dulwich College for lack of finances, Sidney worked for a short while as a teacher in Essex, and then took a post as a junior clerk at London's Marlborough Street police court. He held this clerk's job for many years, while devoting most of his evenings and other leisure time to studying science, especially chemistry.

Bild 354
Sidney Gilchrist Thomas, 1850–1885
Nach R. W. Burnie: Memoirs and Letters of Sidney Gilchrist Thomas,
London 1891

When Bessemer revolutionised steel making with his 'process'* of using a converter to make bulk steel in 1856, he did not know that it could not be used for iron ores that included phosphorous. He had used pig iron from Blaenafon, which was phosphorous-free. Phosphorous made steel very brittle, and was present in over 90% of European iron ores, and around 98% of American ore. The 1856 'basic Bessemer Process' of steel production had been invented by a Welshman, George Parry, chemist at the Ebbw Vale ironworks. It was sold to Bessemer for the enormous sum of £30,000 (-worth £20 million today using the average earnings index.) Parry received £10,000 and the owners of the ironworks received £20,000. Parry had used pig iron from Blaenafon, which was phosphorous-free, which had massive implications.

Henry Bessemer was trying to design guns, and needed to know how to manufacture better quality iron in greater quantities. The 'Bessemer Process' involves a converter where air is blown through molten cast iron to make bulk steel. The violent reaction removed carbon from the iron, making mild steel instead of wrought iron. The process could not be used for iron ores that included phosphorous, so non-phosphoric ores had to be expensively imported from Sweden or Spain for the process.

From 1870, Sidney Gilchrist Thomas had been engaged in experimentation, to solve the problem of de-phosphorising pig iron to make steel. In the other main process used in steel making, the Siemens-Martin process, the problem of brittle steel also occurred, and steel-foundries across the world were employing the greatest scientists of the age to solve the problem. Towards the end of 1875, Sidney Gilchrist Thomas found a provisional solution, and passed his findings to his cousin, the industrial chemist Percy Gilchrist (1851-1935), then working at a large iron-works in Blaenafon.

Both men carried out more experiments. In 1877 the cousins found out how to remove the phosphorous. In 1878 he sensationally announced to the Iron and Steel Institute of Great Britain his invention, and took out his first patent. On 4 April 1879, the experiments carried out by Sidney in his home laboratory, and at Blaenafon by Percy, were confirmed in a demonstration in Middlesbrough with a 15,000 kg converter. Steel producers from all over the world rushed to London to buy the 'exploiting licence' of the new patent. Just one example is The Luxembourg-German producer Metz & Cie, which obtained its licence just 16 days after the successful trial, and immediately built a new steelworks to take advantage of the process.

The basis of Thomas's invention was replacing the acidic fireclay refractory lining in the Bessemer converter. Instead he used a basic lining of calcined dolomite. The addition of limestone then allowed the formation of a basic slag which absorbed the phosphorous, as it was oxidised from the molten metal. Differently-lined Bessemer converters were adopted across Europe, and the process was also used by the open-hearth steelmakers. This was the 'basic process' used across the world until the introduction of the 'Basic Oxygen process', which also relies upon Thomas's invention.

Steel production worldwide soared, which led to a great increase in the amount of slag remaining in converters. Because Thomas's process was known as 'basic', as he had added a chemically basic lining to the converter, the phosphorous-rich residue was called 'basic slag'. Thomas experimented upon it, and discovered that it made an excellent soil fertiliser. This phosphate-rich fertiliser is called *Thomasmehl* (meal of Thomas) in German, and cheaply-produced phosphate-rich fertilisers revolutionised agricultural production.

An obelisk in Blaenafon commemorates the cousins for the 'invention (which) pioneered the basic Bessemer or Thomas process'. Andrew Carnegie (1835-1919) bought the rights to the 'Thomas process', and then made a fortune in the USA and elsewhere from what is known today as his 'Carnegie Process' (replicating George Parry's sale of his 'process' to Bessemer.) Carnegie admitted that the Carnegie Process was not his, stating: 'These two men, Thomas and Gilchrist of Blaenavon, did more for Britain's greatness than all the kings and queens put together. Moses struck rock and brought forth water. They struck the useless phosphoric ore and transformed it into steel, a far greater miracle. Sidney Gilchrist Thomas's invention allowed the manufacture of high-grade steel using ores with phosphorous content, opening up the vast reserves of phosphoric ores to steel production across the world. His discovery vastly accelerated industrial expansion in Europe and America. These refiners of the Bessemer process and inventors of the Carnegie Process had changed the world.'

Sidney Gilchrist Thomas's invention allowed the manufacture of high-grade steel using ores with phosphorous content, opening up the vast reserves of phosphoric ores to steel production across the world. In 1890, Britain was the world's greatest steel producer, but by 1902 this great invention had allowed Carnegie, and Krupp of Essen to propel the USA and Germany into the first two places in steel production. Germany was not a serious rival to Britain in steel production until the *minette*, the phosphoric ores of Lorraine, were made available by the Gilchrist-Thomas process. R.C.K. Ensor stressed that 'the discovery created a gigantic German steel industry which would not have been possible without it; and this, which by 1895 had a larger output than the British, played a very important part in predisposing Germany to aggressive war and enabling her after 1914 to sustain and prolong it.'

Not until 1879 had Thomas resigned his clerkship, and was in extremely poor health owing to his work with chemicals. He pursued health cures overseas in his few remaining years, dying in Paris at the age of 35. He was buried at Passy cemetery, near the Eiffel Tower. His large and accumulating fortune was left on trust to his sister Lilian to be dispersed in charitable causes. Blaenafon Ironworks opened in 1789, was one of the largest in the world, operating until 1900. The remains, the best-preserved in Western Europe, are open to visitors. This historically important site includes a bank of three blast furnaces, casting houses, water balance lift and workers' cottages, and is presently in the care of CADW. Blaenafon is so internationally important in its archaeological remains that it has recently become a 'World Heritage Site'. Blaenafon has also become a Booktown, following the path laid down by the inestimable King Richard Booth of Hay-on-Wye.

* **The Bessemer Process and George Parry**: The Bessemer Process was actually invented by a Welshman, George Parry of Ebbw Vale, who sold it to Bessemer for the enormous sum of £10,000. Steel is a major component in buildings, infrastructure, tools, ships, cables, cars, machines, appliances, and weapons. While blast furnaces produced cast iron with great efficiency, the process of refining cast iron into the far more useful malleable wrought iron remained comparatively inefficient. (It was called 'wrought iron' because it had been usually worked, or wrought, by hand). Demand for wrought iron reached its peak in the 1860s with the building of railways and adaptation of ironclad warships, but then declined drastically as cheaper mild (low carbon) steel became available. Steel had been extremely expensive, having been produced by various inefficient methods long before the Renaissance, but its use had become more common after more efficient production methods were devised in the 17th century.

In 1850 great economy in blast furnace practice was achieved at the Ebbw Vale ironworks. George Parry, Abraham Darby's chemist there, was the first to successfully to adopt the cup and cone on blast furnaces, which was then adopted across Europe. The process had independently discovered in 1851 in the USA by William Kelly (1811-1888), but bankruptcy forced Kelly to sell his patent to Henry Bessemer, who was working along similar lines. Bessemer also paid the Ebbw Vale Company £30,000 for their patents on steel making. George Parry received £10,000 for his steel-making process, which was similar amount to Kelly's. Parry's patented steel process in turn had been purchased in 1855 from the American J.G Martien, and improved. Bessemer used Parry's patents for the patented invention of his 'Bessemer process' 1855, whereby steel soon became an inexpensive mass-produced material, made from molten pig-iron. The key principle is to remove impurities from the iron by oxidation, with air being blown through the molten iron. The oxidation also raises the temperature of the iron mass and keeps it molten. The process of using a basic refractory lining became known as the 'basic Bessemer process' and the later improvement as the 'Gilchrist-Thomas process'. Thus the 'Bessemer Process' was invented by Martien, Parry and Thomas, not Bessemer. Further refinements such as BOS (basic oxygen steelmaking), lowered the cost of production while increasing quality.

DAVID LLOYD GEORGE 17 January 17 1863 - 26 March 1945

ONE OF THE GREATEST STATESMEN OF THE 20TH CENTURY, 'THE MAN WHO WON THE WAR', 'THE GREATEST PRIME MINISTER SINCE PITT,' 'THE GREATEST WELSHMAN... SINCE THE AGE OF THE TUDORS'

He was the son of William George of Pembrokeshire and Elizabeth Lloyd of Llanystumdwy, Caernarfonshire, and was born in Manchester, where his father was teaching. His ailing father took his family and returned to farm in Pembrokeshire three months after David's birth, but died fifteen months later of pneumonia. His widow took her children to live with Richard Lloyd, David's uncle at Tŷ Newydd, Llanystumdwy. David George adopted his uncle Richard's surname to become David Lloyd George. Lloyd was a Welsh-speaking Nonconformist shoemaker, deeply resenting English dominance over Wales, and had a lasting influence upon his nephew. David grew up Welsh-speaking and did well at school, passed the Law Society examinations, and in 1879 was articled to a firm of solicitors in Porthmadoc, before setting up his own law practice in Cricieth. In 1888 he married Margaret Owen, and was an active member of the Disciples of Christ Chapel in Cricieth. His reputation grew as a fiery orator in Welsh and English in church, and as a man who was willing to defend people against those in authority.

Joining the local Liberal Party, David became an alderman on Caernarfonshire County Council. A great supporter of Land Reform, he took part in demonstrations against church tithes. From 1890-96, Lloyd George was leader of the Welsh Home Rule Campaign, but the failure of the Cymru Fydd movement was assured in 1896, when businessmen from Cardiff and Newport blocked the Liberal party's support for Welsh self-government. Lloyd George now turned his attentions from Welsh affairs to 'the country as a whole'.

In 1890, Lloyd George had been selected as the candidate for the Conservative parliamentary seat of Caernarfon Borough. He fought on a platform of religious equality in Wales, land reform, graduated taxation, free trade and a local veto in granting licences on alcohol. He won by just 18 votes, and at 27 became the youngest member of the House of Commons. His great powers of oratory brought him to the attention of Liberal leaders in the House, but because of his radicalism, and his opposition to the Boer War, they felt he would lose his seat in the 1900 election. However, Lloyd George won comfortably - he was seen as the most important figure in Parliament defending Welsh rights. He also incurred the displeasure of the Liberal bigwigs in supporting the 1902 Education Act, in particular for assisting John Clifford's National Passive Resistance Committee. Over 170 Nonconformists had been sent to prison for refusing to pay their school taxes - Lloyd George advocated free schooling for all.

The Liberal Party had surged into power in Wales with its opposition to landlords and anti-establishment policies, and by the turn of the 20th century was virtually in total control. In the 1906 election, the Liberal Henry Campbell-Bannerman became the new Prime Minister, appointing the capable Lloyd George as President of the Board of Trade. David impressed him so much, that in 1908 he was promoted to become Chancellor of the Exchequer. Previously as Minister for the Board of Trade (1905-1908) he had been responsible for the passing of three important acts involving merchant shipping, the production census and patents. He introduced Old Age Pensions (1908) and National Health Insurance (1911) when Chancellor of the Exchequer from 1908-1915. A fierce opponent of the Poor Law, the Chancellor wanted to 'lift the shadow of the workhouse from the homes of the poor.' The rejection of his budget by The House of Lords, with its Conservative majority, in 1909-1910 led to Parliamentary reform and a lessening of the nobility's power.

Lloyd George toured the country, making speeches in working-class areas, against the 'nobles with no nobility' who were using their privileged position to hurt the poor and stop old age pensions.

He called it a 'war budget. It is for raising money to wage implacable warfare against poverty and squalidness.' Because of the ensuing unpopularity of the House of Lords*, the Liberal government managed to cut its powers in the 1911 Parliament Act. The 1911 National Insurance Act gave the British working classes the first contributory system of insurance against illness and unemployment. All wage earners between 16 and 70 had to join the health scheme, the worker paying 4d a week, the employer 3d and the state 2d. In return there was free medical attention and medicine, and workers were guaranteed 7 shillings a week for 15 weeks in any one-year, if they were unemployed. The Conservative opposition and the House of Lords declaimed Lloyd George as a 'socialist'. His measures formed the basis of the Welfare State that until recently gave a reasonable safety net to the disadvantaged in Britain.

A radical Welsh nationalist and a pacifist, he had compared the Boers, in their fight against the Empire, to the Welsh. He only moved from pacifism with the invasion of Belgium by Germany in 1914. Even so, with three other senior members of the Government, he had written to the Prime Minister, Herbert Asquith, that he intended to resign rather than be party to a war declaration. The other three resigned, but Asquith managed to convince Lloyd George to stay on, as the country needed him.

In August 1914, the South Wales Miners' Federation proposed an international miners' strike to stop the outbreak of war, and there continued to be an anti-war movement in the South Wales mining areas. A massive increase in food prices, coupled with record profits for coal-owners, caused a demand for a new wage agreement in 1915, which was refused, so the South Wales miners went on strike. The Government, coal-owners, Great Britain Miners' Federation and the national newspapers, opposed them and the government threatened to imprison any strikers. However, the strike was solid. The then Minister of Munitions, David Lloyd George, intervened and personally settled the strike, acceding to most of the demands of the South Wales Miners' Federation.

As Minister of War from 1915-1916, Lloyd George was put in charge of the total war effort, and found it difficult to control the poor and wasteful tactics of his generals of the Western Front. Lloyd George argued strongly with the dinosaur Field-Marshal Douglas Haig, commander in chief of the BEF, and with General Robertson, chief of the imperial general staff, about their using men as cannon-fodder. When at last Lloyd George's proposal was accepted, that the French and British forces fight under one joint commander, the war turned decisively the allies' way. However, he was more successful with the navy, when he with great difficulty persuaded them to use the convoy system to ensure adequate imports of food and military supplies. The Coalition Government was impressed by Lloyd George's capabilities and began to question Asquith's leadership in these days of crisis.

In December 1916, Lloyd George agreed to collaborate with the Conservatives to remove Asquith, a decision that split the Liberal Party. Lloyd George was now Prime Minister, and his Coalition Party won the 1918 General Election, Asquith losing his seat. In 1916, Lloyd-George was welcomed into No. 10 Downing Steet by Maurice Hankey, later War Cabinet Secretary. 'I congratulated him' said Lord Hankey later, and he replied slowly 'You are shaking hands with the most miserable man on earth.' However, Lloyd George was now virtually a prisoner of the Conservative party after the war, and although he promised progressive reforms in education, housing, health and transport, he was unable to effect them. He was defeated in the 1922 election.

For the rest of his career he was a campaigner, but with no power base - the Tories did not want change, and the Liberals distrusted him as the man who broke up their party. Just two months before his death, he received the title Earl Lloyd-George of Dwyfor.

By his forceful policy he was, as Adolf Hitler later said, 'the man who won the war'. One of the 'Big Three' at the peace negotiations, he was shown to be a brilliant diplomat. Lloyd George mediated a settlement with Germany mid-way between Woodrow Wilson, and the more punitive actions desired by Clemenceau, as France had lost so much in the Great War. His defeat in 1922 was mainly due to his ceding of 'The Irish Free State' - the modern day Eire was given its independence by him against strong opposition by the Conservatives in his government. Lloyd George is also notable in world history for approving the Balfour Declaration, promising the Jews a national state in Palestine. So Wales has had a world statesman who has changed the face of the twentieth century.

* In an editorial for *Udgorn* in 1888, Lloyd George wrote of the House of Lords: 'This institution is at odds with the spirit of the age... the true basis of any government is the voice of the people... the House of Lords has won for itself a reputation as the arch enemy of every reform... a man of the weakest understanding or with the most tarnished of characters may sit in this noble house... it is readily conceded even by Tories that the House of Lords should be reformed, however total abolition of this place is the only reform worth fighting for... to include the fall of this God of oppression among the victories of liberty would give reason to rejoicing for generations to come.'

Footnote:
The only other 'great' British Prime Minister of the 20th century was a war-leader but no reformer, Winston Churchill. On Lloyd George's death in 1945, Churchill told the Commons: 'He was the greatest Welshman which that unconquerable race has produced since the age of the Tudors. Much of his work abides, some of it will grow greatly in the future, and those who come after us will find the pillars of his life's toil upstanding, massive and indestructible.' A

statue of Lloyd George, funded by charitable donations, was erected in Parliament Square in 2007.

FRANK LLOYD WRIGHT 8 June 1867 – 9 April 1959

'THE GREATEST AMERICAN ARCHITECT OF ALL TIME'

Frank Lloyd Wright, the leading 20th century architect, along with Le Corbusier, was so proud of his Welsh heritage that he called the Wisconsin home he built for himself, 'Taliesin'*, after the legendary Welsh bard (q.v.). Another home and school, Taliesin West, was built near Phoenix, Arizona in 1938. A controversial and daring architect, his weekend home of Fallingwater (near Pittsburgh) is famous world-wide, as was the earthquake-proof Imperial Hotel in Tokyo, and the brilliantly designed Guggenheim Museum of Modern Art in New York. His mother had been born in Llandysul and his Welsh upbringing is described lovingly in his sister's book *The Valley of the God Almighty Joneses*** (by Maginel Wright Barney). He used Iolo Morganwg's motto '*Y Gwir yn Erbyn y Byd*', 'The Truth Against the World.'

Franks' mother Hannah (Anna) Lloyd Jones was a teacher before she married William Carey Wright, a widower with three children. Frank was the first child of William and Hannah, born in Richland Center, Wisconsin. Growing up, Frank spent his summer months on the farm of James Lloyd Jones in Wisconsin. He wrote in his autobiography: 'I learned to know the ground plan of the region in every line and feature. For me now its elevation is the modelling of the hills, the weaving and fabric that clings to them, the look of it all in tender green or covered in snow or in full glow of summer that bursts into the glorious blaze of autumn. I still feel myself as much a part of it as the birds and bees are, and the red barns.' He also referred to his immigrant grandfather, Richard Lloyd Jones: 'He was in league with the stones of the  field and he taught his children to work hard until the valley blossomed like a garden. His New Wales. He planted a small world within the world that is again within other worlds, without end.'

In 1885, aged 18, Wright's parents divorced, and his preacher-musician father left the family in Madison, Wisconsin. Wright never saw his father again, and had to help support his mother and two sisters. Frank took a part-time job as a draughtsman with Allan Conover, the University of Wisconsin engineering professor, and from 1886 attended the University as a 'special student'. From 1887-89 Frank worked for Chicago architects Adler and Sullivan, and in 1889 married Catherine Lee Tobin. A year later, their first child, Lloyd Lloyd Wright, was born. Wright recognised Louis Sullivan as a great influence, who based his designs on natural themes, saying 'form follows function'. Wright lated developed this idea further, believing that 'form and function are one.' By now he was designing all residential buildings for Adler and Sullivan, including his own home in Oak Park, Illinois. 1892 saw the birth of John Lloyd Wright.

In 1893, Wright was forced to leave the firm and open his own architectural practice (he was discovered taking on outside commissions), and his first revolutionary masterpiece was the 'Winslow House' in River Forest, Illinois. His 'organic architecture' idea meant that his buildings tried to form a natural link between mankind and his environment. Notable designs followed, called his 'prairie house' phase, where homes reflected the long, low horizontal prairie, with low-pitched roofs, deep overhangs, and long rows of casement windows emphasising the horizontal theme. Native materials were used, and the wood was always stained, never painted, to show the natural beauty. He was the chief practitioner of the 'Prairie School' of architecture.

He held his first exhibition in Chicago in 1894, the year in which Catherine Lloyd Wright was born. Another exhibition followed in 1895, with a son David being born, followed by Frances Lloyd Wright in 1898. His commissions were now becoming grander, and by 1900 he was lecturing upon architecture to the American Architectural League. In 1903, Robert Llewellyn Wright was born. In 1905, Frank and Catherine made their first trip to Japan, accompanied by some clients, and he became a serious collector of Japanese prints. In 1909 Wright took his family to Europe for further inspiration, and in 1911 began work on a new studio and home, Taliesin, near Spring Green, Wisconsin. His publications and buildings gained him international acclaim at this time. 1913 saw the architect in Japan securing the commission for the Imperial Hotel, but in 1914 disaster struck. A crazed servant killed a client's wife, her two children and four others, and set fire to Taliesin. Wright began to rebuild it, as Taliesin II. 1916 saw the building of the Imperial Hotel, with Wright personally supervising in Tokyo, and in 1918 he visited China. His first honour came in 1919, with the citation of 'Kenchiko Ho, Royal Household Japan'. He constructed other buildings there. In 1922, Catherine and Frank divorced and in 1923 he married Miriam Noel. That same year saw the great Kanto earthquake that demolished much of Tokyo, but the Imperial Hotel survived.

Miriam Noel and Wright separated in 1923, and he met Olga Lazovich (Olgivanna), who gave birth to a daughter, Iovanna in 1925. There was another fire at Taliesin, and Taliesin III was built. 1926 was a bad year, as Taliesin was repossessed by the Bank of Wisconsin for debts incurred by Wright in its rebuilding. He and Olgivanna were also arrested near Minneapolis for violating the Mann Act, a law that prohibited taking women across a state border for immoral purposes. In 1927 he divorced Miriam and the following year married Olgivannaa. Also in 1928, a group of friends and admirers clubbed together to buy Taliesin from the bank and return it to Frank. He received honours from Belgium and Germany, but the great stock-market crash of October 29, 1929, halted all his work for a time. He turned more to lecturing, touring and trained young architects at Taliesin.

1932 saw the publication of his autobiography and *The Disappearing City*, influencing several generations of young architects.From now on was a halcyon period for Wright, with honours accruing across the world as his value was recognised. In 1937 he bought 800 acres near

Taliesin West

Phoenix, Arizona and began construction of Taliesin West, and in 1938 was on the cover of *Time* magazine. Taliesin West was his 'architectural laboratory' for the next 20 years, where he experimented with designs and structures, and taught students in winter. 1935's house 'Fallingwater', built on a waterfall in the Pennsylvania countryside, and other designs had brought a new flood of commissions, but World War II again interrupted his work. In 1941, he was made a member of RIBA by King George VI, and in 1951 his exhibition 'Sixty Years of Living Architecture' opened in Florence, before going to Zurich, Paris, Munich, Rotterdam., Mexico, New York and Los Angeles. Although most of his designs had been residential, in 1957, 35 of his 59 new projects were for public buildings. It is remarkable that in 1958, in his 90's, he received another 31 new commissions.

Frank Lloyd Wright spent over 70 years creating designs that revolutionised the art and architecture of the 20th century. Of the 1141 works he designed, from houses to bridges, offices to churches, 532 were built and 409 still stand, many open to the public. Over a third of his buildings are in the USA's National Register of Historic Places or in a National Historic District. He tried to achieve rooms that flowed into each

351

other, moving away from the 19th century 'box-plan' houses. Wright believed that 'A building is not just a place to be. It is a way to be.' His works show an instinctive understanding of social and human needs, with a superb command of the use of natural, local materials. He also designed furniture fabrics, glass, tableware, and was influential in graphic arts. He described architecture as 'frozen music', and an excellent pianist, he experimented with rhythm and composition in his designs. The eminent architect Charles Montooth wrote: 'Frank Lloyd Wright came upon the American scene at precisely the right moment for what his mother had decided he would become - an architect. He was born in a booming, building, expanding nation to which he to bring a philosophical and spiritual message in the form of architecture, just the proper medium for a pragmatic people in a material-oriented society to understand. He was a unique creative force in the world for fine art. It was as if the talents of a Bach, a Beethoven, and a Schoenberg were combined in one person. He can be compared to Bach, a master of geometry, form and tradition; or Beethoven, a bold innovator breaking with tradition; or Schoenberg, an influential teacher of pupils anxious to follow new paths.'

* Taliesin means 'shining brow', and Frank said 'the hill on which Taliesin now stands as "brow" was one of my favourite places when I was a boy, for pasque flowers grew there in March sun, while snow still streaked the hillsides... I began to build Taliesin to get my back against the wall and fight for what I saw I had to fight.... Taliesin was the name of a Welsh poet, a druid bard who sang to Wales the glories of fine art. Many legends cling to that beloved revered name in Wales.' In a later filmed interview in 1953, Lloyd Wright said 'All my people had Welsh names for their places - my sister's place was called Tan-y-Deri (Under-the-Oaks)'. Taliesin was nominated as a World Heritage Site, as well as being a National Historic landmark. On the estate is still the remarkable 'Tan-y-Deri' building.

** On his maternal side, Wright's grandparents were Richard Jones and Mary (Mallie Thomas). His uncle Thomas Lloyd Jones was a builder, who along with a Welsh stone mason David Timothy helped Wright with his early practical construction experience. Thomas married a Welshwoman Esther Evans. Another uncle was John Jones, a miller who married another Welshwoman, Hannah Reese. John bought the property where Taliesin is situated, which Frank's mother Hannah Lloyd Jones later purchased for him. Wright's aunt Margaret Jones first married Thomas Evans, and on his death married another Thomas Jones. Aunt Mary Jones married Welshman James Phillip. Aunts Nany, Jane and Ellen Jones never married. Uncle Enos Jones married Eleanor Jones, eldest daughter of Thomas Jones, Margaret's second husband. Uncle James Jones seems to have been the only member of the family who married an English/American, Laura Hickox. Thus virtually all of Frank Lloyd Wright's extensive maternal family were Welsh and also married into Welsh families.

BERTRAND RUSSELL 1872 – 2 February 1970

THE 3RD EARL RUSSELL, 'THE 20TH CENTURY'S MOST IMPORTANT LIBERAL THINKER, ONE OF TWO OR THREE OF ITS MAJOR PHILOSOPHERS, AND A PROPHET FOR MILLIONS OF THE CREATIVE AND RATIONAL LIFE'*

His grandfather and Prime Minister Lord John Russell was the architect of the Great Reform Bill of 1832, which began to open up voting to the middle classes. Born in Trellech, Gwent, an orphan from the age of 3, Bertrand Russell was brought up by his grandmother, who tried to train him to become Prime Minister like her husband. Educated in virtual isolation, not until he went to Trinity College, Cambridge in 1890 did he mix with his peers, but easily gained firsts in mathematics and moral sciences. Russell had found to his surprise that he was extremely gifted in philosophy and mathematics, and quickly became a world authority, and an FRS in 1908. Between 1910 and 1913 he jointly authored with Alfred Whitehead the groundbreaking *Principia Mathematica*. His work on the foundations of epistemology, logic and mathematics forced English philosophy in a new direction, towards science, despite the reservations of Wittgenstein.

Russell argued for Free Trade in 1903-04, and supported the Women's Suffrage Movement from 1906-1910. For his speaking against the First World War, which he thought would permanently impair European civilisation, he was fined for anti-war activities and dismissed from Trinity College. Two years later, he was imprisoned for five months. He visited Russia in 1920, hoping that the new society would transcend the warlike nature of capitalist society, and returned appalled by what he had seen. Russell also visited China at this time. In the 1920's and 30's, Russell ran an experimental, pacifist school. He was offered a teaching appointment in City College, New York, but the appointment was rescinded in 1940 because of protests that he was 'morally unfit' to teach.

Along with George Orwell, he was one of the few Western intellectuals not to sympathise with Communist Russia in the 1920's and 1930's. He had seen the real Russia at first-hand. Russell abandoned his advocacy for peace, in the face of Hitler's Fascist onslaught, and spent the

Second World War years in America, where he wrote the superb *History of Western Philosophy*. Returning to Britain in 1944, he now campaigned ceaselessly until the end of his life against nuclear weapons, being the Founding President of the Campaign for Nuclear Disarmament (CND). He was also a passionate opponent of American involvement in Vietnam, and he wished to set up a War Crimes Tribunal to indict the Johnson administration's policy-makers.

An inspiration to younger generations who also saw the futility of nuclear aggression, in 1961 he was imprisoned for anti-nuclear protests. Upon appeal, the 89-year-old served one week in the prison hospital. This author remembers vividly the vitriol poured upon him by the British press, who always prefer war to peace – it sells more newspapers. He spent his last years at his home in North Wales, at Penrhyndeudraeth, and died of influenza, aged 98. When asked what he would say to God if he found himself before Him, Russell answered, 'I should reproach Him for not giving us enough evidence'.

Despite a tangled personal life, involving four wives and many mistresses, Russell was 'with Kurt Godel, one of the two most important logicians of the 20th century', the pioneer of logical positivism, as well as being Britain's most important social critic. In 1949 he received the Order of Merit, and in 1950 the Nobel Prize for Literature. The author of over ninety books, beginning with *German Social Democracy* in 1906, Russell imposed himself upon the fabric of 20th century Britain like no other non-politician. According to Simon Blackburn, 'Russell was the last important public intellectual in Britain. With him, the tradition of Jeremy Bentham and J.S. Mill came to an end.'

* source - McMaster University website

Footnotes:
1. *Russell's Paradox*, according to the *Stanford Encyclopaedia of Philosophy*, was discovered in 1901 when he was working on his *Principles of Mathematics*: 'Russell's Paradox is the most famous of the logical or set-theoretical paradoxes. The paradox arises within naïve set theory by considering the set of all sets that are not members of themselves. Such a set appears to be a member of itself if and only it is not a member of itself, hence the paradox. Some sets, such as the set of all teacups, are not members of themselves. Other sets, such as the set of all non-teacups, are members of themselves. Call the set of all sets that are not members of themselves S. If S is a member of itself, then by definition it must not be a member of itself. Similarly, if S is not a member of itself, then by definition it must be a member of itself. Discovered by Bertrand Russell in 1901, the paradox prompted much work in logic, set theory and the philosophy and foundations of mathematics in the early part of the twentieth century.' I do not understand it, either.

2. Ray Monk's biography of Russell, *The Ghost of Madness*, required him to read Russell's extant output of 60,000 letters, 2,000 articles and 70 books. Monk was asked if Russell and Wittgenstein, 'the Towering Twins of early 20th-century philosophy' could have fitted into modern academic life. He answered 'Oh, that's easy. There's not a university in Britain now that would put up with a Wittgenstein. And Russell wouldn't have put up with a modern university. Genius is not rewarded in universities at present.' Freemasons are, however.

BILLY MEREDITH 30 July 1874 - 19 April 1958

'FOOTBALL'S FIRST SUPERSTAR', 'THE WELSH WIZARD', 'OLD SKINNY', 'THE WIZARD OF THE WING', 'THE KING', FOUNDER OF THE PFA

In Football, the oldest international in the world was William Henry (Billy) Meredith from Black Park, near Chirk, who played right wing for Manchester City, Manchester United, and Wales. At twelve-years-old he was working in Black Park Colliery. The conditions marked him for life, and he decided to become a professional footballer, signing for Ardwick (later Manchester City) for a £5 fee in 1894. He had played as an amateur for Chirk, then almost a season in 1894 as a part-timer for Northwich Victoria at the Drill Field, now the oldest surviving football ground in the world. Northwich was a founder member of the Second Division.

Meredith made his debut while still working down the pit. He scored twice on his home debut and quickly became the favourite player of the supporters. One Friday after working he took the 2am train on Saturday morning to Newcastle, arriving at 11am, played a match and was back home at 10.30pm to go to work the next day. This was his City debut on October 27th, 1894. In 1894, 3 November saw the first-ever Manchester Derby football league match, with 'the Heathens' (Newton Heath, which became Manchester United) playing Manchester City at Ardwick. Both teams had met before in Cup and Alliance matches, but this was the first League meeting. It was Meredith's first home fixture, and although he scored both goals, Newton Heath won 5-2.

This moustachioed lynchpin of the Manchester City team took them to promotion in 1899 and in the next year became their captain. He scored

29 goals in 33 games in his first season in the First Division (today's Premier Division), from his position on the right wing. After temporarily dropping down to the second division again (today's Championship), Meredith captained the team again to promotion in 1903. His trademark was that he chewed a toothpick while playing. Originally, he had chewed tobacco to help him concentrate, but the lady who cleaned his kit complained about the difficulty of removing his stained spit from his shirt, and he took up the toothpick.

As captain, he took Manchester City to the Cup Final in 1904, scored the winner, and took the FA Cup back to Manchester for the first time. He had recently been voted the most popular player in the country by readers of *The Umpire* magazine. The team finished second in the First Division. He had started to become a 'star', on a supposed maximum wage of £4 a week. However, a bribery scandal erupted in 1905, as the FA claimed that Meredith had paid an Aston Villa player £10. Also, the players had been paid £6-7 a week instead of the statutory £4, and 17 City players and 5 directors were suspended. Because of the illegal bonuses, Billy was lucky to play again. Meredith always denied the charge, but he and the entire City team were banned for a year before the suspension was quashed.

Billy then stunned the football world by signing for City's newly promoted bitter rivals, Manchester United, in October 1906, along with four other City players who had also been accused of corruption. They became the backbone of an excellent United team. Meredith was signed first of the City players, by the great United manager Charlie Magnall. He thrilled the United crowds for 15 years, and was their best player, drawing record attendance wherever they played. He also holds the 'oldest Manchester United player' record, and has a place of honour in its football museum. Although officially a 'free transfer', Billy received a £500 signing-on fee, a massive amount of money.

His first game was not until against Aston Villa on 1 January 1907, as his ban ran through all of 1906. The inspired Billy teased the Villa defence, and his cross to Turnbull won the match. They were on their way as a great team. By the end of the season, United had climbed from a lowly position in December 1906 to 8th in the table. As Bobby Charlton stated, Billy Meredith was their 'earliest star'. Football at this time was a 'hard man's game', but Meredith missed hardly any matches as United won the League for the first time in 1908.

He was Manchester United's key player when they won the FA Cup for the first time in 1909, and he became soccer's first media personality, with personal appearances and product endorsements - he was football's first 'superstar' in any country in the world. United beat Brighton away, Everton at home, Blackburn away, then were losing at Burnley when a blizzard halted the match. United won the replay and beat Newcastle, the cup-holders in the semi-final. Newcastle won the league that year. In the final against

Bristol City, Meredith was said to be the difference between the two teams at Crystal Palace in front of 70,000 fans. The players went to the Alhambra Theatre after the game to see the great comedian George Robey. Returning on the train to Manchester on Sunday, they were greeted by a brass band and 300,000 people lined the streets. The maximum attendance of 30,000 people also waited in the Clayton stadium for 3 hours to see the team. (Old Trafford was being built). In 1909 the Charity Shield was won, and in 1911 there was another League Championship.

In his position of authority in the game, Meredith formed and chaired the first meeting of the Professional Footballers' Association at the Imperial Hotel, Manchester. Many unionised players were banned from playing by their clubs, however, and drifted back out of the union, to play for their FA clubs. However, Meredith and the United wing-half Charlie Roberts persisted and formed 'The Outcasts FC' with other United players. Manchester United was suspended by the Football Association, but the new players' union survived by the skin of its teeth, and Meredith was the last player to return to play after the strike for better conditions.

For a long time, only the United players had held out, but Tom Coleman of Everton walked out on his team and sided with the Manchester players, and soon after he was followed by the great north-east clubs of Newcastle, Middlesbrough and Sunderland, then the rest of the Everton team and Liverpool. The FA backed down. The PFA, Professional Footballers' Association, was initially known as 'Meredith's Union', and became affiliated to the National Federation of Trade Unions.

However, World War 1 broke up the fine Manchester United side, with football being suspended from 1915-1918. In these years, Billy guested over 100 times for Manchester City and Stalybridge Celtic, with United's permission. In 1920 he had become then oldest international player on record, on the winning Welsh side against England, aged 45 years and 8 months. In that year, Wales won the international championship for the first time, a fitting end to Meredith's international career. It was the first time that Meredith had been in a winning team against England.

After 332 matches for Manchester United, Billy argued with the club because it would not employ him as a full-time manager, and left on a 'free transfer', aged 48, to rejoin Manchester City as player-coach. According to the 'redcafe' website, his departure was 'the beginning of the end' for United, and in the following season they finished 13th in the league, being ejected from the FA Cup in the first round.

Meredith returned to Manchester City in 1921 for the final three years of a glittering career. Appearing for City, he was the oldest player ever in an FA Cup match, aged 49 years and 8 months in 1924 against Newcastle. In all he played 1,568 matches, including 51 for Wales, still playing for Wales aged 45. Extremely quick, lean, and tall for the times (5 foot 9 inches), Meredith was affectionately known as 'The Welsh Wizard' or 'Old Skinny' to the fans.

He played against England aged almost 46 in 1920, and his international career spanned a record 26-six years, and four decades. Meredith was in the team for Wales' first victory against England, and was selected 71 consecutive times for his country from the age of 21, but only played 46 times because Manchester City often stopped him playing. Meredith played for 30 years in the English First Division and hardly missed a game until he was well into his fifties. Obsessed with training and fitness, he scored nearly 500 goals from his position of outside right, and was a sporting celebrity in his seventies. In 1958 he sent a good luck telegram to Jimmy Murphy's United team in the semi-final of the FA Cup, in the weeks following the Munich Air Disaster, which wiped out the 'Busby Babes'. However, he died in that same year aged 83, and sadly is buried in an unmarked grave in Manchester. The great Stanley Matthews was compared with him, but Meredith could also score goals - he said Matthews 'would never have made the grade in my day'. Billy has been compared to 'the (Stanley) Matthews, (Tom) Finney and (George) Best of his day, all rolled into one'.

Upon his retirement, Billy Meredith took over a pub, although he was a teetotaller, and remained close to both Manchester clubs, scouting and also coaching at Old Trafford from 1931. In April 1925, over 15,000 fans turned up for Billy's testimonial, to see a Manchester XI draw 2-2 with a Glasgow XI. Billy played in the game, aged over 50. In 1926, a full-length film was made of his career, with Billy starring and playing himself as a trainer. A fragment of 45 feet of this film was found a few years ago, so we have some footage of the great man.

D.W. GRIFFITH 22 January 1875 – 23 July 1948

'THE PIONEER OF CINEMA', 'THE FATHER OF FILM', THE TEACHER OF US ALL'

The father of the epic movie, David Lewelyn Wark Griffith – always known as D.W. - used to boast of his Welsh ancestry from Gruffudd ap Llewelyn, King of Wales. His father had been a Confederate veteran, who regaled the young Griffith with tales of bravery and the devastation of the Southern States in the Civil War. Both his parents, Jacob 'Roaring Jake' Griffith and Mary Perkins were of Welsh ancestry. Born in Kentucky, a favourite domicile of expatriate Welshmen, he made hundreds of short films before his masterpieces *The Birth of a Nation* (1915) and *Intolerance* (1916). Other major films made between 1918 and 1922 were *Hearts of the World, Broken*

Blossoms and *Orphans of the Storm. Hearts of the World* broke new ground by showing war scenes actually filmed at the front in World War I.

Griffith revolutionised cinema techniques, innovating the fade-in, fade-out ('dissolve'), close-up and flashback. He elevated moving pictures from an invention to an artistic medium, his epics and masterpieces being  seen and copied all over the world. Not happy at just being an actor in a film, Griffith became a director who made over 450 'short' films between 1908 and 1913. Many big stars had their break at this time, and gained their experience with him, Mary Pickford alone appearing in over 100 of his movies. Other stars 'made' by Griffith included Mack Sennett, Mabel Normand, Lionel Barrymore and Dorothy Gish (Lilian's sister). His assistant directors included Erich von Stroheim, W.S. van Dyke, Tod Browning and Raoul Walsh, all who became top directors themselves.

Influenced by European films, Griffith's first full-length movie was *Judith of Bethulia* in 1914, but his next film *The Birth of a Nation* in 1915 aroused massive controversy. The intimate story of a family torn apart by the Civil War, it featured epic war scenes, and was the most ambitious film ever made. Strongly pro-South, he was forced to alter his views to fund future works. *The Birth of a Nation* made pioneering use of advanced camera and narrative techniques, and its immense popularity set the stage for the dominance of the feature-length film in the United States. Filmed at a cost of $110,000, it returned millions of dollars in profits, making it one of the most profitable films of all time.

Griffith wanted to make a historical blockbuster, and 1916's pacifist *Intolerance* wove together Babylon, Christ's Passion, the St Bartholomew's Day Massacre and a story set in contemporary California. The linking theme was man's intolerance to man. He moved away from the linear narrative of *The Birth of a Nation*, pioneering a new type of film-making, with the stories being told in a parallel mode, and moving back and forwards in time. It infuriated many Americans, who expected the type of film that Mack Sennett was making with his *Keystone Cops* - easy-to-follow plot lines with clear-cut heroes and villains. The film was critically acclaimed in Europe and Russia, but made losses in America. As a result, the amazingly opulent and sexy Babylonian sequence was re-cut and released as *The Fall of Babylon* to try to make profits. His vision of peace was not wanted by a nation preparing for fighting the First World War.

After this epic, Griffith focussed on smaller films, with Lilian Gish in the wonderful *Broken Blossoms* in 1919 and in *Way Down East* in 1920.

In the former a drunken father threatens her, and in the second she insists that her dead baby is baptised. These touching films showed that he could handle, with masterful technical efficiency, intimate story lines, but the 'Roaring Twenties' saw a different style of filmmaker take over. Both films were made for United Artists, but after 1921's *Orphans of the Storm* with Dorothy Gish, neither Gish sister ever worked with Griffith again. In 1915, Griffith had linked up with the other producers Mack Sennett and Thomas Ince, to form Triangle Studios, and the venture lasted until 1919. Its biggest stars, William S. Hart and Douglas Fairbanks, walked out in 1917, after which losses started accumulating. In 1919, Griffith was asked to become part of a daring plan to liberate the screen artist from studio control, and the producer-director joined the fledgling United Artists, co-founding it with the mega-stars Douglas Fairbanks, Charlie Chaplin and Mary Pickford.

In the 1920's Griffith made several features for United Artists, focussing upon his protégée Carole Dempster as the leading lady. *America* in 1924 showed the pride and pitfalls of ambitious patriots in America's history. *Isn't Life Wonderful*, also in 1924, gave Dempster her greatest role, desperately trying to survive in the ruins of post-War Germany. W.C. Fields starred in *Sally of the Sawdust*, a comedy-drama in 1925. Griffith had left his three former partners at United Artists to produce this film. Griffith's last film, in 1931, was only his second 'talkie', *The Struggle*, an ambitious film examining the disease of alcoholism. A film before its time, it sealed his fate, and his last years were wasted, as he could not finance more movies.

In 1936, Woody van Dyke, Griffith's apprentice on Intolerance, asked Griffith to help him shoot the famous earthquake sequence for San Francisco, but did not give him any film credit. Starring Clark Gable, Spencer Tracy and Jeanette MacDonald, it was the top-grossing film of the year. In 1948 Griffith was discovered unconscious in the lobby at the famous Knickerbocker Hotel in Los Angeles, where he had been living alone, and died of a cerebral haemorrhage aged 73.

Film makers across the world respect Griffith's contribution, and Charles Chaplin called Griffith 'The Teacher of us All.' As an example of a hugely talented man, an inspiring pioneer lauded in his lifetime and then wilfully ignored, we can compare him to Orson Welles. Orson Welles said 'I have never really hated Hollywood except for its treatment of D. W. Griffith. No town, no industry, no profession, no art form owes so much to a single man.'

EDWARD THOMAS 3 March 1878 - 9 April 1917

WAR-POET, 'THE POET'S POET', 'THE FATHER OF US ALL'

Philip Edward Thomas was a superb poet, and one of the few Welshmen in recent history to promote Welsh heritage and disdain the English - his book *Beautiful Wales*, published in 1905, has been in print ever since. His tragic death in the First World War in 1917 robbed Europe of a major poet. A line of his that always is remembered, from *Early One Morning*, is 'The past is the only dead thing that smells sweet', and the critic F.R. Leavis called him 'an original poet of rare quality.'

Both his parents were Welsh, his father from Tredegar, and Thomas was born in London, spending his school holidays with relatives in South Wales or Swindon. A nature-lover, he had published articles on natural history before he won a history scholarship to Lincoln College, Oxford, in 1897. In 1899, he married Helen Noble, and their first child was born just six months before his finals. Helen's father had encouraged Thomas's writing talent. He was dependent upon his father, who wished Edward to be a civil servant, but Edward never deviated from his intention to become a full-time writer. Upon graduating, Edward precariously supported his family by editing, wiring essays, biographies and reviews, but felt trapped into writing for the sake of relieving poverty, rather than writing what he wanted to. The sheer volume of work he was forced to undertake to survive, depressed him.

His first child was Merfyn, followed by Bronwen in 1904 and Myfanwy in 1910. In virtual slavery to commissioned works, he wrote *The Woodland Life* in 1897, followed quickly by *Oxford, Beautiful Wales, Richard Jeffries, A Literary Pilgrim in England, Feminine Influence on the Poets, Borrow, Swinburne, Marlborough* and many others. Despite the support of the great O.M. Edwards, Thomas failed to find a desired teaching or library post in Wales.

In 1914, on the eve of the outbreak of war, Thomas and his family moved to the village of Dymoke in Gloucestershire, around which a small group of Georgian poets - Abercrombie, Drinkwater and Gibson - lived. The great American poet, Robert Frost, had arrived with his family a few months before, and Frost and Thomas formed a legendary friendship. They went for long walks, and Frost urged Thomas to write poetry. Other friends, such as W.H Davies (the tramp-poet of Newport) and Walter de la Mere, added their weight of opinion, and Edward wrote his first poem in December 1914. All 143 of his poems were written in an astonishing creative spell between that date and January 1917 when he went to France. The poems that were published in his lifetime, were under his pseudonym Edward Eastaway. It is impossible to summarise the feeling that Thomas conveyed in his poems - a placid acceptance of sadness, perhaps. However, one of his loveliest 'little' poems is *Snow*:

'In the gloom of whiteness,
In the great silence of snow,
A child was sighing
And bitterly saying: "Oh,
They have killed a white bird up there on her nest,
The down is fluttering from her breast!"
And still it fell through that dusky brightness
On the child crying for the bird of snow.'

Between August 1914 and July 1915, Thomas agonised over whether to take his family and rejoin the Frosts in New England, or to enlist. As a married man, he had the choice. Finally, in July 1915 he entered the Artists Rifles, followed by Wilfred Owen just two months later. As a lance corporal at Hare Hall Camp, Romford, Essex, Thomas composed 40 poems in the ten months he was stationed there. In August 1916, he was commissioned in the Royal Garrison Artillery, serving in Wiltshire before embarking for France in January 1917. On 9 April, Easter Monday, the first day of the Battle of Arras opened with a massive artillery bombardment. At 7.30 a.m. Thomas was shot and killed.

Thomas's poetry linked his Georgian contemporaries to modern poetry, and for many years he was regarded as 'the poet's poet' by poets as diverse as W.H. Auden, Philip Larkin and Derek Walcott. He is now seen as one of the most influential 20th century poets. The wonderful poem *To Edward Thomas* by Alun Lewis, who himself died in the Second World War, ends with the verse:

'Divining this, I knew the voice that called you
Was soft and neutral as the sky
Breathing on the grey horizon, stronger
Than night's immediate grasp, the limbs of mercy
Oblivious as the blood; and growing clearer,
More urgent as all else dissolved away,
--- Projected books, half-thoughts, the children's birthdays,
And wedding anniversaries as cold
As dates in history --- the dream
Emerging from the fact that folds a dream,
The endless rides of stormy-branched dark
Whose fibres are a thread within the hand ---

Till suddenly, at Arras, you possessed that hinted land.'

Thomas is commemorated at Poet's Corner, Westminster Abbey, and around nineteen of his poems were set to music by the Gloucester composer Ivor Gurney. The British Poet Laureate Ted Hughes called Thomas 'the father of us all.'

JOHN LLEWELLYN LEWIS 12 February 1880 – 11 June 1969

THE CONSCIENCE OF AMERICAN INDUSTRY

'President of the United Mine Workers of America (UMWA) from 1920 until 1960 and founding president of the Congress of Industrial Organizations (CIO), John Llewellyn Lewis was the dominant voice shaping the labor movement in the 1930s. The CIO owed its existence in large measure to Lewis, who was a tireless and effective advocate of industrial unionism and of government assistance in organizing basic industry.' - from the AFL-CIO America's Unions Website.

John L. Lewis was born in Lucas, Iowa, to Thomas H. Lewis and Ann Watkins, both of whom had emigrated from Llangurig. After his father was black-listed for participating in a strike in 1882, the family moved about in constant search for work. The first of seven children, Lewis joined his father in the mines around 1885-86, and two years later returned to Lucas, where he met his future wife Myrta Bell. A burly,  adventurous young man, Lewis travelled to the West in 1901. He 'rode the rails' for four years and experienced firsthand the hardships of workers across the country, working as a miner in Montana, Utah, Colorado, and Arizona. He was in Wyoming in 1905 when a coal mine explosion killed 236 miners, an experience considered crucial in inspiring his devotion to miners' unionism and mine-safety legislation.

In 1907 he married Myrta Bell, and in later life would credit her, with whom he had three children, as the single most important influence on his life. In 1909 they moved to the southern Illinois coalfield, one of the key districts in the United Mine Workers of America (UMWA). Aided by his five brothers who joined him there, Lewis gained control of the local UMWA local. Following an Illinois mine disaster, the astute lobbying by which he achieved improved mine safety and workmen's-compensation

363

legislation brought him recognition. As a result, the President of the American Federation of Labor (AFL) offered Lewis appointment as an AFL field representative and legislative agent.

Travelling on an AFL expense account, Lewis visited the important mining districts and ingratiated himself with local officials through generous use of AFL funds. Thus he was able to construct his own political machine within the UMWA. From 1910 to 1916, he worked closely with the incumbent UMWA president, to defeat socialist and radical insurgents seeking to control the union. Cooperating with federal efforts to regulate mining production and labour relations during World War I, Lewis helped win substantial wage increases for miners in the central bituminous coal fields. In 1916 he became the UMWA's chief statistician, and a year later he was elected vice president.

On 1 November 1919, Lewis as acting president of the UMWA called the first major coal union strike, and 400,000 miners walked off their jobs. President Wilson obtained an injunction, which Lewis obeyed, telling his members, 'We cannot fight the Government.' In 1920, when the 38-year-old Lewis became president of the UMWA, the union claimed 500,000 members. Lewis was the dominant figure in what was then the largest and most influential trade union in America.

The 40-year-old Lewis now led the largest and most influential union in the country. In the early 1920s, Lewis used the nation's dependence on coal to maintain union membership despite severe economic downturns in the industry. He also guided the miners through a successful five-month strike to preserve the wage gains they had won during the war. The unionized mines faced intense competition from non-union operators, however, and the entire industry suffered from the destructive effects of an unregulated boom-and-bust production cycle. With union membership declining from 500,000 in 1922 to 75,000 in 1933, Lewis lobbied hard for federal legislation that would stabilize the industry, guarantee workers the right to organize and 'take wages out of competition.'

Franklin D. Roosevelt was elected president in 1932, and the previously Republican Lewis sought Democratic support for his ideas. In 1933 Congress passed the National Industrial Recovery Act to regulate production, ensure stable employment and guarantee workers the right to organize and bargain collectively over the terms and conditions of their employment. Gambling his union's remaining funds on an all-out drive for membership, Lewis flooded the coalfields with the message: 'The President wants you to join the union!' Just three months after the National Recovery Administration was established, 92 percent of all the country's coal miners were organized. Lewis next sought support from the AFL to organize other mass-production industries. At its 1935 convention, he led an assault on the AFL's leadership, demanding they make good on their promises to organize and charter industrial unions. When his proposals were defeated, Lewis intentionally provoked Carpenters' President William Hutcheson into calling him a name. Lewis leaped a row of chairs and knocked Hutcheson to the ground with a right to the nose. The blow signalled to millions of workers across the country that they had a new champion in John L. Lewis.

Lewis now committed UMWA funds to support organizing drives in the rubber, auto and steel industries. Without this support, and without Lewis's involvement, it is doubtful whether these campaigns would have succeeded. He personally negotiated the agreements with General Motors and U.S. Steel. Under Lewis's wise leadership the CIO proceeded to mount militant and well-financed organizing efforts in the automobile, steel, rubber, and other industries. In 1937, during protracted industrial conflicts, the CIO succeeded in bringing union organization and collective bargaining to the mass-production industries. In 1938, the CIO (Congress of Industrial Organizations) held its founding convention and elected Lewis its first president. Inspired by his oratory and his demands on corporate power, millions of workers revered Lewis as the conscience of American industry, and the embodiment of the new power of labour. Some commentators considered Lewis a contender for the presidency of the United States.

By the end of World War II, however, Lewis' national stature had diminished. In 1940, frustrated with Roosevelt's war policies and his lack of support of labour during the 'little steel' strike of 1937, Lewis endorsed the Republican candidate for president. When American workers failed to follow his lead and abandon Roosevelt, Lewis resigned as president of the CIO. In 1942, he broke with the industrial union movement he had helped create and took the UMWA out of the CIO.

Thereafter, Lewis largely devoted himself to the UMWA, remaining a bold and visionary labour leader. Bitter mine strikes in 1943 and 1946 earned him the enmity of many, but Lewis persisted. As the coal industry slipped into a long, slow decline and oil replaced coal as the nation's No. 1 source of energy, Lewis fought to protect the income and employment security of miners. In 1948, the UMWA won an historic agreement establishing medical and pension benefits for miners, financed in part by a royalty on every ton of coal mined. The union also acknowledged management's right to automate and to close unprofitable operations. In return, it secured high wages and expanded benefits in the remaining mines. In the 1950s, Lewis won periodic wage and benefit increases for miners and led the campaign for the first Federal Mine Safety Act in 1952. Lewis retired as president of the UMWA in 1960 and died at his home in Alexandria, Virginia in 1969.

The United Mineworkers of America website has the following dedication: 'John L. Lewis was president of the UMWA from 1920-1960. He was a giant among American leaders in the first half of the twentieth century, regularly advising presidents and challenging America's corporate leaders. His work to organize the country's industrial workers through the

Congress of Industrial Organzations (CIO) in the 1930s helped raise living standards for millions of American families. In the first year of the CIO, nearly four million workers joined labor organizations and wages were raised by over a billion dollars. Lewis sent hundreds of UMWA organizers to help create some of the nation's leading labor unions, including the United Steelworkers of America (USWA), the United Auto Workers (UAW), the Communication Workers of America (CWA) and many other important labor organizations that continue to speak in behalf of America's workers.

Perhaps Lewis' greatest legacy was the creation of the UMWA Welfare and Retirement Fund in a contract with the federal government, signed in the White House with President Truman in attendance. The UMWA Fund would change permanently health care delivery in the coal fields of the nation. The UMWA Fund built eight hospitals in Appalachia and established numerous clinics. In 1964, Lewis was awarded the Presidential Medal of Freedom, the nation's highest civilian decoration, by President Lyndon Johnson. He remained Chairman of the UMWA Fund until his death in 1969.'

Footnote:
An example of his oratory is seen in his speech Labor and the Nation given at Washington DC on 3 September 1937: 'The workers of the nation were tired of waiting for corporate industry to right their economic wrongs, to alleviate their social agony and to grant them their political rights. Despairing of fair treatment, they resolved to do something for themselves... No tin-hat brigade of goose-stepping vigilantes or bibble-babbling mob of blackguarding and corporation paid scoundrels will prevent the onward march of labor, or divert its purpose to play its natural and rational part in the development of the economic, political and social life of our nation... The organized workers of America, free in their industrial life, conscious partners in production, secure in their homes and enjoying a decent standard of living, will prove the finest bulwark against the intrusion of alien doctrines of government.

Workers have kept faith in American institutions. Most of the conflicts which have occurred have been when labor's right to live has been challenged and denied... I have pleaded your case from the pulpit and from the public platform - not in the quavering tones of a feeble mendicant asking alms, but in the thundering voice of the captain of a mighty host, demanding the rights to which free men are entitled...'

FREDERICK HALL THOMAS 5 March 1886 – 28 July 1927

THE WELSH WIZARD, FREDDIE WELSH, LIGHTWEIGHT CHAMPION OF THE WORLD

Frederick Hall Thomas of Pontypridd was easily one of the finest boxers that Europe has produced. Freddie Thomas was criticised for his 'over-competitiveness', but won the World Lightweight Title in 1914 from Willie Ritchie at Olympia and held it for three years. After 15 rounds, Ritchie knew that he was so far behind on points that he would have to KO Freddie, but the Welshman finished stronger and won the 20-round contest. Freddie 'Welsh' won his title before the multiplicity of titles and weights* that we have today, and remains the only vegetarian ever known to have won a world boxing championship. Standing just 5 feet 7 inches, with a weight that varied between 130 and 140 pounds, he was one of the finest boxing champions of all time. He seemed to be known as 'English' Freddie Thomas, as one of the very few foreign boxers in America, but insisted he was Welsh. To some thereafter he was reported as 'English' Freddie 'Welsh'. He was never a great knockout specialist, as was Jimmy Wilde (q.v.), but had to rely on boxing skills to hold off more powerful opponents. Welsh was the first boxer to win a Lonsdale Belt.

Suffering from tuberculosis as a 16-year-old, Freddie Thomas was lucky to survive his teens, and in his professional career won 77 fights and drew 7. Aged 17, he was working in Pentre iron foundry, when he decided to emigrate to the glittering shores of the USA. In Philadelphia, the young man was gulping down food at a free lunch counter. When pushed over, he became involved in a brawl with a bartender, and defended himself so well that he was offered a job in a nearby boxing booth. He received just two dollars for his first fight there, that afternoon. Turning professional in America, he returned to Britain to fight and henceforth criss-crossed the Atlantic looking for 'work.'

Freddie's first professional fight in America was in Philadelphia, when he knocked out 'Young' Williams in 1905. In 1906 he had 24 fights, mainly in Philadelphia, that most 'Welsh' of all American states, all unbeaten. The majority were 'No Decisions' but the only contests outside Pennsylvania were when he fought a 20-round draw in Dayton, Ohio, and a 17-round knockout of Hock Keys at the same venue. Ohio, after Pennsylvania, probably has the greatest concentration of Welsh people in the

USA. Finding it difficult to get fights, Freddie Welsh came back to fight in boxing booths in Wales, and on one spectacular night knocked out the lightweight Evan Evans, the welterweight Charlie Weber and the heavyweight Gomer Morgan. He also became Champion of Wales, knocking out Johnnie Owen in the 7th round.

1907 saw another 18 unbeaten appearances, starting the year in London, then boxing in Pontypridd and Merthyr, before going to fight in Philadelphia and Boston. In 1908, Freddie Welsh lost his first professional contest on points in his 48th professional fight, to Packey McFarland in Milwaukee, Wisconsin. He was unbeaten in his other 9 fights in the same year, drawing later over 25 rounds with McFarland. He also fought the world featherweight champion, the USA's Abe Attell, which was a 'no decision' - i.e. the 'home' boxer was given a draw. He boxed in Philadelphia, Milwaukee (4 fights), Los Angeles (4 fights), and Vernon, California.

With constantly harder matches, as he rose through the ranks of boxers, 1909 was another invincible year, with 8 wins, 3 no decisions and a draw. After a bout in Los Angeles, Freddie boxed 3 times in New Orleans, twice in New York, then in Boston, before crossing the Atlantic again to fight three times in Mountain Ash, Wales, before going to London to beat Johnny Summers for the Lightweight Championship of Britain, over 20 rounds. In 1910, he knocked out Jack Daniels in London, before yet another draw with Packey McFarland over 20 rounds in London, then won twice in Liverpool, before the infamous match with 'Gentleman' Jim Driscoll in Cardiff. In 1910, he fought the great Jim Driscoll, a featherweight, at the National Sporting Club and beat the lighter man in a display that degenerated into a street-brawl. Driscoll tried to outbox the heavier man, but Welsh used the dubious tricks learned in the boxing-booth. Gentleman Jim appealed to the referee, then eventually lost his temper, hooking Welsh several times in the kidneys and head-butting him, to receive the only disqualification of his career, in the 9th round.

There was an inauspicious start to the year in 1911, when Welsh lost his second fight, the British Lightweight Championship going to Matt Wells over 20 rounds in London. Returning to the USA, after a no decision in New York, the Welshman won two 20-round contests in California. In 1912, there were another 12 unbeaten fights, in Winnipeg, Buffalo, Columbus and Liverpool, culminating in the regaining of his British lightweight championship from Matt Wells over 20 rounds in London. He defended it the same month in London. There was yet another unbeaten year in 1913, appearing in Aberdare, London, Sheffield, Liverpool and Bridgeport before re-crossing the Atlantic to fight in Winnipeg, Edmonton, Saskatchewan, Vancouver, Montana, New York and Montreal. Apart from his two losses, he was unbeaten by now in his other 98 fights.

1914 was a hard year - his greedy manager booked him six fights in January alone. His opponents were Johnny Dundee in New Orleans (no decision - 10 rounds); Frank Whitney in Atlanta (won - 10 rounds); Sam Robideau in Philadelphia (no decision - 6 rounds); Mickey Sheridan in Kansas City (won - 10 rounds); Earl Fisher in Cincinnati (no decision - 10 rounds); and just 3 days later Leo Kelly in St Louis (no decision - 8 rounds). After another no decision in St Louis, Freddie Welsh won two contests in Los Angeles and another in New Orleans before arriving in London to gain the Lightweight Championship of the World off Willie Ritchie, over 20 rounds at Olympia. Ritchie demanded so much money to fight that Welsh virtually fought for free. News hit the Ritchie camp that the Welshman had injured an eye in training, but Freddie 'conned' the American by wearing a plaster over his undamaged eye. He won by staying out of range and outscoring the champion.

In 1914 he was unbeaten in another 7 contests, in Boston, Buffalo, New York, Milwaukee and Syracuse. 1915 saw another 17 unbeaten matches, and in 1916 Welsh again was invincible in another 20 fights, including two draws against Benny Leonard, and World Title defences against Adolph Wolgast in Denver and Charley White in Colorado Springs. Incidentally, Benny Leonard features 5th to Jimmy Wilde's 4th on lists of all-time Boxing 'Greats' on the www.coxscorner website. These two years were spent solely in the USA and Canada, with war raging across Europe.

In 1917, there were another 5 unbeaten bouts, including one in that most 'Welsh' of all American towns, Scranton, Pennsylvania, before Benny Leonard, on his third attempt, beat Freddy Welsh in New York to take the world-championship. Aged 31, against a man 10 years younger, it was the only time that Freddie Welsh was 'stopped' in any fight. Benny Leonard, the 'Ghetto Wizard', is usually rated in the 'best 3' lightweights of all time, and stayed as world champion until 1923.

In this title fight, stopped in the 9th round, Welsh's American manager had staked the entire purse upon Freddie winning. Not only did Freddie lose his world championship, but he left the ring empty-handed. It was only Freddie's 3rd defeat in 166 bouts. In the aftermath of the Leonard defeat, Freddie Welsh won a match in Newark in 1920, and then two in Pennsylvania and Calgary in 1921, before losing in Winnipeg, followed by his final bout, a loss in 1922 in Brooklyn. Before these final two fights, aged 35, Frederick Hall Thomas had lost just three times in 166 contests. Before he fought Benny Leonard in the 3rd contest, over 12 years Welsh had only lost twice in 162 fights! The record is as follows:

Year	Contests	Losses	Cumulative
1905	1	-	1-0
1906	25	-	26-0
1907	18	-	44-0
1908	10	1	55-1
1909	11	-	66-1

1910	5	-	71-1
1911	4	1	76-2
1912	8	-	84-2
1913	16	-	100-2
1914	18	-	118-2
1915	17	-	135-2
1916	21	-	156-2
1917	6	1	163-3
1918	-	-	-
1919	-	-	-
1920	-	-	-
1921	3	1	166-4
1922	1	1	167-5

After the Leonard fight, Freddie joined the US Army as a captain, but after the war his business ventures failed, forcing him to fight again. Freddie had opened a gym, managed a few fighters, lectured on physical education and operated a health farm. He died penniless and alone in a dingy New York apartment, aged just 41. Nat Fleischer rated him the 4th best all-time lightweight, and Charley Rose as the 5th.

* There are not only 3 'world' titles at any weight now, from the WBO, WBA and IBF, but there are also 17 different weight categories compared to the 8 traditional weights of boxing. Thus 8 'true' world champions in Welsh's time, when there were more boxers, have been replaced by 3 organisations multiplied by 17 weights, or 51 'world champions'.

Footnote:

On a table in St. Fagan's Castle at The Museum of Welsh Life, Cardiff, the author spotted a South Wales newspaper with an advertisement for the Welsh-Driscoll fight in Cardiff, the purse being £2,500, and claiming that the bout was due to massive public demand. The 'exhibition' match, at The American Roller Coaster Rink in Westgate Street, Cardiff, was agreed to reluctantly by Driscoll, because a percentage of the proceeds would go to his favourite charity, Nazareth House. Driscoll was the local Cardiff hero, and Freddie Thomas wanted recognition back in his native land. Driscoll was in constant pain from stomach ulcers and had an ear abscess. He bandaged the other ear, so Freddie Welsh would concentrate on it. There was 'bad blood' between the two from the days when Driscoll was working in a boxing booth near Bridgend in 1907. The unknown Freddie Welsh had accepted the barker's offer of £1 if he could 'stay' 6 rounds with Driscoll, and used the rabbit-punching and other techniques that he had learned in America. Freddie Welsh put up his Lightweight title, plus a donation to St Nazareth House, to meet Driscoll, and the match started evenly enough. In the 4th round Driscoll slipped and was helped up by a smiling Welsh. However, by the 5th round Welsh was hurting from the blows of the superior boxer, and his illegal retaliation was disregarded by the female referee. (Referees stayed outside the ring at this time). Driscoll's retaliation turned it into probably the 'dirtiest' British title fight ever staged. The pair elbowed, gouged and butted for another five rounds, until Driscoll head-butted Welsh under the chin so 'outrageously' that the referee Peggy Bettinson entered the ring and awarded the fight to Welsh. There was then a fight between the boxers' seconds. Incidentally and strangely, Freddie Thomas has not been honoured in the 'Welsh Sports Hall of Fame' at St. Fagans. Boxing historian Herb Goldmann spoke when Welsh was inducted into the International Boxing hall of Fame in 1960: 'The Welsh Wizard came to America from England (sic) and won the lightweight title in 1914 and fought legends Johnny Dundee, Battling Nelson, Rocky Kansas and Johnnie Kilbane as well as Benny Leonard, Willie Ritchie and Ad Wolgast. He twice fought a 25-round draw with Packie McFarland... Goldmann talked about these fighters, and their famous fights, as if they happened recently.'

JIMMY WILDE 15 May 1892 - 10 March 1969

THE MIGHTY ATOM, THE TYLORSTOWN TERROR, THE GHOST WITH THE HAMMER IN HIS HAND, THE HARDEST POUND FOR POUND PUNCHER IN BOXING HISTORY, 'THE GREATEST BOXER OF ALL TIME'

His name is inexcusably missing from *The Dictionary of Welsh Biography*, as is that of Freddie Welsh. Born at 8 Station Road, Pontygwaith, Rhondda, he fought the best flyweights in the world, when there were just eight weight categories, and just one world title in each. His natural weight was only 6 stone 4 pounds, and his maximum fighting weight was 7 stone 4 pounds, but nearly all of his opponents weighed around 8 stone. 'He would often weigh in fully clothed, wearing a hat, and carrying weights in his pockets' (*The Western Mail*, 4 November 1998).

In 1904, aged just 12, Wilde went to work underground in a colliery. He turned to boxing in his early teens, but promised his fianee to give up boxing. However, the miners' strike of 1911 meant that Wilde's young wife (both were 19) now acquiesced to his boxing for money. Jimmy knew that he and his new wife had to support his four brothers and sisters, and there was no alternative to starvation. He gatecrashed a boxing booth at

371

Pontypridd, shouting challenges to everyone and making such a commotion that he was allowed into the ring to 'shut him up'. He won five shillings that afternoon, a considerable sum and enough to feed the family for a week, and caught the eye of boxing promoters. Wilde had entered the ring knowing that he had to win. Another source states that Wilde started exhibiting in 1909, and from then to 1914 he appeared in over 500 fights in Jack Scarrott's boxing booth. It is thought that he engaged in at least 700 booth matches up until his retirement. He was sometimes outweighed by up to 60 pounds (27 kg) in boxing matches (e.g. in his 11th fight, against the former middleweight champion, Billy Papke), as from his booth experiences he did not fear heavier men.

Despite the interference of the Great World War, he fought 151 times between 1911 and 1923, winning 132 (101 inside the distance), drawing 2, with 13 no-decisions and only 4 defeats. That is the official record, but Wilde had his own record, including booth and exhibition bouts, of 864 fights from 1910. 'On one day, in a booth in Pontypridd, he knocked over 17 opponents before lunch and, after a cup of tea, demolished another 8 opponents'. This is possibly the day recorded when he knocked out 20 opponents in 4 hours to earn £40, with no fight lasting more than 30 seconds!

On Boxing Day, 1926, Wilde fought a 'no decision' with Les Williams at Pontypridd, and in the following year beat 29 opponents in Pontypridd, Cardiff and Edinburgh. In 1912 he won another 20 fights, in Tonypandy, Cardiff, Merthyr, Swansea, Pentre, Pontypridd, Sheffield, Liverpool and London. In 1912, 'The Tylorstown Terror' won his first title, the Welsh Flyweight Championship, from George Dando in Cardiff. His invincible 1913 saw another 33 fights, in Tonypandy, Merthyr, Swansea, Cardiff, Hanley, Ferndale, Liverpool, Manchester and Glasgow, where he beat Billy Padden for the 98-pound Championship of Great Britain on New Year's Day. In 1914, he beat Eugene Musson of France for the European Championship. In this year he also conquered Young Joe Symonds, but lost in 17 rounds to the stone heavier Tancy Lee. Wilde had been in bed with influenza the previous days. He won 19 of his 20 fights this year, appearing in Tonypandy, Aberdare, Ashton, Liverpool, Leicester, London, Birkenhead, Sheffield, Manchester and Leeds. This was the first year he fought more fights outside Wales, with only three Welsh appearances.

Wilde was twice rejected as unfit for military service in World War I, before being recruited as a sergeant-instructor on the Army PE staff. Meanwhile, the Scot Tancy Lee had lost his British Championship to Young Symonds, and Wilde regained the title in 1915. Four months later he floored Lee after four rounds, avenging his single luckless defeat. In 1915, because of the war, there were only 10 fights, won in London, Liverpool, Sheffield, Dublin, Barrow and Bradford. 1916 saw wins in Swansea, London and Liverpool, before gaining the Flyweight Championship of the World from

Joe Symonds in London, followed by two more wins in London. He then defended his World Title in Liverpool against Johnny Rosner, and beat Benny Thomas in Cardiff. Upon May 13th he beat Darkey Saunders and Joe Magnus on the same day at Woolwich. After another win in London, he fought Tancy Lee for the British, European and World titles and won in London, before another two wins in London and Liverpool. He finally beat Young Zulu Kid in London over 11 rounds to retain his World Flyweight Championship. The Americans had just recognised the Flyweight division, and the match was a unification title, making Wilde the first World Flyweight Champion recognised across the world. For good measure he had defended his British Championship by knocking out Johnny Hughes, and also flattened the Canadian champion in 4 rounds in 1916.

With the Great War at its height, there were only 4 fights in 1917, all in London, and Wilde retained his World, European and British championships against George Clarke. 1918 saw just three wins in London and one in Aldershot. In 1919, he beat the revered American Joe Lynch at the heavier Bantamweight level in London, and also won in Liverpool, London (twice) and Milwaukee against Jack Sharkey. 1920 saw an unbeaten tour of North America, winning in St Louis, Milwaukee, Jersey City, Philadelphia, Toledo, Windsor (Ontario, where he again defeated Young Zulu Kid), Camden (New Jersey), Lawrence (Massachusetts), Philadelphia again, and Toronto. Jimmy had fought an amazing 145 professional fights in 11 years, drawn two in his second year of fighting and lost just one. And previously he had won an estimated 715 amateur fights.

In January 1921, Wilde fought for the World Bantamweight Title in America. Wilde had been suffering from influenza, and was giving 2 stones away to Pete Herman ('one of the all-time great bantamweight champions). Herman had refused to weigh in, knowing he was overweight. Wilde was badly hurt in the 15th round, and in the 17th round was knocked through the ropes three times. The referee carried Wilde to his corner and told him 'I'm picking you up, because you don't know when to lie down.' Jimmy made no excuses, saying after the fight 'I can sincerely say that Herman beat me because he was the better boxer.'

His only other fight that year was a win, a month later in Wales. For the next two years there were no serious challengers for his World Flyweight Title, and he had just one winning bout in London in early 1923. Wilde returned to booth fighting to keep in shape, and had no professional matches for two years. However, in June 1923, he was offered the fabulous amount of £23,000 to then fight the Filipino, 'Pancho Villa', 10 years his junior, and like Wilde one of the greatest fighters of all time. A right to the head floored Jimmy after the bell had ended Round 2, but despite calls from spectators to disqualify the Filipino, the referee did nothing. After that, Wilde was fighting a losing battle. He lost at the New York Polo Ground, being knocked out in the 7th round. Wilde did not recognise his wife until three weeks later. The new champion* burst into tears at the end of the fight, saying 'Me no want to hurt him'. Gene Tunney, the World Heavyweight Champion, called Wilde 'the greatest fighter I ever saw'.

Boxing Illustrated, in April 1993, ran an article upon the '40 hardest punchers, pound for pound in boxing history.' At numbers 9 and 8 were Jack Dempsey and Joe Louis. 3rd and 2nd were Bob Fitzsimmons and Max Baer. Seventy years after his last fight, Jimmy Wilde was rated number one. The great critics Nat Fleischer and Charlie Rose rated Wilde as the 'all-time number one Flyweight', and he was elected in the inaugural class of the International Boxing Hall of Fame in 1990. His other claim to fame is that his is still the longest uninterrupted title reign of any world flyweight champion at 7 years and 4 months.

His record reads: Fought 864 times, Lost 3, including 2 of his last 3 fights. 89% of his wins recorded below were by knockout. His professional KO wins by round were: in round 1 - 3 knock-outs; round 2 - 17; round 3 - 21; round 4 - 10; round 5 - 9; round 6 - 4; round 7 - 4; round 8 - 11; round 9 - 4; round 10 - 4; round 11 - 6; round 12 - 3, and one KO in each of rounds 13, 14, 15, 17 and 18. Wilde's 18th-round knockout was for his 98-pound championship against Billy Padden in 1913. His 101 consecutive fights without a loss is an all-time boxing record at any weight. It is fairly easy to make a case for the Welshman being the greatest boxer of all time, yet few have heard of him.

'The Mighty Atom' retired to Victoria Park, Cadoxton, Barry, where the author as a cub scout was privileged to carry out a 'bob-a-job' weeding his front path, but at the age of 72 he was mugged by some mindless youths on a deserted platform at Cardiff Railway Station. His mind was never the same after, and he spent the last four years of his life in Whitchurch, Cardiff's hospital for the mentally ill, before dying in a coma in 1969 aged 76. The year before his death, Wilde had been voted 'the greatest boxer of all time', by the four leading American boxing commentators and writers.

Date	Fights	Win	Knock-out	Points	No Decision	Draw	Loss
1910	1	-	-	-	1	-	-
1911	29	27	21	6		2	-
1912	17	15	11	4	2	-	-
1913	33	29	19	10	4	-	-
1914	20	20	13	7	-	-	-
1915	10	9	9	-	-	-	1
1916	15	15	14	1	-	-	-
1917	2	2	2	-	-	-	-
1918	3	3	3	-	-	-	-
1919	5	4	2	2	1	-	-

1920	10	6	5	1	4	-	-
1921	2	1	-	1	-	-	1
1922	-	-	-	-	-	-	-
1923	2	1	-	1	-	-	1
	149	132	99	33	12	2	3

* Pancho Villa of Manila died in 1925 of blood poisoning, aged just 25. Nat Fleischer and Charley Rose both ranked Pancho Villa as the second best flyweight of all time after Jimmy Wilde.

(JOHN) SAUNDERS LEWIS 15 October 1893 – 1 September 1985

PATRIOT, INTELLECTUAL, ACTIVIST, FOUNDER OF PLAID CYMRU, 'THE GREATEST FIGURE IN WELSH LITERATURE IN THE 20TH CENTURY'

John Saunders Lewis was brought up in the strong Welsh community of the Wirral, on the west bank of Liverpool's Mersey River. He fought alongside Irishmen in the First World War, which activated his sense of nationalism, being rightly convinced that the survival of the Welsh language was the key to the survival of the nation. His studies at Liverpool University had been interrupted by the war, where he served as an officer with the South Wales Borderers in France, Italy and Greece. He returned to take a first in English, before undertaking a dissertation upon English influences upon classical Welsh poetry. In 1922, he was a lecturer in Swansea University's Department of Welsh. During the National Eisteddfod in Pwllheli in 1925, representatives from *Y Mudiad Cymreig* (The Welsh Movement) and *Byddin Ymreolwyr Cymru* (The Army of the Welsh Home Rulers) met to join and form *Plaid Genedlaethol Cymru* (The National Party of Wales, later *Plaid Cymru*). Saunders Lewis was a founder, and in 1926 became its President.

For Lewis, as president 1926 – 1939, 'the chief aim of the party [is] to 'take away from the Welsh their sense of inferiority... to remove from our beloved country the mark and shame of conquest', and he wished to demonstrate how Welsh heritage was linked as one of the 'founders of

European civilization'. In 1935 the UK Government settled on Llŷn as the site for a bombing training camp after similar proposed sites in Northumberland and Dorset met with protests. However, Prime Minister Baldwin refused to hear the case against building this 'bombing school' in Wales, despite a deputation representing 500,000 Welsh protesters, around a quarter of the population. Protest against the project was summed up by Lewis when he wrote that the UK Government was intent upon turning one of the 'essential homes of Welsh culture, idiom, and literature' into a place for promoting a barbaric method of warfare.

In 1936, with two friends Lewis Valentine and D.J. Williams, he set fire to a hangar at the RAF bombing range of Penberth, at Penrhos on the Llŷn Peninsula. Little damage was caused, and the three turned themselves into police the next day for their token act.

From the dock at his trial in Caernarfon he declaimed 'What I was teaching the young people of Wales in the halls of the university was not a dead literature, something chiefly of interest to antiquarians, but a living literature of the Welsh people. This literature is therefore able to make demands of me as a man as well as a teacher... It is plain historical fact that, from the 5th century on, Llŷn has been Welsh, of the Welsh, and that as long as Llŷn remained un-Anglicised, Welsh life and culture were secure. If once the forces of Anglicisation are securely established behind as well as in front of the mountains of Snowdonia, the day when the Welsh language will be crushed between the iron jaws of these pincers cannot long be delayed. For Wales the preservation of the Llŷn peninsula from this Anglicisation is a matter of life or death.' The Welsh jury could not agree a verdict. The English authorities had the three retried in London, giving them nine months in Wormwood Scrubs.

The Welsh former Prime Minister, David Lloyd-George, railed against the injustice of it all - 'They yield when faced by Hitler and Mussolini, but they attack the smallest country in the kingdom which they misgovern. This is a cowardly way of showing their strength through violence... This is the first government that has tried to put Wales on trial at the Old Bailey... I should like to be there, and I should like to be 40 years younger.' Saunders Lewis was asked if he wanted to see a bloody revolution, and answered 'So long as it is Welsh blood and not English blood.'

He died in 1985, a poet-philosopher-nationalist-pacifist, still without much honour in his own land - the majority of Welsh youngsters have never heard of the man, who did more than anyone since Bishop William Morgan to keep the Welsh language alive. Lewis said 'to acquiesce in the death of a language which was the heritage of our forefathers for 1,500 years, is to despise man. Woe betide the society that despises man.' Saunders Lewis would have hated the fields of holiday home caravans on the Llŷn Peninsula and along the Welsh coastlines, and the massive colonisation in progress for the last four decades.

Saunders Lewis was the major figure of both Welsh-language politics and literature of the 20th century, who in Plaid Cymru set out to create a culturalist nationalist party. He could not see the possibility of creating a Welsh nation-state, unlike Gwynfor Evans (q.v.), but aimed to preserve Welsh language and tradition. He wanted a rural economy rather than large-scale capitalism and socialism, with small-scale private ownership, redistribution of wealth, and deindustrialisation. He saw Wales as part of a European federation of peoples, not a Europe of nation-states.

After Lewis' release from prison and his sacking from his lectureship, Lewis supported himself by farming, occasional teaching, and journalism. He was forced to resign as Plaid Cymru president in 1939, saying that Wales was not yet ready for the leadership of a Roman Catholic. Many Welsh people were angered by the judge's scornful treatment of the Welsh language, by the decision to move the trial to London, and by the decision of University College, Swansea, to dismiss Lewis from his post before he had been found guilty. Dafydd Glyn Jones wrote of the fire that it was 'the first time in five centuries that Wales struck back at England with a measure of violence... To the Welsh people, who had long ceased to believe that they had it in them, it was a profound shock.' Saunders Lewis was shamefully blacklisted by the University of Wales for his nationalism - not until 1952 was he accepted back into acadaemia, at Cardiff University's Department of Welsh. Constantly writing in Welsh, he retired to his home in Penarth in 1957, to devote himself full-time to writing. His astonishing output is listed in detail in *The New Companion to the Literature of Wales*, edited by Meic Stephens. Apart from his contributions to political journalism and literary criticism, the *Companion* notes:

'The writings of Saunders Lewis are informed by a love of Wales seen in the context of European Catholic Christendom. He had a profound knowledge of Latin, French and Italian literature as well as English and Welsh... His own most important contribution to Welsh literature was as a dramatist. Apart from a handful of comedies in which Welsh institutions are gently but tellingly satirised, his plays explore such weighty and often sombre themes as the imperatives of honour, the responsibilities of leadership, the nature of politics and the conflict between "*eros*" and "*agape*"... Apart from *Siwan* (1956), which he described as a poem, Saunders Lewis published no more than 53 poems in all but some of them are undoubtedly among the finest Welsh poems of the 20th century. They deal, in a variety of metres both traditional and innovatory, with the predicament of Wales, the glory of nature, and the call of God.'

A partial translation (by Gwyn Thomas) of Lewis's bleak *Y Dilyw* of 1939 reads:

'The tramway climbs from Merthyr to Dowlais,
Slime of a snail on a heap of slag;

Here once was Wales, and now derelict
Cinemas and rain on the barren tips;
The pawnbrokers have closed their doors,
The pegging clerks are the gentry of this waste;
All flesh had corrupted his way upon the earth.'

In 1979, the Welsh people voted against a National Assembly, fearing another bureaucratic layer of committees and unemployables. In 1997 the tiniest minority passed the referendum for a Welsh Assembly, mainly because Welsh Nationalists threw everything into supporting the proposal - they saw it as a halfway house to full devolution and independence for Wales. Scotland also voted for limited independence, but was given a real Parliament, with far greater powers than the Welsh Assembly. Scotland has, along with Northern Ireland, had billions more poured into it than Wales – the subsidy per capita to Wales is far less, leading to Welsh schoolchildren receiving £600 a year in funding less than their UK counterparts. Without Saunders Lewis, even this small measure of independence from London would not have been achieved.

In 1962, Lewis made his famous radio speech, *Tynged yr Iaith*, forecasting the death of the Welsh language by 2000. This stimulated the formation of *Cymdeithas yr Iaith Gymraeg*, the Welsh Language Society. As much as Gwynfor Evans, Lewis was responsible for the Welsh Language Bill by his incessant work in stemming the twin inflows of ignorance and apathy. Twice nominated for the Nobel Prize for Literature, in 1970 and after his death in 1985, the literary talents of this poet, dramatist, literary historian and critic have been compared to those of T.S. Eliot and W.B. Yeats. The wonderful Idris Davis (q.v.) wrote of Lewis:

'Though some may cavil at his creed
And others mock his Celtic ire,
No Welshman loyal to his breed
Forgets this prophet dares the fire,
And roused his land by word and deed
Against Philistia and her mire.'

And the late, and similarly minded R.S. Thomas (q.v.) wrote:

'And he dared them;
Dared them to grow old and bitter
As he. He kept his pen clean
By burying it in their fat
Flesh. He was ascetic and Wales
His diet. He lived off the harsh fare
Of her troubles, worn yet heady

At moments with the poet's wine.
A recluse, then; himself
His hermitage? Uninhabited
He moved among us; would have led
To rebellion. Small as he was
He towered, the trigger of his mind
Cocked, ready to let fly with his scorn.'

IVOR NOVELLO 15 January 1893 - 6 March 1951

DAVID IVOR DAVIES, FILM STAR AND MUSICAL PLAYWRIGHT, 'THE LAST GREAT ROMANTIC', 'THE WELSH GENIUS', 'THE VALENTINO OF ENGLAND', 'THE BRITISH ADONIS'

Born at Llwyn-yr-Eos (Nightingale Grove), 95 Cowbridge Road East in Cardiff, his Welsh-speaking parents were David Davies and Clara Novello Davies. There is a blue plaque on the house, and there was once a small lilac bush in the garden. The family moved later to nearby 11 Cathedral Road, a far grander property. His mother was named Novello after her godmother, a famous Italian singer, and Clara was the founder and creator of the Welsh Ladies Choir. Ivor was just six months old when he was taken to the 1893 Chicago World Fair with the choir, which won the Ladies Choral Competition and every solo prize for which they entered. On her return Madam Clara was invited to sing before Queen Victoria, and henceforth the choir was known as The Royal Welsh Ladies Choir. Ivor learned music from his mother, before entering the Magdalen College of Music in Oxford.

In 1914, he composed the most popular song of the Great World War, *Keep the Home Fires Burning,* and entertained the troops in war-torn France. In 1916, he became a pilot in the Royal Naval Air Service, surviving two crash landings. David Ivor Davies of Cardiff, Ivor Novello, not only wrote popular songs, but was an actor-manager, taking the romantic lead in his musicals such as *Glamorous Night* (1935), *The Dancing Years* (1939), *Arc de Triomphe* and *Gay's The Word* (1951). He also wrote the operettas

Careless Rapture (1936) and *King's Rhapsody* (1949). His other musicals included *Crest of the Wave* (1937), and *Perchance to Dream* (1945).

He was the leading British silent movie star and a matinee idol through the 1920's, working with the great directors D.W. Griffith (q.v.), Alfred Hitchcock and Louis Mercanton, but the theatre remained his first love.

The Frenchman Mercanton came to London looking for a leading man for his new film *Call of the Blood* and saw a photograph of Novello, exclaiming 'That's the actor I want!' Upon discovering that Novello was a composer, not an actor, he still pursued him to make the film and Novello became a great star. He became the heir to the romantic throne in the cinema left vacant by the death of Rudolph Valentino.

His starring roles were 1919 *The Call of the Blood* (Mercanton); 1920 *Miarka: The Daughter of the Bear* (Mercanton); 1922 *Carnival* (Knoles); 1922 *The Bohemian Girl* with Gladys Cooper (Knoles); 1923 *The Man without Desire* (Brunel); 1923 *The White Rose* (D.W. Grffith); 1923 *Bonnie Prince Charlie* (Calvert); 1925 *The Rat* (Cutts); 1926 *The Triumph of the Rat* (Cutts); 1926 *The Lodger* (Hitchcock); 1927 *Downhill* (Hitchcock); 1928 *The Vortex* (Brunel); 1928 *The Constant Nymph* (Brunel); 1928 *The Gallant Hussar* (von Bolvary); 1928 *The South Sea Bubble* (Hayes Hunter); 1928 *The Return of the Rat* (Cutts); 1930 *Symphony in Two Flats* (Gundry); 1931 *Once a Lady* (McClintie, in the USA); 1932 *The Phantom Fiend [The Lodger]* (Elvey); 1933 *I Lived With You* (Elvey), 1933 *Sleeping Car* (Litvak) and 1934 *Autumn Crocus* (Basil Dean).

Films of his musicals include *Glamorous Night* in 1937; *The Dancing Years* starring the Welsh actor Dennis Price in 1950, *King's Rhapsody* starring Errol Flynn and Anna Neagle in 1955, and *The Dancing Years*, made for TV in 1977. *Glamorous Night* had a West End revival in 1997. Novello also had an 'electrifying stage presence', writing 24 plays and appearing in 14, including *Henry V*. But his favourite genre was the musical - he appeared in six of the eight he wrote and composed over 250 songs. A little-known fact is that he co-scripted *Tarzan the Ape Man* in 1932, and was responsible for the line 'Me Tarzan, You Jane', which was included after he said it in a mix-up in rehearsal, when the female lead accidentally quoted the lead's lines to him.

Novello's songs have survived as classics of musical theatre. Ivor Novello was the toast of the West End in the beginning of the 20th century, and his first 'hit', *Keep the Home Fires Burning* became almost an anthem of the troops suffering in Europe. He was one of the world's greatest songwriters, with *Dreamboat* and *We'll Gather Lilacs* being huge hits. He was probably never knighted because of a legal problem in 1944. An infatuated female fan tried to gain favour by obtaining for him a car licence under false pretences. A particularly vindictive judge gave the unwitting Novello a one-month prison sentence as an example. However, Novello emerged from gaol as popular as ever - he had almost single-handedly kept the theatres open during the dark days of the war years.

Novello was a naturally gifted star of stage and screen, also writing songs, operettas, plays and films. A gifted playwright, his dazzling musical shows helped keep West End London theatres alive in the traumatic years of the 1930's and 1940's. He was described as having 'the most beautiful profile in the world', and the excellent biography by James Harding is now available in paperback from the Welsh Academic Press. A modest, caring, self-effacing man, despite the epithets such as 'the Valentino of England' bestowed on him by the American press, David Ivor Davies was devoted to his 'Mam' until her death. Noel Coward, Novello's friend for 35 years, said in the introduction to 'Ivor Novello, Man of the Theatre', 'His death will be a personal loss to many millions of people... For those who loved him there is no consolation except the memory of his charm, his humour and his loving generosity.' In the same book, Peter Noble wrote: Even those other playwrights, actors and composers who were inclined to be jealous of his continued successes, could not but agree that he was a most charming and kindly man.'

Novello died suddenly of coronary thrombosis in his flat above the Strand Theatre. Just four hours previously he had played the lead in his favourite and greatest musical, *King's Rhapsody* at London's Palace Theatre. 7,000 people attended his funeral, overwhelmingly female. His first biographer, Peter Noble, called him 'the great Welshman who brought more happiness to more people through his many gifts than possibly any other man of our century'. The Ivoe Novello Awards for songwriting, established in 1955 in his memory, are awarded each year by the British Academy of Songwriters, Composers and Authors to British songwriters and composers, as well as to an outstanding international music writer.

DAVID JONES 1 November 1895 – 25 October 1974

POET-PAINTER, ACCORDING TO T.S. ELIOT ON THE SAME LITERARY LEVEL AS EZRA POUND, JAMES JOYCE AND ELIOT HIMSELF

Walter David Michael Jones was born in Brockley, Kent, the son of James Jones, a printer's manager. His father, James Jones, had been born in Flintshire, to a Welsh-speaking family but was discouraged from speaking Welsh by his father, who, in common with many Welsh-speaking parents of the time, believed that habitual use of the language might hold his child back in his career. Jones' knowledge of print, and his remarkable gifts in calligraphy and printing, probably stem from his father's work. Aged just 7, David's *Dancing Bear* sketch gained public attention, and his pictures began to be exhibited at the Royal Drawing Society. At 16, David Jones enrolled at Camberwell Art College. Jones' intention was to become a 'painter of Welsh history' or an animal illustrator, but his teachers opened his eyes to French Impressionists and the Pre-Raphaelites.

However, the Great War interrupted Jones' studies, and he enlisted in January 1915, serving in the horrors of the Western Front with the Royal Welsh Fusiliers, from 1915 to 1918. Jones was wounded at the Somme in the Battle of Mametz Wood in 1916. The regiment was exhausted by forced

marches, and some of the men were barely conscious before the conflict, and Jones was carried unconscious from the front. These experiences forever dramatically affected his later literary output.

After demobilisation, Jones received a grant to study art once more, at the Westminster School of Art. However, his years under fire in the army jarred with the placid environment of the art school, and Jones sought some answer by converting to the Roman Catholic Church in 1921. He met the engraver/sculptor Eric Gill, who wished to form 'a company of craftsmen living by their work and earning such reputation as they had by the quality of their goods', and moved out of London to join him, learning wood and copper engraving.

He illustrated *Gulliver's Travels, The Rime of the Ancient Mariner* and other books, and worked on his watercolours while travelling around Britain, sometimes staying with Gill near Llantony Abbey, sometimes with his parents, and sometimes at Benedictine monasteries. His delicate watercolour washes and elegant calligraphy took him away from the mainstream of British art, and a reassessment of this most multi-talented man is overdue. The late Kathleen Raine describes the 'Turneresque evanescence' of his *Manawyddan's Glass Door* in her wonderful appreciation of his writings, poetry and art in *David Jones and the Actually Loved and Known*. His luminous, visionary watercolours, redolent of Arthurian mysticism and the legends of *The Mabinogion*, can be seen in the Tate Gallery and many other museums.

There is a David Jones Society, and its website relates: 'Having trained as a painter, he continued to paint throughout his life, producing such masterpieces as *Manawydan's Glass Door* (1932) and *Flora in Calyx-Light* (1950). He also created some powerful wood and metal engravings, notably those for Coleridge's poem *The Rime of the Ancient Mariner*. Perhaps his unique contribution to twentieth century visual art was his 'painted inscriptions', where word and image combine in harmonious abstract patterns, which he made in his later years.' Jones had to give up engraving because of the strain on his eyes.

In 1933 Jones suffered a severe nervous breakdown, probably brought on by his war injuries and experience. His drawings and paintings were shown at Chicago in 1933, the Venice Biennale in 1934 and the World's Fair, New York, in 1939. In 1937 he published his long narrative, *In Parenthesis*, an epic poem based on his first seven months in the trenches. The following year it won the Hawthornden Prize, at the time the only important British literary award.

The full title was *In Parenthesis (seinnyesit e gledyf ym penn mameu)*. TS Eliot wrote that he was 'deeply moved' by the typescript and that it was 'a work of genius' in his introduction to it. Part poem, part book, it mingles Jones' cathartic experiences in the First World War with Arthurian legend, Welsh mythology and the Roman occupation of Britain. Eliot places Jones in the same literary representation as himself, Ezra Pound and James Joyce. Jones, a writer, painter, calligrapher and illustrator, was obsessed with the way technocracy has taken us away from faith and sacrament. The intensity of inspiration from his historical roots is possibly only rivalled by Arthur Machen and W.B. Yeats.

The great poet Stephen Spender, in his *New York Times* book review of *In Parenthesis*, said 'This work of a poet-painter has its every word chiselled out of experience, and is probably the World War I monument most likely to survive.' And the review in *The Times Literary Supplement* stated 'This is an epic of war... but it is like no other war-book because for the first time that experience has been reduced to a "shape in words"... the impression still remains that this book is one of the most remarkable literary achievements of our time.' The work is a mixture of poetry and prose, a painting of words which TS Eliot called 'a work of genius... When "*In Parenthesis*" is widely enough known - as it will be in time - it will no doubt undergo the same sort of detective analysis and exegesis as the later works of James Joyce and the *Cantos* of Ezra Pound'. Lines of this WWI poem read:

'You can hear the silence of it:
you can hear the rat of no-man's-land
rut out intricacies,
weasel-out his patient workings
scrut, scrut, scrut,
harrow-out earthly, trowel his cunning paw'

In 1948 he suffered a second severe nervous breakdown, but in 1952 published *The Anathemata*, a dramatic-symbolic anatomy of Western culture. According to the great poet W.H.Auden, David Jones' *The Anathemata* was 'very probably the finest long poem written in English this century'. This considered meditation on the history and mythology of Celtic-Christian Britain was intelligent, ambitious and influenced T. S. Eliot's own work. Jones' *Epoch and Artist* is dedicated to Saunders Lewis, the Welsh Nationalist writer. All his writings show his alienation against the world of machines, existentialism, modernism and the analytical philosophy that eradicates metaphysics and the signposts of history. From *Epoch and Artist* we read 'A man can not only smell roses (some beasts may do that, for lavender is said to be appreciated in the Lion House) but he can and does and ought to pluck roses and he can predicate of roses such and such. He can make a signum of roses. He can make attar of roses. He can garland them and make anathemata of them. Which is, presumably the kind of thing he is meant to do. Anyway, there's no one else can do it. Angels can't nor can the beasts. No wonder then that Theology regards the body as a unique good. Without body: without sacrament. Angels only; no sacrament. Beasts only: no sacrament. Man: sacrament at every turn and all levels of the "profane" and "sacred", in the trivial and the profound, no escape from sacrament.'

In 1974 he published *The Sleeping Lord*, a collection of mid-length poems, and died in that year. On 11 November 1985 Jones was among sixteen Great War poets commemorated on a slate stone unveiled in Westminster Abbey's Poet's Corner. The works of this unknown humble Welsh genius need to be truly celebrated.

ANEURIN BEVAN 15 November 1897 – 6 July 1960

FOUNDER AND ARCHITECT OF THE NATIONAL HEALTH SERVICE

'Nye' Bevan was born in Tredegar, one of the ten children of a miner, David Bevan. A poor performer at school, he was made to 'repeat' a year before he left to work in a colliery, aged 13. Like many other poor youngsters in the Valleys, he received most of his learning from the local Workingmen's Institute Library. He joined the South Wales Miners' federation, and aged just 19 became chairman of his Miners' Lodge. His employers, the Tredegar Iron and Coal Company, saw him as an agitator and sacked him, but with the support of the Miners' Federation, the company was forced to re-employ him, on the grounds that he had been fired because of 'victimisation'. In 1919 he won a scholarship to study at the Central Labour College in London, and spent two years studying economics, politics and history. He read the *Communist Manifesto*, took up the ideas of Marx and Engels, and was also given lessons to cure his stammer.

Bevan returned to Tredegar in 1921, but the company refused to re-employ him, so for three years he was without work. In this time he acted as an unpaid adviser to people with financial and health problems. However, in

1924 Bevan managed to find work at the nearby Bedwellty Colliery, but this lasted only a few months as the colliery closed. In 1925 his beloved father died of pneumoconiosis - the dreaded disease of miners in Wales. Luckily, in 1926, Nye obtained another job, as a union official, his wages of £5 a week being paid by the members of the Miners' Lodge. With the General Strike of May 3rd, 1926, Bevan soon became one of the leaders of the South Wales miners.

The National Health Service, the jewel that was pioneered in Britain and copied in civilised countries all over the world, was largely based upon the example of a Welsh valley community scheme. Tuberculosis and pneumoconiosis were rife in nineteenth-century Wales, but in Tredegar was established the Workmen's Medical Aid Society (with its own doctors), in the 1890s. Workers paid three old pence in the pound, equivalent to just over one per cent of their income, for dentistry services, spectacles and midwives. Its doctors included AJ Cronin, who wrote about the scheme and its effects in *The Citadel*. In 1923, Aneurin ('Nye') Bevan was elected to the Hospital Committee, allied to the Medical Aid Society, and as Minister of Health just over three decades later, he launched the National Health Service. It is thought that Tredegar is the model that inspired the creation of the NHS.

In 1928, Bevan was elected to Monmouthshire County Council, and in 1929 easily beat the opposition in Ebbw Vale to become its Labour candidate in the next General Election. He became a Labour MP in 1931, and in World War II was frequently a 'one-man opposition' to Winston Churchill. His maiden speech in Parliament was an attack upon Churchill, his main enemy in the General Strike, the man who sent troops into South Wales. Churchill had sent the army to restore order after the Tonypandy miners' riots, in 1910. Bevan was just 12 years old, and knew the misery and hunger of the time. One of the most attractive aspects of Nye's personality was that he never tried to disguise his roots - not for him the claret-smooth old boy networks of miner's son Roy 'Woy' Jenkins. Nye Bevan was unequivocal in his attachment to the working classes: 'No amount of cajolery, and no attempts at ethical and social seduction, can eradicate from my heart a deep burning hatred for the Tory Party... So far as I am concerned they are lower than vermin.'

Bevan was one of the most outspoken opponents of Ramsay MacDonald's National Government, violently arguing against 'Means

Testing' for the poor, and in 1934 married a fellow left-wing Labour MP, Jennie Lee. They became active for 'The Relief of the Victims of German Fascism', before the War, and helped set up the left-wing socialist weekly newspaper, *Tribune*. In 1938 he visited the Republican Government in Spain, witnessing the fight against Franco's Fascism. At the start of the War, he campaigned strongly for his once implacable foe, Winston Churchill, to replace *Neville* Chamberlain and his Government. He also used his influence as editor of Tribune and leader of the left-wing MP's in the House of Commons to shape Government policies. He advocated nationalisation of the coal industry, was against heavy censorship and the locking-up of foreign nationals, and spoke for a Second Front to help Russia against Germany.

After the War, Bevan was made Minister of Health, and 1946 saw his revolutionary National Insurance Act, instituting the Health Service from 1948, and beginning compulsory wage contributions to fund sickness, maternity and old age benefits and pensions. Bevan resigned as Minister of Labour from the post-war Attlee Government in 1951, ostensibly over charges being introduced for teeth and spectacles. However, the real reason was the foreign and defence policy of the Labour government. The scale of the arms budget, forced upon Britain by the U.S. government during the Korean War, was unsustainable. (At the time the USA was forcing Britain to pay back its War Loan incurred for WW2, and transferring the money into the rebuilding of Europe and restructuring Japan to stop in falling into Communist hands. In 2013, the Tory Government announced that Britain had paid off loans from America for the First World War, but was 'economical with the truth' – it had merely taken advantage of lower interest rates to reschedule the debt.) Even his enemy Winston Churchill later acknowledged that Bevan was right.

In the last sixty years, political machismo has forced Britain to throw away over 10% of its (borrowed) wealth every year into the bottomless pit of 'defence' spending. Thus less investment, on a cumulatively exponential scale, is available for education, health, science, pensions etc., etc. It is no surprise that the economic success stories since the Second World War, Germany, Japan and Switzerland, have restricted defence budgets. Nye later became Shadow Foreign Secretary to Hugh Gaitskell, and was Deputy Leader of the Labour Party when he died of cancer.

It is odd that major politicians brought up in Wales, such as Michael Heseltine, Michael Howard, Roy Jenkins, and Geoffrey Howe have adopted upper-crust English accents. Bevan refused to do so, and was pilloried in the press of the time as a semi-Communist. Aneurin Bevan is commemorated in a statue at the West end of Cardiff's Queen Street. There are several websites devoted to Bevan's sayings, all of which refer to him as an 'English' politician. Just some are repeated here - they demonstrate the shining wit and unswerving idealism of one of the very, very few politicians who never betrayed the electorate:

'It is an axiom, enforced by the experience of all the ages, that they who rule industrially will rule politically;
I read the newspaper avidly. It is my one form of political fiction;
Freedom is the by-product of economic surplus;
Stand not too near the rich man lest he destroy thee - and not too far away lest he forget thee;
You call that statesmanship. I call it an emotional spasm;
We know what happens to people who stand in the middle of the road. They get run down;
This island is made mainly of coal and is surrounded by fish. Only an organising genius could produce a shortage of coal and fish at the same time;
The Prime Minister has an absolute genius for putting flamboyant labels on empty baggage (on Harold MacMillan);
I am not going to spend any time whatsoever in attacking the Foreign Secretary... If we complain about the tune, there is no need to attack the monkey when the organ grinder is present (In the House of Commons, to Prime Minister Anthony Eden and Foreign Secretary Selwyn Lloyd);

And the following are just some of his comments across the benches, directed at Churchill:

'He is a man suffering from petrified adolescence;
The worst thing I can say about democracy is that it has tolerated the right honourable gentleman for four and a half years;
The Prime Minister has very many virtues, and when the time comes I hope to pay my tribute to them, but I am bound to say that political honesty and sagacity have never been among them;
I welcome this opportunity of pricking the bloated bladder of lies with the poniard of truth;
He never spares himself in conversation. He gives himself so generously that hardly anyone else is permitted to give anything in his presence; and
The Tories always hold the view that the state is an apparatus for the protection of the swag of the property owners... Christ drove the moneychangers out of the temple, but you inscribe the title deed on the altar cloth.
All Tories are vermin... The whole art of Conservative politics in the 20th century is being deployed to enable wealth to persuade poverty to use its political freedom to keep wealth in power.'

LLEWELYN MORRIS HUMPHREYS 1899 - 23 November 1965

MURRAY THE CAMEL, MURRAY THE HUMP, PUBLIC ENEMY NUMBER ONE, THE MAN WHO INVENTED MONEY LAUNDERING, THE MAN WHO MADE LAS VEGAS

This Welshman is eminent is the sense that he made the Mafia what it is today. Some queried his inclusion in a previous version of this book, but he transformed the Mafia for all time. Murray Lewellyn Humphreys was probably the only Welsh mobster in America's gangland. He was initially known as Murray the Hump, and by extension as Murray the Camel. Lean, tall, dapper and handsome, with a brooding manner, he was the first of a new breed of racketeer, part criminal and part businessman. He was Al Capone's favourite sideman, and Capone once said 'anybody can use a gun...the Hump uses his head. He can shoot if he has to, but he likes to negotiate with cash when he can. I like that in a man.' The trademark of the Capone gang was the Thompson submachine gun, affectionately known as the 'Chicago Chopper' or the 'Chicago Tie-Breaker'.

However, Humphreys believed in killing only as a last resort as he was known to place great trust in the corruptibility of authority figures; a favourite saying being 'The difference between guilt and innocence in any court is who gets to the judge first with the most'. His ruthless streak was shown in his statement: 'Any time you become weak, you might as well die'. Humphreys main role in the Chicago Outfit was to do everything in his power to ensure its members attracted as little press attention as possible. Whereas some mobster welcomed the limelight, most gangsters took their cue from Humphreys, conducting themselves behind the scenes out of public view. He lived most of his life in a nondescript bungalow in Chicago's South Shore.

Brian Humphreys and Ann Wigley married in a Methodist chapel in China Street, Llanidloes. Both were from Carno, just 9 miles from Newtown, and they struggled to make a living there, on a hilltop farm called Y Castell. After a few years they emigrated, and Llewelyn Morris Humphreys was born in their small house in North Clark Street, Chicago. He was named after his uncle Llywelyn Humphreys, a JP, chapel deacon and county councillor back home in Wales. By the age of 7, Llewelyn had left school and was selling newspapers on a street corner, during a time of great violence between newspaper proprietors in the city.

He had a benefactor, however, Judge Jack Murray, and in his youth Humphreys adopted Murray as his Christian name, as no one could say Llywelyn properly. Murray Humphreys, as he was drawn in from the streets into Al Capone's ubiquitous Mob, became Murray the Hump, then Murray the Camel, either because of the association of Hump with Camel, or from his penchant for wearing elegant camel-hair coats and always carrying a walking stick. His first position was as a 'torpedo' (hired gunman or assassin), and it is believed that he shot-gunned to death Roger Touhy, a bootlegger and Capone's enemy, just 23 days after Touhy's release from prison.

The Camel was the architect of the infamous St Valentine's Day Massacre of 1929.

There was a power struggle in Chicago between Bugsy Moran's North Side Irish Gang and Capone's South Side Italian Gang. Moran was hijacking Capone's illicit liquor shipments bound for Detroit. Tony Accardo was Capone's chief bodyguard, nicknamed 'Joe Batters' by Capone after he had beaten a rival mobster to death with a baseball bat. Accardo and 'Tough Tony' Capezio were given the contract to kill Weiss after the Weiss-Moran gang had made an attempt to kill Capone. They machine-gunned him on the steps of the Holy Name cathedral.

Bugsy Moran was now the main target. The Camel discovered that Bugsy Moran bought his liquor stocks from the Genna Brothers, and got Angelo Genna to call Moran to take a delivery on 14 February, at 10.30 in the morning. To ensure the whole Moran Gang would be there, Genna told them it was an extra large delivery, requiring many men to shift it for distribution. The Hump then borrowed a police paddywagon from the captain of the police auto-pound, and two uniforms from a corrupt officer. 'Machine Gun' Jack McGurn and Louis 'Little New York' Campagna wore the police outfits, and 'Joe Batters' Accardo and 'Tough Tony' Capezio wore overcoats. Believing that it was a police raid, Bugsy's men dropped their weapons and faced the wall, knowing that Moran's connections would make sure any charges were dropped. The 5-man assassination squad dressed as policemen wiped out 7 members of Bugsy Moran's opposition gang at the garage warehouse, in the street where 'The Hump' was born. Bugsy missed it because he had luckily overslept, while Capone had a safe alibi at his Florida holiday-home.

One of Moran's 'enforcers', Frank was still alive when police first arrived on the scene, despite reportedly having fourteen bullets in his body. When questioned by the police about the shooting, his only response was 'Nobody shot me.' His brother Peter had been killed, and Frank died three hours later.

In 1931 Capone was in Cook County Jail for income tax evasion, receiving visits from senators and city dignitaries. A newspaper report mentioned Murray 'The Camel' Humphreys calling on 'Snorky' Capone in his new 'office' to bring him up-to-date on the latest 'take'. Prohibition was repealed in 1933, and the Syndicate's best source of illegitimate income died up overnight. Some mobsters went legitimate and stayed in the distilling business, but others returned to their core businesses of vice and gambling.

1933 saw Humphreys take an 11-year 'rap' for tax evasion, but he only served 3 years. In 1936, Humphreys, the youngest member of the Capone Syndicate, left Leavensworth Jail, returning to his rightful place as a gang leader in the rackets. In 1943 his colleague Frank 'The Enforcer' Nitti was charged with tax evasion and committed suicide. In 1944 'Big Bill' Thompson, the most colourful and corrupt Mayor Chicago had ever seen, died. Thompson left more than $2 million in shoe-boxes, but his highest salary had only been $22,500 p.a.

Aged 48, Alphonse Capone died of syphilis in 1947, and the Hump attended the funeral as the 'heir apparent', along with Jack 'Greasy Thumb' Guzic. Eliot Ness of the 'untouchables', his main enemy Capone gone, drifted into alcoholism by 1948, and died heavily in debt in 1957, aged just 54. Bugsy Moran had lost power. Many other racketeers managed to dodge the law under Capone's protégé Murray the Camel, who now succeeded Al Capone as Public Enemy No. 1. Under Humphreys, the rackets continued to thrive in Chicago. With the demise of bootlegging, Humphreys led the mob into the semi-respectability of liquor distribution and running saloons. However, he held on to the control of gambling and prostitution via political pay-offs. While more respectable and discreet, Humphreys moved the mob into the control of unions and financial institutions, moving also into thoroughly legitimate spheres and entertainment. Capone's 'syndicate' was now called 'the outfit', the name by which the Chicago rackets are known today. He was in control of 70% of racketeering in Chicago, making about $80 million a year.

The FBI credits Murray the Camel with the technique of money laundering, investing crooked money in legitimate business, and it was certainly Humphreys behind the introduction of gambling into Las Vegas, Nevada. *The Godfather* films are an excellent depiction of this period). In 1959 the mob accountant husband of the 37-year-old Betty Jean Vine found out that she was having an affair with the 60-year-old Humphreys. Allegedly Humphreys murdered him with an ice pick, then divorced his part-Cherokee wife Mary and married the younger woman. He visited Wales just once, in 1963, under an assumed name. Two years later he died, just after the FBI issued a warrant for his arrest. His daughter Luella lived on a fortified ranch outside Oklahoma City, and remembered him as a loving and devoted father. For one of her teenage birthday parties at the swish Humphreys' residence in Chicago, the guest singer was Frank Sinatra.

Footnote:

1. Nicknames are a Mafia phenomenon. Apart from 'the Hump', or 'the Camel', there was Vincenzo de Mora, known as 'Machine-gun' Jack McGurn. Other well-known mobsters were Paul 'the Waiter' Ricca, 'Tough Tony' Capezio, 'Bugsy' Moran, Louis 'Little New York' Campagna, Frank 'The Enforcer' Nitti, Jake 'Greasy Thumb' Guzik, Tony 'Joe Batters' Accardo, 'Big Jim' Colosimo, Sam 'Mooney' Giancana (also known as 'Momo', he shared a mistress with President Kennedy), Frank 'Strongy' Ferraro, Sam 'Teets' Battaglia, Felix 'Milwauke Phil' Alderision, Joey 'O'Brien' Aiuppa, Joey 'The Clown' Lombardo, Carl 'Tuffy' Deluna, Tony 'The Ant' Spilotro, Sam 'Wings' Carlisi, John 'No Nose' DiFronzo, 'Trigger' Mike Coppola, Frankie 'The X' Esposito, Sammy 'The Bull' Gravano, John 'The Dapper Don' Gotti, 'Big Paul' Castellano, 'Jackie 'Nose' D'Amico, 'Tony Roach' Rampino, 'Jelly Bean' DiBono, 'Gas Pipe' Casso, Vincente 'Chin' Gigante, Benny 'Eggs' Mangano, 'Fat Tony' Salerno, 'Fat Tony' Pronto, 'Fat Angelo' or 'Fatso' Ruggiero, 'Crazy Joe' Gallo, Joey 'The Check-Casher' Ingrassia, Jimmy 'The Weasel' Fratianno, Angelo 'The Ape' Annunciata, 'Tony Ducks' Corallo, Vincent 'Jimmy Blue Eyes' Alo, 'Short Pants' Cacioppo, Frankie 'The German' Schweihs as well as Al 'Scarface' Capone.

2. *The Dark Side of Camelot* by Seymour Hers claims that the Kennedys 'bought' the 1960 Election with Mafia help. Jeanne Humphreys, the Camel's widow, claimed that of the five Mafia leaders who agreed to a deal with Joe Kennedy, to financially support his sons win crucial votes against Nixon, the Hump was the only one who dissented. He regarded Joe Kennedy as a 'four-flusher' from Prohibition days, who could not be trusted. His fears were justified as the mobster Sam Giancana, who shared a mistress with John F. Kennedy, was wiretapped by the FBI in the 1960s, which recorded him saying that he had been double-crossed by the Kennedys.

IDRIS DAVIES 6 January 1905 – 6 April 1953

THE MINER-POET, THE WORKING-CLASS POET

In 1926, the miners refused to work an extra hour a day, coupled with large pay cuts of 16-25%. On 30 April 1926, those miners refusing the terms were locked out and the pits stopped producing. On 3 May, the General Strike, called by the TUC, began. The mood in South Wales was almost revolutionary at this time, and when the TUC called off the strike just 9 days later, the Welsh were left to fight on, alone and betrayed. Almost a quarter of a million men stayed away from the pitheads. Police were called in from outside Wales to keep order, until the starving miners were forced back to work at the end of 1926. The effects on that South Walian generation solidified a feeling of 'us against the world' for decades.

The problem here is that death wipes out memories. Young people at university have absolutely no idea of German and Japanese atrocities of two generations ago. The horrors of the First World War, the terrible poverty of the 1920's and the like simply do not exist for many people. It is 'cogito, ergo sum' in action - 'I think therefore I exist' but the corollary is that 'It only matters if I know about it'. Knowledge is the only weapon ordinary people have in their armoury against pollution, unnecessary wars, corrupted politicians, multinational over-pricing and the like. Davies could see this, and cared for his fellows.

He was born at 16 Field Street, Rhymney to Colliery Winderman Evan Davies and Elizabeth Ann in 1905. From a Welsh-speaking home, Rhymney-bred Idris Davies learned English in the local elementary school,

and having left school at 14 he worked underground at Abertysswg and Rhymney Mardy Pits.

At the colliery, a fellow-miner introduced Davies to the works of Shelley, and Davies realised that he could use the poetic medium to politicise people, proselytising socialism and human dignity. In 1926, aged 21, he lost a finger in a pit accident, and in a 1937 notebook he mentions the accident: 'I looked down and saw a piece of white bone shining like snow, and the flesh of the little finger all limp. The men supported me, and one ran for an ambulance box dwon the heading, and there I was fainting away like a little baby girl.'

Almost immediately the Great Strike started. With no work, Davies matriculated via a correspondence course to gain acceptance at Loughborough College and then at Nottingham University, qualifying as a teacher. Between 1932 and 1947 he taught in the East End of London and at schools evacuated from wartime London. After many attempts, he managed to be transferred back to Rhymney Valley to teach in 1947 in a junior school at Cwmsyfiog. Davies was found to be suffering from stomach cancer in 1951, and died aged 48 in 1953, being buried at Rhymney Cemetery. His first volume of published poems, *Gwalia Deserta* (1938) focused on the impact of the depression on south Wales.

Along with David Jones and R.S. Thomas, Davies is this author's favourite Welsh poet. His *Gwalia Deserta* (the Wasteland of Wales) was recommended as follows by T. S. Eliot... 'They are the best poetic document I know about a particular epoch in a particular place, and I think that they really have a claim to permanence.' The long and unified dramatic poem described the desert that industrial South Wales had become in the 1920s and 1930s. *Gwalia Deserta* shows a socially and politically committed poet, full of the imagery of mining-valley life in the terrible days of the 1930's.

Much of his work describes the impact of the Industrial Revolution, and its terrible decline, upon his beloved countryside and people. A Celtic Christian Socialist, he epitomised Welsh bardic tradition with a respect for fellow mankind, rather than for wealth based upon prosperity... 'Any subject which has not man at its core is anathema to me. The meanest tramp on the road is ten times more interesting than the loveliest garden in the world. And instead of getting nearer to nature in the countryside I find myself craving for more intense society'.

Idris Davies is the most approachable of all Welsh poets writing in English, and verse XV of his *Gwalia Deserta* was set to music by Pete Seeger and also recorded by The Byrds amongst many others -

O what can you give me? / Say the sad bells of Rhymney.
Is there hope for the future? / Cry the brown bells of Merthyr.
Who made the mineowner? Say the black bells of Rhondda.
And who robbed the miner? Cry the grim bells of Blaina.
They will plunder willy-nilly, Say the bells of Caerphilly.
They have fangs, they have teeth! Shout the loud bells of Neath.
To the south, things are sullen, Say the pink bells of Brecon.
Even God is uneasy, Say the moist bells of Swansea.
Put the vandals in court! Cry the bells of Newport.
All would be well if - if - if - Say the green bells of Cardiff
Why so worried, sisters, why? Sing the silver bells of Wye.

His other great work was *The Angry Summer: A Poem of 1926,* published in 1943. It graphically illustrates the plight of the miners and their families during the six-month-long miners' strike of 1926:

'Do you remember 1926? That summer of soups and speeches,
The sunlight on the idle wheels and the deserted crossings,
And the laughter and cursing in the moonlit streets?
Do you remember 1926? The slogans and the penny concerts,
The jazz-bands and the moorland picnics,
And the slanderous tongues of famous cities?
Do you remember 1926? The great dream and the swift disaster,
The fanatic and the traitor, and more than all,
The bravery of the simple, faithful folk?
"Ay, ay, we remember 1926," said Dai and Shinkin,
As they stood on the kerb in Charing Cross Road,
"And we shall remember 1926 until our blood is dry."...'

Not until 1994 were Davies' complete poems collected in hardback, and are now available in paperback. *The New Welsh Review* recorded their publication as follows: 'the poet, who in his lifetime, was usually treated with condescension and frequently accused of being merely a propagandist for socialism and of writing journalism, is central to the study of Anglo-Welsh poetry - more crucial, in fact, than Dylan Thomas or even R.S. Thomas... this splendid volume... must be saluted: it is surely a major landmark in Anglo-Welsh studies.' And *Poetry Review* said 'he has a claim to be recognised as one of the outstanding working-class poets of the century... an important work of publishing and scholarship'. Ignoring the slightly derisory connotations of 'working-class', we can see that Davies is slowly receiving the acclaim that he deserved in life.

He brilliantly summed up the hypocrisy of some of the stricter Nonconformist sects in his poem *Capel Calvin*...

'There's holy holy people
They are in capel bach -
They don't like surpliced choirs,
They don't like Sospan Fach.
They don't like Sunday concerts,
Or women playing ball,
They don't like Williams Parry much
Or Shakespeare at all.

They don't like beer or bishops,
Or pictures without texts,
They don't like any other
Of the nonconformist sects.

And when they go to Heaven
They won't like that too well,
For the music will be sweeter
Than the music played in Hell.'

A diary entry reads: 'I am a socialist. That is why I want as much beauty as possible in our everyday lives, and so I am an enemy of pseudo-poetry and pseudo-art of all kinds. Too many poets of the left are badly in need of instructions as to the difference between poetry and propaganda... These people should read William Blake on Imagination until they show signs of understanding him. Then the air will be clear again, and the land be, if not full of, fit for song?' 'He is perhaps the most authentic socialist poet of the inter-war years to write in English, because he speaks out of the experience of his own working-class community.' *The Collected Poems of Idris Davies* is a truly wonderful and moving book, ending with his *Psalm*, which begins with the lines which could have been inscribed on the new Millenium Theatre:

'Make us, O lord, a people fit for poetry,
And grant us clear voices to praise all noble achievement.'

GWYNFOR EVANS 1 September 1912 – 21 April 2005

'ONE OF THE GREAT SOULS OF TWENTIETH-CENTURY WALES', PLAID CYMRU'S FIRST MP

President of Plaid Cymru - The Party of Wales - for 36 years from 1945 until 1981, and its 'Honorary President' until his death, Gwynfor was the first member of his party to be elected to Parliament, in 1966. A trained solicitor, a devout Christian and a pacifist, he was almost treated as a pariah in the House of Commons because of his insistence that Wales was a nation which needed to preserve its language, and which needed its own parliament. Fortunately, Gwynfor Evans knew the history of Wales, what had been done to it, and its remarkable culture, heritage and contribution to Christianity and civilisation. This compares dramatically with a later Welsh political leader, Neil Kinnock, who sadly believed that Wales did not have 'much of a history'. The problem, as always, is that people only believe what they are told - the inquiring mind will find that history is always written by the conquerors. From the anti-Druid propaganda of the Romans via the Hanoverian apologist Bishop Stubbs to today's times, the media follows the masters, and what went before is wiped out.

Gwynfor Evans graduated at Oxford and Aberystwyth, and took over as President of Plaid Cymru in 1945. He married Rhiannon, had seven children and mainly worked as a commercial gardener in Llangadog until his retirement. To some extent the Conservative government of the 1950's helped the growth of Plaid. Responding to its election pledges, it attempted to create a sinecure phantom Ministry of Welsh Affairs in that decade, headed by the first of a long line of English Tories, Sir David Maxwell Hamilton-Fyfe. His strange attitude towards Wales and the Welsh earned him the epithet across Wales was 'Dai Bananas'. He was followed by others of the ilk of Sir Henry Brooke, Sir Keith Joseph, the miming John Redwood and the adolescent William Hague. Wales was given a Secretary of State position in the Cabinet in 1964. Evans during this time had moved away from Saunders' Lewis vision of Plaid Cymru, towards more political activity, environmentalism, European federalism and social democracy based on the Scandinavian model.

Born in Barry, Glamorgan, a town of few Welsh-speakers, his father owned the department store, Dan Evans, which stood in the run-down main street (Holton Road) of the town*. Gwynfor was a pacifist in World War II, which turned many local people against him, and his father helped him move

to Carmarthenshire and start a market garden, which was an occupation which did not require one to go to war. (This last statement was queried in previous editions of this book, but all I am repeating is what my parents and their friends and relatives told me, people who lived in Barry and knew the Evans brothers). Imprisoned several times for trying to keep the language alive, his daughter Meinir was also twice imprisoned herself in London's Holloway gaol, and her husband Ffred Ffrancis himself spent five years in prison.

Ffrancis was leader of Cymdeithas yr Iaith Gymraeg (the Welsh Language Society), the formation of which by a younger generation in the 1960's Gwynfor called 'one of the proudest chapters in the history of Wales'. The movement, by court protests at wishing trials to be held in Welsh, by daubing English road-signs in Wales, and by a programme of civil disobedience, eventually was rewarded with Welsh being awarded official language status.

The Welsh Language Act of 1967 has not secured the language, but will help slow its destruction. Some readers should probably be made aware that Welsh was 1,400 years old when Chaucer was trying to write the first barely recognisable English. If we say the Shakespeare's language is the beginning of modern English, it is around a fifth of the age of Welsh. The language is dying because for four decades, 90% of then population growth of Wales has come from outside. In the last Census, only 2 million of the 3 million inhabitants called themselves Welsh, and many of those were the children of incomers. The heartlands of the language, rural unspoilt areas, have been filled with retirees, the unemployed and people upon benefits. They do not come to Wales for work – there is none. No politician will address the threat to the true British language, for fear of being termed racist. There was a favourable review in *Planet* in April 2010 of my 2009 A Historical Companion to Wales, but included the statement: 'Few political commentators would agree that Plaid Cymru, which apparently flourished under the leadership of Dafydd Wigley in the 1990s, "in this millennium seemingly has become moribund"!' The 2015 General Election results prove my contention.

Gwynfor was the first Plaid Cymru MP to be elected, in a stunning victory at Carmarthen in July 1966, following the death of Lady Megan Lloyd George. He constantly campaigned for better road networks between Wales and the rest of the UK, which promoted the cause of the M4 motorway across South Wales. For this he became known as 'Gwynfor Dual-Carriageway' in some quarters. Apart from his other efforts to raise the profile of the Welsh language, Gwynfor knew that it was necessary to be a language of the media - there simply had to be a Welsh television channel. The author was in Galway in 1995, speaking to a Gaelic radio station, and realised that Ireland needed a Gaelic 'soap-opera' on TV to help its dying language. *Pobol y Cwm* has that distinction on *Sianel Pedwar Cymraeg* (Welsh Channel 4), and people should remember that Gwynfor Evans threatened to go on a hunger strike in 1980 to get a Welsh language TV channel. The bellicose Prime Minister, Mrs Thatcher, had promised one, but reneged. After her U-turn, someone scrawled in letters three feet high, on the wall of the Thames Embankment facing Westminster, 'GWYNFOR 1 - THATCHER 0'.

Another of Gwynfor's achievements is the popularity of Welsh-medium schools, in which teaching is carried out in the Welsh language. As he said in 1996, 'the way to annihilate a nation is to obliterate its culture. The way to delete its culture is to destroy its language'. He also believes that 'the nation-state is now so powerful it can kill a culture merely by ignoring it.' This author, however, believes that nation-states are increasingly powerless, and that stateless multinational companies control economies, labour forces and politicians.

His greatest sorrow was the drowning of Trywerin, 'except for the campaign for a Parliament for Wales, Trywerin was the most important of our battles'. The beautiful valley of Cwm Trywerin was made into a reservoir for Liverpool, despite overwhelming opposition from the Welsh people**. Presently the Welsh pay more for water than the English who use water from Welsh reservoirs. As Trywerin is now surplus to Liverpool's requirements, perhaps it could be drained and the land returned as National Park to Wales. Passive demonstrations, encouraged by Gwynfor, were no good, and there was some sabotage against transformers used in the dam's construction, and against the following Clywedog dam for Birmingham's needs.

The Lord Mayor of Liverpool opened the Trywerin Dam and Reservoir in October 1963, with a strong police presence, and stones and fireworks being thrown. Suddenly the shouting died down as the crowds joined in with a small group of youths who had begun singing an old hymn. There were new words, repeated over and over, and the Lord Mayor and his councillors respectfully listened in peace. The words were '*Twll din pob Sais'* – 'Arseholes to all Englishmen'.

All Welsh MP's voted against the Trywerin tragedy and the wiping out of the 100%-Welsh-speaking community of Capel Celyn, except for Sir Henry Brooke, the Tory Minister of Welsh Affairs. Gwynfor's pamphlet, *Save Cwm Trywerin for Wales* was published by Plaid Cymru in 1956, and the cover features an illustration of Bob Roberts Tai'r Felin, the renowned Welsh ballad singer who lived near the site of the dam.

Even the conservative *Western Mail* commented 'There has been every appearance of complete contempt for Welsh opinion on the part of both the Liverpool Corporation and of Parliament.' The present water situation as regarding Trywerin, the Elan and other reservoirs, is scandalous, and needs addressing by the Welsh Assembly Government as a priority. I wrote this last sentence 15 years ago, and it is repeated. Wales gets nothing in return from the imposition of reservoirs.

It is fair to say that the precarious survival of the language, despite the consistent cries from English settlers in their last colony, and the existence of a 'National Assembly' since 1999 ***, have been in no small part due to Evan's influence and stance. Because of him, Plaid Cymru for some time became a real opposition to the Millbank-controlled Labour Party in Wales. Welsh schools and colleges are massively under-funded compared to those in England, and the wealth per person (GDP per capita) is around three-quarters that of England's. Wales has always been neglected by the Tories when in power at Westminster, because it is not a source of parliamentary power for them. Labour has ignored it for exactly the opposite reason - it can count upon Wales for seats in Parliament, and does not need to offer 'sweeteners'.

For the Sake of Wales: the Memoirs of Gwynfor Evans has been translated by Meic Stephens, and is a marvellous book. Its reviewer in the American-Welsh newspaper *Ninnau* said 'there are not enough superlatives in my vocabulary to express what I believe to be the value of "*For the Sake of Wales*", especially to the North American Welsh, or others of the Greater Welsh Nation throughout the world, who want to come home to their Welshness'. And Manon Rhys, in her preface to the original publication in Welsh in 1982 wrote 'This is the story of one of the great souls of Twentieth-century Wales.' The memoirs reveal his feelings about the influx of English retirees and holiday homeowners into the Welsh language heartland of north and west Wales. He says 'just to talk about it risks being seen as anti-English but I'm not at all. I'm anti-English government... I'm not very optimistic (about the future of the language), but I'm not without hope... only when the community is Welsh-speaking is the language secure.'

* The author grew up in Barry - the beautiful Town Hall and Carnegie Library on the main King Square was semi-derelict and mainly unoccupied for over 20 years, since the council moved into grand new offices. The roof of the once-

superb library, which forms part of the building, collapsed. Only by an unlikely coalition of Plaid and the Tories replacing the perennial Labour Council was anything done about it. Barry has huge infrastructural problems, which politicians seem unable to face. One of the main problems of Cardiff's growth and popularity is that it has sucked resources from its neighbouring hinterland - to the east Newport, to the north Caerffili and the valleys, and to the west Barry. All have been ill-served by their elected representatives for decades.

** A copy of a letter sent to the Prime Minister by the President of Plaid Cymru (Welsh Nationalist Party), Alderman Gwynfor Evans, M.A., Ll.B., upon July 28th 1957 was printed as a pamphlet by Plaid Cymru, and reads as follows: 'The Trywerin issue has been widely understood to be crucial for the future of the national language and way of life. Therefore the Third reading on Wednesday of Liverpool Corporation's Bill to drown the Valley is a fateful occasion for Wales. No national issue during this century has united the Welsh people as strongly as this. Over a long period, their will has been clearly and forcefully expressed by hundreds of representative assemblies. The biggest cities in England have seen Welsh men, women and children from Cwm Trywerin pleading for their right to live in their homes undisturbed, and in the Bill's Second Reading not a single Welsh MP gave it support. There can be no doubt about the conviction of Wales in this matter. Wales stands firm in the defence of its heritage.

Liverpool Corporation demands a huge quantity of water from Merioneth, not because its reasonable needs cannot be met elsewhere – there are a dozen possible sources in England – but because Cwm Trywerin is the cheapest and most profitable source to exploit. In these circumstances to force the Bill through Parliament by an English majority, with the incongruous help of The Minister for Welsh Affairs, can do no more than give a veneer of legality to an immoral act of aggression. It would be a declaration by the English majority in Parliament that it has the power to destroy Wales and will not refuse to do so if it thinks this would be in the interests of a part of England. Liverpool will have enlisted the power of the strong to force the weak into submission, and its success may soon be emulated by other corporations and bodies who will have observed how powerless Wales is to protect her community and resources. If we Welshmen accepted this passively, it would be an act of betrayal on our part. If all legal and constitutional endeavour to defend the Welsh heritage is ignored, despite the unity and depth of Welsh conviction, the defence must continue, but by other means.'

*** The Scottish Assembly had far more power than the National Assembly (which should be called the 'British Assembly'), because the Prime Minister and Cabinet which agreed to the legislation were overwhelmingly Scottish at the time. Of the 22-man cabinet, the only Welshman was the placid Alun Michael as the ineffectual Minister for Wales. The Prime Minister (Blair), Chancellor of the Exchequer (Brown), Foreign Secretary (Cook), Minister of Defence (Robertson), Lord Chancellor (Irvine) and Defence Minister (Robertson) were all Scottish, filling 6 of the 7 most powerful Cabinet places (-the Home

Secretary, Straw, was English). If we add Dewar (Scotland), the Scots had 7 of the 22 Cabinet places.

Footnote: (From this author's *Wales: A Historical Companion*)
WATER
In 1892, the British government passed the Birmingham Corporation Water Act allowing the council to compulsory purchase almost seventy square miles of Wales. This was the water catchment area of the Elan and Claerwen Valleys. The Act also gave Birmingham the powers to move more than a hundred Welsh-speaking people living in the Elan Valley. All the buildings were demolished; these included three manor houses, eighteen farms, a school and a church founded by the Knights Hospitallers. Only landowners were given compensation. There are four main dams and reservoirs (constructed 1893–1904 in Elan Valley, and 1946–1952 at Claerwen) with a potential total capacity of nearly 100,000 megalitres. The Claerwen dam was the last to be finished in 1952, is almost twice the size of the other dams in the Elan valley, and was opened by Queen Elizabeth. Claerwen reservoir is leased for 999 years to the Midlands for 5 pence a year.

Lake Efernwy (Vyrnwy) was constructed in the 1880s in Montgomeryshire, with its stone-built dam being the first of its kind in the world. It was built to supply Merseyside and Liverpool with fresh water. It submerged the small village of Llanwddyn, with its population of 450. Two chapels, three inns, ten farmhouses, and 37 houses were all lost under reservoir. Also lost under the water was Eunant Hall, a large house and estate. It was the largest man-made lake in the world. The people were forcibly moved to new houses down the valley to accommodate its construction, and the village now numbers only 300 people. The reservoir is Severn Trent Water's largest, being eleven miles in circumference. In common with all the reservoirs built across Wales, there was no proper archaeological survey of what was being covered. The Alwen Reservoir in Conwy is a 3-mile long reservoir built to supply Birkenhead, Liverpool, built between 1909 and 1921.

Faded graffiti, *'Cofiwch Drywerin'* (Remember Trywerin) can still be seen in parts of Wales. In the Valley of Trywerin, the village of Capel Celyn was drowned to satisfy the water needs of Liverpool. This was despite the fact that water from a valley of a tributary of the Trywerin could have been taken without destroying any homes. A plaque near Trywerin reservoir car park reads: '*Under these waters and near this stone stood Hafod Fadog, a farmstead where in the seventeenth and eighteenth centuries Quakers met for worship. On the hillside above the house was a space encircled by a low stone wall, where larger meetings were held, and beyond the house was a small burial ground. From this valley came many of the early Quakers who emigrated to Pennsylvania, driven from their homes by persecution to seek freedom of worship in the New World*'.

All the people of the doomed village marched through Liverpool, but the English Parliament voted by 175 votes to 79 in 1979 to kill the community. Thirty-five of thirty-six Welsh MPs opposed the bill, with one abstention, but the bill was passed in 1957. Wales has never had a say in the Parliamentary affairs of England. Five hundred members of Plaid Cymru, led by Gwynfor

Evans, badly disrupted the reservoir opening ceremony in 1965, but Capel Celyn is rotting beneath the waters. In 1956, a private bill sponsored by Liverpool City Council had been brought before Parliament. By obtaining authority via an Act of Parliament, Liverpool City Council would not require planning consent from the relevant Welsh local authorities. This, together with the fact that the village was one of the last Welsh-only speaking communities, ensured that the proposals became deeply controversial. The members of the community waged an eight-year effort, ultimately unsuccessful, to prevent the destruction of their homes. This is similar to every local community fighting against the threat of wind follies at present, with little hope.

When the valley was flooded in 1965, the village and its buildings, including the post office, the school, and a chapel with cemetery, were all lost. Twelve houses and farms were submerged, and 48 people of the 67 who lived in the valley lost their homes. In all some 800 acres, 2.5 miles by a mile, were submerged. The opening ceremony lasted less than 3 minutes, for protesters had cut the microphone wires, and the chants of the hundreds of protesters made the speeches inaudible. In October 2005, Liverpool City Council passed a public apology for the incident. Its full statement reads: '*The Council acknowledges its debt to the many thousands of Welsh people who have made their homes in the City. They have, in so many ways, enriched the life of the City. We know that Liverpool, especially in the fields of medicine and education, has been of real service to the people of Wales. We realise the hurt of forty years ago when the Tryweryn Valley was transformed into a reservoir to help meet the water needs of Liverpool. For any insensitivity by our predecessor Council at that time, we apologise and hope that the historic and sound relationship between Liverpool and Wales can be completely restored.*' It is difficult to understand the weasel words of Liverpool's reciprocal value '*in the fields of medicine and education*' to Wales in the above apology. It would be wonderful to see Llyn Celyn emptied and used as a national memorial of some sort.

The Clywedog reservoir near Llanidloes was completed in 1967 to supply water to Birmingham and the English Midlands. It is the tallest concrete dam in the UK, with a height of 72 metres and a length of 230 metres. Construction of the dam commenced in 1963 after an Act of Parliament. Local opposition was strong against the construction of the reservoir as it would result in the flooding of much of the Clywedog valley and the drowning of 615 acres of agricultural land. On top of several disruptions and protests, during construction in 1966 a bomb was detonated within the construction site, setting work back by almost 2 months. The political extremist group *Mudiad Amddiffyn Cymru* (MAC) was responsible. Their bomb delayed work by 8 weeks, and John Jenkins was imprisoned.

Llyn Brenig was completed in 1976 on the borders of Conwy and Denbighshire, particularly for the needs of Liverpool and its surrounding area. The reservoir has a perimeter of fourteen miles. Welsh MP's could not stop any of these reservoirs being built via compulsory purchase. Because of continuing shortages in the south-east of England, there are plans to divert water from the Severn and Wye into England. The third biggest river in England and Wales, after the Welsh Severn and Wye rivers, the Trent, has had no reservoirs built on it.

R. S. THOMAS March 29 1913 - September 25 2000

THE POET-PRIEST, 'THE SOLZHENITSYN OF WALES'

 Ronald Stuart Thomas was a poet-priest, nominated for the 1996 Nobel Prize for Literature. Born in Cardiff in 1913, he studied classics at Bangor University and theology at Llandaff. 'R.S.' became an Anglican priest in 1936, retiring in 1978. Ending his days on the Llŷn Peninsula, he was to my mind the finest poet writing in English, with no sign of any weakness in his powers to transfix the reader, with visions of bleakness and beauty. He represents the uncompromising conscience of a Wales, under ceaseless alien attack, and tries to work out our difficult relationship with God.

He was born in Cardiff, the only son of Huw and Margaret. In 1914, his family moved to Holyhead, and he was ordained as a priest in 1936 after graduation from Bangor. He was curate of Chirk and Hanmer from 1936-40, then moved to Manafon as rector and in 1943 began to learn Welsh. In 1940 he married Mildred Eldridge, an English artist. After learning Welsh he scoured the country for parishes in which to preach and perfect his knowledge of the language, but always regretted that his linguistic skills in poetry were better in English.

He published collections of poems, *The Stones of the Land* (1946), *An Acre of Field* (1952) and *The Minister* (1953) before moving to Eglwys-fach outside Aberystwyth in 1954. He was disappointed at Eglwys-fach that there were so many English in his parish – he wanted to be immersed in a Welsh-speaking community. He said that there were as many 'retired tea-planters and ex-army officers' as there were Welsh speakers. His *Song of the Year's Turning* won the Royal Society of Literature's Heinemann Prize for Poetry in 1955. John Betjeman wrote the preface to this work, stating 'The name which has the honour to introduce this fine poet to a wider public will be forgotten long before that of R.S. Thomas.' *Poetry for Supper* was published in 1958, and with *The Bread of Truth* in 1963, he was Stratford-upon-Avon's 'Poet of the Year.'

In 1966, Thomas won the Queen's Gold Medal for poetry, and in 1967 became vicar of the ancient church of St Hywyn, Aberdaron, overlooking the 'Isle of Saints', Ynys Enlli (Bardsey Island). He was happiest here, in what was a truly Welsh community at the very end of the Llŷn peninsula. (However, it is now mainly incomers and holiday-homes). In 1972, he became vicar of Rhiw with Llanfaelrhys, and published *What is a Welshman* (1974), *Laboratories of the Spirit* (1975) and *The Way of It* (1977). Aged 65, in 1978 R.S. retired from the church, won the Cholmondely Award and published *Frequencies*. From 1981 to 1986 he published *Between Here and Now, Later Poems, Ingrowing Thoughts, Destinations, Neb* (*Nobody* - an autobiography), and *Experimenting with an Amen*. In *Neb* he stated 'There is no such thing as an Anglo-Welshman... you have to make a stand, and that is the stand I have chosen to make.' His only prose work apart from *Neb* was *Blwyddyn yn Llŷn*, (*A Year in Llŷn*). In the latter he noted his sadness over Welsh acceptance of English imperialism, 'worrying continually for a dying nation, and tortured by the unanswerable question: is she being killed or does she want to die? A mixture of both I'd imagine.'

His worries about the future of Wales were evident in these lines from 'Welsh History'... 'We were a people bred on legends, / Warming our hands at the red past. /
The great were ashamed of our loose rags / Clinging stubbornly to the proud tree / Of blood and birth, our lean bellies / And mud houses were a proof / Of our ineptitude for life.
We were a people wasting ourselves / In fruitless battles for our masters, / In lands to which we had no claim, / With men for whom we felt no hatred.
We were a people, and are so yet. / When we have finished quarrelling for crumbs / Under the table, or gnawing the bones / Of a dead culture, we will arise, / Armed, but not in the old way.'

R.S.Thomas incurred the wrath of the police in 1988, when he said of a fire-bombing campaign that it would be better for someone to die as a result of the campaign, than for the language to die out. His wife Mildred was always known as 'Elsi' Thomas, and she died in 1991. In 1992 and 1995, *A Mass for Hard Times* (dedicated to his deceased wife) and *No Truce with the Furies* appeared, and in 1996 he won the Lannan Literary Prize for Lifetime Achievement, the same year as his Nobel nomination. He lost out on the Nobel Prize for Literature to his friend Seamus Heaney, who read the eulogy at Thomas's memorial tribute in Westminster Abbey, just five years later. In 1999 he won the *Western Mail* and Welsh Books Council 'Book of the Century' Award for his collected poems. He wrote of her:

His poem *Reservoirs* sums up his disgust with abandoned communities ('smashed faces of farms'), with the alien Sitka Spruce of the Forestry Commission ('gardens gone under the scum of forests'), with tourist 'strangers' to whom the reservoirs have 'the watercolour's appeal to the mass'. He had become, over time, a committed Welsh Nationalist. RS displays a scorn for those complicitous in the loss of language, and the turning of Wales into some quaint theme parks for the richer, more sophisticated English: 'Where can I go, then, from the smell / Of decay, from the putrefying of a dead / Nation? I have walked the shore / For an hour and seen the English / Scavenging among the remains / Of our culture, covering the sand / Like the tide and, with the roughness / Of the tide, elbowing our language / Into the grave that we have dug for it.'

Ted Hughes, himself of Welsh stock and a great admirer, described R. S. Thomas' poetry - it 'pierces the heart', and Thomas' indignation at the way history has treated the Welsh demonstrates this in the concluding lines of his 1955 poem *Welsh Landscape*: '

There is no present in Wales,
And no future;
There is only the past,
Brittle with relics,
Wind-bitten towers and castles
With sham ghosts;
Mouldering quarries and mines;
And an impotent people,
Sick with inbreeding,
Worrying the carcass of an old song.'

The Eton-educated Scot Lord Gowrie, Chairman of the Arts Council of Great Britain, has found Thomas's work 'offensively nationalistic'. Gowrie was in touch with the real world, being previously chairman of Sothebys from 1985-1994, after resigning from the Cabinet in 1995 because 'it was impossible for him to live in London' on a £33,000 salary (the equivalent of £95,000 today) and expenses. People who live upon different planets should never pass comment upon reality. The rightful bitterness present in much of Thomas's work can be explained in an interview he gave to Nia Griffith, when he was aged 82. 'The anger born out of the exile that Thomas has felt in Wales and with an expanding Welsh culture, has, however, calmed in later years. "It was all part of this hyphenated person that I am, thinking myself Welsh, learning the language, but with an English upbringing, always being on the outside. Now, though, I feel completely integrated... Also, my move from the Llyn to Anglesey, where there are less caravans, and less political stirrings has caused me, along with my age, to become less involved... But I still stand for the de-Anglicisation of Wales and for the true Welsh identity to re-emerge. I just don't think it's going to happen. My words have been misinterpreted. I've always been a pacifist and never encouraged violence. The language is the one thing we have left, and if that goes, everything goes.'

Thomas retired to the remote village in northwest Anglesey, Llanfairynghornwy. In 1996, Thomas married again, a Canadian widow called Elisabeth (Betty) Vernon. R.S. Thomas died at home in Llanfairynghornwy and is buried in St John's Church, Porthmadog. His widow and his son Gwydion survive him.

The Guardian obituary of 27 September 2000 reads: 'The poet RS Thomas was embraced by the admiration of Wales and a wider world when his death was announced yesterday. Thomas, one of the most uncompromising, purest and most sustained lyric voices of his century, died at his virtual hermit's home at Pentrefelin, near Cricieth. He was 87 and had been ill with heart trouble. He was being treated at Ysbyty Gwynedd hospital until two weeks ago. The unchanging themes of his poetry were God and the sparse natural world of the north Wales parishes, which he served for 40 years as a Church in Wales priest. He was still railing like a prophet against "the technological smugness, the awful atheism, the political sleaze" of the contemporary world in one of his last interviews late last year. But his views were felt modern enough for a line from one of his poems to be quoted two years ago on the cover of the Manic Street Preachers album *This is My Truth, Tell me Yours*. In another poem, he wrote that he hated the Welsh "for your irreverence, your scorn even/of the refinements of art and the mysteries of the church". He accused them of committing their own cultural suicide, as "an impotent people/sick with inbreeding/worrying the carcass of an old song."

But in the Principality yesterday he was hailed as a greater poet than Dylan Thomas. For the Welsh language Society, Dafydd Lewis said, "He was probably Wales' most outstanding poet of the 20th century. He was a very good friend of ours. He was quite a character and did not mind supporting unpopular causes if he thought they were correct. Even if you didn't agree with his views, they were interesting and thought-provoking." But the society disagreed with him over his support for the campaign of arson attacks on holiday homes in Wales. Praising those who were fire-bombing English-owned property, Thomas asked in 1998, "What is one death against the death of the whole Welsh nation?"

Rhodri Morgan, first secretary of the Welsh National Assembly, said the country had lost a grand man of letters, a fierce and passionate man who had a unique knowledge of Wales and Welshness. "He leaves behind a rich legacy; a fascinating vision of an idyllic Welsh rural past and spirituality which will be read with admiration for generations." The Plaid Cymru President, Ieuan Wyn Jones, called Thomas one of Wales's greatest literary voices. He had helped put it on the cultural map of the world. "His profound spirituality and unashamed patriotism made his poetry unique and gained him an international audience," Mr Jones said yesterday. "His work will remain with us as a testament to the flowering of Welsh writing in English and the emerging Welsh identity in the latter part of the 20th century." M. Wynn Thomas, a professor at the University of Wales, Swansea, said, "He was the Solzhenitysn of Wales because he was such a troubler of the Welsh conscience. He was one of the major English language and European poets of the 20th century." Al Alvarez, the English poetry critic, poet and author who first promoted Thomas's work in the 1950's - along with that of Ted Hughes and Sylvia Plath - said last night: "He was wonderful, very pure, very bitter but the bitterness was beautifully and very sparely rendered. He was completely authoritative, a very, very fine poet, completely off on his own, out of the loop, but a real individual. It's not about being a major or minor poet. It's about getting a work absolutely right by your own standards and he did that wonderfully well". Mr Alvarez said Thomas's work would survive as securely as that of Henry Vaughan, the 17th century metaphysical poet who wrote: "I saw Eternity the other night/like a great ring of pure and endless light".'

Footnotes:
1. It is indicative of the way that Welsh people think of their greatest heroes – their names invariably get shortened to RS, Dylan, Pantycelyn, Glyndŵr, Bleddyn, Gareth and JPR – that is three poets, a warrior and three rugby players.

2. *The Daily Telegraph* obituary is as follows: 'R.S. Thomas, Poet, 1913-2000. R.S. Thomas was a fervent defender of Wales and the Welsh language, which made it odd that he should have been one of the best poets writing in English since the Second World War. The style of his verse - spare, harsh, austere (though lit by sudden flares of lyrical splendour) - reflected the appearance of the man. But the economy of the phrasing carries complex meanings and the surface clarity deep resonance.

Ruthlessly unsentimental, he did not hesitate, in his fiercer moods, to depict the hill farmers as vacant, miserly and mean-spirited. There were no newspapers in his house; still less television. To feed his intellect he read philosophy. Thomas's defence of Wales and the Welsh language became ever more extreme, until in 1990 he called for "non-violent night attacks" on English properties. He could not support Plaid Cymru because it recognised Westminster. "Britain does not exist for me," he explained. "It's an abstraction forced upon the Welsh people." But he also castigated the Welsh themselves who, "through indifference, lack of backbone, snobbishness and laziness", had chosen to speak English and cast away their inheritance. He received the Queen's gold medal for poetry in 1964, and the Cheltenham prize in 1963. "Prizes are irrelevant," he said.'

DYLAN MARLAIS THOMAS 27 October 1914 - 9 November 1953

WALES' BEST-KNOWN POET, THE SELF-STYLED 'RIMBAUD OF CWMDONKIN DRIVE' 'THE GREATEST LIVING POET IN THE ENGLISH LANGUAGE'

His place of birth at 5 Cwmdonkin Road, in Swansea's Uplands district, has been a place of pilgrimage by admirers from all over the world, including Mick Jagger and ex-President Jimmy Carter. Famously, a less salubrious future President, Bill Clinton, attempted to drive there, but drove to Bristol instead of Wales. Dylan's best work was accomplished when he was young - he extensively 'quarried' from his schoolboy notebooks, and worked, and reworked lines of poems constantly to achieve the right feeling and flow. In 1927, aged just 13, he had a poem published in *Boys Own*, and in 1931 left

Writing shed, Laugharne

school to work as a journalist on the *South Wales Evening Post* in Swansea. In 1933 *And Death Shall Have No Dominion* became the 19-year-old's first poem to be published in a London magazine, the *New English Weekly*. In 1933 he visited London for the first time and the

following year won a competition, which ensured the publication of his first book, *18 Poems*. He was now living in London, and in 1936, *25 Poems* was printed.

Dylan's mother, Florence, was from the Llansteffan peninsula, a short ferry-ride from Laugharne. Although she moved to Swansea, many relations stayed in the Llansteffan area, and her sister's farm of Fernhill, near Llangain, is the setting for one of Thomas's most celebrated poems. In 1937, Dylan made his first radio broadcast and married Caitlin MacNamara, then the mistress of Augustus John*. They lived in Laugharne, in 'Sea View', paying a rent of ten shillings a week. Their first child, Llywelyn Edouard, was born in 1939. Richard Hughes allowed Dylan access to a gazebo in the castle grounds where he wrote *Portrait of the Artist as a Young Dog*. Dylan habitually wrote in the gazebo from 2-7 pm each day, after which he would 'reward' himself by going to Browns Hotel for some beers.

In 1939, his third book, *Map of Love* was published and he toured the USA to read his poems. At the outset of War, Thomas was worried about conscription and tried to avoid it because coughing sometimes confined him to bed. After initially seeking employment in a reserved occupation, he managed to be classified Grade III, which meant that he would be among the last to be called up for service. From 1941 he and Caitlin and their two children lived in London. In early 1943 Thomas began a relationship with Pamela Glendower, one of several affairs he had during his marriage. In March 1943 Caitlin gave birth to a daughter, and Aeronwy Bryn. They lived in a run-down studio in Chelsea, made up of a single large room. In 1944, with the threat of German flying bombs, Thomas moved to the family cottage in Blaen Cwm near Llangain where he resumed writing poetry. In September Thomas and Caitlin moved to New Quay in Ceredigion, which inspired Thomas to pen the radio piece *Quite Early One Morning*, a sketch for his later work, *Under Milk Wood*. The family then moved back to Blaen Cwm.

In 1948 Hughes had given up the lease on Castle House, and Dylan hoped against hope that he would be able to live there - 'dreamily grinning, hopelessly shaking our heads, then beaming and gabbling together again as we think of the great house at the end of the cherry treed best street in the world, bang next to the Utrillo tower, with its wild gardens and owly ruins, the grey estuary, forever linked to me with poems done and to be.' However, it was not to be, and an admirer, A.J.P. Taylor's wife Margaret, bought him the now-famous Boathouse overlooking the estuary in 1949. The Thomas family moved to the Boathouse, Laugharne in 1949, when another boy, Colm Garan Hart, was born. Dylan acquired a garage a hundred yards from the house on a cliff ledge which he turned into his writing shed, and where he wrote several of his most acclaimed poems – it can be seen today, as he left it. His pattern of work remained the same, rounded off with late night 'stop-ins' at Browns Hotel. When Dylan was touring in America, Caitlin, possibly jealous, embarked upon a series of affairs with local men.

Inside of writing shed, Laugharne

In 1950, 1952 and 1953 Dylan toured America, performing *Under Milk Wood* for the first time in New York in 1953. Thomas's last collection *Collected Poems, 1934–1952*, published when he was 38, won the Foyle poetry prize. Reviewing the volume, Philip Toynbee wrote that 'Thomas is the greatest living poet in the English language.' On his fourth reading tour, in 1953, he died allegedly of alcoholic poisoning, and Caitlin emigrated to Italy. He was possibly burnt out as a poet. Controversy about Thomas's death has arisen. He was supposed to have supped 18 straight whiskies at his favourite bar, the White Horse Tavern in Greenwich Village, and mumbled 'I think that's the record'. However, there is other evidence that he was a diabetic, and was in an undiagnosed diabetic coma when his New York doctor gave him a lethal dose of morphine. He died before the BBC could record his radio play *Under Milk Wood*, and Richard Burton starred in its first broadcast.

Dylan Thomas is the Welsh poet in essence, throwing words around like confetti, unlike the more restrained (and Christian) R. S. Thomas. His *Under Milk Wood* was later filmed in Lower Fishguard with Elizabeth Taylor and Richard Burton. The boathouse near Laugharne Castle, where he wrote much of his work, is open to the public. Buried at Laugharne in a simple grave, many visitors go to Browns Hotel where he used to become famously drunk.

Strongly influenced by Gerard Manley Hopkins, his writings are emotive, and a link to Wales for anyone who leaves the country to find work. The free-form thought processes, refined by dozens of rewrites, have given us poetry that will last forever. Dylan throws thoughts, ideas and words into a magical blender. His *Do Not Go Gentle Into That Good Night* was recently voted the second most popular poem written in English - he asked his dying father to 'rage, rage against the dying of the light', as 'old age should burn and rave at close of day.' In his short life before he succumbed in the States, he kick-started Welsh poetry into word plays hardly ever seen in the English language. I could pick just about any passage from Dylan's prose and poetry and be thrilled with its spine-tingling joie de vivre... from *A Child's Christmas in Wales*: 'Years and years and years ago, when I was a boy, when there were wolves in Wales, and birds the colour of red-flanneled petticoats whisked past the harp-shaped hills... when we rode the daft and happy hills bareback, it snowed and snowed.'

Or, the first lines from *Under Milk Wood*: 'It is spring, moonless night in the small town, starless and bible-black, the cobblestreets silent and the hunched, courters'-and-rabbits' wood limping invisible down to the sloeblack, slow, black, crowblack, fishing-boat bobbing sea.'

Or, 'The force that through the green fuse drives the flower / Drives my green age; that blasts the roots of trees / Is my destroyer. / And am I dumb to tell the crooked rose / My youth is bent by the same wintry fever'.

The great Idris Davies, in 1946, wrote of Thomas:
'He saw the sun play ball in Swansea Bay,
He heard the moon crack jokes above the new-mown hay,
And stars and trees and winds to him would sing and say:
Carve words like jewels for a summer's day.'

* The Welsh artist and court-painter Augustus John (1878-1971) said to another artist, Nina Hamnett, 'We are the sort of people our fathers warned us against'. His lecherous reputation was such that it was said that, whenever he walked down Chelsea's King's Road, he used to pat the heads of all the children, just in case it was one of his. He was supposed to have 'forced' himself on his female models, including a 16-year-old Irish dancer, Caitlin MacNamara, when he was

52. Whatever the truth of the matter, she rapidly became his mistress. Augustus John and Caitlin were to visit Richard Hughes at Laugharne's Castle House, and Dylan Thomas engineered an invite to meet the great man in July 1936. The day deteriorated on a trip to Carmarthen, with John becoming increasingly irritated with the behaviour of Dylan and Caitlin. After a drunken fight, Dylan was left in a car park in Carmarthen while John and Caitlin returned to Castle House for dinner. This was the first meeting of Dylan Thomas and his wife-to-be. It was thought that Dorelia John would have been tired of Augustus' many affairs and their Bohemian lifestyle, but the Welsh novelist Richard Hughes once heard her say 'There's one thing about John that I've never got used to, not after all these years... I don't know what to do about it... Time after time... he's late for lunch'.

TOMMY COOPER   March 9 1922 - April 15 1984

THE COMEDIAN'S COMEDIAN

Possibly the greatest British comedian of all time, he was held in massive regard by contemporaries such as Eric Sykes, 'who bowed to no-one when it came to comedy'. Born in Caerphilly, he moved with his parents to the West Country at an early age. He had not been expected to survive as a premature baby, but his grandmother helped keep him alive of a mixture of brandy and condensed milk. Aged 8, his auntie Lucy bought Tommy a magic set, and he spent the next eight years perfecting tricks. His first job was on board a boat as an apprentice shipwright, and he gave his first public performance there. It was disastrous. The coloured handkerchiefs, which were supposed to pour from a cylinder, were steadfastly stuck, no matter how he tugged them. A card fell out of his sleeve, and Cooper fled the stage in tears. However, he calmed down and analysed what went wrong, recalling years later 'I got stage fright. That's why it all went wrong. But then I thought to myself, well it might all have gone wrong but I got a laugh. Perhaps I should concentrate on that.'

Aged 18, Tommy Cooper was called up in 1940 for the Second World War. The sickly baby was now 6 feet 4 inches, with size 13 boots when he joined the Horse Guards. He remembered 'On the first day there I put my foot in the stirrup but the saddle slipped and I ended up underneath the horse's belly. Everyone was sitting on their horse except me.' In the Middle East, Cooper was wounded in the arm, and joined the concert party entertaining the troops. While entertaining the troops in NAAFI in Cairo, he had forgotten the pith helmet that he usually used for his act. To improvise, Cooper whipped off the fez of a passing waiter, and used that instead. This raised such a laugh, that the red fez became his trademark ever after.

He left the Army in 1947, to concentrate upon becoming a professional, incompetent buffoon (and thus could have had an alternative career in politics). As a full-time music-hall comic, he made his television debut on December 24th 1947 on the *Leslie Henson Christmas Eve Show.* Television did not really take off in Britain until the late 1950's, and Cooper honed his skills in live Variety Theatre, living hand-to-mouth at stages. After this initial break-through, it was almost a year before Cooper had a booking, in November 1948 at the Collins Music Hall, Islington. He toured the variety circuit, low on the bill, supplementing his income by working as a barrow boy in the Portobello Road market until 1950. His next break was at the famous Windmill Theatre, where so many of Britain's post-war comedians learned their trade, competing with the main attraction, half-naked stationary ladies. In one week in 1950 he performed 52 shows there. Between 1951 and 1952 he was at the London Hippodrome, and also starred in the BBC TV series *It's Magic*.

However, by the mid-50's his act had developed to the extent that he was appearing in television specials such as *Sunday Night at the London Palladium* and *Saturday Showtime*. In 1957, his first TV series, *Life with Cooper* appeared. This was 'live' on a Monday night for a trial of 12 weeks. Of course, Tommy Cooper's act was ideal for live television - it did not matter if things went right or wrong, as his persona and professional training in the music halls enabled him to easily 'paper over the cracks'. The series was such a success that halfway through ATV offered him another series, *Cooper's Capers*, which ran in 1958. He was thereafter a constant feature of British television with guest appearances and his own shows such as *Cooper's Half-Hour* and *Life with Cooper*. During all this time, he kept touring the country appearing in clubs and perfecting his act as 'the comedian's comedian'.

1957 had seen a successful debut season at the Hotel Flamingo in Las Vegas, and he turned down a season at America's famed *Radio City Music Hall* because he was 'booked solid' for two years in England. Cooper returned to America in 1967 to record two *Ed Sullivan Shows*. At the time this was the most influential show on American television, and Sullivan introduced him as 'the funniest man to ever appear on this stage.' For years, Cooper was the most impersonated man in the UK, as he was so famous.

Cooper could make an audience howl with laughter just by appearing on the stage, with his big, clumsy persona, and perspiring face which could switch from joyful to lugubrious in an instant. His act revolved around magic tricks going wrong (- he was, incidentally, a superb magician and member of the Magic Circle), and simple, slightly corny, jokes. Paul Daniels, the leading British magician, reminisced: 'He did a great after-

411

dinner speech at the Water Rats (the charity sponsored by entertainers). This great big man just stood up. That's all he did. He just stood up and the place was in absolute hysterics and a man standing up. Now, I don't care how much you study comedy, you can't define that, the ability to fill a room with laughter because you are emanating humour. After several minutes of laughter he turned to his wife and said, "I haven't said anything yet." And the whole place went up again.'

He was given a Variety Club lunch by his peers in 1977 in honour of his 30 years in show biz. As mentioned, this huge man always wore his red fez when performing. Cooper stood up in front of the 400 honoured guests from the entertainment industry, and on cue, each one reached into their pockets and pulled out a hidden fez that they placed on top of their heads. Cooper stared at them, puzzled, for a few minutes, waiting for the laughter to die down, reached into his pocket, pulled out a fisherman's yellow 'sou'wester' hat and donned it. 'Everyone fell about again.'

It is impossible to summarise the act - it was a one-off by a much-loved man in his favourite element, and his enjoyment shone through any kind of material. 'Unforgettable' is the best word to describe him, and there are several websites devoted to his jokes. Fellow-Welshman Anthony Hopkins' favourite party act is to adopt the Cooper persona and run through a string of his one-liner gags. Some of the author's favourite Cooper jokes are:

'I'm on a whisky diet - I've lost three days already.'
'I was cleaning out the attic the other day with the wife. Filthy, dirty and covered with cobwebs... but she's good with the kids.'
'I slept like a log last night - I woke up in the fireplace.'
'So a fella goes to the Doctor and he says "I keep thinking I'm a dog". The Doctor says "Well lie on the couch". The fella says "I'm not allowed!"'
'I was in Margate last year for the Summer Season. A friend of mine said, "You want to go to Margate, it's good for rheumatism." So I did... and I got it.'

There are at least 12 videos easily available of Cooper, plus the film *The Plank* in which he starred with Eric Sykes, possibly the best British comedy short film ever. One problem with Cooper, is that in line with his shambolic personality, he was terribly unpunctual, driving directors to despair in rehearsals. Sykes, a known stickler for professionalism and time keeping, and incidentally probably the most under-rated British comic ever, said that they had decided to meet at a pub near the film studios at 12 noon. 'So noon comes and goes and there's no sign of Tommy.' Eric Sykes told the producer that he was very annoyed, and that he was going to have harsh words with Cooper if he turned up at all for the production meeting. The pub had filled up to maximum capacity by 12.45, when the front door swung open, and standing there was Tommy Cooper, wearing just a bowler hat and pair of pyjamas. He walked up to their table in the crowded pub, ordered a drink, and simply said 'I'm sorry I'm late. I couldn't get up.' Sykes and the producer dissolved with laughter.

However, Cooper's other problem was more serious - alcohol - and his long-suffering wife said once 'There's only one trick that Tommy always does successfully. It's making a drink disappear.' His fatal coronary, on stage during a live television broadcast at Her Majesty's Theatre, had the audience believing it was part of the act. He fell back gracefully, disappearing through the curtains and died ten minutes later on his way to hospital. Jimmy Tarbuck, the show's host, commented 'As usual, he was supposed to make a mess of the last trick. He was wearing a long cloak from which he was supposed to start bringing out large objects. Then a ladder would come through his legs, followed by a milk churn and a long pole. When Tommy fell backwards, I thought he'd put another gag in. I thought he was going to do some levitation trick from under his cloak. We all expected him to get up and we waited for the roar of laughter. It was terrible when he didn't.'

In 1977 in Rome, Tommy Cooper had previously a heart attack, and after lung trouble had had to give up his beloved cigars. It is impossible to do justice to Cooper in words, but there is a true story which sums the man up, when he met the Queen after a Royal Command Performance. The dialogue went as follows:

Cooper 'Do you think I was funny?'
Queen 'Yes, Tommy.'
Cooper 'You really thought I was funny?'
Queen 'Yes, of course I thought you were funny.'
Cooper 'Did your mother think I was funny?'
Queen 'Yes, Tommy, we both thought you were funny.'
Cooper 'Do you mind if I ask you a personal question?'
Queen 'No, but I might not be able to give you a full answer.'
Cooper 'Do you like football?'
Queen 'Well, not really.'
Cooper 'In that case… do you mind if I have your Cup Final tickets?'

DONALD WATTS DAVIES CBE FRS 7 June 1924 – 28 May 1999

'THE COMPUTER PIONEER WHO MADE POSSIBLE THE INTERNET', 'THE SCIENTIST WHO ENABLED COMPUTERS TO TALK TO EACH OTHER'

Born in Treorchy, the son of a clerk at the coalmine, his father died a few months later. His mother took Donald and his twin sister back to her hometown of Portsmouth. Davies is remembered as 'the scientist who enabled computers to talk to each other, and thus made possible the Internet'. At Imperial College, London Davies gained a first in physics in 1943, and a first in mathematics in 1947, (being awarded the London University Lubbock Memorial Prize as the leading mathematician of his year). Between the two degrees he was working with the famous Klaus Fuchs on atomic research at Birmingham University.

Davies started his career in a small team at the National Physics Laboratory, under the scientific genius Alan Turing, the man who first conceptualised computer programming. Turing's group developed one of the first stored-programme digital computers in the world in 1950. Commended for a Commonwealth Fund fellowship in 1954, Davies' senior officer described him as 'outstanding not only in intellectual power but also in the range of his scientific, technical and general knowledge. He is equally unusual in his ability to apply this knowledge to mechanical and electrical design and even to the actual construction of complex equipment. He is, for example, one of the very small number of persons who could draw up a complete logical design of an electronic computer, realise this design in actual circuitry, assemble it himself (with a high probability that it would work as designed) and then programme it and use it for the solution of computational problems.' In 1955, Davies married Diane Burton, and they raised a daughter and two sons.

Working at the National Physical Laboratory, Davies coined the term 'packet switching' in 1966 for the data transmission that is fundamental to the workings of the Internet. Davies gave the name 'packet' to a chunk of data. Davies said I thought it was important to have a new word for one of the short pieces of data which travelled separately. This would make it easier to talk about them. I hit upon the word packet in the sense of the small package.' He also led a team that built one of the first functioning networks using packet data. He was reported in *The Guardian* in 1997 as saying that it was inefficient for a computer to send an entire file to another computer in an uninterrupted stream of data, 'chiefly because computer traffic is "bursty" with long periods of silence. So, in November 1965, I conceived the use of a purpose-designed network employing packet-switching in which the stream of bits is broken up into short message, or "packets", that find their way individually to the destination, where they are reassembled into the original stream."

The work of his team was presented at a 1967 conference in Tennessee where Lawrence Roberts (also of Welsh extraction) of the Advanced Research Projects Agency (part of the US Department of Defence) presented a design for creating a computer network. This led to the Internet prototype, the ARPANET. Unfortunately, like most British breakthroughs, funding was not available for a wide area network experiment by Davies, but his scientific papers were used world-wide, especially in America by Roberts and others to develop the technology. (The British are excellent at invention, but finance for innovation to market has always been the greatest problem - in a high interest rate economy, which favours financial institutions making easy profits, there is no desire to 'risk' investments outside the financial sector. Britain is now a foreign-owned service-sector economy).

Davies developed a UK version of the ARPANET, mainly laboratory-based. His packet-switched network, Mark 1, served the NPL from 1970, replaced with his Mark II in 1973, which remained in operation until 1986, but it never was assisted in any way to develop the scale of the ARPANET. ARPA's designers used his self-routing method for messages, as the transport mechanism of the ARPANET, and the ARPANET evolved into the Internet. Paul Baran at RAND had also been working on computer networks, and one of his

With the pilot ACE team, 1950

parameters was the same as Davies' packet size of 1024 bits, which became the industry norm. Although Tim Berners-Lee has been called 'the father of the internet', it was the serendipitous marrying-up of the independent work of Davies, Roberts and Baran that made the Internet a practical proposition.

Davies later moved into data-security systems, working for teleprocessing systems, financial institutions and government agencies. He was among the first to realise that malicious interference had to be prevented for the Internet and secure transaction to succeed. He received the British Computer Society Award in 1974, was made a Distinguished Fellow of the BCS in 1975, and published several books upon communication networks, computer protocols and network security. *Communications Networks for Computers* (1973) was groundbreaking. *Computer Networks and their*

Protocols (1979) and *Security for Computer Networks* (1984, written with fellow-Welshman Wynne Price) remain classic references. He was made a Fellow of the Royal Society in 1987, and also was visiting professor at Royal Holloway and Bedford New College. He pioneered work in the 1980's on Smart Cards, as he believed they would be useful components in the secure operation of financial services over open networks. Retiring in 1984, Davies continued working as a data security consultant.

Smart Cards were derided in the USA at the time as a French aberration, and as being only usable in off-line situations. The chip card with metal contacts was newly invented, and seen as unreliable and expensive, compared to established contact-less portable data carriers like the magnetic stripe card and the bar code label. Disagreeing, Davies and his team at NPL managed to get substantial funding from the banks, EFTPOS, American Express, The Post Office, Texas Instruments and other companies. By the mid-80s the TTCC (Tokens and Transactions Control Consortium) had moved quickly into delivering solutions, focusing on high-speed encryption and authentication of sender and recipient. Regulation of secure access to, and private communication across, an open network by authorised users was enabled by what we now call an Intranet. An early application of the PC encryption card was found in the EFTPOS (Electronic Funds Transfer at Point of Sale) terminals in supermarkets. Of course, supermarkets can now use this payment method build up databases of customer needs and patterns of shopping, and also to directly input these retail purchases, to trigger their own stock fulfilment systems. This unknown Welshman has helped to change the face of our world.

RICHARD BURTON 19 November 1925 - 5 August 1984

RICHARD WALTER JENKINS Jr. - 1960'S FILM SUPERSTAR

Born Richard Jenkins, he came from the same neighbourhood as Anthony Hopkins and after Oxford University trained at RADA. A superb stage actor, he also received seven Academy Award nominations and twice-married Elizabeth Taylor prior to his death from a stroke and brain haemorrhage in 1984. His villa where he was buried, on Lake Geneva, was called *Pays de Galles* (French for Wales), and *Sospan Fach* was played at the funeral of this hard-drinking Celtic genius. Burton was survived by Sally Hay (Burton) whom he married a year before his death. His first wife was Sybil Williams, to whom he was married from 1948-1963. He married Elizabeth Taylor twice, from 1964-1974 and 1975-1976. He was also married to Susan Hunt, the former wife of the racing driver James Hunt, from 1976-1982.

The second youngest of a Welsh miner's 13 children, he grew up Welsh-speaking in Pontrhydyfendigaid near Port Talbot, Glamorgan. His former schoolteacher Philip Burton, who discovered and nurtured Burton's acting talents, and helped him win a scholarship to Oxford, adopted him. By 1949 he was seen as one of Britain's most exciting theatrical talents, and film director Phillip Dunne remembers him in London in *The Lady's Not for Burning*: 'He "took" the stage and kept a firm grip on it on every one of his brief appearances', eclipsing the star, John Gielgud.

His performances in the West End in the early 1950's, notably as *Hamlet*, made his name, but he is better known for his total of around 60 films. Apart from his brooding good looks and pale blue eyes, Burton had a marvellously rich speaking voice. 20th Century Fox signed Burton, hoping to make him into the 'new Olivier'.

He began an affair with Liz Taylor, the wife of the crooner Eddie Fisher, while filming *Cleopatra* in 1962. Taylor was critically ill, postponing the filming, and the star playing Antony, Stephen Boyd, walked away from the film. When Liz Taylor's heart stopped after an emergency tracheotomy, she had a near-death experience, when she 'knew there was a new love awaiting my return'. Burton was brought in for Boyd, and the greatest love affair Hollywood has ever known was ignited.

Burton's own cabal of Welsh drinking partners, the actors Stanley Baker and Donald Houston, the opera singer Geraint Evans, the harpist Osian Ellis and the singer-comedian Harry Secombe, all tried to make Burton stay with his Welsh wife, Sybil. All five met Burton and Taylor in a bar near Borehamwood film studios to make him see sense, but ended up singing Welsh  songs instead. A cable from Laurence Olivier to Burton at the height of the *Cleopatra* scandal read 'make up your mind, dear heart. Do you want to be a great actor or a household word?' Burton tersely cabled back 'Both'.

With Elizabeth Taylor he starred in *Cleopatra* (1963), *The VIP's* (1963), *The Sandpiper* (1965), *Who's Afraid of Virginia Woolf* (1966), *Doctor Faustus* (1967 - Burton also directed), *The Comedians* (1967), *The Taming of the Shrew* (1967), *Boom* (1968), *Hammersmith is Out* (1972) and *Under Milk Wood* (1973).

Burton's 'best' films are possibly *Becket, Equus* and *Who's Afraid of Virginia Woolf*, with his role as a fallen priest opposite Ava Gardner in *Night of the Iguana* possibly his greatest screen performance. Burton once said 'I want an Oscar - I've won all kinds of little Oscars but not the big one.' Sadly, despite a record seven nominations (along with Peter O'Toole), he never was awarded the accolade. He had been nominated for Best Supporting Actor for *My Cousin Rachel* in 1952. Then came a run of six nominations for Best Actor - *The Robe* (1953), *Becket* (1964), *The Spy Who Came in from the Cold* (1965), *Who's Afraid of Virginia Woolf* (1966), *Anne of the Thousand Days* (1969) and *Equus* (1977). For *Anne of the Thousand Days* he received the colossal sum of a million dollars and a percentage of the gross take, up from just half a million dollars for *The VIP's* in 1963.

We can see here just how much of a Hollywood 'superstar' he was in the 'Swinging 60's' For the 1966 Oscar Awards ceremony, Taylor and Burton had co-starred in *Who's Afraid of Virginia Woolf*. Liz Taylor was awarded her second Best Actress Oscar, but Burton was beaten by Paul Scofield in *A Man for All Seasons*. Burton refused to attend the awards, having been let down in the two previous years. Other notable 1960's films which included Burton were *Where Eagles Dare*, *The Comedians*, and *What's New Pussycat*. His awards included Best Actor for *Virginia Woolf* in the British Academy Awards, and Best Actor for *Becket* and *Look Back in Anger* given by the New York Film Critics Circle.

He made many mediocre films, being 'driven' a little like today's Michael Caine. Both came from humble backgrounds and felt that it was somehow not normal to be working full-time. Burton admitted 'I've done the most awful rubbish in order to have somewhere to go in the morning... I've played the lot: a homosexual, a sadistic gangster, kings, princes, a saint, the lot. All that's left is a *Carry On* film. That's my ambition.' He admitted to a drink problem all his life, and said 'My father considered that anyone who went to chapel and didn't drink alcohol was not to be tolerated. I grew up in that belief... When I played drunks I had to remain sober because I didn't know how to play them when I was drunk.'

However, it was on the stage that Burton really commanded, being seen as the true heir to Laurence Olivier. Sir John Gielgud said 'He was marvellous at rehearsals. There was true theatrical instinct. You only had to indicate. Scarcely even that.' In his last film, *1984*, released in Burton's final year, we can glimpse what a truly great actor he was. At the funeral service, Brook Williams read that most moving of Dylan Thomas's poems, written to his dying father, *Do not go gentle into that good night*. Paul Scofield read 'Death is Nothing at All', by an unknown author:

'Death is nothing at all;
I have only slipped away
Into the next room.
Whatever we were to each other,
That we still are.
Call me by my old familiar name,
Wear no forced air of solemnity
Or sorrow;

Life means all that it ever meant.
Why should I be out of mind
Only because I am out of sight?
I am waiting for you
For an interval,
Somewhere very near,
Just around the corner.
All is well.'

'CLIFF' MORGAN CVO OBE 7 April 1930 – 29 August 2013

'THE BEST FLY-HALF THERE CAN EVER HAVE BEEN'

It is a wonder how this wonderful man was never knighted. I was lucky to see him a few times as a boy, and also fortunate to see many, many times the great Barry John. Clifford Isaac 'Cliff' Morgan was born in Trebanog, from a mining family in the Rhondda valley, and joined Cardiff Rugby Club straight from Tonyrefail Grammar School in 1949, playing at fly-half. He had loved football, but was converted to rugby by a teacher and Morgan moved from school to village rugby, turning out on a windy hillside for Coedely Coke Ovens XV at Llantrisant. He said: 'Before the game we had to drive a herd of cows from the pitch; there was little we could do about the cow pats. That is how we learned to swerve and sidestep. Those who failed to develop these skills smelled horribly for weeks.'

He was soon talent-spotted for Cardiff, where he used to arrive by double-decker bus with his boots in a brown cardboard case. Those boots had been cleaned by his father, who also helped him on his way by giving Cliff a copy of a rugby manual by Wavell Wakefield, the former England captain, which the fly-half treasured all his life. Blessed with natural balance and strength, together with an astute line-kicking ability and searing acceleration, he

Playing the Springboks

quickly made an impact. Cliff scored 38 tries in 202 appearances for Cardiff between 1949 and 1958 and helped them to beat the 1953 All Blacks and the 1957 Wallabies. He made the first of his 29 Welsh appearances against

Ireland in 1951 and was an ever present in the 1952 Grand Slam side. When Wales won the Triple Crown in that year by beating Ireland in Dublin, Cliff's miner father became so excited that he spat his false teeth 15 rows in front, and never saw them again. His mother said to Cliff: 'You are no longer ours. You belong to everyone now.'

He played against South Africa for Wales in the unlucky 6-3 defeat in 1951 and then helped Wales beat the All Blacks two years later in the famous 13-8 victory at Cardiff Arms Park - still the last time Wales beat New Zealand. He helped Wales to share the Five Nations title in 1954 and 1955 and was captain in 1956 when they won the title outright, losing only to Ireland in Dublin. He also played club rugby in Ireland for Bective Rangers in the 1955–56 season, with the club being dubbed the 'Morgan Rangers' as a result.

Morgan recalled of his first international, against Ireland in Cardiff: 'I felt a hand gently touch my shoulder. It was the man I was having to mark, the maestro [fly-half] Jackie Kyle. He put an arm around me and whispered as fondly and genuinely as an uncle would: 'I hope you have a wonderful, wonderful first cap today, Cliffie'. Frank Keating wrote of this episode: 'Thus, like all true romances, was the baton passed on.' Kyle, who became a missionary in Zambia, has described Morgan as 'the best fly-half there can ever have been, thrusting, darting, always unexpected'.

Morgan resisted the temptations of Rugby League. One chairman arrived at his parents' terraced house in a white Rolls-Royce and placed £5,000 in fivers on the kitchen table, along with a cheque for £2,500. Cliff's mother told him money was not important and she wanted her son to stay at home. She cooked the chairman breakfast, then sent him on his way, saying: 'It's been lovely to have you down here, but on Sundays we go to chapel.' This was in the days when rugby union players were not paid.

During the 1955 Lions tour to South Africa, when Morgan became a global star as the tourists shared the series 2-2 against the mighty Springboks, and he became the tour choirmaster both on an off the field: 'We came to the decision that we were going to be a singing team. I was appointed choirmaster, with first call on the hotel piano, and every day for a week we practiced, English, Scottish and Irish songs in English, Welsh songs in Welsh and, in a four-part harmony, *Sarie Marais* in Afrikaans, which we thought would go down well with the people over there. We learned this parrot-fashion, and the words of the Welsh songs I wrote on a blackboard... Coming down the steps of the plane [on arrival in Johannesburg], we were amazed at the crowds who had waited so long to greet us. I turned round and said, "OK lads, look at the people". So we all came to a stop and sang practically our full repertoire from *Sospan Fach* to *Sarie Marais*, cheered on by the crowd. And that was the spirit of that trip, everybody together... Later that week the *Rand Daily Mail* carried a front page headline: "This is the greatest team ever to visit South Africa'. And we hadn't even played a match!";

His most famous moment on the rugby field came on this tour, when he played a starring role in the Springboks' first defeat since the Second World War in an epic match at Ellis Park, Johannesburg, played in front of a crowd of 96,000. The Lions won 23-22 in what was described as 'without question one of the greatest Test matches ever played anywhere in the world in any era'. Clem Thomas, later captain of Wales, played in that game and recalled: 'Cliff Morgan weaved some of his magic. I can still see him sticking his neck out and rocketing past the great Basie van Wyk with a devastating outside break to score an inspirational try.' A local rugby writer said afterwards: 'Cliff Morgan is the best fly-half to have played in South Africa in the past 50 years. I have yet to see his equal.'

The South African newspapers dubbed him 'Morgan the Magnificent' and the level to which his influence was thought key was reflected in the frenzy of coverage his injured ankle received as the fourth Test came around. Although he played, he was not fully fit and the Lions could not prevent the Springboks squaring the series. But his reputation was already made and the memory of that tour - still known in South Africa as 'the Cliff Morgan tour' - proved long-lived. His last game of first-class rugby was for the Barbarians in May 1958 against East Africa in Nairobi.

Although his playing career came to an end aged just 28, Morgan continued to be involved in sport through his television and radio work with ITV and the BBC. He made a successful career in broadcasting, both as a commentator and presenter and also as a programme-maker and BBC executive. Morgan. He spent 30 years in broadcasting, becoming Head of Outside Broadcasts at BBC Television, and on radio his voice became familiar in millions of households during his 11 years as presenter of Sport on 4.

In 1964 he moved to independent television to produce the cultural affairs programme *This Week* for two years, working with figures such as James Cameron, Ludovic Kennedy and Robert Key. Morgan once said that for him the greatest pleasures in life were a Welsh choir in full song, watching Gareth Edwards play for Wales, working on television with James Cameron, and Richard Burton reading Dylan Thomas. Later, in Hollywood, he and Burton astonished staff who had placed them at the best table at the Beverly Hills Hilton by proceeding to order egg and chips.

In 1972, at the age of 41, Morgan suffered a stroke which temporarily left him speechless and paralysed down one side. Alarmed financially for the future, he and his wife, Nuala, wrote down a list of everything they owned, and decided to sell the family car and her engagement ring. Friends gave them money, which they immediately returned, and refused a large sum offered by Burton. Cliff fought to overcome his illness, and nursing a slight limp, rejoined the BBC as Editor of Sport, Radio.

Just a year later, in 1973, he made one of his most celebrated contributions in the commentary box, stepping in for Bill McLaren, who was ill, for the match between the Barbarians and New Zealand at Cardiff Arms Park. New Zealand scored two great tries, but could not match the Barbarians, who scored four, including a Gareth Edwards touchdown that completed a flowing move that had run the length of the pitch. Morgan's commentary communicated the genius of the play unfolding in front of him:

'Brilliant... oh, that's brilliant', he exclaimed as Phil Bennett sidestepped a clutch of tackles to start the counter-attack almost from under his own posts. Seconds later, Morgan seemed barely able to credit the progress of the Barbarians down the pitch: 'This is the halfway line,' he gasped, an instant before the team's famous scrum-half appeared at a sprint, from out of the television shot, to collect a short pass on the left wing. 'This is Gareth Edwards... A dramatic start. What a score!'

He was one of the original team captains on a *Question of Sport*, alongside boxer Henry Cooper, and rose to the positions of Head of BBC Radio Outside Broadcasts in 1974 and Head of Sport and Outside Broadcasts for BBC Television from 1976 to 1987. He then began his 11-year stint as presenter of Sport on 4, but his controversial sacking in 1998, on the grounds of his being too old-fashioned and sentimental for a modern audience, brought a deluge of complaints from the public. In retirement he was an outstanding public speaker, often travelling many miles to speak free of charge, and raising large amounts of money for charities, especially for the disabled and mentally handicapped. Audiences warmed to his humour and humility and to his rich fund of anecdotes.

Cliff was appointed OBE in 1977 and CVO in 1986. His autobiography, *Cliff Morgan: Beyond the Fields of Play*, was published in 1996. When the International Rugby Hall of Fame was created in 1997, Morgan was among the inaugural inductees, alongside his Lions contemporary and great friend Tony O'Reilly and Barry John, Gareth Edwards and J.P.R. Williams. He married, in 1955, Nuala Martin, with whom he had a daughter and a son. Nuala died in 1999. In 2001 he married Pat Ewing, a former Head of Sport on Radio 4, and settled at Bembridge, on the Isle of Wight.

Cliff Morgan possessed what Des Lynam called 'one of the best broadcasting voices of all time' but tragically Cliff lost his voice to cancer. Des Lynam recalled him: 'Cliff was one of the most charismatic men I ever met. I knew him as a brilliant rugby player for Wales and the British Lions only through those grainy black and white images from the 50s but later he was my boss at BBC Radio, became my mentor and we formed a friendship that lasted for 40 years. A brilliant broadcaster himself, his advice to those of us trying to make our way in the business was wise and invaluable. But underlying it all was his great sense of fun. "Enjoy yourself" he would say, "It's not working down the mine, is it?" Many of his family had done precisely that. His generosity of spirit was legendary. He would travel the length and breath of the country at his own expense for charitable causes until in recent years he suffered the tragic indignity of losing his voice to cancer and that wonderful, mellifluous instrument would be heard in public no more. Cliff himself once wrote of the untimely passing of another old friend and colleague "I won't believe it if I don't want to." That's exactly how I feel right now.'

JOHN CHARLES 27 December 1931 – 21 February 1994

THE GENTLE GIANT, *IL GIGANTE BUONO*, 'THE BEST IN THE WORLD'

Like Cliff Morgan, Charles should have received a knighthood. Charles rivals George Best and Billy Meredith as the greatest footballer produced in the British Isles, and could play in attack or defence, standing almost 6 foot 3 inches and weighing nearly 14 stone. His preferred position was centre forward, but he was equally proficient as a centre-half, and may be unique in sometimes playing centre forward for a club and centre-half for his country, and vice-versa.

Aged 14, he left school to join Swansea City's ground staff, but never played for his home town's first team because of his age. Playing for Gendros Youth Club, he was spotted by a scout, given a trial and left Swansea for Leeds in 1948, being chosen personally by the Leeds manager Major Frank

Playing for Juventus

Buckley. Buckley played him at right back, centre-half and left half for the reserves, before John made his first team debut in 1949 aged 17. His first team debut was a friendly against Queen of the South soon after. He was told to mark the Scotland centre-forward Billy Houliston, the man of the match when Scotland had beaten England at Wembley, ten days previously.

The score was 0–0, and after the game Houliston said 17-year-old Charles was 'the best centre half I've ever played against'.

From 1950-52 John did National Service, but still played for Leeds and the Army, winning the Army Cup but having operations upon his cartilages. From November 1951 Charles played at centre-forward and centre half for Leeds and remained at centre-half until the 1952–53 season. In October 1952, he was switched to centre forward and immediately started to score, with 11 goals in 6 games. In 1955 he was appointed club captain and during the 1955-56 season, Leeds won promotion to the first division with Charles scoring 30 goals in 42 appearances. In the following season in the first division he hit a record tally of 38 goals in 40 league appearances as Leeds secured an 8th-place finish in the first division. His influence on Leeds' success during his final season was so strong, reporters nicknamed the club 'John Charles United'. In total he scored 150 league goals in eight years for Leeds

In 297 league games he scored 151 goals for Leeds, including a club record 42 goals in 39 appearances during the 1953–54 season. He remains the second highest all time goal scorer after Peter Lorimer. Lorimer scored 255 goals in 779 games, a goal every three matches, compared to Charles a goal every other match. He joined as a left-half, was switched to right-back and then centre-half, but moved to centre forward with the emergence of Jack Charlton. John scored 30 goals in his first season as centre forward in 1952-53, and a club record 42 goals in 1953-54, his second season in the position. In his first season in the old First Division, he scored 38 goals, but Leeds were forced to sell him to Juventus because the club was on the verge of bankruptcy after a fire destroyed its main stand. In 2002, Leeds fans voted Charles their best player of all time. England's famous captain and centre-half, Billy Wright, was asked who was the best centre forward he had ever played against. He answered, 'John Charles'. Then he was asked who was the greatest centre-half he had played against. He gave the same answer.

This superb Welsh footballer was the first British transfer over £50,000 when he left Leeds in 1957 for a distinguished career with Juventus from 1957, where he was nick-named *'il Giante Buono'*, 'the gentle giant', and is still remembered with affection. £67,000 was a record transfer fee for a British player at the time. Charles scored the winner in his first three matches. Of his 28 goals in his first season, in the toughest league in the world at the time, he scored hat-tricks against Verona, Udinense and Atalanta. He scored 93 goals at Juventus in just 155 games, contributing to the winning of three championships and two Italian Cups. Charles scored 28 goals in his first season, being crowned *capocannoniere* (top scorer *in Serie A*). This was in a defensive-oriented game, where goals were hard to score. A statue of him stands outside the ground, and he also played for AS Roma, scoring 4 goals in 10 games in 1962.

His appearance on the streets of Turin used to be greeted with spontaneous applause, and he said 'If you go to play in another country and you don't reach out to the people, you are going to make your life a misery. I took to the Italians right away, and they took to me. I got on well with my teammates and I liked to mix with the supporters in the little cafes. It was a wonderful slice of my life and I still have strong relationships from that time. In 1958 Charles was voted Italy's Footballer of the Year after his first season's performances, and was also one of the few non-Italian players chosen to play in the Italian National League XI. In this year, Juventus valued him at £150,000; over twice what they paid a year earlier, making John Charles the most valuable player in the world. His 105 goals in 178 appearances as a scoring ratio can never be bettered, in a league was was notoriously defensive in nature.

A Newspaper headline in Italy of April 14th, 1959 read alongside a picture of John: 'A Magnificent 6'3" Chunk of Welsh Marble bestriding the pitch in the No. 9 Zebra shirt of Juventus'. 40 years later, Italian supporters of Juventus still voted John Charles as one of the ten greatest foreigners ever to wear the famous black and white stripes. A canvas portrait of him still hangs in the players' lounge in the club. In Italy, all players were treated equally, but there were win bonuses. Charles said 'Everybody got the same wage but when you played against Torino, Milan and Inter the president would come in and say "Right, you're on £500 bonus if you win." I had four kids. I couldn't bring up four kids on £18 a week. So we put that little bit extra into it to win matches.'

Agnelli offered Charles the massive sum of £18,000 to stay with Juventus instead of returning to Leeds, but Charles said 'At the time I was thinking of my kids' education - I didn't realise they were better off in an English school in Italy and being able to speak Italian. We got used to Italy. I never had to wear an overcoat there.' A fluent Italian speaker, he was voted Juventus' finest ever foreign player in 1997. His scoring record is incredible, because in the words of Michael Parkinson, 'John Charles was the complete footballer. In Italy they would play his centre forward until he scored, then switch him to centre half to stop the other side scoring. That seems to me the perfect all-rounder.' As Jack Charlton said, 'John Charles was a team unto himself' and his is Charlton's choice of the most effective footballer in history. Major Frank Buckley, the Leeds manager, called Charles 'the best in the world.'

Following his time at Juventus, Don Revie paid a club record £53,000 to secure the return to Yorkshire of John Charles. As a result of the excitement this created, Leeds United raised admission prices for the start of the 1962-63 season. However, his second spell at Elland Road was less successful. After five years in Italy he found it difficult to adjust to life and football back in England. After 11 games and three goals - a shadow of his former strike rate - Charles was sold for £70,000 to Roma. Initially, the move was a success and Charles scored within fifteen minutes of his first game against Bologna. The early promise was never fulfilled, however, and Charles was on the move again a year later. He left to join Cardiff City (where this author saw him play) where he stayed until 1966, which marked the end of his league career.

Charles was capped for Wales in 1950, aged just 18. He would have made more than 38 appearances for Wales, but Juventus were always reluctant to release their leading scorer. Charles scored Wales' first ever World Cup goal, in the 1958 1-1 draw with Hungary. He was not fit for the Wales team that narrowly lost in the World Cup quarter-finals in 1958, 1-0 to Brazil. He had been severely and constantly kicked in the preceding game, because of his influence on the Welsh team. It is fair to say that if he had been able to play, and get on the end of the constant stream of crosses served up by Cliff Jones, Wales could have won and been known world-wide. Such is the power of football.

Brazil went on to win this World Cup in Sweden, starring the young Pelé. John Charles' brother Mel was a noted international who played against Brazil, voted the best half-back in the tournament, and a long-time Arsenal player. John Charles returned to Wales to play for Cardiff in 1963, aged 32, and scoring on his debut on August 24 against Norwich City. He scored 19 goals in 66 games, leaving in 1966. It is impossible to recall any other player in history who could play centre-forward and centre-half, with equal distinction at international and top club level, he rivals Billy Meredith as the greatest footballer ever produced by Wales, and is possibly the greatest sportsman of the nation. At the same time as banging in 42 goals as centre forward for Leeds United, in the same season he was Wales' centre-half.

There will never be another player like him. At 18, he had been the youngest player to pull on a Welsh shirt. In 1997, 25 international football writers assembled to draw up a list of the greatest footballers ever. No one else in the top 25 had regularly played in two positions. He was never booked or sent off in his long career. John Charles was voted 9th in Football's Hall of Fame. If he had been Brazilian, he would have been voted first. In 1999, the respected *Football Weekly* placed Charles in its top 50 players of the century.

Also in 1999, Swansea University gave John Charles an honorary MA. Charles said 'I had to leave school young, so it's unbelievable that I'm here today. You see things like this on television then it happens to you. It's unbelievable. I feel honoured because it's come from my hometown. It's all so unexpected, and I am surprised. Football is football, but to have an honour from outside football, I think, is terrific.' John Charles was not in the best of health, and there was a campaign for him to receive a knighthood for his services to the game. He was living on a state pension in Leeds, having given away all his mementoes and awards to charities over the years.

However, he still tried to return to Italy every year to stay with old friends. He commented in 1999: 'They still recognise me over there. Last year I was sitting in a car and a boy, who was about 14, said, "Giovanni, come sta?" (John, how are you?)' In 1995 the author was trying to explain to several female pensioners at an outside café table in Reggio Emilia, near Bologna, that he was from Wales, in reasonable Italian. Thwarted, he tried the usual litany of 'Tom Jones', 'Shirley Bassey' and 'rugby', with no joy. At last one of the old ladies realised, and said 'Ah, John Charles' and the others happily repeated the name, realising that the author came from the same area as *Il Gigante Buono*. This was 35 years after John Charles had left a rival club over a hundred miles away.

Sir Alex Ferguson chose his all-time World XI – John Charles was the only Briton to feature, alongside Schmeichel, Santos, Maldini, Beckenbaur, Cruyff, Di Stefano, Maradona, Platini and Pele. On his last visit in 2004 to Juventus as an honoured guest, John was taken gravely ill, and the club paid his expenses and flew him home in the club jet, for treatment. From 1999 he had been battling with cancer, and in June 2001 was awarded a CBE, not the knighthood he deserved. A blood clot led to part of John's foot being amputated, but he died in February, leaving a widow and four sons.

Footnotes:

(1) It is worth mentioning the matches in the 1958 World Cup. Wales had finished second to Czechoslovakia in their qualifying group, and beat Israel 2-0 home and away to reach the final rounds. Their manager was Jimmy Murphy, Matt Busby's assistant coach at Manchester United, and the team left London not expecting very much. That superb Tottenham Hotspur winger Cliff Jones said 'We were badly organised for a competition like the World Cup where preparation is half the battle. Jimmy hadn't been able to study any of our opponents, we'd had very little practice together and when we flew out we weren't even sure John Charles would [be allowed by Juventus] to play for us.'

In the three seasons before John Charles had joined Juventus, the club had finished 7th, 9th and 9th in Serie A. In Charles' first season, they won the Championship, so the owner Umberto Agnelli did not want to lose him to Wales, and forbade him playing in the qualifying rounds. At the very last minute, Agnelli and the Italian FA relented and let Charles join the Welsh team in Sweden. The Swedish organisers wanted the great man to play, to help ticket sales, and Jimmy Murphy snapped 'How can I stage proper rehearsals without knowing whether he will turn up?. Three days after the Welsh team arrived in Sweden, John Charles turned up in their hotel for breakfast, having caught an overnight flight. He walked into a rapturous and incredulous reception. His brother Mel remembered 'I'll never forget it. John walked in. he looked like a Greek god because he was so tall and bronzed. The selectors saw him; threw down their knives and forks, stood up and started singing "For he's a jolly good fellow, for he's a jolly good fellow". It was like a kids' party.'

The first match was against the 1954 finalists, Hungary, who were expected to win comfortably. They took the lead after five minutes, and spent the rest of the match chopping down the danger man, Charles, from behind. However, the much-abused centre forward scored a brilliant header 20 minutes from time, and then Wales were mysteriously refused an obvious penalty when the great Ivor Allchurch was felled in the penalty area. Although Wales should have won, Murphy was ecstatic about the result. Wales 1 - Hungary 1.

The second match, in Stockholm, pitted Wales against Mexico, and most of the Swedish crowd supported the exotic Mexicans. Charles remembered 'We came out on to the pitch and saw all these people wearing sombreros. All you could hear was Messico! Messico! It didn't really affect the players though. Once you get started you don't notice the crowd.' In a poor game, Allchurch volleyed a goal from a Webster cross, and Mexico equalised in the last minute. Wales 1 - Mexico 1.

The next game was against the World Cup hosts, Sweden, and although Wales should have won the previous two matches, they knew they needed only to draw to go through to the next stage. Packing their defence, Wales survived in another poor game. Wales 0 - Sweden 0.

Faced with a barrage of criticism after the Swedish match, Jimmy Murphy stated 'Those people who say we can't attack can expect a shock.' However, again against Hungary Wales were 1-0 down at half-time, but dominated the second half. After two penalty appeals by the Welsh, Ivor Allchurch scored one of the best goals of the tournament. John Charles chipped the ball forward and Allchurch curled the ball into the top corner of the net. Again Charles was being savagely attacked, with no protection from the referee, and Wales needed to win to go through. With just 14 minutes left, Terry Medwin of Tottenham Hotspur scored to progress. Wales 2 - Hungary 1.

The quarter-final was against the eventual winners, Brazil, and Charles, the Welsh talisman and Europe's best footballer, was too injured to play. The Brazilian team featured the household names of Pelé, Didi, Garrincha and Zagalo. Wales attacked from the kick-off, with Webster missing two simple chances. Medwin and Jones, the wingers from the remarkable Spurs double-winning side of 1961, supplied a constant stream of crosses into the penalty box, but there was no John Charles to convert the opportunities into goals. Extra time looked a distinct possibility, but just 17 minutes from the end the 17-year-old Peléscored his first World Cup goal, which he later called the most important of his whole career. His shot was not clean or hard, but deflected off right-back Stuart Williams past the goalkeeper Jack Kelsey of Arsenal. To go out of the World Cup to a poor goal was terrible. Mel Charles commented 'I felt terrible. If it was a great goal I wouldn't have complained, but it wasn't - it was like a golf putt.' Thus Wales lost its greatest chance in the modern age of international recognition. Wales 0 - Brazil 1.

(2) Juventus wore black armbands after John's death, in their next match against Bologna. 'We are crying for the loss of a great champion and a great man', said Juventus vice-president Roberto Bettega. 'He was a person who represented in the best way the Juve spirit and who personified the sport in the purest and most

beautiful manner. The thoughts of everyone at Juventus are with his wife Glenda and the children of the unforgettable Gentle Giant.' Giampiero Boniperti, a former teammate of Charles at Juventus and later the club's honorary president, said he was 'an extraordinary person, a great friend and a remarkable teammate. Charles was one of the most loyal and correct men that I ever met, as well as being a great footballer. He kept the whole squad together, whenever there was a row things calmed down as soon as he was present on the field or in the dressing room. I remember John Charles with enormous affection and great sadness. There is no longer the man who always did things for the best, a person who offered so much to learn from.' Marcello Lippi, the Juventus coach, said Charles had produced some magnificent performances in combination with Omar Sivori. 'From the human aspect, we have lost a great man. I was able to get to know him during his trips in Italy, when he came to visit the team during our summer training camp at Chatillon and here in Turn. He left a special impression on me, whenever he spoke of Juventus, past or present, his eyes lit up.'

SIR ANTHONY HOPKINS CBE 31 December 1937 -

PHILIP ANTHONY HOPKINS, HOLLYWOOD SUPERSTAR

Filming Shakespeare's violent *Titus Andronicus* in 1999, Anthony Hopkins was quoted as saying 'To Hell with this stupid business, this ridiculous showbiz, this futile, wasteful life. I look back and see a desert, a wasteland, all those years in a false environment.' His Welsh co-star Matthew Rhys spoke of the pressure of filming, saying that Hopkins' part was 'horrendous', trying to find reasons for the actor's decision to take a 'long, long rest' and leave acting completely. However, a quality cast and $15,000,000 made him reconsider his decision, to star once again as as Hannibal Lecter. 2001's *Hannibal* was the long-awaited follow-up to the film *The Silence of the Lambs*, which had catapulted Hopkins into the big league in 1991. In it, he played a psychopathic cannibal. His other 2001 films included *Hearts in Atlantis* and *The Devil and Daniel Webster*.

The voice of Port Talbot-born Hopkins has an uncanny resemblance to that of Richard Burton, born just a few miles away. His films since *Silence* in 1991 include *Dracula* (1992), *Howards End* 1992, *Freejack* (1992), *Chaplin* (1992), *Spotswood* (1992), *Shadowlands* (1993), *The Trial* (1993), *The Innocent* (1993), *The Remains of the Day* (1993), *Legends of the Fall* (1994), *The Road to Wellville* (1994), the title role in *Nixon* (1996),

Surviving Picasso (1996), *August* (1996), *Amistad* (1997), *The Edge* (1997), *Meet Joe Black* (1998), *The Mask of Zorro* (1998), *Instinct* (1999), *Mission Impossible 2* 1999 and *Titus Andronicus* in 1999. With such a punishing schedule of starring in 22 films (and TV work) in 9 years, it is little wonder that Hopkins considered taking time out.

The only son of a baker, he did not enjoy his time at at Cowbridge Grammar School, and still considers himself as a 'loner' and 'outsider'. His father was Richard Arthur Hopkins and his mother Muriel Phillips. When the soon-to-be actor met Richard Burton, the course of his life would dramatically change. Encouraged and inspired by Burton, Hopkins enrolled at the Royal Welsh College of Music and Drama when he was only 15 years old. After graduation in 1957, Anthony Hopkins spent two years in the British Army before moving to London to begin training at the Royal Academy of Dramatic Art, where by his own admission he had a drink problem that persisted for many years. After training and working for several years, he became almost a protégé of the legendary actor Sir Laurence Olivier. In 1965, Olivier invited Hopkins to join the Royal National Theatre and become his understudy. The famed actor wrote in his memoir, 'A new young actor in the company of exceptional promise named Anthony Hopkins was understudying me and walked away with the part of Edgar like a cat with a mouse between its teeth. When Olivier came down with appendicitis during a production called *Dance of Death*, the young Hopkins stepped in, making waves with his performance.

His breakthrough movie role had been as the scheming future Richard the Lionheart in *The Lion in Winter* in 1968, and other films included *Hamlet, The Looking Glass War, When Eight Bells Toll, Young Winston, A Doll's House, All Creatures Great and Small, A Change of Seasons, Juggernaut, A Bridge Too Far, Magic, International Velvet, The Elephant Man, The Bounty, 84 Charing Cross Road, The Good Father, A Chorus of Disapproval*, and *Desperate Hours*. He was knighted in 1993, having received the CBE in 1991. Upon 13 April 2000, he officially became a resident of the USA, which caused some controversy in Wales.

Beginning as a theatre actor, he played *Julius Caesar* at the Old Vic, and starred in a Broadway production of Peter Shaffer's *Equus* (1974) even as he devoted more and more attention to developing his talents for television and film. He was awarded a British Theatre Association and Observer Award for his role in the National Theatre's *Pravda* in 1985. He won Emmies for his TV work in *The Lindbergh Kidnapping Case* (1976) and *The Bunker* in 1981. *The Tenth Man* drew a Golden Globe nomination, a National Board of Review Award and a New York Film Critics Association Award. *The Lion in Winter*, his second film, drew a British Academy Award nomination, as did *Magic* in 1978, which also had a Golden Globe nomination. *The Silence of the Lambs* won Hopkins his Oscar, a British Academy Award, various critics' awards and a Golden Globe nomination.

He was also nominated for an Oscar for *Shadowlands* and *Nixon*. His role in *Nixon* also won him a Golden Globe nomination and a Screen Actors Guild award nomination. For *The Remains of the Day* he received a British Academy award. For *Amistad* where he played the American-Welsh president John Quincy Adams he was nominated for an Oscar, and said that he felt a real affinity with the man and the role. 'You can't go anywhere with the character until you know the lines. I go over my lines 200, 250 times. Learn it so cold so that you can do it, almost parrot-fashion. And in the process of doing that, you learn the rhythms of the speeches, and from reading the text of the actual speech he gave to the Supreme Court, you can hear how he must have said it and you can begin to feel like John Quincy Adams.' In this film, he impressed Spielberg and his crew by his memorisation of a seven-page speech for the courtroom finale. His method of preparation for roles has always been a source of fascination to critics and young actors alike. Hopkins prefers to memorize his lines in extremis, sometimes repeating them more than 200 times. The finished product typically reveals a naturalness that skillfully hides the massive amount of rehearsal the actor has done. Because of this style, Hopkins prefers fewer, more spontaneous takes.

2002 saw the films *Red Dragon* and *Bad Company*. In 2003, Hopkins appeared in *Edgardo Mortata* and *The Human Stain*, and in 2005 in Oliver Stone's *Alexander* and *Proof*. He was also in *Beowulf* (2007), *Thor* (2011), and was cast as Alfred Hitchcock in the 2012 biopic *Hitchcock*.

Hopkins was married to his first wife, Petronella Barker, from 1967 to 1972. The couple had one daughter, Abigail Hopkins, born in 1968. Hopkins then married again, to Jennifer Lynton, from 1973 to 2002. The actor long battled alcoholism, once saying, 'I led a pretty self-destructive life for a few decades. It was only after I put my demons behind me that I was able to fully enjoy acting'. In 1975, Hopkins began attending Alcoholics Anonymous, blaming his drinking for breaking up his first marriage. He gave up alcohol upon Christmas Day. In April 2000, he became a naturalized citizen of the United States and, in 2002 he married his third wife, Colombian-born Stella Arroyave. In 2000, he donated £1,000,000 to help save a large part of Snowdonia National park from development. In 2006, he was awarded the Golden Globes' Cecil B. DeMille Award for lifetime achievement.

GARETH OWEN EDWARDS 12 July 1947 -

THE GREATEST RUGBY PLAYER OF ALL TIME

'Kirkpatrick to Williams. This is great stuff. Phil Bennett covering, chased by Alistair Scown. Brilliant, oh that's brilliant. John Williams, Bryan

Williams, Pullin, John Dawes, great dummy, David, Tom David, the halfway line. Brilliant by Quinnell, this is Gareth Edwards, a dramatic start, what a score! Oh that fellow Edwards'. Every Welshman remembers Cliff Morgan's increasing crescendo of a commentary on that day, when the Welshmen in the Barbarians team magically carved through the invincible All Blacks' defence on January 27th, 1973. From Phil Bennett fielding a

 long kick and dangerously sidestepping and jinking three times under his posts, the ball went to the truly great JPR Williams, who was high-tackled around the neck by Bryan Williams. However, JPR managed to pass the ball to the English hooker John Pullin who immediately transferred to Dawes. Gareth Edwards at this time is near the ball, but not involved Welsh captain John Dawes took the ball on, with a dummy cutting through defenders, then that wonderful flanker Tommy David received his pass, and burst over the half-way line. He is forced to flip the ball one-handed to his left. Derek Quinnell, the father of the current internationals Scott and Craig, caught the very low pass at speed and flipped it up to wing John Bevan near the touchline. However, the pass is intercepted by Edwards, who has joined the movement like a guided missile from nowhere, sprinting outside the New Zealand fullback and just making it over the try-line near the corner flag.

25 seconds of magic, which the referee later admitted he could have stopped because of two New Zealand high tackles. Because of the preponderance of Welshmen in the Barbarian team against the unbeaten All-Blacks, in the final match of their tour, it seemed like a home match at Cardiff Arms Park. The Baa-Baa's won 23-11 in a fabulous game of open aggressive rugby, the like of which we shall never see again unless rugby returns to the understandable laws of the 1970's. (The great game has been radically altered by law changes to make it a contest between battering rams, with hard-contact thuggery being the aim of the game rather than ball-movement and grace. The lock-picker's toolbox of amateur rugby, where we can analogise the screwdriver, pliers, spanner etc. to the swerve, scissors, pace-change, dummy, side-step etc., has been replaced by the Irish hammer of heavily padded professional men simply crashing into each other and becoming arthritic before their time).

Gareth Edwards of Gwaun-Cae-Gurwen made a record 53 consecutive appearances for Wales from 1967 to 1978, when he retired after scoring a remarkable 20 tries for his country. *Rugby World* published a poll of 200 players, coaches, managers and writers across the globe, to find the greatest rugby player of all time, in October 1996. The highest Englishman, at 12th, is Fran Cotton. Top was Gareth Edwards, (followed by Serge Blanco) and three other members of 'the golden team', Gerald Davies, Barry

John and J.P.R. Williams, are all in the top 10. Another poll, of internationals and coaches, carried out across the world before the 1999 World Cup, also placed Edwards as the 'greatest-ever', over 20 years after his leaving the game. Edwards won three Grand Slams, 5 successive Triple Crowns, captained Wales 13 times and scored 20 tries. He went on three British Lions tours, including the successes of New Zealand in 1971 and South Africa in 1974. He won 5 triple Crowns and 3 Grand Slams. His try mentioned previously, in the 1973 Barbarians defeat of New Zealand, was manufactured almost entirely by Welsh players, and is arguably the most memorable try in recorded history. Edwards was also a key member of the British Lions team that beat New Zealand in 1971 and South Africa in 1974, winning 10 Lions' Caps. Both tours featured some of the greatest flowing rugby ever seen, which makes it all the more odd that the rules were altered to make the game more like rugby league, and far more unattractive as a spectacle in the last decade. (The impetus for rule changes has always come from the Southern Hemisphere, and rugby is becoming less popular every year as a playing sport, because of the increased emphasis upon brute force.)

Remembered for the 1971 and 1974 Lions Tours, Edwards was a youngster on the 1968 tour to South Africa. However, he believes it was the true turning point in his personal career. He had a long pass, but he knew that it could be bettered, so tended to run with the ball sometimes when a pass was a better option. On his first appearance with the legendary John outside him at fly half, Edwards has asked 'The King' how he wanted the ball given to him. John famously responded, 'Just throw it, I'll catch it', which did not really help Edwards much. At this time, Cardiff played on the old Cardiff's Arms Park, which was also used by the international team, and by Cardiff Athletic (the Rags), with games never being called off because of 'bad conditions'. As a result it was like a quagmire for most of the rugby season, and the old leather (non-coated) balls became increasingly heavy in wet conditions. Edwards recalled that he had no confidence in his passing, and that Ken Catchpole (Australia) and Chris Laidlaw (New Zealand) could put spin on the ball. South Africa gave him his first opportunity to learn to pass like these maestros - I had three months in perfect conditions and could practise virtually every day. From that time, I never looked back and it changed my game almost overnight. Though it took me quite a long time to perfect the long spinner, my confidence came right back. I did not have to worry about my pass any longer. Everything was right for me after that tour.'

Edwards' Cardiff and Wales partnership with Barry John heralded the 'Golden Age' of Welsh rugby in the 1970's. From 1969-1979 there were only three seasons when Wales did not finish top of the 5 Nations Championship, winning 3 Grand Slams, 6 Triple Crowns and never losing at the Arms Park. In 1971 at Stade Colombes, tries from John and Edwards gave Wales a 9-5 victory (3 points for a try) after being down 5-0. This gave Wales their first Grand Slam since 1952. Edwards greatest individual try is thought to be against Scotland in 1972. Wales were leading 16-12, with Edwards already having scored, when Gareth broke from a scrum in his own 25-yard area, near the touchline. He passed the Scottish wing-forward and scorched up the touchline until faced by the Scottish fullback, chipping over him. Kicking the ball on through the mud as the cover closed on him, he just made the try-line by the corner-flag. The great comedian Spike Milligan remembers standing up and roaring at his television set, willing Edwards on to score. It turned into Wales' biggest victory for 41 years.

The author recently met Edwards, now a director of Cardiff Rugby Club, and used to watch him and Barry John play for Cardiff. Both were amateurs in those days, and received nothing for playing for Wales or Cardiff. Edwards told me 'you had to win for Wales - you couldn't go home otherwise', and that crowds did not realise that often players played when suffering injuries. There was no alternative to winning. The Welsh Rugby Union has since consistently ignored the men whose skills, intelligence and backbone made Welshmen everywhere stand tall. Not just Edwards and John, but of their era the sublime Gerald Davies, the invincible J.P.R. Williams, the 'Pontypool Front Row', Mervyn 'Merve the Swerve' Davies, the grafting Dai Morris, the inestimable John Taylor - the list goes on. Even today's players know all their names and grew up in their shadow - why cannot these legends, for that is their value to Wales, meet the Welsh team before every match to help motivate them?

Edwards has had a successful career since his 1978 retirement from the game, in business, broadcasting and writing. His most beloved pastime apart from his family is fly-fishing on the Welsh rivers. A natural athlete, he won the All England Schools 400-yards hurdles when at Millfield. He could break out of rugby tackles, seeing them as a personal affront, and went fearlessly for the try line like a terrier when other scrum-halves would pass or kick. The author watched Gareth Edwards and Barry John in their pomp for Cardiff and Wales. Other players have been able to match Edwards in parts of his game, but none in its totality - he simply had no weaknesses as a rugby footballer. To appreciate Gareth Edwards, one has to watch videos - writing cannot do him justice.

5-Nations Champion 1969, 1970, 1971, 1975, 1976, 1978
Triple Crown 1969, 1976, 1977, 1978
Grand Slam 1971, 1976, 1978
British Lions 1968 South Africa, 1971 New Zealand, 1974 South Africa

Footnotes:
(i) The great player and coach Carwyn James spoke to the Barbarians players on the morning of their match against the unbeaten All-Blacks, probably the most unpopular touring side ever to visit the British Isles. The following is taken from a Stephen Jones' article in The Sunday Times, June 13, 1999, entitled 'The Try for All Seasons': 'People expected us to win, but also in a certain style' said

Edwards. 'I have never felt so weak at the kick-off, because of the pressure'. 'I remain convinced' JPR Williams said, 'that the whole thing really was Carwyn's try...He soothed us, told us to enjoy it. And I'll never forget his last words - to insist to Phil Bennett, who was full of trepidation, to go out and play just like he did for Llanelli'. Bennett was told by James that he could 'sidestep this lot off the park'. Jones goes on to describe the build up to Edwards' participation in the try '...David had made his boisterous surge, Quinnell had handled the ball delicately, on his fingertips and handed it on towards John Bevan on the left wing. More dazzling microseconds as Bevan shaped to catch the ball, still with the defence in reasonable shape; and suddenly, Edwards came to the scene from nowhere, at a pace so blistering that he added another gear to a movement that was already at high speed.

But where had he been? Why so late at the party? 'Even though the game was only a few minutes old I was feeling weak with the pressure. I was running round like I had no legs and never really feeling part of it. When Phil fielded the ball I was 50 yards away in the other corner, running back towards our line'. Indeed, the first contribution which Edwards made to the move lay in avoiding his own onrushing colleagues. At one stage, he was probably as much as 25 yards behind the ball. 'I was still asking myself why didn't someone kick the ball out, so I could get my second breath'.

But instincts were quickly aroused. 'John Dawes got the ball, and like the poacher I was, I thought that if I chased there could be something on'. There was. Edwards spotted a running line down the left wing and the ball gradually moved back towards that flank of the field. Edwards is the greatest rugby player that I have seen in my life. He was also one of the fastest, a marvellous athlete and sprinter. Bennett and the others have conjured marvellously. But that final ingredient, which takes the try from possible to certain, is raw pace. Suddenly, it is as if all the rest had been treading in treacle after all. Edwards snatches the ball from the outstretched fingers of Bevan and covers the final 33 yards at searing speed. 'I was 20 yards back initially but when I caught up I was in full stride. I know John Bevan was screaming for it and maybe he was earmarked by some of the defence. But it doesn't matter who Derek was trying to pass to. I was in full sprint stride when I caught it. By the time I got round Joe Karam, the only thing I thought about was my hamstrings. Never before had I felt I had run so fast.' A later try in that game, by JPR Williams passed through more pairs of hands, but this was the try that everyone always remembers.

(ii) Cardiff Rugby Football Club was the most famous rugby club in the world, still playing at the Cardiff Arms Park, and mention should be made here of its record against the 'Big 3' touring teams. Cardiff always plays the 'first team' of South Africa, New Zealand or Australia, as the match is regarded very much as an 'international' by these teams. Other British teams often play the touring team's 'seconds'. Against South Africa, the statistics are skewed because the author saw the 13-0 defeat in 1960, where the Cardiff fly-half Tommy McCarthy was stretchered off early on to a horrible, and unpunished late tackle, forcing Cardiff to play with 14 men (no substitutes, then) in the mud against the dirtiest team ever to tour Britain. However, that caveat aside, the record against South

Africa is Won 1, Lost 6, average score 8-10 (taking out the 1960 match, the average score would be 8-8). Against New Zealand, Cardiff has Won 1, Lost 8, average score 8-15. However, against Australia, Cardiff have never lost - Won 6 Lost 0, average score 15-8. (The full Welsh team's record against Australia is Won 8, Lost 11). So in all matches, Cardiff have won 8, lost 14, with an average score of 8-10. This is why touring teams wanted to play their best sides at the Arms Park - no other team in Britain can touch Cardiff's record. It is a tragedy that professionalism and new Southern Hemisphere rules have disfigured the game, and that some current Cardiff players do not realise the heritage of the club. The new regional Cardiff Blues team can never repeat the success of its amateur forebears.

(iii) It is well worth recording in full *The Times* report of Edward's first Triple Crown win. The reader may note that Wales scored 7 tries, worth 3 points each, with just three converted, a drop goal and two penalties, to three penalties by a good English team. Scorers were not included, except for the superb Cardiff centre and wing, Maurice Richards, who scored 4 tries in this match before joining rugby league. In today's scoring, the result would be (on a poor pitch) Wales 50: England 9. Anyone who believes that rule changes, enforced on rugby by the Southern Hemisphere countries (to favour prolonged contact by massive players on the Rugby League pattern), have improved the game, should watch a video of this match. No child watching the 1999 World Cup in Wales would wish to take up rugby, or come away with a set of heroes to emulate - it was incredibly boring, and featured more incredibly stupid refereeing errors than the author has seen in a lifetime of watching rugby. Two of the tries scored by Australia against Wales make one think that match fixing has not been confined to football and cricket. Awesome incompetence by the referee and his linesmen is the most Christian way to view any recording of that match. The other point about the new rules is that there is not one child in Britain who came away from watching that World Cup with any hero to emulate. The game is simply no longer attractive, the only interesting game being the semi-final upset where France beat New Zealand. The most recent Rugby World Cup also featured very little attacking rugby, except for some remarkable Welsh performances. The 'hero' was a kicker, Johnnie Wilkinson, which says it all for the way rugby has gone downhill. However, let us return to better days. Wales had not won the 5-Nations Championship since 1966, and went on to dominate the game for a decade:

'WALES WIN THE TRIPLE CROWN April 14 1969
At last Wales proved on Saturday that they were unquestionably the best rugby team in this year's international championship by winning it for the first time since 1966 and the Triple Crown into the bargain. Hitherto they had suggested it, but three goals (converted tries), a drop goal, two penalty goals and four tries to England's three penalty goals at Cardiff, stamped them with that priceless quality of being able to pull out their best when it was needed.

Now the Welsh dragon can at least embark upon its south Pacific tour with its tail up. This morale booster must have been doubly sweet to the Welsh coach, D.C.T.Rowlands, who was their captain when they last won the Triple Crown in 1965. The congratulations showered upon him were well earned. He will be the first to admit, however, that he has had currently exceptional quality to mould without which the best teaching in the world can fail.

This was Wales's biggest victory over England for 47 years, and in the championship they have scored 79 points, including 14 tries, or an average of three and a half a match. Nobody could deny that this was positive stuff, a capacity which made their kicking in some earlier matches rather puzzling. On Saturday they let rip with some authority, and four tries for Richards alone were more in an international match than most people can remember.

The pattern of victory was set by the Welsh forwards, well led by Brian Thomas, and with Delme Thomas, who came in for Brian Price, in outstanding form. From the first scrummage their pack, in which the front five were entirely predominant over their opposite numbers, pushed England all over the place. They had command of the lineout, and as a whole were more effective in the loose.

No wonder therefore that Wales were well set up for their glorious spree in the second half, after appearing a little low in the first period against a wind off the Taff violent enough to send bandsmen's caps bowling down the field.

Edwards, captain and scrumhalf, again showed how he has already perfected most of the tricks of his trade. John's intuitive directional sense, which threads him through apparently impenetrable defensive jungles, was a great nuisance to England.

Both wings were in form, and the quick-witted swift-moving Richards had help with some of his tries from the centre where Jarrett also kicked a dozen points and Dawes brought with him his usual air of orderly rationality.

Quite simply England did not have enough of the ball to have much of a chance. When they did have possession for some time in the first half, with the wind behind them, they wasted too many opportunities to run the ball. In this Wales taught them a most painful lesson after the interval.'

ABERFAN 21 October 1966

This entry replaces that of 'The Miner' in my previous book. As of completing this work in July 2015 there has been no movement whatsoever to commemorate the horrifying moments of Aberfan and its terrible consequences. Perhaps such events should be swept under the carpet, but in England the Hillsborough and Bradford football disasters of 1989 and 1985 have been remembered publicly in 2014 and 2015, with a combined total of 152 dead. The Labour Government was responsible for 144 deaths at Aberfan, and still Welsh Labour hopes it is forgotten. If Aberfan had happened in England, it would be a national shrine, commemorated every year. The Welsh still seem to be treated as, and accept being treated as, second-class citizens. The Welsh keep accepting whatever is thrown at the nation, lacking any political leaders to unite against wrongs.

On 21 October 1966, it took five minutes for the coal tip above Aberfan to slide down the mountain and engulf a farm, 20 terraced houses and a school. Children at Pantglas Junior School were just beginning their first lessons of the last day of term. A landslide of slurry, up to 40 feet high, smashed into their classrooms. Some children were able to escape, but 116 infants were killed. There was no counselling for the survivors and families of those who died. The tip had been placed upon known springs, and the Labour Government immediately took money from the disaster appeal funds donated by the public. No one in the National Coal Board lost his job, despite a damning report. The shame of the story of Aberfan seems to have been quietly airbrushed from history. It is the saddest place in Wales.

In 1961 No 7 Pantglas Tip had been started, on top of a mountain stream, next to six other slag heaps on boggy ground on the side of a hill.

Directly underneath it was Pantglas School. There were local protests at the time. No 7 Pantglas Tip grew quickly. The National Coal Board - a nameless, faceless, ignorant bureaucracy - used the dangerous site to deposit 'tailings', tiny particles of coal and ash. In 1963 a Merthyr Council official wrote to the National Coal Board: 'You are no doubt aware that tips at Merthyr Vale tower above the Pantglas area and if they were to move a very serious situation would accrue.' When wet, tailings formed a consistency identical to quicksand.

Aberfan, 1966

On 21 October 1966, after three inches of rain in the week, men working on No 7 Pantglas Tip arrived at work at 7.30 am. A 30-foot crater had developed in the centre of the tip. At 9 am, the tip slowly started moving. At 9.15, within seconds it rolled down the hillside, over twenty sheep, covered some walkers on the canal bank, smashed through 8 terraced houses in Moy Road, and buried the village school. It was just 3 hours before the half term holiday was to begin at Pantglas Junior School, Aberfan. One in two families in the village was bereaved. 116 children and 28 adults, including 5 teachers, were crushed. The deputy headmaster was uncovered, and seen to have tried to use the blackboard to shelter the children in his class - all 34 were killed. A lady in the village recalled: 'See those rows of

438

white arches? Each one's a child. One of the rescue workers recounted: 'My supervisor called me out of the mine and we went to help. A farmhouse near the school had been pushed right through it. I didn't cry until I saw them bring a little baby from the farmhouse, suffocated by the dust.' Apart from the baby, the village lost a three year old, 7 seven year olds, 25 eight year olds, 35 nine year olds, 35 ten year olds, 5 eleven year olds, 1 twelve year old, 3 thirteen year olds and 3 fourteen year olds.

Most villagers will still not talk about it. Mothers died of broken hearts. Front rooms are their children's shrines. The greatly honoured Chairman of the NCB, Lord Robens, immediately lied that it was not known that the tip was placed on a stream. An Appeal Fund raised £1.75 million from the British public. The National Coal Board asked for £250,000 from it and accepted £150,000, to meet the costs of clearing the remaining slurry from the hilltops around the town. The families of the bereaved were offered £500 each, regardless of how many children the National Coal Board had killed.

Eventually, the NCB gave £1,500 per family, taking it from the Appeal Money it had disgracefully taken from the disaster fund raised by the public. Other parts of the fund were used to build a new, necessarily smaller, school and make a memorial cemetery. No one in the National Coal Board lost his job, despite a damning report. The shame of the story of Aberfan seems to have been quietly airbrushed from history. This is the saddest place in Wales. The 4,236 page enquiry began legislation to remove all tips from the edges of mining villages. The mine closed in 1989. As part of her Jubilee celebrations in April 2012, Queen Elizabeth visited Aberfan. In 1966, she did not visit until nine days after the event. One believes that if a disaster on such a scale had occurred in Surrey or Hampshire, the Queen might have found an earlier space in her packed social diary. There was no counselling for the trauma.

Some readers may think that this entry upon Aberfan is given too much prominence in a book upon great Welshmen, but mining is part of Welsh heritage since the copper and gold mines of pre-Roman times, and events like this have shaped the Welsh view of the world. Cockneys and Geordies and Irish all have different perspectives on their regions, but the Welsh viewpoint is particularly affected by grief and oppression. If any Welshman did not shed a tear over Aberfan, it is difficult for him to understand Welsh history and heritage.

In 2001, on BBC Radio Wales, I was promoting my *100 Great Welshmen*, in a 3-way link with Gareth Edwards and Tanni Grey-Thompson, when a caller said that I should have included the former Speaker of the House of Commons, George Thomas, aka Viscount Tonypandy, in the book. I replied, fairly soberly, that it was not his sexual persuasion which had led to his exclusion, but the fact that no resident of Aberfan would think that he should be anywhere near a book about great Welshmen. In secret Cabinet

Papers, released in 1996 under the 30-year rule, it had been revealed that it was George Thomas's recommendation that the publicly-raised fund for the villagers should be used by the Labour government to clear the coal-tips. A producer at the BBC congratulated me after the programme, stating that the BBC Wales top brass always laid out the red carpet a special welcome for Thomas, treating him like royalty on his visits. BBC Llandaff 'went into melt-down' in the words of another BBC worker. I could never, ever understand the near-hagiography of Thomas's admirers, even before the news of his betrayal was released – apart from his sexual deviations involving children, he was a deeply devious, anti-nationalist, Royalist sycophant, and the very antithesis of a Socialist. Only in 1997, after 30 years of campaigning by Plaid Cymru, did the Labour Government repay the money into the fund. However, it did not repay the £3,000,000 it was worth after 30 years of inflation, only the original £150,000. The paltry £150,000 was paid back to the charity fund in 1997 by the newly appointed Secretary of State for Wales Ron Davies, who was quoted as saying: 'It was a wrong perpetrated by a previous government – a Labour secretary of state. I regarded it as an embarrassment. It was a wrong that needed to be righted.'

There was obviously no apology as it was an 'embarrassment'. To put it into context, £150,000 in 1966 would be worth £250 million as of writing this book.

This terrible event, when a whole school was wiped out, seems to have been airbrushed from British history. Today, few people under forty have ever heard of Aberfan, the greatest tragedy to hit the British people since the Second World War. (In the Lockerbie plane bombing in 1988, 270 passengers were killed, of which just 43 were British citizens). No blame was attached to anyone involved for Aberfan – politicians, the National Coal Board, anyone – and no apology has ever been given to the people of Aberfan. If the disaster had happened in Nottingham

Aberfan disaster, 1966

or Metz or anywhere else in Europe, it would be a place of pilgrimage. The disaster has been so effectively covered up that it is passing from both written history and human remembrance.

As a footnote, on the evening of the disaster of 31 October, the National Coal Board's chairman, Lord 'Alf' Robens, celebrated his installation as Chancellor of the University of Surrey at a party. The uneducated 'Lord' began his career as an errand-boy. Miners at the same time were desperately working under floodlights hoping to find survivors, but only digging out the bodies of children. They used their bloodied, bare hands to dig, instead of picks and shovels as they did not wish to harm any body they found. Initially the National Coal Board tried to minimise its responsibility by offering £50 compensation to each of the bereaved families (- 2014's value was just £800!) It later settled for what it called a 'generous settlement' of £500 for every child killed - a pathetic £8,000 in today's money. As noted above, Lord Robens ensured that the NCB recovered nearly all this compensation money by taking £150,000 from the Aberfan Disaster Fund to pay for the removal of the remaining coal tips. Only under the 30 years rule, it was also discovered that the NCB exaggerated the cost of removing the tips, and also deliberately obstructed a private contractor's offer to do the work far more cheaply. The 1967 Report on the disaster was devastating, but as usual in Britain, no-one was made to suffer, only the villagers: 'The Aberfan Disaster is a terrifying tale of bungling ineptitude by many men charged with tasks for which they were totally unfitted, of failure to heed clear warnings and of total lack of direction from above.'

More information has emerged from a 1999 study by Nuffield College, Oxford, sponsored by the Economic and Social Research Council. Professor Iain McLean stated: 'The Charity Commission and outdated charity law obstructed the Aberfan Disaster Fund in its attempts to help bereaved parents and other victims. At one point the Charity Commission wanted to insist that the fund should only pay grants to those parents shown to have been close to their dead children.' Please re-read that last sentence – the Charity Commission wanted in effect to set up a slide rule and put grieving parents under scrutiny to see who deserved what from the deaths of their children. The Commission also stopped any payments being made to families where children were not injured. The Commission would not back the trustees of the Disaster Fund who wanted the Labour government to remove the remaining dangerous tips overlooking their village. Thus the trustees were literally forced to hand over the exaggerated cost of £150,000 for the removal of those slag-heaps.

Jeff Edwards, a magistrate, was a survivor when the school was covered, and stated in 1999 that it was 20 years before his family received any payment. He had seen his classmates die. In other cases, many families received nothing. He stated 'Parents of uninjured children also went through the trauma – they had to live with the sleepless nights, the nightmares and the tantrums for years afterwards.' There is a collective consciousness that wants to forget Aberfan – to forget means that it will be repeated, and some politician or official will yet again be in the media stating the pathetic and perpetual mantra that 'Lessons will be learnt'. To forget something like Aberfan means that the guilty will always escape justice. To forget breaks one's ties with truth and honesty, and means colluding with the perpetrators of injustice. To forget means that those who died meant nothing. Some may believe that this is an over-long entry in this book, but the purpose of historical non-fiction is not to regurgitate other books, but to question the given version of events and to highlight what is being deliberately lost.

The following poem describes some mining disasters and Aberfan, and was published in my *The Path To Inexperience* in 2002. Even then there had been consistent rumours about George Thomas' paedophilic tendencies, shared with other political leaders of his era. He is still 'honoured' in Wales, and his name attached to the George Thomas Hospice. As of writing, just over a year before the fiftieth anniversary, there is nothing planned to commemorate the tragedy except that the composer Karl Jenkins is collaborating with the poet Mererid Hopwood upon an hour-long musical tribute to those who died and suffered.

CHALICE

'For the sculptured novelist and bon viveur Martin Amis, as quoted in discussion with A.N. Wilson, *The London Evening Standard*, 17 July 1991... this was before he spent over £20,000 upon having his rotten teeth transformed into humanoid ones and left his wife for a younger model... To joke about Aberfan is not the action of any civilized human being... '*The South Waleyans are a particularly bitter and deracinated breed*". *He began a bad-taste joke about Aberfan causing a "ripple of pleasure" through the mining valleys, but he choked it back with a giggle... Martin does the Welsh voice with an accuracy which reflects real loathing'.*

The Lordship of Senghenydd
Green on Grey on Black
Betrayed by Norman Englishmen
A Thousand-Year Attack

On the only nation
Which has never
Declared war
On anyone

We were your first and last colony
And a prototype of ethnic and ethical cleansing
You almost killed our language
Because it was fifteen-hundred years older than yours
With your 'Welsh Not' just out of living memory
You killed our Church at the Synod of Whitby
Taking it away from the people and giving it to Rome

You gave us a higher density of castles and forts
Than anywhere in the world
You killed the old laws of Hywel Dda
Because they looked after the people and accepted women as equal
And instead gave all rights
        in ascending importance
                to people with property and titles
You tried to kill our countryside with water on villages
Like Trywerin and charge us more than your Middle Saesneg for it
You tried to kill our culture by using our best in your wars
And you stripped out all our minerals…

In return you gave us nystagmus and insanity;
Emphysema, silicosis, pneumoconiosis - slow death

And fast death…

And slower deaths…

In the 19th century, children under 8 spent hours in the pitch black, opening and closing the trapper doors of ventilation tunnels. If over 8, they dragged baskets of coal to the bottom of the shaft.

In 1840, 6-year-old Susan Reece said *'I have been below six or eight months and I don't like it much. I come here at 6 in the morning and leave at 6 at night. When my lamp goes out or I am hungry I go home. I haven't been hurt yet'*. Her mission was to open and close the ventilator at Plymouth Colliery, Merthyr Tydfil.

The boys who, with chains around their waist, pulled trucks of coal through galleries too low for pit-ponies, were called *'carters'*. James Davies, an 8-year-old carter, reported that he earned 10 pennies a week, which his father took from him. John Saville, a 7-year-old carter, said that he was always in the dark and only saw daylight on Sundays.

Listen to our inventory of lost human capital:

1825   Cwmllynfell 59 men and children killed in an explosion
1842   The English Parliament under Lord Shaftesbury forbids the employment underground of women, girls and boys under 10 years old as miners. The mine owners opposed the bill and there was little inspection
1844   Dinas Middle, Rhondda,   12 men and boys killed
1849   Lletyshenkin, Aberdare,   52 men and boys killed in an explosion

| 1849 | Merthyr, Dowlais, Rhondda, | 884 people killed by cholera |

1849   Merthyr, Dowlais, Rhondda,   884 people killed by cholera
1852   Middle Duffryn, Aberdare,   65 men and boys killed in an explosion
1856   Cymmer, Porth,   114 killed, 7 of the 114 were under the age of 10, 7 were 10, and 7 were 11 years old
1867   Ferndale, Rhondda,   178 killed
1869   Ferndale, Rhondda,   another 60 killed
1877   Tynewydd   5 killed in a flooded pit
1880   Naval Colliery, Rhondda,   96 killed in an explosion
1885   Maerdy   81 killed in an explosion

The first 'firemen' were covered with water-soaked rags and crawled towards seepages with a naked flame on a long stick to explode the gas.

Some survived

Methane   = Firedamp
Carbon Monoxide   = Afterdamp
Carbon Dioxide   = Blackdamp
Hydrogen Sulphide = Stinkdamp

In 1889, there were no major disasters - it was a good year, just 153 deaths in the pits. Among them...

John Evans age 14 killed in a roof fall at Ocean Colliery, Treorchy
Thomas Evans age 16 killed in a roof fall at Seven Sisters, Neath
James Minhan age 13 fell from shaft at Great Western Colliery, Pontypridd
Thomas Jones age 17 rushed by trams at Cwmheol Colliery, Aberdare
Thomas Jones age 17 knocked down by tram at Duffryn Main, Neath
Morgan Harris age 16 run over by a coal wagon at No 9 Pit, Aberdare
James Webber age 17 killed by falling stone at No 1 Pit, Ferndale
Richard Jones age 17 killed in roof fall at Abercanaid Colliery, Merthyr
Thomas Cooper age 15 killed by a roof fall at Albion Colliery, Cilfynydd
Joseph Grey age 17 crushed between tram and coal face Gendros Colliery, Swansea
John Howells age 13 crushed by trams at Penrhiwceiber Colliery
Thomas Davies age 17 head crushed between crossbar and tram at Cwmaman Colliery
Thomas Pocket age 16 killed in roof fall at Brithdir Colliery, Neath
Thomas Evans age 17 killed in roof fall at Dunraven Colliery, Treherbert
Richard Martin age 15 killed in roof fall at Coegnant Colliery, Maesteg
David Jones age 17 crushed by tram at North Tunnel Pit, Dowlais
William Meredith age 15 crushed by pit cage at Maritime Colliery, Pontypridd

Aaron Griffiths age 14 crushed by tram at Clydach Vale Colliery

W.R. Evans age 15 died in roof fall at North Dunraven Colliery, Treherbert

Henry Jones age 14 killed in roof fall at Blaenclydach Colliery, Clydach Vale

Samuel Harris age 14 killed in roof fall at Fforchaman Colliery, Cwmaman

Joseph Jones age 16 killed in roof fall at Ynyshir Colliery

John Barwell age 13 fell into side of tram at Clydach Vale Colliery

Thomas Welsh age 15 killed in roof fall at Nantymelyn Colliery, Aberdare

Walter Martin age 15 killed in roof fall at Albion Colliery, Cilfynydd

Robert Thomas age 17 killed in roof fall at Treaman Pit, Aberdare

David Thomas age 17 killed in roof fall at Old Pit, Gwaun Cae Gurwen

Thomas Evans age 13 run over by trams at Glamorgan Steam Colliery, Llwynypia

David Arscott age 14 run over by tram at Abercanaid Colliery, Merthyr

Ben Rosser age 14 killed by fall of rock at Gadlys New Pit, Aberdare

William Osborne age 14 crushed in engine wheels at Albion Colliery, Cilfynydd

1892   Parc Slip   114 killed - in a gas blast - the school had a half day holiday for the funerals

1893   A Health Report on the Rhondda Valleys stated *the river contained a large proportion of human excrement, pig sty manure, congealed blood, entrails from slaughterhouses, the rotten carcasses of animals, street refuse and a host of other articles - in dry weather the stink becomes unbearable*

1894   Albion Colliery, Cilfynydd - 290 killed of the 300 on the shift - 11 could not be identified. One miner's head had been blown 20 yards from his body. *'All through the darkness the dismal ritual of bringing up the dead continued, illuminated only by the pale fitful glare of the surrounding oil lamps... each arrival of the cage quenched the glimmer of hope that lived in the hearts of those who waited'* - A court case was brought against the mine owners and managers but all serious charges were dropped.

There is no compensation
For the dust of our land
Now in our lungs
And in every pore of our bodies
Except our white eyes

A solitary
        disfigured
                maddened
                        cripple

445

Was unlucky to survive
The 1901 explosion
At Universal Colliery, Senghenydd
When 81 miners died

A forewarned accident
But never responsibility
So back to work, it is lads
Serene immutability
For the company,
Lewis Merthyr Consolidated Collieries Ltd.,
All charges were of course dismissed

1901   Morgan Morgans died in a fall at Cymmer Colliery, Porth, which pushed him onto a pick axe, which went through his head. His son, Dai Morgans, aged 13, witnessed the accident and was so traumatised that he never worked again

1905   National Colliery, Wattstown, 109 killed and the first disaster at Cambrian Colliery, Clydach Vale, 31 killed

14 October 1913, 12 years later, let us return to Senghenydd

Same pit, different scale
Cover their faces with their coats
There are plenty more Welsh males

The Universal was known as a '*fiery*' pit, full of hidden methane-filled caverns.
A miner went to the lamp room to light his wick, a roof-fall nearby released methane into the tunnel, the explosion ignited the coal dust, and the fire caused a massive second explosion that roared up the Lancaster Section of the pit, smashing through the workings.

The fires could not be put out for a week, during which all but 18 of the survivors died of carbon monoxide poisoning.

The pit cage was blown right out of its shaft
Into the clear blue air

Aged a little over 14 years
Harry Wedlock's first day
As a colliery boy was spent in tears
With cracking timber falling away

Fire and foul air filled his chest
While Sidney Gregory cwtched him best
As he could in the black smoke and dust
2,000 feet under the management offices

Upon October 14, 1913, at the Universal Colliery
The dead included:

> 8 children of 14 years
> 5 children of 15 years
> 10 children of 16 years
> 44 children of 17 to 19 years
> And 377 other miners

8 bodies were never identified and 12 could not be recovered

Of the 440 dead, 45 men were from Commercial Street, Senghenydd and 35 from the High Street

Not one street in Senghenydd was spared -

Parc Cottages	1 dead
Gelli Terrace	2 dead
School Street	2 dead
Windsor Place	2 dead
Cross Street	2 dead
Clive Street	3 dead
Kingsley Place	4 dead
The Huts	6 dead
Alexandra Terrace	8 dead
Station Road	8 dead
Brynhyfryd Terrace	8 dead
Phillips Terrace	9 dead
Coronation Terrace	10 dead
Station Terrace	11 dead
Woodland Terrace	12 dead
Graig Terrace	14 dead
Parc Terrace	15 dead
Grove Terrace	19 dead
Stanley Street	20 dead
Cenydd Terrace	22 dead
Caerphilly Road	39 dead
High Street	40 dead
Commercial Street	44 dead

Some women lost their husbands in 1901 - and their sons in 1913

Mrs Benjamin of Abertridwr lost her husband and both her sons, aged 16 and 14

At 68 Commercial Street, the widowed Mrs Twining lost each one of her 3 sons, the youngest aged 14

Richard and Evan Edwards, father and son, of 44 Commercial Street, were found dead together

Half the village rugby team died - they changed their strip from black and white to black

"For weeks, there was no rugby on Saturday
...only funerals"

In 12 homes, both father and son died

'When Edwin John Small died
with his 21 year-old son
it left his 18 year-old daughter Mary
to rear 6 children
the youngest 3 years old'

A survivor, William Hyatt, recalled:
'My father always said
That there was more fuss
If a horse was killed underground
Than if a man was killed...

Men come cheap
...they had to buy horses"

We know of a price, not a value

It was 75 years ago today
That the pit boss brought the band to play
But it didn't help him
They've been going in and out of style
But they're guaranteed to raise a pile
The manager was found guilty on 8 charges
So let me introduce to you
The one and only real scapegoat
Of breaches of the 1911 Coal Mines Act
And fined £24...

Five-pence ha'penny a corpse
In old money to us
2p to you

There was no compensation
Wrth gwrs

For the company,
Lewis Merthyr Consolidated Collieries Ltd.,
All charges were
Of course
Dismissed

But we appealed, we showed 'em

And Lewis Merthyr Consolidated Collieries Ltd.
Were fined £10
With costs of £5 and 5 shillings
The copper content of the bodies

There was no compensation

'We slunk to the biblical parlours to stare in shock
At the coke of flesh in the coffin, the ashes of a voice;
There we learned above the lids screwed down before their time
Collects of red rebellion, litanies of violence'

In Senghenydd and Abertridwr
The graves are brambled now
Monuments overgrown
The 14 year-old's place
Into the ground is sewn

Death rolls around this country
A skull with dust in its sockets

1915   Thomas Williams was killed at Lucy Drift Mine, Abercanaid,
leaving a widow and seven children, five of whom were still at home. No
compensation was paid.

St David's Day, 1927   Marine Colliery, Cwm, Ebbw Vale - 52 dead

Half a mile underground
1934 Gresford

262 colliers dead
And 3 of the rescue brigade
Despite the shotfirer's premonition
About the gas in Dennis Deep Section

'The fireman's reports are all missing
The records of 42 days,
The colliery manager had them destroyed
To cover his evil ways'

Charges? What charges?

The dust comes out of the ground
Into our silicotic lungs
To be vomited near to death
Not hootering death
But doubled-up suffering wheezing darkness before our time death

Buckets of death feed the flames
More dust goes on the slag heaps

Fear of tears, insider squealing, new markets, Newmarket and
The Falklands hide the blameless obscenity of pulverised spines

The Great War hid Senghenydd
A slag heap hid the school
Can hate fade like pain?

Who wants to know?

Between 1837 and 1934 there were more than 70 disasters in Welsh mines,
And in 11, more than 100 were killed in a single day

Who worries, Lord Bute?
Fill the boneyards and build mock castles over them

1931 Cilely Colliery, Tonyrefail, John Jones killed. Wife and four children receive £6 compensation

1937 - from the notebook of Idris Davies, miner and poet - '*I looked at my hand and saw a piece of white bone shining like snow, and the flesh of the little finger all limp. The men supported me, and one ran for an ambulance box down the heading, and there I was fainting away like a little baby girl.*'

Davies understood the sullen slavery of his fellow colliers -
'There are countless tons of rock above his head,
And gases wait in secret corners for a spark;
And his lamp shows dimly in the dust.
His leather belt is warm and moist with sweat,
And he crouches against the hanging coal,
And the pick swings to and fro,
And many beads of salty sweat play about his lips
And trickle down the blackened skin
To the hairy tangle on the chest.
The rats squeak and scamper among the unused props
And the fungus waxes strong.

And Dai pauses and wipes his sticky brow,
And suddenly wonders if his baby
Shall grow up to crawl in the local Hell,
And if tomorrow's ticket will buy enough food for six days,
And for the Sabbath created for pulpits and bowler hats,
When the under-manager cleans a dirty tongue
And walks with the curate's maiden aunt to church...

Again the pick resumes the swing of toil,
And Dai forgets the world where merchants walk in morning streets,
And where the great sun smiles on pithead and pub and church-steeple.'
1941   Coedely Colliery - Hugh Jones was killed and his mother received £15 compensation, of which the coffin cost £14 14s. She went to the pit with the £15 and waved it at miners, shouting *'Look, boys, get out of this pit as quick as you can - because this is all your lives are worth!'*

1941   Markham Colliery - Leslie James killed, family also receives £15 for the funeral

1947   Lewis Merthyr Colliery - George Waite killed - wife and five children receive £500 compensation

1947   Lewis Merthyr Colliery - 18 year old Neil Evans suffocated in roof fall. His family receives £200 compensation, but the National Coal Board takes away their entitlement to free coal in return

Between 1931 and 1948, of the 23,000 men who left mining because of pneumoconiosis, almost 20,000 came out of the South Wales pits.

1950   Maritime Colliery, Pontypridd - John Phillips dies - no compensation for family

1951   Wern Tarw Colliery - two brothers, Aaron and Arthur Stephens were killed in a roof fall - Aaron's widow received £200 compensation, and Arthur's widow £250. The differential was explained by the fact that Arthur had two children.

1957   Bedwas Colliery - Bobby John killed - parents receive £300 compensation

1960   Six Bells Colliery, Abertillery, 45 dead

In 1961 No 7 Pantglas Tip was started, on top of a mountain stream, next to 6 other slag heaps on boggy ground on the side of a hill. Directly underneath it was Pantglas School. There were local protests.

1962   Tower Colliery, 9 dead - Dai Morris was decapitated. The miner with him reminisced *'when the nurse pulled my shirt off, she pulled away half my skin with it'.*

Ken Strong died at Tower - his wife Mary was only 32 and then never left her home for 15 years until she died in 1977

No 7 Pantglas Tip was getting bigger - the National Coal Board - a nameless, faceless, ignorant bureaucracy, used it to deposit *"tailings"*, tiny particles of coal and ash.

1963 a Merthyr Council official wrote to the National Coal Board *'You are no doubt aware that tips at Merthyr Vale tower above the Pantglas area and if they were to move a very serious situation would accrue'*

When wet, tailings form a consistency identical to quicksand

1965   Another disaster at Cambrian Colliery, Tonypandy, with 31 dead in the explosion

But we digress, it was only a *'small'* disaster - hardly touched the *'Nationals'*

Let us instead return to Merthyr Vale and Pantglas

After three inches of rain in the week, men working on No 7 Pantglas Tip arrived at work at 7.30 am…

A 30-foot crater had developed in the centre of the tip. Just after 9 the tip moved.

452

Within seconds it rolled down the hillside, over 20 sheep, covered some walkers on the canal bank, smashed through 8 terraced houses in Moy Road, and buried the school.

9.15 am
21st October
1966
Just three hours before
The half term holiday was to begin
at
Pantglas Junior School
Aberfan

1 in 2 families bereaved

There were warnings, of course

As always

The Lord helps them now as helps themselves
[Thanks to Lady Thatcher]
They are the rich men, the hollow men, stuffed with air
Whispering no meanings, to show they really care…
Soft-talking, seductive, motionless promises,
They have the answers, the questions and the messages
Made-up, but not so false, for we know what they are:
Powdered faces, 5 houses and a Minister's car.

Aberfan
A round gross of crushed Taffs -
A lovely cemetery with a white arch
For each of the 116 children
And 28 adults
Was built

The deputy headmaster tried to use the blackboard to shelter the children in his class - all 34 were killed

On a tombstone
'Richard Goldsworthy, Aged 11,
Who loved Light, Freedom and Animals'

On another
The parting was so sudden

One day we will know why
But the saddest part of all
We never said goodbye"

'I'r Rhai a Garwn ac y
Galarwn o'u colli"...

Today's your birthday
Happy birthday to you

To ease the pain
But not the hate
Or *'The Dust'*

'See those rows of white arches?
Each one's a child.
You can't imagine what it was like.
It was as if someone took the roof off your house,
Filled it up to the top with dust and dirt,
And then put it back on.
They found 6 of the children still standing up around their teacher,
It happened so fast"

What a joke
Sup your brandy, Kingsley
Suck your rusk, Martin - how are the new teeth?

Intelligentsia, it's funny
It makes your brain go runny

'My supervisor called me out of the mine
And we went to help.
A farmhouse near the school
Had been pushed right through it.
I didn't cry until I saw them
Bring a little baby from the farmhouse,
Suffocated by the dust'

Apart from the baby, the village lost a three year old, 7 seven year olds, 25 eight year olds, 35 nine year olds, 35 ten year olds, 5 eleven year olds, 1 twelve year old, 3 thirteen year olds and 3 fourteen year olds - 116 potential novelists

Let the children sing

'I can still remember the noise,
a tremendous noise, like a thunder
but magnified a thousand times;
it sounded frightening

Some instinct made me jump from my seat and try to run for the door.
After that,
nothing,
till I came round and found
myself buried up to my waist
in black slurry.

The walls and roof of the classroom
had caved in
and beside me,
under the rubble,
was a little boy I knew,
lying
dead.
Another child's hand was hanging above me,
poking through from the next class where the wall had given way.
I took hold of the hand
and squeezed it.
I still don't know whose hand it was -
a child who was already
very probably dead.

On that day
116 children were killed,
my younger brother Carl, 7,
my sister Marilyn, 10,
among them.

I was eight years old
and spent the months
following the tragedy
in hospital with hip
and leg injuries.

The world mourned for Aberfan,
but the focus was on the children
who had been lost
rather than those who had survived.
Everyone was so busy looking for someone to blame,

we were chucked aside,
forgotten.

It was about 30 years ago,
and nobody thought about
our traumas and nightmares
then.

The attitude was that you should be grateful
that you were alive. For years I never spoke
about what had happened.

At that age I was too embarrassed to talk about how I felt.
I thought I would be laughed at.
All of us were brought up then to bottle up emotions,
to bury what had happened and
get on as best we could.
But I needed to get it out of my system.
At 12, I wrote it all down in a blue school exercise book, every detail of what
I had seen and how I felt at the time and afterwards.
Nobody saw it but my family and one teacher.
After he had read it he did not even speak to me, he seemed so shocked.
My parents were horrified.
It was another 20 years before I took it out and showed it to a woman who
was writing a book about Aberfan. In the meantime, I had tried to forget and
I was shocked at how forcibly it all came back to me. I realised I still had a
great deal of suffering inside me, that I needed to talk and to think about
how Aberfan had affected all of us who were involved. A lot of people had
breakdowns, probably because they were never adequately able to share
their grief.'

No individual was to blame
For a tip
Smothering
A school

The Chairman of the NCB
Lord Robens
Claimed that they did not know
That the tip was placed on a stream

What a scream
If you had but the chance
Who bloody cares as long as Income Tax is under 25 pence?

That seems to be the going rate for discussion -
Of course we'll be forced to leave the country if taxes rise.
[Thank you, Messrs Caine, Lloyd-Webber and Collins - be sure you take your muzak and money with you as you close the door]

'And in the end
The love you take
Is equal to the
Love you make'

It has started
The white arches
are becoming overgrown tombstones
in abandoned graveyards in our memories

Without a knowledge of history
One is condemned
To repeat the mistakes
Of the past'

Who realises that ALL wealth
stems from some poor bastard
digging something out of the ground ?

It never ends
every night
in tears
the *nightmare never dies*

Mothers still die of broken hearts
Front rooms are their children's shrines

Miners used bare, bleeding hands to remove tons of slurry off the buried children
- in the black slime
they were afraid of driving a spade into a child's body

'When the tip collapsed on October 21, 1996, Idris Cole had been at work since 7.30am. He recalls that he and his colleagues were struck by an uncanny silence in the air just before the calamity. Here, (thirty years later) he reveals for the first time what happened next.
Suddenly, someone shouted to my workmates that the tip had collapsed and was on the move. The main water pipe carrying water to Cardiff had been crushed with the weight of the tip and torrential rain, until

it was like a wafer, causing the tip to slide down the mountain. We rushed to the school, wading through slurry which had gone through the houses over a large area and on down to the river. The whole tip had moved silently, like a volcano spewing lava, but this was horrible black slurry. The scene as we approached the school was horrendous and frightening beyond description - screams and shouts of mothers and fathers, some of them who had just taken their children to school and had stopped for a chat. It was all so terrifyingly unbelievable. In their panic, people were unable to think what to do.

Their screams have never gone away. My workmates and myself waded on through the slurry and the rubble of the crushed building. I dived down to where I could see some of the children, the ones who had not been completely buried. Some, like rag dolls, were crushed against a radiator. And a teacher with outstretched arms, as if to protect the little ones. I was one of the first people to get right in the middle of it, and I couldn't believe what I was seeing. I recall one distraught father frantically searching for his two children. He was hysterical and kept pushing me away from what I was trying to do. He was out of his mind with anguish and had to be led away and physically restrained.

I think I went mad myself, from what I was seeing. But I just had to get on with using my skills and trying to keep the slurry back. Some part of the roof was still there, but hanging dangerously. The skills of the building trade enabled my mates and myself to jack it up to prevent further falls. We worked late in the night by the light of lamps which were brought in. I have never done so much crying as that day; we all did. The slurry was so deep, at one point I almost got sucked down into it. They had to pull me out and strip off my denims and my shirt, but I just wanted to carry on. Eventually, I collapsed from exhaustion and was carried off. I had double pneumonia and was given an injection which put me to sleep for many, many hours. I didn't know where I was by then; all I remember is seeing the doctor bending over me to give me the injection.

I don't think I have ever felt completely normal since that day. I had experienced many horrors during the war, from the beaches of Dunkirk, to a naval battle on the battleships taking us to Malta where I served for three years. Malta was under siege, continuously being bombed, and on very meagre rations. From there, I went to Minterno and Cassino, where we had to bury many of our comrades who were slaughtered. But nothing can ever erase the memory of that fateful morning at Aberfan and the loss of 116 little children. It was much worse, because it was the children who died. Their laughter would never ring out again in that sad, sad, village. I can never forget it. Let no-one ever forget that terrifying, sad day - or the lesson to be learned.'

It is almost forgotten
Deliberately so

By those on high

Most villagers will still not talk about it
Grief is private
And unrewarded
The proud humility
Of non-acceptance

An Appeal Fund raised £1.75 million from the British public.
The National Coal Board asked for £250,000 from it
And accepted £150,000
To meet the costs of clearing the remaining slurry
From the hilltops around the town

The families of the bereaved were offered £500 each
Regardless of how many children
The National Coal Board had killed.
Eventually, the generous NCB
Gave £1,500 per family
From the Appeal Money
It had taken

Tiny front rooms in the packed terraces
Are shrines to the dead generation
And the generation of broken-hearted deaths

The mine closed in 1989
'What becomes of the broken-hearted
Who had love that's now departed...'

The 4,236 page enquiry
Banished all tips
From the edges of mining villages

There is no money left
From the Appeal Fund
To restore the Portland Stone Monument
Or maintain the Memorial Gardens
The White Arches
Of the dead children

The Fund built an expensive community centre
With no monies for its upkeep
So the local council took it over

£1,500 per family
The Royalties of Murder

As bitter as he's ugly
Just like his scabby daddy
This pox-scarred whelp
Needs some real help
Because he's his mummy's babby

No Iranian torturer could have elicited a greater variety of winces and
flinches
states Amis fils, being forced to endure the whole of the screening of
Four Weddings and A Funeral with one of his fellow illuminated glitterati,
Salman Rushdie.
They cannot leave early because of security reasons.
The great Rushdie explains that
The world has bad taste. Didn't you know that?

Blest are those with choice and no contempt

Listen to John Evans, a miner aged just 47 and looking into darkness:
'I'm glad I haven't a son ...
It must be a heart-breaking business to watch your boy
Grow into manhood and then see him deteriorating
Because there is no work for him to do....
I've been out of work now for eight years,
And I've only managed to get eleven days work
In all that time.
Work used to shape the whole of my life
And now I've got to face the fact
That this won't be so any more.
I am really glad I live in the Rhondda.
There's real kindness and comradeship here,
And that just about makes life worth living.
The spirit here in this valley helps to soften
Many of the hardships of unemployment.'

Crush our language
Crush our men
Crush our youth
Crush our children
Turn the babies back to dust

Parfait gentil knights

Sir Galahad and *Sir Tristram*
1982 The Malvinas
43 Welsh Guards
Sitting ducks
In another futile English war
No-one was to blame
Although the captain was implored
To disembark

'After all, it never would have happened if Mark Thatcher had been in the army instead of secreting millions of pounds in his Swiss bank accounts and why should multimillionaires fight for their country anyway they are far too valuable of course and just why should we pay taxes in Britain and what do you think of the claret, perhaps a teensy robust?' warbles the acclaimed novelist, wit and raconteur

Unlike Simon Weston
The name with no face
Or skin

Sing along now in your English cathedrals:
Glory Glory Maggie Thatcher
Glory Glory Maggie Thatcher
Glory Glory Maggie Thatcher
Hide all the cripples away

Only complete heroes sit in the front, please,
You'll upset the voters

'Everywhere there's lots of piggies
Living piggy lives
You can see them out for dinner
With their piggy wives'

The pits have gone
Except for one
The dust is going
The wealth has gone
The slag heaps are going
The breed is still here
Uproot us if you can

Our brightest and best
Are forced to leave

But they sometimes come back

You are in our country
You changed it
We made the money
You spent it
We held together
You used us
Take what's left
And leave us

Never understand

... Real ghosts.

Deracinate intrenchant cultures, now!
And place fresh holly on sweet Jesus' brow,
Slit sad sores, suck old pus,
And abetting of such sights,
Lose starving blue bridges of the sky,
Regretting rien for our plight, forgetting in the laxer light,
Shame washed with blood, disputes with death,
The hurdling towards night.

Norman bastards…'

This poem was originally written in 1991 while working in London, in response to Martin Amis' opinion of Aberfan - that event was too painful to write about before I felt the anger inspired by Amis. It was updated in 1996 and 2000 and finally published in 2002. Quotes are from eyewitnesses, Lennon-McCartney, D. Gwenallt Jones, 'The Dead', Santayana, Gwalia Deserta Verse VII by Idris Davies, and The Western Mail article upon Idris Cole upon the thirtieth anniversary of Aberfan. Martin Amis' comments upon watching a popular film being worse than castration, rape and murder were in his New Yorker column in January 1996, and also reported in Private Eye, 9 February 1996. The remembrances of a survivor were reported in The Sunday Times, 15 September 1996, and Gaynor Madgwick's book of dealing with the horrors of memory is Struggling Out of the Darkness, published locally by Valley and Vale in September 1996. John Evans is quoted in Time To Spare 1935, by F. Green.

Footnote:
There seemed to be a wish to ignore the 50th anniversary of this terrible time. The brilliant stainless steel statue of Llywelyn ap Gruffydd Fychan by the Peterson brothers should be a template for historic venues across Wales. I

contacted the studio with the idea of a commemorative stainless steel waterfall for Aberfan. It would consist of 144 weeping stainless steel tears, 116 (representing the children) resting upon 16 larger tears (representing the adults). A letter was sent to all Welsh press in June 2106, suggesting this, but it seems that Aberfan is not worth remembering, compared to the publicity over the Hillsborough disaster. Welsh television had far more programmes dedicated to the event than that of England. Aberfan must never be forgotten. '*Cofiwch Aberfan*' has been written under the '*Cofiwch Drywerin*' inscription near Llanrhystud.

BOOKS BY T.D. BREVERTON

AN A-Z of WALES and the WELSH (300 pages) March 2000 ISBN 0715407341 - published Christopher Davies – *'the first encyclopaedia of Wales'; 'a comprehensive anthology'*

THE SECRET VALE OF GLAMORGAN (230 pages) June 2000 ISBN 190352900X supported by a Millennium Commission grant for local parishes *'a historian's delight'*

THE BOOK OF WELSH SAINTS (606 pages) September 2000 ISBN 1903529018 hardback – *'this book is a really extraordinary achievement: a compilation of tradition, topography and literary detective work that can have few rivals. I have enjoyed browsing it immensely, and have picked up all sorts of new lines to follow up'* – Archbishop Rowan Williams; *'an enormous work of research'*

100 GREAT WELSHMEN (376 pages) May 2001 ISBN 1903529034 Welsh Books Council **Welsh Book of the Month** *'painstaking research'; 'a fascinating compendium'* (New Edition 2005)

100 GREAT WELSH WOMEN (304 pages) ISBN 1903529042 September 2001 *'an absolute must for all those who value their Welsh heritage'*

THE PATH TO INEXPERIENCE (158 pages) ISBN 1003529077 March 2002 *'magnificent, compassionate and moving'*

THE WELSH ALMANAC (320 pages) ISBN 1903529107 WBC **Welsh Book of the Month** July 2002 hardback *'a tremendous undertaking'; 'it will take its place on the bookshelf with other important works of reference'*

THE BOOK OF WELSH PIRATES AND BUCCANEERS (388 pages) ISBN 1903529093 WBC
Welsh Book of the Month April 2003 *'exemplary'; 'an immense work of great scholarship'; effectively a study of the whole genre of piracy'*

GLAMORGAN SEASCAPE PATHWAYS (144 pages) ISBN 1903529115 June 2003 supported by a Millennium Commission WCVA Arwain grant. **Fellow of the Millennium Award** (FMA) *'fascinating'*

BLACK BART ROBERTS – THE GREATEST PIRATE OF THEM ALL (254 pages) ISBN 1903529123 March 2004 (published abridged as BLACK BART ROBERTS – THE GREATEST PIRATE OF THEM ALL by Pelican

Publishing USA [166 pages] ISBN 1-58980-233) *'a must read for anyone interested in pirates'*

THE PIRATE HANDBOOK (290 pages) ISBN 1903529131 Autumn 2004 (published abridged in USA by Pelican Publishing 2004 as THE PIRATE DICTIONARY [192 Pages] ISBN 9781589802438) - WBC **Welsh Book of the Month** *'this wonderful sourcebook is an absolute must'; 'a vitally important addition to the canon of naval literature'*

Introduction and 3 major poems in 600th anniversary commemorative book on Owain Glyn Dŵr, SONGS FOR OWAIN (98 pages) ISBN 0862437385 published by Y Lolfa June 2004.

SIR HENRY MORGAN – THE GREATEST BUCCANEER OF THEM ALL (174 pages) ISBN 1903529174 Spring 2005 – WBC **Welsh Book of the Month** - published abridged by Pelican USA as ADMIRAL SIR HENRY MORGAN – KING OF THE BUCCANEERS [120 pages] ISBN 9781589802773

100 GREAT WELSHMEN (NEW EDITION) (432 pages) ISBN 1903529034 2005 *'a veritable goldmine of a book'; 'a massive treasure chest of facts and figures which no collector of books on Wales can overlook'* 2006

WELSH SAILORS OF WORLD WAR II (with Phil Carradice) (448 pages) ISBN 9781903529195 March 1st, 2007 - WH Smith Welsh **Book of the Month** *'an account worthy of the pen of Xenophon'*

THE FIRST AMERICAN NOVEL: THE JOURNAL OF PENROSE, SEAMAN BY WILLIAM WILLIAMS, & THE BOOK, THE AUTHOR AND THE LETTERS IN THE LILLY LIBRARY BY TERRY BREVERTON (446 pages) ISBN 9781903529201 August 30th 2007. This is 'The Journal of Lewellin Penrose – Seaman', and an autobiography of William Williams - **Everett Helm Visiting Fellowship Award** of Indiana University.

Introduction and Annotated Edition of Exquemelin's 'THE BUCCANEERS OF AMERICA' (192 pages) August 2008 – commissioned July 2007 for Quarto Publishing. Consultant editor and writer: translation four different language versions of Exquemelin's Buccaneers of America as THE ILLUSTRATED PIRATE DIARIES: A REMARKABLE EYEWITNESS ACCOUNT OF CAPTAIN MORGAN AND THE BUCCANEERS, hardback for worldwide distribution by Apple Press (UK 9781845433000), New Holland (Australia) and Collins (USA 0061584487 and

9780061584480). *Das Piraten-Tagebuch* (trans. Karen Schuler & Henning Dedekind; *Dzienniki Piratow* etc.

IMMORTAL WORDS: HISTORY'S MOST MEMORABLE QUOTATIONS AND THE STORIES BEHIND THEM (978-1-84866-0045) 384pp hardback Quercus History/Borders – August 2009

OWAIN GLYNDŴR – THE STORY OF THE LAST PRINCE OF WALES (978-1-84868-3280) – 192pp July 2009 Amberley hardback *'Accessible and Highly Readable'*

WALES - A HISTORICAL COMPANION – (978-1-84848-3264) 360pp November 2009 Amberley

BREVERTON'S NAUTICAL CURIOSITIES – A BOOK OF THE SEA (978-1-84424 – 7766) 384pp April 2010 Quercus hardback: published as BREVERTON'S NAUTICAL COMPENDIUM Globe Pequot USA 2010

IMMORTAL LAST WORDS – HISTORY'S MOST MEMORABLE DYING REMARKS, DEATHBED DECLARATIONS AND FINAL FAREWELLS (978-1-84916-478-8) 384pp Quercus/Borders hardback September 2010 (published in Holland as *Onsterfelikje Laatste Woorden*)

WALES' 1000 BEST HERITAGE SITES (978-1-84868-991-6) 224pp – Amberley – October 2010

BREVERTON'S PHANTASMAGORIA (978-0-85738-337-2) – A COMPENDIUM OF MONSTERS, MYTHS AND LEGENDS Hardback 384pp Quercus 7 July 2011

BREVERTON'S COMPLETE HERBAL – A BOOK OF REMARKABLE PLANTS AND THEIR USES – BASED ON NICOLAS CULPEPER'S THE ENGLISH PHYSITIAN OF 1652 AND COMPLEAT HERBALL OF 1653 (978-0-85738-336-5) Hardback 384pp Quercus 29 September 2011

I HAVE A DREAM – INSPIRING WORDS AND THOUGHTS FROM THE WORLD'S GREATEST LEADERS (978-1-84866-134-9) Hardback 384pp Quercus January 2012

BIRD WATCHING: A PRACTICAL GUIDE WITH PHOTOS AND FACTS (978-1-4454-8868-4) Parragon – the largest non-fiction illustrated book publisher in the world 2012

BACKYARD BIRDS – THE BIRDS OF AMERICA Parragon USA 2012

BREVERTON'S ENCYCLOPEDIA OF INVENTIONS – A COMPENDIUM OF TECHOLOGICAL LEAPS, GROUNDBREAKING DISCOVERIES AND SCIENTIFIC BREAKTHROUGHS THAT CHANGED THE WORLD (978-1-7808-72391) Hardback 384pp Quercus May 2012

THE WELSH – THE BIOGRAPHY (978-1-4456-0808-2) *'Breverton's breadth, generosity and sheer enthusiasm about Wales are compelling'* 400pp Amberley – 28 November 2012

THE PHYSICIANS OF MYDDFAI – CURES AND REMEDIES OF THE MEDIEVAL WORLD – The first new and unexpurgated translation for 150 years, with a biography of physicians to the present day (978-0-9572459-9-0) 292pp Cambria Books November 2012

RICHARD III – THE KING IN THE CAR PARK: The Real Story of 'the Hunchback King' (978-1-4456-2105-0) Hardback 192pp Amberley 2013 [This is in fact a comparative analysis of Richard III and Henry Tudor]

THE JOURNAL OF PENROSE, SEAMAN - THE NEW ROBINSON CRUSOE (978-0-9576791-1-5) 548pp Cambria Books 2013/2014 – a rewrite of the original manuscript, with explanatory text

BREVERTON'S FIRST WORLD WAR CURIOSITIES (978-1-4456-3341-1) 320pp - Amberley June 2014

JASPER TUDOR – DYNASTY MAKER 320pp hardback Amberley September 2014

EVERYTHING YOU EVER WANTED TO KNOW ABOUT THE TUDORS BUT WERE AFRAID TO ASK 320pp Amberley hardback October 2014

RICHARD III – THE KING IN THE CAR PARK Feb 2014 paperback re-edition

THE TUDOR KITCHEN: HOW THE TUDORS ATE AND DRANK, WITH OVER 500 AUTHENTIC RECIPES OF THE TIMES Amberley hardback autumn 2015

THE TUDOR COOK BOOK: OVER 400 RECIPES FROM THE TIMES Amberley Spring 2016

JASPER TUDOR – DYNASTY MAKER 320pp paperback Amberley 2016

HENRY VII – THE MALIGNED TUDOR KING 320pp hardback Amberley 2016

OWEN TUDOR – FOUNDING FATHER OF TUDOR DYNASTY 320pp hardback Amberley 2017

CONFESSIONS OF THE WELSH SMUGGLER WILLIAM OWEN Gwasg Carreg Gwalch 2018

WELSH PIRATES AND PRIVATEERS Gwasg Carreg Gwalch 2018

A GROSS OF PIRATES Amberley 2018

BOOKS EDITED AND PUBLISHED BY TERRY BREVERTON
The Dragon Entertains, Alan Roderick 2001
A Rhondda Boy, Ivor Howells 2001
Glyn Dŵr's War: The Campaigns of the last Prince of Wales', Gideon Brough 2002
From Wales to Pennsylvania: the David Thomas Story', Dr Peter Williams 2002
The Man from the Alamo, John Humphreys 2004 WH Smith **Book of the Month**
Heroic Science – the Royal Institution of South Wales and Swansea 1835-1865, Ronald Rees 2005
Gringo Revolutionary – The Amazing Adventures of Carel ap Rhys Pryce, John Humphreys 2005

A big thanks to Dave Lewis of **Publish & Print**, who formatted the manuscript, designed the book cover and without whom this book could not have been published.

www.publishandprint.co.uk

Made in the USA
Columbia, SC
13 October 2017